SOCIAL SCIENCE DIVISION
CHICAGO PUBLIC LIBRARY
400 SOUTH STATE STREET
CHICAGO, IL 60605

D0138500

CHICAGO PUBLIC LIBRARY

SOCIAL SCIENCE DIVISION
CHICAGO PUBLIC LIBRARY
400 SOUTH STATE STREET
CHICAGO, IL 60605

HUMAN MEMORY AND COGNITION

HUMAN MEMORY AND COGNITION

SECOND EDITION

MARK H. ASHCRAFT
Cleveland State University

HarperCollins*College*Publishers

Acquisitions Editor: Catherine Woods
Project Editor: Marina Vaynshteyn
Design Supervisor: Heather A. Ziegler
Cover Photo: Elle Schuster
Production Manager: Mike Kemper
Compositor: University Graphics, Inc.
Printer and Binder: R.R. Donnelly & Sons Company
Cover Printer: The Lehigh Press, Inc.

For permission to use copyrighted material, grateful acknowledgment is made to
the copyright holders listed on pp. 735–741, which are hereby made part of this
copyright page.

Human Memory and Cognition, Second Edition

Copyright © 1994 by HarperCollins College Publishers

All rights reserved. Printed in the United States of America. No part of this book
may be used or reproduced in any manner whatsoever without written permission, except in the case of brief quotations embodied in critical articles and
reviews. For information address HarperCollins College Publishers, 10 East
53rd Street, New York, NY 10022.

Library of Congress Cataloging-in-Publication Data
Ashcraft, Mark H.
      Human memory and cognition / Mark H. Ashcraft.—2nd ed.
          p.   cm.
      Includes bibliographical references and index.
      ISBN 0-673-46789-9
        1. Memory.   2. Cognition.   I. Title.
BF371.A68   1993
153—dc20   93-32908
                                            CIP

97 98 99   9 8 7

R03061 93846

SOCIAL SCIENCE DIVISION
CHICAGO PUBLIC LIBRARY
400 SOUTH STATE STREET
CHICAGO, IL 60605

To my parents,
J. Morris Ashcraft and Bernice Haley Ashcraft,
who made sure I learned to read, write, and type.

Contents

▼ **Chapter 11**
Decisions, Judgments, and Reasoning   519

Preface

To the Student

The psychology of human memory and cognition is fascinating, dealing with questions and ideas that are inherently interesting—how we think, reason, remember, and use language, to name just a few. When cognitive psychologists "talk research" at conventions, they are agitated, intense, and full of energy. In contrast to this enthusiasm, however, our undergraduate texts often portray the field as rather dull, too concerned with the minutiae of experimental method and technical jargon, and not concerned enough with the interesting issues.

Without slighting the empirical foundation of the field, I have tried to capture some of the excitement of the area. All professors want their students to understand the material, of course, but I also want you to appreciate cognitive psychology as one of the most interesting and memorable topics of your student career. Several features of the book are designed to accomplish this.

- To engage your interest and understanding, I have included examples and demonstrations throughout the text. Most of the chapters have a demonstration "box" that lists suggestions for reasonably quick "miniature experiments" you can conduct, with only moderate effort and a minimum of equipment. Trying several of these will be one of the best ways to see memory and cognition "in action."

- Students often have difficulties with the terminology of a new field. To help you with the "jargon problem," critical terms are boldfaced in the text and defined immediately in italicized print. Each chapter's terms are listed at the end of the chapter, and the entire collection of terms and definitions appears in the Glossary at the end of the book. Try studying for exams by playing a Jeopardy-like game with the glossary; one person reads a definition, the other names the defined term.

- Each major section of a chapter ends with a brief list of Summary Points, naming the ideas and issues you have just studied. There is a longer Summary at the end of each chapter. Get in the habit of using these as study guides. Note that it is sometimes helpful to read the Summary first, as an abstract of the chapter's content, then return to it after you have read the whole chapter, as a review.

- I have quite intentionally adopted a more colloquial style than is customary in the field (or in texts in general), using the first person, posing direct questions to the reader, inserting parenthetical commentary, and so on. My own students have told me that these features make the book more enjoyable to read; one said "It's interesting—not like a textbook," which I took as a compliment. Some professors may expect a more formal, detached style, of course. I would rather have you read and remember the material than have you cope with a book selected because of a carefully pedantic style. Besides, you will have plenty of time to deal with boring books in graduate school.

To the Instructor

This book is directed primarily toward undergraduates at the junior–senior level, who are probably taking their first basic course in Memory and Cognition. It has also been used successfully in introductory graduate surveys, especially when first-year students lack a thorough undergraduate background in memory and cognition. The supplementary readings suggested at the end of each chapter may be particularly useful in such classes. I have also noted which readings are appropriate for undergraduates and which are frankly too difficult for students at that level.

At my university, the typical quarter contains 10 weeks of instruction, sufficient to cover all but about two or three of the chapters. I have organized the book so that an instructor can either omit certain chapters, because of time or interest constraints, or omit distinct sections of the chapters. Some instructors may have a curriculum that covers the topic of language in other courses, and they would want to omit Chapters 8 and 9 and the aphasia section of Chapter 10. Others may view the material in Chapters 11 through 13 as less central to the core of cognitive psychology. Below are five groupings of the chapters that suggest appropriate reading assignments for courses tailored to one or another focus within the field of cognitive psychology.

Chapter Titles

1. Cognitive Psychology: An Introduction
2. The Human Information Processing System

3. Perception and Attention
4. Short-Term, Working Memory
5. Episodic Long-Term Memory
6. Semantic Long-Term Memory
7. Interactions in Long-Term Memory
8. Language
9. Comprehension: Language and Semantics Together
10. Neurocognition
11. Decisions, Judgments, and Reasoning
12. Problem Solving
13. Current Directions

Focus	Suggested Chapter Assignments
Cognitive survey	1–4, 6, 7, 9, 11–13
Memory survey	1–10
Cognition with language	1–3, 6–10, 12, 13
Cognition without language	1–7, 11–13
Cognitive science	1–3, 6–10, 12, 13

This book is written so that certain chapters may be omitted without seriously disrupting the continuity of topics. On the other hand, I have not forced the chapters to "stand alone" completely. In my view, the distinct disadvantage to such an approach is that the interconnections among topics are slighted. When I refer to a discussion elsewhere in the book, I have either provided enough information so that the interconnection is obvious or referred to the specific section in the other chapter that a student might want to review quickly.

As in the first edition of the book, I have attempted to strike a balance between basic, core material and "cutting edge" topics. As cognitive psychology matures, it is important to maintain some continuity with our older topics and evidence. Students need to understand "how we got here," and instructors cannot be expected to start from scratch each time they teach the course again. On the other hand, revising the book was a very revealing exercise in how cognitive psychology has evolved in the past few years. Connectionism, research on implicit versus explicit memory, and developments in what I have called *neurocognition* are merely the most prominent of the several new directions that characterize cognitive psychology. These receive substantial treatment in this edition as well. Also new to the second edition is an *Instructor's Manual,* which contains multiple choice and essay questions keyed to the book; ask your HarperCollins sales representative for a copy.

I hope that the balance between classic research and current topics, the style I have adopted, and the relatively standard organization I have used will make the text easy to teach from, and easy for students to read and remember. More important, I hope that my portrayal of the field of cognitive psychology will be viewed as useful in the education of our students. I would be delighted to receive the comments and suggestions of those who use this book, instructors and students alike. Write in care of the Psychology Department, Cleveland State University, Cleveland, OH 44115. My BitNet address is r0599@csuohio. My Internet address is m.ashcraft@csuohio.edu.

Acknowledgments

In the first edition, I said that writing a book is similar to riding a roller coaster: the ride is longer than expected, full of ups and downs, and the author alternates between having a good time and wishing he or she had never gotten on in the first place. Working on the second edition was also a larger enterprise than I anticipated—not as large as the first version to be sure, but long enough nonetheless. Individuals who helped to shape the first edition continue to deserve mention here: for editorial support and assistance, Jane Sudbrink, Denise Workman, Rebecca Strehlow, and Jean Dal Porto; for professional advice, R. Reed Hunt, John Jonides, Michael Masson, James S. Nairne, Marjorie Reed, and Gregory B. Simpson; and for class testing, my several undergraduate Cognition classes. The suggestions and comments contributed by these people made the book easier to study, more balanced, and ultimately more useful.

For the second edition, several additional people provided assistance. Catherine Woods and Marcus Boggs were responsible for the project at HarperCollins, my new publisher; they knew just when to offer help, when to leave me alone, and when to make critical decisions about the form of the second edition. The manuscript was reviewed carefully by several individuals, to whom I express my gratitude: Richard Griggs, University of Florida; Richard Jackson Harris, Kansas State University; Donald Homa, Arizona State University; and Paul Whitney, Washington State University. On a moment's notice, colleagues like Tom Carr, Frances Friedrich, Dave Geary, and Mike McCloskey were willing to email suggestions, comments, opinions, and recommendations. Several researchers, including Morti Gernsbacher, Art Graesser, Keith Holyoak, George Kellas, Mark Marschark, and Paul Whitney, responded quickly and generously to my requests for reprints and other information. David Fleck, on the local scene, provided invaluable help with chores ranging from printing and photocopying to reading and critiquing. And finally, as before, I must thank my wife and children, who again put up with an absentee husband and father, and now welcome me back into the family.

Mark H. Ashcraft

HUMAN MEMORY AND COGNITION

Chapter 1

COGNITIVE PSYCHOLOGY: AN INTRODUCTION

▼ **Thinking About Thinking**

▼ **Memory and Cognition Defined**

▼ **An Introductory History of Cognitive Psychology**

> Anticipations of Psychology
> Early Psychology
> Behaviorism and Neobehaviorism
> Dissatisfaction with Behaviorism: The Winds of Change

▼ **Cognitive Psychology and Information Processing: The New Direction**

> The Assumptions of Cognitive Psychology

What a piece of work is man. How noble in reason! How infinite in faculty! In form and moving how express and admirable! In action how like an angel! In apprehension, how like a god! (Act 2, scene 2, of Shakespeare's Hamlet*)[1]*

One difficulty in the psychological sciences lies in the familiarity of the phenomena with which they deal. A certain intellectual effort is required to see how such phenomena can pose serious problems or call for intricate explanatory theories. One is inclined to take them for granted as necessary or somehow "natural." (Chomsky, 1968, p. 24)

T his book is about human memory and cognition, and specifically about the scientific study of human memory and cognition. Let's start with a quick definition of terms, then return later for the more formal definition. For the moment, consider the topic of this book to be *the mental events and knowledge we use when we recognize an object, remember a name, have an idea, understand a sentence, and solve a problem.* In this book, we will consider a very broad range of subjects, from basic perception through complex decision making, from seemingly simple mental acts such as recognizing a letter of the alphabet to very complicated acts such as participating in a conversation. We'll be asking questions like: How do we read for meaning? How do we memorize facts? What does it mean to "forget" something? How do we know that we *don't* know something? The unifying theme behind all this is one of the most fascinating and important questions of all time: How do people think?

Note right away that we are interested in an empirical, scientific approach to human memory and thought. This places us in the branch of modern psychology usually labeled *cognitive psychology.* What drives the field, in short, is research, the results of experiments and the explanations of models and theories. We will be dealing with many of these experiments, explaining why they were done, what sorts of questions they answer, what directions they suggest for future studies, and so on. By contrast, this book does not deal in any serious way with nonempirical or philosophical approaches to the human mind. Of course, we do not deny the profound influence that philosophy has had on psychology; indeed, psychology began as an offshoot of philosophy. And it is obviously true that we all—cognitive psychologists included—have been shaped and influenced by our culture and intellectual history in countless ways. Nonetheless, the discipline of psychology has largely accepted the empirical, scientific approach to the study of mind and behavior; purely philosophical approaches are viewed rather skeptically, at least until put to the test in empirical research. Thus one of the central features of modern cognitive psychology is its allegiance to objective, empirical methods of

---

[1]Unlike Shakespeare, modern writers have been sensitized to the sexist bias implied by the generic terms *man, he,* and so on. I have attempted to avoid such usage whenever possible. On those stylistic occasions where the generic term couldn't be avoided, or when I simply grew tired of the plural or collective terms, I have tried to alternate between the generic *he* and *she,* on a section-by-section basis.

investigation: this is one of the shiniest badges we wear. We are experimentalists, and this is the approach you'll read about in this book.

After reading the previous paragraph, a few of you may be thinking "Well, that's the bad news. Now, where's the good news?" Here it is. Within the boundaries of objective scientific methods, cognitive psychology is asking an enormous range of fascinating questions. Since the beginnings of modern cognitive psychology some 35 to 40 years ago, there has been a true explosion of interest in cognition and in the cognitive approach to human behavior and thought. Questions that had been on the back burner for too long—such as "How do we read?" or "How do we use language?"—have become active areas of investigation. The pent-up interest in these questions, unleashed during the "cognitive revolution" of the late 1950s, has yielded tremendous progress. Furthermore, we now acknowledge—and even seek—the important contributions that can come from disciplines like linguistics, computer science, and the neurosciences. This interdisciplinary approach, this joining of diverse forces, is called *cognitive science,* the scientific study of thought, language, the brain—in short, the mind.

The most basic purpose of this book is to tell you what has been discovered about human memory and cognitive processes, and to share cognitive psychology's conclusions and insights about that particularly human activity called thought. The most highly sophisticated, flexible, and efficient "computer" available today is your memory, with its collection of mental processes. How does it work? As amazing as electronic computers are, their capabilities are literally kid's stuff compared to what you routinely do in even a single minute's worth of thinking. The need to understand ourselves is basic, and this includes an understanding of how our own mental apparatus operates.

Another purpose of this book is to describe how cognitive psychology has made these discoveries. Your appreciation of the information in this book will be amplified if you also understand how cognitive research is done, how new knowledge is acquired in the scientific pursuit of cognition. Relatively few of you will become cognitive psychologists yourselves, but presumably most of you who are reading this book have decided to major in psychology or a cognate field. Since the cognitive approach has come to influence many areas in modern psychology, your mastery of psychology as a whole will be enhanced by an understanding of cognitive psychology. (And—trust me on this—you'll need to know the material for your GREs!)

A final purpose of this book is to illustrate the pervasiveness of cognitive psychology and its potential impact on other fields outside psychology proper. As you read a moment ago, cognitive psychology is already a multidisciplinary field, under the name cognitive science. This fusion of disciplines represents the conviction that researchers in linguistics, artificial intelligence, the neurosciences, and even anthropology can contribute important ideas to psychology and vice versa. Psychology has a long tradition of influencing educational practice, and the potential for cognitive psychology to continue these contributions is both obvious and important. We expect that even such diverse fields as medicine and law may incorporate some of cognitive psychology's findings (some of these contributions, real and potential, are discussed in Chapter 13). But in a way, we should not be at all surprised that cognitive psychology is relevant to so many other fields. After all, what human endeavor doesn't involve thought?

▼ Thinking About Thinking

Let's begin to develop an intuitive feel for our topic by considering some examples, coming back later to improve our quick definitions of the terms *memory* and *cognition*. For all three of the examples that follow, you should read the question and come up with the answer, but more importantly you should try to be as aware as possible of the thoughts that pass through your head as you consider the question. The first question is easy:

(1) How many hands did Aristotle have?[2]

For such a ridiculously easy question, we're of course not particularly interested in the correct answer "two." We are tremendously interested, however, in the thoughts you had as you considered the question. Most students I've tried this demonstration with report a train of thoughts something like this: "Dumb question, of course he had two hands. Wait a minute—why would a professor ask such an obvious question? Maybe Aristotle had only one hand. Nah, I would have heard of it if he had had only one hand—he must have had two."

Let's attempt a bit of informal cognitive analysis to uncover some of the different activities you engaged in while arriving at your answer. We'll keep track of the analysis with the listing in Table 1-1; as you read the later questions, refer to Table 1-1 to see which processes and steps apply to all the questions, and what new ones need to be added. Bear in mind that Table 1-1 merely illustrates the intuitive analysis; it does not substitute for the full description of these processes and steps found later in the book.

First of all, although you were no doubt totally unaware of it, a large group of perceptual processes were brought into play to deal with the written words of the question. Highly overlearned visual processes focused your eyes on the printed line, then moved your focus across the

---

[2]The Aristotle question is not original; I got it from someone else. My difficulty is that I don't remember who. I strongly suspect it originated with Allan Collins, who gave a talk on "Reasoning from Incomplete Knowledge" several years ago. On the other hand, knowing that Collins did this kind of research, I may just be attributing the Aristotle question to him because it makes sense to do so; after all, he did use several especially compelling examples in his talk. Then again, it may have been someone else; since I've used the example in describing Collins's research, I suppose it's even possible that I generated the question, then by association have awarded it to him. In any event, this rather ironic situation is a good example of uncertainty in everyday reasoning and remembering.

Table 1-1   SUMMARY OF THE INTUITIVE COGNITIVE ANALYSIS

Processes	Topic and Chapter
Sensory and Perceptual	
Focus eyes on print Encode/perceive the printed material	Visual perception and sensory memory— Chapter 3 Pattern recognition—Chapter 3 Reading—Chapter 9
Memory and Retrieval	
"Look up" letters and words in memory Identify words Retrieve word meanings and connections	Memory retrieval—Chapters 4–7 Semantic memory—Chapter 6 Comprehension—Chapters 7, 9
Comprehension	

Combine word meanings to yield sentence
  meaning
Evaluate overall sentence meaning
Consider alternate word/phrase meanings
  if necessary
	Semantic retrieval and comprehension—
	Chapters 7, 8, 9

Judgment and Decision	
Determine answer to the question Determine "reasonableness" of the question Judge speaker's intent Judge own knowledge of topic	Semantic retrieval—Chapters 7, 8 Comprehension/conversation—Chapter 9 Decision making/reasoning—Chapter 11
Computational (Question 2 only)	
Retrieve knowledge of "how to divide" Carry out the procedure of long division	Procedural knowledge/problem solving— Chapter 12

line bit by bit, registering the printed material into some kind of memory system. Smoothly and rapidly, another set of processes "looked up" the encoded material in memory and identified the letters and words. Of course, few if any of the readers of a college text need to pay conscious attention to the nuts and bolts of perceiving and identifying words, unless the vocabulary is unfamiliar or the printing is faint. Yet your lack of awareness of these stages doesn't mean they didn't happen: ask a first-grade teacher about the difficulties children have in learning to identify letters and their sounds, and in putting these components together into words.

We've encountered two important lessons of cognitive psychology already. First, mental processes can occur with hardly any conscious awareness at all. This is especially (or maybe only) true of processes that have received a great deal of practice, as in reading skills. Second, even though these processes can operate very quickly, they are nonetheless quite complex, involving difficult motor, perceptual, and mental acts. Their complexity makes it even more amazing how efficient, rapid, and seemingly automatic they are.

As the individual words in the first question were being identified, you were also *accessing* or "looking up" the meanings of those words and then fitting those meanings together to understand the question. Surely no one was consciously aware of looking up the meaning of the word *hands* in a mental dictionary. Just as surely, however, you did search for and find that entry in memory, stored with all your other general knowledge about the human body. A few students often insist that they wondered whether the question might be referring to a different Aristotle—maybe Aristotle Onassis?—since a question about the philosopher Aristotle's hands seems so odd.

Now we're getting to the meat of the process. With little effort, we retrieve the information from memory that the word *Aristotle* refers to a human being, a historical figure from the distant past. Many people know little else about Aristotle beyond the fact that he was a Greek philosopher. Yet this seems to be enough, combined with what we know to be true of people in general, to decide that he was probably just like everyone else—he had two hands. Those who consider Aristotle Onassis seem to reach the same stage as well. Even though they may know a few facts about this more contemporary person (Greek shipping magnate, married Jacqueline Kennedy), they probably find no specific information in memory concerning the number of hands he had, so they make the default assumption that it was two. Think of the uncertainty you might have felt if the question had been "How many hands does Aristotle have?" Tipped off by the present tense, would you have searched your memory for a still-living person named Aristotle? Would you have explicitly asked yourself if Aristotle Onassis was dead or not; or would you have tried to find some unusual, maybe metaphorical way of interpreting the question?

At a final (for now) stage, people report a set of thoughts and judgments that involve the "reasonableness" of the question, similar in many respects to the interpretations of remarks in a conversation. In general, people do not ask obvious questions, at least not to other adults. If they do ask an obvious question, however, it is often for another reason—a trick question, for instance, or sarcasm. Consequently, students report that for a time they decided that maybe the question wasn't so obvious after all. In other words, there was a return to memory, to see if there was some special knowledge about Aristotle that pertains to his hands. The next step is truly fascinating. The majority of students claim to have thought to themselves "No, I would have known about it if he had had only one hand," and they decide that indeed it was an obvious question after all.

This "lack of knowledge" reasoning process is itself a fascinating topic in cognitive psychology, since so much of our everyday reasoning is done without benefit of complete knowledge. In an interesting variation, I have asked students "How many hands did Beethoven have?" Knowing of Beethoven's musical fame typically leads to the inference that "since he was a musician, he probably played the piano, and he couldn't possibly have been very successful at it with only one hand; therefore he must have had two." An occasional student will even go further, with the intriguing answer "Two—but he did go deaf before he died."

Now *that's* interesting! Someone found a connection between the physical handicap implied by the question "How many hands?" and a related shred of evidence in memory, Beethoven's deafness. Such an answer shows how people can also consider implications, inferences, and other unstated connections as they reason and make decisions: it shows what a great deal of knowledge can be considered even for a relatively simple question. The answer also illustrates the role of prior knowledge in such reasoning, where the richer body of information about Beethoven can lead to a more specific inference than was possible for the Aristotle question.

While this informal analysis does not in any way exhaust the discussion of cognitive processes in reading, memory retrieval, or comprehension, it does serve to orient you to some of the important features of cognitive psychology and its subject matter. Let's continue with the other questions to see what else is in store for you in this book.

(2) What is 723 divided by 6?

This question clearly relies on a different kind of knowledge than the Aristotle question, the knowledge of arithmetic that you learned in grade school. Just as was true in reading the words in the first question, many of your mental processes happened more or less automatically for the division problem—identifying the digits, accessing your knowledge of arithmetic procedures, and so on. Yet you were also no doubt consciously aware of the problem-solving steps in doing long division—divide 6 into 7, subtract 6 from 7 to get the first remainder, bring down the 2 and then divide 12 by 6, and so on. These steps suggest that we should add a different kind of process to Table 1-1, something on the order of "computational processes" that would include your knowledge of how to do long division. Cognitive psychology is no less interested in your mental processing of arithmetic problems, or in the knowledge you acquired in school, than it is in the informal reasoning processes you used for Question 1. In other words, the fact that you were explicitly taught how to divide doesn't make your mental processes less interesting to study. If anything, it may make them more interesting, since we might be able to find parallels between teaching methods and people's mental processes.

The third question is in many ways more typical of cognitive psychology's interests and research than the first two. For reasons that will become more convincing throughout the book, a great deal of research in cognitive psychology has timed people as they make simple yes/no decisions about questions such as the following:

(3) Does a robin have wings?

Unlike the first two examples, most adults find themselves unable to say much of anything about the train of thoughts they considered when answering this question. Indeed, many people insist, "I just knew the answer was yes." (In honesty, many people also question the sanity of an investigator who asks such trivial questions.) One purpose of the informal analysis for Question 1 was to illustrate just how much of our cognitive processing can occur below the level of awareness; in other words, automatically. As you can no doubt guess by now, cognitive psychology does not find the notion that "I just knew it" to be particularly useful, however certain you are that no other thoughts occurred to you. Clearly, you had to read the words, find their meanings in memory, check the relevant facts, and make your decision in a similar fashion to the previous examples. Each of these steps (and there are many more steps involved here) is a bona fide mental act, the very substance of cognitive psychology. Furthermore, each step takes some amount of time to be completed. A sentence such as Question 3 takes adults about 1.3 seconds to answer; the question "Does a robin have feet?" takes longer, around 1.5 seconds. Even such small time differences can give us a wealth of information about mental processing and human memory.

What does seem strikingly different for Question 3 is that virtually none of the mental processes required much awareness or conscious activity: the question seems to have been processed automatically. Because such automatic processes are so pervasive in mental activity, cognitive psychologists are particularly interested in understanding them.

Summary Points: scope of cognitive psychology; contribution of automatic processes

▼ Memory and Cognition Defined

Now that you have developed an idea of the topics we are concerned with in cognitive psychology, we need to state more formal definitions of the terms *memory* and *cognition*. It will also be useful to spend a moment discussing the topics you will and will not find covered in this text. Most of us have a reasonably good idea of what the term *memory* means, something like "being able to remember or recall" some information. As defined in *Webster's New World Dictionary*, memory consists of "the power, act, or process of recalling to mind facts previously learned or past experiences." Note that both of these definitions are hopelessly circular; memory is "being able to remember" or "the process of recalling to mind." While this circularity is unfortunate, the definitions do point to several critical ideas.[3]

---

[3]Etymologically, the circularity may be unavoidable. The words *memory, remember, mental,* and *mind* all developed from related Indo-European bases, meaning "to think" and "to remember." The base of the word *cognition* means "to know." In our modern usage, cognition refers more to the processes of thinking, and memory more to the knowledge we have acquired and stored. (All etymological sources throughout the book are from *Webster's New World Dictionary of the American Language* unless otherwise noted.)

First, the event or information being recalled from memory is one from the past. In other words, we "remember" things from the past but "experience" things in the present. Quite literally, any past event that is currently recalled is evidence for memory—even those very recent events of the last second or two. Second, memory usually refers to a process, a mental act in which stored information is recovered for some current use. It is this recovery or retrieval of what has been placed in memory that specifies the process of interest, a "getting out" of what was previously "put in." Note that the term *retrieval* here includes both varieties of remembering, the conscious, intentional "recalling to mind" implied in Webster's definition, as well as the more automatic (or even unaware) kind of retrieval discussed in the examples above.

Finally, the term *memory* also refers to a place, a location where all the events, information, and knowledge of a lifetime are stored. This sense of the word is especially evident in those models and theories of cognition that rely on divisions such as short-term and long-term memory. While it is obviously true that there is indeed some physical location within your brain where facts and processes are stored, we are not necessarily trying to pinpoint a physical structure or mechanism in the brain that corresponds to the various memory systems or processes. Instead, this "location" sense of the word is usually taken somewhat metaphorically; regardless of anatomy and physiology, there is some "memory system" that holds information for later retrieval. On the other hand, the neurosciences are making truly remarkable progress in exploring functions and processes as they occur—or occasionally are disrupted—in the brain. (Chapter 10 focuses directly on the work of brain–cognition relationships, based on research in the neurosciences.)

Let's offer a formal definition of the term *memory* now, one that captures the essential ingredients of the discussion above. Consider **memory** to mean *the mental processes of acquiring and retaining information for later retrieval, and the mental storage system that enables these processes.* Operationally, memory is demonstrated when the processes of retention and retrieval influence your behavior or performance in some way, even if you are unaware of the influence. Furthermore, we understand this definition to include not just retention across hours, weeks, or years, but even across very brief spans of time, in any and all situations in which the original stimulus event is no longer present. Note also that *memory* is referring to three different kinds of mental activities in this definition: initial acquisition of information (usually called learning or encoding), subsequent retention of the information, and then retrieval of the information (Melton, 1963). Because all three activities are logically necessary to demonstrate that remembering has taken place, we include them in our broader definition of the term *memory* as well.

The term *cognition* is considerably richer in its connotations and indeed is almost an umbrella term for any and all of the "higher mental processes." Webster's defines it as "the process of knowing in the broadest sense, including perception, memory, judgment, etc." (*Webster's New*

World Dictionary, 1980). *Cognitive Psychology,* Neisser's (1967) land-mark book, claimed that cognition "refers to all the processes by which the sensory input is transformed, reduced, elaborated, stored, recovered, and used [including] terms as *sensation, perception, imagery, retention, recall, problem solving,* and *thinking*" (p. 4). For the present, we will use a definition that is somewhat easier to remember, but just as broad: **cognition** is *the collection of mental processes and activities used in perceiving, remembering, thinking, and understanding, as well as the act of using those processes.*

While our definition of the term *memory* is relatively specific, note that the definition of *cognition* is still somewhat slippery. A term such as *thinking* in a scientific definition virtually begs for clarification, or at least a catalog of examples. You might, in good faith, decide that dreaming is a perfectly valid act of cognition, according to the definition. You would then be puzzled that cognitive psychology generally ignores dreaming (but see G. Mandler, 1984, and also Chapter 13 here). Why do we include some topics but ignore others?

One purpose of the examples in the previous section was to suggest that cognitive psychology is largely, though not exclusively, interested in what might be considered everyday, ordinary mental processes. The processes by which we read and understand, for instance, are entirely commonplace—not simple by any means, but certainly routine. On the other hand, we should not amend the definition to include only "normal" mental activities. It is true that cognitive psychology generally does not deal with the psychologically "abnormal," such as the varieties of thought disturbance associated with schizophrenia (but a cognitive approach to these problems is certainly possible). The problem with excluding the "nonnormal" processes is that the unusual or rare may also be tossed out, impoverishing our science in the process. Rather than change the definition then, we will merely assume that cognition usually refers to those customary, commonplace mental activities that most people engage in as they interact with the world around them. As you'll see, this still casts a rather broad net as we fish for topics to investigate and interpretations to explain our results.

Nonetheless, there are still omissions, sometimes glaring and sometimes not. To the distress of some (e.g., Neisser, 1976), most of our research deals with the sense modalities of vision and hearing, rather than other sensory ways of knowing the world, and focuses very heavily on language; as Keil (1991, p. 287) quipped, "Minds talk a lot . . . they see a little, but they don't feel much else." More disturbing, probably, is our reliance on seemingly sterile experimental techniques and methods (this is Neisser's more substantive criticism), techniques that ask rather simple questions and may therefore yield overly simple views about the operation of cognitive systems. In Neisser's term, much of our cognitive research lacks **ecological validity,** meaning that it is not representative of the real-world situations in which people think and act. As a simple example, imagine how different your reading and comprehension processes would be if you were shown this paragraph one word at a time, each word for only a fraction of a second. The method would prevent you from slowing down when your comprehension lagged, from returning your gaze to a previous word or sentence you may have misinterpreted, and so on. And yet, this method has been used to investigate reading and comprehension.

While Neisser's criticism was sensible, it was also possibly premature. We find great complexity in cognitive processing, even when artificially simple tasks are performed. At our current level of sophistication, we truly might be overwhelmed if our tasks were also permitted to be more complex, or if we tried to investigate the full range of a behavior in all its detail and nuance. In other words, in the early stage of investigation it is reasonable for scientists to take a *reductionistic approach* to complex events, attempting to understand them by investigating their components. After all, an artificially simple situation can sometimes reveal rather than obscure a process, and sometimes we gain insight by preventing a process from occurring in its regular fashion (see Mook, 1983, for a fine discussion of the entire issue of ecological validity). Of course, it is also reasonable to expect that scientists will eventually put the pieces back together again and deal with the larger event as a whole. In fact, recent developments seem to hold just that sort of promise.

Summary Points: definitions of memory and cognition; ecological validity versus reductionism

▼ An Introductory History of Cognitive Psychology[4]

Having presented cognitive psychology to you first by example, then by definition, we now present it in terms of its history and development. This treatment should give you a better appreciation of what cognitive psychology is, and how it became so (more thorough presentations of this material are listed in the Suggested Readings at the end of the chapter). Figure 1-1 summarizes the main patterns of influence that produced cognitive psychology. As you read, study the figure to decide which pathways indicate positive influences, where ideas and questions from an earlier movement continued to inspire the approach that followed, and which pathways indicate negative influences, where the later approach specifically rejected elements of its predecessor.

To a remarkable extent, the scientific study of human memory and cognition is quite new. Although elements of our explanations, and cer-

---

[4]I have relied extensively on Leahey's fine book *A History of Psychology* (1992a) in this section. And my intellectual debt to Lachman, Lachman, and Butterfield (1979), especially on the development of cognitive psychology, is especially apparent. Readers should consult both sources to flesh out my sketchy summary of this fascinating story.

FIGURE 1-1

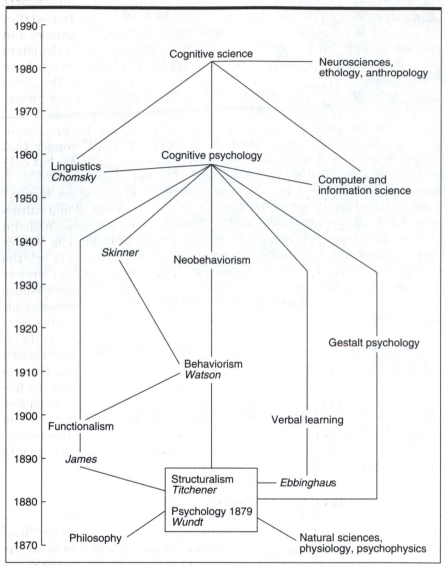

tainly many of our experimental tasks, appeared even in the earliest years of psychology, the relevant body of work and theorizing has been created since the 1950s. And yet, as is true of most topics in psychology, interest in human memory and cognitive processes is as old as recorded history. Aristotle, born in 384 B.C., considered the basic principles of human memory and proposed a theory of memory in his treatise *De Memoria* [Concerning Memory] (Hothersall, 1984). Even a casual reading of ancient works such as Homer's *The Iliad* or *The Odyssey* reveals that people have always wondered about how the mind works and how to improve its functioning (as told in Plato's *Phaedrus,* Socrates fretted that the invention of written language would weaken reliance on memory and understanding, much the way modern parents worry that calculators will weaken children's learning of math). Philosophers of every age have considered questions of the nature of thought and memory. Descartes even decided that the ultimate proof of human existence is our awareness of our own thought—*Cogito ergo sum,* "I think therefore I am" (Descartes, 1637, p. 52, in Hothersall, 1984, p. 28). Given this preoccupation with thought and mind in Western culture, it is no wonder that Ebbinghaus's (1908, p. 1) comment, "psychology has a long past but only a short history," is so widely repeated in histories of psychology.

The critical events at the beginning of psychology's "short history" were in the late 1800s. It was as if the important intellectual and cultural influences of the day converged most strongly on one man—Wilhelm Wundt—and on one place, Leipzig, Germany. In 1879, Wilhelm Wundt established the first laboratory for psychological experiments, at the University of Leipzig. Of course, several notable individuals had already begun what was later seen as research on psychological topics—Weber and Fechner's work in psychophysics and Helmholtz's discoveries about the speed of neural impulses, for instance. There was even a laboratory established by William James, the American psychologist, in 1875, although it apparently was used largely for classroom demonstrations rather than experimental studies.[5] Despite these developments, there is a general consensus that the date of 1879 marks the beginning of the formal academic, empirical discipline of psychology, a separate discipline from either philosophy or physiology. Wundt, of course, built his work on the advances that came before him, developments that gave rise to psychology and psychological research. It is these developments we turn to now.

Anticipations of Psychology

Let's begin with Aristotle, who for two reasons is the historical "first" we typically point to in psychology. Aristotle is generally viewed as the first philosopher to have advocated an empirically based "natural science" approach to understanding. While he was certainly not the only great thinker to have insisted on observation as the basis for all science, he did "get there first" with this fundamentally important idea. Second, Aristotle's inquiry into the nature of thought and mind by his own natural science method led him to a reasonably objective explanation of how

---

[5]Watson (1968) points out that James and Wundt both established their labs in 1875 and insists that the 1879 date is notable only "for the appearance of the first student to do publishable psychological research with Wundt" (p. 266). Hothersall, on the other hand, suggests that the 1875 Wundt lab was largely for class demonstration purposes, with experiments independent of such demonstrations beginning only in 1879. The American Psychological Association gave its blessing to the 1879 date, and we celebrated the centennial of Psychology in the year 1979.

learning and memory take place. This explanation could not truly be considered a theory of memory, by modern standards, nor should we expect it to be. On the other hand, the basic principle that Aristotle identified, that of *associations,* has certainly figured prominently in most psychological theories of the past century.

Equally important to psychology as a whole was Aristotle's insistence that the mind is a "blank slate" at birth, a *tabula rasa* or clean sheet of paper (Watson, 1968; this term is also frequently translated as the "blank wax tablet"). This notion claims that the experiences of the individual are of paramount importance, since experience, rather than inborn factors, "writes" a record onto the blank paper. It is possible that no other issue has so preoccupied philosophers of all ages, an issue we refer to as the "nature/nurture" or "heredity/environment" debate. In cognitive psychology, we encounter the controversy in several places, most notably when we discuss theories of language and its acquisition (see Chapter 8).

Most of the other anticipations of psychology date from the Renaissance and later periods and largely consist of developments in the area of scientific methods and approaches. By the mid-1800s, positions such as Descartes's "rational" approach had been discarded by scientists, in favor of observational or empirical methods. Thus by the time psychology appeared, the general procedures of scientific inquiry had been developed and were, for the most part, accepted by all scientific disciplines and areas. There was widespread agreement on the need for science to be based on objective procedures and methods such as careful quantification and definition, empirical observation, and so on (obviously, the agreement continues through the present). Given the notable progress made in scientific fields such as physics, biology, and medicine by the mid-1800s, it is not surprising that the early psychologists thought the time was ripe for a true "science of the mind."

Early Psychology

Four early psychologists are of particular interest in our study of cognitive psychology. They are Wilhelm Wundt, Edward Titchener, Hermann von Ebbinghaus, and William James.

Wilhelm Wundt To a large extent, the early psychologists were students of Wilhelm Wundt (1832–1920); this was especially true for the early American psychologists (Benjamin, Durkin, Link, Vestal, & Acord, 1992). Beginning in 1875, when he moved to the University of Leipzig, he directed over 100 doctoral theses on psychological topics. Such important psychologists as William James, Hugo Munsterberg, Charles Spearman, James McKeen Cattell, and Edward Titchener studied with Wundt, investigating primarily those topics that Wundt felt were appropriate to

Wilhelm Wundt

the new "science of the mind." Wundt continually updated his book *Principles of Physiological Psychology,* reporting new results obtained in his laboratory, and also founded the first journal devoted to psychological research, *Philosophical Studies* (neither of these titles seems to match modern connotations of the terms). His influence was far reaching, since his was the first truly psychological system. In fact, Leahey (1992b) credits Wundt with starting the first—and only—true scientific revolution in psychology. Unfortunately for the future of psychology, Wundt's interests in the last 20 years of his career went largely unrecognized until quite recently. His work on language, child psychology, and other topics was virtually rejected by the influential Titchener, who believed these topics simply did not belong in psychology (even Wundt questioned how adequately they could be studied experimentally). American psychologists may have even found an additional excuse for their narrow and biased attitudes; Wundt was an enthusiastic German nationalist during World War I (Benjamin et al., 1992).

Wundt believed strongly that the proper topic for psychology to study was "conscious processes and immediate experience"; today, we would place these topics somewhere near the areas of sensation, perception, and attention. To study such processes in a scientific manner, an approach to which Wundt was thoroughly dedicated, he devised the methodology of *selbst-beobachtung.* Translated literally as "self-observation," this method of investigation is generally known in English as **introspection,** a method in which one looks carefully "inward," reporting on inner sensations and experiences. By all accounts, Wundt intended this to be a careful, reliable, and, above all else, scientific method. For instance, Hothersall (1984) notes: "Wundt's introspection was a rigidly controlled, arduous, experimental procedure. . . . To yield valid introspections Wundt insisted that certain rules be enforced: the observer had to be 'master of the situation,' that is, in a state of 'strained attention'. . . . All observations were to be repeated many times; and finally, experimental conditions were to be varied systematically to allow a general description of mental contents" (pp. 88–89). The observers in these experiments required a great deal of training in the method, so that they would report only those elements of experience that were "immediate" and conscious. Reports in which memory intruded— Wundt's term was *mediate experience*—were excluded.

Edward Titchener   For American psychology in Wundt's tradition, the most important figure was Edward Titchener, an Englishman who came to Cornell University in 1892 to direct its psychology laboratory. Titchener's work with Wundt had convinced him that psychology's knowledge was obtainable only with the introspective method. As his career at Cornell progressed, Titchener became even more firm in this conviction and even more narrow in his definition of psychology. Concerns with mental illness, educational applications, social psychology, and other areas (including Wundt's broader interests as well) were "impure," since they could not be studied with introspective methods. Like Wundt, Titchener insisted on careful control and rigorous training for his introspectors, who were required to avoid what he called "the stimulus error" of describing the physical stimulus rather than the mental experience of that stimulus. Moreover, "certain introspections were defined as correct, and certain others as in error, with the final authority being Titchener himself" (Hothersall, 1984, p. 105). By these means, Titchener studied the structure of the conscious mind, the sensations, images, and feelings that were the very elements of the mind's structure. The term he used to describe this psychology was **structuralism,** the first major movement or school of psychological thought (see Figure 1-1).

As you might expect, such an exclusive system of psychology, relying as it did on the ultimate authority of Titchener to validate its observations, was destined for difficulties. As other researchers applied the introspective methods in their own laboratories, differences and contradictory results began to crop up. For instance, a controversy developed over "imageless thought." Researchers of the Würzburg School found evidence for imageless thought in their studies. When Titchener found no such evidence in his own studies, he claimed that the Würzburg researchers' findings were wrong, merely the product of sloppy methods and poorly trained observers. (In a similar dispute, over sensory and motor reaction times, Titchener's methodological criticism was that the subjects had been untrained observers. He would surely have disapproved of modern insistence on naive volunteers from Intro Psych.) These disputes, along with other developments, hastened the decline of Titchener's once-powerful structuralism.

Hermann von Ebbinghaus   In contrast to the doomed structuralism of Wundt and Titchener, there was the theoretically modest but

Hermann von Ebbinghaus

eventually more influential work of Hermann von Ebbinghaus (see Chapter 5). Ebbinghaus was a contemporary of Wundt in Germany, although he never studied with Wundt in person. In fact, Ebbinghaus's achievements in studying human memory and forgetting are all the more impressive largely because he worked outside the "establishment" of the time. Watson (1968) notes that Ebbinghaus was familiar with Wundt's writings but, if anything, viewed Wundt's pessimism about studying higher mental processes as a challenge rather than a deterrent to pursuing that work. Historical accounts suggest that Ebbinghaus read Wundt's book, decided instead that a study of the mind by objective methods *was* possible, and set about the task of figuring out how to do it.

Lacking a formal laboratory and serving in a nonpsychological academic position with no similar-minded colleagues, Ebbinghaus was forced to rely on his own resources to study memory, even to the extent that he alone served as a subject in his research. Ebbinghaus's goal was to study the mind's process of association formation, using thoroughly objective methods. He reasoned that for this goal to be accomplished, he needed to use materials that had no preexisting associations. Thus the first step in his method involved the construction of stimulus lists of "nonsense syllables," C-V-C (consonant–vowel–consonant) triads that seemingly by definition were of uniform meaningfulness: to wit, they had no meaning whatsoever. Following this, Ebbinghaus would learn a list, say, of 16 items, to an arbitrary criterion of mastery, say, two perfect recitations, then set the list aside. On some later occasion, he would relearn the same list, noting how many fewer trials he needed for relearning to the same criterion. The measure of learning in these studies was the "savings score," the number (or proportion) of trials that had been "saved" in memory between the first and second sessions. By this method, Ebbinghaus examined forgetting as a function of time that intervened between the two learning sessions, degree of learning or over-

William James

learning, and even the effect of nonsense versus meaningful material (he compared forgetting curves for nonsense syllables versus meaningful poetry).

Ebbinghaus's methods and results, described in his 1885 book, were acclaimed widely as the very model of scientific inquiry into the processes of memory; for instance, Titchener praised Ebbinghaus's work as the most significant progress in studying associations since Aristotle (1919; cited in Hall, 1971). Indeed, it is difficult to point to another psychologist of his day, aside from Freud, whose specific contributions or methods continue to be used. It is certainly true that the field of verbal learning, throughout the 20th century, owed a great deal to Ebbinghaus; after all, he was the first to invent a reasonably scientific, enduring method to study memory and mental processes. The Ebbinghaus tradition, depicted in Figure 1-1, is in many ways the strongest of all the influences on cognitive psychology. No other influence in the figure is as positive as this century-old tradition begun by Ebbinghaus.

William James   The American philosopher and psychologist William James, a contemporary of Wundt, Titchener, and Ebbinghaus, provided at Harvard an alternative to Titchener's rigid system. His approach to psychology was a kind of **functionalism** in which the functions of consciousness, rather than its structure, were of interest. Thus James asked questions such as "How does the mind function?" and "How does it adapt to new circumstances?"

James's rather informal analyses led to some strikingly useful observations on a variety of topics in psychology. To note one of interest to us, he proposed that memory consists of two parts, an immediately available memory of which we are currently aware, and a larger memory, usually hidden or passive, that is the repository for past experience. The notion of a memory system divided into several parts, based on their different functions, is a widely popular idea today. Indeed, the first serious models of human information processing, in the 1950s and 1960s, included exactly the two kinds of memories that James discussed in 1890.

Probably because of his personal distaste for experimentation and his far-reaching interests beyond the topic of memory, James seems not to have espoused the Ebbinghaus methods of studying memory, although he apparently had high regard for Ebbinghaus's work. Titchener no doubt dismissed James and his writings, since James was only a "half hearted" researcher (Boring, 1950) and interested in topics Titchener found inappropriate. Ultimately, however, James's far-reaching thought was far more influential to the whole of psychology than any of Titchener's work (see Miller's introduction to the 1983 edition of James's 1890 book).

Given other developments at the time, however, James's influence on the psychology of human memory and cognition was considerably delayed. For it was John B. Watson, in 1913, who stridently proclaimed—and possibly solidified—the new direction that American psychology was taking, a direction that specifically rejected both the structuralist and functionalist approaches as well as many of their concerns. This new direction, of course, was behaviorism.

Behaviorism and Neobehaviorism[6]

To begin with, it is a mistake to suggest that all American psychology from 1910 through the 1950s was completely and thoroughly behaviorist in its viewpoint. During this period, the fields of clinical, educational, and social psychology, to name just a few, continued in their own development, pursuing their own agendas. In a sense, these other branches of psychology developed in parallel to behaviorism: they were contemporary fields with little contact or mutual influence. Furthermore, Leahey (1992a) notes that there were significant changes within behaviorism itself, changes that eventually smoothed the transition to cognitive psychology. Nonetheless, experimental psychology has traditionally been the discipline of researchers concerned with learning, memory, perception, thought, and related topics. It was these psychologists, mostly in

---

[6]I am treating behaviorism and neobehaviorism here as if they were identical, which is clearly an oversimplification. The basic difference between behaviorism and neobehaviorism was that the neobehaviorists included a limited number and kind of "internal" and unobservable mechanisms in their theories, while the earlier behaviorists (and Skinner, for that matter) restricted themselves only to observables. A classic example was Hull's (1943) intervening variable of habit strength, sHr, an unobservable, *mediating* variable between the observable stimulus and the overt response. While such variables were clearly not the mental mechanisms or processes of cognitive psychology, their necessity in neobehaviorist theories set a strong precedent for theorizing about the unobservable. According to Leahey (1992a), it was this "mediated" nature of neobehaviorism that paved the way for cognitive science.

academic settings, who were responsible for the birth and rearing of behaviorism and for its eventual dominance in American experimental psychology.

Everyone who has taken introductory psychology knows of John B. Watson, the early behaviorist who offered: "Give me a dozen healthy infants, well-formed, and my own specified world to bring them up in and I'll guarantee to take any one at random and train him to become any type of specialist I might select—doctor, lawyer, artist, merchant, chief and, yes, even beggarman and thief, regardless of the talents, penchants, tendencies, abilities, vocations, and race of his ancestors" (Watson, 1924, p. 104). Although Watson admitted in his very next sentence that he was exaggerating, he made it clear that he viewed experience as the primary factor in determining even the largest aspects of one's behavior. Rarely in the history of science has anyone taken so extreme a position on the nature/nurture issue as Watson did (histories of psychology note that this extreme position of "environmentalism" was not typical of his early, scholarly works, but only of his later writings).

Watson's firm belief, stated unequivocally in his 1913 "manifesto," was that observable, quantifiable behavior was the proper topic of psychology, not the fuzzy and unscientific concepts of thought, mind, and consciousness. He viewed any and all attempts to understand the "unobservables" of mind and thought as inherently and hopelessly unscientific and pointed to the unresolved debates in structuralism as evidence. Thus psychology was redefined as the scientific study of behavior, the program of **behaviorism.** There was no room here for hidden or internal mental processes, since behavioral laws were supposed to relate observable behavior to objective, observable stimulus conditions within the environment. To Watson then, being a doctor was merely a matter of learning appropriate "doctor behaviors." No appeal to the mind, to innate abilities, or to mental activities was at all necessary, and no important limitations on the learning process were acknowledged.

Why did such a radical redefinition of psychology's interests have such broad appeal, gain so many adherents, and become so dominant? There is no doubt that part of the enthusiasm for a psychology of behavior, and the belief that a science of behavior was a reasonable goal, was the work that Pavlov and others were doing on learning. Here was a definite, scientific methodology and approach that was going somewhere, in contrast to the seemingly endless debates in structuralism. (Strangely, Watson seems to have been unaware of Ebbinghaus's careful, empirical studies of learning and memory, work that even the dogmatic Titchener saw as valuable.) Furthermore, the measurement and quantification that accompanied behaviorism seemed to be a hallmark of the already successful sciences like physics. By modeling psychology on their methods and quantification, psychology might gain acceptance as a true science as well (Leahey, 1992a, refers to this mentality as "physics envy").

Beginning in the late 1890s (Leahey, 1992a), the new behaviorism attracted many practitioners and adherents; in a sense then, Watson's paper in 1913 was not a rallying point but instead marked the final triumph of the behaviorist approach. Not all were eager to climb on this bandwagon, however. There was, naturally enough, an early wait-and-see attitude on the part of some. For instance, Titchener's loyal student Edwin G. Boring, whose definitive book *A History of Experimental Psychology* appeared in 1929, condescended in his preface that behaviorism was "as yet undignified by the least trace of antiquity." In his 1950 edition, however, Boring admits that "for a while in the 1920s it seemed as if all America had gone behaviorist" (p. 645, although this admission is contained in a chapter somewhat pejoratively called "Behavioristics"). And other research traditions, especially the *verbal learning* tradition begun by Ebbinghaus (see below), continued their work. But these traditions became "second class citizens," in a sense, as behaviorism's emphasis on observable stimuli and responses came to dominate American experimental psychology.

From the standpoint of cognitive psychology, this period of behaviorism and then neobehaviorism was one of relative inactivity, owing to the influence of Watson and the other leading behaviorists. For instance, note that the word most commonly used to describe Watson is *antimentalistic.* Any concept or idea that smacked of mentalism, such as *consciousness, memory,* and *mind,* was to be excluded from psychology, according to Watson's view. This restriction in the scope of psychology, in hindsight, seems almost a willful and deliberate blindness to the existence of obviously important phenomena. And it certainly produced some curious and convoluted explanations. For instance, because of the need to explain such ostensibly mental activities as thought and language in nonmentalistic terms, Watson developed the notion of "implicit behavior." Implicit or covert behavior was a reduced, inner version of the normally observable behavior that psychology investigated. Thus "thought" to Watson was "nothing more than subvocal talking or muscular habits learned in overt speech which become inaudible as we grow up" (Watson, 1968, p. 427; no relation to John B.).

While a few psychologists continued to pursue cognitive topics—Bartlett of Great Britain being a notable example—the most visible part of American experimental psychology focused instead on observable, learned behaviors, especially those of animals. Even the decidedly cognitive approach of Tolman, whose paper "Cognitive Maps in Rats and Men" (1948) is still worth reading, included much of the behaviorist tradition—concern with the learning of new behaviors, animal studies, and interpretation based closely on the observable stimuli in an experimental situation. Gestalt psychology, which emigrated to the United States in the 1930s (Mandler & Mandler, 1969), always maintained an interest in human perception, thought, and problem solving but never captured the loyalties of many American experimentalists (although we look back now at some of their research with greater respect).

Thus the behaviorist viewpoint continued to dominate American experimental psychology until the 1940s, when B. F. Skinner emerged as one of its most vocal, even extreme, advocates. Much in keeping with Watson's earlier sentiments, Skinner also argued that mental events such as thought have no place in the science of psychology—not that they are not real, necessarily, just that they are unobservable and hence unnecessary to a scientific explanation of behavior.

Dissatisfaction with Behaviorism: The Winds of Change

As we saw earlier, it is difficult, if not impossible, to determine precisely when historical change takes place, when a movement or trend gains sufficient recognition to be proclaimed a *fait accompli*. We agree that 1879 saw the founding of academic, empirical psychology, yet we point to important research, and even to books with "psychology" in their titles, that predate 1879. Watson's 1913 paper has been viewed as the agent of change in instituting behaviorism, yet it just as clearly can be viewed as the culmination of two decades of gradually shifting allegiances. It is even more difficult to pinpoint historical change when it is recent and somewhat controversial. Many current psychologists look kindly on the idea that there was indeed a "cognitive revolution" in the mid- to late 1950s—an abrupt change in research activities, interests, and scientific beliefs on the part of experimentalists, a definitive break from the previously dominant behaviorism. And indeed, it is indisputably true that the experimental psychology of today is radically different from that of the 1940s and 1950s. Psychology seemed to "lose its head" during behaviorism's day in the sense that memory, thought, and other mental activities were largely ignored. To continue the figure of speech, our psychology of today has "come back to its senses," and to its memory and mental activities as well.

Because of the nature and scope of these changes, many psychologists regard the current cognitive approach as a revolution, a revolution in which behaviorism was rejected due to its lack of progress on—or even interest in—important questions. It was replaced with cognitive psychology and the information processing approach. Lachman et al. (1979) provide an especially compelling account of the cognitive revolution, from the standpoint of Kuhn's (1962) classic work on the history of science. Some historians, however, claim that the cognitive revolution was not a true scientific revolution at all, but merely "rapid, evolutionary change" (see Leahey, 1992a,b, for this lively counterargument). In either case, the years from 1945 through 1960 were a period of crisis for American neobehaviorism and of rapid reform in the thinking and research of experimental psychologists. The serious challenges to neobehaviorism came both from within its own ranks and from outside, prodding psychologists along toward the new direction to be taken.[7]

Challenges and Changes: The 1940s and 1950s   To neobehaviorism, the ultimate importance of learning—the acquisition of new behaviors by means of conditioning—was an absolute article of faith. This *was* psychology. While some behaviorists paid lip service to the notion of instincts, species-specific behaviors, and other nonlearned sorts of behavior, none of the important theories of learning gave serious consideration to these ideas. Speaking anthropomorphically, the animal subjects often thumbed their noses at such theoretical purity and proceeded to behave according to their own laws. Researchers began finding significant instances in which conditioned behaviors, supposedly under the control of reinforced learning, would begin to change in the direction of instinctive behavior. For instance, "the Brelands found instances in which animals did not perform as they should. In 1961, they reported their difficulties in a paper whose title, 'The Misbehavior of Organisms,' puns on Skinner's first book, *The Behavior of Organisms*. For example, they tried to teach pigs to carry wooden coins and deposit them in a piggy bank. Although they could teach the behaviors, the Brelands found that the behavior degenerated in pig after pig. The animals would eventually pick up the coin, drop it on the ground and root it . . . [as if] 'trapped by strong instinctive behaviors' that overwhelm learned behaviors" (Leahey, 1992a, p. 422).

For the theoretical system of behaviorism, committed to the *tabula rasa* position that exalts learned behaviors, this was a serious difficulty. No ready explanation was available to account for this instinctive drift by means of the principles of reinforced learning. And incorporating instincts into the theories would have been a blunt admission that the laws of conditioning and learning were not general, that they were modified by other overpowering, central factors. To make matters worse, Skinner asserted that a theory of behavior was not even necessary, finding theory building to be somewhat of a distraction from the main business of gathering data. Such a position seemed to undermine the intense efforts that had been exerted in developing and testing theoretical posi-

---

[7]It is not clear what definition Leahey uses to distinguish "revolution" from "rapid evolutionary change." He credits Wundt with the one and only scientific revolution in psychology, despite the intellectual movements that predated the 1879 lab, and the lack of an accepted paradigm prior to that date. The situation in the 1940s and 1950s would appear to be similar, yet does not qualify as "revolution" for Leahey. Just as he asserts that the American revolution was "not a revolution at all" (1992a, p. 458), he claims that "cognitive scientists believe in a revolution because it provides them with an origin myth, an account of their beginnings that helps legitimize their practice of science" (p. 458), a psychological "radical chic" of the 1960s and 1970s.

tions such as Hull's (1943) or Tolman's (1948). What an unpleasant time to have been a behaviorist, beset by significant nonlearned behaviors, by unresolvable theoretical disputes, and by a position that asserted that theorizing was a waste of time!

World War II   Lachman et al. (1979) make an additional point concerning this growing dissatisfaction within the ranks of the neobehaviorists. They note that many academic psychologists were involved, in one capacity or another, with the U.S. war effort during World War II. Psychologists accustomed to studying animal learning in the laboratory were "put to work on the practical problems of making war . . . trying to understand problems of perception, judgment, thinking, and decision making" (p. 56). Many of these problems arose because of soldiers' difficulties with sophisticated technical devices—skilled pilots who crashed their aircraft, radar and sonar operators who either failed to detect or misidentified an "enemy blip," and so on.

Lachman et al. (1979) are quite succinct in their description of this situation: "Where could psychologists turn for concepts and methods to help them solve such problems? Certainly not to the academic laboratories of the day. The behavior of animals in mazes shed little light on the performance of airplane pilots and sonar operators. The kind of learning studied with nonsense syllables contributed little to psychologists trying to teach people how to operate complex machines accurately. In fact, learning was not the central problem during the war. Most problems arose after the tasks had already been learned, when normally skillful performance broke down. The focus was on performance rather than learning; and this left academic psychologists poorly prepared" (pp. 56–57). As Bruner, Goodnow, and Austin (1956) put it, the "impeccable peripheralism" of stimulus–response (S-R) behaviorism became painfully obvious in the face of such practical concerns.

To deal with these practical concerns, wartime psychologists were forced to conceive of human behavior in a different fashion. The concepts of attention and vigilance, for instance, were important to an understanding of radar operators' performance; experiments on the practical and then theoretical aspects of vigilance began (see especially Broadbent, 1958, Chapter 6, and Wickens, 1984, on the emergence of Human Factors as a distinct area of psychology). Decision making was a necessary part of this performance too, and from these considerations came such developments as signal detection theory. Beyond this, these wartime psychologists also rubbed shoulders with professionals from different fields—those in communications engineering, for instance, from whom new outlooks and perspectives on human behavior were gained. They had seen firsthand how relatively empty the behaviorist "toolbox" was, and how other approaches held promise for their own work. Thus these psychologists returned to their laboratories after the war deter-

THE FAR SIDE   By GARY LARSON

THE FAR SIDE copyright 1985, 1986 & 1991 FARWORKS, INC. Distributed by UNIVERSAL PRESS SYNDICATE. Reprinted with permission. All rights reserved.

"Stimulus, response! Stimulus, response!
Don't you ever *think*?"

mined to broaden their own research interests and those of psychology as well.

Verbal Learning   The term *verbal learning* is the label attached to that branch of experimental psychology that dealt with human subjects as they learned "verbal material," items or stimuli composed of letters or sometimes words. Earlier, the ground-breaking research of Hermann von Ebbinghaus was mentioned, in which desirably objective methods for studying human memory were invented and used. This work started the verbal learning tradition within experimental psychology (see Chapter 5). Even casual examination of published articles during the 1920s and 1930s reveals a fairly large body of verbal learning research, with reasonably well-established methods and procedures. Tasks such as serial learning, paired-associate learning, and to an extent free recall were the accepted methods of investigation, using Ebbinghaus-inspired nonsense syllables.

Verbal learning held many beliefs that were similar to those of the behaviorists. For example, those in verbal learning agreed on the necessity of using objective methods; although an occasional allusion to subjects' introspections was made, this was usually in the sense that they "confirmed" the conclusions drawn from more objective measures. There was widespread acceptance of the central role of learning as well, conceived as a process of forming new associations. And yet, much like their forefather Ebbinghaus, the verbal learners were curiously atheoretical, interested more in pursuing "fruitful" avenues of research than building theoretical edifices. They were "behavior*alists*," in Leahey's (1992b) description, committed to the methods of observing behavior to be sure, but not bound to either the "empty organism" view of radical behaviorism or any other theoretical movement: they were theoretical agnostics, as it were.

Lachman et al. have argued that this atheoretical viewpoint in verbal learning circles made it quite easy for psychologists to accept the new cognitive psychology of the 1950s and 1960s: if you're not committed to a theory, you don't mind switching to another when the time comes. It clearly also made them more open-minded, to be frank. There were many indications in their results that an adequate psychology of human learning and memory needed more than just observable behaviors. For instance, the presence of meaningfulness in virtually any "nonsense" syllable had been acknowledged early on; Glaze (1928) entitled his paper "The Association Value of Nonsense Syllables" (and apparently did so with a straight face). At first, such troublesome associations were merely controlled in the experiments, to avoid contamination of the results. Later, it became apparent that the memory processes that yielded those associations were in fact more interesting to study than to control. Hall (1971) termed this the "new look" in verbal learning, with its greater emphasis on memory rather than learning processes.

In this tradition, Bousfield (1953; Bousfield & Sedgewick, 1944) reported that, under free recall instructions, words that were associated with one another (e.g., *car* and *truck*) tended to "cluster together" in recall, even though they had been arranged randomly in the stimulus list. In this research, there was clearly the implication that existing memory associations led to the reorganization of the words during recall. Such obvious evidence for processes occurring *between* the stimulus and the response—in other words, mental processes—slowly led verbal learning to propose a variety of mental operations such as rehearsal, organization, storage, and retrieval. The lack of theoretical commitment to the behaviorist canon of antimentalism facilitated this change.

We can point to one outstanding achievement of the verbal learning tradition, however theoretically undeveloped the work was. To a very large extent, the researchers in the verbal learning area devised laboratory tasks of learning and memory that remain useful today. In their acceptance of the scientific need for objective procedures and methods, the verbal learners borrowed from Ebbinghaus's example of careful attention to rigorous methodology. From this they developed tasks that, we still agree, seem to measure the outcomes of mental processes in valid and useful ways. Some of these tasks, naturally, were more closely associated with behaviorism than others, for instance, the paired-associate learning task. Because these tasks lent themselves to tests of S-R associations in seemingly direct ways, they became somewhat overused. (Some have noted the popularity of the paired-associate task and the verbal learners' tendency to study performance on the task rather than the principles of human memory revealed by the task. A professor of mine likened this situation to "an archaeologist who studies his shovel.") Nonetheless, verbal learning gave cognitive psychology an objective, reliable methodology for studying mental processes, research that would be built upon later (e.g., Stroop, 1935), and a set of inferred processes such as storage and retrieval to begin investigating. As such, the influence from verbal learning to cognitive psychology, as shown in Figure 1-1, was almost entirely positive.

Linguistics   The changes in verbal learning from its early work to its emergence as cognitive psychology around 1960 seem to have been quite evolutionary, a gradual shifting of interests and interpretations that blended almost seamlessly into cognitive psychology. In sharp contrast to this, the year 1959 saw the publication of an explicit, defiant challenge to behaviorism. Watson's 1913 paper has been called a "behaviorist manifesto," crystallizing the view against introspective methods and those who practiced them. To an equal degree, Noam Chomsky's 1959 paper was a "cognitive manifesto," an utter rejection of purely behaviorist explanation of that most human of all behaviors—language.

A bit of background is necessary in order to appreciate the significance of Chomsky's paper. In 1957, B. F. Skinner published a book entitled *Verbal Behavior,* a treatment of human language from the radical behaviorist standpoint of reinforcement, stimulus–response associations, extinction, and so on. His central point in this book was that the psychology of learning, that is, the conditioning of new behavior by means of reinforcement, provided a useful and scientific account of human language use. In oversimplified terms, Skinner's basic notion was that human language use, "verbal behavior," followed the same laws of learning that had been discovered in the animal learning laboratory: a reinforced response is expected to increase in frequency, a nonreinforced response should extinguish, a response conditioned to a certain stimulus should be emitted to the same stimulus in the future, and so on. In principle then, human language, obviously a learned behavior, could be explained by the same sort of mechanism as *any* learned behavior—with knowledge of the current reinforcement contingencies and past reinforcement history of the individual.

Noam Chomsky, a linguist at M.I.T., reviewed Skinner's book in the

Noam Chomsky

journal *Language* in 1959. The very first sentence of his review notes that many linguists and philosophers of language had "expressed the hope that their studies might ultimately be embedded in a framework provided by behaviorist psychology" and as such were interested in Skinner's formulation. Chomsky alluded to Skinner's optimism that the problem of verbal behavior would yield to behavioral analysis, since the reinforcement principles discovered in the animal laboratory "are now fairly well understood . . . [and] can be extended to human behavior without serious modification" (Skinner, 1957, cited in Chomsky, 1959, p. 26).

And yet on the third page of his review, Chomsky states that "the insights that have been achieved in the laboratories of the reinforcement theorist, though quite genuine, can be applied to complex human behavior only in the most gross and superficial way. . . . The magnitude of the failure of [Skinner's] attempt to account for verbal behavior serves as a kind of measure of the importance of the factors *omitted* from consideration" (p. 28, emphasis added). The fighting words continued. Chomsky asserted that if the critical terms *stimulus, response, reinforcement,* and so on are used in their technical, animal laboratory sense, then "the book covers almost no aspect of linguistic behavior" (p. 31) of interest. His central theme was that Skinner's account used the technical terms in a non-technical, metaphorical way, which "creates the illusion of a rigorous scientific theory [but] is no more scientific than the traditional approaches to this subject matter, and rarely as clear and careful" (pp. 30–31).

To illustrate his criticism, Chomsky noted the careful operational definitions that Skinner provides in the animal learning laboratory, for instance, for the terms *response* and *reinforcement.* But unlike the distinct and observable pellet of food in the Skinner box, Skinner claimed that reinforcement for verbal behavior can be administered by the person emitting the behavior, that is, self-reinforcement. In some cases, Skinner continued, reinforcement could be delayed for indefinite periods, or never be delivered at all, as in the case of a writer who anticipates that her work may gain her fame for centuries to come. When an explicit and immediate reinforcer in the laboratory, along with its effect on behavior, is generalized to include nonexplicit and nonimmediate (and even nonexistent!) reinforcers in the real world, it truly does seem, as Chomsky argued, that Skinner had brought along the vocabulary of a scientific explanation but left the substance behind. As Chomsky bluntly put it, "A mere terminological revision, in which a term borrowed from the laboratory is used with the full vagueness of the ordinary vocabulary, is of no conceivable interest" (p. 38). The explanation was merely dogmatic, and not at all scientific.

Chomsky's own position on language, emphasizing the novelty of human language and the internal rules for language use, will be discussed in Chapter 8; there, the strong influence of linguistics on cognitive psychology (Figure 1-1) will be described in some detail. For now, the essential message involves the impact that Chomsky's review had on experimental psychology (not to mention the impact on linguistics itself; see Wasow, 1989). As Lachman et al. (1979) point out, this was not a dispute that could easily be dismissed by psychologists as irrelevant. No, language *was* an important behavior—and a learned one at that—to be understood by psychology. A dominant approach that offered no help in understanding such an important behavior was useless, not to mention embarrassing.

To a significant number of individuals, Chomsky's arguments summarized the dissatisfactions with behaviorism that had become so very apparent. For these individuals, the irrelevance of behaviorism to the study of language, and by extension to the study of any significant human behavior, was now painfully obvious. In combination with the other developments, the wartime fling with mental processes, the expansion of the catalog of such processes by verbal learning, and the disarray within behaviorism itself, it was clear that the new direction for psychology, growing in influence throughout the 1950s, would take hold.

Summary Points: associations from Aristotle to Skinner; the establishment of psychology by Wundt; Watson's behaviorism; dissatisfactions with behaviorism; verbal learning; Chomsky's attack

▼ Cognitive Psychology and Information Processing: The New Direction

If we had to pick a date that marks the beginning of cognitive psychology, one that indicates as accurately as possible when cognitive psychology started, we might pick 1960. This is not to say that significant developments in the study of cognition weren't present before this date, for they were. This is also not to say that most experimental psychologists who studied humans "became" cognitive psychologists that year, for they didn't. As with any major change, it takes a while for the new approach to catch on, for people to learn the new rules, to feel free to speak the new language, and, indeed, to decide that the new direction is worth following.[8] Several significant events clustered around the year 1960, however, events we look back on from our short period of hindsight as having been significant departures from the mainstream that came before. Just as 1879 approximates the formal beginning of psychology, and 1913 the beginning of behaviorism, so 1960 seems to approximate the beginning of cognitive psychology in its modern form.[9]

Let's pick up the threads of what came before this date, to see what the new cognitive psychology and information processing approaches were all about. One of the most significant threads, of course, was Chomsky's 1959 review; such a forceful argument against a purely behaviorist position could not be ignored. Chomsky argued that the truly interesting part of human language, indeed the very key to understanding it, was exactly what Skinner had omitted from his book—mental processes. Chomsky also argued that language users follow rules when they generate language—rules that are stored in memory, rules that imply mental processes. The so-called empty organism psychology of stimulus–response connections was empty in the sense that behaviorists did not deal with properties of the organism that come between the physical stimulus and the behavioral response. In Chomsky's view, it was exactly there, in the organism, where the key to understanding language would be found.

To a large extent, researchers in verbal learning and other fields were making the same claim. As noted, Bousfield (1953) found that subjects cluster or group words together on the basis of associations *among the words*. Memory and a tendency to reorganize on the part of the subject were clearly involved in this performance. Where were these associa-

---

[8]Skinner, for one, was certain that this new direction was absolutely wrong and maintained this conviction up until his death in 1990 (e.g., Skinner, 1990). "Cognitive psychology is causing much more trouble [than humanistic psychology], but in a different way. . . . The word *cognitive* is sprinkled through the psychological literature like salt—and, like salt, not so much for any flavor of its own but to bring out the flavor of other things, things which a quarter of a century ago would have been called by other names [like learning]. . . . Cognitive psychology is frequently presented as a revolt against behaviorism, but it is not a revolt; it is a retreat [to unscientific language]" (Skinner, 1984, pp. 948–950).

[9]Gardner (1985) states, "There has been nearly unanimous agreement among the surviving principals that cognitive science was officially recognized around 1956. The psychologist George A. Miller . . . has even fixed the date, 11 September 1956" (p. 28). Miller recalls a conference from September 10 to 12, 1956, at M.I.T., attended by leading researchers in communication and psychology. On the second day of the conference, there were papers by Newell and Simon on the "Logic Theory Machine," by Chomsky on his theory of grammar and linguistic transformations, and by Miller himself on the capacity limitations of short-term memory. Others that Gardner cites suggest that, at a minimum, the five-year period 1955 to 1960 was the critical time during which cognitive psychology emerged as a distinct and new approach. By analogy to psychology's selection of 1879 as the starting date for the whole discipline, however, 1960 is special in Gardner's analysis: in that year, Jerome Bruner and George Miller founded the Center for Cognitive Studies at Harvard University.

tions? Where was this memory? And where was this tendency to reorganize? They were in the subject, of course, in human memory and mental processes. A particularly clear statement of the involvement of a subject's mental processes appeared in Tulving's 1962 paper, "Subjective Organization in Free Recall of 'Unrelated' Words." Even when the words to be learned were unrelated, subjects still reorganized them, a strategy for recall that was clearly coming from within the organism. During the 1950s, there were reports on human attention, first from English researchers such as Cherry and Broadbent, that were thematically related to the wartime concern with attention and vigilance. Again, fascinating attentional and perceptual processes were being isolated and investigated, processes whose unseen, mental nature could not be denied, and yet whose existence could not be denied either. A classic paper in this area, Sperling's monograph on visual sensory memory, appeared in 1960. (MacLeod, 1992, notes that there was a marked increase around 1960 in citations to the rediscovered Stroop [1935] task.)

Possibly the single most startling development of this period, certainly in terms of its impact on society, was the invention of the computer. Initial work had begun in the 1930s and 1940s on what we now call computer science, although philosophers had conceived of such a machine in general terms long before the technology existed to build one (e.g., Haugeland, 1985). At some point during the 1950s, a few psychologists realized the possible relevance of computing machinery to issues in psychology. It dawned on psychology, in a sense, that in some interesting and possibly useful ways, computers behave much like people.[10] They take in information, do something with it internally, then eventually produce some observable product. The product, to a greater or lesser extent, reflects what went on during the "internal" phase. The various operations performed by the computer were not unknowable merely because they occurred internally, of course. They were in fact under the direct control of the computer program, the instructions given to the machine to tell it what operations to perform.

The realization that human mental activity might be understood by analogy to the seemingly intelligent (or at least intelligent-acting) machine was a significant breakthrough. Especially important to the analogy was the notion of symbols and their internal manipulation. That is, the computer is a symbol-manipulating machine: its operation involves interpreting the symbols fed to it in the computer program, then performing the operations that those symbols specify. The insight that the human mind might also be fruitfully considered as a symbol-manipulating "machine" or system is usually attributed to Allen Newell and Herbert Simon. Their conference in 1958, according to Lachman et al.

---

[10]The similarity, according to Norman (1986), is not at all surprising, since the "architecture of the modern digital computer . . . was heavily influenced by people's (naive) view of how the mind operated. . . . Everyone . . . consciously and deliberately claimed to be modeling brain processes" (p. 534).

(1979), had a tremendous impact on those who attended, for at this conference Newell and Simon presented an explicit analogy between information processing in the computer and information processing in humans. This important work, probably as much as anything he did in the field of economics, was the basis for the Nobel Prize awarded to Simon in 1978.

Among the many indirect results of this conference was the publication, in 1960, of a book by Miller, Galanter, and Pribram, entitled *Plans and the Structure of Behavior*. The book suggested that human problem solving could be understood as a kind of planning, in which mental strategies or plans guide behavior toward its eventual goal. Why was this book viewed as a scientific contribution, involving as it did such mentalistic ideas as plans, goals, and strategies? Because the mentalistic plans, goals, and strategies weren't just unobservable, hypothetical ideas. They were instead ideas that could be *exactly* specified, in a program running on a lawful, physical device—the computer. (We will have much more to say about computers and computer models of cognition throughout the book.)

The Assumptions of Cognitive Psychology

We turn finally to three assumptions that pervade the field of cognitive psychology: (1) that mental processes exist, (2) that people are active information processors, and (3) that mental processes and structures can be revealed by time and accuracy measures.

Mental Processes Exist   Surely by now you know what the single most defining feature of the new cognitive psychology was—a scientific interest in human mental activity and processes. Whereas the behaviorists intentionally avoided any theorizing about the higher mental processes, these processes are exactly what cognitive psychology investigates. Our most basic assumption in cognitive psychology is that human mental processes exist, that they are lawful, systematic events, and that they can be studied scientifically.

We are of course very mindful of the checkered history of investigations into the higher mental processes. We fault the structuralists, such as Wundt and Titchener, not for their interests but for their methods. Note that our biggest lesson from the behaviorist period, and also from the example set by verbal learning, was the lesson about scientific methods and procedures. Unlike the structuralists, we in cognitive psychology rely on measures of behavior that are as objective and reliable as possible. That is, we attempt to unravel the complex questions of mental activity with tasks and measures of behavior that are quantifiable, open to scientific scrutiny, easily replicated by other investigators, and, in short, faithful to the scientific empirical tradition. As best we can, we avoid measures that are colored by subjective bias or influence, as the old introspectionism was.

Active Information Processors A second basic assumption, implied by the first assumption that mental processes exist, is the notion that the human subject is an *active* participant in the world of thought and behavior. The behaviorist, in contrast, viewed the subject as a largely passive creature, one who essentially waited around for a stimulus, then responded to it in ways determined by previous conditioning. Cognitive psychology specifically rejects this outlook as it applies to humans. We firmly believe that humans actively process the environmental stimuli around them, selecting some parts of that environment for further processing, relating those selected parts to already known information in memory, then doing something as a result of processing. And if no external stimulation is present, we occupy ourselves with internal, mental stimulation. (To prove the point, try this. Stop reading for a moment, and try to keep your mind *completely* inactive and blank for a full minute—no thoughts, recollections, or even daydreams.)

We believe that people do not passively respond on the basis of simple conditioning or reinforcement. Instead, people respond actively on the basis of their mental processing of events and information. And, as you saw in the examples at the beginning of the chapter, an enormous amount of mental activity can underlie even very simple question answering. All this mental processing is evidence for the active nature of people and their cognitive processes.

These two features form the core of cognitive psychology: our assumptions that human mental activities exist, and that the person doing the relevant mental activities is an active information processor. These ideas have a *metatheoretical* status in cognitive psychology; that is, they are above and beyond any particular theory of cognitive processes. In other words, they are so central to our discipline that they are assumed to be true. It is the various implications drawn from them that are tested in our experiments.

Time and Accuracy Measures Aside from these two important ideas, there is one other common theme that runs through the research and theorizing in cognitive psychology. We assume that the mental processes and structures we are investigating can be revealed by two general classes of behavior: the *time* it takes to perform some task and the *accuracy* of that performance. Since these measures are so pervasive in our research, it's important to discuss them here at the outset.

Psychologists from different persuasions than cognitive psychology (and, indeed, a few within cognitive psychology as well) bemoan our heavy reliance on measures such as *reaction time* (abbreviated RT), simply a measure of the time elapsed between some stimulus and the person's response to the stimulus (RT is almost always measured in milliseconds, abbreviated *msec*, i.e., thousandths of a second). Why is a time-based measure so important, especially when the actual time differences can be so small, say, on the order of 40–50 msec? Consider the following reasons. It has been known for a considerable time that individual differences among people can often be revealed by RT measures. In 1868, the Dutch physiologist Donders pointed out that the measure is potentially much more informative than this, in a proposal for studying the "Speed of Mental Processes" by means of reaction time (1868/1969). A moment's reflection should reveal why cognitive psychology uses reaction time measures so frequently: *mental events take time.* Consequently, one way of "peering into the head" is to examine how long a certain set of mental processes takes to be completed. As Donders and many others have observed, careful comparisons of people's reaction times to different stimuli can often give a strong clue to the mental processes going on internally. (Remember the robin question earlier in the chapter?)

Here's a quick example of the kind of reasoning that flows from measuring RTs. Ask yourself the following question: How do people read? That is, what perceptual and memory processes are going on as you read this very sentence? But before you construct a theory of reading, note the following: in general, it takes less time to recognize a word than it does to recognize a single printed letter, the "word superiority effect" (e.g., Wheeler, 1970). Now, is one of the necessary or even unavoidable components of reading skill a letter-by-letter process? No! How could it be, since we read words faster than the letters that compose the words?

It is a mistake to think that all of cognitive psychology's research is based solely on time measures. Often we are interested instead in some measure of the subject's *accuracy,* broadly defined. Sometimes we simply note which words a subject recalled correctly and which were omitted in recall. In a variation of such a simple list learning experiment, it might also be of interest to examine the incorrect responses, not just the words that were omitted but also any recalled words that were *not* on the studied list. Did the subject "recall" a related word, rather than the exact word that was studied, "apple" instead of "pear"? Or, was an item recalled because it resembles the target stimulus in some other way, say, remembering "G" instead of "D" when a string of letters was studied?

In more complex situations, the term accuracy takes on richer connotations. For instance, if we ask subjects to read and then paraphrase a paragraph, we don't score the paraphrase according to verbatim criteria (although the lack of verbatim memory for a paragraph is interesting in its own right). Instead, we need to score the paraphrase on its meaning, on how well it preserves the ideas and relationships of the original. Accuracy and inaccuracy here are a bit harder to pin down but are still informative. Particularly interesting in some research situations is an explicit consideration of the errors that people make, again as a way of peering in on the mental processes. Of course, this approach is quite similar to the Piagetian tradition of examining children's errors in reasoning, such as failure to conserve quantity or number, to examine their cognitive processes.

Summary Points: the impact of computers; the three assumptions of cognitive psychology; time and accuracy measures

CHAPTER SUMMARY

1. Cognitive psychology is the scientific study of human memory and mental processes, including such activities as perception, remembering, using language, reasoning, and solving problems.

2. Intuitive analysis of examples such as "How many hands did Aristotle have?" and "Does a robin have wings?" indicates that many important mental processes can occur *automatically,* that is, very rapidly and below the level of conscious awareness; experimental evidence presented later in the book supports these intuitive conclusions.

3. *Memory* refers to the mental processes of retaining information for later use and retrieving such information, and the mental storage system that allows this retention and retrieval. *Cognition* refers to the collection of mental processes and activities used in perceiving, remembering, and thinking, and the act of using those processes.

4. The modern history of cognitive psychology began in 1879 with Wundt, and his use of introspection. The behaviorist movement rejected the use of introspections and substituted the study of observable behavior as the true goal of psychology. Modern cognitive psychology, which dates from approximately 1960, rejected much of the behaviorist position but accepted many viewpoints, assumptions, and methods from fields such as verbal learning, linguistics, and computer science. Depending on your definition, this was at least a rapid, evolutionary change in interests, if not a true scientific revolution.

5. The three most basic assumptions of cognitive psychology are: (1) mental processes exist and can be studied scientifically; (2) humans are active information processors; and (3) time and accuracy measures can provide important information on the nature of human mental processing.

Glossary Terms: behaviorism/neobehaviorism; cognition; ecological validity; functionalism; introspection; memory; metatheory; reaction time; reductionism; retrieval; structuralism; *tabula rasa;* verbal learning

SUGGESTED READINGS

Leahey's (1992a) *A History of Psychology: Main Currents in Psychological Thought* (3rd edition) gives particular emphasis to the development of cognitive psychology. The most thorough treatments of the cognitive revolution—if there was one—are contained in the book by Lachman et al. (1979), especially the first five chapters, and in Baars (1986). In this material you will find very careful analysis of the positive and negative contributions of the various influences on cognitive psychology and a complete account of the assumptions and beliefs of cognitive psychologists. Chomsky's 1959 paper is difficult reading at times, but the combative flavor of the behaviorist versus cognitive debate over language and the substantive issues of the debate are highlighted in the paper. A very approachable statement of the new direction versus the old is contained in Jenkins's paper, "Remember That Old Theory of Memory? Well, Forget It," reprinted in the *American Psychologist,* 1974, pp. 785–795. Gardner's *The Mind's New Science: A History of the Cognitive Revolution* (1985) is an absolutely fascinating analysis of the historical roots, present activities, and future prospects of the study of cognition. And finally, the February 1992 issue of the *American Psychologist* is a special issue devoted to the history of American psychology, commemorating the 100th anniversary of the American Psychological Association.

For relatively brief introductions to cognitive psychology, see Richard Mayer's 1981 book, *The Promise of Cognitive Psychology,* and the more recent "Essay in Cognitive Science" by Mandler (1985a). Kuhn's (1962, 1970) book is required reading for anyone interested in the philosophy and history of science. For an interesting application of Kuhn's and others' ideas to cognitive psychology, see Gholson and Barker (1985); for the counterargument, again, see Leahey (1992a,b).

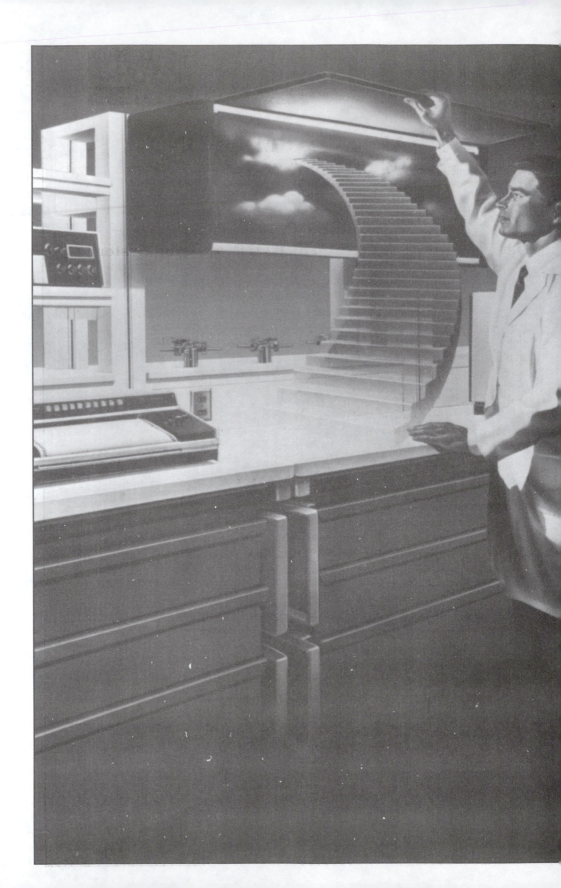

Chapter 2

THE HUMAN INFORMATION PROCESSING SYSTEM

The basic reason for studying cognitive processes has become as clear as the reason for studying anything else: because they are there. . . . Cognitive processes surely exist, so it can hardly be unscientific to study them. (Neisser, 1967, p. 5)

If we are to have any kind of reasonable theory about human thought and action, we must have a system that represents what the organism knows. Thus, representation becomes a necessary part of any mental theory. . . . Representation in the widest sense of the term is the central issue in cognitive psychology. (Mandler, 1984, p. 4)

The human operates as an information processing system [IPS] . . . a system consisting of a memory containing symbol structures, a processor, effectors, and receptors. . . . There is no evidence that the human LTM [long-term memory] is fillable in a lifetime, or that there is a limit on the number of distinguishable symbols it can store. Hence, we assume that the IPS has a potentially infinite vocabulary of symbols, and an essentially infinite capacity for symbol structures. (Newell & Simon, 1972, pp. 19–20, 792)

T his chapter, like the first, is largely introductory. In Chapter 1, you got a very general idea of what cognitive psychology is all about, and you read a bit of the history of this approach. The purpose of that material was to make cognitive psychology a living, breathing *thing* for you—not some obscure, academic quest that only PhDs can be interested in, but a dynamic and vibrant approach to questions of human memory and thought. I tried to give you some of the flavor of the field and a sense of the excitement that cognitive psychologists feel for their topic by describing some of the shouting matches that gave birth to cognitive psychology. A student 30 years ago, fired with curiosity about how memory works, would have been sent off to study retroactive interference, paired-associate learning, and forgetting curves. The same student today is sent off to study human reasoning, comprehension of paragraphs, brain processes, and the like. This is certainly a more rewarding set of questions to study: there *has* been progress (Simon, 1992).

Nonetheless, it's also true that these newer questions and interests are often quite difficult to pin down in a scientific fashion. The practitioners of a science need more than just the questions to tell them what experiments ought to be done and how they ought to do them. In particular, scientists need some sort of general framework to guide them, a set of assumptions that tells them where to start, what to look for, what to beware of. This general framework is sometimes referred to as a *metatheory,* where *meta* means above or beyond. A **metatheory** is this *set of assumptions and guiding principles,* a kind of Michelin guide that helps us find our way through unknown territory.

To a large extent, cognitive psychology's Michelin guide, our metatheory, has been the **information processing approach.** This broadly defined approach describes cognition as *the coordinated operation of active mental processes within a multicomponent memory system.* The human information processing system that is described is thus a general model of the human memory and cognitive systems, a model that goes hand in hand with the broad approach known as information processing. Note that as it was originally used, however, the term *information processing* had a rather narrow connotation, one that emphasized a one-by-one sequence of mental operations where one operation was assumed to end before another could begin. You'll read about this so-called strict information processing approach, how it generated some important discoveries and ideas, what its drawbacks and limitations were, and how these led to the broader, less restrictive approaches of contemporary cognitive psychology.

A second goal of this chapter is to alert you to some of the important themes and ideas that you will encounter in this book. Some of these are rather new ideas in cognitive psychology and so are not reflected in the general information processing model of the early 1970s: the distinctions among automatic, conscious, and unconscious processing are good examples. Some are perennial issues that continue to be important to our theories and research: attention is, without doubt, the best example of this kind of issue. And finally, some are overriding issues, not specific to any one theory or approach, but general questions that cognitive psychology must consider. A good example of this is the issue of "the representation of knowledge," how we organize or structure the information that we store in the memory system. You won't find sections throughout this book with these titles, however. Instead, the themes are recurring issues that contribute to *several* areas of cognitive psychology. If you can read a chapter and identify and discuss the themes that pertain to it, then you probably have achieved a good understanding of the material.

▼ Getting Started

As you read in Chapter 1, a growing number of psychologists in the 1940s and 1950s became disenchanted with the behaviorist approach to psychology: it seemed too narrow and rigid to cope with complex human behavior and performance. During this period, the seemingly unrelated fields of communications engineering and computer science supplied psychology with some particularly intriguing ideas, ideas that were instrumental in developing the human information processing approach. To highlight just one, psychologists became fascinated with the issue of "channel capacity" borrowed from communications engineering. In the design of a telephone communications system, for instance, one of the built-in limitations is that any channel—any physical device that transmits messages or information—has a limited capacity. In simple terms, one telephone wire can carry just so many messages at the same time and loses information if the capacity is exceeded. Naturally, communications engineers tried to design equipment and techniques to get around these built-in limitations, thereby increasing the overall capacity of a channel.

At some point, psychologists noticed that in several important ways, humans could be thought of as limited-capacity channels, transmitters of information with a "built-in" limitation in the amount of information that could be handled at one time. This insight lent a fresh perspective to human experimental psychology. Suddenly it made sense to ask questions such as: How many sources of information can humans pay attention to at one time? What information is lost if we overload the human system? Where is the limitation, and how can we overcome it? We will describe some of this research and thinking in this chapter and the next two, since much of the impact of the capacity limitation idea was on the areas of attention, sensory memory, and short-term memory. For now, note how this pollination of ideas from communications engineering helped the budding cognitive psychology determine its new approaches and directions.

More influential than the "message" that psychology received from communications engineering, however, was the "input" from computer science. While the limited-capacity channel idea is important, it is just one part of the general information processing approach to human performance. Computer science, on the other hand, had a machine that in many ways reflected the very essence of the human mental system. This machine, in its own way, did many of the things that humans do, things that cognitive psychologists very much wanted to understand. Because those "things" are unseen both when computers and humans do them, there is good reason for drawing "the computer analogy" to human cognition. Basically, this analogy says that human information processing may be similar to the sequence of steps and operations in a computer program. As such, maybe thinking of how a computer accomplishes various tasks will give us insight into the way humans process information.

A second reason for our reliance on computers is also important. By far the most serious, ambitious theories in cognitive science are usually written as computer programs: the formalities of computer programming force the theorist to be very explicit in devising the pieces of a psychological theory. Interestingly, some theories require such a huge number of computations that they could not exist without high-speed computers to do the processing. A prime example of this is the *connectionist modeling* approach discussed later. Thus it seems more than appropriate to begin our study of human information processing by taking a detour through computer science.

▼ The Computer as an Information Processing System

Early in the development of high-speed electronic computers, scientists in that field needed a term to describe what it was that these computers did. Their term was *data processing:* computers take in data and then "process" those data in some fashion or another.[1] The term *processing,* of course, is pretty vague, but that level of abstraction was necessary because of the multiple kinds of processes one might want to apply to the data. For someone doing statistics, the processing would involve arithmetic and mathematical operations. The computer on an airliner, on the other hand, performs different processes such as figuring flight paths, fuel reserves, and so on, while computers with engineering, military, or business applications need still other kinds of processes. Thus *processing* was an appropriately general term to use.

It turns out that the *data* part of *data processing* was too restrictive. The word *data* usually implies numbers, but by the late 1950s, developments in computer science rapidly outgrew the early "number crunching" limitations. All sorts of nonnumerical data are routinely processed by computers now, adding substance to the claim that the computer is in fact a "universal machine." Thus the computer field switched to the even more neutral term *information processing.* Computers process information: they take in information of all varieties, perform internal operations on that information, then spew out the results for us.[2]

But what is it that justifies the claim that there is a useful analogy between human and computer information processing? There are two ways of looking at this question, the first involving the computer's **hardware,** *the physical machinery of the computer,* the second involving the **software,** *the computer programs that direct the machine to perform certain operations, processes, and tasks.* We'll take a simple example of using the computer for a statistical analysis in order to explore both sides of computerized information processing. Refer to Figure 2-1 for a schematic diagram of a typical computer installation.

Hardware

Say, for example, I want the computer to reanalyze some numerical data from an experiment I did a year ago. I tell the computer what kind of analysis I want, what set of data it should use for the analysis, and how I want it to report the results. Think of how the physical computer apparatus manages to perform an analysis of variance when I request it. First, I must speak to it in a language it understands, formerly the lan-

---

[1]If "those data" seemed strange, read on because I can't resist this opportunity. *The word "data" is plural* (ditto for "phenomena"); "datum" is the singular form of the word and is hardly ever used. It drives me crazy to read a psychology major's paper with ungrammatical sentences like "The data shows that . . . ," especially because the very foundation of psychology is data. It may seem like a picky detail, but Please, Don't Leave College Without It.

[2]*Information* has a quite technical definition in computer and information science, referring to *uncertainty* as measured in bits of *information.* To illustrate, I'm thinking of a number between 1 and 8. It takes only three yes/no questions to determine the number: Is it in the first half? (yes) Is it one of the first two? (no) Is it the number 3? (no). The three yes/no questions necessary to figure out the number I picked, the number 4, mean there were three bits of uncertainty or information in the situation. Computer memory operates on this principle of binary, two-choice (yes/no) representation of information. This technical version of the word *information* was tested as an approach to human memory early on in cognitive psychology but was abandoned in favor of a general meaning for the term.

FIGURE 2-1

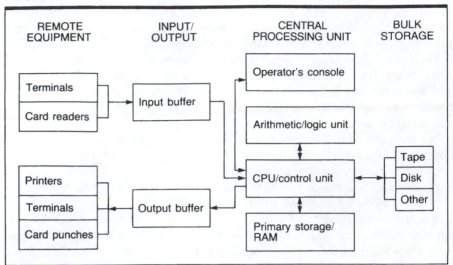

A schematic diagram of the hardware components in a modern computer installation. Remote terminals and card readers are the input devices that send information to the input buffer, an input device that holds information and then transmits it to the central processing/control unit. The CPU has access to four distinct resources for input and output: primary storage (random access memory—RAM); bulk storage devices (tape, disk, other); the arithmetic/logic unit; and the operator's console. Output from the CPU is directed to the output buffer, and from that device to whichever responding device has been selected (printer, terminal, etc.). (Adapted from Klieger, 1984.)

guage of punched holes on a card, but now the electronic impulses on a remote terminal. The computer has a device that responds to the physical patterns of electronic impulses, taking in those patterns and translating them into the internal language that *it* speaks. Once this translation is done, the transformed message is sent along to a central processor (the *central processing unit* or *CPU*), a place in the main computer where the operations of the analysis are conducted. This is the physical place that holds the retrieved data and then applies the computational formulas to those data. Once this is done, the results are sent back out to some responding unit such as a printer, which displays to me the evidence that the analysis was done. In general terms then, the computer system has a device that receives information, a central processor where the symbols in the computational formulas are applied to the data, a memory that stores the formulas, and a device that communicates to the outside world by generating output.

Compare this last sentence to the Newell and Simon quotation at the beginning of this chapter. You'll understand more clearly now what that quotation means and why the information processing approach came to be the metatheory of cognitive psychology. Analogous to physical com-

Workers at computer terminals in a mainframe computer room.

puter systems, humans have mental devices, mechanisms, and processes that receive and hold information, that apply mental symbols and instructions to information held in memory, and that then report the results of the processing to the outside world. In a sense then, these two information processing systems are similar at the level of hardware.

Software

While this hardware analogy is interesting, it is *not* the computer analogy for which we are looking. Instead, it is the similarity or analogy between human and computer *processes* that are instructive, the activities and operations that are performed by the two systems. Let's focus on those processes and activities, the software, to find the true value of the human computer analogy.

I sit down at a terminal and enter a series of statements that specify "analysis of variance on data set ABC." I then transmit these electronic impulses to the computer, which reads the impulses and converts them to a usable form. This input operation—*encoding*—literally translates the electronic patterns into the internal representation that the computer will use for its computations. The translated patterns are then sent to the computer's central processor, which retrieves the instructions for doing an analysis of variance from its program library, retrieves the appropriate set of data from the data library, and then performs the sequence of calculations specified in the programmed instructions. Besides doing the computations, the processor also has instructions and procedures—software—for keeping track of where it is in the sequence of calculations, for recalling quantities from earlier in the sequence, and so on.

Eventually (an extremely brief "eventually" for the computer), the analysis is finished. At this point, the computer generates for me a printed copy of the outcome of the analysis, formatted in the fashion that I requested. I know exactly what information was given to the computer— it's contained in the statements I typed on the terminal—and I know exactly what the computer gave to me as output—it's printed on paper. I can infer from the output that the computer indeed did what I asked. I can also infer, again from the output, what operations the computer can perform, what kinds of things it "knows how to do." It doesn't bother me that I never see any of those operations as they happen. Literally watching the physical hardware of the computer as it works would be of no help at all in figuring out what it does. I can simply infer, based on the input I supplied and the output it supplied, that computers can do analysis of variance.

Right here, in a nutshell, is some important thinking in the information processing approach to human memory and cognition. Obviously we cannot watch the human mind as it processes information, for instance, as it figures out the answer to a question. Yet, we know what the input was, the question we gave to a human subject, and what output was given back, the answer the subject gave to us. If I ask "What is 7×3?" and you answer "21," I can draw inferences and conclusions about *your* information processing, just as a computer user can draw the same inferences about the *computer's* information processing. I infer from your response that you know how to do multiplication, or at least that you know the answer to that particular multiplication problem.

This focus on *software* in the computer analogy is particularly apt for cognitive psychology. We are interested in the mental processes of thought, how they happen, how they're learned, and how they're modified by experience. Assume for the sake of argument that human thought consists of applying various operations and instructions to the symbols held in some "central processor," much as this occurs in the computer. By attempting to specify some of those operations, just as we would in writing a computer program, we try to reach a better understanding of how human mental processes occur. We understand how information "flows" through the computer system by understanding the computer program, the software. Can we try to understand human cognition in a similar way, examining the flow of information through the human information processing system? Can we make progress in cognitive psychology by investigating the "human software" of mental processes?[3]

---

[3]Increasingly, the data structures used in computer modeling are treated as analogous to neural structures in the brain, for example, the units and linkages among them in a connectionist model. This is a much more specific analogy, in that it involves both the operations specified in the program and the data structures operated on by the program.

Measuring Information Processes

There is one remaining gap in this computer analogy. To understand how the computer processes information, we merely sit down with a listing of the computer program and follow step by step through the instructions that it performs. But we have no equivalent listing for the operations and steps that the human information processing system follows. We do have a few strong hints, however, as to what those operations might be, and how they might function. As was mentioned in the previous chapter, cognitive psychology frequently relies on measures of time in order to infer the underlying steps and operations. To continue the informal example above, we might present the problem $7 \times 3 = ?$ *and* the problem $9 \times 7 = ?$ When this is done, it generally takes adults about 900 msec (milliseconds) for the larger problem, but only about 750 msec for the smaller one (e.g., Campbell, 1987). The nature of our inference here should be clear—something about the human mental processes for larger arithmetic problems takes longer than for smaller problems. Maybe there are more steps involved, maybe the larger problem is more difficult to find in memory—these are questions we can grapple with as we work *within* the information processing approach.

While this time-based approach to cognition is very popular and useful, other measures of behavior are also appropriate in our investigations. Since human memory is fallible—even error-prone in some settings—it isn't surprising that cognitive psychology continues to use the venerable accuracy measures that date from Ebbinghaus. In other words, correct recall from memory, errors, and incomplete memory performance are all highly important indicators of mental processes. And especially in situations that require a great deal of time and active problem solving, the subjects' spoken reports of their thoughts can also be used as a way of studying cognition (Ericsson & Simon, 1980; but see Nisbett & Wilson, 1977, and Russo, Johnson, & Stephens, 1989, for some difficulties with spoken reports). In short, we measure any and all human behaviors that can provide glimpses of the mental processes and activities that are the "software" of human cognition.

Summary Points: information processing as our metatheory; the computer as an analogy for human cognition; the software of human thought; ways to measure information processes

▼ The Human Information Processing System: An Overview

Enough of computers for a while—it's time to explore the human information processing system more carefully. We will examine both the original, rather narrowly defined strict information processing approach as well as the current, broader approach that most cognitive psychologists adopt. We are going to present the standard theory of human information processing, along with various examples of everyday experience that lend support to it. This is a general description of the human information processing system, the major outlines of which are still widely accepted. When we get to the section on process models, however, we'll be discussing the strict information processing approach and how research was conducted within this framework. Process models were an important adjunct to the standard theory but turned out to be too dependent on some assumptions that proved to be unwarranted. So, as the story unfolds, you'll read about more recent developments, ideas that don't "fit" into the strict approach very well. Some of these ideas have led to a modification and elaboration of the standard theory and the process model approach. Others offer new insights or perspectives and are useful because they are continual reminders of the complexity of the human information processing system.

By the end of this chapter, you should have a reasonably complete, intuitive idea of (1) what the current information processing approach is all about, (2) the architecture of the human IPS, (3) some of the general mental processes that have been investigated, and (4) the methods we use to investigate other, more specific processes. You'll also be ready to go back to these issues from an empirical standpoint, studying the research results that give us the detailed information we need in cognitive psychology. The intuitive grasp you develop here, in other words, will provide a context for you, letting you see where the many different topics later in the book fit into the human information processing system.[4]

The Standard Theory

Figure 2-2 illustrates the "standard theory" of human information processing, as it existed in the early 1970s. It is adapted from one of the first such models to receive widespread acceptance, the Atkinson and Shiffrin (1968, 1971) model of human memory. Note first the hardware of the Atkinson and Shiffrin system. There are three memory components: **sensory memory, short-term memory,** and **long-term memory.** In computer systems, these three correspond, respectively, to the receiving or input buffer device, the central processor, and the library of programs and data that are stored and available for use. At the input end of the human system, environmental stimuli flow into the system, each sense modality having its own sensory register or memory. At the output end, responses are assumed to come most directly from the short-term or

---

[4]I do not want to elevate intuitive or introspective approaches above the empirical, scientific approach. On the other hand, an account of cognitive psychology that never makes contact with your own awareness and knowledge, or one that belittles the role of everyday, intuitive understanding, strikes me as both sterile and educationally misguided.

FIGURE 2-2

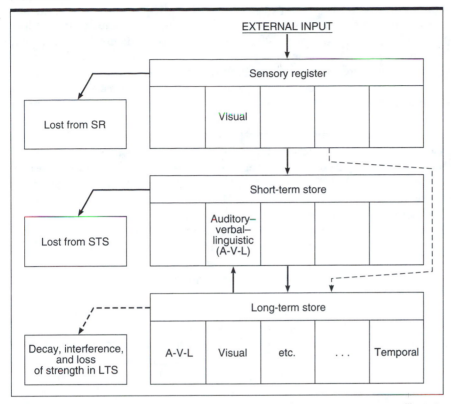

The three memory components—sensory, short-term, and long-term memory—are illustrated along with the pathways of information flow, from sensory to short-term memory, from short-term to long-term memory, and from long-term to short-term memory. Note that all responses are assumed to come most directly from short-term/working memory. (From Atkinson & Shiffrin, 1968.)

working memory system, making the outcome of the internal processes observable.

Let's briefly review the multiplication example from above, now tracing the flow of processing through Figure 2-2. I ask you "What is 7 × 3?" The sound wave patterns you hear are encoded into auditory sensory memory; the term **encode** means *to take in information and convert it to a usable mental form*. Since you were paying attention to the question, the encoded stimulus is passed almost immediately to the short-term store or memory (STM). This STM is a working memory system where the information you are consciously aware of is held for further mental processing. For the multiplication example, the system determines that it needs to call on long-term memory (LTM) for the answer to the problem. One of the control processes in working memory initiates this search, while others maintain the problem until processing is completed. After the relevant memory search has occurred, long-term memory "sends" the 21 to short-term memory, where the final response can be prepared and sent to the appropriate device (the speech mechanism). Thus the environmental input has been encoded into the human information processing system, a series of mental operations has occurred, and a final output has been generated.

In this example, we focused on how the hardware and software of the human information processing system enable us to retrieve already known information from long-term memory. A slightly different example will illustrate another aspect of the model in Figure 2-2: how new information is learned or stored in long-term memory.

Consider a third-grade child who has learned only part of the "times table" and is now trying to master the rest of the table. The teacher or textbook states that $7 \times 3 = 21$. The same sensory and attentional processes operate as before, so the stimulus is in short-term memory. Some other process must operate now to store the problem in long-term memory. A likely candidate here is rehearsal: the child repeats over and over that 7×3 is 21, either silently or aloud as part of classroom drill. A few other "seven times" facts may be practiced too, integrating 7×3 into a memorized sequence. Each repetition should do two things. First, the repetition maintains the item in short-term memory, temporarily preventing it from slipping away; Craik and Lockhart (1972) call this recycling kind of rehearsal **maintenance rehearsal,** a *refreshing of the memory trace through repetition.* Second, repetitions serve to promote transfer of the information into long-term memory. Of course, once it's stored there, then the information can be recalled as needed, as in the preceding example.

Finally, other working memory processes may be employed here as well. One principle covered throughout the book concerns the influence of already known information and its (usually) positive effects on retrieval from memory. For now, assume that our third-grader compares the fact she's trying to learn with related knowledge about arithmetic. She may recall or discover that adding 7 together three times is the same as multiplying 7×3. Or, if she already knows 3×7, she may use the inverse rule to help learn 7×3. Craik and Lockhart term this **elaborative rehearsal,** a *more meaningful kind of rehearsal, using related knowledge from long-term memory.*

While dozens of other examples could also be described, this is probably enough to reveal the usefulness of models like that in Figure 2-2. With these models, we have an idea of how to investigate mental activities such as learning and remembering. By devising experiments that test the characteristics of the three different memory components, cognitive psychology has discovered much about the hidden mental processes of human cognition. Given the broad outlines of the human system, we know where to look for more particular processes and skills.

Let's now go back and consider each memory component a bit more deeply, from the standpoint of three important questions. (1) How is information encoded into each memory component? (2) What is each component's size or capacity for holding information? (3) How long does information remain in the component? In keeping with the introductory flavor of this chapter, this overview will focus more on intuitive demonstrations and everyday examples than on empirical evidence. After this introductory discussion, you'll be ready to plunge into the more detailed and specific topics that form the rest of the book.

Sensory Memory

The two varieties of sensory memory we will discuss are auditory and visual. So few investigations have been done on the other sense modalities that there is little point in speculating about olfactory, kinesthetic, or other sensory memory systems. At this point, we merely assume that memory registers exist for these other senses, and that in important but unspecified ways they resemble auditory and visual sensory memories. In contrast, a great deal of research has been done on auditory and visual sensory memory, starting at the very dawning of cognitive psychology. In addition to considering the sensory memory registers from the standpoints of encoding, capacity, and duration, we will also deal repeatedly with the role of attention in sensory memory processes. We'll begin with auditory sensory memory.

Auditory Sensory Memory   As you talk with a friend in an airport, bus terminal, or other noisy place, you are bombarded with an enormous amount of auditory stimulation. While you can pay attention to that roar of sounds if you wish, more commonly you continue your conversation with the friend and try to ignore the auditory confusion around you. It is tempting to conclude from this that you really receive only the conversation message from your friend in this situation, and that the rest of the sensations are never even encoded in the first place. Of course, receiving the friend's message may be quite difficult, depending on factors such as the loudness of both the friend's voice and the background noise, as well as your intent or determination to follow what the friend is saying. Nonetheless, in routine situations we can generally overcome the nuisance of background noise and listen to the primary message we're trying to receive.

Yet, as we all know, if some nearby stranger happens to say your name, you typically *do* hear that message: your head jerks around as you try to hear that other conversation, and you miss what your friend was saying in the meantime. If you'll think about it for a moment, you'll have to agree that even the background messages surrounding you in the noisy place must be entering your memory system to some degree. If they weren't, how could you possibly have detected your name being spoken by someone to whom you weren't listening? What does an example like this tell us about auditory sensory memory?

Auditory sensory memory, also termed **echoic memory** by Neisser (1967), is *the sensory memory component that receives auditory stimulation from the external environment.* Since even those messages we weren't paying attention to can cause a reaction, we must suppose that any and all auditory stimuli that are sufficiently loud will be entered or encoded into auditory sensory memory. This does not mean we can identify or understand every speech message that is encoded—this is clearly not the case. It simply means that at the very earliest stage of information processing, auditory messages or signals are all encoded into the memory system, where they are then available for further processing.

Input into auditory memory appears to be quite automatic. That is, deliberate attention is not required for receiving a message—if the message is loud enough, it will be received. Furthermore, we usually cannot avoid the wholesale encoding of everything audible around us. We've already covered our first two questions, encoding and capacity. Encoding into auditory sensory memory appears to be universal: any sound loud enough to be perceived gets encoded. Since any one of the encoded sounds might, in principle, prompt the redirection of attention that your name causes in the airport, we further conclude that the capacity of auditory sensory memory is probably very large.

Note another implication of this redirection of attention. There is some lag, however short, between the time the stranger nearby happened to say your name and the time you reacted to that sound. This means that the auditory sensory memory system is a true *memory* register or device: it holds information beyond the physical duration of the stimulus. In the case of sounds, this is especially sensible. An auditory stimulus such as spoken speech is inherently spread across time. We obviously need to remember the auditory message across some time period in order to have it available for further processing.

The time period during which information in auditory sensory memory is available is probably no more than 2 or 3 seconds, at least for speech sounds. Nonetheless, even this short duration gives the memory system enough time to review the last few seconds' worth of auditory input, permitting a virtual rehearing of those sounds. (Did you ever have a friend say "Huh?" to your question, then proceed to answer it before you've repeated yourself? Do you understand how this happens now?)

Visual Sensory Memory Whereas auditory messages are inherently spread out across time, visual stimulation is inherently spread out across space, across a huge array of spatial locations. Glance up from the book now and focus on a single spot across the room (or on your fingertip, held at arm's length). Then, without shifting your focus or attention, note all the other information that is visible in your peripheral vision. To be sure, you can focus precisely only on the information that is projected onto the central region of the eye, the fovea. On the other hand, our peripheral vision is sufficiently sensitive to receive a great deal of visual information and to prompt a redirection of the eyes and/or visual attention when movement, light, and so on are detected. We're talking now about information received into **visual sensory memory,** also known as **iconic memory** (Neisser, 1967). Just as is the case for hearing, we have a *brief-duration, sensory memory system specially designed to receive and hold visual stimulation*—visual sensory memory. During the time that visual stimulation is being held in this memory, other cognitive processes, largely those related to attention, must act to process this visual information further, say, by forwarding it to short-term memory.

So, in terms of our basic questions, it would seem that any and all visible stimulation can be registered or encoded into visual sensory memory, again by apparently automatic processes, while merely gazing on a visual stimulus or scene. The capacity of visual sensory memory, likewise, must be quite large, since there would be little point in receiving tremendous amounts of information, only to be unable to hold but a fraction in the actual memory system.

This is not to say that the visual information is held a long time, however—it is not. We estimate that the functional duration of information held in iconic memory is about one-quarter to one-half of a second. That is, visual sensory memory holds information for no longer than one-half of a second, during which time the other attentional and cognitive processes must act. If attention is not devoted to the contents of visual sensory memory, then the information is lost very rapidly, just as unattended auditory messages are lost. In other words, when we attend to the contents of sensory memory, the contents are transferred via attention into short-term memory. When we fail to attend, the contents are lost or forgotten, quickly replaced by the new sensory messages being encoded into the system. (The verb *attend* simply means "pay attention to." While the dictionary claims this sense of the word to be archaic, it is used almost universally in psychology to convey this meaning.)

A useful example of visual sensory memory is the perception of a flashlight swung in a circle in a darkened room (it's not a precise example, since we obviously devote attention to the flashlight display). What you see in this situation is remarkably like a time-lapse photograph of car traffic, that is, a connected path of light. Since the flashlight is in only one physical location at a time, the visual experience of a path suggests that there is visual memory for the just-previous locations. These memories are combined across time in some way to yield the perceived path of light. Think of visual sensory memory in this sense, a memory register that holds visual sensations for a very brief duration, combining them into something like a time-lapse photograph. The contents of this photograph, of course, will disappear quickly without attention, but at least the memory record is there long enough for attention to be shifted to it.

Short-Term Memory/Working Memory

Being consciously aware of sensory memory is virtually impossible, since its duration is so brief and since the attention we devote to sensory stimuli automatically transfers them to the next memory component, **short-term memory (STM).** Being aware of short-term memory is much easier, however, since short-term memory can be loosely equated with consciousness. If you are paying attention right now, for instance, you may remember, without looking back, what the last word in the last sentence was: Remember "consciousness"? And right now, you're conscious of the experience of having just been asked what that last word was. You were aware of reflecting for a moment, then remembering what it was. And if you weren't able to remember it, you're probably conscious of the implication that you're not attending carefully enough as you read. All this—your recent thoughts and experiences, the information you have recently attended—is being held in your short-term memory system. So short-term memory is the *memory buffer or register that holds current and recently attended information.*

Unlike the sensory memories, which receive information from the external world, short-term memory receives its information from the internal, mental world: it encodes information from sensory memory and from long-term memory. When a sight or sound is attended, then the mechanism of attention transfers the attended message into short-term memory almost instantly and automatically (and during that time, the unattended information in sensory memory is being lost). Residing in short-term memory, the information is now available for conscious, deliberate processing. And when you're asked a question—Who was the first president of the United States?—successful retrieval from long-term memory "places" or encodes the answer into conscious, short-term memory.

The traditional view of short-term memory claims that it is a relatively small memory buffer or register, with the capacity to hold up to 7 plus or minus 2 *units* of information (Miller, 1956). Note what a cripplingly small amount this is, a mere 7 units of information. This limitation in capacity (recall the "channel capacity" idea from before) has been likened to a bottleneck. Just as traffic across a bridge is slowed because of a construction bottleneck, so the bottleneck in processing capacity permits only a relatively few items or units of information to be held in short-term memory.

The term *units* here is intentionally nonspecific, because the person and the situation determine what a unit is, how big it is, and how much information it contains. A phone number, encoded or recalled one digit at a time (six-eight-seven-two-five-four-five) essentially uses up the 7 ± 2 capacity. A powerful device for overcoming this limitation is called **recoding,** *grouping or chunking together some of the information into* *larger units.* Your memory for phone numbers will improve if you merely group the last four digits into twos (six-eight-seven, twenty-five, forty-five). Two and five were separate units before but are now grouped into just one unit, thus saving capacity and avoiding possible overload. If the exchange portion of the number is familiar enough (687 is my university's exchange), it may be retrieved from long-term memory as a single unit, further reducing the drain on short-term memory capacity.

A different control process operates to preserve the short-term memory record, that is, the recycling or rehearsal processes mentioned above. As an example, directory assistance gives you a phone number, and since you don't have a pencil, you repeat the number over and over until you can dial it. Once it's dialed, you can now breathe a sigh of relief and think of other things while waiting for the call to go through. Of course, if the number is busy, the newer things you've been mulling over may have destroyed your short-term memory record of the phone number, within a fairly short period of time.

A newer conception of short-term memory uses the term **working memory** as a rough synonym. Under this newer connotation, working memory is the "scratch pad" of the memory system, the dynamic place where intermediate results of the memory processes are "scribbled down" so they'll be available for later processing. The limitation of the scratch pad is not due to the size of working memory, however. Instead, it is due to the limited amount of *processing resources* available to working memory. There seems to be an upper limit on the number of processes that can

Toll booths force a bottleneck in a highway's traffic flow.

occur simultaneously, or on the accuracy of processes that occur simultaneously, because of the limited resources of the system. Examples of this limitation are common, of course. It is very difficult to talk with someone if you're driving in heavy traffic; to use my favorite example, you cannot (and should not!) listen to the radio or watch TV while studying for your Memory and Cognition class.

Concluding with short-term/working memory, let's mention a couple of facts you already know. If you've ever had to call directory assistance *again,* you know that information held in short-term memory isn't there for very long. We mentioned earlier the idea of maintenance rehearsal, a recycling of the data in short-term memory. This is the repetition of the phone number until you dial it—refreshing the short-term memory trace to prevent it from being forgotten. Research suggests that the functional duration of short-term memory information is about 15–20 seconds—longer if you rehearse it, but no longer than that if you start attending to something else entirely.

A second fact you already know concerns the fate of short-term memory information when other things happen in the meantime. Which will be more difficult, rehearsing the phone number when someone asks your name, or when someone asks your social security number? The latter, of course—saying the numbers in your social security number will surely destroy the short-term memory trace more completely than responding fairly automatically with your name. So interference from other sources, including other components of your memory, may depress your performance—interference may cause forgetting. This is particularly true if the interfering message is highly similar to the trace you're rehearsing, or if the interfering message requires significant mental resources. Furthermore, you demonstrate your sensitivity to the threat of interference by engaging in rehearsal; your self-monitoring control processes alert you to the need to do something in order to avoid the interference.

Long-Term Memory

How do we encode information into **long-term memory?** We learn it! Well, what is learning and how does it happen? In some fashion, learning involves taking information that is currently being processed and attended and storing some version of it in long-term memory. Thus long-term memory is the ultimate destination for information we want to learn and remember, *the memory system responsible for storing information on a relatively permanent basis.*

One method of accomplishing this storage into long-term memory has already been mentioned—rehearsal. Rehearsal is a deliberate mental process that can form a long-term memory trace, a record or representation of the information. Another method, one that probably involves the essentials of straightforward rehearsal, might be comprehension. That is, if you're listening to a fascinating speaker, interested in her lecture, and comprehending what she's saying, you're probably forming a long-term memory record of the lecture. You're not "memorizing" her exact words, of course, unless you specifically rehearse that one sparkling figure of speech or that one especially pertinent joke. Instead, you're forming a long-term memory trace of the gist, the general idea about which the speaker is talking. With adequate attention, interest, and comprehension, we seem to be able to store information in long-term memory with minimal extra effort.

Who was that phone call from last night? You'd surely have to say that you didn't deliberately rehearse that person's name after the call was over ("I'm storing in memory the fact that Karen called just now"). On the other hand, the conversation took some amount of time, during which you were paying attention, understanding what was said, and contributing your point of view. All this requires attention and comprehension, of course. Furthermore, the topic of the conversation with Karen probably fits in with what you already know about Karen: in a sense, it merely continues the "Karen story" you already have stored in memory. The fact that you attended and comprehended, and that you already have a great deal of information about Karen stored in memory, suggests that storing the gist of last night's conversation will not require that much additional effort. It will probably be integrated into your existing knowledge (depending on the situation, it may also become virtually indistinguishable from the other knowledge about Karen that's already in memory).

Encoding into long-term memory, then, would seem to require some active attention on your part. Rehearsal certainly requires an active learner, not only to perform the rehearsal but also to realize that rehearsal is necessary in the first place. Deliberate attention or concentration also seemed necessary to store the gist of the lecture in long-term memory. For a fascinating lecture topic, or a phone call from a friend, the attention and concentration do not seem unpleasant or difficult. As you know only too well, however, a more ordinary lecture, on a less engrossing topic, is harder to remember later: the necessary attention and concentration weren't there to begin with, so surely you store less information in long-term memory in such situations.

What about the capacity and duration questions? The issue of capacity is an easy one. No serious theorist has ever suggested there is a limit on how much information can be stored in long-term memory. While the number of brain cells we have is certainly finite (but enormous), as is the number of interconnections among the neurons (even more enormous), we might as well admit that for practical purposes there is no limitation on long-term memory's capacity. What often limits us is our unwillingness to do the hard work of storing information there in the first place.

The duration and forgetting question is not answered so easily. One strong implication of the traditional research on interference theory was that any information stored in long-term memory is subject to loss, by virtue of competing, interfering information that is also stored there. More current theories suggest that no information is truly lost from long-term memory, except for cases of physical damage to the brain itself. Instead, it's almost as if information gets lost *in* long-term memory: it's still there, but it can't be located or retrieved. (For example, who was the first person to walk on the moon?) Other current research, focused on memory for real-world events, indicates that integrating new knowledge into existing information structures may set up a situation where old knowledge is replaced, revised, or updated by new information. In other words, old knowledge is altered, and therefore lost, as it is modified by new inputs.

Apollo 11 astronaut Edwin E. Aldrin, Jr. walks on the surface of the moon, July 20, 1969. The photograph was taken by astronaut Neil A. Armstrong. Which one was the first to walk on the moon?

In any event, the current debate over forgetting from long-term memory always involves a careful consideration of retrieval processes: Was the item truly lost from memory; was the attempt at retrieving it unsuccessful, possibly because the knowledge was stored too weakly to begin with; or was retrieval unsuccessful because the information had been altered or revised in the meantime? Thus while we do truly lose information from sensory memory, by mere decay or replacement, and we do lose information from short-term memory, most probably by interference, it is questionable whether we truly lose information from long-term memory.

Summary Points: the "standard theory" of information processing; encoding, capacity, and duration in the three memory components; auditory and visual sensory memory; rehearsal and processing resources in short-term, working memory; permanence in long-term memory

A Process Model

Say that I want to investigate how people read. In particular, I'm interested in how they "look up" words in memory when they see them on the printed page and how long this process takes. I might be interested in this for any of several reasons; for instance, maybe the speed of finding words in memory is centrally important in determining how rapidly a person can read or how high the person's comprehension is during reading. Maybe the results on speed of retrieval will give me a new way to understand why learning to read is difficult for some children.

Regardless of my particular interests, I need something much more specific to guide my research than the illustration in Figure 2-2. That doesn't look like a theory I might test when doing my research. It tells me only in very general terms what components are involved in reading. Frankly, it doesn't help me, in any detailed way, to know that reading involves sensory, short-term, and long-term memory systems. I want to know *how* the process of reading takes place, how the various mental activities are accomplished. I need something that specifies the mental processes in much more detail than Figure 2-2, helping me to isolate the potentially difficult or time-consuming phases of the activity we call reading.

For this purpose, we need another illustration, a figure that depicts the sequence of mental processes in a task related to reading speed. Figure 2-3A shows such a model, a **process model** or *hypothesis about the specific mental processes that take place when a particular task is performed.* Part B of the diagram gives a rough indication as to which components and activities from Figure 2-2 go with which stages in the process model. Models such as this represent one way that cognitive psychologists apply the information processing approach to their research. Often as not, such process models also characterize the strict information

FIGURE 2-3

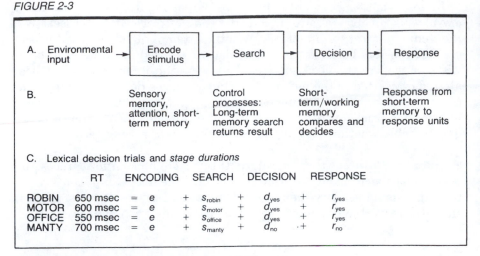

A. A general model, adapted from Sternberg (1969).
B. A listing of the memory components and processes that operate during the separate stages of the process model.
C. A process analysis of the lexical decision task, where RT to each letter string is shown to be the sum of the durations of the separate stages. Note that for the three word trials, the only systematic difference arises from the search stage; encoding, decision, and response times should be the same for all three word trials, according to the logic of process models and the assumptions of sequential and independent stages of processing.

processing approach mentioned earlier, because of two rather strong assumptions that usually accompany this kind of model.

A Process Model for the Lexical Decision Task   Let's pick a task that is quite typical of research in cognitive psychology, to explore the usefulness of process models and to see some of the limitations that paved the way for the more flexible, broadly defined information processing approach. The task we're interested in here is the **lexical decision task,** or sometimes simply the "word/nonword task" (see Meyer, Schvaneveldt, & Ruddy, 1975). In this task, we show a series of stimuli, where each stimulus is a string of letters. On each trial, the subject must look at the letter string and decide if the letters form a word or not: that is, "Is this letter string in your 'lexicon,' your mental dictionary?" On any given trial, the letter string might either be a true word, for example, MOTOR, or it might be a nonword (usually called a pseudoword), for example, MANTY. Subjects are asked to respond rapidly but accurately, and the reaction time to each letter string is the main performance measure. (Note that the pseudowords are "word-like" in their appearance, spelling patterns, pronounceability, and so on, so that subjects won't judge all the stimuli on such tangential factors.)

Logically, what sequence of processes or events must happen in this task? In the process model of Figure 2-3, the first step or stage of processing involves *encoding* the stimulus, taking in the visually presented letter string and transferring it to the holding mechanism of short-term or working memory. Now that the stimulus resides in the mental system, working memory calls long-term memory, asking if the stimulus is stored there. A *search* through long-term memory takes place, either finding the letter string or not. In either event, the outcome of the search is returned to working memory and forms the basis for the subject's *decision,* either "yes" it's a word, or "no" it's not. If the decision is yes, then one set of motor *responses* is prepared and executed, say, pressing the button on the left; the alternate set of responses is prepared and executed for pressing the other button.

Lexical Decisions and the Word Frequency Effect   Say that our results revealed a relationship between RT and the frequency or commonness of the words (this is not just a hypothetical result; word frequency is virtually always an important influence on RT in the lexical decision task). For instance, we might have tested words at low, medium, and high levels of frequency in the language; ROBIN occurs quite infrequently, only twice per (approximately) million words, MOTOR is of moderate frequency, occurring 56 times per million, and OFFICE is of high frequency, occurring 255 times per million (all word frequencies from the Kucera & Francis, 1967, tabulation; for comparison purposes, the most frequent printed word in English is THE, occurring 69,971 times). It takes significantly longer to judge words of lower frequency than it does to judge high-frequency words (Whaley, 1978). This is, in essence, the **word frequency effect.** While other variables are also known to affect the latencies or times, the word frequency effect is enough here to develop our example of a process model and interpretation.

For the sake of argument, say that our low-frequency words such as ROBIN took an average of 650 msec, our medium-frequency words such as MOTOR took an average 600 msec, and our high-frequency words such as OFFICE averaged 550 msec. What does the process model in Figure 2-3A tell us about such a result? Logically, we would not expect that encoding the various words would be influenced by the frequency effect: otherwise we'd have to make the improbable assumption that high-frequency words are more perceptible, are literally easier to see. Since this is unlikely, we instead make the assumption that the encoding stage is unaffected by word frequency. The normal time required for encoding, whatever that might be, should be the same for low-, medium-, and high-frequency words alike (and for pseudowords too). So encoding time for all trials should be a constant.

Likewise, all three of these trials will yield a successful search, so the same message is being sent to the decision stage in all three cases—"yes, it's a word." We would therefore not expect any time differences in the decision stage for the low-, medium-, or high-frequency word trials, since they would all require the same decision (yes). And finally, "yes" responses should all take the same amount of time for the response stage: it shouldn't take any longer to press the "yes" key for ROBIN or MOTOR than for OFFICE, since all three words require the same response. Thus encoding, decision, and response stage times should all be constants, regardless of word frequency.

The only stage left is the search stage. And, on reflection, the search stage of processing seems very likely to be influenced by word frequency. It seems possible, for instance, that the words in our language that are used more frequently are stored more strongly in memory: stronger memory traces could easily yield faster search times. Alternatively, the more frequent words in our language might be encountered earlier, on the average, when we search through the mental lexicon. This would also produce faster RTs to higher frequency words. On these logical grounds, then, we might tentatively conclude that word frequency has an effect on the search stage of processing, because word frequency is somehow embedded into people's long-term memory record for the words of their language. Any factor that affects the long-term memory search should influence the search stage of processing and should produce a time or accuracy difference due to the altered operation of that stage. Using the numbers supplied earlier, it would seem that the search process takes an extra 50 msec for each change from high to medium to low word frequency.

The Two Strong Assumptions   It's not appropriate now to develop a full-blown theory of long-term memory storage as a function of word frequency. Instead, you need to appreciate the nature of the process analysis or stage analysis that we just performed. Only when you understand this kind of analysis, and the assumptions embedded in this approach, will you then be able to understand the important criticisms of the strict information processing approach, and where the current information processing approach has relaxed or discarded some of the strong assumptions in the typical process model.

The first assumption in such process models is the assumption of **sequential stages of processing.** It is generally assumed under this approach that there is a sequence of stages or processes, such as those depicted in Figure 2-3, that occur on every trial. Importantly, the order of the stages is considered to be fixed, on the grounds that each stage provides a result that is necessary for the operation of the next stage. More to the point, this assumption of sequential stages usually implies that one and only one stage or process can be performed at any one time. In other words, sequential processing not only means that the sequence of stages is fixed but also implies strict "one after the other" operation.

The influence of the computer analogy is especially clear here. Modern computers may have achieved extremely high speeds of operation, but most are still *serial processors:* they still perform operations one-by-one, in a sequential order. And yet, there is no a priori reason to expect that humans are limited to one-by-one processing in any and all situations. Thus, to foreshadow just a bit, this is the place where critics of the strict information processing approach tend to cluster, at the assumption of sequential, one-at-a-time stages of processing.

The second assumption, really an extension of the first, was that the stages were **independent** and **nonoverlapping.** That is, any single stage was assumed to finish its operation *completely* before the next stage in the sequence could begin, and the duration of any single stage had no bearing or influence on the other stages. Thus, at the beginning of a trial, the encoding process starts, completes its operations entirely, and then passes its result along to the next stage in sequence, the search stage. Then and only then could the search stage begin, followed after its completion by the decision and then the response stages. With these assumptions, the total time for any trial could be interpreted as the sum of the durations for each independent stage; since mental processes take time, and since each stage was a separate mental process, the total time for a trial could be viewed as the sum of the times for all the individual stages.

In our earlier example then, the 50 msec differences between ROBIN, MOTOR, and OFFICE would be attributed to the search stage. In other words, because encoding, decision, and response all take constant amounts of time, only the search stage is left to account for the time differences to the three levels of word frequency. The memory search for these words, then, is presumably slowed down when the words are of lower frequency.

Summary Points: the stages in a process model; the strict information processing approach; word frequency and the lexical decision task; assumptions of independent, nonoverlapping stages

▼ Beyond the Information Processed: Seven Current Themes

The information processing approach just described was a dominant way of "doing business" in cognitive psychology until the mid-1970s. Much of the research in cognitive psychology up to that point proposed process models, such as the one in Figure 2-3, and often used a particular statistical and interpretive approach called "the additive factors technique" (Sternberg, 1969), which was based on such models. While this was, and occasionally still is, a very productive technique for studying cognitive processes (see Chapter 4), more recent developments have called into question some of the assumptions of the approach. As in any science, new questions and new discoveries have shown us some of the limitations of earlier conceptions and have broadened our awareness of the issues that need further study.

This final section of the chapter discusses seven current themes found in cognitive psychology; Table 2-1 provides brief summaries of the seven

Table 2-1　SEVEN CURRENT THEMES IN COGNITIVE PSYCHOLOGY

1. **Attention**　Attention is a topic of overriding concern in cognitive psychology. Attention is assumed to transfer information from sensory to short-term memory and is also assumed to be a critical mental resource necessary for the operation of any conscious or partly conscious process. All theories that discuss attention assume that it is a limited mental resource and that the upper limits of this resource pool determine how many separate processes can occur simultaneously.

2. **Automatic and Conscious Processing**　Mental processes are assumed to fall on a continuum, with "fully conscious" at one end and "fully automatic" at the other end. Extensive practice and overlearning are generally viewed as the necessary means by which a conscious process becomes more automatic. Whereas conscious processes are assumed to require attentional resources, automatic processes are assumed to require little if any of those attentional resources for their operation. Detection of your name is presumed to be fully automatic; lengthy and difficult problem solving is presumably fully conscious.

3. **Data-Driven Versus Conceptually Driven Processes**　A data-driven mental process is one that relies almost exclusively on the "data," that is, the stimulus information being presented in the environment. Whereas data-driven processes are assisted very little, if at all, by already-known information, conceptually driven processes are those that rely heavily on such information. Thus a conceptually driven process uses the information already in memory, and whatever expectations are present in the situation, to perform the task; data-driven processes use only the stimulus information.

4. **Representation of Knowledge**　Cognitive psychology is concerned with how information is represented or stored in memory. For instance, is long-term knowledge of the words in our language represented or organized randomly in memory, or in some more orderly, systematic fashion? The issue also orients us to different kinds of knowledge, such as knowledge of how to do something, as well as how the different kinds of knowledge might be represented in memory.

5. **Metacognition**　The term refers to the awareness and monitoring of one's own cognitive system and its functioning. Metacognitive awareness is thus a prompt that we need to rehearse information that we want to remember, is a checking mechanism by which we assess our level of comprehension or performance, and is a source of strategies and plans to be used for improving memory performance.

6. **Unconscious Processing**　Not all cognitive operations are conscious; unconscious processes include registration of incoming stimuli without any conscious awareness, and the lack of introspective awareness about some mental processes, especially those that are automatic. The term implicit memory refers to performance that shows the influence of a stimulus even though there may be no conscious, explicit awareness of that stimulus.

7. **Levels of Analysis in Cognitive Science**　The major level of analysis we're concerned with is the cognitive level, focusing on what the cognitive processes are, how they are organized, and how they interact. To this level we add two others, the neuroscience level, concerned with the neurological structures and functioning that supports cognition, and the computer science level, concerned with modeling intelligent, cognitive processes by means of computer programs and systems.

themes. To differing degrees, each of these themes questions the generality, or at least the completeness, of models such as those presented in Figures 2-2 and 2-3. In my view, it is a mistake to conclude that these newer questions and discoveries support the cynical evaluation that there has been little if any progress in cognitive psychology (e.g., Neisser, 1976). Instead, it is likely that no one would have ever noticed the issues and questions if it hadn't been for the earlier process models. Furthermore, we do not throw out all earlier research merely because there are newer ways of studying cognitive processes. We merely acknowledge that those conclusions pertain to certain kinds of mental processes and situations, and that other processes and situations require different concepts of the human information processing system.

Attention

Turn back to Figures 2-2 and 2-3 and study them very carefully. What's missing from these two illustrations? Attention. It's not surprising that attention isn't listed in the three-component memory model of Figure 2-2, because the figure shows the *structure* or architecture of the memory system, not the processes. Note though that a slightly revised version of this model (Atkinson & Shiffrin, 1971) expanded the description of short-term memory, by calling it temporary working memory, and listed several of STM's control processes—rehearsal, coding, decision, and retrieval strategies. But again, there was nothing directly labeled as attention, and there was no component in the system that encompassed attention either.

By rights, since attention is a process of the memory system, we should expect it to show up in process models—but it doesn't. Why isn't it there, given that the entire overview section you've just read repeatedly discussed the process of attention as a central and fundamental feature of human information processing? After all, isn't there some part of the cognitive apparatus that directs and coordinates the components and processes of cognition? And furthermore, *where* should it be, given that the influence of attention seems to pervade the entire range of memory systems and processes? Where is this process that directs activity? Who's in charge here?

One answer to this question is depicted in Figure 2-4, a substantially revised version of the traditional approach. In the figure, there are the same information flow pathways as in the Atkinson and Shiffrin model, but several new ones have been added.[5] The extra pathways essentially

---

[5]The traditional linear arrangement of sensory, short-term, and long-term memories implies a left-to-right sequence, the first-next-and-then-finally order characteristic of serial, data-driven processing. Thus I have borrowed Neisser's (1976) triangular "perceptual cycle" notion here, because it displays the continually interacting nature of the cognitive system.

FIGURE 2-4

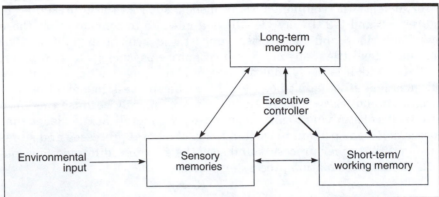

Two important aspects of the revision are (1) there are bidirectional pathways of information flow among all components, and (2) executive controller has been added to coordinate the sequence of processing and the management of attentional/processing resources.

allow for each of the three components to influence each other component: long-term memory can now influence sensory memory, short-term memory can act on sensory memory, and so on. Thus the revised model eliminates the heavily sequential nature of the original information processing models, in that there is no inherent order of operation for the stages or components. Also eliminated here is the notion of strict independence of stages and components. Within the structure diagrammed in Figure 2-4, it is easy to see how one component might enter into the activities of another, how the components can continually interact and influence each other.

Furthermore, there is an added component in the figure called the **executive controller.** This component has the responsibility of parcelling out the mental resources of attention, in reaction to changing demands for processing resources by the three memory components. It coordinates the processing activities and steps, directing the various components in the system toward some eventual goal or behavior. In computer science terms, the executive controller here is the "executive routine" in a computer program, that part of the program that keeps track of what has already happened and what still needs to be performed, deciding which activity or process should come next.

In psychological terms, proposing an executive control mechanism or process is often viewed as highly suspect. To suggest that there is a mechanism in the memory system that directs and controls activity strikes some people as highly unscientific, or at least evasive. The gist of the criticism is that in attempting to explain how the whole system works, we propose a new component, an executive endowed with the mental powers of making decisions and causing mental activities to happen. Haven't we just reinvented the mental system we were originally trying to explain—haven't we merely put "a little thinking person," a *homunculous*, inside the "thinking person" we started out to understand? Haven't we merely awarded the homunculous with just the right mix of abilities and powers needed to "explain" the system?

The executive controller, however, need not be endowed with majestic powers. For example, in Baddeley's (1981, 1992a,b) *Working Memory* system, the central executive was a limited-capacity attentional system that could call on a variety of other working memory components to accomplish a task. One of the components available to the central executive was Baddeley's articulatory loop, the subsystem responsible for verbal rehearsal. Rehearsal, not surprisingly, uses some of the executive's processing capacity, that is, attention. And an earlier discussion of executive control by Greeno and Bjork (1973) is also quite similar to the present proposal: in these authors' view, the existence of an executive control component could not be doubted, given "the importance of attention and decision processes in the storage, rehearsal, and retrieval of information" (p. 84; see Kahneman, 1973, for a similar consideration of attentional capacity and central control mechanisms).

So for this discussion of attention, consider the executive controller to be the component of the information processing system that doles out attention for the completion of various tasks. In response to some goal state, say, remembering the phone number that directory assistance has just given you, the executive calls a verbal rehearsal process and devotes some conscious, attentional resources to that rehearsal.

Automatic and Conscious Processing

In Chapter 1, we mentioned several mental processes that seem to occur without any conscious awareness or involvement. For skilled readers, one such automatic process is the identification of words. You don't have to decide consciously to identify a word you see printed on the page in front of you: in fact, you usually can't *avoid* identifying it, can't avoid becoming aware of its meaning as an automatic by-product of perceiving it (e.g., Stroop, 1935; this fail-safe task is described in the Demonstrations section). Just as obviously, though, many mental activities depend quite heavily on conscious decision and processes, such as long division, writing a term paper, learning a foreign language, or even understanding a textbook. What causes some processes to become automated while others remain conscious? Can any process eventually become automatic, or are some so complex or lengthy that they will always require conscious effort?

The details of "diagnosing" automaticity, of determining whether or not a process is performed automatically, need not bother us yet. For now, it is useful to propose a general rule about automatic and conscious processing. If we ignore innate reflexes, it seems that most mental processes begin at a conscious level. That is, they require conscious attention and processing resources at the outset. With extensive practice, however, some of these mental processes can migrate toward the automatic end of the continuum. Thereafter, the mental activity can routinely happen at a very automatic, effortless level under normal circumstances, requiring little if any attention. If the situation changes dramatically, however, then some greater involvement of conscious processing may be required temporarily.

Consider examples of motor control to clarify these remarks. When a baby begins to take her first steps, it requires intense concentration—conscious processing, in other words. Even with this conscious involvement, however, performance will not be flawless. If you call the baby's name out, she's likely to look toward you, lose her balance, and keel over onto the floor. The distraction of hearing her name took away attentional resources that were being devoted to the job of walking. With enough practice, however, the baby can now walk with little or no conscious effort involved and is not thrown off balance when attention shifts to another task. Conscious control may still be necessary under unusual circumstances, though, such as walking on the uneven surface of the backyard or climbing stairs. Mastering the coordination for the accelerator, clutch pedal, and gear shift in a manual transmission car is another excellent example—you eventually are able to pay attention to other things, like the traffic around you, because your foot and hand movements are now under automatic control.

There is a subtle but tremendously important contradiction between what you just read about automaticity and what you learned earlier about the strict information processing approach. You just read that processes can become automatic, enabling you to do *other* things that require attention while the automatic processes (walking, shifting gears) occur automatically. In simple terms, you *can* do more than one thing at the same time, subject to available mental resources. The psychological term for this is *parallel processing,* performing at least two separate processes simultaneously. And yet a central assumption in the strict processing models was that the mental stages of information processing occur one at a time, with no overlap. This is *serial processing,* in which mental processing is a series of one-after-the-other stages. But something is wrong here; how can we say that mental processing is serial, then turn around and say that two (or more) processes can occur in parallel if one of them is automatic?

To resolve this apparent contradiction, think of the assumptions of serial processing in terms of automatic and conscious control. Under conscious control, it seems likely that only one highly resource-consuming process can occur at a time—the baby must concentrate on those early steps and will fall if her attention is diverted. Under automatic control, however, when few if any mental resources are necessary for a process to occur, then presumably other processes *are* free to occur. After all, adults routinely walk and talk at the same time, because walking is so automatic that it requires none of the "talking resources" for efficient performance (for that matter, most of us know people who talk without benefit of conscious processing as well). Thus serial processing and conscious processing seem to go together; processes requiring conscious control tend to occur serially. Likewise, when performance is quite automatic, then several processes can co-occur, can be performed in parallel. As an example, Salthouse (1984) has analyzed skilled typing and found evidence for four separate processes, all of which occur in parallel during normal, rapid typing.

What about purely cognitive tasks, where two or more mental processes must occur? It seems safe to conclude that virtually any cognitive task, except the very simplest ones, will involve some balance of automatic and conscious processing. The faster the performance in the task, the more exclusively it uses automatic processes. Slower performance is the product of both kinds of processes, with conscious processing taking the dominant role. The examples in Chapter 1—"Does a robin have wings?" and "How many hands did Aristotle have?"—illustrate this balance or proportion idea fairly clearly. Processing is largely automatic for the robin question. Part of the processing for the Aristotle question was also quite automatic, the perceptual/reading part, for example. Other aspects of processing were quite conscious for this question, however (e.g., when you asked yourself "Why would he ask such an obvious question?").

As Eysenck (1982) has noted, subjects typically have little or no conscious awareness of the nature of their mental processes during so-called **fast process tasks,** tasks that typically last no more than one or two seconds. Such tasks tend to ask for more elementary information, often require only yes/no decisions, and generally involve fewer, somewhat simpler, and highly practiced mental processes. For the most part, it is these tasks that have been studied within the process-model framework of information processing—the lexical decision task is an excellent example of a fast process task. It is also these fast process tasks that tend to focus on the automatic components of mental activities (e.g., Posner, 1978). And, importantly, this is where we tend to lose our introspective awareness: automatic processes are too fast, and too highly overlearned and practiced, to be accessible to conscious awareness.

Slow process tasks take from several seconds up to several minutes or more to be completed. These tasks generally rely very heavily on conscious processes, and often are of a problem-solving nature, either literally or figuratively. Since conscious processing is required, the subject is more able to introspect about those activities during the actual performance. Naturally, the accompanying automatic processes will remain out of awareness in slow process tasks. They will be masked by the more time-consuming, effortful conscious activities that capture our awareness.

DEMONSTRATIONS

In my own Memory and Cognition classes, I require students to conduct a small project or "mini-experiment," one that tests some cognitive principle or result in a fairly straightforward way. My purpose in this assignment is to help students realize the countless ways that the principles of cognitive psychology apply to our everyday mental lives.

With very few exceptions, each chapter in this book will have one of these Demonstration sections, with suggested projects and activities relevant to such an assignment. Many of the ideas have come from student projects; many more are simple adaptations of research studies you'll read about. Unfortunately, some topics such as attention are quite difficult to test without elaborate timing and stimulus presentation apparatus. For these, I've described a situation or two to which introspective or diary methods might be applied. I would encourage you to try some of these demonstrations on your own. Most require only the bare minimum of equipment, and you can usually determine the result by simply computing the subjects' means.

1. A fail-safe demonstration of automaticity, in particular the automatic nature of accessing word meaning, involves the Stroop task. With several different colors of marker pens, write a dozen or so color names on a sheet of paper, making sure to use a *different* color of ink than the word signifies (e.g., write "red" in green ink). Make a control list of noncolor words (e.g., "hammer, card, wall"), again in colored inks. Explain to your subject that the task is to name the *ink color* as rapidly as possible. Time the subject (the second hand/display on your watch is more than sufficient) on each kind of list. The standard result is that the color word list will require substantially longer for ink color naming than the control list. Other useful control lists are simple blotches of color, to check on the speed of naming the colors, and nonwords ("manty," "zoople," etc.) written in different ink colors.

Data-Driven Versus Conceptually Driven Processes

Neisser's (1967) landmark book, considered by many to have signaled the coming of age of cognitive psychology, popularized a progressive and compelling theoretical notion about the everyday operation of the human information processing system. This notion was called **analysis by synthesis,** a concept borrowed from work in speech perception. As Turvey (1978) put it, however, "analysis by synthesis was to become, in the hands of Neisser (1967), a provocative account of many visual phenomena, both common and exotic" (p. 101). The specific term has fallen by the wayside, but the idea is still forceful throughout cognitive psychology. Ignoring many of Neisser's detailed remarks, the *analysis by synthesis* phrase suggested largely the same combination of mental efforts as the more current terminology, *data-driven* and *conceptually driven mental processes*; a completely synonymous set of terms is *bottom–up* and

2. Several variations are possible with the Stroop task. Construct displays of different numbers of visual stimuli like those shown below. Use note cards, and have the subject go through the deck of cards stating, as rapidly as possible, how many patterns are displayed on a card. Record the total time to get through the entire deck.

3. Test other "special" kinds of subjects, to see if they show the Stroop effect, that is, the slowdown on experimental lists. For instance, test someone learning French by writing French color words in contrasting inks. A child in early first grade might not show the standard Stroop effect on words, whereas a second or third grader might; children who know their numbers might show the effect on the tests illustrated below.

A Modified Stroop Task

For panel A, begin with the upper left square and call out the number of digits in each square as rapidly as possible. Ignore the names of the digits. Panel B represents a control condition, for which calling out the number of letters in each square is considerably easier. (Adapted from Howard, 1983.)

top–down processing. A compelling, revered example of these distinctions is illustrated in Figure 2-5.

If you've never seen this photograph before, your attempt at figuring out what is depicted is probably an excellent example of data-driven, or bottom–up, processing. You're confronted with an odd collection of black and white splotches. Since it's an illustration in a textbook, your general knowledge of these things tells you it has to be an illustration of *something*—it's probably not just random splotches—but beyond that, you haven't got a clue. As you slowly study the picture, you eventually start to perceive some distinguishable forms. In a manner of speaking, you begin to "try on" some interpretations of the picture, much as you would try on several pairs of shoes to see which pair fits the best. Eventually— it usually strikes people quite suddenly—something in the picture "fits," and you realize you're looking at a rather unusual picture of a dalmatian

FIGURE 2-5

First identification of the pattern relies almost exclusively on data-driven processing, whereas later identification relies heavily on conceptually driven processing.

dog, his nose down to the ground, standing in a shady, mottled patch of ground. Your shifts of gaze back and forth to different portions of the picture, your very conscious puzzling over the picture, and the final identification of the pattern, were rather unusual, in the sense that so much effort is usually not necessary to process ordinary pictures.

What happened here was largely **data-driven processing**. You were working from the bottom up, *using only the features and clues in the stimulus—the data in the environment—to identify the pattern*. Little of your existing knowledge was of any use as you looked at the picture, so you had to rely almost exclusively on just the stimulus itself, just the *data* afforded you by the picture. With only a little help from your "higher" conceptual knowledge, you slowly pieced together some ideas about the picture. Rarely in our everyday world are we confronted with so isolated a situation, with data so lacking in helpful context and familiarity. But data-driven processing is just that—attempting to process a stimulus with none of the supporting context and knowledge that we usually bring to bear on the data around us. (Listening to fluent speakers of another language is a good example of data-driven processing—our mental processes have only the unfamiliar sounds of those strange data to drive them toward understanding.)

If you *had* seen the dalmatian photograph before, then you probably only glanced at the picture briefly. You realized "Ah, it's that strange dalmatian picture again." This abbreviated set of mental processes comes very close to illustrating purely **conceptually driven processing,** where your *mental processing is guided by means of the "top" level of knowledge stored in memory*. In this case the top level of knowledge exerted an influence "down" toward the actual perceptual processes of scanning the picture. You needed only a bare minimum of information or data from the illustration, just enough to trigger the relevant knowledge in memory. From this point, your conceptual processes took over and likely did not even call for any more perceptual processing of the figure. You relied almost exclusively on the context supplied to you by your knowledge of the picture, a clear case of the mental processes being driven by conceptual knowledge. (Failing to notice typograpical errors, such as the one you just passed over, is another good illustration of top–down processing.)

Standard information processing approaches, such as those illustrated in Figures 2-2 and 2-3, generally imply bottom–up processing—the sequence of mental processes, triggered by the stimulus, is driven or "powered" by the features and characteristics of that stimulus. A symptom of this data-driven emphasis is that the majority of pathways in such figures point inward, *from* out there in the environment *into* the memory system. The serious shortcoming of this approach is that it neglects mental processing that is triggered or assisted by *internal* events, by knowledge you already possess. If you were already familiar with the dalmatian example, you needed only a small bit of processing of the picture before you recognized the pattern. In other words, you do not repeat the slow, effortful understanding of the pattern each time you see it. Once you've identified the pattern, then your next encounter with it benefits from that previous experience: knowledge in long-term memory assists you with subsequent encounters. Significantly, once you're familiar with the pattern, it's quite difficult to *avoid* seeing the dalmatian when you view the picture again. Even consciously trying to see it again "from the bottom up" fails, because you know where to look for the dalmatian, and you can't help but see it there.

Accordingly, a major modification of the standard information processing approach involved the additional pathways shown in Figure 2-4 (see Neisser's "perceptual cycle" notion, 1976), pathways that enable each component to influence each other component in an interactive fashion. In the normal course of events, any significant mental task will involve both data-driven and conceptually driven processing. Elements of the data will be identified in long-term memory, prompting a change in the ongoing activities of sensory and short-term memory. Sometimes, because of these changes, the nature of the operations can be influenced quite radically, with startling results. As an example, read the following sentence, taken from Reed (1992).

FINISHED FILES ARE THE RESULT OF YEARS
OF SCIENTIFIC STUDY COMBINED WITH THE
EXPERIENCE OF MANY YEARS.

Now, read it a second time, counting the number of F's. If you counted fewer than six F's, try again—and again if necessary. Why is this difficult? Because your knowledge of English, that function words like "of" carry very little meaning, prompts your perceptual processes to read only the content words in the sentence, a clear-cut example of conceptually driven processing.

Representation of Knowledge

An important theme in cognitive psychology, especially since the early 1970s, has been an interest in the different information *types* that must be stored in long-term memory. For instance, the Atkinson and Shiffrin model suggested that certain *physical* characteristics of an input would be recorded in long-term memory, whether the input was visual, linguistic, kinesthetic, and so on. On the other hand, the model did not distinguish among other kinds of long-term memory records. As an example, all of the following are probably stored in the "A-V-L" (auditory–verbal–linguistic) mode: your mother's maiden name, your street address, your concept of a robin, your knowledge that people generally have two hands. These kinds of knowledge are relatively undifferentiated in the Atkinson and Shiffrin model: all of them are simply A-V-L memories. Yet they *seem* quite different, ranging from very personal and specific to very cultural and generic.

Furthermore, our generic knowledge itself varies from rather simple and limited concepts, such as the name of a letter in the alphabet or the meaning of a single word, all the way up to very global knowledge, such as the typical sequence of events when you eat at a restaurant or travel by airplane. The question then is how these *different* types of information are stored. Is there a different representation for different kinds of information, or are all kinds represented in some common format?

One of the basic distinctions that has been proposed is the distinction between *semantic* and *episodic* knowledge (Tulving, 1972). In this dichotomy, **semantic memory** contains a person's *general world knowledge, including knowledge of language*. Semantic memory is conceived to be the all-purpose, permanent repository of generic information that is usually quite similar across individuals. Thus your concept of a robin is largely the same as mine, and the same as anyone else's in the culture and society we all share. On the other hand, **episodic memory** is characterized as an *autobiographical memory storehouse*, containing all of the personally experienced and stored information that is particular to the individual. Thus while the concept of "dinner" is common to all of us, that is, a semantic memory, what you ate for dinner last night is an episodic memory, specific to you and your experiences.

Other long-term memory distinctions have also become more important across the last 15 years or so. For example, we now speak of the differences between *declarative* and *procedural* knowledge (e.g., Anderson,

1976, 1982; Squire, 1987).[6] According to this dichotomy, *basic facts and conceptual knowledge* are stored in a **declarative long-term memory system**, whereas *knowledge of how to do something* is part of one's **procedural knowledge base**. Declarative knowledge here is "knowing *that*," for example, "I know that 2 + 3 is 5, I know that robins have wings." Procedural knowledge, on the other hand, is "knowing how to." This includes the various mental procedures used for thought and also other kinds of "how to" knowledge; for example, "I know how to ride a bicycle, how to shift gears in a car."

Many reasons make this an attractive distinction, including the growing evidence that various forms of brain damage have different effects on procedural and declarative knowledge. For example, Squire (1987) has found that people with *amnesia*, permanent memory loss due to some kind of brain damage, often show an impairment in tasks that require declarative knowledge performance (e.g., recall a list of words), despite little if any impairment in their procedural performance (e.g., learning a new motor skill; see Chapter 10 for a full discussion of this topic). To repeat the earlier idea, nothing in the older models of information processing suggested questions about how complex ideas and skills might be learned or stored in memory, or even that long-term memories of different *kinds* might exist. Newer approaches to human information processing have inquired about these more complex issues, however, and have helped revise the older models to provide a more complete account of human cognitive processes.

Metacognition

A now-important issue in cognitive psychology came originally from research on the development of children's memory and cognitive processes. This contribution is usually labeled **metacognition** and refers to an *awareness and monitoring of one's own cognitive state or condition*. Our ability to reflect on our own cognitive condition, to assess how successfully our own memory and thought processes are operating, is metacognition. A simple example of metacognition involves rehearsal. In many situations, adults show a high degree of metacognitive awareness—we know we have to recycle the phone number in short-term memory until we dial it.

Interestingly, small children show very little sensitivity to the need for rehearsal. They act as though they are unaware of the need to rehearse the phone number, unaware that deliberate effort is necessary to store information in memory. Their predictions about their own mem-

---

[6]The term *declarative*, I suspect, is borrowed from computer programming, where a variable is "declared" at the beginning of the program, to set up the initial state of the system that contains (or will contain) certain information. Anderson's declarative knowledge (e.g., 1983) is similarly set up as the basic factual memory that will be used by various procedures in different problem-solving situations.

ory performance are sometimes wildly optimistic; and when confronted with their poor performance, they sometimes are genuinely puzzled. In short, small children are often quite unaware of how their own memory system works, of how to assess the difficulty of a task and respond appropriately to that assessment. This research implies quite clearly that we have to learn how our memories work and what has to be done to ensure successful remembering.

This self-examining aspect of thought is an important influence on mainstream cognitive psychology, because it addresses the topic of awareness and self-assessment. You read earlier that awareness tends to accompany mental events that are performed consciously, that is, events that require attentional resources for their completion. And we suggested that the *executive controller* is the component that doles out these attentional resources. In a sense then, it stands to reason that the executive controller is the aspect of the cognitive system that accounts for metacognition. That is, in order for the executive system to respond to cognitive demands, it has to be aware of those demands, at least at some level. Thus the executive controller not only instigates mental processing to achieve different goals, it is also the most likely component to explain our awareness of the goals and of at least some of the mental processes being used to achieve them.

Why do we rehearse information, like a telephone number? Because the executive controller is responding to the goal "Learn the phone number" by supplying attentional resources to a major "learning" process, rehearsal. In such an explanation, realizing that you need to rehearse implies awareness, a self-monitoring act of the cognitive system. Why do you occasionally re-read sections of this book? Because your self-assessment suggests that you may not have devoted sufficient effort to understanding the material. This self-assessment, and the processing that results, is the essence of metacognition.

Unconscious Processing

Don't let that last section mislead you. Yes, we are aware of many of our cognitive processes and often know how to improve our performance when self-monitoring indicates the need for additional processing.[7] But in ways just now coming into clear focus in cognitive psychology, a significant number of important mental processes and operations appear to operate entirely out of conscious awareness. These varieties of mental processing illustrate what is being called *unconscious processing*.

We are not speaking of the classical, Freudian-style unconscious here, however important that might be to an understanding of personality and behavior (see Erdelyi, 1974, 1992, for comparisons between the Freudian

---

[7]Whether we follow our own metacognitive advice or not ("I should read that section again if I really want to understand it") is of course another issue entirely. Maybe our cognitive theories need yet another component, the one that corresponds to the effects of "cognitive laziness."

and cognitive concepts of "unconscious"). Instead, we are interested in mental processing that we are "unaware of" in two senses of that phrase (see Greenwald, 1992). First, some processes are unconscious in that they occur outside of attention, without the involvement of normal attentional processes. As Greenwald (1992) notes, if you are selectively attending to certain stimuli—the conversation you're listening to—then *other* stimuli that enter sensory memory but are not attended are "outside of attention." Unless you happen to hear your name spoken in some other conversation, for example, those other noises are simply not paid attention to: they enter sensory memory but are quickly lost. Interestingly, even surprisingly, recent research is showing how unattended stimuli can sometimes have an effect on later mental processing.

The second kind of unconscious process reflects a lack of or failure of introspection and is more familiar to you at an intuitive level. Recall the earlier section on automatic and conscious processing. When a process occurs automatically, you generally have no introspective awareness of it: you cannot accurately describe *how* you look up a word's meaning in memory, *how* you read the black marks on a page as words, and so on. In this sense of the term, procedural knowledge seems to be unconscious—it is "verbally unreportable," in Greenwald's (1992, p. 767) words. Stated differently, we have no useful metacognitions about such knowledge.

An umbrella term for much of the current interest in unconscious processing is *implicit memory*, memory performance that is "assessed with tasks that do not require conscious recollection of specific episodes" (Schacter, 1992). For example, subjects might be asked to complete a word fragment like TAB___. Their completion, say, forming the word TABLET, is affected by having seen that word on an earlier list, even though they may not have recalled TABLET from the list, and even though TABLE would normally be a more common way of completing the word fragment. Such demonstrations can be even more fascinating in studies of patients with brain damage: an amnesia patient will complete the fragment as TABLET and yet have no explicit memory whatsoever of having seen *any* list of words at all (see Chapter 10).

In short, there are more cognitive processes, and more influences on those processes, than we are aware of. Some of those processes are called unconscious because of their automaticity, and some because we lack the ability to introspect about them. But the newest research is also showing a different kind of unconscious effect: experiences that never seemed to enter conscious awareness, or that could not be explicitly remembered later on, nonetheless can have important effects on performance.

Levels of Analysis in Cognitive Science

Did you notice that the last section contains the second reference in this chapter to the topic of brain damage? While this may not seem odd to you, it represents a rather major change in the scope of cognitive psy-

"No GOOD. IT'S STILL NOT WORRYING ABOUT HOW IT'S DOING."

chology, compared to, say, 10–15 years ago. Far more than previously, we are now open to evidence about human cognition that is gleaned from research in the neurosciences. Indeed, there is now an entire chapter (10) devoted to such evidence in this book, compared to only 12 pages in the first edition.

In addition to this change there is the ever-increasing importance of computer-based modeling approaches to cognition. The specific development of interest here is the rise of *connectionist* models (also called neural net models, or parallel distributed processing models), introduced at some length in Chapter 3. These models go substantially beyond the computer analogy that was important in the early days of cognitive psychology, because they are deliberately designed in many cases to resemble important aspects of the human brain and its functioning. Thus it's now necessary for cognitive psychology to understand and benefit from these computer-based approaches too.

These are the strong interdisciplinary forces in modern cognitive science—the neurosciences and computer science are informing, shaping, and enriching cognitive psychology. (In many cases, linguistics and other behavioral sciences also contribute to this broadened approach to the mind. See Figure 1-1, for example, where ethology and anthropology are listed as contributors to cognitive science, based on Johnson-Laird's [1988] analysis.) Most theorists would agree that this interdisciplinary approach is valuable, even necessary for a full understanding of human

Table 2-2   MULTIPLE LEVELS OF ANALYSIS IN LANGUAGE

Level of Interest	Questions and Issues
Cultural	How cultural factors influence one's mode of speech
Interpersonal	The influence of social status, setting, and level of acquaintance on one's speech
Long-term memory	The speed of word retrieval; tip-of-the-tongue failures during speech; storing "gist" in memory
Short-term memory	How ideas are held in short- term memory; maintaining topic in conversation
Auditory, visual perception	Long-term memory's influence on speech perception; storing input mode in short- and long-term memory
Brain structures	Specialized brain structures for oral speech, aural comprehension, word retrieval
Neurons	Neuronal change when new words are stored in long-term memory; patterns of neural activity in speech comprehension and production

cognition. This is the same as saying that human cognition can be studied at several levels of analysis, all the way from the microscopic level of the brain cell and its functioning up through the complexities of cultural and social influence on thought (as an example, see the questions illustrated in Table 2-2, concerning levels of analysis for language).

Obviously, this book will focus more heavily on the distinct *cognitive level* than the others, at the level that focuses on the functions of memory, the ways that various mental processes and components interact, and the results of those processes and components. This level, along with the contributions of the neurosciences, linguistics, computer science, sociology, and the rest of the behavioral sciences, is all important in the study of the greatest, most complex system that science has ever investigated, the human cognitive system.

Summary Points: seven current themes; fast and slow process tasks; implicit memory

CHAPTER SUMMARY

1. The information processing approach has been the dominant metatheory in cognitive psychology. The original "strict" information processing approach was responsible for some important developments and insights. This strict approach has now been largely rejected in favor of a more broadly conceived approach, which describes cognition as the coordinated operation of active mental processes within a multicomponent memory system.

2. The computer has provided cognitive psychology with its richest analogy for understanding human cognition. There is a rough analogy between human and computer systems at the level of hardware, the physical devices and mechanisms, but this is far less important than the analogy based on the software of the two systems, the actual processes and activities that occur within the human and computer information processing systems.

3. The human information processing system consists of three major memory components: the sensory memory, short-term or working memory, and long-term memory. The three basic issues of encoding, information capacity, and the duration of storage are discussed for each memory component; the processes of attention, rehearsal, and retrieval, for the most part, account for the transfer of information among these three components.

4. To understand performance in some information processing task, we often devise a *process model*, a step-by-step breakdown of the entire task into separate processing components. As an example, the lexical decision task is analyzed in terms of a process model, and a result known as the *word frequency effect* is interpreted as being due to the operation of a long-term memory search stage. This process analysis reveals the two strong assumptions that characterized the strict information processing approach and that forced cognitive psychology to revise and elaborate this approach.

5. Seven overriding themes are described, issues and ideas that reappear frequently throughout cognitive psychology. The seven themes take us beyond the strict information processing approach and reveal some of the fascinating complexity and flexibility of the broadly conceived human information processing system. The seven themes are attention, automatic and conscious processing, data-driven versus conceptually driven processes, representation of knowledge, metacognition, unconscious processing, and levels of analysis in cognitive science.

Glossary Terms: attention; automatic/conscious processing; channel capacity; conceptually driven/data-driven processes; connectionist models; declarative/procedural knowledge; elaborative and maintenance rehearsal; encoding; episodic and semantic memory; executive controller; hardware/software; independent, sequential stages; information processing approach; lexical decision task; long-term memory; metacognition; metatheory; process model; recoding; representation of knowledge; sensory memory—auditory and visual; serial/parallel processing; short-term memory; unconscious processing; word frequency effect; working memory

SUGGESTED READINGS

Read about modern computer systems and artificial intelligence, for instance, Klieger's (1984) *Computer Usage for Social Scientists* or Haugeland's (1985) *Artificial Intelligence: The Very Idea*. It's fascinating to realize how extensively computer science and cognitive psychology have borrowed each other's terms. Computers have memory, "talk" to one another, "shake hands," and store and retrieve data; people have central processors and "memory banks." Haugeland's (1981) collection of papers in *Mind Design* contains one of my favorites, McDermott's "Artificial intelligence meets natural stupidity." Johnson-Laird (1988, Chapter 19) has a wonderfully thought-provoking discussion of the relationships among metacognition, self-reflection, and free will.

Chapter 5 in Lachman et al. (1979) presents a detailed discussion of the elements of the information processing approach. Newell and Simon's (1972) "Historical Addendum" provides a first-person account of the development of the general information processing framework and discusses the connections between psychology, computer science, and information theory. The September 1991 issue of *Psychological Science* is devoted entirely to the topic of "cognitive science"; see Gardner (1985) for a full-length treatment.

Chapter 3

PERCEPTION AND ATTENTION

If, then, by the original question, how many ideas or things can we attend to at once, be meant how many entirely disconnected systems or processes of conception can go on simultaneously, the answer is, not easily more than one, unless the processes are very habitual; but then two, or even three, without very much oscillation of the attention. Where, however, the processes are less automatic . . . there must be a rapid oscillation of the mind from one to the next, and no consequent gain of time. (James, 1890, p. 409)

Attention either shifts with great agility from one activity to another, or some of the activities are so automatic and habitual that they do not enter consciousness at all. (Hunter, 1923, pp. 137–138)

Perception seems so effortless and instantaneous, however rich and varied the visual scene may be, that it is hard to imagine the complexity of the analysis on which our experience depends. (Treisman, 1988, p. 201)

L et's get right to it—an in-depth discussion of perception, the sensory registers, pattern recognition, and the pervasive role of attention in the functioning of the human perceptual system. As the above quotation from James indicates, sensation, perception, and attention were among the very first interests of psychology in the late 1800s. Wundt and Titchener's concern with "the elements of consciousness" was largely an interest in the contents of the attentive mind: What are we aware *of* when we're attending to something? Since consciousness and attention were so wholly *mental,* not to mention troublesome from a scientific standpoint, it is not surprising that these topics were rather systematically ignored by American behaviorists. In tribute to their importance, however, they were among the very first cognitive topics to reappear in the 1950s. And despite their "old" age, you'll find that perception and attention are still among the most active of cognitive psychology's interests.

We'll begin with a basic study of perception, first visual and then auditory. We will focus especially on the mechanisms and properties of the visual and auditory sensory registers, because they are at the important intersection between the environment and the human cognitive system. Several theories of perception and pattern recognition will be covered, including your first major exposure to a *connectionist* model of cognition. In the final section of the chapter, we consider attention and its role in perceptual processing, and we merge the visual and auditory systems into an overview of human perception.

▼ Visual Perception

Figure 3-1 illustrates the basic sensory equipment involved in human vision. Light waves enter the eye, are focused and inverted by the lens, and are projected onto the **retina.** The retinal surface is composed of three basic layers of neurons: *rods and cones, bipolar cells, and ganglion*

FIGURE 3-1

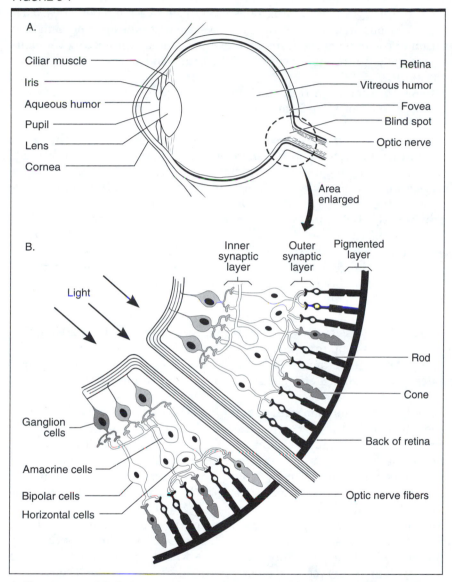

A.

Ciliar muscle

Iris

Aqueous humor

Pupil

Lens

Cornea

Retina

Vitreous humor

Fovea

Blind spot

Optic nerve

Area enlarged

B.

Inner synaptic layer

Outer synaptic layer

Pigmented layer

Light

Rod

Cone

Ganglion cells

Back of retina

Amacrine cells

Bipolar cells

Horizontal cells

Optic nerve fibers

A. The structure of the human eye, foveal pit, the optic nerve, and other structures.
B. The retina, rods and cones, bipolar cells, and ganglion cells. (From Hothersall, 1985.)

cells (see Figure 3-1B). The rods and cones form the back layer of neurons on the retina and are the neurons that are first stimulated by light. Thus these photosensitive neurons begin the process of vision. Patterns of neural firing from the rods and cones are forwarded to the second layer of neurons, the bipolar cells, which collect the messages and then pass them along to the third layer, the ganglion cells. The extended axons of the ganglion cells converge at the rear of the eye, forming a bundle known as the *optic nerve.* This nerve exits the eye and continues back through various structures in the optic system (e.g., the optic chiasm, the junction of the optic nerve from each eye), eventually projecting the neural message onto the visual cortex of the brain, in the lower rear portion of the skull.

Of special interest in this quick physiology lesson is the idea of *compression,* a kind of transformation that both analyzes and summarizes the visual input. That is, the message that finally reaches the visual cortex represents an already processed and summarized record of the original stimulus. As Haber and Hershenson (1973) point out, only a fraction of the original light energy is registered on the retina, the rest being absorbed and scattered by the fluid and structures within the eye. Furthermore, the three-layered retina also loses information. There are approximately 120 million rods on each retina, and about 7 million cones. Most of the cones lie in the small area known as the **fovea** (or foveal pit), which provides us with our most accurate, precise vision. At least some of the cones in the fovea seem to have their own "private" bipolar cells for relaying impulses—only *one* cone connecting with *one* bipolar cell, instead of many cones funneling their information into one bipolar cell (technically, we say that a cone *synapses* onto a bipolar cell). This is not the case in peripheral vision, however. About 20 degrees away from the fovea, tens or even hundreds of rods in the periphery will converge on a single bipolar cell. Such many-to-one convergence clearly implies a loss of information, since a bipolar cell cannot "know" which of its many rods triggered it.

Finally, only about one million ganglion cells combine to form the optic nerve. Here is still more compression and summarization of the neural impulses, now transmitted from the bipolar cells (again, there is evidence of the "private" pathway from some of the foveal cones and bipolar cells). Thus even the relatively "raw" messages reaching the brain, not yet processed by the cognitive system, have been reduced and summarized to a great degree.

Despite this summarizing, human vision is still amazingly sensitive and acute, enough so to perceive a candle flame on a clear, dark night at a distance of 30 miles (Galanter, 1962). As with all good summaries, the visual system preserves the most useful information, the edges, contours, and any kind of change, and omits the less useful, the unchanging, or steady-state information.

We've been talking about visual **sensation,** the *reception of stimulation from the environment and the initial encoding of that stimulation into the nervous system.* On the other hand, our primary interest concerns what happens next, what we *do* with this encoded information once the optic nerve has transmitted it to the visual cortex. In other words, we want to understand visual **perception,** *the process of interpreting and understanding sensory information.* In Levine and Shefner's (1981) words, "*Perception* refers to the way in which we *interpret* the information gathered (and processed) by the senses. In a word, we *sense* the presence of a stimulus, but we **perceive** what it is" (p. 1, emphasis added). Since doing something mentally with the raw sensory information is our primary focus, we need to explore the stages of visual perception and information processing. We begin by asking how the eye gathers information from the environment, then turn to the memory system that registers that information, visual sensory memory.

Gathering Visual Information

It is easy to believe, naively, that we take in visual information in a smooth and continuous fashion whenever our eyes are open. After all, our visual experience is of a connected, coherent visual scene that we can scan and examine at will. This is largely an illusion, however—one that you can easily disconfirm by a simple observation. Have someone watch your eyes as you read. Your friend will tell you that your eyes do not sweep smoothly across a line of print. Instead, they jerk across the line, bit by bit, with pauses between the successive movements.

Here are the facts. The eye sweeps from one point to another in fast movements called **saccades** (French for "jerk"), movements that are interrupted by pauses or **fixations.** While the eye movement itself is fairly rapid, on the order of 50–100 milliseconds (msec), it takes about 200 msec to trigger the movement (Haber & Hershenson, 1973). During the saccade, there is suppression of the normal visual processes. Thus, for the most part, the eye takes in visual information only during the 200 msec fixation pause. It's as if we are blind during the actual sweeping of the eye (if the eye did encode information during the saccade, we'd see a blur). If we assume something in the range of 250–300 msec for an entire fixation-then-saccade cycle, there is enough time for about three or four complete visual cycles per second. Each cycle registers a distinct and separate visual scene, although only a radical shift in gaze would make one cycle's input completely different from the previous one.

A final important detail concerns the triggering of saccades themselves, and more generally the engagement of visual attention. As Allport (1989) notes, there is a competition-like situation in visual attention. On the one hand, attention must be "interruptible." That is, we need to be prepared to react quickly to the unexpected, for example, when sudden movement alerts us to a possibly dangerous situation (a car running a red light as you drive through the intersection). Thus while you are focusing your visual attention on one stimulus, the visual system must be able to process *other* visual inputs, those outside the focus of visual attention, to at least some degree. As you'll read later, much of this low-level processing appears to occur in parallel with other visual processing and involves detection of simple visual features (e.g., Treisman & Gelade, 1980). On the other hand, visual attention should not be *too* interruptible. We cannot constantly be switching from one input to another—from the words in this sentence to your desk lamp to the scene outside your window to the color of the wall. If attention switched that frequently and erratically, visual (and mental) continuity would be destroyed. Balancing these competing tendencies then is an ongoing process of monitoring; we evaluate the importance of current activity, of maintaining visual attention, and we judge that relative to the importance or urgency of stimuli outside the current attentional focus.

Visual Sensory Memory

We turn now to visual sensory memory, the memory register that receives the visual input from the eyes. Since this memory system is so very brief, we generally have few useful intuitions about its operation. Unusual circumstances, however, can give us some clues. Thus we begin with such a circumstance.

Everyone has seen a flash of lightning during a thunderstorm. Think about that for a moment, then make a guess as to the duration of the light we see in an otherwise darkened backyard (or other visual scene) when a bolt of lightning strikes. Most people guess that the flash of light lasts a little more than a half second or so, maybe closer to a whole second sometimes. If your estimate was in this neighborhood, then it's reasonable—but not as an estimate of the physical duration of the lightning. The bolt of lightning is actually three or four separate bolts. Each bolt lasts about one millisecond, and there is a separation of about 50 milliseconds between each bolt. Thus the entire lightning strike lasts no more than about 2/10ths of a second, or 200 msec, and is composed of several individual flashes (Trigg & Lerner, 1981).

What was reasonable about your estimate? It was your *perception* of a

Our perception of lightning is a mental event that reflects visual persistence.

flash of light extended in time. This phenomenon is called **visual persistence**—the *apparent persistence of a visual stimulus beyond its physical duration.* This phenomenon usually includes the subjective feeling that you can "look around" the scene and that the scene "fades away" rather than being "switched off." In terms of the physiology of the visual system, the neural activity on the retina that is caused by the lightning flash does not outlast the flash itself. The eye itself does not continue to send "lightning" messages into the system after the flash is over (unless a retinal afterimage is involved). Your perception of the lightning, however, is a mental event that reflects visual persistence: you *perceive* a lighted scene that then begins to fade away. Since any persistence of information beyond its physical duration defines the term *memory,* the processes of visual perception (as opposed to sensation) must begin with a visual memory system, some sort of *temporary visual buffer that holds visual information for brief periods of time.* This memory is termed **visual sensory memory;** Neisser's (1967) term **iconic memory** is entirely equivalent.

Amount and Duration of Storage The classic cognitive research on the characteristics and processes of visual sensory memory was that reported by Sperling and his co-workers (1960; Averbach & Sperling, 1961). Sperling used a special apparatus for presenting visual stimuli, the *tachistoscope,* commonly known (and more easily pronounced) as a *T-scope.*[1] By using this apparatus, an investigator can present a visual stimulus for a carefully controlled period of time, usually on the order of milliseconds, and in a carefully controlled position, usually so that the stimulus is projected on the subject's fovea. The T-scope also permits the experimenter to control what is seen before and after the stimulus, the *preexposure* and *postexposure* fields. As investigators before him had, Sperling wondered about "the information available in brief visual presentations," the title of his important monograph in 1960.

A typical iconic memory experiment by Sperling presented arrays of letters and digits to subjects on a T-scope for very brief durations. In all cases, the subject's task was to report what could be remembered from the display. For example, subjects would be shown a series of trials, each with a 3 × 4 array of letters (three rows, four letters per row). The array was shown for 50 msec and was followed by a blank postexposure field. Finally, a signal was given to the subject to report the letters from the display. See Figure 3-2 for a schematic diagram of a typical trial.

Sperling found that subjects generally reported no more than four or five items correctly in this kind of test. When fewer than five items were shown, performance was essentially perfect, but when more than five were shown, subjects averaged about 4.5 letters correct; for a display of 12 letters, this is 37% accuracy. Furthermore, he found that this level of

---

[1]The stem *tachisto* is from Greek, meaning very swift or rapid, as in the word *tachometer.* The suffix *-scope* refers to an instrument for seeing or observing.

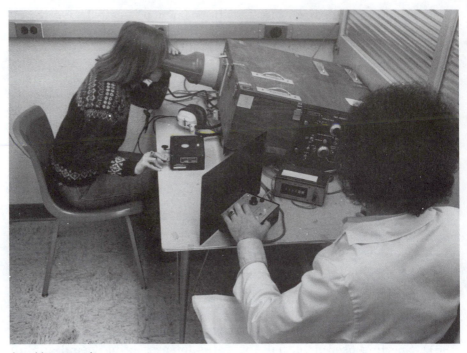

A tachistoscope in use.

FIGURE 3-2

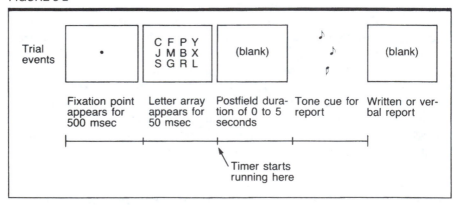

A schematic diagram of a typical trial in Sperling's (1960) experiments. After a fixation point appears for 500 msec, the letter array is displayed. The visual field after the display is blank. The tone cue can occur at the same time as the postfield, or it can be delayed up to 5 seconds.

accuracy remained essentially the same for exposures as long as 500 msec, and even as short as 5 msec (1963). It appeared to Sperling that subjects' average of 4.5 items correct reflected a kind of "default" strategy. That is, subjects said they couldn't possibly remember all 12 letters because the display seemed to fade from view too rapidly: even though they had genuinely seen the entire display, it disappeared too quickly. Consequently, subjects seemed to be deciding before the trial began that they would focus or concentrate on just one or two of the rows, trying to maximize their performance on at least a part of the display. Their level of performance, about 4 or 5 items, was what would be expected based on the **span of apprehension,** *the number of individual items recallable after any short display* (also known as the *span of attention* or the *span of immediate memory;* see Chapter 4).

What distinguished Sperling's research from the many studies that preceded it was the ingenious condition he developed to contrast with these results. The condition described above, where subjects are to report any and all letters they can, is termed the **whole-report condition,** for the obvious reason that the whole display was to be reported. The contrasting condition Sperling dreamed up is called the **partial-report condition.** The logic behind this condition was absolutely elegant.

Sperling reasoned that *all* the letters of the display might be available initially, but then might fade more rapidly than subjects could report them. If this is true, then subjects should be highly accurate on any *one* of the rows that the experimenter might choose at random, if they are told which row to report before too much fading has taken place. So in the partial-report condition, he prearranged a special signal for the subjects: a high tone, sounded right after the display went off, was a cue for reporting the top row; a medium tone cued the middle row, and a low tone cued the bottom row. The crucial ingredient here is that the tone cues were presented *after* the display went off. Subjects had no way of knowing ahead of time which row they would be responsible for, so they had to be prepared to report *any* of them.

Say that on a particular trial the low tone sounded right after the display went off. Given that the array should still be visible to the subject, because of visual persistence, the subject should be able to focus mental attention on the bottom row and read out those letters accurately while they are still visible. Sperling found that this was exactly what happened. When the tone followed the display immediately, subjects' performance was 76% correct; that is, 76% of the cued row (about three of the four items) could be reported accurately. By logical extension, if performance was 76% on any randomly selected row, then the subjects' visual memory of the *entire* display must also be around 76%.[2]

This rather startling result suggested that immediately after a visual

---

[2]Professors use the same logic. I tell my class, "You are going to be tested on Chapters 1 through 3," then I *only* ask questions from Chapter 2. If you score 76% on this test, I infer that you also could have gotten about 76% on either of the other two chapters. Thus it seems that 76% of the total amount of information was available to you on the test.

stimulus is displayed, a great deal of the stimulus information is available in visual sensory memory—much more than could be reported out loud. On the other hand, we would not expect this much of the display to remain visible and reportable for very long. After all, the whole-report condition almost never exceeded four or five items, averaging 37% of the whole display. As expected, performance in the partial-report group began to decline as the information in iconic memory began to fade. As the blank postfield interval got longer—more and more time passed until the tone—performance dwindled further. With a one-second delay, partial-report performance was 36%, almost exactly what the whole-report condition achieved on the same materials (Sperling, 1960).

These important results are shown in Figure 3-3, in the curve for light pre- and postfields. In Sperling's own words, "The explanation for these results is that the visual image of the stimulus persists for a short time after the stimulus has been turned off, and that the subjects can utilize this rapidly fading image. In fact, naive subjects typically believe that the physical stimulus fades out slowly" (1963, p. 22). This, of course, was our naive impression of the flash of lightning as well. As the fading continues, however, less and less of the original display is still visible in iconic memory, until by one second the only reportable items are those

FIGURE 3-3

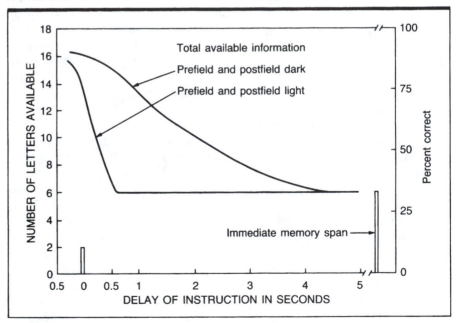

One subject's results on the number of letters available for report, as revealed by the partial-report condition. The number of reportable letters drops sharply within 0.25 seconds when the postfield is light; the information persists considerably longer when the postfield is dark. The vertical bars on the abscissa show the number of letters reported under whole-report.

few that were transferred into the more durable short-term memory store.

In other experiments, Sperling determined some of the limits of this visual sensory memory and some of its more detailed characteristics. For instance, in one study he presented 18 letters in the display; partial-report performance indicated that at least 17 of the letters were available in the initial **icon** (the contents of iconic memory are often merely referred to as the icon, *the visual image that resides in iconic memory*). This study (Averbach & Sperling, 1961) also varied the visual characteristics of the stimulus, to demonstrate the particularly *visual* (as opposed to mental) nature of the icon and iconic memory storage. Dark pre- and postexposure fields lengthened the useful readout period of iconic information, when compared to light pre- and postexposure fields (just as a lightning bolt is more visible in a nighttime storm than a daytime storm, because of the contrast with the background illumination). Over 50% of the letters were still available after a two-second cue delay when dark fields were used (see Figure 3-3). In contrast, accuracy dropped to 50% with light fields after only a quarter of a second. As would be expected of a visually based memory, the light and dark contrast of the stimulus display itself also affected the results, with better iconic visibility for sharper contrasts.

Finally, in all cases, the actual reporting of the letters was due to a "readout" or transfer process; recall from the last chapter that the subject's response is always assumed to come most directly from the short-term memory system. In this readout process, the available letters are transferred, by means of attention, to short-term memory, where the actual written or spoken response is generated (note that long-term memory is implicated here as well, since the names of the letters have to be "looked up" in memory in order to be written or spoken). Just as we would expect from short-term memory, Sperling found that subjects' errors were often *auditory* rather than visual, for example, substituting a letter or digit that sounded like the stimulus (B or 3 for T, for instance). Since the auditory nature of short-term memory was well known by this time (see Chapter 4), this was especially convincing evidence that iconic memories were shunted through short-term memory in order to be reported.

Erasure of Visual Information   A related series of experiments by Sperling and others explored the loss of information from iconic memory more carefully. The original research suggested that forgetting was a passive process like fading. That is, the mere passage of time degraded iconic memory for the display, rendering it illegible after some short interval. This must certainly be true, in and of itself, since care was taken to prevent subsequent stimuli from entering the visual store (the blank postexposure fields). But of course, in normal vision, no such blank field follows the visual input to our eyes: we look around continuously, shifting visual gaze from one stimulus to another all the time. What happens to iconic memory when a second stimulus is presented to the subject, when one visual scene is immediately followed by another?

A well-known study of this more elaborate situation was done by Averbach and Coriell (1961; reprinted in Coltheart, 1973). These investigators presented a display of two rows of letters, eight letters per row, for 50 msec. A blank white postexposure field, varying in duration, followed the display and was then itself followed by a partial-report cue. Unlike Sperling, however, Averbach and Coriell used a *visual* cue, either a vertical bar marker or a circle marker. The bar marker was positioned just above (or below) the position of the to-be-reported letter, while the circle marker was presented so as to surround the position where the to-be-reported letter had just disappeared. As in the Sperling procedures, subjects did not know ahead of time what letters would appear in the display or which letter they would have to report.

In their bar marker study, Averbach and Coriell found results that were very close to those obtained by Sperling; for example, high performance with short delays of the cues, lower performance with longer delays, an effective duration of about one-quarter of a second. But the results from the circle marker study were somewhat different. When the circle marker cued the position to be reported, subjects were considerably less accurate than they were with the bar marker. In a second study, the circle marker was filled with grid lines and produced an even more dramatic decline in performance.

These results suggested strongly that the identical positioning of the circle had in some way "erased" the memory trace for the letter in that position. Note what a seemingly unusual event this is: *"a later visual stimulus can drastically affect the perception of an earlier one"* (Averbach & Coriell, cited in Coltheart, 1973, p. 16, emphasis added). This effect is called **backward masking.** The masking stimulus, if it occurs soon enough after the letter display, interferes with the perception of the earlier stimulus presented at the same position. In some backward masking studies, subjects literally claim that they saw *only* the mask, even though their other performance indicates that the sensory system did indeed register the first stimulus (data on this go back as far as Werner, 1935; see Kahneman, 1968, for a review). In general then, *when the contents of visual sensory memory are degraded by subsequent visual stimuli,* the loss of the original information is termed *erasure.*

The Argument About Iconic Memory

The evidence collected by Sperling, Averbach and Coriell, and others, led cognitive psychology to propose that iconic memory was the initial step in visual information processing. The phenomenon of visual persistence, as revealed in the quarter-second duration of information presented by the T-scope, was replicated many times. This convinced cognitive psychology that iconic memory existed, and that it was the important first phase in visual perception (e.g., Neisser, 1967). Theories of visual perception therefore included iconic storage as an integral part of visual perception.

An alternate view, however, was expressed most strongly by Haber (1983) in his paper "The Impending Demise of the Icon." Haber did not doubt the evidence on visual persistence, nor did he quibble with the term *icon* as a label for the mental image or "snapshot" preserved by visual persistence. What he claimed, however, was that this static icon is quite irrelevant to an understanding of normal visual perception. As he put it, only somewhat facetiously, "The notion of an icon as a brief storage of information persisting after stimulus termination cannot possibly be useful in any typical visual information-processing task except reading in a lightning storm" (p. 1).

The logic behind Haber's conclusion was based in part on the concept of ecological validity (see Chapter 1). As Haber noted, no ordinary visual experience is even remotely similar to lab tasks using the T-scope. We do not normally see only brief flashes of visual stimuli in our environment, followed by a blank field. The only real-world circumstance that even comes close to resembling this is the brief illumination provided by a bolt of lightning. Instead, the visual environment *remains* in view as long as we fixate our eyes on it. We have *continuous,* rather than momentary, exposure to visual scenes, and we can extract information from those scenes across as much time as we care to devote to them. In short, Haber argued that while iconic memory and visual persistence are real, they are irrelevant to the normal task of perceiving continuous visual information.

Haber's paper was followed by a string of replies, some in favor of his conclusion, some opposed. Several (e.g., G. R. Loftus, 1983) attacked the philosophical basis of Haber's argument. Haber maintained that the visual stimulation provided by a T-scope is so artificial as to be ungeneralizable to real perceptual environments. Loftus, among others, criticized this view on the grounds that science has traditionally taken exactly this kind of reductionistic approach and has generally been well served by it. According to this counterargument, cognitive psychology's task is not to throw out the concept of iconic memory, but instead to flesh it out and to determine how it contributes to normal visual perception.

A second criticism leveled by Haber involves the notion of the continuously available visual environment. Why would we build a theory of visual perception based on brief, discrete flashes of stimulation, he asked, when the normal visual environment is continuously present? As it happens, it may be rather unimportant for normal vision that the environment *is* continuously present, strangely enough—at least if we consider printed text to be a normal visual environment. Coltheart (1983), for example, pointed out that Sperling's original experiments included an examination of different durations of presentation; some trials presented the letter grid for only 5 msec, and some presented it for up to 500 msec. Interestingly, accuracy in these two extreme conditions was not appreciably different. In other words, subjects' reports were as accurate with only 5 msec of time to extract information from the display as they were with a full 500 msec.

A similar—and very powerful—demonstration was reported by Rayner, Inhoff, Morrison, Slowiaczek, and Bertera (1981), who examined performance during a text-reading task. After subjects had fixated a word for 50 msec, the word was *replaced* with a completely irrelevant stimulus, which remained in view for another 175 msec in order to "fill up" the rest of the fixation time. Surprisingly, this replacement did not affect reading performance at all. In Coltheart's (1983) words, "Continuous . . . sampling of the text throughout a fixation does not occur. Once the text has been fixated for 50 msec or so, its presence during the remainder of the fixation is *irrelevant* and makes *no* contribution to reading" (p. 18, emphasis added). Thus Haber's point about the environment—that we can continuously sample information from it—may in fact be irrelevant to the way the eye actually extracts visual information.

Finally, Haber noted that the static "snapshot" character of the icon seems irrelevant to the issues of how people perceive movement, and how perception functions when our eyes, heads, and bodies move in relation to the visual environment. In response to such criticisms, several investigators have collected evidence on what might be called "dynamic icons," that is, iconic images that contain movement. For instance, Treisman, Russel, and Green (1975) presented a brief (100 msec) display of six moving dots to their subjects and asked them to report the direction of movement. Partial-report performance was superior to whole-report performance, and accuracy under partial report declined across time. In short, the moving images of the dots were decaying just as the static letter grid had in Sperling's procedures (see also Finke & Freyd, 1985; Irwin, 1991, 1992; Loftus & Hanna, 1989). Thus visual perception is not a process of flipping through successive "snapshots," with three or four snapshots per second. Instead, it may be more accurately described as a process of focusing on the visually attended elements of successive fixations, where each fixation encodes a dynamic segment of the visual environment. As Irwin (1991) put it, our "perceptual representation of the environment is built up via the integration of information across [several] saccadic eye movements" (p. 420).

A Summary for Visual Sensory Memory

How do all these different results make sense, the wholesale input of visual stimulation, the persistence, decay, and erasure of information, the concept of visual attention?

Consider the following integration. Under normal viewing conditions, one moment's visual input replaces the just-previous visual input, by means of erasure or "writing over." Under unusual circumstances, say, the single brief glimpse afforded by a T-scope, even the shortest of stimulus displays will seem to last about $1/4$ sec (250 or 300 msec) due to visual persistence, the duration of a normal iconic memory. With a blank post-exposure field, which artificially prevents any subsequent stimulus at all, the perceptual fading of the icon is even visible. The continuous stream of successive glimpses in normal vision, however, serves as the eraser under more normal viewing conditions. Under those normal circumstances, we're not aware of any fading. Note here that the rapid extraction of information during the first few milliseconds of exposure appears to be critical to the perception of continuous vision. Indeed, it may be that the first 50 msec or so are all that's needed to encode visual information; during the remaining time, we then read out the information and begin to replace that icon with new information from the next fixation.

The entire sequence of encoding visual information—selecting part of it for further processing, planning subsequent eye movements, and so on—is highly active and very rapid. The visual continuity we experience, our feeling that we see continuously, without breaks, pauses, or blank intervals, is due to the constant updating of visual sensory memory and to our focus on attended information. As we pay attention to a visual stimulus, we seem to be examining the "readout" from iconic memory. In the meantime, a new visual scene is being registered in sensory memory. Our mental processes then pick up the thread of visual information in the newly registered scene, providing a smooth transition from one attended display to the next.

Focal attention was Neisser's (1967) term for this *mental process of visual attention,* for instance, the mental redirection of attention when the partial-report cue is presented. It would seem that focal attention, now more commonly referred to simply as **visual attention,** might be the "bridge" between successive scenes registered by visual sensory memory. This bridging process prevents us from sensing the blank space of time occupied by the eye's saccades, by directing focal attention instead to elements of the icon. While we *sense* a great deal of visual information, what we *perceive* is the part of a visual scene selected for focal, visual attention. To exaggerate just a bit, what you are perceiving right now is not the printed page in front of you. Instead, you are perceiving the processed and attended portion of the displays that were registered in sensory memory, your iconic trace, as processed by visual attention. And, to anticipate an important idea about attention itself, think of this focused visual attention as a "visual spotlight," shining on just a fragment of the visual world at any moment, but encoding the spotlighted fragment into visual sensory memory.

Summary Points: anatomy of vision; sensation versus perception; visual sensory memory, amount and duration; decay and erasure; the dynamic icon; focal "spotlight" attention

▼ Auditory Perception

Auditory stimuli consist of sound waves traveling through the air. The human auditory mechanism that responds to these stimuli is an amazingly awkward combination of components, a Rube Goldberg-like mechanism that translates the sound waves into a neural message. First, the sound waves are funneled into the ear, causing the tympanic membrane, or eardrum, to vibrate. This in turn causes the bones of the middle ear to move, which in turn sets in motion the fluid in the ear's inner cavity. The moving fluid then moves the tiny hair cells along the basilar membrane, generating the neural message, which is then sent along the auditory nerve into the cerebral cortex (e.g., Forgus & Melamed, 1976). Thus from the relatively unpromising elements of funnels, moving bones, and the like (see Figure 3-4) arises our sense of *hearing* or **audition.**

The sensitivity of our sense of hearing is of particular interest, since it defines the limits of our auditory world. A pure tone, such as that generated by a tuning fork, is a traveling sound wave with a regular *frequency,* a smooth pattern of up-and-down cycles per unit of time (see Figure 3-5A). Generally, humans are sensitive to patterns as low as 20 cps (cycles per second) and as high as 20,000 cps. Most of the sound patterns we are interested in, such as those generated by spoken speech, are of great complexity, combining dozens of different frequencies that vary widely in intensity or loudness. In terms of the sound-wave patterns, these different frequencies are more or less superimposed and can be summarized in a "spectrum" (see Figure 3-5B). Thus Figure 3-5A shows a wave with a frequency of 100 cps; this 100 cps value is the first vertical component of the spectrum in the bottom illustration, a spectrum of frequencies in a piano's middle C note.

In one sense, human hearing is not particularly impressive: dogs, for instance, are sensitive to much higher frequencies than we are. In quite a different sense, our hearing is almost unbelievably complex. For instance, our hearing is sufficiently sensitive to detect, from a distance of about 20 feet, the ticking of a watch in a quiet room (Galanter, 1962). More impressive yet, we can discriminate accurately between highly similar sounds even from birth: the slight difference between the sounds "pah" and "bah" is noticed by newborn infants (e.g., Eimas, 1975). And most impressive of all, we routinely convert the continuous stream of sounds known as speech into a comprehended message with little or no apparent effort, at a rate of about two or three words per second. How does this auditory system work? How does it coordinate with our knowledge of language to yield recognition and comprehension so rapidly?

FIGURE 3-4

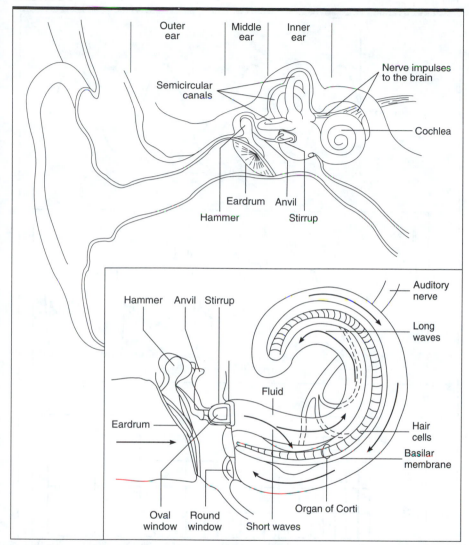

The gross structure of the human ear and a close-up of the middle and inner ear structures.

Auditory Sensory Memory

The term **auditory sensory memory** is used interchangeably with Neisser's (1967) term **echoic memory.** Both terms refer to a *brief memory system that receives auditory stimuli and preserves them for some amount of time.* Neisser's argument on the existence of echoic memory is

FIGURE 3-5

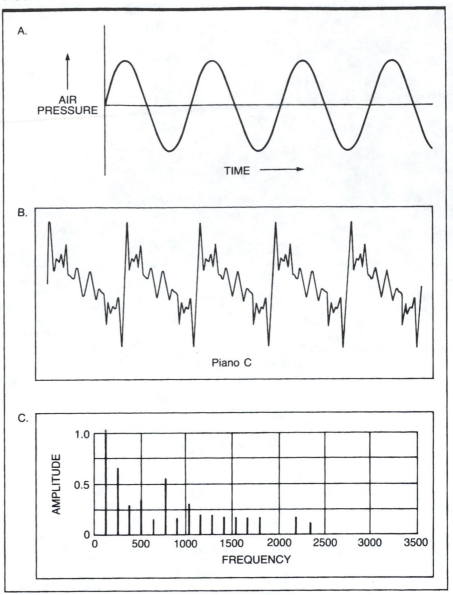

Panel A illustrates a simple sound wave of regular frequency. The sound wave pattern of a piano's middle C is illustrated in panel B, and a spectrum of this pattern is illustrated in panel C.

still airtight: "Perhaps the most fundamental fact about hearing is that sound is an intrinsically temporal event. Auditory information is always spread out in time; no single millisecond contains enough information to be very useful. If information were discarded as soon as it arrived, hearing would be all but impossible. Therefore, we must assume that some 'buffer,' some medium for temporary storage, is available in the auditory cognitive system" (1967, pp. 199–200).

On the other side of the coin, it's equally clear that the memory system cannot (and should not) preserve the raw echoic memory trace forever. As was the case in iconic memory, only confusion would result if all auditory traces were held indefinitely. Thus the function of echoic memory is to encode the sensory stimulation into the memory system and hold it just long enough for the rest of the mental system to gain access to it.

Amount and Duration of Storage   What is the effective duration of information stored in echoic memory? How long will encoded information reside there before it is lost? To answer these questions, we need a task that is the auditory analogue to Sperling's work. That is, we need a task that presents auditory stimuli briefly, in different auditory "locations," and in such a way that we can cue selected parts of the auditory "display" for partial report.

Such a task was devised by Darwin, Turvey, and Crowder (1972; see also Moray, Bates, & Barnett, 1965). Darwin et al. devised what they called the "three-eared man procedure," in which three different spoken messages came from three distinct locations. The subjects heard tape-recorded letters and digits through stereo headphones, with the tape engineered so that one message was played only into the left ear, one message was played only into the right ear, and the final message was played into *both* ears. Of course, the message played into both ears seemed to be localized in the middle of the subject's head, at the "third ear." Each of the messages contained three stimuli, say, *T 7 C* on the left ear, *4 B 9* on the right ear, and so on. Each sequence lasted one second on the tape recording, and all three sequences were presented simultaneously. Thus in the space of one second, three different sequences of letter and digit combinations were played, for a total of nine separate stimuli.

After the auditory messages were presented, subjects in the whole-report condition had to report as many of the nine items as they could remember. Their performance averaged about four items correct, as shown in Figure 3-6. Subjects in the partial-report condition were shown a visual cue, prompting recall of the left, right, or middle message. When the visual cue was presented immediately after the stimuli had been heard, performance on the cued ear was well above 50%, suggesting that nearly five items out of the original nine were still available. The advantage of partial report over whole report was maintained even with a four-second delay in presenting the cue, although performance did decline during that waiting period (see Figure 3-6). Thus the decline in accuracy suggested a decrease in the useful contents of auditory sensory memory, presumably due to a passive fading of information across longer delays.

Note two differences in these results, compared to those for visual sensory memory. First, the estimated amount of information originally stored in auditory memory—estimated by partial report, of course—was not as impressive as the 75–90% values found for iconic memory. Dar-

FIGURE 3-6

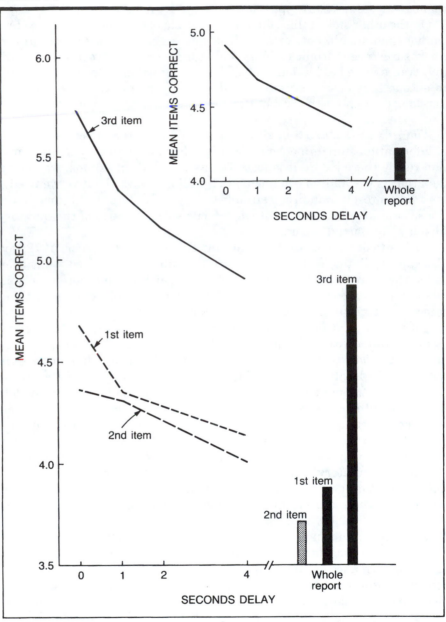

Partial-report performance, the average number of items recalled correctly, is shown for the first, second, and third items in the three lists, across varying delays in the presentation of the partial-report cue. The inset shows overall performance, along with the vertical bar that shows whole-report accuracy. (Data from Darwin et al., 1972.)

win's subjects exceeded the level of about five items available out of the presented nine only on the third position items, those presented last in the sequences. Second, there is the distinct possibility that sensory traces reside in auditory memory for a longer time if they represent simpler information. In general, the four-second duration found by Darwin et al. (1972) is longer than most estimates, probably due to the simplicity of the stimuli they used (most of the studies described below used coherent spoken language). In contrast, the four-second estimate is considerably shorter than the 10-second storage found by Eriksen and Johnson (1964)—but Eriksen and Johnson's subjects merely had to detect a simple tone while performing an attention-capturing task (they read novels for two hours; see also Watkins & Watkins, 1980).

Persistence and Erasure of Auditory Information   Without the process of redirected attention, the auditory trace in sensory memory will simply vanish with the passage of time, the auditory equivalent of passive fading in iconic memory. Recall, however, that there is also evidence of another kind of forgetting in iconic memory, due to erasure by subsequent stimuli. Is there any evidence of this kind of forgetting in auditory sensory memory, based on the interference of stimulus information encoded *after* the target information?

In a word, yes, although recent research indicates that a straightforward parallel with iconic persistence and erasure may be misleading, or even that a straightforward, purely auditory basis for what we've called auditory sensory memory may be somewhat inaccurate. We'll consider the original evidence, then discuss the controversy over the current status of, and understanding of, auditory sensory memory.

The best-known evidence on auditory persistence was presented by Crowder and Morton (1969; also Crowder, 1970, 1972). In their research, a list of nine digits was presented to all subjects in written form, at the fairly rapid rate of two items per second. In their Silent Vocalization condition, subjects merely saw the nine numbers and read them silently as they appeared. In the Active Vocalization condition, subjects not only saw the list, they were also asked to name the digits out loud as they appeared on the screen. In the Passive Vocalization condition, subjects heard an accompanying tape recording that named the viewed digits for them. When Crowder and Morton examined subjects' recall performance, they found hardly any errors on the last item in the list when there was an auditory trace of that letter, that is, in the Active and Passive Vocalization groups. Errors here, as shown in Figure 3-7, were below 10%. These subjects had literally heard that last item, so presumably could perform simple *readout* on it from auditory sensory memory (in fact, the last three positions showed the auditory advantage). In other words, there appeared to be a lingering sensory trace for the last sounds that were heard. The Silent group, however, showed substantial errors on the last items, around 50%, because there was no auditory sensory memory

FIGURE 3-7

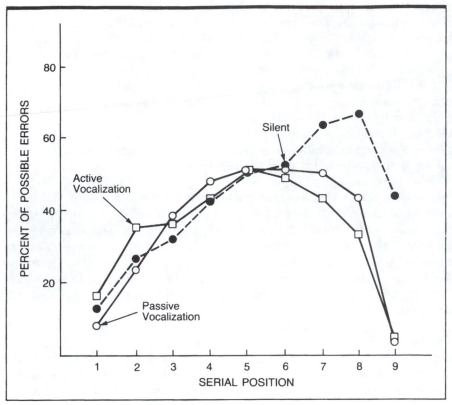

The number of errors in recall as a function of position in the list of items to be recalled. Note that the two Vocalization groups show virtually no errors on the last item, compared with the Silent group, which had no auditory trace of the list.

trace for them. (Recall for the earlier positions was presumably due to some combination of short- and long-term memory factors—rehearsal of some sort—and so is not of primary interest here.)

Thus Crowder suggested that the Vocalization conditions' recall for the last items was assisted by still-present traces in auditory sensory memory. This effect is generally known as the **modality effect,** *superior recall of the end of the list when the auditory mode is used instead of the visual mode of presentation.* Crowder (1972) argued that these results supported two distinct ideas: first, the existence of auditory sensory memory, and second, the persistence of auditory traces in sensory memory across some short interval of time. Crowder's term for auditory sensory memory was **precategorical acoustic storage,** usually abbreviated **PAS.** Since *categorization* implies recognition of the pattern, Crowder was claiming that this acoustic storage mechanism was *precategorical;* that is, it occurred *prior* to categorization or pattern recognition.

Having established that auditory traces persist across time, even in an unrecognized form, Crowder went on to investigate another important point, auditory erasure. After they heard the items in the list, subjects in the *suffix* groups then heard one additional auditory stimulus, either the word "zero" or a simple tone. Both groups were told that this final item was merely a cue to begin recalling the list. In reality, of course, the auditory *suffix* was intended to erase or interfere with the lingering auditory trace for the last items in the list.

As predicted, the "zero-suffix" group showed a high error rate on the last items, essentially the same error rate as the Silent group showed in the earlier study. The "tone-suffix" group, however, had very few errors on the last positions, just as with the Vocalization groups mentioned earlier. It seemed as though the auditory suffix had indeed degraded or erased the auditory trace for the last digits in the list when the suffix was similar to the list. Figure 3-8 summarizes this program of research. The result is quite similar to the erasure effect in vision, in that it varies depending on speech versus nonspeech suffixes, physical differences, and so on. Other research (Morton, 1970) found the suffix effect is strong when the sound arrives from the same physical location in auditory space; when the sound comes from a different location, the effect is reduced.

Summary Thus auditory sensory memory is similar to the visual sensory memory system at a general level, but the details of storage duration and amounts are rather different. Both systems register sensory information and hold it for a brief period of time; $1/4-1/2$ sec in vision, but 2–4 sec in audition. This duration for auditory sensory memory, however, may vary with the complexity of stored information. Generally, more information is encoded in both systems than can be reported; capacity in auditory sensory memory, however, may be proportionately lower than visual sensory memory, although this issue is not an easy issue to pin down. The items held in both sensory systems are subject to loss over short periods of time, either by fading, when no other stimuli are encountered, or by erasure, when interfering auditory stimuli are processed. Finally, if attention is redirected during the critical interval, information can be sent to short-term memory, preventing it from being lost. Just as in vision, our normal auditory world is usually one of continuous auditory stimulation, not discrete "bursts" of sound followed by unfilled, blank intervals.

A Note of Controversy

There has been some controversy around the issue of modality and suffix effects recently, and how critical it is that we are testing these effects with *language* stimuli, that is, spoken letters and digits. For example, Greene and Crowder (1984) found both a modality effect and a suffix effect when subjects silently "mouthed" the list items (also Greene

FIGURE 3-8

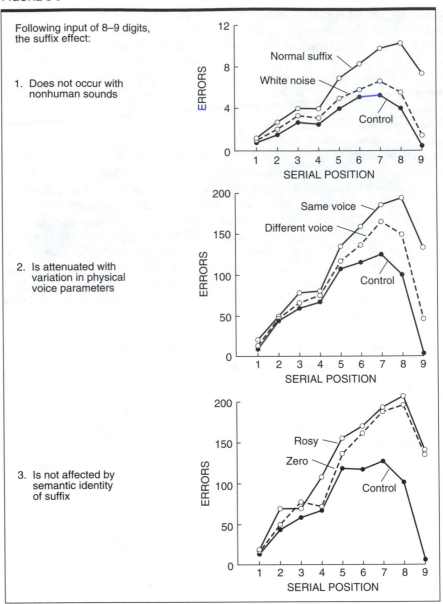

Following input of 8–9 digits, the suffix effect:

1. Does not occur with nonhuman sounds

2. Is attenuated with variation in physical voice parameters

3. Is not affected by semantic identity of suffix

The effect of various manipulations on the size of the stimulus suffix effect. (From Crowder, 1972.)

& Crowder, 1986). Of course, this suggests that having an auditory suffix *per se* is not important, a seemingly strange conclusion when the topic of the research was auditory sensory memory.

The interpretation offered by Greene and Crowder, however, seemed to resolve this apparent contradiction. In particular, they suggested that the mouthing of the list items generated some internal "gestural" code that was also stored in auditory sensory memory. This code would be related to the mouth and vocal *gestures* necessary for the generation or enunciation of the list items. In other words, even though mouthing the list items doesn't involve sound, mouthing would produce a speech-like mental code that is retained in sensory memory. It would be this code, rather than a literal auditory code, that accounts for the modality and suffix effects. Thus, by this account, auditory sensory memory can contain not only sound but also sound-related codes that are involved in speech and language. It would be this more generalized, sound-related code that is responsible for the typical effects, not just truly auditory information. As Greene and Crowder put it, "It is becoming clear that PAS is more than simply an 'echo box.' ... Experiments such as the present ones complicate our earlier models for PAS, but they also draw it more convincingly into an important role in language perception" (p. 381).

Summary Points: anatomy of audition; auditory sensory memory, amount and duration; erasure; modality and suffix effects

▼ Pattern Recognition: Vision

You've now studied the basics of vision and audition, the sensory systems and the sensory memories they imply. Let's turn to the next logical topic. Now that environmental stimuli are "in" the mental system, how do you recognize what you're perceiving? Because the answers to this question are similar for vision and audition, we'll focus just on vision here; the final section of the chapter will cover auditory pattern recognition in connection with attention.

Deciphering Written Language

We turn now to one of the most intriguing and debated topics in visual perception, the recognition or identification of visual patterns. The role of visual sensory memory in this process is that of encoding the visual information into the memory system. And yet, we need to go more deeply into the memory system in order to understand how a visual stimulus is processed to a level where it can be recognized as a familiar pattern. How does your cognitive system manage to input visual stimuli such as "G" or "tree" and end up recognizing them as familiar, meaningful symbols? How do we recognize patterns of handwriting, despite incredible variability (see Figure 3-9)?

The Template Approach As Neisser (1967) pointed out, recognition of patterns would be a simplified problem—though still thorny—if all the equivalent patterns we saw were identical. That is, if there were

FIGURE 3-9

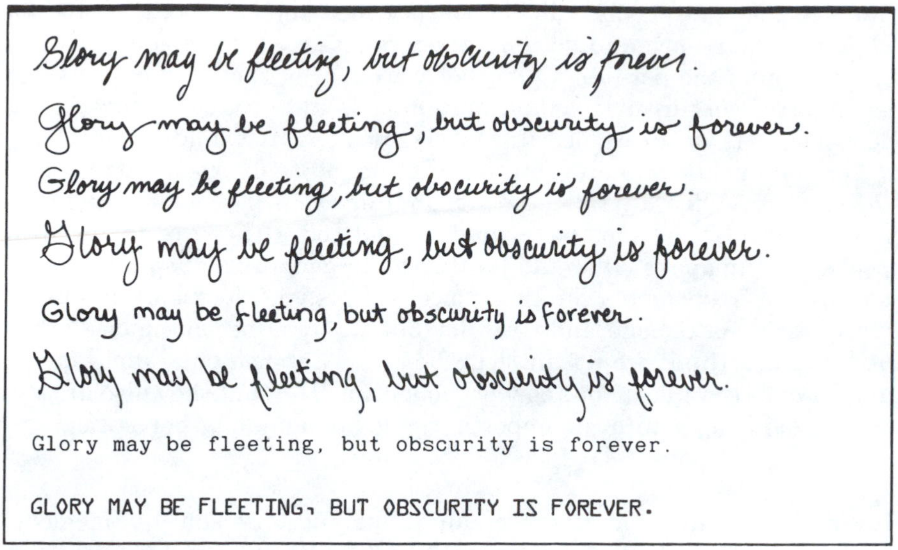

Glory may be fleeting, but obscurity is forever.

Glory may be fleeting, but obscurity is forever.

Glory may be fleeting, but obscurity is forever.

Glory may be fleeting, but obscurity is forever.

Glory may be fleeting, but obscurity is forever.

Glory may be fleeting, but obscurity is forever.

Glory may be fleeting, but obscurity is forever.

GLORY MAY BE FLEETING, BUT OBSCURITY IS FOREVER.

An illustration of the variety of patterns that are easily categorized by adult readers.

one and only one way for the capital letter G to appear, then the mental process that determines "ah, it's a G" would be more tractable to investigate. Figure 3-9 shows the obvious point, however, that the visual environment is not so conveniently organized. An enormous variety of visual patterns, in essentially infinite combinations of orientation and size, will all be categorized as the capital letter G, and of course likewise for all other letters, figures, shapes, and so on.

Perhaps this categorization is done by means of **templates,** *stored models of all categorizable patterns.* After all, when the computer at your bank reads your checking account number, it is performing a *template matching* process. Its visual input system attempts to make physical identity matches between the numbers on your check and its stored templates for the digits 0 through 9. Those templates are from the ANSI-OCR typeface (American National Standards Institute—Optical Character Recognition), as are the letters in the bottom line of Figure 3-9. When the computer "recognizes" a pattern, it has matched it to one of its stored digit or letter templates.

While the template approach has simplicity and economy on its side, it has very little else to recommend it. Quite obviously, it is a seriously flawed explanation of human pattern recognition. We've already covered the primary reason for this, the enormous variability in the patterns that we can nonetheless recognize. Other reasons exist too; for example, how long would it take you to learn the infinite number of possible patterns that you can recognize, or to search through them in memory? Would you have room left in memory for anything else?

Visual Feature Detection A distinct improvement over the template approach is the notion of **feature analysis** or **feature detection.** A feature, in this approach, is a *very simple pattern, a fragment or component that can appear in combination with other features* across a wide variety of stimulus patterns. A good example of such a visual feature might be a single straight, horizontal line, a feature that appears in capital letters A, G, H, L, and so on; another might be a circular segment, open to the right, as in capital letter C, diagonals as in V, and so on. In general, feature theories claim that we recognize whole patterns by breaking them apart, by analyzing them into the building-block features they contain. Rather than matching an entire template-like pattern for capital G then, maybe we simply analyze the G into its features. When "circle opening right" and "horizontal straight" segments are detected, the features match with those stored in memory for capital G. Successful feature matches, of course, are the necessary evidence for categorization, for deciding that the pattern is indeed a G.

This feature approach has been popular enough that several investigators have proposed rather elaborate theories of feature-based pattern recognition and have carefully worked out the "catalog" of features, so to speak, in written or printed letters (e.g., Gibson, 1965). We'll discuss one such model in some detail, since it represents a particularly clear example of feature-detection models, and since it was described in a rather entertaining (for psychology) fashion. It is also important because it provides some necessary building blocks for understanding the current rage in cognitive science, *connectionist models.*

Pandemonium

Selfridge, an early advocate of feature detection, described a model of pattern recognition he called Pandemonium (1959); an illustration of the model is shown in Figure 3-10. In Selfridge's imaginative description, "Pandemonium reigns" in the process of pattern recognition because of the mental mechanisms that process a visual stimulus. These mechanisms were *demons* in Selfridge's model, little mental demons who shout out loud as they attempt to identify patterns. As the figure shows, a pattern is encoded by a set of *data demons*. Next, the *computational demons* begin to act. These computational demons are the feature analyzers in Selfridge's model—each one has a single, simple feature it's trying to match in the stimulus pattern. For instance, one demon might be trying to match a simple horizontal line, another would try to match a vertical line, another a complete circle, another a curve opening to the right.

FIGURE 3-10

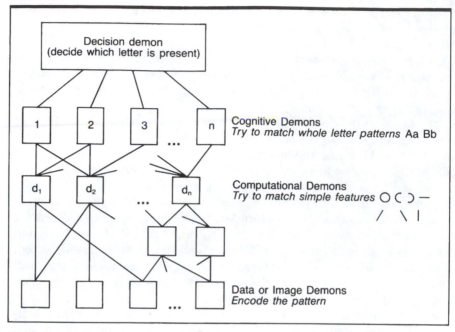

The data or image demons encode the visual pattern. The computational demons try to match the simple features present in the pattern. Cognitive demons represent the combinations of features that are present in different letters of the alphabet; each tries to match the several computational demons that match the stimulus input. Finally, the decision demon identifies the pattern by selecting the loudest cognitive demon, the one whose features most nearly match the pattern being presented.

When a computational demon matches a stimulus feature, it begins to shout excitedly.

At the next level up, listening to the shouting of all the noisy computational demons, is a set of *cognitive demons*. These cognitive demons represent the different letters of the alphabet, one for each letter. Each one is listening for a particular combination of demons to shout: for instance, the G-demon is listening for the "open curve" and the "horizontal bar" feature analyzers or demons to shout. Any evidence from the computational demons that suggests a match with the stimulus causes the cognitive demon to begin shouting as well: it thinks, based on the feature analysis evidence, that *it* is the matching pattern. Several of the cognitive demons will be shouting at once, since several letters will usually share some features (e.g., C and G). Thus the one who shouts the loudest is the one whose pattern is most nearly matched by the input stimulus. The loudest cognitive demon is finally heard by the *decision demon,* the highest level demon in the model. This demon, of course, has the final say in recognizing and categorizing the pattern.

Aside from the vividness of the model's description—scores of shouting demons producing a noisy Pandemonium—Selfridge's model incorporated several ideas that are important to the entire issue of pattern recognition. First, at base, it was a feature-detection model. The features that were detected and reported by the demons were elementary, simple features—components that in different combinations represent the letters of the alphabet being recognized (Selfridge's model was not limited to letters, but the process is more easily described using letters as examples).

There are now several related lines of evidence for feature detection in visual pattern recognition (e.g., Pritchard, 1961). Especially convincing are the neurophysiological studies, showing that specialized visual cortex cells exist for various simple visual features and patterns. The most widely known evidence of this kind comes from research done by Hubel and Wiesel (1962). Using sophisticated electrode implant procedures, these researchers found neurons in cats' brains that respond only to vertical lines, other neurons that respond only to diagonals, and so on. On the assumption that the human brain is not radically different from a cat's at the level of neuronal functioning, this would suggest that feature detection may even have a physiological status in the nervous system (for similar evidence in monkeys, see Maunsell & Newsome, 1987). Furthermore, it means that psychological theories of pattern recognition must be compatible with this neurological evidence.

A second important notion in Selfridge's model was the idea of parallel processing; the computational demons, for instance, all work at the same time, each one trying to match its own feature while all the others are doing the same thing. Selfridge was pointing out, with this aspect of his model, that feature detection or analysis is most probably a simultaneous or parallel process, instead of a serial, "one after the other" process. This would seem to be a very reasonable position, even if we use printed text as our only evidence. That is, the number of individual feature tests needed to recognize all the letters across a single line of print must be quite large. Given the speed with which adults can read a single line, we would have to assume an impossibly fast rate of feature detection if the process is occurring serially. Neisser, Novick, and Lazar (1963) found evidence consistent with the proposal of parallel processing of features when their subjects could scan for the presence of ten different letters just as quickly as they could scan for one. Indeed, there is physiological evidence of parallel processing within the visual cortex (e.g., see Lennie, 1980).

Beyond Features: Conceptually Driven Pattern Recognition

How adequate is the feature-detection approach as an explanation of visual pattern recognition? Does it do justice to our performance on various visual perception tests? Let's examine some data that support the feature theory approach, but that at the same time suggest an extra ingredient that is missing from our description.

Consider the now classic research conducted by Neisser (1964) on visual search. Neisser presented pages of characters, 50 lines of printed letters, with four to six letters per line. The subject's task was to scan the page as rapidly as possible in order to find the one occurrence of a pre-specified letter (in other tasks, he asked people to find the line *without* a certain character). As an illustration of the task, do the visual searches presented in Figure 3-11, timing yourself as you find the several different targets. You'll notice how hard it is to find a line without a specified letter, and to find a letter that is physically similar to the distractor letters in the display.

Can a pure feature-detection theory, such as Selfridge's, account for these results? A feature-detection theory claims that the subject scans down the columns of letters, extracting the elements or features from each pattern, then classifying the letters as targets or distractors. Finding the K in the angular-letter column will be difficult, of course, because the features that define K are also sprinkled liberally through the rest of the angular letters. But if the display contains mostly rounded-feature letters, then most of the detectable features in the display can be ignored: the pattern recognition system can "shut off" the curve-detecting features when it's searching for the K in this kind of display (see Duncan & Humphreys, 1989, for careful consideration of visual search when the similarity of targets and nontargets varies).

There's the shortcoming—we have to "shut off" some feature detectors to explain fast search for K in the round-letter condition (analogously, in Duncan and Humphreys's [1989] approach, variations in the nontarget letters influence the speed of search for targets). But where did the instruction to shut off those detectors come from? Not from the feature detectors themselves, of course; feature detectors do only one thing—they detect visual features. Instead, this instruction came from someplace "higher up," something like your realization that you could ignore all dissimilar letter shapes.

Thus the missing ingredient in pure feature-detection models is *top–down* or *conceptually driven processing,* one of the basic themes in cognition you read about in Chapter 2. In other words, some higher, more thoroughly cognitive process is assisting in the nuts and bolts of basic pattern recognition, something beyond straightforward feature detection. In fact, this cognitive process is *altering* basic visual recognition. The source of the top–down influence, of course, is your knowledge—your knowledge of letter shapes; in other examples, it is your knowledge of language that supplies the top–down effect.

You encountered an example of this in the last chapter, when you failed to notice the typograpical error that was just repeated here (did you fall for it again?). If we identify words by first recognizing simple features then individual letters, you should not recognize "typograpical" as a word. And yet you do, because of **context,** the influence of *surrounding*

FIGURE 3-11

A. SEARCH FOR K	B. SEARCH FOR LINE WITHOUT Q	C. SEARCH FOR Z	D. SEARCH FOR Z
EHYP	ZVMLBQ	ODUGQR	IVMXEW
SWIQ	HSQJMF	QCDUGO	EWVMIX
UFCJ	ZTJVQR	CQOGRD	EXWMVI
WBYH	RDQTFM	QUGCDR	IXEMWV
OGTX	TQVRSX	URDGQO	VXWEMI
GWVX	MSVRQX	GRUQDO	MXVEWI
TWLN	ZHQBTL	DUZGRO	XVWMEI
XJBU	ZJTQXL	UCGROD	MWXVIE
UDXI	LHQVXM	DQRCGU	VIMEXW
HSFP	FVQHMS	QDOCGU	EXVWIM
XSCQ	MTSDQL	CGUROQ	VWMIEX
SDJU	TZDFQB	OCDURQ	VMWIEX
PODC	QLHBMZ	UOCGQD	XVWMEI
ZVBP	QMXBJD	RGQCOU	WXVEMI
PEVZ	RVZHSQ	GRUDQO	XMEWIV
SLRA	STFMQZ	GODUCQ	MXIVEW
JCEN	RVXSQM	QCURDO	VEWMIX
ZLRD	MQBJFT	DUCOQG	EMVXWI
XBOD	MVZXLQ	CGRDQU	IVWMEX
PHMU	RTBXQH	UDRCOQ	IEVMWX
ZHFK	BLQSZX	GQCORU	WVZMXE
PNJW	QSVFDJ	GOQUCD	XEMIWV
CQXT	FLDVZT	GDQUOC	WXIMEV
GHNR	BQHMDX	URDCGO	EMWIVX
IXYD	BMFDQH	GODROC	IVEMXW
QSVB	QHLJZT		
GUCH	TQSHRL		
OWBN	BMQHZJ		
BVQN	RTBJZQ		
FOAS	FQDLXH		
ITZN	XJHSVQ		
VYLD	MZRJDQ		
LRYZ	XVQRMB		
IJXE	QMXLSD		
RBOE	DSZHQR		
DVUS	FJQSMV		
BIAJ	RSBMDQ		
ESGF	LBMQFX		
QGZI	FDMVQJ		
ZWNE	HQZTXB		
QBVC	VBQSRF		
VARP	QHSVDZ		
LRPA	HVQBFL		
SGHL	HSRQZV		
MVRJ	DQVXFB		
GADB	RXJQSM		
PCME	MQZFVD		
ZODW	ZJLRTQ		
HDBR	SHMVTQ		
BVDZ	QXFBRJ		

In list A, the target is the letter K; in list B, the target is a line without the letter Q; in lists C and D, the target is the letter Z.

information and your own knowledge. To be sure, pattern recognition is tremendously influenced by the actual pattern being presented. Such an influence, recognizing patterns by analyzing the stimulus features, embodies the notion of *data-driven* or *bottom–up processing.* No one doubts that the cognitive system is triggered by the physical data or pattern, and that it identifies patterns on the basis of stimulus features. Nonetheless, this bottom–up emphasis slights the contribution made by the cognitive system. We often identify a pattern that is literally *not* in original stimulus at all, such as the "the" in the last clause. If you misread that sentence, if you saw the missing "the," where did that "the" come from? Stated simply, it came from you, from your knowledge of the grammatical structure and meaningfulness of language. Thus top-level conceptual knowledge stored in memory is being used for lower-level processes such as pattern recognition.

We believe strongly that conceptually driven *and* data-driven processes are combined in most pattern-recognition situations, not to mention more complex cognitive processes such as comprehension of language. It was the top–down aspect that was missing from Selfridge's Pandemonium model. Let's explore a model that includes top–down effects now, and in the process learn about what's called the *connectionist* approach to cognitive science.

Connectionism

The approach to cognitive theories known as **connectionism** or **connectionist models** has two other commonly used names, **neural net models** and **parallel distributed processing models;** the latter is usually abbreviated simply as **PDP models.** The "connectionist" and "PDP" terms will be used interchangeably here; in Chapter 10 you'll read about the neurological connotation often implied by the "neural net" term. The connectionist approach achieved a critical level of visibility in the mid-1980s, when a set of two books on PDP modeling was published (Rumelhart & McClelland, 1986, for Volume 1, and McClelland & Rumelhart, 1986, for Volume 2). Within a very short period of time, this PDP approach to theorizing has become a dominant force in cognitive science, with symposia at conventions and special issues of journals devoted to the topic (several are listed in the Suggested Readings). In short, connectionism is now an important part of cognitive science and the most important format for computer-based theory development and testing.

In a moment, you'll read about a connectionist model of visual pattern recognition, the substantive topic we're interested in now. But first, let's cover the basics of PDP models, to get an idea of the general approach. Table 3-1 provides a list of basic terminology and assumptions, with explanations so that the jargon doesn't prevent you from understanding

Table 3-1   A PRIMER OF CONNECTIONIST TERMINOLOGY AND ASSUMPTIONS

Basic Statement of PDP Principles

1. Complex mental operations are the combined effects of the "massively parallel processing" that characterizes the network. The processing is distributed across all the levels of the network (hence "parallel distributed processing").
2. The network is composed of (usually) three levels of units—the input level, hidden level, and output level; the internal "hidden" layer is invisible to an outsider. Units in each of these levels are interconnected (hence "connectionism"). The connections are either positively or negatively weighted.
3. Positive connection weights pass "excitation" or excitatory activation to the connected unit; negatively weighted connections pass "inhibition" or inhibitory activation. A unit transmits its activation to connected units if it has received enough positive activation to reach threshold.
4. Connection weights are assigned as a function of "training," in which feedback as to correctness/incorrectness leads to a mathematical adjustment of weights. When a network is given this procedure, and the weights have stabilized, the network is said to have been "trained up." Backpropagation is the most commonly used training method, although others exist.
5. The obvious similarities between PDP models and the neurological structures and activities in the brain are usually quite intentional; connections are sometimes referred to as synapses, excitation and inhibition are parallel to those processes in the neocortex, and the entire approach is also commonly known as *neural net modeling*.

Lexicon of Other Connectionist Terms

Backpropagation   The most commonly used training procedure, in which the weight-adjusting phase proceeds from the output units back in to the other layers, each unit propagating a series of computations.
Delta Rule   The mathematical rule for adjusting weights during training, where delta (Δ) stands for "change."
Distributed Representation   The representation for a letter, word, concept, and so on is said to be distributed because the knowledge is spread widely across the units and their weights.
Local Minima   Occasionally in the training procedure, the system seems to have found the most stable "baseline" values for the weights, the *global minimum;* think of the global minimum as the deepest "valley." But instead, it may just be trapped in a local minimum or valley.
Massively Parallel Processing   Virtually all the units in the system have some role in each step of processing, and all the units are operating simultaneously.

the approach.[3] Consult the table, and Figure 3-12, frequently as you read the next section.

The Basics of Connectionism

Connectionism is a theoretical *and* computational approach to some of the most challenging issues in cognitive science. By *computational* we mean essentially "how the human cognitive system performs its mental

---

[3]This is probably your first serious encounter with connectionism, so I've simplified many aspects of the treatment here. I am more interested in your understanding the approach than with presenting its full complexity and theoretical foundations at the outset. Later sections in the book delve more deeply into some of the details, and some of the debate over the ultimate value of connectionist models.

FIGURE 3-12

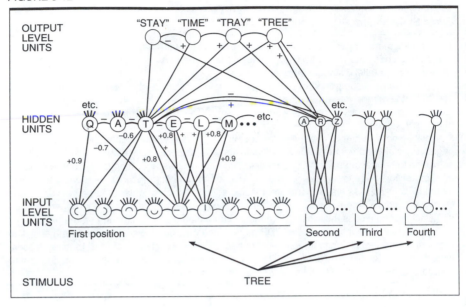

operations." We use the term **compute** here in the verb sense of "process"; putting it colloquially, "compute" means to "figure out." Thus when you read and understand the sentence "The lightning snaked across the sky," we say that you have "computed" the meaning of the sentence; you have determined, figured out, "computed" what the sentence means. It is in this sense that we say that pattern recognition—or any other cognitive operation—involves the process of computation.

Equally true of connectionism is that it involves a *massive* number of computations, real, honest "number crunching" mathematical computations. A connectionist PDP model is *always* implemented as a computer model, with a set of computational formulae that perform computations on the model's basic units. Even though the number of units may be fairly small, the number of separate computations in a single "run" of the model is staggeringly large. Thus we rely on high-speed computers to perform the calculations and to report the outcomes to us at the end of a "run."

An Example of Connectionism

Sounds pretty vague, doesn't it? It's not, of course—no model that can be programmed and run on a computer is vague. But the terminology is admittedly abstract, which is actually an advantage for a scheme that can be applied as broadly as connectionism can. But for a moment, let's get very concrete, to flesh out the meanings of these abstract terms. The situation we're considering is a model that can recognize four-letter words, for instance, TREE.

Input Units   Let's build the relatively simple connectionist framework illustrated in Figure 3-12, piece by piece. In this structure there are three levels of units. First, at the bottom, there are the *input units*. These are extremely basic, elementary "cells" in the structure, which receive the inputs from the environment. Our example is visual word recognition, so our input units are simple visual detectors. That is, we have a set of nine input units, each of which responds to the different basic visual features in the letters of the alphabet. To build on what you already understand, consider the input units to have exactly the same function as the data and computational demons in the Pandemonium model, shown in Figure 3-10. Our input units here encode and then respond to simple visual features in letters of the alphabet. Thus the input unit level in this illustration is the "feature-detector" level.

Hidden Units   How do these input units work? When a stimulus is presented to the input device, one or more of the input units will match the features in the stimulus. When this happens, each unit that matches activates a set of connected units in the middle level of the structure, the *hidden unit* level; "hidden" here simply means that this level is completely internal, always one step removed from either input or output. In our diagram, the hidden units correspond to the "letter" level. Note that the activation is sent across the pathways or connections that link the units together: *these* are the connections in *connectionism*.

The connections *always* have a weight attached to them, a weight that represents the relationship between the linked units. Some of the weights are *positive,* and some are *negative.* For example, in the figure, the horizontal straight bar feature has positive weights connecting it to the letters T, E, and L, since those letters all contain that feature (to minimize confusion in looking at the figure, many of the connections have not been fully drawn, and only a few numerical weights are given). Conversely, the weights between the horizontal straight bar feature and the letters C, O, Q, and so on will be negative. Likewise, all the curved features at the input level have positive weights to curved letters and negative weights to angular letters.

Hidden units that receive enough positive activation—called *excitation*—will govern the outcome of processing. Units receiving negative activation—*inhibition*—end up having little control over the outcome. Eventually, after all the weights have been factored into the computational formulae, activations at the output level come into play.

Output Units   Where is this getting us, you ask? Imagine that you were trying to build a machine (program a computer) that could identify visually presented words, for instance, the four-letter words we're considering here. What you see in Figure 3-12 is primarily the connectionist network for the *first position* in the four-letter words. Three more sets of connections, shown in reduced form at the right of the figure, essentially duplicate the same connections again, once for each position in the four-letter word. Given these additional positions, we can now talk about the *output units,* the units that report the system's response to the question "What is this word?"

For simplicity, only a handful of four-letter words are shown at the level of output units in the figure. Note, however, that three of the word-level units are consistent with the letter detection performed on T in the first position; that is, three of the words begin with a T. Now think about the fuller representation of such a model, a model that identifies four-letter words. Each of the four input unit segments will perform as described above, forwarding both positive and negative activation to the hidden units, these in turn forwarding positive and negative activations to the output units. At the end of the "run" of the model, presumably one of the several output units will have received enough positive activation to exceed its threshold. When this happens, that unit "responds," in other words, outputs its word as the answer to the question "What is this word?"

One more complexity is needed now, the one that gets top–down effects into the model. Reflect for a moment on how likely the spelling pattern "TZ" is at the beginning of English words. Not very likely, is it? On the other hand, "TA," "TE,", "TI," and so on *are* quite likely, as are a few consonant–consonant pairings like "TH" and "TR." These likelihoods are also represented in the network; to distinguish them visually from the other connections, they're shown with curve-shaped connections. The overall effect of these letter-to-letter weights is that the activations in the system can make up for missing features at the perceptual level.

Figure 3-13, taken from Rumelhart and McClelland's (1986) work, shows the final levels of activation for three possible words, given the partially obscured stimulus pattern shown at the bottom. The illustration shows an important feature of connectionist models; enough knowledge is represented in the system, by means of the weights for letter-to-letter sequences, that the model identifies the word "work" even when the last letter could also be an R.

Why is this so important? It's important because it is a concrete illustration of the general theme you read about in the last chapter, top–down or conceptually driven processing. If you saw the partially obscured pattern in Figure 3-13, you would identify the word as "work," based on your knowledge that "worr" is not a word in English. Quite literally, your higher-level knowledge of English words would be assisting your perceptual process here, in service of identifying the word. This is *exactly* what's happening in the connectionist model; higher-level knowledge, coded as simple weighted connections in the massive network, is participating in the lower-level task of identifying letters.

FIGURE 3-13

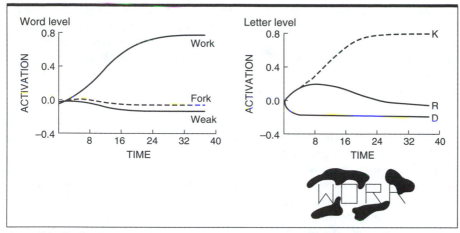

A possible display that might be presented to the interactive activation model of word recognition, and the resulting activations of selected letter and word units. The letter units are for the letters indicated in the fourth position of a four-letter display. (Adapted from Rumelhart & McClelland, 1986.)

Training a PDP Network One critical detail has been left out of this presentation, to simplify your first exposure to a connectionist model. We spoke as if the weights connecting the units in the model were fixed, as if they somehow existed at the outset. This is *not* the case. The various weights assigned to the connections are the end result of a long *training* procedure, a procedure that takes a basic network in the "naive" state and transforms it into one that "knows," for example, how to recognize letters of the alphabet. Here is an (extremely) abbreviated idea of this training procedure.

Start from scratch—all units are connected to all others, and each of the connections has a weight varying within some small, rather insignificant range, say, from −0.05 to +0.05 (e.g., McCloskey & Lindemann, 1992). Now, present a stimulus for the system to identify, say, TREE. Obviously, the system has essentially no knowledge, so when all its activations have been computed, and when the output level responds with a word (say, GIRL), it has made an error. Now we begin the training. We give the system feedback; putting it very roughly, we "tell it" that TREE was the correct answer. A complex set of mathematical formulae are now applied to all the weights in the network, adjusting them—"nudging them" in Churchland's (1990) description—a small amount toward a pattern that would be more likely to identify TREE correctly.

Now we present another stimulus, and another, and another, each time applying the adjustment procedure to the connection weights. Although several different algorithms exist for these adjustments, the *backpropagation* method—working backward from output units to hidden to input units—is the most widely accepted method. The end result of this training procedure is a pattern of connection weights among the units (e.g., all in the range between −1.0 and +1.0) that represent the features and spelling regularities of the training stimuli. Once the network has been "trained up," as the expression goes, it can then be tested. In our example, we'd present a whole series of four-letter words, including some the system has never seen, to see if they can be identified.

In a very real sense, such connectionist models satisfy the difficulty you read about just a few minutes ago, the need for top–down processing in the Pandemonium model. In the figure, the top–down effect is especially prominent in the curved connections, which represent mutual excitation and inhibition of units. But the approach has far more important consequences than merely providing a way to repair Pandemonium. As you'll read at several points in this book, connectionist accounts of a whole range of cognitive operations are becoming popular and are providing new insights into ways of modeling and understanding human cognition.

Summary Points: templates, feature detection, and top–down processing; connectionism/neural net models/parallel distributed processing models

▼ Pattern Recognition: Audition

Since our auditory mechanism resembles the visual perception mechanism in many ways, it is not surprising that theories of auditory pattern recognition are also similar. Of course, one very important difference is that vision is spatially distributed, while audition is temporally distributed. Thus it is not surprising that pattern-recognition theories for hearing have stressed the input of stimulus information *across time,* compared to visual pattern-recognition theories. Nonetheless, we have progressed to the same point in studying auditory pattern recognition that we reached in vision: simple template approaches are rejected, feature approaches are accepted as far as they go, but the still-missing ingredient of conceptually driven processing must be added. In brief, template and feature-detection theories of auditory recognition are data-driven, bottom–up processing approaches. They neglect the enormous contribution of the listener, who brings knowledge of language and the world to recognize meaningful patterns. They neglect the active, mentally involved role played by the person doing the recognizing.

Conceptually Driven Recognition

We need discuss only one widely appreciated set of results to illustrate this point. Warren and Warren (1970) presented subjects with specially tape-recorded speech messages and asked them to report what they heard. Their tape-recording technique permitted them to locate a particular speech sound on the recordings and to replace that sound with some other nonspeech sound, usually white noise (the sound of a cough works just as well). Table 3-2 illustrates the several sentences that were tape-recorded, altered, then presented to the subjects. In all cases, the same nonspeech sound was substituted, yet the subjects always perceived the "right" sound, the sound that best completed the meaning of the sentence. Apparently, none of the subjects even noticed anything unusual about what they heard. When *context* prevails—that is, when the surrounding information supplies you with enough information to know what the sentence is about—then pattern recognition will "fill in the blanks" in a top–down, conceptually driven fashion. Note the tremendous power of this context effect: the topic of the sentence isn't even mentioned until the last word, yet it exerts a perceptual influence back to the earlier, missing sound.

Selective Attention in Auditory Perception

When you look at a visual scene, there is an obvious correlate of visual attention: you move your eyes, thereby *selecting* what you'll pay attention to. Attention in hearing, however, has no outward, behavioral component analogous to eye movements, so the process of selective attention in hearing seems more thoroughly cognitive, and less transparent. This accounts for cognitive psychology's heavy investment in **filter theories of auditory perception.** If we cannot avoid hearing something, we then must *select* among the stimuli by some mental process, filtering out the unimportant and attending to the important. We turn now to investigations of selective attention in audition, and in the process collide directly with modern theories of attention itself.

A general aspect of most sensory memory experiments, whether on vision or audition, involves the procedure of overload. In brief, we can overload the sensory system by presenting more information than it can handle at once and then test accuracy for some part of the information. In studies of auditory perception, this has usually involved a **dual task** or **dual message** procedure. *Two tasks or messages are presented, making sure that one task or message captures the subject's attention almost completely.* Since the subject's attentional resources are so consumed by

---

Table 3-2   ALTERED SENTENCES IN WARREN AND WARREN (1970)

It was found that the *eel was on the axle.
It was found that the *eel was on the shoe.
It was found that the *eel was on the orange.
It was found that the *eel was on the table.

The asterisk (*) denotes the replaced sound.

In a classroom situation, students must constantly filter out the unimportant from the important details. This is an example of selective attention in auditory perception.

this primary task, there are few if any resources left over for conscious attention to the other information being presented.

In most instances, these dual task or dual message experiments are doubly informative. That is, we can vary the auditory characteristics or the actual content of the two messages being presented to the subject, making the subject's job easier or harder. For instance, paying attention to a message spoken in one ear while trying to ignore the other ear's message is especially difficult when both messages are spoken by the same person. We can conclude from this that auditory sensory memory is quite sensitive to purely auditory features such as pitch and intonation. Thus when we examine performance to the attended task, we can discuss selective attention and perception: How does the subject manage to attend to one of the messages selectively? How accurately is the message perceived? How much does the other message interfere? We can also look at the subject's accuracy for information that was not in the primary message, the so-called unattended message in the other ear. If the subject shows any evidence of remembering that unattended message, or even some of its auditory features, we can discuss the operation of sensory memory when its contents are not attended.

The Shadowing Experiments

Some of the earliest cognitive research on auditory pattern recognition and selective attention was performed by E. Colin Cherry (1953; Cherry

ZIGGY

HOW COME
...WHEN PEOPLE ARE WHISPERING.. THE ONLY THING YOU CAN HEAR IS YOUR NAME ?

ZIGGY copyright ZIGGY AND FRIENDS, INC. Distributed by UNIVERSAL PRESS SYNDICATE. Reprinted with permission. All rights reserved.

& Taylor, 1954). Cherry was interested in the basic phenomena of speech recognition and attention. Cherry characterized his research procedures, and for that matter the question he was asking, as "the cocktail party problem": How do we pay attention to and recognize what one person is saying when we are surrounded by other spoken messages? To simulate this real-world situation in the laboratory, Cherry (see also Broadbent, 1952) devised the workhorse task of auditory perception research, the **shadowing task.** In this task, Cherry recorded spoken messages of different sorts on tape, then played the tape to a subject who was wearing headphones. The subject's task was to "shadow" the message coming into his right ear, that is, to *repeat it out loud as soon as it was heard.* In most of the experiments, subjects are also told to ignore the other message, the one coming to the left ear. It makes no difference which ear is shadowed and which is ignored, of course. For simplicity, we'll assume that the right ear always receives the to-be-shadowed *attended message* and the left ear receives the *unattended message.*

While this procedure sounds simple enough, it requires a surprising amount of attention and concentration to shadow a message accurately. On the one hand, subjects were quite accurate in producing "shadows" and reported that the task was relatively easy. Nonetheless, Cherry found that subjects' spoken shadows were usually produced in a monotone voice, with little emotional content or intonational stress, and generally lagged behind the taped message by a second or so. Interestingly, subjects seem rather unaware of the strangeness of their spoken shadows and usually cannot remember much of the content of the shadowed message once the task is over.

Assured that the task consumed enough attention to leave little, if any, left over for other purposes, Cherry then began to vary the unattended message. In a typical session, the tape would begin with a continuous coherent message presented to the right (attended) ear and another coherent message to the left (unattended ear). Once the subject had begun to shadow, the message in the left ear would be changed. At the end of some amount of time, subjects were interrupted and asked what, if anything, they could report about the unattended message.

Generally, subjects could report accurately on a variety of physical characteristics of the unattended message. They noticed, for instance, if it changed from human speech to a tone. They usually detected a change from a male voice to a female voice. On the other hand, when the unattended message was changed to reversed speech, only a few subjects noticed "something queer about it." Changes from English to a different language generally went unnoticed, and, overall, the subjects were unable to identify words or phrases that had been on the unattended message. In a dramatic confirmation of this last result, Moray (1959) found that even a word presented 35 times in the unattended message was never recalled by the subjects.

Selection Models

It would appear that virtually *any* physical difference between the messages permits the subject to distinguish between them and eases the job of selectively attending to the target message (Johnston & Heinz, 1978). Eysenck (1982) has called this *Stage 1 selection;* the first stage of perception is an acoustic analysis, based on physical features of the message. The evidence is that people can select a message based on Stage 1 sensory information, based on loudness, location of the sound source, pitch, and so on (e.g., Egan, Carterette, & Thwing, 1954; Spieth, Curtis, & Webster, 1954).

This evidence, indicating that subjects could somehow "tune" their auditory mechanism to one message and then ignore the other, prompted Donald Broadbent (1958) to propose a filter theory of auditory perception (actually, Broadbent's theory also covered memory, learning, and other more complex topics). In Broadbent's view, the auditory mechanism acts as a selective filter, as shown in Figure 3-14. Regardless of how many competing channels or messages are coming in, the filter can be tuned, or switched, to any one of the messages, based on characteristics such as loudness or pitch. Note that only *one* message can be passed through the filter at a time, in Broadbent's theory. In other words, despite the many incoming signals, only one message can be sent along through the filter into the "limited-capacity decision channel," essentially the same as short-term memory. Only the information on the attended, "passed along" message can affect performance, in Broadbent's view, since only it gets past the filtering mechanism.

It was realized very quickly that Broadbent's filter approach had some serious shortcomings. For one, common intuition tells us that we often

FIGURE 3-14

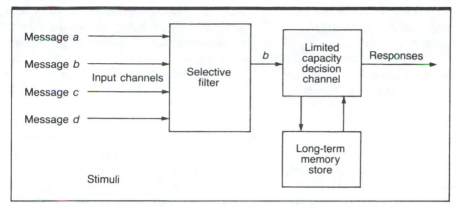

A depiction of Broadbent's (1958) filter theory of selective attention. Four messages are presented, yet only one is selected and passed to the limited-capacity decision mechanism. (Adapted from Broadbent, 1958.)

notice information from a message we are not attending, for instance, when you hear your name spoken in a crowded, noisy place. Moray (1959) found an exact laboratory parallel to this intuitive example; while people did not recall a word presented 35 times to the unattended ear, they invariably heard their name spoken on the unattended channel. If Broadbent's theory were correct, then only the attended and passed-along information should be available for further cognitive processing, where attention is directed by physical cues. And yet, clear evidence was available that unattended information could somehow slip past the filter.

An important series of investigations was performed by Treisman (1960, 1964) to explore this "slippage" more closely. Treisman used the standard shadowing task but varied the nature of the unattended message across a much more subtle range of differences. She first replicated Cherry's findings that selective attention was easy when various physical differences existed between the messages. Then she turned to the situation where physical differences were absent: both the attended and unattended messages were tape-recorded by the same speaker. Since the same pitch, intonation, stress, and so on should be on both messages, Stage 1 selection should not be possible. And yet, she found that subjects were still able to shadow quite accurately: they were able to attend selectively to one message while ignoring the other. The basis for the selection, however, was not any physical characteristic of the messages. Instead, subjects now performed their selection on the basis of *message content*—what the message was about rather than what it sounded like. Eysenck (1982) terms this *Stage 2 selection,* where the grammatical and semantic features are the basis for selection ("semantic" refers to meaning).

To show the power of selection based on the content of the message,

Treisman conducted a study now considered a true classic (1960); the set-up for the experiment is depicted in Figure 3-15. Treisman arranged the tape recording so that the coherent message being shadowed by the subject was unexpectedly *shifted* to the unattended channel. Quite literally, the sentence the subject was saying switched from the right to the left ear. Despite a high degree of practice in shadowing the right ear and the high level of concentration required, subjects routinely switched to the left ear message, the one that completed the meaning of the sentence they were shadowing. While the subjects did not continue to shadow the "wrong" ear for very long, the fact is that when the meaningful sentence switched to the other ear, they also switched. Clearly, there must be some consideration of the unattended message, unlike the prediction from Broadbent's theory. Semantic elements of the unattended channel must be receiving some analysis, Treisman reasoned, or there would be no basis for preferring it when the sentences switched ears.

Based on such results, Treisman rejected the "early selection" notion embodied in Broadbent's theory, what Eysenck called Stage 1 selection. Instead, she claimed that *all* incoming messages receive some amount of low-level analysis, including an analysis of the physical characteristics of the message. In the process of shadowing, we arrive at an identification of the words and phrases on the attended message. Treisman (1965) felt that it was *during* this process of semantic analysis that we make our selection among messages—Stage 2. This scheme places selective attention well within the cognitive apparatus, of course, and permits attention to be affected by the semantic aspects of the message, that is, a top–down effect. (A more extreme view, proposed by Deutsch and Deutsch [1963],

FIGURE 3-15

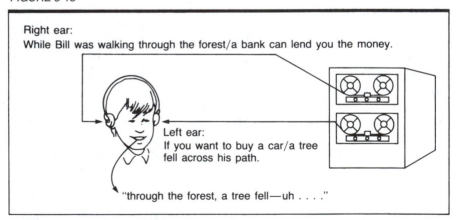

An illustration of the shadowing task. Two messages are played simultaneously into different ears, then, at the slash, the ear-of-arrival is switched for the two messages. (Adapted from Lindsay & Norman, 1977.)

claimed that selection takes place only after *all* messages have received full acoustic and semantic analysis; in other words, just before the response stage. This was a "late selection" theory, at Stage 3 in Eysenck's [1982] terminology, where the outcomes of all earlier analyses become conscious.)

Where does this leave us, you may be wondering? We can certainly select a message based on physical characteristics. But the evidence is that much more information is getting into the cognitive system than strict selection or filtering would permit—the meaning of the words on the unattended channel, for example, in Treisman's study (1960; see also Lewis, 1970; Carr, McCauley, Sperber, & Parmelee, 1982, found comparable results for visually presented stimuli). Intrusion of "tree" into the subject's shadow, as shown in Figure 3-15, makes sense only if "tree" has been recognized as related to the "forest" theme of the shadowed message, an effect that implies some quite rapid process of accessing the meanings of words. Can such spoken patterns truly be processed to the level of meaningfulness in the absence of explicit attention, with no conscious attention whatsoever? How?

Summary Points: selective attention and filtering; shadowing task; selection stages

▼ Attention: Mechanism, Process, and Mental Resource

As usual, William James (1890) was on the right track. The quotation at the beginning of this chapter claims that probably only one "process of conception" can occur at a time, but that we may seem to do more than one thing at a time if the other processes are "habitual." When processes are "less automatic," however, then attention must oscillate among them if they are done simultaneously, with "no consequent gain of time." And Hunter was blunter: since attention is the same thing as consciousness, any activities beyond the limit of one must be "automatic."[4]

The key point in James's and Hunter's remarks involves the idea of automatic processes, that some mental events can happen automatically without draining the pool of mental resources we call attention. In simple terms, the germ of James's idea—automaticity—has become central to cognitive psychology's views on attention, pattern recognition, and a host of other topics as well. And cognitive science has devoted a huge amount of effort to recasting James's ideas about automaticity, and attention, into more formal, quantifiable concepts.

---

[4]I've included this very noticeable—even jarring—rhyme in order to set up an example for Chapter 9. The point being made is that even silent reading may contain an auditory or acoustic component.

Automatic and Conscious
Processing Theories

In place of the former approach, the limited-capacity attentional mechanism and the need for filtering in selective attention, the current view is that a variety of perceptual and cognitive processes can be executed in an *automatic* fashion, with no necessary involvement of a conscious, limited-attention mechanism. Two such explicit theories of **automaticity** have been proposed, one by Posner and Snyder (1975) and one by Shiffrin and Schneider (1977; Schneider & Shiffrin, 1977). These theories differ in some of their details but by and large are similar in their overall message. A related theory of pattern recognition by Rumelhart and McClelland (1982; also McClelland & Rumelhart, 1981) meshes very nicely with the distinction between automatic and conscious processes and provides us with an integration of perception, pattern recognition, and attention processes.

Automatic Processing Posner and Snyder describe three characteristics that are necessary for the "diagnosis" of an automatic process, listed for convenience in Table 3-3. First, an automatic process *occurs without intention;* in other words, an automatic process occurs whether you consciously want it to or not. Recall from the first chapter the short discussion of Stroop's (1935) research. Words such as RED GREEN BLUE YELLOW were presented visually to subjects, written in mismatching colors of ink (e.g., RED printed in green ink). When subjects have to name the ink color, they must try to ignore the printed words themselves. This leads to tremendous interference given the mismatching colors (this is an extraordinarily easy demonstration to perform).

In Posner and Snyder's terms, accessing the meaning of the written symbol RED is automatic: it requires no intention, it happens whether you want it to or not. In the research that demonstrates automatic access to word meaning, the term we use is **priming.** A word automatically *activates* or primes its meaning in memory and, as a consequence, primes or activates meanings closely associated with it. This priming then makes related meanings easier to access: because of priming, they've been boosted up, or given an extra advantage or head start (just as well water is pumped more easily when you "prime the pump"; see Dunbar & MacLeod, 1984, and MacLeod, 1991, for an explanation of Stroop interference based on priming). This is quite obviously the mechanism underneath Treisman's "tree–forest" result in the shadowing task, as well as the Lewis (1970) and Carr et al. (1982) results.

Second, an automatic process *does not reveal itself to conscious awareness.* Stated another way, you are unable to describe the mental processes of looking up the word RED in memory. The look-up processes are automatic and are not available to conscious awareness. You are not aware of the operation of automatic processes, for instance, the perceptu-

The demands on attention and memory in flying a jet airplane are enormous. The pilot must simultaneously pay conscious attention to multiple sources of information while relying on highly practiced, automatic processes and overlearned actions to respond to others.

Table 3-3   DIAGNOSTIC CRITERIA FOR AUTOMATIC AND CONSCIOUS PROCESSES

Automatic	Conscious
1. The process occurs *without* intention, without a conscious decision.	1. The process occurs only *with* intention, with a deliberate decision.
2. The mental process is not open to conscious awareness or introspection.	2. The process is open to awareness and introspection.
3. The process consumes few if any conscious resources; that is, it consumes little if any conscious attention.	3. The process uses conscious resources; that is, it drains the pool of conscious attentional capacity.
4. (Informal) The process operates very rapidly, usually within one second.	4. (Informal) The process is relatively slow, taking more than a second or two for completion.

Partial Autonomy/Automaticity
A process is said to be partially autonomous if it can *begin* automatically but requires a more conscious set of operations for completion (see Zbrodoff & Logan, 1986).

al mechanisms of looking at the visual pattern T and recognizing what it is. Contrast this, for instance, with the awareness you had when you answered the Aristotle or division questions in Chapter 1.

Finally, the third criterion of automaticity, according to Posner and Snyder, is that a fully automatic process *consumes little or no conscious resources*. Such a process should not interfere with other tasks, certainly not those that do use conscious resources. Walking, to take an obvious example, is so automatic for adults that it simply does not interfere with other processes: you can walk and talk at the same time. (A fourth criterion, quite informal but nonetheless useful, is that automatic processes tend to be very fast; a good rule of thumb is that a response requiring no more than one second is heavily automatic.)[5]

Conscious Processing   Let's contrast these diagnostic criteria for automaticity with those for conscious processing (again, refer to Table 3-3). First, conscious processes occur only *with intention*. They are optional, and can be deliberately performed or not performed by the subject. Second, conscious processes are *open to awareness;* we know they are going on, and within limits we know what they consist of. Finally, and of greatest importance to the research, conscious processes *require attention*. They consume some of the limited attentional resources we have in the cognitive system. A demanding conscious process should leave very few resources still available for use by a second conscious process. Of course, if a second process is automatic, then both processes may proceed without interference. As mentioned above, you can walk and talk at the same time. Walking is so automatic that it does not interfere with any other ongoing activity. Contributing to a conversation should require a fair amount of conscious processing, however, and should prevent you from simultaneously doing other attention-consuming activities (e.g., playing the piano or Nintendo, studying for an exam).

Integration with Conceptually Driven Processes   Let's go one step further now, integrating this explanation into the notion of conceptually driven processing. Attending to one of two incoming messages and shadowing that message out loud require conscious, deliberate attention. Such a process is under the subject's direct control, the subject is aware of performing the process, and the process consumes most of the available mental resources that can be allocated. Presumably, no other conscious process can be performed simultaneously with the shadowing task without showing poor performance in one or the other task (or both). When the messages are acoustically similar, then the subject must rely

---

[5]Note that the interference in the Stroop task is because the two automatic processes, reading the words and detecting the color of ink, eventually compete with one another when it's time to make a response: both processes are trying to output their results to the same speech mechanism. When we say that an automatic process generally does not interfere with other processes, it is assumed that we are speaking of situations where the two processes are not competing for the same response mechanism.

on differences of content or meaning to keep them separate. But note that, by tracking the meaning of a passage, the person's conceptually driven processes will come into play in an obvious way. Just as subjects "restored" the missing sound in "the *eel was on the axle" (Warren & Warren, 1970), the shadowing subject "supplies" information about the message from long-term memory. Once you have begun to understand the content of the shadowed message, then your conceptually driven processes assist you by narrowing down the possible alternatives, by "suggesting" what might come next.

Saying that conceptually driven processes "suggest" what might come next is an informal way of referring to the important process of priming. You shadow "While Bill was walking through the forest." Your semantic analysis primes related information and thereby "suggests" the likely content of the next clause in the sentence; it's likely to be about trees, and it's unlikely to be about banks and cars. At this instant in time, your "forest" knowledge has been *primed* or activated in memory. It's ready (indeed, almost *eager*) to be perceived, since it's so likely to be contained in the rest of the sentence. Then *tree* occurs on the unattended channel. Since we seem to access the meanings of words in an automatic fashion, the extra boost given to *tree* by the priming process pushes it over into the conscious attention mechanism. Suddenly, you're saying "a tree fell across . . ." rather than sticking with the right-ear message. Automatic priming of long-term memory has exerted a top–down influence on the earliest of your cognitive processes—auditory perception and pattern recognition.

The Role of Practice and Memory If accessing word meaning is automatic, then you might be wondering about some of the shadowing research described earlier in which subjects were quite *insensitive* to the unshadowed message, failing to detect the word presented 35 times, the reversed speech, and so on. If word access is automatic, why didn't these subjects recognize the words on the unattended channel? A very plausible explanation, in view of recent research, is *practice*. It now seems very likely that subjects' inability to detect or to be influenced by the unattended message was due to their relative lack of practice on the shadowing task. As several studies have shown, with greater degrees of practice even a seemingly complex and attention-consuming task becomes easy, or less demanding of attention's full resources. In fact, Logan and Klapp (1991; see also Zbrodoff & Logan, 1986) suggest that the effect of practice is to store the relevant information in memory; that is, that the necessary precondition for automatic processing is memory.

One of the most compelling strengths of the Shiffrin and Schneider (1977) theory of automatic and conscious processing (actually, they use the term *controlled* instead of *conscious* processing) is the role they award to old-fashioned, repetitive practice. Their experiments asked subjects to detect one or more target stimuli in successively presented displays—for example, hold the targets 2 and 7 in memory, then search for either of them in successively presented displays of stimuli. For some subjects, the targets were consistent across hundreds of trials, always digits, for instance. This was called Consistent Mapping. For subjects in the Varied Mapping groups, the targets were varied across trials—for example, 2 and 7 might be targets on one trial, 3 and B on another, M and Z on yet another.

The essential ingredient here is practice on the stimuli and task. Unlike the Varied Mapping groups, subjects who received Consistent Mapping had enormous amounts of practice in scanning for the *same* targets. Across many experiments, subjects in the Consistent Mapping conditions developed quick, automatic-detection processes for their unchanging targets, to the point that they could search for any of four targets in about 450 msec, even in the largest display size, four characters shown at once. Subjects in the Varied Mapping conditions, on the other hand, required greater search times for larger displays. At the large display size, their four-target search time was 1300 msec (Experiment 2, Schneider & Shiffrin, 1977). These subjects, in the authors' interpretation, had not developed automatic detection processes because the stimuli they had to detect kept changing from trial to trial. Their search, in short, required conscious or controlled processing.

Rounding out their evidence on the effect of prolonged practice, Shiffrin and Schneider administered 2100 detection trials to another group of subjects, consistently using one set of letters for the targets and a different set for the distractors. In the authors' words, "The subjects all reported extensive, attention-demanding rehearsal . . . during the first 600 trials of Experiment 1, but they gradually became unaware of rehearsal or other attention-demanding controlled processing after this point. . . . [They] gradually shifted to automatic detection" (1977, p. 133). After this lengthy procedure, Shiffrin and Schneider then *reversed* the target and distractor sets, forcing subjects to search for targets that were previously distractors and to ignore distractors that were previously targets. Shiffrin and Schneider suspected that "automatic detection would prove impossible and that the subject would be forced to revert to controlled search" (p. 133). This is indeed what happened; it took 2400 trials after the reversal to equal the detection speed originally achieved after only 1500 trials.

A Synthesis for Perception and Attention

Attention, in its usual, everyday sense, is essentially equivalent to conscious mental capacity or conscious mental resources. We can devote these attentional resources to only one demanding task at a time—or to two somewhat less demanding tasks simultaneously, as long as the two together do not exceed the total capacity available. This devotion of resources means that few, if any, additional resources will be available for other demanding tasks.[6] Alternately, if a second task is performed largely at the automatic level, then it can occur simultaneously with the first, since it does not draw from the conscious resource pool (or, to change the metaphor, the automatic process has achieved a high level of skill; see Hirst & Kalmar, 1987). The more automatically a task can be performed, the more mental resources will be available for other processes.

The route to automaticity, it would appear, is practice and memory. With repetition and overlearning comes the ability to perform in an automatic fashion what formerly required conscious processing. A particularly dramatic illustration of the power of practice is the Spelke, Hirst, and Neisser (1976) demonstration. With massive practice, two subjects were eventually able to read stories at normal rates, and with high comprehension, while they simultaneously copied words at dictation, or even categorized the dictated words according to meaning. The Shiffrin and Schneider results tracked the changes in performance across practice, showing a steady shift or migration from conscious to automatic. Significantly, once practice has yielded automatic performance, it seems especially difficult to undo the practice, to overcome what has now become an automatic and, in a sense, autonomous process (Zbrodoff & Logan, 1986).

Different degrees of practice, and therefore different degrees of automaticity, probably account for the varied results from the shadowing studies as well. As subjects gain more experience with the shadowing task, their shadowing presumably requires less and less conscious attention. This would of course release some of their conscious resources for other purposes. Among those other purposes would be the conscious detection of related information, as Treisman found, or even detection of unattended channel information while shadowing (Moray himself, with presumably much practice at shadowing, outperformed less practiced subjects in reporting unattended channel information).

Returning now to the models of perception and pattern recognition, we need to indicate how conceptually driven processes such as priming exert their influence. Consider visual pattern recognition: for instance, the patterns that form the letters of the alphabet. Young children, with virtually no significant practice, have to labor consciously over identifying which pattern corresponds to which letter. With practice, however, the perceptual processes become more automatic, eventually achieving the status of fully automatic, nonoptional processes. As an adult, you cannot look at a pattern such as T without automatically accessing it in memory. Your feature-detection processes, by virtue of practice, have become automatic.

---

[6]On this point, Kahneman (1973) has suggested that attentional resources or capacity might be "elastic," in that increasing the task load may lead to an increase in the subject's arousal, which in turn makes additional mental resources available. As Eysenck (1982; Eysenck & Calvo, 1992) notes, this is a plausible idea but certainly complicates matters when trying to determine how much of the mental resource pool is consumed by a particular task.

Furthermore, when the T is embedded into a larger unit such as TREE, we begin to see the full effect of conceptually driven pattern recognition. Rumelhart and McClelland (1982, 1986) suggest that the basic feature-detection phase—extracting the horizontals, open circles, and so on—can be understood as a process assisted by priming, by the information-carrying weights that connect basic units in the mental network. As one feature—say, horizontal bar—is extracted, it activates other features that signify A, H, T, and so on. This activation then becomes the top–down priming that influences further perceptual activities. Feature detectors, in their scheme, begin to activate related features and inhibit unrelated ones; as composites these begin to activate letter and then word detectors. In simplified terms, activations from higher levels feed into the feature-detection phase itself, altering the process because of context (see McClelland & Elman, 1986, for an analogous model of speech perception, the TRACE model). By such top–down means, you fail to notice typographical errors, you accidentally read words ("the") that aren't there, and you categorize patterns that are otherwise ambiguous (see Figure 3-16).

FIGURE 3-16

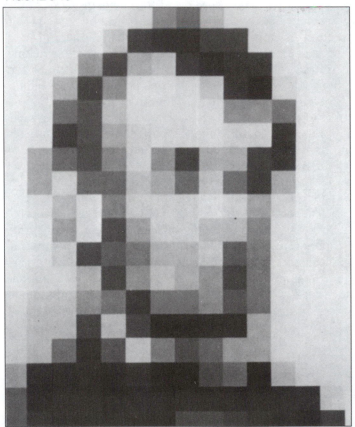

Two Kinds of Attention

The word "attention" normally has exactly the connotations we've been using here: it refers to awareness, it involves the conscious deployment of mental resources to accomplish some task, and it exists in limited quantity. We might call this *conscious attention*. But there is also another kind of attentional process, one operating at a more microscopic and automatic level. It is basically the same as the idea called *focal attention* earlier in this chapter, a process likened to a mental "spotlight." As distinct from relatively deliberate, conscious attention, this second kind of attention—let's call it *"spotlight" attention*—seems extremely rapid, nearly automatic, and responsible for rather simple operations.

A distinguished series of studies by Treisman and her associates (e.g., Treisman, 1982, 1988, 1991; Treisman & Gelade, 1980) has examined "spotlight" attention in terms of visual pattern recognition. Typically, subjects in the experiments were told to search the visual display for

---

DEMONSTRATIONS

Data collection projects relevant to this chapter typically involve rather elaborate and specialized equipment, given that a great deal of precision is necessary to capture the rapid phenomena of perception and attention. Unless you're a whiz at programming your PC to present visual stimuli, you'll probably have to be content with an informal self-assessment or diary kind of project. A few such suggestions follow.

1. Capture of attention. Take an introspective approach to the question of what kinds of stimuli capture your attention. For example, during class, your attention to the lecture can be interrupted by sudden or unexpected noise, or movement in your peripheral vision. Keep a tally of how many times such disruptions occur. More interestingly, tally how frequently "stray thoughts" interrupt your attention to the lecture; for instance, remembering related information, thinking about a recent experience or planned activity, and daydreaming.

2. Attention and interest. In a similar vein, try tallying the frequency of events that disrupt your attention under different conditions of interest or concentration, for example, during a lecture versus a movie, studying from a boring text versus reading a novel.

3. Interview people about their own selective and divided attentional processes, when they can "go on autopilot" and when they have to concentrate. (For example, minor disturbances like whispering often don't disturb my lecturing in Intro Psych, but usually do in Memory and Cognition.)

4. Shadow some significant sample of speech (e.g., a television or radio newscast) to see how attention consuming the shadowing process is. Once you've gotten reasonably good at shadowing, try doing a second task simultaneously, for instance, crossing out the vowels in a passage of written text.

either a simple feature, say, letter S or a blue letter, or a conjunction of two features, say, a green T. The search for a simple feature was called the disjunction condition: subjects responded "yes" when they detected the presence of either one of the specified features, either a letter S or a blue letter. In the conjunction condition, they had to search for the combination of two features, T *and* the color green.

In the typical result (e.g., Treisman & Gelade, 1980, Experiment 1), subjects could search rapidly for either color or shape, and it made little if any difference whether they searched through a small or a large display; for instance, subjects were able to search through as few as five patterns or as many as 30 in about the same amount of time, approximately 500 msec. Because there was no increase in RT across the display sizes in the disjunction search condition, Treisman and Gelade concluded that visual search for a dimension like shape or color occurs in parallel across the entire region of visual attention. Such a search, they suggested, must be largely automatic and further must represent very early visual processing.

But when subjects had to search for a *conjunction* of features, for example, a green T, they took considerably more time, up to 2400 msec as more and more distractor items filled the display (distractors for both conditions were brown T's and green X's). Such conjunction search, Treisman and Gelade reasoned, must be occurring in a more serial, one-by-one fashion, and seemed to be a far more conscious, deliberate act.

There is some debate, to be sure, about these interpretations. For example, Duncan and Humphreys (1989) showed that visual search rates depend critically on the kinds of distractor patterns through which subjects are searching, and the similarity of those patterns to the targets (see also Duncan & Humphreys, 1992; Treisman, 1992). Regardless of which specific theory of feature detection turns out to be more viable, there is an important message here that deserves mention—there's *another* kind of attention.

Two Attentions   Consider the early, rapid stages of feature detection as *"spotlight" attention,* a process operating very early in perception (e.g., Posner & Cohen, 1984). The "spotlight" is directed toward a visual display and "enhances the detection of events within its 'beam' " (Kanwisher & Driver, 1992). It provides the encoding route into the visual system. It is this attentional focus mechanism that provides early, extremely rapid feature detection for the ensuing process of pattern recognition. It is especially *visual;* for instance, it has been referred to as "posterior attention," given that the earliest stages of visual perception occur in the posterior region of the brain, in the occipital lobe (see Chapter 10, and the color illustration of neural activity in the occipital lobe when a visual stimulus is presented).

The *"spotlight" attention* we're talking about—and, of course, we presume there is an equivalent attention mechanism for audition too—

would appear to be quite rapid, automatic, and perceptual. It is thereby distinguished from the slower, *conscious attention* process that matches the more ordinary connotation of the term attention. The "regular" kind is the conscious attention that we have loosely equated with awareness. Based on some neurophysiological evidence, we might even call this "frontal" or "anterior attention," since activity in the frontal regions of the brain seems to accompany elements of conscious awareness, for instance, awareness of the meaning of a word (e.g., Posner, Kiesner, Thomas-Thrapp, McCandliss, Carr, & Rothbart, 1992).

Conscious attention prepares us to respond in a deliberate way to the environment. It is slower, operates in a more serial fashion, and is especially influenced by conceptually driven processes. Spotlight attention, however, is a basic, rapid attentional mechanism that seems to operate in parallel fashion across the visual field, in a highly automatic fashion. It is largely a data-driven process, serving to funnel aspects of the environment into the cognitive system. Conscious attention then enables us to respond to that environment.

Summary Points: automatic and conscious processing; criteria of automaticity; practice and memory; spotlight versus conscious attention

CHAPTER SUMMARY

1. The eye sweeps across the visual field in short movements known as saccades, taking in information during brief fixations. The information encoded in these fixations is stored in visual sensory memory for no more than about $1/4$ second. This iconic image, which may include movement, fades rapidly or can be erased by subsequent visual stimulation. Considerably more information is stored in visual sensory memory than can be reported immediately. Information that is reported has been transferred to short-term memory by the process of focal attention.

2. Auditory stimulation is stored briefly in auditory sensory memory, for periods up to 4 seconds or so for language-based information. While auditory sensory memory lasts longer than visual sensory memory, its capacity may not be as large as that of visual sensory memory. Generally, the last items in a list presented auditorially will be recalled better than items presented visually, an effect known as the modality effect; furthermore, an auditory suffix added to the end of the list will degrade performance on the last list items, demonstrating erasure from auditory sensory memory. Recent evidence suggests that language-related codes, such as gestural codes involved in the enunciation of words, may be stored in auditory sensory memory, as well as true sounds.

3. Recognition of visual patterns is certainly not a process of matching stored templates to a visual stimulus. Feature detection provides a much more convincing account of visual recognition, where the

features being detected are elementary patterns that can be combined to form letters and other visual stimuli. A feature-detection account of pattern recognition must be augmented by conceptually driven processes to account for the known effects of context in visual recognition. Current models of this sort include the powerful new connectionist approach.

4. Recognition of auditory patterns, especially spoken language, reveals again the importance of conceptually driven processes. In the shadowing task, the meaning of the shadowed material can override the deliberate direction of attention to one or the other ear. Selection models explaining the process of selective attention have claimed that we filter out unwanted auditory messages on the basis of physical characteristics, meaning-based characteristics, or at a late stage just prior to making a response. These approaches bear directly on the general topic of attention.

5. Recent theories of attention claim that mental processes range from highly conscious to highly automatic. Automatic processes occur without intent, are not revealed to conscious awareness, and consume no conscious processing resources; conscious processes occur only with intention, are open to conscious awareness, and do consume attentional resources. With extended practice, many mental processes can become more automatic. A complete understanding of perceptual phenomena, both visual and auditory, requires an integration of the notions of automaticity and conceptually driven processes, and a distinction between lower-level rapid "spotlight" attention and slower, more deliberate conscious attention.

Glossary Terms: auditory sensory (echoic) memory; connectionism/PDP models; conscious attention; decay; dual task method; erasure; feature detection; Pandemonium; priming; selective attention; shadowing; "spotlight" attention; templates; visual sensory (iconic) memory; visual persistence; whole–partial report

SUGGESTED READINGS

Norman's (1976) excellent book *Memory and Attention* contains particularly readable fragments of the important papers in pattern recognition and selective attention (see especially Chapters 2 through 4). Norman's commentary furthers the discussion, showing how the theories and ideas evolved from simple filtering approaches through conceptually driven models. The book also contains a useful chapter on the effect of practice, particularly for motor skills such as playing the piano and juggling (Chapter 9). See Kanwisher and Driver (1992) for a brief overview of what we've called "spotlight attention" here.

The topics of visual and auditory sensory memory are still surprisingly controversial. In iconic memory, two different viewpoints on this issue are represented by Sakitt's work (e.g., 1975), which suggests that iconic memory is located at the rods of the retina, and Haber's work (1983), which discusses the irrelevance of iconic storage to normal perception. Haber's provocative article is followed by no fewer than 32 comments, both pro and con, many of which make fascinating reading. Since the concern with ecological validity is central to Haber's thesis, this collected set of papers is an excellent, though somewhat advanced, baptism into this important issue as well. For auditory sensory memory, papers by Greene and Crowder (1984, 1986) serve as an instructive guide to the arguments about echoic memory and its relation to auditory perception and language.

Finally, Neisser's *Cognition and Reality* (1976) deals largely with perceptual issues and includes the intriguing notion of the "perceptual cycle." In this continuously interacting process, existing knowledge directs further visual exploration, sampling more information from the viewed object, with this information then modifying the existing knowledge, which then directs further exploration, and so on. A consistent emphasis throughout this very approachable book is the ecological validity issue, as applied to Neisser's view of cognitive psychology.

Chapter 4

SHORT-TERM, WORKING MEMORY

> *Elementary memory makes us aware of . . . the* just *past. The objects we feel in this directly intuited past differ from properly recollected objects. An object which is recollected, in the proper sense of that term, is one which has been absent from consciousness altogether, and . . . is brought back . . . from a reservoir in which, with countless other objects, it lay buried and lost from view. But an object of primary memory is not thus brought back; it never was lost; its date was never cut off in consciousness from that of the immediately present moment. In fact it comes to us as belonging to the rearward portion of the present space of time, and not to the genuine past. (James, 1890, pp. 643–647)*

Primary memory, elementary memory, immediate memory, short-term memory (STM), short-term store (STS), temporary memory, working memory—all these terms refer to the same memory component, to the same aspect of the human information processing system. It is this component where the "immediately present moment," in James's explanation, is held in consciousness. It is the "location" of the conscious attentional system discussed in Chapter 3. It is this component where active mental effort is expended, whether to remember a phone number from directory assistance or to help in memorizing your own new phone number. This is where comprehension "takes place," the short-term, working memory system. What it is, what it does, and how it does it are the topics of this chapter.

Note that James's term *primary memory* suggests wrongly that it's the *first* memory stage. It's not the first, of course; a stimulus first encounters the sensory memory components on its way into the information processing system. But short-term memory is the first memory system we are conscious of, sufficiently aware of that we can offer intuitions and introspections about its functioning. Many—but not all—of those intuitions and introspections match what has been discovered empirically, not surprising given adults' metacognitive awareness of their own memories at work. On the other hand, some mental processes that occur in short-term, working memory are not revealed to consciousness: they are automatic. Naturally, these processes yield no useful introspections; indeed, people often naively feel that they don't exist. (This is why I've said that short-term memory is only *roughly* the same as consciousness. While we are aware of the contents of short-term memory, we are not necessarily aware of the *processes* that occur in short-term memory.)

Modern cognitive research on short-term memory came hard on the heels of the selective attention studies of the mid-1950s.[1] George Miller's

---

[1]There was also some research on short-term memory prior to the behaviorist period. For instance, Mary W. Calkins, the first woman to serve as president of the American Psychological Association, conducted such work in the 1890s, and in fact reported several important effects that were "discovered" in the 1950s and 1960s. See Madigan and O'Hara (1992) for an account of the "truly remarkable legacy" (p. 174) of this pioneering woman.

(1956) classic paper, which we'll discuss shortly, is an excellent example of the upsurge in interest in short-term retention. A commonplace observation, that we can remember only a small number of isolated items presented rapidly, began to take on new significance as psychology groped toward a new approach to the human memory system. Miller's insightful remarks were followed shortly by the surprising Brown (1958) and then Peterson and Peterson (1959) reports. An amazingly simple three-letter stimulus, such as CHJ, was forgotten almost completely within 15 seconds if the subject's attention was diverted by the distractor task of counting backward by threes. Such reports were convincing evidence that the limited capacity of the memory system was finally being pinned down and given an appropriate name—short-term memory.

As we proceed chronologically through the research, we'll shift from the term *short-term memory* to *working memory*. Why do we need two terms here? After all, at a rather general level, both terms refer to the same memory system, the same system discussed as far back as James. Wouldn't it make more sense to settle on one term?

I think there is good reason for keeping the two names separate. Stated simply, the terms have historically different connotations. *Short-term memory* is the older of the two terms and carries a somewhat simpler, less elaborate sense to it. It is the label we usually use when the focus is on the *input and storage of new information*. When a rapidly presented string of digits, for example, is tested for immediate recall, we generally refer to short-term memory and imply a simple "recycling" kind of mental activity as an explanation of recall. Likewise, when we focus on the role of rehearsal we are examining how short-term memory assists in the memorization of new information, highlighting the "control processes" (Atkinson & Shiffrin, 1971) in STS. Operationally, short-term memory is observed whenever relatively short retention is being tested—no more than 15 or 20 seconds—and when little, if any, transfer of new information to long-term memory is involved.

The term *working memory,* on the other hand, is the newer term for this "short" component of the memory system and has been the subject of substantial research over the past 20 years or so. The term generally has the connotation of a mental workbench, a place where conscious mental effort is applied (Baddeley, 1992a,b; Baddeley & Hitch, 1974). The term usually refers to *the mental workplace for retrieval and use of already known information*. Thus when word meanings are retrieved from long-term memory and then put together to understand a sentence, working memory is the place where this "putting together" happens. It is the location of conscious, attention-consuming mental effort. Traditional immediate memory tasks may be a component of working memory research but usually are only a secondary task to the reasoning, comprehension, or retrieval task. Indeed, Baddeley has proposed that the short-term memory responsible for digit span performance is but a single component of the more elaborate working memory system.

Finally, the terms themselves imply a somewhat different set of characteristics, and consquently a somewhat different set of empirical questions. Short-term memory is *short*—it doesn't last very long. The very term embodies the notion of a limited-capacity system. Where is the limitation in capacity? It's in short-term memory. Why is short-term memory limited? It's too short! Working memory, on the other hand, uses the active verb *work*. This is an action-packed, busy place, a place where mental activity happens. Where is the limitation in this system? It's in *how much work* can be done at one time, how much working memory capacity there is to share among several simultaneous processes.

▼ Short-Term Memory: A Limited-Capacity "Bottleneck"

If you hear a string of about ten single digits, read at a constant and fairly rapid rate, and then are asked to reproduce the string, you generally cannot recall more than about seven or so of the digits; this is roughly the amount you can say out loud within about two seconds (Baddeley, Thomson, & Buchanan, 1975). Likewise, you can reproduce only about seven unrelated words, presented in a comparable fashion (see the Demonstration projects for sample lists for immediate memory tests, and try testing a few willing volunteers). As Miller (1956) put it, "Everybody knows that there is a finite span of immediate memory and that for a lot of different kinds of test materials this span is about seven items in length" (p. 91). Indeed, this limit has been recognized for so long, it was included in the earliest intelligence tests (e.g., Binet's 1905 test; see Sattler, 1982). Small children and individuals of subnormal intelligence generally have a shorter "span of apprehension" or *memory span,* so digit span is a reasonable diagnostic test in intelligence testing. In fact, in the field of intelligence testing, it's almost unthinkable to devise a test *without* a memory span assessment.

The Magical Number Seven, Plus or Minus Two

For our purposes, the importance of this limitation is that it reveals something absolutely fundamental about the human memory system. Our immediate memory cannot encode or input vast quantities of new information and hold that information accurately. Instead, there is a rather severe limit on how much can be encoded, held, and reported immediately. Miller stated that limit aptly in the title of his article: "The Magical Number Seven, Plus or Minus Two: Some Limits on Our Capacity for Processing Information." We can take in large amounts of stimulation into the sensory memories, and we can hold truly vast quantities of information in the permanent long-term memory system. And yet, the transfer of information between sensory and long-term memory is troublesome. Immediate memory is the narrow end of the funnel, the four-lane bridge between sensory and long-term memory with only one tollgate, the bottleneck in our information processing system. It imposes "severe limitations on the amount of information that we are able to receive, process, and remember" (Miller, p. 95).[2]

And so the limitation remains . . . unless the seven items we are trying to remember are richer, more complex items than seven single digits, or unless the items are grouped in some fashion, as in the 3–4 grouping of a telephone number or the 3–2–4 grouping of a social security number. In Miller's terms, *the richer, more complex item* is properly referred to as a **chunk** of information, a **unit** that can hold something as impoverished as a single digit or letter, or as complex and elaborate as a word or phrase. By chunking individual items together into groups, we can overcome this limitation and "break (or at least stretch) this informational bottleneck" (Miller, p. 95).

What follows is a simple example of the power of chunking, of forming larger units:

BYGROUPINGITEMSINTOUNITSWEREMEMBERBETTER

No one can remember these 40 letters correctly if they are treated as 40 separate, unrelated letters in a string. But the effect of the *chunking* process is that grouping together the isolated items into a richer chunk enables us to retain more information. You can easily remember the eight words in the phrase above because they are familiar words that combine grammatically to form a coherent thought. You can remember a social security number more easily by grouping the digits into the arbitrary 3–2–4 pattern. And you can remember a telephone number more easily if you further group the last four digits into two, two-digit numbers.

Recoding Miller's central point, then, was that our short-term memories are inherently limited in the total amount of information that can be held at any one time. The limit seems to be seven units or chunks, plus or minus two. Any quantity greater than this, if it is to be retained successfully, must be grouped or chunked, again with a limit of about seven of these enriched chunks. The technical term for this process of *grouping items together, then remembering the newly formed groups* is **recoding.** By recoding, a novice begins to hear not the isolated *dit* and *dah* sounds of Morse code, but whole letters, then words, and so on.

The principle behind recoding schemes is very straightforward: recoding reduces the number of units to be held in short-term memory by increasing the richness of each individual unit. Short-term memory is therefore not as heavily loaded with units after recoding, although the

---

[2]Miller was using the technical definition of **information,** related to uncertainty, measured in bits; see footnote 2 in Chapter 2 for an explanation of "bits of information."

individual units are of course packed with more information than before. Forming these enriched units requires some difficult mental effort, however. Try recoding the longest digit list in the Demonstrations lists into two-digit numbers (28, 43, etc.), trying to remember these enriched units. This will illustrate the mental effort required for this kind of recoding (in fact, Brooks & Watkins, 1990, suggest that there is already a subgrouping effect in the memory span, with the first half of the span enjoying somewhat of an advantage over the second half).

Given the active, attention-consuming nature of recoding, you might feel that the BYGROUPINGITEMS example you saw earlier isn't quite fair. After all, the meaning and grammar serve to make the sentence easily understood and eliminate the need for much of that hard mental work.[3] Actually, the example clarifies the goal of any recoding scheme—to make the newly formed units as meaningful and as related to easily retrievable information as possible. A string of 40 digits, obviously longer than the capacity of short-term memory, can still be recalled accurately if your recoding scheme is powerful enough and if you can apply it flexibly and quickly. Miller, in fact, described an individual who could recall 40 binary digits (1's and 0's) without errors, by means of such a recoding scheme. He then noted: "If you think of this merely as a mnemonic trick for extending the memory span, you will miss the more important point that is implicit in nearly all such mnemonic devices. The point is that recoding is an extremely powerful weapon for increasing the amount of information that we can deal with. In one form or another we use recoding constantly in our daily behavior" (p. 95).

Note an implicit but vitally important point about recoding: it requires the active involvement of the subject to recode the stimulus items into richer groups and then maintain those groups in short-term memory. The bottleneck in the system is in short-term memory's capacity, according to Miller. We can overcome that limitation by the process of recoding, but only under either of two conditions, it seems. First, we can recode if there is sufficient time to apply the recoding scheme, or more accurately, if there are sufficient mental resources such as attention still available to do the recoding.

Long-Term Memory Involvement in Recoding   Alternatively, we can recode if the recoding scheme is highly overlearned, as the Morse code or binary digit schemes become with practice. Here, a well-learned **mnemonic device,** a *rehearsal or recoding strategy,* is used as the basis for grouping the stimulus items to be recalled. As an example, one of Chase and Ericsson's (1982) subjects was able to recall 82 digits in order after extensive practice by recoding the digits into groups on the basis of

---

[3]The hard mental work isn't revealed very clearly with the written example. In my classes, I present the string of 40 letters orally, at the same rapid rate as shorter lists, making sure no inflection or stress gives away the fact that the letters form words. Generally, by about halfway through the list, the students catch on that the letters spell words. It usually takes a second reading of the list, however, before many of them can figure out the whole message.

a personally meaningful scheme (the subject was a runner, so remembered the digits by relating them to known facts about running; e.g., 351 as "the former world record time for running the mile"). Thus specialized long-term memory knowledge enabled recoding of the digits and in turn helped overcome the limitations of short-term memory. Note, in general, that two kinds of information are stored in long-term memory here—the specific facts as well as the overlearned recoding strategy. Thus the term **mnemonic** in the above quotation refers to any kind of *remembering strategy, especially when long-term memory is involved.*

One of Miller's soundest insights followed immediately from the above quotation about mnemonic "tricks": "In my opinion, the most customary kind of recoding that we do all the time is to translate into a verbal code. When there is a story or an argument or an idea that we want to remember, we usually try to rephrase it 'in our own words' " (p. 95). As you have probably deduced by now, an adult's language comprehension skills are highly overlearned and have surely migrated toward automaticity. This makes rephrasing an excellent, flexible, and overlearned recoding scheme in the present context. Indeed, it's exactly this long-term memory/language-based recoding that assisted your memory for BYGROUPINGITEMS.[4]

But what about situations when no automatic recoding scheme is available, such as in the relatively less meaningful situation (for most of us) of remembering numbers instead of words? What is the fate of items in short-term memory when there is insufficient time or attention available to apply a more conscious scheme? Can we merely hold the usual 7 ± 2 items?

The Brown–Peterson Task: Decay from Short-Term Memory

Under some circumstances, we can't even hold *half* that many items in short-term memory. The research by Brown (1958) and Peterson and Peterson (1959) provided psychology with a compelling demonstration of this and is still viewed as trend-setting for the study of cognition. We'll spend a few moments discussing the task and results, since you'll encounter the same kind of empirical hypotheses and tasks several more times in this book.

The central idea in the Brown and the Peterson and Peterson papers was that some forgetting might take place even during the course of learning new material, and that this forgetting might be due simply to the passage of time before testing—in other words, forgetting due to decay. In the experiments, a simple three-letter stimulus was presented to the subjects, followed by a three-digit number. Subjects were instructed first to attend to the stimulus, then to begin counting backward by

---

[4]In the oral classroom example with BYGROUPINGITEMS . . . , a typical recall is "By grouping items together, we remember better." QED.

threes from the number they'd been shown. The counting was to be done out loud, in rhythm with a metronome clicking twice per second. At the end of a variable-length period of counting, the subjects were asked to report the three-letter stimulus they had heard. The results of these studies were apparently so unexpected, and the number of researchers eager to replicate the study so large, that the task acquired a nickname that is still in use—the "Brown–Peterson task."

The surprising result was that memory for the simple three-letter stimulus was only slightly better than 50% after three seconds of backward counting; accuracy dwindled to about 5% after 18 seconds of counting (see Figure 4-1). The essential ingredient in this finding, of course, was the distractor task, the backward counting. As Peterson and Peterson put it, "It was considered that continuous verbal activity during the time between presentation and signal for recall was desirable in order to minimize rehearsal behavior. The materials were selected to be categorically dissimilar and hence involve a minimum of interference" (p. 194).

This distractor task clearly requires a great deal of attention (if you doubt this, try it yourself from any three-digit number, making sure to

FIGURE 4-1

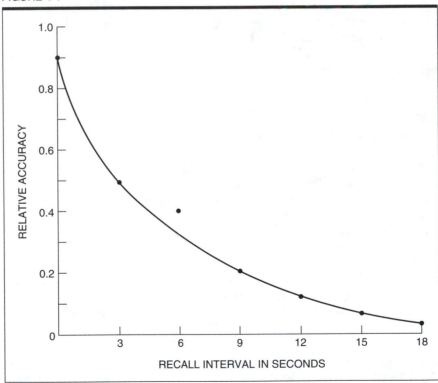

Relative accuracy of recall in the Brown–Peterson task, across a delay interval from 0 to 18 seconds. Subjects had to perform backward counting by threes during the interval. (From Peterson & Peterson, 1959.)

count backward twice per second). Furthermore, it surely prevents rehearsal of the three letters, since rehearsal requires the same attention mechanism as the backward counting. What was surprising was that the letters were forgotten so quickly even though short-term memory was not overloaded—a 50% loss after only *three* seconds (assuming recall would have been perfect with a zero-second delay). On the face of it, it seemed that the Petersons had presented evidence of a simple decay function in short-term memory: with an increasing period of time, less and less information still resided in short-term memory.

Interference Versus Decay in Short-Term Memory

Later research, especially that presented by Waugh and Norman (1965) in their paper "Primary Memory," questioned one of the assumptions made in the Peterson and Peterson report. Recall that the Petersons suggested that there should have been little, if any, interference from the distractor task to the memory test—from counting backward to recalling the three-letter stimulus—since letters and digits are "categorically dissimilar." As such, the forgetting functions they observed were interpreted as evidence for simple decay of information from short-term memory. Waugh and Norman, however, felt that the distractor task might very well have been a source of interference. They noted that if the numbers spoken by the subjects during backward counting had interfered with the short-term memory trace, then longer counting intervals would have provided more opportunity for interference, since subjects would have produced more numbers during the longer interval.

Waugh and Norman's reanalysis of several short-term memory studies confirmed their suspicion. Especially convincing were the results from their own "probe digit task." Subjects heard a list of 16 digits, read at a rate of either one digit or four digits per second. The final item in each list was a repeat of an earlier item, and it served as the subjects' probe or cue to write down the digit that had followed the probe in the original list. For instance, if the sequence 7 4 6 9 had been presented, then the probe digit 4 would have cued recall of the digit 6.

For the issue of decay versus interference, the important part of their experiment was the time it took to present the 16 digits. Presentation of the entire list took 16 seconds for one group, but only 4 seconds for the other group. If forgetting were due to decay from short-term memory, then the groups should have differed markedly in their recall, since so much more time had elapsed in the 16-second group. Yet as Figure 4-2 shows, the two groups barely differed at all in their recall accuracy.

The Waugh and Norman result suggested strongly that forgetting had been influenced by the number of intervening items between the critical digit and the recall test, and not merely by the passage of time. In other words, forgetting in short-term memory was due to interference. Thus

In retroactive interference, new information (Aunt Grace's address) interferes retroactively with older information (number of pennies). (The Born Loser cartoon reprinted by permission of Newspaper Enterprise Association.)

the Peterson and Peterson distractor task had not only prevented rehearsal, as it was supposed to, it had also produced interference with the critical digit to be remembered, as it was *not* supposed to. The short-term memory trace had experienced interference from the events that followed it during the trial.

Note that it's virtually impossible to test the simple decay theory in an adequate fashion. To do so, we'd have to present the stimulus material followed by a blank interval of time during which decay could take place, then the recall test. Yet, as the Petersons suspected, subjects *will* use a blank retention interval for rehearsal. And preventing rehearsal by introducing a distractor task yields interference. A straightforward test of decay theory would seem to require an interval of time during which *neither* interference *nor* rehearsal takes place. Putting it bluntly, this goal can never be reached. On the other hand, the decay theory would have to predict the same amount of forgetting for the same interval of time,

FIGURE 4-2

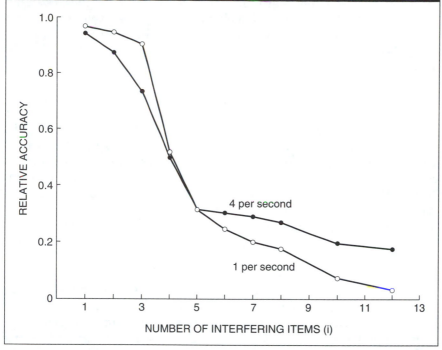

Relative accuracy in the Waugh and Norman (1965) probe-digit experiment, as a function of the number of interfering items spoken between the target item and the cue to recall; rate of presentation was either 1 or 4 digits/second.

regardless of what kind of distractor task was being used; after all, the mere passage of time is *the* cause of forgetting according to decay theory.

A variety of experimental tests used this reasoning to examine the relative inadequacy of simple decay theory for short-term forgetting. In one study, Talland (1967) used the Brown–Peterson task with two different distractor activities. One group did subtraction during the retention interval; the other group merely read the same numbers they *would* have spoken if doing subtraction. Not surprisingly, the group that actually had to do subtraction performed worse on recall than the reading group (see also Dillon & Reid, 1969), despite the same retention interval for both groups. Similarly, Peterson, Peterson, and Miller (1961) tested different kinds of stimulus materials, nonsense syllables versus words, while holding the retention interval constant. After six seconds of backward counting, word recall was significantly higher than recall of a three-letter nonsense syllable, again in disagreement with simple decay explanations.

In short, different kinds of interference tasks and different kinds of stimuli produced different amounts of forgetting. Such results are virtually impossible to explain by means of decay theory but are clearly sensible if forgetting from short-term memory is due to interference. (In a later section, we'll reinterpret these effects as being due to competition for processing resources in working memory, with different degrees of forgetting due to different amounts of leftover resources available for rehearsal.)

Release from PI   We will discuss one other famous line of research on this interference effect, a series of studies by Wickens (1972; also Wickens, Born, & Allen, 1963). Very shortly after the Peterson and Peterson report, Keppel and Underwood (1962) reported a startling effect that also challenged the Petersons' interpretation of decay. It seems that subjects forgot at the dramatic rate reported by the Petersons only *after* they had been tested on several trials in the short-term memory task. On the first trial, memory for the three-letter stimulus was virtually perfect. Keppel and Underwood pointed out the straightforward reason for this result. As you experience more and more trials in the Brown–Peterson task, recalling the stimulus becomes more difficult because the *previous* trials are generating interference.

This form of interference is called **proactive interference (PI),** *when older material interferes forward in time with your memory for (recollection of) the current stimulus.* This is the opposite of **retroactive interference (RI),** in which *newer material interferes backward in time with your memory for (recollection of) older items.* In other words, short-term memory loses information rapidly, say, within 15 seconds, when similar material has already been presented and tested. The loss of information in the Brown–Peterson task, according to Keppel and Underwood, was due to proactive interference.

The importance of Wickens's research was in his adaptation of the interference task, and especially in the way he turned proactive interference to his advantage. Wickens would present three Brown–Peterson trials, using three words per trial as the stimulus. On the first trial, accuracy was near 90%, but it drifted down to about 40% on Trial 3. At this point, Wickens then changed to a different kind of stimulus for Trial 4. Subjects who had heard three words per trial were given three numbers on the fourth trial, and vice versa. The results were dramatic. When the nature of the stimulus was changed, performance on Trial 4 returned to the 90% level of accuracy (of course, Wickens also included a control group of subjects who received the same kind of stimulus on Trial 4 as they had gotten on the first three trials, to make sure their performance continued to dwindle, which it did). Figure 4-3 illustrates this result.

The interference interpretation here is very clear. Performance deteriorates across trials because of the buildup of proactive interference. If the to-be-remembered stimulus changes, however, then you are "released" from the interference. Your performance is no longer depressed by the growing amount of interference, so you once again recall with about 90% accuracy. Wickens's (1972) research over a lengthy

FIGURE 4-3

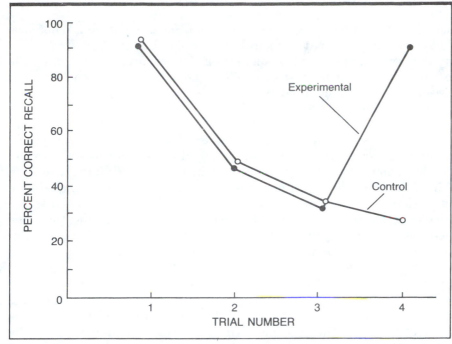

Recall accuracy in a release from PI experiment by Wickens, Born, and Allen (1963). Triads of letters are presented on the first three trials, and proactive interference begins to depress recall accuracy. On Trial 4, the control group gets another triad of letters; the experimental group gets a triad of digits and shows an increase in accuracy, known as release from PI.

period demonstrated conclusively the effect of proactive interference, and then the release from PI when the stimulus materials are changed.

For now, the importance of the Wickens's research was that it showed clearly the influence of interference in the process of forgetting information in short-term memory. While it is possible that simple decay also occurs in short-term memory, it seems virtually impossible to give this hypothesis a fair test. But from the practical standpoint, interference due to intervening material surely characterizes our everyday experiences with short-term memory. As Howard (1983) put it, "Unrehearsed material is seldom allowed to remain in working memory long enough to decay, because there is usually something else—if only some daydreaming—to be done with the limited capacity available. To convince yourself of this, try keeping your mind completely blank for 15 seconds" (p. 109).[5]

Summary Points: short-term and working memory; limited capacity; chunking or recoding; decay versus interference; release from PI

---

[5]At a purely introspective level, the way a dream seems to "slip out of your grasp" as you wake in the morning certainly feels like the fading predicted by the decay theory. What's always intrigued me is that the dream fades away so rapidly and completely despite seemingly great effort to remember it.

▼ Short-Term Memory and Recall

"Unrehearsed material," the quotation from Howard just said. What does that phrase imply? What happens to material sitting in short-term memory that goes unrehearsed? It undergoes interference, usually, and so is lost from the short-term store. Let's explore this now from the other direction, not from the direction of interference, but from the more positive direction of rehearsal. What happens when the material sitting in short-term memory *is* rehearsed?

Of course, we've nibbled at the edges of this question, and you've encountered some indirect answers to it already. *Rehearsal* is a term that has been tossed in occasionally, for instance, in the form of Miller's (1956) recoding, but it has not yet been really defined or explored as a vital, short-term memory process. Furthermore, if you remember the topic of rehearsal from your introductory psychology course, you may have wondered why you've read this far in the chapter without yet running into a **serial position curve,** a *graph of item-by-item accuracy on a recall task*. The term *serial position* simply refers to the original position an item had in the list that was studied; for example, serial position #3 refers to the item presented third in a list being learned. I wanted to save this discussion until dealing with the decay and interference approaches to forgetting, since they provide insight into the particular shape of the serial position curve. But now the time has come to talk about serial position. Figure 4-4 shows several time-honored, traditional serial position curves.

Free Versus Serial Recall

Before studying the evidence in these serial position curves, let's consider the two basic tasks we use to test subjects, **free recall** and **serial recall.** In free recall, subjects are free to *recall the list items in any order,* whereas in serial recall we ask subjects to *recall the list items in their original order of presentation.* Not surprisingly, serial recall is the more difficult task to perform: to recall the items in order, subjects must rehearse the items as they are shown, trying to store not only the stimulus but also its position in the list. As more and more items are shown, subjects are less and less able to do this rehearsal, so they tend to show poorer performance later in the list.

In contrast, free recall provides the opportunity to recall the items in any order. As Atkinson and Shiffrin (1968, 1971) argued, this final recency portion of the list is generally held only in short-term memory and is "spewed out," so to speak, as soon as the signal to recall is given to the subjects. This recall strategy works because the recency of those last items ensures that they are still in short-term memory. Clearly, you cannot capitalize on recency in a serial recall task; you must start recalling

FIGURE 4-4

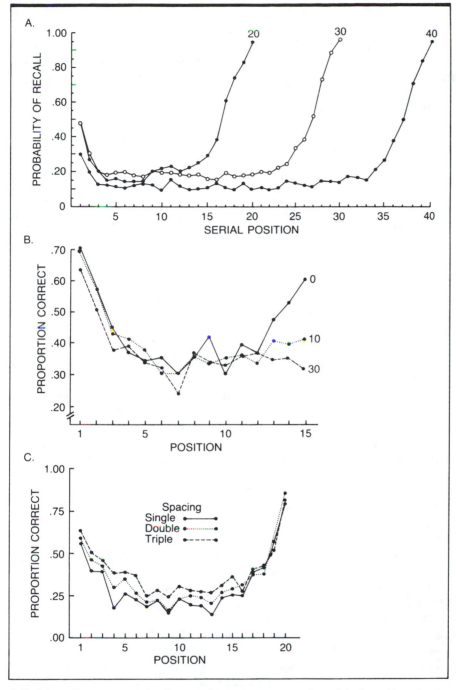

A. Serial position curves, showing recall accuracy across the original positions in the learned list. Rate of presentation was one item per second.

B. Serial position curves, showing the decrease in recency when either 10 or 30 seconds of backward counting is interpolated between study and recall.

C. Three different rates of presentation: single (3 seconds), double (6 seconds), and triple (9 seconds).

with the first item in the list. Since you cannot rely on immediate recall for any of the items in serial recall, you must rehearse them as they are shown, in order to store them in a more enduring form.

Serial Position Effects

We generally refer to the early positions of the list as the "primacy portion" of the serial position curve; these are the early serial positions plotted across the bottom of the figure. "Primacy" here has its usual connotation of "first"—it's the first part of the list that was studied. The term **primacy effect,** then, always refers to the *accuracy of recall for the early list positions.* A strong primacy effect means good, accurate recall of the early items on the list, usually due to rehearsal. A weak primacy effect, low accuracy on the early items, is usually due to insufficient rehearsal. The final portion of the serial position curve is known as the "recency portion." A **recency effect** refers to *the level of correct recall on the final items of the originally presented list.* "High recency" means high accuracy, and "low recency" means that this portion of the list was hardly recallable at all.

As Figure 4-4A shows, a strong recency effect is obtained across a range of list lengths, 20, 30, or 40 items (Murdock, 1962); these lists were presented at a rate of one item per second. Note further that there is a slight primacy effect for each list length, but that the middle portion of the lists showed very low recall accuracy. Apparently, the first few items were rehearsed enough to make them recallable from long-term memory, but not enough time was available for rehearsing the items in the middle of the list. For all lists, though, the strong recency effect can be attributed to recall from short-term memory.

The experimental manipulation that eliminates the recency effect should be no surprise to you. Glanzer and Cunitz (1966), for instance, showed their subjects 15-item lists, required them to do an attention-consuming counting task for either 10 or 30 seconds, and then finally asked them to recall the items. In contrast to the group that was asked for immediate recall (0-second delay), the groups that had to perform the counting task before recalling the list showed very low recency (Figure 4-4B). On the other hand, the primacy portion of the list was essentially unaffected by the counting task. The early list items, in other words, must have resided in a more permanent, long-lived memory store for them to endure the 30 seconds of counting that was interpolated between study and test. These items seemed quite immune to the interference effects of the distractor task. The most recent items, however, were dramatically susceptible to interference, so they must have been stored in a shorter-term, more fragile memory—STM.

Other manipulations, summarized by Glanzer (1972), showed how the two portions of the serial position curve are indeed influenced by different factors. For our consideration of short-term memory, note that providing more time per item during study ("spacing" of 3 versus 6 versus 9 seconds, in the figure) had virtually no effect on the recency portion of the list but did alter the primacy portion to a significant degree (Figure 4-4C; from Glanzer & Cunitz, 1966). Additional time for rehearsal enabled subjects to store the early items more strongly in long-term memory, it seemed. On the other hand, additional time was not necessary or even helpful for the sort of immediate recall used for the most recent items. These items were presumably held in short-term memory and recalled rapidly before interference could take place.

Rehearsal Buffer

The notion of short-term memory as a *rehearsal buffer,* a mental recycling system for holding information temporarily, was clearly a dominant idea through the 1960s. Waugh and Norman's (1965) model explicitly showed rehearsal as a recirculating loop within primary (short-term) memory. The typical interpretation was that rehearsal was an optional control process invoked by short-term memory. Rehearsal was thought to have two properties; it could maintain information in short-term memory, by recirculating it through the rehearsal buffer, and at the same time it could increase the likelihood that the rehearsed information would be transferred to long-term memory for more permanent storage (Atkinson & Shiffrin, 1968; Waugh & Norman, 1965). Bear these two properties in mind—recycling and transferring to long-term memory—since they are crucial to what follows.

We will discuss this second function of rehearsal, transferring information into long-term memory, in the next chapter. At that time, we will take up the distinction between maintenance and elaborative rehearsal (Craik & Lockhart, 1972) more thoroughly. For now, note that the rehearsal function was established as a short-term memory process, a characteristic *activity* of the short-term memory system. Rehearsal was said to be an optional control process, which could both maintain items in STM by recycling the information *and* help transfer them to LTM. The results revealed by serial position curves are in agreement with these ideas, with "recycling" rehearsal responsible for the recency effect and "transferring" rehearsal responsible for the primacy effect. Yet this evidence is rather indirect.

Further research has provided straightforward evidence that the kind of rehearsal subjects perform during the primacy portion of the list is quite different from their rehearsal on the recency portion. That is, differences in primacy and recency effects are due to differences in the kind of rehearsal subjects perform. An illustrative study was performed by Kellas and Butterfield (1971). Some subjects had to perform the usual free recall task, while others were held to a serial recall requirement. The nine-item lists that had to be learned were either single letters, letter pairs, or letter triples; the triples ("trigrams" in the figure) were the most difficult, of course, but also illustrate the rehearsal point the best, so we'll consider only these results. The interesting difference between

Kellas and Butterfield's procedures and those discussed above was that these investigators permitted the subjects to study the items in the list for as long as they wished.

Figure 4-5 shows two kinds of serial position curves: first, the results on study time (how long subjects looked at each item), and second, the accuracy results. Note how the subjects in the serial recall condition spent an ever-increasing amount of time studying the items, all the way through the list. This pattern of study suggests a genuine, laborious attempt to rehearse all items in order and to add the next list item to the growing set already being rehearsed (see also Kellas, McCauley, & McFarland, 1975b). Recall of the letter triples showed a declining serial position effect with no recency. Of course, the requirement to recall the items in order prevented the subjects from taking advantage of the recency of the last items, much as interpolated counting had done in the study described above.

On the other hand, the free recall group showed steadily increasing study times until the last few items in the list, at which point they *decreased* their study time, as shown in the figure. Their recency effect was intact when accuracy was scored, because they had been able to take advantage of the rapid, "spewing out" kind of immediate recall. Indeed, the fact that they could begin their recall with these last items affected the way they studied—as if they had said to themselves, "I don't need to spend much time on the last items, since I can name them first." This is, of course, an illustration of metacognitive awareness on the part of the subjects, a tailoring of their rehearsal strategy to the particular task. (How often have you tailored your study time and habits to fit the kind of exam you're going to have?)

A final kind of support for the notion of two kinds of STM rehearsal comes from developmental studies of children's learning and short-term memory performance. A second study by Kellas, McCauley, and McFarland (1975a) examined performance of children in third, fifth, and seventh grades. In support of several earlier studies, their results showed an increase in laborious rehearsal across the grade levels: seventh-graders rehearsed much more than fifth-graders, and fifth-graders rehearsed more than third-graders (see also Flavell, 1970). The important point here, however, concerns the recency effects that were found. As Figure 4-6 shows, there were virtually no differences among the grades on the recency items in the lists—immediate recall from STM did not differ. However, the more deliberate kind of rehearsal responsible for primacy effect differences did vary with ages.

It seems very clear from these several studies that two distinct kinds of rehearsal can be performed in short-term memory, a deliberate kind that transfers information to long-term memory, and a simpler, less effortful kind that is responsible for recency effects. The deliberate, strategic rehearsal responsible for primacy effects will be discussed further in the next chapter, since its effect seems to be one of transferring

FIGURE 4-5

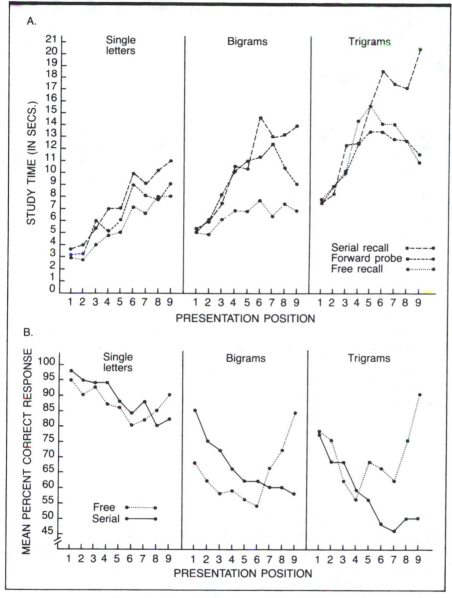

A. Serial position curves showing study time during presentation of the list, for serial and free recall tasks; subjects studied single letters, letter pairs (bigrams), or letter triples (trigrams).

B. Recall accuracy across serial positions for the two recall tasks and the three types of list items. Note that under free recall, the serial positions in the recency effects correspond to those positions in panel A on which subjects decreased their study time.

FIGURE 4-6

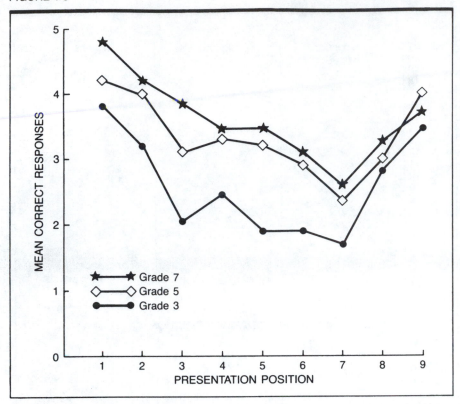

Recall accuracy across serial positions for free recall, subjects from grades 3, 5, and 7. Note that the primacy effects differ by age, but that recency is nearly the same for all three groups.

information to long-term memory. For our consideration of short-term memory, however, note two things. First, the recency effect remains fairly constant across ages and across differing amounts of study. Second, the recency effect is eliminated under conditions of interference, either by distraction from rehearsal (the counting task) or by the need to recall other information first (the serial recall task).

What is short-term memory for? Part of the answer is rehearsal— rehearsal that can transfer information to long-term memory, and rehearsal that maintains a short-term memory trace for a brief period of time.

Summary Points: free and serial recall; serial position; primacy and recency; rehearsal buffer

▼ Short-Term Memory Scanning and Sternberg's Reaction Time Paradigm

You've just read many important facts about short-term memory, about its limited capacity and susceptibility to interference, about rehearsal and recoding. These effects are absolutely basic to short-term memory. And yet, in terms of sheer impact on the field of cognitive psychology, a series of short-term memory studies by Saul Sternberg has probably had at least as great an influence as any of the reports already discussed. Although the specific conclusions about short-term memory that Sternberg offered have been called into question, it is important nonetheless to study the task and results. The major reason for this is that Sternberg showed the way for countless cognitive studies to ask much more sophisticated questions about memory than had been asked before, questions about long-term as well as short-term memory. Sternberg's research asked three fundamental questions: How do we search through information stored in the memory system? How rapidly and accurately can this search be performed? What is the structure or format of the information through which we search?

Let's begin with the logic of this whole enterprise, a logic for "inferring mental processes from reaction time measures" (Sternberg, 1966, 1969, 1975). Sternberg began by noting (1966) that the use of reaction time (RT) tasks to infer mental processes had a venerable history, dating back at least to work by Donders in the 1800s.[6] Donders had proposed a general method called the "subtractive method" for determining the time necessary for simple mental events. In simple terms, if you're interested in the duration of Process B in a task that involves A, B, and C, then you must devise a comparison task that has only Processes A and C. Test your subjects under both tasks, measure how long the combination of A + B + C is, and then subtract the time for the combination of A + C. The difference, by the subtractive method, should be the time for Process B.

Sternberg pointed out the difficulty of applying the Donders subtractive method. It is virtually impossible to make sure that the comparison task, the A + C task, truly contains *exactly* the same A and C processes as the complete task. There is always the likelihood, Sternberg reasoned, that by eliminating process B, you have inadvertently simplified the A and C components. If so, then the time for A + C will be shorter than it would be in the full, three-process task.

---

[6]Donders (1868/1969) apparently tested the personnel at an observatory, to try to determine why some of their records disagreed. The observatory set Greenwich Mean Time by having an individual press a button when a certain star was centered on the cross hairs of the telescope sight. A few of the individuals, it seemed, responded more slowly to the "target," so their time to press the button was longer than others'. Donders was able to convince the observatory that these individuals were not being sloppy, but that their "personal equation" was longer because of slower motor response time due to advancing age.

Sternberg's solution to this knotty problem seems quite straightforward in retrospect; apparently, at the time he proposed it, virtually no one would believe that it might work. His solution was to stop trying to eliminate one step from the sequence of processes, as the subtractive method tries to do. Instead, he suggested that the experiment be arranged so that the process of particular interest, say, Process B, would have to *repeat* one or more times during a single trial. Across an entire experiment there would be many trials on which Process B had occurred only once, many on which it occurred two times, three times, and so on. Naturally, we can then examine the reaction time for these successive conditions. We can figure out how long Process B takes by determining how much time is added to the subjects' responses when an extra cycle through Process B is required. The term Sternberg chose for this logical and statistical system was "additive factors logic." [7]

The Sternberg Task

Sternberg applied his additive factors logic to the question of retrieval of information from short-term memory. To investigate this question he devised an appealingly simple task that he called "short-term memory scanning." In a typical experiment, Sternberg's subjects would be shown several hundred trials, each consisting of two parts. First, the subjects would be shown from one to six letters (or digits in some experiments) and would be asked to hold that set of items in short-term memory. These items are referred to as the **memory set.** Sternberg always presented fewer than seven items in the memory set, to make sure that all could be held accurately in short-term memory.

After a short pause, a test letter was presented to the subjects, termed the **probe item;** this was the second part of each trial. The subjects' task was simply to make a yes/no judgment as to whether the probe item was one of the letters in the memory set. While the accuracy of the subjects' judgments was of course important, the speed of their judgments, their RT as measured in milliseconds, was even more important. Thus subjects were instructed to respond as quickly as possible while maintaining high accuracy.

Table 4-1 shows the memory sets and probe items for several trials in a typical Sternberg task and the typical sequence of events in the task. You might try a few of these, covering the probe item until you've stored

---

[7]It's a useful mnemonic to remember the term "additive factors logic" by noting that Sternberg's task *added* cycles through a certain stage, rather than trying to subtract a stage altogether. The only difficulty with this mnemonic is that it is wrong. "Additive factors logic" refers to the factors or independent variables in an analysis of variance that are manipulated in the Sternberg task, and the statistical pattern of interactions in the results (if two factors do not interact in the statistical analysis, then they are additive—their effects add together). In Sternberg's logic, two such additive factors must be influencing separate stages in the encoding, search, decision, and response sequence. Alternatively, if two factors interact (i.e., if they are not additive), then they must be influencing at least one stage in common. Considerable research after Sternberg has called this original logic into question, however.

Table 4-1

Trial	Memory Set Items	Probe Items	Correct Response
1	R	R	Yes
2	LG	L	Yes
3	SN	N	Yes
4	BKVJ	M	No
5	LSCY	C	Yes
Before timing starts, store memory set in STM	Timing starts here Probe item	Scan STM	Timing stops here Make response
e.g., E Q H D	J	Compare J to E, compare J to Q, etc.	No

the memory set in short-term memory, then uncovering it and making your yes/no judgment. Pay attention to your introspections as you do the task, so you can compare them with the actual results (for a better demonstration, have someone read the memory set, then the probe item, to you).

If you're reading carefully, you've already figured out the connection between the Sternberg task and the goal of forcing Process B to happen once, twice, and so on. The connection is the memory set, the set of one to six items held in short-term memory. What was the subjects' task? It was to encode the probe item, then scan through the contents of short-term memory to see if the probe matched any of the letters in the memory set. If we call Process B the scanning or comparison process, then doesn't B have to happen again and again, once for each item scanned in the memory set? By comparing reaction times for trials with one, two, three (and so on) comparisons, we should be able to determine how long the RT is for any one of them: it should be the amount of extra scanning time when one more item is added to the memory set. (If this logic is still vague to you, reread the last four paragraphs now before going any further.)

False Trials

The condition in Sternberg's experiments that illustrates this logic most clearly is the condition in which a "false" judgment is correct: that is, when the probe item is *not* contained in the memory set (needless to say, subjects did not know ahead of time that the correct response would be "false"). Consider the fourth trial in Table 4-1, a memory set of B K V J, followed by the probe item M. Sternberg assumed, reasonably enough,

FIGURE 4-7

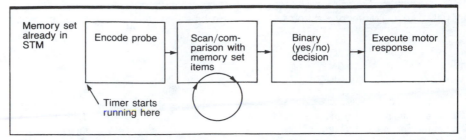

The four-stage process model for short-term memory scanning. (Adapted from Sternberg, 1969.)

that the total time for a response to the probe consisted of individual times for four separate stages, illustrated in Figure 4-7. First, as the timing apparatus begins running with the presentation of the probe, the first stage of information processing is encoding. Simply put, the probe has to be encoded into memory so it can then be compared to items in the memory set. Encoding happens just once per trial, of course.

The match or comparison process, which happens after the encoding stage, consists of the mental scanning or searching process, trying to match the probe item by examining each item in the memory set. If a single comparison takes m amount of time, then the four comparisons necessary for set B K V J should take $4m$ amount of time.

The yes/no decision stage and the motor response stage are more like encoding, on the other hand, in that each of them occurs only once per trial. Furthermore, there is no reason to suspect that encoding, decision, or motor response time will *change* in duration from one trial to another. In other words, the probe item M should be no faster or slower to encode than any other probe letter. Deciding "false" should take about the same amount of time on each "false" trial. And making the correct response—either saying "false" out loud or pressing a button labeled "false"—should not change in speed either. Thus encoding, decision, and response time should all be constants for all trials.

Scanning time, on the other hand, should *not* be a constant for all trials, because on some trials only one search is necessary, on some two searches are necessary, and so on, up to memory set size six, requiring all six comparisons. The basic Sternberg result for false trials is presented in the open circles of Figure 4-8A. Nearly 400 msec are required for the combination of encoding, decision, and response time, since the *y*-intercept for the graphed function is about 400 msec (the hypothetical time necessary for a memory set size of zero, when only encoding, decision, and response would occur). Adding one item to the memory set, plotted across the *x*-axis, added 37.9 msec to overall reaction time; adding yet another item to the memory set boosted RT by another 37.9 msec, and so on.

FIGURE 4-8

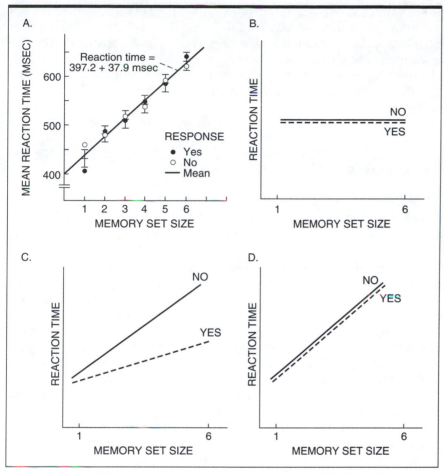

A. Reaction time in the short-term memory scanning task, for yes (shaded circles) and no (unshaded circles) responses. Reaction time increases linearly, at a rate of 37.9 msec per additional item in the memory set.
B. The predicted RT effects if short-term memory is scanned in parallel fashion.
C. The predicted RT effects if short-term memory is scanned in a serial self-terminating fashion.
D. The predicted RT effects if short-term memory is scanned in a serial exhaustive fashion, the prediction that matches the obtained results.

In other words, loading short-term memory with one more item necessitated one more comparison operation and added another increment of about 38 msec to overall RT. How quickly can the contents of short-term memory be scanned when no match is found? Apparently, based on Sternberg's classic results, the contents can be scanned at a rate of 38 msec per item.

This result seems to rule out one of the logically possible ways that short-term memory might be scanned. That is, we might hypothesize that scanning takes place *in parallel,* with all items in the memory set being scanned simultaneously. If this were the case, then the simplest predictions would be that reaction time should not increase at all with larger and larger memory sets: if short-term memory is searched in parallel, then any number of scans (up to six or seven) will occur simultaneously. The predicted outcome of such a search is graphed in Figure 4-8B. Clearly, this simple parallel processing hypothesis does not match the data (although a complex parallel process might; see the discussion below).

True Trials

When the probe *does* match an item in the memory set, the "true" trials, subjects must make a "yes" decision. This is the condition in which the specific nature of the scanning process is revealed most clearly.

Self-Terminating Search   Consider next the kind of search that seems most plausible, at least from an intuitive standpoint—the "serial self-terminating search." This kind of search is the mental equivalent of a physical search, say, looking for your lost car keys. If there are five places you normally leave your keys, then you begin searching in the first place, continuing to the next location and the next until you finally find your keys. Once you find the keys, then you stop searching. In other words, you search the locations one by one, *serially,* and you stop searching, in *self-terminating* fashion, when you find what you were looking for. Maybe short-term memory is searched in the same way; maybe we search serially, one memory set item at a time, in a self-terminating fashion, stopping when the probe matches the item with which it is compared.

If this were the way that short-term memory were scanned, then the results for such a serial self-terminating search would resemble those in Figure 4-8C. "Yes" trials should show a shallower slope, in other words faster average RT for serial self-terminating search than "no" trials. The reason for this is quite straightforward; you can often stop searching part-way through the memory set on "yes" trials, but you must search all the way through the set on "no" trials. For example, in Table 4-1, on Trial 2, you could stop scanning short-term memory after the first position was searched, because the probe L matches the first position of the memory set. You'd have to search both positions on Trial 3, however.

Serial Exhaustive Search

Instead, the results Sternberg obtained matched the pattern in Figure 4-8D, the pattern derived from the hypothesis of *serial exhaustive search* (compare Figure 4-8D to the actual data in 4-8A). However implausible it may seem to you, it appeared that short-term memory was searched in a serial exhaustive fashion: you search through *all* memory set positions, even if the probe matched an early position. Sternberg drew this inference because of the overwhelming similarity of the "yes" and "no" curves. Search *has* to be exhaustive on "no" trials; you have to look in all five locations for your keys before you're sure they're not there. Thus finding the same pattern, and virtually the same RTs, for "yes" trials implies that they too are performed via an exhaustive search. Even when a match occurred in an early position, subjects apparently continued their search through the remaining positions before making their decision.

However ridiculous it would be to search for your car keys in this way, Sternberg argued persuasively that **serial exhaustive search,** *scanning all positions on all trials,* might in fact be more efficient in the domain of short-term memory. Consider the search rate of 38 msec per item. This is incredibly fast: after all, it's less than ¹⁄₂₀th of a second. Sternberg (1969) suggested that the search process is so rapid that it might be impossible to stop it once it begins. In other words, maybe once the high-speed scanning process is triggered, it "runs to completion" more or less automatically and cannot be voluntarily stopped (as Zbrodoff & Logan, 1986, have described an "autonomous" mental process).

Sternberg also pointed out a second efficiency of exhaustive search. Under exhaustive search, you scan short-term memory, then merely make *one* yes/no decision at the completion of scanning. In contrast, if you searched in a self-terminating fashion, you'd scan one position, decide if the probe matched, scan the next position, decide if the probe matched that one, and so on, cycling back and forth between comparison and decision. In the end, you will have made many extra decisions that could have been avoided just by postponing the decision stage until your search was completed.

The basic Sternberg results can be summarized in three points. First, it seems that short-term memory is a searchable memory system; that is, the contents of short-term memory reside as separate elements that can be examined one by one during a mental search. Second, it seemed that our search process is a serial one, rather than a parallel search through all items simultaneously, and a very rapid serial one at that—38 msec per comparison for adults. Finally, the method of searching seemed to be exhaustive, rather than self-terminating. However implausible an exhaustive search is for lost keys (or, for that matter, for long-term memory), it seems to characterize the mental process operating in short-term memory, a rapid, exhaustive, and highly automatic search process. (Our lack of awareness for rapid, automatic processes is especially obvious in this task. If you try it yourself, you're tempted to say that there is no search at all, only a simple decision. Clearly, logic and Sternberg's results disconfirm that introspection.)

After Sternberg's research was published, a large number of researchers jumped on the bandwagon of short-term memory scanning, and a variety of intriguing results were obtained. Hunt (1978) reviewed much of this research, studies that used the Sternberg task to examine short-term memory processes in different kinds of people. In general, the *nature* of search usually turned out to be serial exhaustive, while the *rate* of search was found to change dramatically depending on who is tested; for example, mentally retarded individuals, who showed a much slower rate of scanning short-term memory than normal children (e.g., Dugas & Kellas, 1974), and high-school students, who were slower than normal adults. See Figure 4-9 for a summary of these results. In a very different use of the Sternberg task, Darley, Tinklenberg, Hollister, & Atkinson (1973) found that search rate was unaffected, although overall reaction time was slower, for subjects under the influence of marijuana. In other words, the fundamental memory process of scanning was unaffected by the drug, but other processes such as encoding, decision, and motor response were altered.

As stated in Chapter 2, there have also been detractors of the Sternberg method, in particular, of the notion that increasing reaction times necessarily mean serial exhaustive search. For instance, one proposal explains this pattern of results as the product of a parallel search, where each additional item to be scanned slows down the rate of scanning for all items (much as a battery will run several motors at once, but each will run more slowly than if fewer motors were connected; see Baddeley, 1976, for a review of such criticisms). Others have objected to a different aspect of Sternberg's work, the embedded assumption that the several stages or processes are sequential, and that one must be completed before the next one begins. For instance, McClelland (1979) proposed that the mental stages might overlap partially, in "cascade" fashion. In a general way, our earlier discussions of automaticity and parallel processing should suggest the nature of this criticism to you. With practice, a process becomes more automatic, thus releasing attentional and processing resources to be devoted to other mental processes. Such outcomes, of course, suggest that the assumption of sequential and independent stages of processing is incorrect, or, at best, incomplete.

Disputes such as these indicate an active, probing science. It's a bit disconcerting to students that cognitive psychology doesn't have the solid answers they were expecting (one of my professors in graduate school routinely commented, "Hey, you chose psychology. You're just going to have to learn to live with uncertainty"). On the other hand, balancing out Sternberg's critics, note the following: the fact that we might interpret his results as parallel rather than serial search is a tremendous advance over the former state of affairs, never having conceived of short-term memory search in the first place.

Summary Points: short-term memory scanning; memory set, probe item; serial versus parallel search; self-terminating versus exhaustive search

FIGURE 4-9

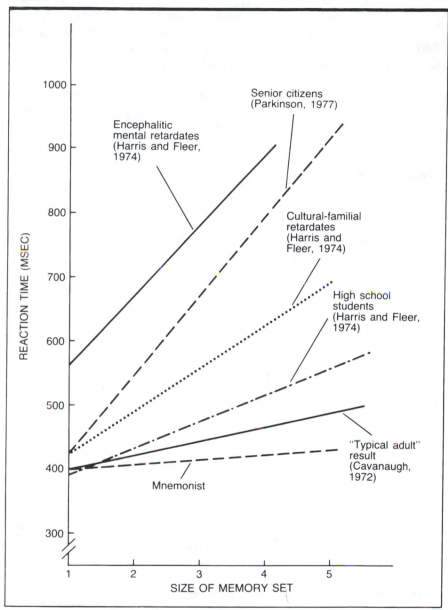

Results from short-term memory scanning experiments from differing groups of subjects. The figure shows that there are group differences in the rate of scanning through short-term memory, with senior citizens and encephalitic mental retardates showing the slowest rates, and typical adults and a mnemonist (person skilled at the use of mnemonic devices) showing the fastest rates.

▼ Codes in Short-Term Memory

We turn now to a somewhat different question about short-term memory. What is the *form* of the stored information? If the information stored in visual sensory memory is based on a visual code, and the information stored in auditory sensory memory is based on a sound code, then what is the code for short-term memory? Are there in fact several different kinds of codes that can be held in short-term memory? (Note that this is another way of stating one of our seven themes, the one concerning the representation of knowledge in memory.)

Verbal Codes

Most of the early research on short-term memory, if it considered this question at all, merely assumed that the information code in short-term memory was probably an acoustic, verbal code. If the experiment asks subjects to report a spoken triad of letters, or scan through a short list of letters, it seems only natural to suppose that the memory code for the letters is related to the letter names themselves, a verbal, almost speech-like code.

To be sure, several reports demonstrated that short-term memory represents information in an acoustic, verbal-based form. Conrad (1964), for instance, presented a string of letters visually to his subjects and then recorded their errors in immediate recall. He found that when they made mistakes, they were quite likely to "recall" a letter that *sounded* like the correct one, substituting D for E, for example. Visual confusions, such as substituting F for E, were rare. In other words, even though the letters were presented visually, they were apparently stored in short-term memory in an acoustic, sound-based fashion. In a similar study, Wickelgren (1965) presented four letters to his subjects, then distracted them by having them copy down eight different letters. Finally, when asked to recall the original four letters, his subjects did poorly when the eight copied letters rhymed with the four target letters. (Note here that Wickelgren used a retroactive interference task, where the later material, the eight letters, interfered backward in time with memory for the earlier four letters.)

It appeared from this research that the code in short-term memory is verbally based, related to the spoken names of the stimulus items. This code is usually referred to as an **acoustic–articulatory code,** since either the actual *sound (acoustic code) or the pronunciation (articulatory code)* could be important. Subsequent research, however, showed that the acoustic–articulatory code was not the only format for storage in short-term memory. In particular, several *other* codes can be held in short-term memory, for instance, semantic- or meaning-based codes, visual codes, and even physical movement codes.

Semantic Codes

How might we test the hypothesis that semantic codes can be used in short-term memory? We need to devise a short-term memory task in which the meanings of the stimulus words might influence retention. An obvious choice is the Wickens *release-from-PI* paradigm. Use a Brown–Peterson task, including a distractor during the retention interval. Vary the semantic characteristics on the "switch trial," the trial on which the nature of the stimulus is changed.

Wickens and his colleagues performed many such experiments and commonly found that switching word class or meaning resulted in a dramatic increase in accuracy on the switch trial (reviewed in Wickens, 1972). Figure 4-10 illustrates a representative study (Wickens &

FIGURE 4-10

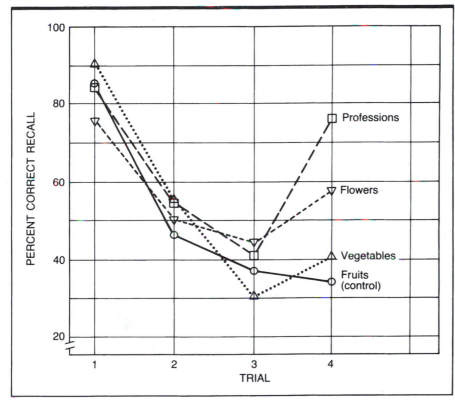

Recall accuracy in a release from PI experiment by Wickens and Morisano (reported in Wickens, 1972). All subjects received word triads from the fruit category on Trial 4. On Trials 1–3, different groups received triads from the categories fruits (control condition), vegetables, flowers, and professions.

Morisano, reported in Wickens, 1972). All subjects had four successive Brown–Peterson trials. The control group saw three trials, with three words on each trial, from the fruit category. The other groups saw three trials, again with three words each, but from the categories of professions, flowers, or vegetables. All groups saw three fruits on trial 4. Thus the control group saw a total of four trials of fruit names, whereas the other groups experienced a semantic shift from some different category to the fruit category on Trial 4.

As you would expect, accuracy for all the groups declined across the first three trials, due to the buildup of proactive interference. This decline in recall continued on Trial 4 for the control group, because they got yet another triad of fruit names. The other groups, however, showed release from PI on Trial 4, higher recall on the "switch trial." Furthermore, the amount of release depended on the similarity of the categories. Because switching from professions to fruits is a major change in category, those subjects showed strong release from PI, compared to the small effect for subjects switched from vegetables to fruits.

This result showed conclusively that semantic factors can influence the amount of release from PI. Furthermore, as the semantic change from the earlier category to the fruit category became more pronounced, there was greater release from PI. Since the triads are always being held in short-term memory in this task, the improvement on Trial 4 indicates a short-term memory sensitivity to meaning. Can semantic codes be part of the short-term memory representation of information? Yes.

Visual Codes

A variety of experiments might be described to support the claim that short-term memory can contain visual codes (e.g., Posner 1978; Posner & Keele, 1967). We'll look at just two classic demonstrations of the visual-code hypothesis. In addition to showing how visual information influences short-term memory, these studies begin to suggest why cognitive psychology started shifting from the traditional term *short-term memory* to the more current notion of *working memory*.

A fascinating study by Brooks (1968) used a variation on the dual task method we discussed in the last chapter: ask the subjects to do two things at once, and see if the two tasks interfere with one another. Brooks asked two groups of subjects to hold a visual image in short-term memory, and then to do a second task that also consumed attention. Both groups were asked to form a mental image of a block letter, a capital F. One group was then asked to scan mentally along the edges of the imagined F, saying yes if the corner they reached mentally was at the extreme top or bottom of the figure, saying no if the corner was not at the extreme top or bottom. See Figure 4-11, and note where the beginning point is, at the asterisk. Try doing this yourself for a moment, to get a feel for the task.

FIGURE 4-11

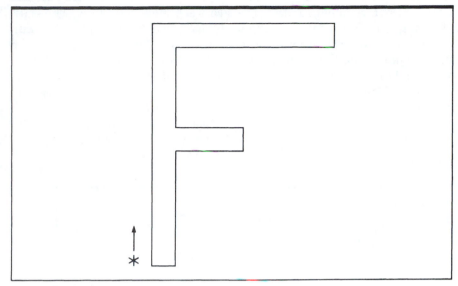

The block capital F used in Brooks's experiments (1968). Form a mental image of the F. Beginning at the star, mentally scan around the image, saying yes if the corner you reach is at the extreme top or bottom of the letter.

The second group, while still holding the visual image of a block F, was asked to do a *spatial* or visual task. They had to point to the column on a sheet of paper that had the correct sequence of *yes* and *no* responses for the "extreme top/bottom" judgments. Brooks made this second visual task particularly demanding by using only "y" and "n" for yes and no, and by staggering the columns so that the lines of responses were jagged.

The results were clearcut. Requiring the subject to scan a visual image in short-term memory *and* to perform another visual task simultaneously, reading then pointing to the correct jagged line, resulted in very low accuracy. On the other hand, the group that scanned the visual image and simultaneously made a *verbal* report of yes and no responses had much less difficulty. Seemingly, short-term memory can hold visual codes but cannot support two simultaneous visual tasks. If the two tasks require *different* modes, visual image and auditory response, then there is little conflict or interference. Segal and Fusella (1970) found comparable results: subjects holding a visual image in short-term memory were poor at detecting a visual signal, compared to those who detected auditory signals. Conversely, subjects who held an *auditory* stimulus in short-term memory detected visual signals quite well, but auditory signals quite poorly.

The most dramatic evidence of visual codes in short-term memory, however, were the demonstrations of *mental rotation* by Shepard and Metzler (1971) and Cooper and Shepard (1973). In the Shepard and Metzler paper, subjects were shown a complex perspective drawing in two forms and had to judge whether the two were the same shape. The critical factor here was that the second drawing was depicted as if it had been rotated from the orientation of the first drawing. Clearly, to make accurate judgments, the subjects had to perform some transformation on the second drawing, mentally rotating it into the same orientation as the first so they could judge it "same" or "different." Figure 4-12 displays several such pairs of drawings and the basic findings of the study.

The overall result was that people took longer to make their judgments as the angular rotation needed for the second drawing increased.

FIGURE 4-12

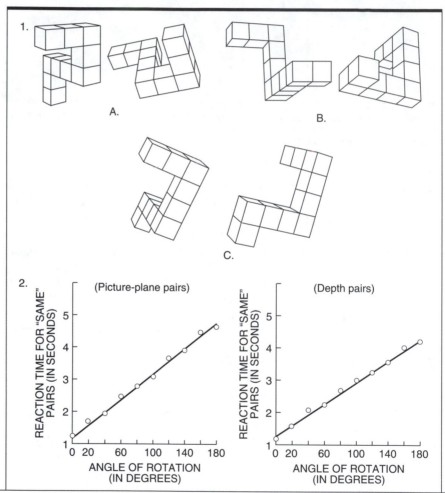

1. Three pairs of drawings are shown. For each, rotate the second drawing and decide if it is the same figure as the first drawing. The *A* pair differs by an 80-degree rotation in the picture plane, and the *B* pair differs by 80 degrees in depth; the patterns in *C* do not match.
2. The RTs to judge "same" are shown as a function of the degrees of rotation necessary to bring the second pattern into the same orientation as the first. Reaction time is a linear function of the degree of rotation.

In other words, a figure that needed to be rotated 120 degrees to bring it back to the orientation of the first drawing took longer to judge than one needing only 60 degrees of rotation. In the Cooper and Shepard (1973) report, subjects were shown the first figure and were told how much rotation to expect in the second figure. This advance information on the degree of rotation permitted subjects to do the mental rotation ahead of time; in other words, it allowed them time to prepare for the later-presented second figure.

Note that in both studies the subjects were performing a complex, visually based mental task—holding a mental image in short-term memory, then doing difficult, attention-consuming mental *work* on that image. It is almost inconceivable, especially for the shapes shown in Figure 4-12, that such performance could be achieved if short-term memory has *only* acoustic or verbal-based codes. (Ask yourself, what sort of verbal code would be sufficiently detailed to permit such regular rotation without benefit of visual information?)

Instead, the mental image and rotation studies demonstrated rather conclusively that, when we give subjects the chance, they can generate and use visual codes in short-term working memory. And, considering the *kind* of mental processing required, it certainly seems more natural to refer to the workplace for this rotation process as working memory. Somehow, the notion of 7 ± 2 chunks of information seems quite irrelevant to the process of mental rotation, doesn't it?

Other Codes

To conclude this discussion of short-term memory codes, note that other formats for information storage in short-term memory are also possible. For example, most people can conjure up the "kinesthetic" image of riding a bicycle, in a manner similar to Brooks's capital F study. Similarly, Shand (1982) reported a fascinating set of results that demonstrate that short-term memory *can* hold information for physical movement. (See the Demonstrations for a visual plus physical movement test of memory span.)

Shand's subjects were congenitally deaf, and quite skilled at American Sign Language (ASL). He administered a short-term memory test to these people, requiring serial recall (recall in order) of five-item lists. One kind of list contained English words that were phonologically similar (SHOE, THROUGH, NEW), and one contained ASL "words" that were *cherologically* similar, that is, similar in the hand movements necessary for forming the sign (e.g., wrist rotation in the vicinity of the signer's face). The subjects' recall showed confusions based on the cherological relatedness of the list items, *even* when the list was presented as a series of written, English words. In other words, Shand's deaf subjects were recoding the written words into an ASL-based code in short-term memory, then basing their performance on that code.

In a manner of speaking, cognitive psychology used to be "certain"

DEMONSTRATIONS

Several tests of short-term, working memory can be given with very little difficulty, to confirm the various effects you're reading about in this chapter. Below are suggestions, along with a few sample lists.

1. *Simple Memory Span.* Make several lists of the following kinds, being sure that the items don't form unintentional patterns. Read the items at a fairly constant and rapid rate (no slower than one item per second) and have the subject name them back *in order*. Your main dependent variable will be the number or percentage correct.

List types: single digits, consonants, nonsense syllables, unrelated words, simple line drawings

Several easy variations on this procedure are possible:

a. To illustrate the importance of interference, have your subjects do an interference task on half of the trials. On an interference trial, give them a number like 437 and have them count backward by threes, out loud, for 15 seconds, before recalling the list items.

b. Keeping list length constant, give different retention intervals before asking for recall (e.g., 5 seconds, 10 seconds, 20 seconds), either with or without backward counting.

c. Vary the presentation rate, say, 1 word/second versus 1 word/3 seconds, to see how the additional time for rehearsal influences recall.

d. See if your subjects notice anything different about lists that *do* have some special pattern to them, like the starred lists here:

870314
71505436
2864612975
584393482561
TSYLQP
CIMWODXA
*QWERTYUIOP
KWUCRALNYWGSJ
*LABONNEMAISON
LEAF GIFT CAR FISH ROCK
PAPER SEAT TIRE HORSE FILM BEACH FOREST BRUSH
BAG KEY BOOK WIRE BOX WHEEL BANANA FLOOR BAR PAD
   BLOCK RADIO BOY
*LOVE EMOTION PLAN ATTEMPT RULE LAW ANALYSIS SYSTEM
   FINE PAYMENT
*WHILE I WAS WALKING THROUGH THE WOODS A RABBIT RAN
   ACROSS MY PATH

2. *Release from PI.* To do this demonstration, have four or five lists of materials ready; use nonsense letter triads, unrelated words, or related words as shown below. Present three or four of the similar lists one after the other, using the Brown–Peterson task (present the three list items, give a number, have the subjects count backward by threes before recall). Then switch the type of list on the next trial, also illustrated below.

TRIAL # 1	2	3	4	5
APPLE	BLUEBERRY	GRAPE	ORANGE	BEEF
LIME	PEAR	LEMON	STRAWBERRY	CHICKEN
APRICOT	BANANA	PEACH	GRAPEFRUIT	PORK

3. *Nonverbal STM.* This is a nonverbal analog to a verbal memory span task, sometimes used in neuropsychological testing for patients who are unable to speak. The stimulus lists are sequences of "taps" on a visual array of four locations. You tap out a sequence of length 8, for instance, and then the subject "recalls" by tapping the sequence back to you.

    a. Draw four squares on a piece of paper, in a row. You'll present the lists of "items" to the subject by tapping the squares in a predetermined random sequence. Make lists of the digits 1 to 4 in random order; tap the squares in those orders as if the leftmost square was #1, next to left #2, and so on. Obviously, do not tell the subject the square numbers, or suggest that the sequence can be recoded into numbers. As in the straightforward memory span demonstration, the percentage correct will be the main measure of performance.

LISTS

1 4 3 4 2 1 3
3 1 2 1 4 3 1 2
4 3 1 4 2 3 1 1 2
etc.

    b. Variations might include grouping your "taps" in 2s, as if you were tapping 14, 34, 21, slowing down the rate of tapping, and suggesting to the subject that the sequence can be recoded into the numbers 1–4.

4. *Dual Task Procedures.* You can adapt any of these tests by selecting a "secondary task" to be performed simultaneously. For example, while the subjects listen to the list items, have them scan a page of words, crossing out the vowels, words beginning with K, or animal names. Find out which combinations are the most difficult. Try one of the verbal short-term memory tasks while having the subjects perform a visual task, for example, counting the number of "outside corners" on a mentally imaged capital F (see the discussion of Brooks's study). Or use the verbalization tasks listed in Figure 4-14, from Baddeley and Hitch's (1974) studies, while the subjects do the nonverbal memory span task.

that short-term memory relied only on acoustic–articulatory coding. It turned out, however, that we had tested short-term memory only with acoustic or verbalizable stimuli: the mistaken "certainty" was a by-product of the kinds of stimuli we tested. In Shand's words, arguing for a "preference for phonological coding in short-term memory processes may reflect the *audiocentricity* of the experimenters" (p. 11, emphasis added), rather than an inherent tendency of short-term memory. In other words, short-term memory indeed seems able to hold information in *any* format that can be sensed—auditory, visual, kinesthetic, and so on—and in any format used in the mental system—semantic, imaginal, and so on.

▼ Working Memory

So what kind of system should replace this short-term memory? Adding semantic, visual, and other codes is a step in the right direction, to be sure, but still seems inadequate. After all, think of Brooks's study again. Two simultaneous tasks were pitted against one another, in one case the visual image task (capital F) plus verbal yes/no, in the other the visual image task plus a *visual* search. The latter combination was more disruptive. How could the simple "7 ± 2" short-term memory explain that?

More generally, by the early 1970s, cognitive psychology had awarded all sorts of roles and functions to short-term memory, in tasks involving problem solving, comprehension, and the like. And yet, as Baddeley and his colleagues pointed out (e.g., Baddeley, 1976; Baddeley & Hitch, 1974; Baddeley & Lieberman, 1980), very little research had tested those kinds of demands; in Baddeley and Hitch's (1974, p. 48) words, "The empirical evidence for such a view is remarkably sparse."

To illustrate those demands intuitively, solve the following problem:

$$[(4 + 5) \times 2] / [3 + (12/4)]$$

The problem-solving nature of your mental activity, including the "load" on memory, cannot be denied here—and yet, this is barely addressed by issues like 7 ± 2 units, recency, release from PI, and so on, right? Likewise, little that you've studied about short-term memory so far seems to capture how difficult it is to comprehend a sentence like

> *I know that you are not unaware of my inability to speak German.*

Let's go beyond intuitive examples, however. To document their position on the need for an elaborated short-term memory, Baddeley and Hitch (1974) described a particularly dramatic case study, reported by Warrington and Shallice (1969; also Shallice & Warrington, 1970; Warrington & Weiskrantz, 1970). A series of reports by these authors described a patient "who by all normal standards, has a grossly defective STS. He has a digit span of *only two items,* and shows grossly impaired performance on the Peterson short-term forgetting task. If STS does indeed function as a central working memory, then one would expect this patient to exhibit grossly defective learning, memory, and comprehension. No such evidence of general impairment is found either in this case or in subsequent cases of a similar type" (Baddeley & Hitch, 1974, pp. 48–49, emphasis added; also Baddeley & Wilson, 1988; Vallar & Baddeley, 1984).

How can working memory and short-term memory be the same thing, Baddeley and Hitch reasoned, when a patient with grossly defective STM performance exhibits *no* memory deficiencies in other tasks attributed to STM? To anticipate the conclusions in their paper, the problem lies with the theory of an undifferentiated STM. In Baddeley's view, traditionally defined STM is but one component of a larger, more elaborate system, **working memory.**

The Dual Task Method Applied to Working Memory

Let's spend some time reviewing the evidence that Baddeley has presented to support this view (see Baddeley, 1992a, for an excellent retelling of the development and support of the working memory hypothesis). To begin with, Baddeley and Hitch noted that evidence about short-term memory has typically come from two quite different results: first, the limited memory span, and second, the recency effect in free recall tasks. They noted that the one common characteristic between these results was the notion of limited capacity, that memory span and the recency effect both imply a memory system with rather severe limits. Of course, this idea has been common at least since Miller's characterization of short-term memory as an information processing "bottleneck."

They then designed a series of experiments based on the dual task procedure, similar in many respects to some of the research on visual codes (e.g., Brooks's "capital F" study, 1968). In general, they asked subjects to perform two tasks at a time, both of which were thought to make significant demands on the limited-capacity working memory system. Most commonly, one of the tasks was a memory span task—hold some number of items in a short-term buffer, then recall those items after the other task has been completed. The critical aspect here is that some amount of processing is necessary to maintain the items in the recycling buffer. With many items (i.e., a heavy memory load), enough mental resources may be used that performance on the other task will deteriorate. Thus, as in all dual task settings, Baddeley and Hitch were interested in the competition or interference effects that might be produced when two attention-consuming tasks had to be performed simultaneously. See Table 4-2 for a description of the conditions in the Baddeley and Hitch experiments.

As you read, remember the purpose of the dual task procedure and the kind of interpretations it permits. Any two tasks that are performed

The difficulty of language comprehension when working memory is overloaded.

simultaneously may show either complete independence, complete dependence, or some intermediate level of dependency. If neither influences the other, then we infer that the two tasks rely on separate mental mechanisms, or on separate pools of mental resources. If one task always disrupts the other, then the two tasks presumably require the same mental resources while they are being performed. That is, some common memory component or pool of capacity is being tapped by both. Finally, if the two tasks interfere with each other in some circumstances but not others, then there is evidence for partial overlap between the two, partial sharing of mental resources.

Working Memory and Reasoning In the Baddeley and Hitch experiments, subjects were asked to hold from one to six randomly chosen letters or digits in the short-term "buffer," the system responsible for memory span. Naturally, subjects' recall for those items was always tested. The other activity in the dual task procedure varied; in some experiments, it was a reasoning task, in others it involved language comprehension, and still others used a free recall learning task. Baddeley and Hitch's first three experiments used a concurrent (simultaneous) reasoning task. That is, while several items were being held in short-term memory, subjects also had to do a mental reasoning procedure. Stimuli

Table 4-2   DESCRIPTION OF THE CONDITIONS TESTED IN BADDELEY AND HITCH (1974)

Experiment 1

Short-term buffer task	then	Concurrent task	then	Memory span recall
Hold 1 or 2 items in buffer.		See AB, and decide true or false to sentence "B does not precede A."		Recall items in buffer.

Experiment 2

Short-term buffer task	then	Concurrent task	then	Memory span recall
Hold 6 items in buffer.		See AB, and decide true or false to sentence "B follows A."		Recall items in buffer.
or (control condition) Hold 0 items in buffer.		(same concurrent task)		Recall 6 items for memory span task.

Experiment 3

Articulatory suppression task	then	Concurrent task
Control condition—no articulation		See AB, and make same kind of decision.
Condition 1— repeat "the the the" out loud for duration of trial		Simultaneously see AB, and make same kind of decision.
Condition 2—repeat "one two three four five six" out loud for duration of trial		See AB, and make same kind of decision.
Condition 3—hold 6 randomly ordered digits and repeat out loud for duration of trial		See AB, and make same kind of decision.

such as AB were presented, and subjects had to respond true or false to an accompanying sentence. For a stimulus like AB, true sentences might be "A precedes B," a passive-voice "B is preceded by A," a negative "B does not precede A," one using the alternate verb "B follows A," or any combination of these (e.g., passive negative "A is not preceded by B"). As you would expect, the time it took to make the true/false judgments increased as the test sentence became more complex. The slowest and most difficult sentence type to judge was the passive negative type.

More to the point, however, was the way reasoning speed depended on the memory span task. In Experiment 1, only one or two items were "preloaded" into memory—stored and held in the short-term rehearsal buffer throughout the reasoning task. There was no interference under these conditions (see Table 4-3). Subjects' recall of the "preloaded" letters was essentially perfect and did not depend on hearing versus seeing the preloaded letters.

In Experiment 2, however, subjects were preloaded with either zero or six letters; in the "zero preload" condition, subjects were given the six letters *after* they had answered the reasoning question, thus placing no memory demand on them during the reasoning task. But with a six-item memory load, reasoning time jumped from 2.73 seconds to 4.73 seconds when correct recall of the letters had been stressed. And not only was reasoning speed slower in this condition, but recall of the six letters also suffered. In contrast, the "equal stress" group, whose instructions did not stress memory at the expense of reasoning, showed only a small increase in reasoning time when they held six letters in working memory—but their recall dropped to only 3.7 items on the memory span task.

The Working Memory Interpretation   Overall, it seemed that holding six items was a significant drain on working memory. If you were holding six items, there was insufficient extra mental capacity for doing the reasoning task "up to speed." Subjects could sacrifice reasoning speed and manage to do well on the memory span task, or could sacrifice

Table 4-3   REASONING TIMES AND LETTER RECALL UNDER VARIOUS MEMORY LOAD CONDITIONS

	Experiment 1		
	Memory load (number of letters held in memory)		
	0	1	2
Reasoning times	3.20 sec	3.31 sec	3.31 sec
Letter recall	Essentially perfect		

	Experiment 2		
	Memory load		
	0	6	
Reasoning times	3.27 sec	3.46 sec	"Equal stress"
Letter recall	5.5	3.7	
Reasoning times	2.73	4.73	"Memory stress"
Letter recall	5.8	5.0	

Note: In both experiments, a memory load of 0 was a control condition. In these conditions, subjects performed the reasoning task, and only then were they given the set of letters for the memory span task. Thus letter recall of 5.8 in the 0 Memory load condition means that 5.8 letters were recalled immediately after their presentation, where presentation followed the reasoning task.

Adapted from Baddeley & Hitch, 1974.

memory span and do well on reasoning speed. But they seemed unable to do well on both tasks *unless* the span task made minimal demands on the working memory system.

Baddeley's interpretation here is quite important. The reasoning task seemed to be dependent on the capacity of working memory, a limited-resource system. One- or two-item memory loads caused no disruption in working memory, so holding these memory loads was probably dependent on a *different* component of the overall working memory system. On the other hand, the component that was used for memory span performance could be overloaded by asking it to hold six items. Under this overloading condition, Baddeley suggested that the memory span component tends to drain mental resources from the larger, multipurpose working memory system. Baddeley called the component responsible for memory span the *articulatory loop* (e.g., Salame & Baddeley, 1982; also called the phonological loop; Baddeley, 1992a). The articulatory loop is a subcomponent of working memory that is specialized for the verbal-based recycling of items; it's the component that can prevent forgetting, via rehearsal. Under small memory loads, the articulatory loop functions independently and does not disrupt working memory. With heavy memory load, however, it shows partial overlap with the general working memory component used for reasoning. This partial overlap is evidenced by the interference between memory span and reasoning speed.

The Components of Working Memory

A description of Baddeley's proposed working memory system will provide a useful context for the studies described later; a diagram of the proposed working memory system is shown in Figure 4-13. In Salame and Baddeley's (1982) words, "The articulatory loop [is] part of a broader conceptualization of short-term memory . . . termed Working Memory. The Working Memory system was assumed to comprise a central executive which was responsible for initiating control and decision processes, and which was assisted by [two] subsidiary slave systems. The articulatory loop was one of these, and was assumed to comprise a modality-free store which used the process of articulatory rehearsal in order to maintain items in short-term storage" (p. 151).

Note first that working memory was a three-component memory system. The main part of the system is the *Central Executive* or *Executive Control* system. This executive is in charge of directing attention and mental resources, of starting the rehearsal procedure when it is necessary, and of making decisions. It also carries out the bulk of the reasoning task. One of the assistants to the executive, a "slave system" in Baddeley's terms, is the *Articulatory Loop,* the component responsible for memory span performance; the other slave system is the *Visuo-Spatial Sketchpad,* described by Baddeley and Lieberman (1980). These slave systems can operate on their own, once triggered by the central execu-

FIGURE 4-13

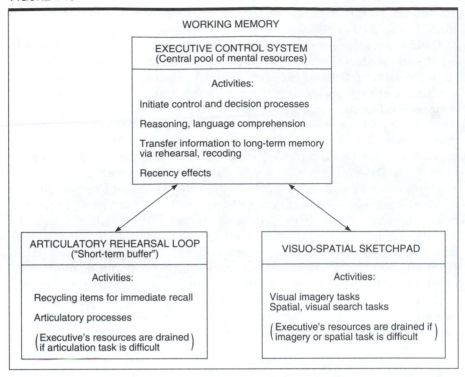

WORKING MEMORY

EXECUTIVE CONTROL SYSTEM
(Central pool of mental resources)

Activities:

Initiate control and decision processes

Reasoning, language comprehension

Transfer information to long-term memory
via rehearsal, recoding

Recency effects

ARTICULATORY REHEARSAL LOOP
("Short-term buffer")

Activities:

Recycling items for immediate recall

Articulatory processes

(Executive's resources are drained
if articulation task is difficult)

VISUO-SPATIAL SKETCHPAD

Activities:

Visual imagery tasks
Spatial, visual search tasks

(Executive's resources are drained if
imagery or spatial task is difficult)

The executive control system supports reasoning, language comprehension, and other such tasks by using resources from the central pool. Both the articulatory rehearsal loop and the visuo-spatial sketchpad have their own mental resources, but these are insufficient for especially demanding tasks. When necessary, each of these can drain resources from the central pool in the executive control system.

tive, without disrupting the executive's functions at all; such is the situation with only one or two memory span items. On the other hand, we can have the slave system do a very demanding task, such as holding six items in a memory span task. In this situation, the slave system can either drain off some of the executive's resources for its own performance, or can simply do poorly on its task. Of course, when the slave drains resources from the executive, we would then expect the task being performed by the executive to suffer.

The Articulatory Loop   To test the characteristics of the articulatory loop, Baddeley and Hitch conducted a third experiment. In this study, they asked subjects to perform the standard reasoning task while doing one of three "articulatory suppression" tasks (there was also a control task that required no other processing); the experimental conditions are summarized in Table 4-2, Experiment 3. One of the articulatory suppression tasks required fast repetition of the word "the." The idea here was that saying "the the the" would not require *memory,* per se, but would consume the articulation resources of the articulatory rehearsal loop. As such, saying "the the the" should suppress any articulation that is a normal part of the reasoning process. The second suppression task required rapid repetition of the sequence "one two three four five six." This form of articulatory suppression might be a bit more difficult than "the the the," Baddeley and Hitch reasoned, but still not as difficult as a true memory span task.

The last suppression task, however, involved a memory span procedure, with strings of six digits. In this task, subjects had to repeat aloud the random digit string over and over while answering the reasoning sentences—obviously, a combination of articulation *and* memory span. Note how the amount of articulation in the three suppression tasks was about the same (a speaking rate of four to five words per second was enforced), but the demands on memory steadily increased from "the the the" through the digit memory span task.

The reasoning speed results for different sentence types are presented in Figure 4-14. In general, reasoning time increased as the sentences became more complex. Furthermore, reasoning time also increased as the suppression task grew more difficult. It seemed clear that both the reasoning and the articulation tasks could share the same pool of mental resources or attention if necessary. Enough resources were available for a minimal memory load of one or two items while reasoning (Experiment 1), but certainly not enough were available for a heavy memory load task combined with reasoning (Experiment 2). And when an articulatory suppression task was required, the greater drain on working memory slowed down the reasoning task even more (Experiment 3). By far the most dramatic condition in the figure is the last group, passive negative reasoning problems ("A is not preceded by B"). When no other task was required (control condition), these sentences took slightly over 3 seconds to judge. But if a random string of six digits had to be recycled through memory at the same time, the difficult sentences required nearly 6 seconds to judge.

Language Comprehension   The results found by Baddeley and Hitch on language comprehension tasks were largely the same as those on reasoning problems: holding six digits in memory significantly disrupted comprehension scores and also significantly impaired the subjects' memory span performance. In companion experiments, reasoning and comprehension speed were tested when the stimulus sentences were phonetically similar ("B precedes P"; "Redheaded Ned said Ted fed in bed") versus dissimilar ("M precedes C"; "Dark-skinned Ian thought Harry ate in bed"). Of course, the fact that short-term memory often relies on an acoustic–articulatory code means that phonetically similar items should be more difficult to process (recall the acoustic confusion results described earlier). This was exactly what happened.

FIGURE 4-14

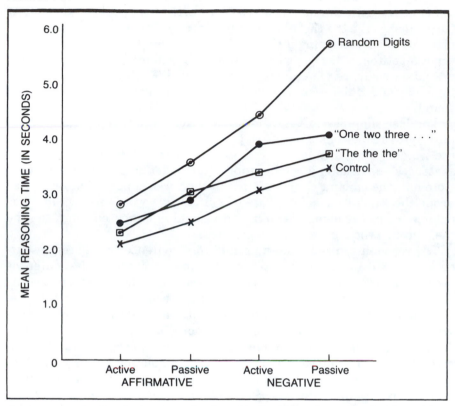

Average reasoning time is shown as a function of two variables: the grammatical form of the reasoning problem and the type of articulatory suppression task that was performed simultaneously with reasoning. In the "random digits" condition, a randomly ordered set of six digits had to be repeated out loud during reasoning: in the other two suppression tasks, either "the the the" or "one two three four five six" had to be repeated out loud during reasoning.

The Visuo-Spatial Sketchpad   In the Baddeley scheme, the second major slave system is the **visuo-spatial sketchpad.** This subsidiary system is dedicated to maintaining visual and spatial information in working memory and thus is the basis for tasks involving visual imagery and visual or spatial performance (Baddeley & Lieberman, 1980; earlier accounts called it a "scratch pad," with the unintended connotation of the written, verbal notes you'd write on a scratch pad). Analogous to studies on the articulatory loop, Baddeley and Lieberman (1980) tested the visuo-spatial sketchpad idea by the dual task procedure.

In particular, they were directly inspired by Brooks's (1967) rather difficult visual task. Subjects saw a 4 × 4 matrix, with one of the squares marked as the starting point. The subject then heard and was required to repeat back a sequence of sentences like "In the starting square put a 1, in the next square to the right put a 2, in the next square down put a

3" (Baddeley, 1992a, p. 10), and so on. As Baddeley noted, "Subjects almost invariably remember the sentences by creating an imaginary path through the matrix" (p. 10). In a contrasting task, the words "left," "right," "up," and "down" were replaced with "good," "bad," "weak," and "strong" (e.g., "in the next square to the good put a 2"). In this condition, subjects simply relied on rote verbal recall; that is, they did *not* rely on visual information.

At this point, Baddeley and Lieberman then introduced the second task, the venerable *pursuit rotor task*. In this task, subjects track a moving spot of light with a pencil-like pointer, trying to keep the pointer on the spot of light for as long as possible. The heavily visual nature of the pursuit rotor task disrupted performance on the visual "next square to the right" task. But pursuit rotor performance did *not* interfere with the verbal version of the task, remembering sentences like "in the next square to the good put a 2." Thus the experiment showed the independence of visual–spatial performance from verbal performance. In other words, the study demonstrated the existence of a separate, visually based system within working memory. In fact, more recent work has even suggested that the visuo-spatial sketchpad is itself a combination of two subdivisions, one each for visual and spatial information (Baddeley, 1992a, cites especially the neuropsychological work by Farah, Hammond, Levine, & Calvanio, 1988, in this regard).

Overview

The general conclusion from Baddeley's research is that *working memory* is a more suitable name for the attention-limited "workbench" system of memory. Working memory is responsible for the active mental effort of reasoning and language comprehension, as well as for the transfer of information into long-term memory by means of rehearsal. Aside from the central executive of working memory, there is a separate articulatory loop component and a separate visuo-spatial component. The articulatory loop is partially autonomous, in that it can recirculate a small amount of information without interfering with the central executive's performance. When overloaded, however, it begins to drain extra mental resources from the executive component. This disrupts the ongoing executive activity, whether it is reasoning, comprehending, or learning. Likewise, the visuo-spatial sketchpad can do a small amount of processing independently but, when faced with a demanding task, can siphon off mental resources from the executive.

Importantly, there is an overall limitation in the mental resources available to working memory: it's a "closed" system, with only some fixed quantity of mental resources to spread around. In other words, when extra resources are drained by the slave systems, they are not replaced into working memory by some other component. Instead, the central executive merely suffers along with insufficient resources for its own work. Naturally, as processes become more automatic, fewer of working memory's resources will be tied down by the task (see Hirst & Kalmar, 1987, for an analysis of the "pools of resources" metaphor).

A Working Memory Interpretation of the "Classic" STM Effects
A final strength of Baddeley's proposed working memory system is that it can accommodate most, perhaps all, of the standard short-term memory effects you read about earlier in the chapter. For instance, a working memory reinterpretation of simple memory span would suggest that the articulatory loop can hold about seven plus or minus two units of information, but a heavier load is not possible because of restrictions in the available pool of mental resources. Likewise, interference in STM, say, in the Brown–Peterson task, can be attributed to insufficient mental resources. Backward counting uses enough resources that those remaining are insufficient for recycling the three-letter stimulus in the articulatory loop. Similarly, because holding three words in working memory should drain fewer resources than holding three letters, the superior recall of words after an attention-consuming distractor task is understandable. Note also that counting backward at a rapid rate was enforced in all the experiments that used the Brown–Peterson task. This means that the other task, remembering the stimulus, would suffer instead of the counting performance. Clearly, if subjects had been permitted to slow down their counting, recall would have improved.

Finally, Baddeley's dual task has been applied to a study of primacy and recency effects (Baddeley & Hitch, 1974). Increasing the memory load from zero to three to six items depressed primacy effects in free recall but, rather surprisingly, did not alter the recency effect. Apparently, the articulatory loop responsible for memory span performance is a separate system from the one that generates the recency effect. As such, recency effects may provide evidence of a separate recall mechanism, one not tied to the active rehearsal and recycling that is characteristic of the articulatory loop.

Summary Points: verbal, semantic, visual, and movement codes; components of working memory; dual task procedure; central executive, articulatory loop, and visuo-spatial sketchpad

CHAPTER SUMMARY

1. Short-term or working memory is an intermediate memory system between the sensory memories and long-term memory. Its capacity for holding information is rather severely limited, on most accounts to only 7 ± 2 units of information. The process of recoding, grouping more information into a single unit, is the means of overcoming this limitation or "bottleneck" in the information processing system.

2. Whereas decay as an explanation of forgetting from short-term memory is logically possible, most of the research implicates a process of interference or competition as the reason for short-term forgetting. With an attention-consuming distractor task, such as counting backward by threes, even a very simple stimulus can be lost from short-term memory. The research suggests that this loss is a product of two kinds of interference: retroactive interference from the distractor task, and proactive interference from multiple trials on the same kind of material.

3. Serial position curves reveal the operation of two kinds of memory performance. Early positions in a to-be-recalled list are sensitive to deliberate rehearsal that transfers information into long-term memory, whereas later positions tend to be recalled with high accuracy in the free recall task; this latter effect is termed the recency effect and is due to the subjects' strategy of recalling these most recent items first. Asking subjects to perform some distractor task before recall usually eliminates the recency effect, since the distractor task prevents the subject from maintaining the most recent items in immediate memory. The rehearsal that is necessary to transfer information into long-term memory is a short-term, working memory activity.

4. Sternberg's important paradigm, "short-term memory scanning," provided a technique for investigating how we search through information held in short-term memory. Sternberg's results indicated that this search is accomplished in a serial exhaustive fashion, at a rate of about 38 msec per item to be scanned or searched. The Sternberg task illustrated how the short-term memory search processes of different kinds of people (children, adults, people under drug influences) might be investigated, as well as how other kinds of memory search processes might be investigated (e.g., long-term memory).

5. The release from PI task, which illustrates interference effects, has been used to document a different point, that short-term memory can hold a variety of informational codes. The evidence suggests that short-term memory often relies on an acoustic–articulatory code, but can also hold visual information, semantic information, and even information related to physical movement.

6. Working memory, a broader conceptualization of our short-term, immediate memory abilities, consists of a central executive system and two major slave systems. The most commonly investigated subsystem is the articulatory rehearsal loop, the system responsible for memory span performance. Baddeley's results suggest that when the memory span task is difficult, the articulatory loop can drain off mental resources from the central executive component. When this happens, then the task being performed by the executive will suffer either in speed or accuracy. The same arrangement applies to the visuo-spatial sketchpad, the other major slave system. On this theoretical account, the memory span performance tested in "classic" STM research is the articulatory loop, merely one component of the flexible, multipurpose system known as working memory.

Glossary Terms: articulatory loop; "bottleneck"; Brown–Peterson task; central executive; chunk; decay; free recall; interference; mental rotation; mnemonic device; primacy; PI—proactive interference; recency; recoding; rehearsal buffer; release from PI; RI—retroactive interference; serial exhaustive search; serial position curve; serial recall; Sternberg task; visuo-spatial sketchpad

SUGGESTED READINGS

The Atkinson and Shiffrin *Scientific American* paper in 1971 should be high on your outside reading list, if for no other reason than it was one of the first contributions to that prestigious journal by cognitive psychologists (authorship of a *Scientific American* article is by invitation only). Sternberg's original 1966 paper is also interesting to read, partly because its "modesty" is an interesting contrast with the eventual high regard the paper achieved. For current views, see the March 1993 issue of *Memory & Cognition,* devoted entirely to short-term memory.

Baddeley's (1992a,b) recent papers provide excellent and very approachable summaries of the entire program of research on working memory. In the 1992a article (the written version of his "Bartlett Lecture"), he also considers disruption of the central executive as a major consequence of Alzheimer's disease. In the 1992b paper, he summarizes work on the relationship between working memory and reading comprehension (see also Baddeley, Logie, Nimmo-Smith, & Brereton, 1985; Just & Carpenter, 1992; King & Just, 1991; MacDonald, Just, & Carpenter, 1992). Others have considered working memory and the difficulty of reasoning (e.g., Scribner, 1975), the nature of our contributions to a conversation (e.g., Norman & Rumelhart, 1975), and skill in mathematics problem solving (e.g., Geary, 1993). Evidence also suggests that working memory capacity is an important consideration in the process of aging (see Hasher, Stoltzfus, Zacks, & Rypma, 1991; Salthouse, 1992).

Chapter 5

EPISODIC LONG-TERM MEMORY

Memory is the most important function of the brain; without it life would be a blank. Our knowledge is all based on memory. Every thought, every action, our very conception of personal identity, is based on memory. . . . Without memory, all experience would be useless. (Edridge-Green, 1900)

We must never underestimate one of the most obvious reasons for forgetting, namely, that the information was never stored in memory in the first place. (Loftus, 1980, p. 74)

If X is an interesting or socially significant aspect of memory, then psychologists have hardly ever studied X. (Neisser, 1978, p. 4)

There has been more than a decade of passionate rhetoric claiming that important questions about memory could be tackled if only researchers looked to the "real world" for hypothesis validation. Yet, no delivery has been made on these claims. . . . We argue that the movement . . . has proven itself largely bankrupt. (Banaji & Crowder, 1989, p. 1185)

This is the first of three chapters specifically devoted to long-term memory, the relatively permanent storage vault for a lifetime's worth of knowledge and experience. Why do we need three separate chapters? The first reason, as indicated in the Edridge-Green quotation above, is obvious: long-term memory is fundamental to nearly *every* mental process, to virtually *every* act of cognition. Clearly, you're not going to understand human cognition unless you understand long-term memory. The second reason follows from the first: long-term memory is an enormous area of research, with a long (for psychology) history. In fact, the area is so large that it is impossible to do it justice unless some divisions and subtypes are used to organize the material. Thus this chapter and the next focus on two broad classes of knowledge that humans store in long-term memory, a two-part classification that was explicitly discussed by Tulving in his influential chapter "Episodic and Semantic Memory" (1972). Chapter 7 will then integrate these two types of knowledge and consider several other distinctions of growing importance to the field.

In Tulving's classification, **episodic memory** refers to a person's *autobiographical memory, to the personally experienced and remembered events of a lifetime.* A sampling of episodic memories would include remembering your current psychology professor's name, what you had for dinner last Tuesday, and the color of your bedroom walls. Most of the traditional research on memory, say, up through the mid-1960s, tested episodic memory; for example, the words you learn and recall in an experiment are stored in episodic memory. The critical aspect here is that the memories are part of your own personal history and are not generally shared by others.

Semantic memory, conversely, refers to your *general world knowledge, including your knowledge of the vocabulary and rules of language,*

and the general knowledge that relates concepts and ideas to one another.
For instance, you know what a bird is, you know how to use the word
"bird" in a sentence, and you know that robins and sparrows are typical
of the category, whereas ducks and penguins are less so. While it's obviously true that much of your semantic memory knowledge originally
came from personal experience, the particulars of that experience tend to
be either forgotten or irrelevant. You probably don't remember the first
time someone said to you "That's a bird. It's a kind of animal that flies."
And even if you do, that memory is fairly unimportant when you glance
out the window, see a bird, and effortlessly realize that it's a robin.

Episodic and semantic memory are highly interdependent, to be sure.
In fact, there is a recurring professional debate over whether or not they
are truly separate types of memory (e.g., McKoon & Ratcliff, 1986; Tulving, 1989). Regardless of this debate, separating episodic and semantic
memories is a useful organizational device. Thus we will devote this
chapter almost exclusively to episodic memory principles and processes.
These are the more traditional issues in the study of human memory,
including phenomena such as rehearsal, recall, and forgetting. Chapter 6
is then devoted to the semantic memory system, its organization and
principles of operation. Because semantic memory includes such a vast
array of topics, a good deal of the rest of the book is about semantic memory as well. As you'll begin to see, however, the principles and processes
investigated in episodic memory research are highly relevant to our later
consideration of semantic issues.

▼ Preliminary Issues

Let's start our discussion of episodic memory by considering what people
know about their own memory systems. This is the topic of **metamemory,** *knowledge about (= meta) one's own memory, how it works, and how it
fails to work.*[1] While the research and theoretical treatments of metamemory originally came from studies of children's memory performance, they
are quite relevant and important to the study of adult cognition as well.

Metamemory

Flavell and Wellman (1977) described "four broad, partially overlapping categories of memory-related phenomena" (p. 3) that we need to
consider; see Table 5-1 for a listing and description. The list begins with
basic mental operations and processes, such as recognition and the ability to retrieve information, and continues to the second category, the

---

[1]*Metamemory* refers to knowledge about our own memory systems. It is the memory component of
the more global *metacognition,* which includes not only knowledge about one's own memory, but also
about the functioning of one's entire cognitive system.

Table 5-1   FOUR CATEGORIES OF MEMORY PHENOMENA

Category	Description
1. Basic mental processes	The basic mental operations, such as storage and retrieval from memory, ability to recall and recognize, to compare and decide
2. "Knowing"—memory	The basic storehouse of information in memory; for example, 2 + 4 = 6
3. "Knowing how to know"—metamemory	Knowledge of how to learn or acquire new information, including rehearsal strategies and mnemonics
4. "Knowing about knowing"—metacognition	Knowledge and awareness of one's own mental system, how it functions, when it's likely to falter, and so on.

From Flavell & Wellman, 1977.

actual knowledge stored in memory. The third and fourth categories correspond to Brown's (1975) labels of "knowing how to know" and "knowing about knowing," the topics of *metamemory* and *metacognition*. These categories reflect a person's knowledge of how to learn or acquire new information, knowing *how* to know, and a person's awareness of how the whole memory system functions, knowing *about* knowing.

From the standpoint of development, these are obviously important issues. That is, as we grow from childhood to adulthood, we do more than merely learn more information. We also learn *how* to acquire new information, how to memorize, understand, and so on, and we come to appreciate *how* the cognitive system functions, when it's likely to fail, and what to do to minimize such failures. It is actually somewhat surprising to learn that young children are relatively unaware of the *need* to engage in deliberate rehearsal; there is an absence of self-monitoring as they perform a learning task (e.g., Leal, Crays, & Moely, 1985).

What may not be quite so obvious, however, is that adults often display a similar lack of awareness, or achieve that awareness only by realizing how poorly they have performed on some task. For example, Pressley, Levin, and Ghatala (1984) asked their subjects to learn new vocabulary words. They found that their adult subjects favored an associative method over a simple repetition method, *but only* after practice had revealed how inadequate simple repetition was. In contrast, the 11- and 13-year-olds not only required this practice but also required explicit feedback on their performance before showing the preference. In other words, the younger subjects were not spontaneously aware of their metacognitive functioning, but needed some direct hint or prompt.

Note the twin issues raised by such reports. First there is the importance of self-monitoring and awareness—metacognitive awareness, in other words. A fair number of studies have focused directly on metacognitive judgments, for instance, people's "ease-of-learning" estimates or "feeling-of-knowing" judgments (e.g., Leonesio & Nelson, 1990; Nelson, 1988), and how those relate to performance. Second is the issue of what to do about your metacognitive awareness. That is, if you become aware that you're not performing some task particularly well, what mental processes or procedures do you follow to improve your performance? This is largely the issue of **rehearsal,** *a deliberate and planned strategy for practicing and learning material that needs to be remembered later.* Adults are fairly proficient at generating strategies for remembering, at developing methods to rehearse material they realize will be hard to learn. Furthermore, they aren't surprised when unrehearsed material can't be remembered (you're not really surprised when you can't remember someone's name shortly after being introduced, particularly if you made no special effort to remember the name in the first place). Your metamemory processes include the awareness that things don't merely "get into" memory. You must "get them in" by performing some intentional activity.

This intentional mental activity and its effects on remembering make up the study of rehearsal. Rehearsal was the major *control process* that Atkinson and Shiffrin (1968, 1971) had in mind in their model of human memory, and not surprisingly their work prompted much of the research on rehearsal (e.g., Rundus & Atkinson, 1970). But the whole story on metacognitive awareness and rehearsal begins much earlier, with the ancient Greeks and the topic of *mnemonics.*

Mnemonic Devices

The term **mnemonic** (the first m is silent; ne-mahn'-ick) means "to help the memory."[2] It always refers to *an active, strategic kind of learning device or method, a rehearsal strategy* if you will. Formal mnemonic devices rely on a preestablished set of memory aids and considerable practice on the to-be-remembered information in connection with the preestablished set. Informal mnemonics, such as those you invent yourself, are generally less elaborate, are more suited to smaller amounts of information that you're trying to remember, and are more idiosyncratic and personalized. The strengths of such mnemonic techniques are many and include the following important principles: (1) the material to be remembered is practiced repeatedly; (2) the material is integrated into an existing memory framework; and (3) the device provides an excellent means of retrieving the information. We'll study two of the traditional mnemonic devices first, then turn to the issue of inventing new mnemonics as the need arises.

---

[2]In ancient Greek mythology, Mnemosyne (ne-mahs'-uh-nee) was the goddess of memory, hence the term "mnemonic." Furthermore, she was the mother (by Zeus) of the Muses, the nine goddesses who presided over and inspired literature, the arts, and the sciences. Interestingly, the word "muse" comes from an Indo-European base meaning "to pay attention to." "Mnemonic" and "Mnemosyne" come from the same base as "remember," "mind," and "think."

Classic Mnemonics   The first historical mention of mnemonics is in Cicero's *De oratore,* a Latin treatise on rhetoric (the art of public speaking, which in Greek and Roman days meant speaking from memory). In this work, Cicero describes a technique based on visual imagery and memorized locations, ascribed to the Greek poet Simonides (circa 500 B.C.). The mnemonic is now commonly referred to as the **method of loci** ("loci" is the plural of "locus," meaning "a place"; pronounced low'-sigh). The source of Simonides's inspiration, as the story goes, was a personal experience. Simonides was performing a lyric poem at a banquet when he was called out of the hall for a message. While he was outside, the roof of the hall caved in. The disaster was so bad that the bodies of the guests, mangled by the falling roof, were unidentifiable. Simonides, however, realized he could identify the dead by visualizing the banquet table where they had been sitting. Apparently, the scene was impressed strongly enough in Simonides's memory that he was able to remember the faces as they were arranged around the banquet hall locations.[3]

There are two keys to the method of loci: first, the memorized physical locations, and second, the mental images of the to-be-remembered items, one per location. In other words, decide on a set of places or locations, a set that can be recalled easily and in order. You might select a set of 10 or 12 locations you encounter in a walk across campus, or those you encounter as you arrive home, as your preestablished memory aids. Now form a mental image of the first thing you want to remember, and then mentally place that thing into the first location, continuing with the second item in the second location, and so on. Form a good, *distinctive* mental image of the item in its place (McDaniel & Einstein, 1986). (Although people often believe that a more bizarre image is more memorable, it is apparently true that it's the distinctiveness of the image, not its bizarreness per se, that is important [Kroll, Schepeler, & Angin, 1986]. Others [e.g., Hirshman, Whelley, & Palij, 1989] have suggested that the "surprise response" of encountering something that violates your expectations is part of this distinctiveness effect: Wouldn't you be surprised to see a horse up in a tree?) When it's time to recall the items, all you need to do is mentally stroll through your set of locations, "looking" at the

---

[3]The more impressive mnemonic feat performed by Simonides, reciting a lyric poem from memory, is usually overlooked in psychological accounts of the mnemonic device. Orators in ancient Greece recited in the oral tradition for the obvious reason—books were not available. The art of rhetoric, or oration, involved extensive memorization, for example, committing to memory the entire *The Iliad* or *The Odyssey.* To make this task somewhat easier, these heroic poems were filled with mnemonic aids, including easily recalled structure or organization, rhyme and meter, images, repeated phrases ("the rosy-fingered dawn" was one of our favorites in college), and of course a regularly progressing plot. As I recall from freshman literature, *The Iliad*'s 24 chapters progress "into" the story up until Chapter 12, at which point the order of the chapter topics reverses to progress "out of" the story. In the middle chapters, the intricate designs on Achilles' shield are described; the successive designs essentially summarize the plot of the 12 ordered chapters. Thus a poet who was reciting *The Iliad* would call to mind the visual image of the shield, and remember the next part of the story by looking at the next picture or scene in his visual image. We usually simplify our treatment of the classic mnemonic devices as if they were only useful for remembering unrelated sets of words like grocery lists and so on. At least as they were applied in ancient Greece, the mnemonic devices were immensely more useful than this.

Table 5-2   THE METHOD OF LOCI

Set of Loci	Words to Be Remembered	Grocery List and Images
Driveway	Grapefruit	Grapefruit instead of rocks along side of driveway
Garage door	Tomatoes	Tomatoes splattered on garage door
Front door of house	Lettuce	Lettuce leaves hanging over door instead of awning
Coat closet	Oatmeal	Oatmeal oozing out the door when I hang up my coat
Fireplace	Milk	Fire got out of control, so spray milk instead of water
Easy chair	Sugar	Throw pillow is a 5-lb bag of sugar
Television	Coffee	Mrs. Olson advertising coffee
Dining-room table	Carrots	Legs of table are made of carrots
.	.	
.	.	
.	.	

places and "seeing" the items you have placed there. Table 5-2 gives an example of this technique.

Another mnemonic device is worth mentioning here as well, partly because it is so commonly known and easy to use. The technique is known as **the peg-word mnemonic** (e.g., Miller, Galanter, & Pribram, 1960), in which *a prememorized set of words serves as a sequence of mental "pegs" onto which the to-be-remembered material can be "hung."* The peg words rely on rhymes with the numbers one through ten, such as "One is a bun, two is a shoe," and so on (see Table 5-3). The material being learned is then "hung" on the pegs, item by item, making sure that the rhyming word and the to-be-remembered word form a mental image.

For the list "cup flag horse dollar . . . ," create a visual image of a flattened tin cup, dripping with ketchup, inside your hamburger bun; for flag, conjure up a visual image of your running shoes with little American flags fluttering in the breeze as you run a marathon; and so on (go ahead and form images for the rest of the list as an exercise to under-

Table 5-3   THE PEG-WORD MNEMONIC DEVICE

Numbered Pegs	Word to Be Learned	Image
One is a bun	Cup	Hamburger bun with smashed cup
Two is a shoe	Flag	Running shoes with flag
Three is a tree	Horse	Horse stranded in top of tree
Four is a door	Dollar	Dollar bill tacked to front door
Five is a hive	Brush	Queen bee brushing her hair
Six is sticks	Pan	Boiling a pan full of cinnamon sticks
Seven is Heaven	Clock	St. Peter checking the clock at the gates of Heaven
Eight is a gate	Pen	A picket fence gate with ballpoint pens as pickets
Nine is a vine	Paper	Honeysuckle vine with newspapers instead of blossoms
Ten is a hen	Shirt	A steaming baked hen on the platter wearing a flannel shirt

stand the principles of mnemonic devices). Now at recall, all you have to do is first remember what peg word rhymes with one, then retrieve the visual image of bun that you created, looking inside to see . . . a cup. Similarly, what peg word rhymes with "two," and what image do you find along with "shoe"?

Bower's (1970) classic article noted that cognitive psychology had begun to supplement the anecdotal evidence of the usefulness of these mnemonic devices with experimental evidence. To illustrate the effectiveness of such mnemonic devices, he described a study by Ross and Lawrence (1968), in which subjects used a set of 40 campus locations as their loci, then had to learn several 40-item lists using the method of loci. The items were presented about one every 13 seconds and were followed by an immediate recall test; subjects also returned the next day for a delayed recall test. Average performance on immediate recall, using the method of loci, was 38 out of 40, *in their correct order!* One day later, subjects averaged 34 correct, again in order. These levels of accuracy are surely a testimony to the effectiveness of such mnemonic techniques.

Bower concluded by noting the two essential ingredients involved in the successful use of the method of loci: first, that imaginal associations are formed between the memorized loci and the words to be learned; and second, the loci are used as cues for guiding recall. In contrast to the subject who merely attempts to learn 40 unrelated words, the subject using the method of loci has "a known bank of pigeonholes or file cabinets in which he stores the list items. At recall, the person knows where to start his recall and how to proceed from one unit to the next; he has a way to monitor the adequacy of his recall; he knows when he has forgotten an item; and he knows when he has finished his recall" (p. 502). The systematic mnemonic device forces you to learn the material well, provides a memorable, durable record in memory, then guides you during retrieval.

The Three Mnemonic Principles

Read that last sentence again— it contains the crux of the argument for *all* mnemonic effectiveness. What three things does a mnemonic device do to improve memory?

First, it provides a structure for learning, for acquiring the information. The structure may be relatively elaborate, as a set of 40 loci would be, or it may be simple, for example, rhyming peg words. It may even be highly arbitrary if the material is not particularly extensive. (The mnemonic for the names of the five Great Lakes, remembering the word HOMES for Huron, Ontario, Michigan, Erie, and Superior, isn't especially related to the to-be-remembered material, but it is quite simple.)

Second, by means of visual images, rhymes, or other kinds of associations, the mnemonic ensures a durable record of the material in memory, one that won't easily be forgotten (what's sticking out of your running shoes?). As such, the mnemonic seems to safeguard against interference in storage, or against other kinds of loss within memory itself.

Finally, the mnemonic guides you through retrieval by providing effective cues for recalling the information. As we'll discuss extensively later on in the chapter, this function of the mnemonic device is critically important, since much of what we casually call "forgetting" seems often to be a case of retrieval difficulty.

This three-step sequence should sound familiar to you; it's essentially the same sequence we mentioned in Chapter 1, defining memory as the acquisition, retention, and retrieval of information (Melton, 1963). Logically, your performance in any situation that requires memory is dependent on all three of these steps. Any one of the three might be the faulty process that accounts for poor performance, and all three must be accomplished successfully for good performance. A good mnemonic device will ensure success at each of the three stages (see the Suggested Readings at the end of this chapter for sources that describe mnemonics for remembering names, faces, and so on).

Invented Mnemonics   Before turning to the research on this three-step sequence, take a moment to develop your own metacognitive awareness, and your own mnemonic skills. We become increasingly sophisticated, as we grow older, in our abilities to monitor our own memory performance, and in our abilities to invent ways of learning new material. It is also true, however, that everyday adult memory could stand some improvement too: people probably complain more about their forgetfulness than about any other perceived cognitive problem. And college students in particular face stiff demands on memory; you are continually faced with the need to learn and remember new information, and often that information is quite unfamiliar and unrelated to things you already know. How do you deal with these memory demands?

Start first with what you know about metamemory and metacognition. How aware are you of your own state of knowledge about new information? Do you spend more time studying when the material is unfamiliar, or when you judge it as more difficult to learn (e.g., Nelson & Leonesio, 1988)? Do you monitor your performance as you read a text, testing your memory as you go along, or do you merely read through a chapter, treating all the information in the same, undifferentiated way? The self-monitoring and self-correcting aspects of metamemory are vital here. You should be able to point to aspects of your performance that signal this kind of metamemory awareness—a slower reading rate on unfamiliar material, more note taking on difficult lecture topics, and so on. If you can't find any behavioral way to prove your metamemory awareness, then you are probably as deficient on complex memory tasks as small children are on simple ones.

Second, when you are consciously aware of the need for special effort on difficult material, what do you do? Do you "think about knowing," that is, think of how difficult it will be to learn the material and what you might do to actually learn it? Do you ever invent your own mnemonic devices to make sure you'll remember something? Recall the HOMES example and how a simple acronym or word can function as a retrieval cue for the needed information. Other principles come into play here as well, especially rhymes and rhythm. To use a common example, if I ask you how many days there are in June, don't you rely on the "30 days hath September" mnemonic?

As a lesson to yourself, pick something from this book to learn by an invented mnemonic. Try to come up with a mnemonic based on images, rhymes, or acronyms so that you can remember the list easily. The very act of inventing the mnemonic will probably ensure that the material is stored strongly in memory, and the image or rhyme will help assure that it remains in memory until you test yourself. Make sure your mnemonic itself is memorable, so that it can guide you through retrieval by cueing the several items you're trying to remember.[4]

Finally, be on the lookout for "ready-made" mnemonics, or situations in which a mnemonic association is almost built into the material. As an example, did you notice in Chapter 3 that Cherry did research on the cocktail party phenomenon, and can't you "see" that maraschino cherry in the cocktail glass? The more you notice such easily associated items, the easier it will be to come up with invented mnemonics for other material as well. (One of the most stunning descriptions of mnemonic effectiveness is a report by Ericsson and Polson [1988], which describes "a waiter (JC) who can take up to 20 complete dinner orders without taking notes" [p. 305].)

Summary Points: episodic and semantic memory; metamemory, metacognition; mnemonic devices; three mnemonic principles

▼ The Ebbinghaus Tradition of Memory Research

Let's turn now to the first systematic research on human learning and memory, conducted by the first serious human memory investigator, the German psychologist Hermann von Ebbinghaus.

As indicated in Chapter 1, the Ebbinghaus tradition of scientific research on human memory began over 100 years ago, with his publication of *Uber das Gedachtnis* (1885; the English translation is *Memory: A Contribution to Experimental Psychology,* first published in 1913, then reprinted in 1964). As is commonly known, Ebbinghaus used only him-

---

[4]My graduate student, David Fleck, devised two excellent mnemonic sentences for remembering the seven themes listed in Chapter 2, inspired by a similar mnemonic reported in the first edition of this book. The initial letter in each word stands for one of the themes. "Awesome—actually did retain my understanding (of) learning!" for the themes **A**ttention, **A**utomatic/conscious processes, **D**ata- versus conceptually driven processes, **R**epresentation of knowledge, **M**etacognition, **U**nconscious processing, and **L**evels of analysis. Or, if you're momentarily fed up with the topic: "Another awful day reading Memory until late!"

self as a subject in his studies. In the process of his investigations, he had to invent his own memory task, his own experimental stimuli, and his own set of procedures for testing and data analysis. Few, if any, could do as well today without guidance from research and colleagues. As Hilgard put it, in his introduction to the 1964 edition, "For the beginner in a new field to have done all of these things—and more—is so surprising as to baffle our understanding of how it could have happened" (p. vii).

Furthermore, Ebbinghaus anticipated a variety of important issues in human memory research, not to mention developments in general scientific methodology. For instance, Nelson (1985) notes that the relearning task Ebbinghaus invented was a "radical idea that was far ahead of its time, both methodologically and conceptually" (p. 472), in that it recognized the possible influence of nonconscious factors (versus Wundt's concern with the conscious mind). Ebbinghaus carefully laid out his method of measuring retention of information and thus anticipated Bridgman's (1927) influential notion of the operational definition (Nelson, 1985, p. 474). In devising ways to analyze his results, he even came close to inventing what we now would call a correlated- or within-groups *t* test (Ebbinghaus, 1885/1964, footnote 1, p. 67).

The Ebbinghaus Research

Among the psychological issues that Ebbinghaus investigated were the time course of forgetting, the length–difficulty relationship, and an explanation of serial (ordered) learning. Probably more important than these contributions, as Murdock (1985) observes, were the general methodological developments for which Ebbinghaus was responsible. We tend to think of Ebbinghaus merely as the inventor of the nonsense syllable, the "meaningless" consonant–vowel–consonant (C-V-C) triads like XIG or BEF, which he used as stimuli in all his studies. As you'll see, this is a seriously impoverished view of Ebbinghaus's pioneering contributions.

To begin with, it is instructive to consider *why* Ebbinghaus felt compelled to invent a "meaningless stimulus" to be used in his studies of memory.[5] His rationale was that he wanted to study the properties of memory and forgetting—the fundamentals. It was clear to him that words, if used as experimental stimuli, would hopelessly complicate his results. Had he acquired and remembered a list of items by the simple exercise of memory, or had his performance been altered by his existing knowledge of the words? Putting it simply, *learning* seems to imply acquiring *new* information using whatever mental processes are

---

[5]Hoffman, Bringmann, Bamberg, and Klein (1987) point out that Ebbinghaus didn't truly use "nonsense syllables," but instead lists of syllables, where the syllables varied individually in meaningfulness but overall were unrelated to one another. American psychology was apparently misled by a poor translation from the original German. I use the term "nonsense syllables" here to avoid confusion.

required. Yet words are not new, so "learning" a list of words in some sense involves a misnomer.

Other features of Ebbinghaus's procedures are important to note as well, since they exhibit the care and forethought he devoted to his work. For instance, his insight led him to control for possible mental and physical changes, by testing himself at the same time of day; for different degrees of learning, by setting a fixed learning criterion of one perfect recitation without any hesitations (the criterion was two such recitations in some studies); and for the possible intrusion of mnemonic or nonrote factors, by adopting a rapid presentation rate of 2.5 items per second. His only experimental task was the **relearning task,** in which *a list is originally learned, set aside for some period of time, then later relearned to the same criterion of accuracy.* The **savings score** he derived from this task was *the reduction, if any, in the number of trials (or the time, in other studies) necessary for relearning, compared to original learning.* Thus if a list required ten original learning trials, but only six upon relearning, there was a 40% savings (four fewer trials on relearning divided by the ten original trials).

As noted previously, the invention of this task revealed an amazing sensitivity to fundamental states of memory. That is, Ebbinghaus wanted to study memory per se, not just the conscious memory of past events that is measured by a recall task, but even seemingly unretrievable memories that might influence performance. By the method of relearning, *any* information that was left over in memory from original learning could presumably have an influence, conscious or not, during relearning (see Nelson, 1978, 1985; Schacter, 1987). Recent work by MacLeod (1988) indicates that the influence of relearning is on the recall of the material; that is, relearning seems to help retrieve information that was stored in memory yet is not recallable.

Having standardized his testing situation, he then turned to the task of actually collecting data. Slamecka's (1985a) description of the studies illustrates Ebbinghaus's dedication to scientific inquiry: "In an experiment on retention as a function of the number of repetitions (Ebbinghaus, 1964/1885, Chapter 6), he learned and relearned 420 lists of 16 syllables each. For the learning phase alone, with an average of more than 34 trials per series, he went through 14,280 trials. Again, to obtain the data for his famous forgetting curve (Chapter 7), he acquired and then relearned more than 1,200 lists of nonsense syllables" (p. 416). Dedication hardly seems a strong enough word, in view of this heroic effort!

Figure 5-1 presents the famous forgetting curve, showing the reduction in savings as a function of time until relearning. Ebbinghaus relearned the lists after one of seven intervals—20 minutes, one hour, nine hours, one day, two days, six days, or thirty-one days. As is clear from the figure, the most dramatic forgetting occurs early after original learning. This is followed by a decrease in the rate of forgetting; a full 42% was forgotten at one-third of an hour, 56% at one hour, 64% after

FIGURE 5-1

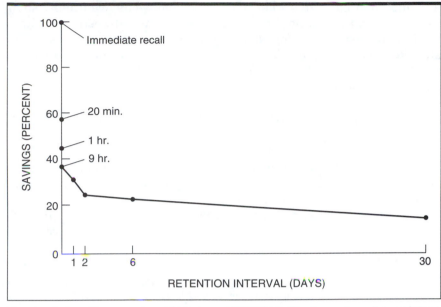

The classic forgetting curve from Ebbinghaus (1885/1913). The figure shows the reduction in savings across increasing retention intervals, time between original learning and relearning.

nine hours, and so on (note that Ebbinghaus necessarily tested himself at different times of the day in this study, in contrast to the situations in which the time of day was kept constant). Quite recently, these forgetting functions have been reanalyzed, finding that they follow the same decreasing function as obtained in a variety of other memory tests (technically, a power function; e.g., Wixted & Ebbesen, 1991).

Some other fundamental results obtained by Ebbinghaus were impressive not necessarily because they were surprising, but because they were the first empirical demonstrations of the effects. For example, he investigated the effects of repetitions, studying one list 32 times and another 64 times, where the 32-trial condition approximated the standard learning criterion of one perfect recitation. Upon relearning, the more frequently repeated list showed about twice the savings of the less frequently repeated list: in other words, overlearning yields a stronger record in memory. Longer lists were found to require more trials to learn than shorter lists. While this was certainly not surprising, the more interesting result was that longer lists then showed higher savings upon relearning. In essence, while it is harder to learn a long list originally, the longer list is then remembered better, simply because there was more opportunity to overlearn it (there were more trials in learning before eventual mastery of the whole list).

Finally, in one experiment (Chapter 8), Ebbinghaus continued to relearn the same set of lists across a five-day period. The savings scores he obtained showed a trend that, if extrapolated, would eventually show perfect savings, that is, no forgetting at all. As an interesting contrast here, Ebbinghaus also reported his results on relearning passages of poetry (kept at 80 syllables in length). After the fourth day of learning, the savings was 100%.[6] (Is it any wonder that actors overlearn their parts through multiple *rehearsals?*)

Evaluating the Ebbinghaus Tradition

There is no doubt or disagreement whatsoever that Ebbinghaus had a tremendous impact on what came to be known as the field of Verbal Learning, and later, cognitive psychology. In a recent set of papers commemorating the 100th anniversary of the 1885 publication (see Suggested Readings), a consensus began to emerge concerning the value of Ebbinghaus's work (with some passionate dissenters, of course). In Mandler's (1985b) words, Ebbinghaus's contribution represented "a door being opened into the human mind, the realization—contrary to then established wisdom—that it is in fact possible to gain positive knowledge about human memory" (p. 464). Slamecka (1985a) called him "the founder of our discipline" and summarized his influence by saying: "He set out to show that an empirical science of memory was possible. . . . He succeeded admirably in this enterprise" (Slamecka, 1985b, p. 497).

Disagreement does exist, however, on the balance between Ebbinghaus's positive and negative influences. No one claims that the general methodological aspects of his work exerted a negative influence; the care he took in controlling extraneous factors, the meticulous way he investigated the effects of variables, and the example he set of inventing an objective task with which to assess memory were all tremendously positive influences.

On the other side of the coin, however, he did exclude meaning from his studies, by using nonsense syllables almost exclusively. Much subsequent research, up through the 1960s (and even the 1970s), continued to use nonsense syllables as the items to be learned and remembered (see Chapter 1, where Glaze's 1928 tabulation of the "meaningfulness" of nonsense syllables is discussed). The problem with this, it is generally conceded, is that for the most part people will not deal with a truly meaningless stimulus. Instead, they will attempt all sorts of mediating, mnemonic, or other rehearsal strategies to render a "nonsense" syllable sensible—mentally turning BEF into BEEF, for example. Ebbinghaus

---

[6]Throughout the book, Ebbinghaus also reported learning and relearning passages from Byron's *Don Juan*. He found repeatedly that learning the poetry was faster, as was relearning, and noted several reasons for this, all of them amounting to the meaningfulness of the poetry compared to the lack of meaningfulness in the nonsense syllables.

seemed able to avoid such mnemonic strategies, partly because of the rapid rate of presentation and partly because of his desire to study only rote learning. It is doubtful that most subjects in psychological research can behave in that pure a fashion, however. Indeed, the fact that Noble's (1952) subjects found their rating task sensible (judging "How meaningful is this nonsense syllable?") confirms that people will attribute or even invent meaning if none is there.

It is clear from Ebbinghaus's own discussion that the nonsense syllable was a deliberate effort on his part to avoid the complications of uncontrolled meaningfulness. In Slamecka's (1985a) analysis, this was understandable and even praiseworthy when we consider that Ebbinghaus was the first to attempt to deal with any of these issues in a scientific way. Contemporary criticism of the artificiality of laboratory research (see the Neisser quotation at the beginning of this chapter) often asserts that Ebbinghaus's example misled psychology and inspired decades of ungeneralizable, even irrelevant, results. To quote Kintsch's (1985) evocative remark, "What a terrible struggle our field has had just to overcome the nonsense syllable! Decades to discover the 'meaningfulness' of nonsense syllables, and decades more to finally turn away from the seductions of this chimera. Instead of the simplification that Ebbinghaus had hoped for, the nonsense syllable, for generations of researchers, merely screened the central problems of memory from inspection with the methods that Ebbinghaus had bequeathed us" (p. 461).

The Ebbinghaus tradition, in short, has been understood (or *mis*understood) as an admonition, to the effect that "meaning complicates matters, so eliminate it from the stimuli." A more temperate view might note that, in the absence of previous research, Ebbinghaus quite properly simplified the experimental situation so as to get interpretable results, a view that Kintsch (1985) also stated. We might further suggest that the fault lies less with Ebbinghaus than with his successors, who slavishly stuck to his methods without questioning their intent or usefulness.

The Current Position   If we consider the quite different position that is accepted today and contrast it with the model of Ebbinghaus's research, we arrive squarely at the empirical research on episodic long-term memory. Today's position consists of at least three parts. First, the fact that people invent meaning, regardless of the experimenter's wishes, is taken as evidence that human memory relies very heavily on meaning. To put it bluntly, if people deal so heavily in meaning, then perhaps we should *investigate* how they invent meaning rather than try to prevent them from doing it.

The second element of this position is implied by the first, that the subject in our memory experiments is an active participant, not content to recite syllables passively and have them eventually make an impression on memory, as Ebbinghaus did, but instead intent on applying mental resources and strategies to virtually every learning situation. The active subject assumption, in other words, is quite the opposite from the Ebbinghaus model, although he himself was aware of the tendency (after all, he took great pains to *prevent* such activity).

The third part of the current position, implied by some of the critics mentioned before, is that results based on meaningless stimuli are themselves meaningless when we attempt to understand how people learn and remember. This is the issue of ecological validity again, saying in essence that our traditional laboratory results do not apply to real-world situations that involve memory for meaningful material. We'll pursue this debate further at the end of the chapter, where research on memory for truly autobiographical knowledge, "everyday memory," is presented.[7]

Summary Points: nonsense syllables; relearning task and savings scores; positive and negative influences

▼ Storage of Information in Episodic Memory

How do people store information in episodic memory, the long-term memory system for personally experienced events and information? How is new information recorded in this long-term memory system so that it will be preserved until some future time when it is needed? And how can we measure this storage of information? Ebbinghaus's research investigated one principal kind of storage variable—repetition—and one memory task—relearning. He found that an increase in the number of repetitions led to a stronger memory, a *trace* of the information in memory that could be relearned more quickly. This would suggest that frequency is a fundamental variable in learning: information that is presented more frequently will be stored more strongly in memory. (As a quick example, do you remember from Chapter 1 the year that the first psychological laboratory was established by Wundt? The date was intentionally repeated several times, to permit this kind of example.)

---

[7]Another aspect of Ebbinghaus's methods that became "standard operating procedure" has largely escaped criticism, which is strange in view of the visibility of the ecological validity issue. Ebbinghaus paced himself at 2.5 items per second during learning; the overwhelming majority of subsequent studies, even those conducted now, have maintained this "experimenter-paced" aspect of the learning task. A strong conviction of my graduate school mentor was that we learn more about human learning if we let subjects pace themselves through a list they are trying to learn; see the description of the Kellas et al. study that accompanies Figure 4-5, for instance. Kellas's procedures were to record unobtrusively the amount of time a subject spent studying each item in the list, then to observe the dependency of recall on study time. While there are some interpretive complexities involved in this method (as there are when meaningful stimuli are used, or when learning is experimenter-paced), it is certainly a sensitive method for understanding subject-controlled factors such as rehearsal and clearly resembles real-world learning situations more closely. See, for example, an experiment by Nelson and Leonesio (1988) for a direct study of the effects of self-pacing, or one by Johnson and Kieras (1983) where self-paced study brought subjects up to the level of a group that was already familiar with the material. I find no inherent difference in the status of the nonsense syllable issue and the experimenter-paced learning issue, at least in terms of generalization to more realistic learning situations. How peculiar that our memory studies still routinely use this part of Ebbinghaus's technique, while critics rail against the "meaningless stimuli" aspect of his procedures.

A corollary of this idea is that people should be good at remembering *how frequently* something has occurred. Hasher and Zacks (1984) have summarized a large body of research on how sensitive people are to the frequency of events. Because people's estimates of relative frequency are generally quite good, these authors proposed that frequency information is encoded into memory in an automatic fashion, with no deliberate effort or intent. While the automaticity of such a mechanism has been disputed (e.g., Greene, 1986; Hanson & Hirst, 1988; Jonides & Jones, 1992), there is no doubt that the frequency with which information or events occur has a large impact on long-term memory. (See Anderson and Schooler [1991] for the intriguing relationship between the need to retrieve some information from memory and the frequency and/or recency of that information in the environment. For example, in their data, the probability that a word occurred in the headlines on Day 101 correlated .997 with its frequency of occurrence in the previous 100 days.)

These effects are interesting, of course, but of limited use if you need to learn and remember something truly new, like a list of words in an experiment or a list of seven themes in a cognition textbook. How do we acquire *this* kind of information? We will consider three important "storage" effects here: rehearsal, organization, and imagery. A summary of these three will then lead us to the topic of retrieval and a discussion of forgetting.

Rehearsal

A fundamental statement on storage was made by Atkinson and Shiffrin (1968) in their influential model of human memory. In their formulation, information that resides in short-term memory may be subjected to **rehearsal,** *a deliberate recycling or practicing of the contents of the short-term store.* Atkinson and Shiffrin proposed that there are two effects of rehearsal. First, rehearsal maintains information in the short-term store, preventing it from being lost or displaced by other information. Second, the longer an item is held in short-term memory by rehearsal, the greater the probability that the rehearsal will also store the item in long-term memory. Basically, this position states that rehearsal "copies" the item into long-term memory, with the strength of the long-term memory trace depending on the amount of rehearsal. In short, rehearsal *transfers* information into long-term memory (see also Waugh & Norman, 1965). Of course, in most experimental situations, the items being transferred are words that the subject already knows. Thus "transferring information" is generally taken to mean storing some "tag" or other indication that a certain word was an item in the list being learned.

What evidence is there of this transfer function for rehearsal? Aside from the classic Ebbinghaus study on repetition, many experiments have shown that rehearsal of information leads to better long-term retention.

For example, Hellyer (1962) used the Brown–Peterson task to examine the effects of rehearsal. Subjects were shown a C-V-C trigram, as usual, and were asked to perform an arithmetic task between study and recall, also as usual. The difference in this study was that on some trials the trigram had to be spoken out loud once, on some trials twice, four times, or eight times. Figure 5-2 shows the results of this experiment. The more frequently rehearsed the item was, the better it was retained across the distracting period of arithmetic. Using a somewhat different approach, Hebb (1961; cited in Loftus & Loftus, 1976) presented strings of digits for recall. Whereas performance remained stable and low on those strings that changed from trial to trial, performance improved significantly on the string of digits that was periodically repeated in the learning trials. Although the task seemed to be testing only short-term retention of digit strings, mere repetition of a string led to some transfer of the information into long-term memory.

While these studies and many others confirmed the general notion that rehearsal leads to an improvement in long-term memory performance, the evidence they presented was somewhat indirect. After all, for evidence about long-term memory, it was slightly odd that two short-term memory paradigms had been used, the Brown–Peterson task and a digit recall task. More direct evidence on rehearsal was soon to follow,

FIGURE 5-2

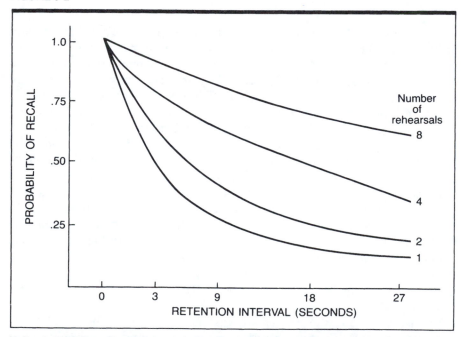

Hellyer's (1962) recall accuracy results as a function of the number of rehearsals afforded the three-letter nonsense syllable and the retention interval.

however. Among the many such studies, the standard citation on rehearsal is to a series of studies performed by Rundus (1971; Rundus & Atkinson, 1970).

Rehearsal and Serial Position Effects In his experiments, Rundus had his subjects learn 20-item lists of unrelated words, presenting them at a rate of 5 seconds per word. Subjects were asked to rehearse out loud as they studied the lists, repeating whatever words from the list they cared to during each 5-second presentation. Rundus then tabulated the number of times each of the words had been rehearsed and compared this tally to the likelihood of recalling the word correctly in the free recall task. Figure 5-3 shows his most telling results. In the early primacy portion of the serial position effect, there was a direct positive relationship between the frequency of rehearsal and the probability of recall. In fact, Rundus also examined a proportional measure of rehearsal and found that "for a given amount of rehearsal, items from the initial serial positions have no better recall than items from the middle of the list" (Rundus, 1971, p. 66). In other words, the *primacy effect*—higher recall of the early items—was viewed as entirely dependent on rehearsal; the early items can be rehearsed more frequently (no doubt because of the experimenter-paced task; see footnote 7) and so are then recalled better.

FIGURE 5-3

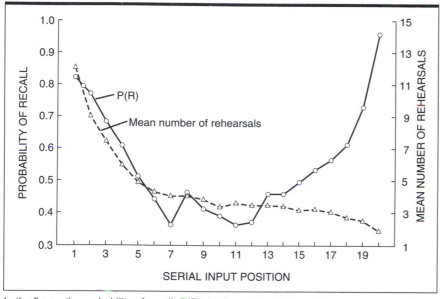

In the figure, the probability of recall, P(R), is plotted against the left axis, and the number of rehearsals afforded an item during storage is plotted against the right axis. The similar pattern of these two functions across the primacy portion of the list indicates that rehearsal is the factor responsible for primacy effects.

Think for a moment about how this research fits in with the serial position effects we discussed in the last chapter. In that section, several variables were shown to have an effect only on the recency portion of the serial position curve, the portion generally viewed as dependent on short-term memory. For instance, requiring subjects to count backward by threes for a period of time seemed to destroy their short-term memory record of the last items in the list. Importantly, this manipulation did not alter the primacy portion of their recall, the portion due to long-term memory. Conversely, a different set of variables left the recency effect alone but had a big effect on primacy. For instance, increasing the study time per item from 1 to 2 seconds improved recall of the early positions but did not change recall from the end of the list. Thus the typical U-shaped serial position curve (showing that "memory sags in the middle," as Martin and Noreen quipped in 1974) is generally taken to indicate two kinds of memory performance: primacy effects due to recall from long-term memory, and recency effects due to short-term memory recall. As a logical extension, Rundus's results showed that deliberate, overt rehearsal improved the accuracy of recall in primacy, the portion of the list influenced by long-term memory. Recall for the recency items, however, was high despite the fact that they had been rehearsed very little.

Later research has focused on the rehearsal activity per se, rather than on the general issue of whether rehearsal stores information in long-term memory or not. Kellas, McCauley, and McFarland (1975b), for instance, compared a group of subjects who rehearsed out loud, as Rundus had tested, to one that rehearsed silently. Among other results, they found that the group that rehearsed out loud had a tendency to rehearse and recall the items in order, whereas the silently rehearsing subjects showed greater flexibility in rehearsal and recall order. It seemed as if rehearsing out loud had led those subjects to use the rather unimaginative strategy of merely repeating the words out loud. In contrast, subjects in the silent rehearsal group were able to use more elaborate and complex kinds of rehearsal, for instance, devising sentences or images to help remember the words. Since these elaborate kinds of rehearsal couldn't be vocalized easily, they did not appear in the groups that rehearsed out loud.

Two Kinds of Rehearsal

The theoretical position behind the notion of "more elaborate and complex" rehearsal claims that there are in fact two major kinds of rehearsal, each with different effects on storage (Craik & Lockhart, 1972). According to this position, **maintenance rehearsal** (or **Type I rehearsal**) is a *low-level, repetitive kind of information recycling*. This is the kind of rehearsal you'd use to recycle a phone number to yourself until you dial it. The essential idea here is that once you've stopped rehearsing the information, it has left no permanent record in memory at all. In Craik and Lockhart's view, maintenance rehearsal merely maintains information at a particular level in the memory system, without storing it more permanently or deeply. As long as an item of information is subjected to maintenance rehearsal, it can be retrieved. Once the maintenance rehearsal stops, however, the item should vanish without a trace.

Elaborative rehearsal (or **Type II rehearsal**), on the other hand, is a more complex kind of *rehearsal that uses the meaning of the information* to help store and remember it. When information is subjected to elaborative rehearsal, according to Craik and Lockhart, the information is stored more deeply in the memory system, at a level that makes contact with the meaning of the information. As a consequence, material that was rehearsed elaboratively should be more permanently available for retrieval from memory—in short, should be remembered better. Among other things, you might include imagery or mnemonic elaboration in your elaborative rehearsal; you might try to construct sentences from the words in a list you're trying to learn; you might impose some organization or structure on the list; you might even try to convert "nonsense syllables" like BEF into more meaningful items, like BEEF. Stating it differently, maintenance rehearsal maintains an item at its current level of storage, whereas elaborative rehearsal moves the item more deeply, and stores it more permanently, into the memory system.

Depth of Processing

Craik and Lockhart (1972) advanced a notion of the memory system quite different from the "stage" approach of sensory, short-, and long-term memory to which we've become accustomed. They embedded their proposal of two kinds of rehearsal into what they termed a **levels of processing,** or **depth of processing,** framework. The essence of this framework goes as follows. Any perceived stimulus receives some amount of mental processing. Some stimuli, which receive only incidental attention, are only processed to a very "shallow" level in memory, possibly no deeper than a rather sensory level (as in hearing the sound of the words without attending to meaning, as a daydreamer might do during a lecture). Other stimuli, on the other hand, are subjected to more intentional and meaningful processing. This deeper processing *elaborates* the representation of that item in memory, for example, by drawing relationships between already-known information and the item currently being processed.

Thus superficial kinds of processing, which require little attention to the meaning of an item, correspond to maintenance rehearsal, or "shallow encoding" into memory; Nairne (1983) has drawn a strong parallel, in fact, between Type I rehearsal and the articulatory loop of working memory. Meaningful processing, which requires much more attention and effort, corresponds to elaborative rehearsal, in other words, a "deep encoding" of the material. An important theme in this depth of processing framework is that the mental activities a subject engages in *during* processing are as important for understanding memory as a determination of the "final resting place" of the information (what we've termed short- or long-term memory).

Several predictions from the depth of processing framework were tested with a fair degree of initial success. For example, if information is processed shallowly, with only maintenance rehearsal, then the information should not be particularly memorable on a later recall test—if it was only maintained, then it should not have been stored in long-term memory by that maintenance (technically, according to the Craik and Lockhart position, we should say that it is not stored at a deep, meaningful level).

This was exactly the result reported by Craik and Watkins (1973). The subjects in this experiment heard a long series of words on a tape recording. Their task was to monitor the words, listening for those that began with some critical letter, say, G. When a new "G-word" was presented, they were to remember the new one and forget the previous one. At the end of the list, subjects merely had to report the last G-word they had heard. This procedure was followed across several trials, with each trial having a different critical letter. Because of the way the lists had been constructed, Craik and Watkins could specify exactly how long each of the critical words had been maintained by Type I rehearsal. Table 5-4 gives an example of a list like those used by Craik and Watkins and illustrates what they termed the "i-value," the number of intervening items across which a critical word was maintained.

As you might expect, at the end of the set of trials, subjects were given a surprise recall test, in which they were to recall any and all words they

Table 5-4   SAMPLE LIST OF WORDS IN THE CRAIK AND WATKINS STUDY

Word List	The "i-Value" for Critical Words	
	SUBJECT MAINTAINS CRITICAL WORD	
Goat	Goat	
Daughter	Goat	
Oil	Goat	
Rifle	Goat	$i = 4$
Garden	Garden	$i = 1$
Grain	Grain	
Table	Grain	
Football	Grain	
Anchor	Grain	$i = 4$
Giraffe	Giraffe	
Brush	Giraffe	$i = 2$
End of list		

G is the critical letter. The "i-value" is the number of intervening words during which the critical words were held.

had heard from all the lists. As you might *not* expect, the amount of time an item had resided in short-term memory (the i-value) had no effect on the subjects' recall. Craik and Watkins did find that memory was better for lists that had been presented at a slower rate, in agreement with earlier research, but this effect was independent of simple time in short-term memory. As they put it in their conclusion, "Time in short-term store will only predict later long-term store performance when the subject has used the time to encode the items elaboratively" (Craik & Watkins, 1973, p. 603; see also Craik & Tulving, 1975).

Challenges to "Depth of Processing"

Now that you understand the Craik and Lockhart notion of depth of processing, it's time to pull the rug out from under you—enthusiasm for the depth of processing approach dimmed considerably within several years. Much of this dimming was due to Baddeley's (1978) important review paper "The Trouble with Levels."

A major point in this review concerned the problem of defining "levels" independently of retention scores, for example, defining and manipulating Types I and II rehearsal (see Glenberg & Adams, 1978; Glenberg, Smith, & Green, 1977). In essence, this criticism was that no method existed for deciding ahead of time whether a particular kind of rehearsal would prompt shallow or deep processing. Instead, we simply had to wait and see if it improved recall or not: if it did, it must have been elaborative rehearsal, if it didn't, it must have been maintenance rehearsal. The circularity of this reasoning should be obvious; the evidence that elaborative rehearsal had occurred, higher recall, was also used as the evidence showing that elaborative rehearsal improves recall.

Task Effects   A second point in Baddeley's (1978) review concerned task effects. That is, a genuine difficulty arose with the levels of processing approach when slightly different memory tasks were used. The reason for the difficulty was, simply, that very different results were obtained using one or another task.

We have known since the time of Ebbinghaus, of course, that different memory tasks will shed different kinds of light on the variables that affect performance. Ebbinghaus used a relearning task instead of simple recall, so that even material that was difficult to retrieve might have a chance of influencing performance. In a similar vein, a substantial difference is generally found between performance on recall versus **recognition tasks.** In recognition tasks, subjects are shown items that were originally studied, known as "old" or *target* items, as well as items that were not on the studied list, known as "new" or *distractor* items. They must then decide which items are targets and which are distractors. Accuracy on a recognition task is usually much higher than on a recall task (see Table 5-5 for a helpful listing and description of all these tasks).

The reason that recognition is easier, it is generally agreed, is that

Table 5-5 STANDARD MEMORY TASKS AND TERMINOLOGY

I. Relearning Task

1. "Original learning." Learn list items (e.g., list of unrelated words) to some accuracy criterion.
2. Delay after learning list 1.
3. Learn list 1 a second time.

Dependent Variables: Main dependent variable is the "savings score": how many *fewer* trials during relearning relative to number of trials for original learning. If original learning took 10 trials, and relearning took 6, then relearning took 4 fewer trials. S score = $^4/_{10}$; expressed as a percentage, savings was 40%.

Independent or Control Variables: Rate of presentation, type of list items, length of list, accuracy criterion.

II. Paired-Associate Learning Task

1. A list of pairs is shown, one pair at a time. The first member of the pair is termed the "stimulus," and the second member is the "response" (e.g., for the pair "ice–brush," "ice" is the stimulus term, and "brush" is the correct response).
2. After one study trial, the stimulus terms are shown, one at a time, and the subject tries to name the correct response term for that stimulus.
3. Typically, the task involves several successive attempts at learning, each attempt including first a study trial then a test trial; the order of the pairs is changed each time. In the "anticipation method," there is just one continuous stream of trials, each consisting of two parts, presenting the stimulus alone, then presenting the stimulus and response together. Across repetitions, subjects begin to learn the correct pairings.

Dependent Variables: Typically the number of study-test trials to achieve correct responding to all stimulus terms ("trials to criterion") is the dependent variable.

Independent and Control Variables: Presentation rate, length of list, the types of items in the stimulus and response term lists, and the types of connections between them. Very commonly, once a list had been mastered, then either the stimulus or response terms would be changed, or the item pairings would be rearranged (e.g., ice–brush and card–floor in the first list, then ice–floor and card–brush on the second list).

III. Recall Task

Serial Recall Task: Learn list information, then recall the items in their original order of presentation.
Free Recall Task: Learn list information, then recall the items in any order.
1. Learn list items.
2. Optional delay/optional distractor task during delay.
3. Recall list items.

Dependent Variables: Main dependent variable is the number (or percentage) of list items recalled correctly. If multiple lists are presented, recall accuracy is often scored as a function of the original position of the items in the list. Occasionally, other dependent variables involve order, speed, or organization of recall (e.g., items recalled by category—"apple, pear, banana, orange"—before a different category is recalled in a free recall task).

Independent or Control Variables: Rate of presentation (usually experimenter-paced), type of list items, length of list.
See Chapters 7–9 for examples of free recall extended to passages of text.

IV. Recognition Task (Episodic)

1. Learn list items.
2. Optional delay/optional distractor task during delay.
3. Make yes/no decisions to the items in a test list: "yes" the item was on the original list, "no" it was not on the original list. This is often referred to as deciding if the item is "old," that is, on the original list, or if it is "new," not on the original list. Old items are also called "targets," and new items are also called "distractors" or "lures."

Dependent Variables: In episodic tasks, the dependent variable is usually a measure of accuracy, for example, the percentage correct on the test list. Correct decisions on old items can be called "hits," and incorrect decisions on new items can be called "false alarms."

Independent or Control Variables: Same as in recall tasks.

recognition tasks require much less retrieval effort than recall tasks; indeed, recognition doesn't seem to require deliberate retrieval at all, since the to-be-retrieved answer is presented to the subject, who then only has to make an old/new decision. Since more information is stored in memory than can easily be retrieved, recognition generally shows greater sensitivity to the influence of stored information.

The relevance of this effect to the issue of depth of processing is simply that most of the early research that supported the levels of processing approach relied on recall tasks. A distinct possibility then was that recognition tests might prove more sensitive in testing the effects of Type I and Type II rehearsal.[8]

The clever set of studies by Glenberg et al. (1977) can be taken as a definitive confirmation of this possibility, and as one of the more serious challenges to the depth of processing position. Glenberg et al. used a standard Brown–Peterson task but asked subjects to remember a four-digit number as the (supposedly) primary task. During the variable-length retention intervals, subjects had to repeat either one or three words out loud as a distractor task (don't confuse the distractor task here with "distractor items," items tested in recognition that were not shown originally). Since the subjects were led to believe that digit recall was the important task, they presumably devoted only minimal effort to the word repetitions; that is, they probably used only maintenance rehearsal or Type I processing.

At the end of the 60 experimental trials of Experiment 1, the subjects were surprised with a free recall test on the *words* they had spoken during the distractor periods. Consistent with the levels of processing view, recall of the words showed no effect of the varying amount of rehearsal, that is, of the period of time (2, 6, or 18 seconds) during which subjects had repeated the words out loud. But in Experiment II, the final memory test was a recognition task. Words that had been repeated during the retention intervals were mixed together with words not used in the experiment, and subjects had to indicate if they had or had not encountered each of the words in the experiment. In this surprise test, the rehearsal interval *did* influence performance: words rehearsed for 18 seconds were recognized significantly better than those rehearsed for shorter intervals. And, to ice the cake, Experiment III showed the same beneficial effects of rehearsal in the recognition task, but this time using C-V-C triads instead of meaningful words; the longer an item had been rehearsed, the better it was recognized. (Given what you know about

---

[8]In fact, even standard recognition memory tasks may be somewhat insensitive. Jacoby and Dallas (1981) found that regardless of whether subjects could recognize a passage as one they had read before, those passages were read more rapidly the second time. There is now substantial evidence that there may be lingering traces in memory even when subjects have no conscious recollection of having experienced the information before. See Chapter 7 here (also Graf & Schacter, 1987; Kolers & Roediger, 1984) for a discussion of this "memory without awareness" phenomenon, now commonly called *implicit memory*.

nonsense syllables and about maintenance rehearsal, why was this study "icing on the cake"?)

Of course, in the depth of processing view, shallow processing (e.g., merely repeating words) should always lead to poorer retention than deep, semantic processing. And yet, the Glenberg et al. studies disconfirmed this central prediction; "mere" repetition and time in short-term memory *did* affect retention (see Wixted, 1991, for a report on the positive effects of maintenance rehearsal and the metacognitive effects of deciding which type of rehearsal to use). "Shallow" processing *can* result in equal or even superior performance.

On Balance   How should we view the depth of processing idea? Baddeley (1978) concluded that, all things considered, the depth notion is valuable only at a rough, intuitive level, and that other, more detailed approaches deserve careful study rather than the broad and general principles that Craik and Lockhart attempted to identify. While Baddeley was undoubtedly correct in terms of scientific theories of memory, at the more everyday level the depth of processing approach is probably a good rule of thumb. That is, think of maintenance and elaborative rehearsal, loosely, as corresponding to simple recycling in short-term memory versus more complex, meaningful study and transfer into long-term memory. Apply this now to your own learning. When you're introduced to someone, do you merely recycle that name for a few seconds, or do you think about it, use it in conversation, or try to find mnemonic connections to help you remember it? When you read a text, do you merely process the words at a fairly simple level of understanding, or do you elaborate what you're reading, searching for connections and relationships that will make the material more memorable (as in the "icing on the cake" question above)?

Summary Points: rehearsal; primacy and recency effects; maintenance and elaborative rehearsal; depth of processing; effects of different tasks

Organization in Storage

Another vitally important piece of the "storage puzzle" involves the role of **organization,** the *structuring or restructuring of information as it is being stored in memory.* Part of the importance of organization is derived from the powerful influence it exerts: well-organized material can be stored and retrieved with impressive levels of accuracy. Another part of its importance (at least in my view) is that the topic furnished dramatic confirmation, during the critical 1950s and 1960s, of the "active-subject" assumption—the notion that we are not passive recipients of stimulation but, rather, are active participants in learning situations, intentionally seeking ways of making information more memorable.

The earliest program of research on organization (or *clustering*) was conducted by Bousfield. In his earliest study (Bousfield & Sedgewick, 1944), Bousfield had asked subjects to name, for example, as many birds as they could. The intriguing result was that the subjects tended to name the words in subgroups, for instance, "robin, bluejay, sparrow—chicken, duck, goose—eagle, hawk."

To investigate this further, Bousfield (1953) designed a study in which subjects were given a free recall task, with a 60-item list to be learned. Unlike other work at that time, however, Bousfield used related words for his lists. In particular, the 60-item list was made up of 15 words each from four distinct categories: animals, personal names, vegetables, and professions. The subjects were presented these list items in a randomized order. Yet in free recall, they tended to write the items down by category; for instance, "dog, cat, cow, pea, bean, John, Bob." How can we explain this, sensible though it may be? Bousfield's modest interpretation was that the greater-than-chance grouping of items into clusters "implies the operation of an organizing tendency" (p. 237).

From where did this "organizing tendency" come? It was not in the words themselves, to be sure. While the words were drawn from categories that were assumed to exist in the subjects' memories, it would be foolish to say that the words exerted the tendency to organize themselves. No, the tendency was in the *subjects,* in the unseen mental activities that went on during the learning of the list. Obviously, subjects noticed at some point during input that several words were drawn from the same categories. From that point on, they used the reasonable strategy of grouping the items together on the basis of category membership (there's a nice metamemory effect here as well). This implies that subjects were reorganizing the list as it was presented, by means of rehearsal. The consequence of this reorganization during storage would be straightforward: the way the material had been stored governed the way it was recalled.

Investigations of category clustering became very common following Bousfield's initial reports for several important reasons. A widely shared viewpoint, expressed neatly by Mandler (1967), was that "memory and organization are not only correlated, but organization is a *necessary condition* for memory" (p. 328, emphasis added). In this view, *any* information that was stored in memory was, almost by definition, organized. Furthermore, standard storage strategies, most prominently rehearsal, came to be viewed as organizational devices with the consequence that anything rehearsed was also organized (at least, anything rehearsed elaboratively). Mnemonic devices, in this view, were no different; for instance, "all organizations are mnemonic devices" (Mandler, 1967, p. 329), and likewise, all mnemonic devices provide organization. We will discuss two of the reasons for the rash of studies on clustering here, along with examples of the research that supported those reasons. Chapter 6, which covers semantic memory, delves still more deeply into the topic of organization. Indeed, the clustering research, with its focus on how word meaning affects recall, was probably the most important experimental bridge to studies of long-term semantic memory.

Relationship to "Chunking"   First, researchers came quickly to the realization that category groupings were merely another form of *chunks* of information, essentially similar to Miller's (1956) famous units of information. Thus clustering research was seen to fit in particularly well with another important set of results, those related to the capacity of short-term memory and the formation and transfer of chunks into long-term memory. Clustering was seen as a powerful *recoding* strategy, a means of making a mass of information memorable. Items like "dog, cat, cow" could be grouped together into a chunk, with the category name "animal" serving as a *code* for that chunk. Thus memory for a long list could be described in terms of a *hierarchical structure,* with a code high in the structure serving as the "label," in a sense, for the individual items at the bottom of the structure. Mandler (1967) extended the similarities between clustering and chunking even further. He noted that in his studies of clustering, where subjects were free to use as many categories as they wished, there was a strong preference for using approximately 5 ± 2 categories, a particularly obvious connection to Miller's (1956) work.

The power of such organizational schemes for improving the storage of information into long-term memory was demonstrated convincingly by Bower, Clark, Lesgold, and Winzenz (1969). Four hierarchies of words were presented to subjects in the "organized" condition; Figure 5-4 shows one of these sets of words (the words were arranged as shown in the figure but were shown without the boxes and connecting lines). The control group was shown words in the same physical arrangements, but the words were randomly assigned to their positions. Subjects got four trials

FIGURE 5-4

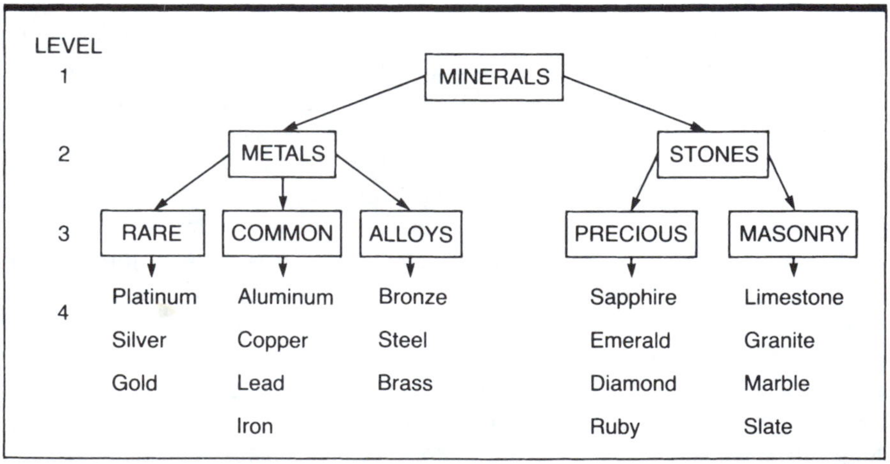

One of the hierarchies presented by Bower et al. (1969).

Table 5-6   AVERAGE NUMBER OF WORDS
RECALLED OVER FOUR TRIALS AS A
FUNCTION OF ORGANIZATION

Conditions	1	2	3	4
Organized	73.0	106.1	112.0	112.0
Random	20.6	38.9	52.8	70.1

Adapted from Bower et al., 1969.

to learn the words, with a total possible recall score of 112. Table 5-6 shows the results. Presenting the words in the hierarchically organized fashion led to 100% accuracy on Trials 3 and 4, an amazing feat given the number and relative unfamiliarity of the words. In contrast, the control group only managed to recall 70 words out of 112 by Trial 4, 62% accuracy. As Anderson (1985) has pointed out, a chapter outline can serve much the same function as the Bower et al. hierarchies, with obvious implications for students' study strategies (*there's* a strong hint).

Rehearsal Strategies   A second reason for the popularity of clustering studies was that they demonstrated subjects' strategies for learning in an obvious and objective fashion. Many different methods were used to examine these strategies. For example, Mandler (1967) gave his subjects a deck of index cards with the list items printed one per card. Subjects then were asked to sort the cards into groups, using as few or as many groupings as they cared to. Naturally, recall tended to mimic the sorting structure the subjects had adopted. More commonly, however, researchers relied on the free recall task and examined the effects of different list structures—organized versus random—different numbers of categories, different numbers of items within categories, and so on. Clustering and organization were then examined in terms of a creative array of dependent variables; for instance, order of recall, degree of clustering, speed and patterning of pauses during recall, and rehearsal (see reviews by Johnson, 1970; Mandler, 1972). Such studies led to productive generalizations between the areas of organization and rehearsal.

As an example, Ashcraft, Kellas, and Needham (1975) asked subjects to rehearse out loud as they studied clustered or randomized lists of words. They found, of course, that subjects tended to recall the words by category, the usual effect. The study went further, however, by relating this result to rehearsal, to the order of recall, and to the time pauses during recall. In particular, subjects tended to rehearse by category; for instance, when "horse" was presented, this would trigger the rehearsal of "dog, cat, cow, horse" together. Apparently, when sufficient time is provided during input, subjects can thoroughly reorganize the words as they store them in memory. Furthermore, the number of times a word had been rehearsed during study was predictive of recall order: more frequently rehearsed categories, as well as words within those categories, were recalled earlier than categories and words that received relatively little rehearsal. In other words, rehearsal and organization are intimately related to the nature of recall from memory.

Subjective Organization   Don't misunderstand the above section: organization during rehearsal is *not* limited to lists of words that belong to obvious, known categories. In fact, some of the earliest and most provocative evidence for organization came from a classic study by Tulving, in 1962, on the organization of unrelated words.

Tulving used what was called the "multitrial free recall task," in which the same list of words is presented repeatedly across several trials, where each trial had a new reordering of the words. His analysis looked at the regularities that developed in the subjects' recall orders, that is, the consistent groupings of otherwise unrelated words that subjects adopted over trials. As an example, a subject might recall the words "dog, apple, lawyer, brush" together on several successive recall trials. This consistency, despite the experimenter's reordering of the list items from trial to trial, suggested that the subject had formed a cluster or chunk composed of those four items based on some idiosyncratic basis. For example, a subject might link the words together in a kind of sentence or story: "The dog brought an apple to the lawyer, who brushed his hair." Regardless of how these links were formed, the clusters were then used repeatedly during the recall trials, serving subjectively as the same kind of organized unit that "dog, cat, horse, cow" would in an experimenter-defined cluster.

Tulving termed this **subjective organization,** that is, *organization developed by the subject, for structuring and remembering a list of items without experimenter-supplied categories.* In other words, Tulving pointed out that even "unrelated" words become organized because of the mental activity of the subject who imposes this organization. As he put it, "Perhaps paradoxically this suggests that a list of completely *unrelated* words is probably as fictional as is a truly nonsensical nonsense syllable" (p. 352).

Imagery

The last storage variable to be considered here involves **visual imagery,** *the mental picturing of a stimulus that then affects later recall or recognition.* Of course, we've discussed two prominent visual imagery effects already, the mental rotation studies, which suggest an imaginal code in working memory, and the imagery-based mnemonic devices. What we are focusing on now, however, is the effect that visual imagery has on the storage of information into long-term memory, the possible boost that imagery gives to material you're trying to learn.

The name most closely associated with early research on imagery is Alan Paivio. In his book, Paivio (1971) reviewed scores of studies that illustrated the generally beneficial effects of imagery on learning and retention. These beneficial effects are over and above those due to other variables, such as word- or sentence-based rehearsal, or meaningfulness (e.g., Bower, 1970; Yuille & Paivio, 1967).

As just one example, Paivio described a **paired-associate learning** study by Schnorr and Atkinson (1969; see Table 5-5). In such a study, items are presented in pairs, the first item designated the "stimulus" item, the second the "response" item. The subject's task here is to *learn the list so that the correct response item can be reproduced whenever the stimulus item is presented.* Thus, if you saw the pair "elephant–book" during study, you would be tested during recall by seeing the term "elephant" and your correct response would be "book" (the later section on interference describes this task in more detail). Schnorr and Atkinson had their subjects study half of a paired-associate list by means of imagery, forming some visual image of the stimulus and response terms together. The other half of the list was studied by means of rote repetition. On immediate recall, the pairs learned by imagery were recalled at better than 80% accuracy, compared to about 40% for the rote repetition pairs. The superiority of the imagery condition was found even after a one-week retention interval.

Studies such as this one led Paivio to propose the **dual coding hypothesis** (e.g., Paivio, 1971). This hypothesis states that *words that denote concrete objects, as opposed to abstract words, can be encoded into memory twice,* once in terms of their verbal attributes and once in terms of their imaginal attributes. Thus a word like "book" enjoys an advantage in memory studies. Because it can be recorded twice in memory, once as a word and once as a visual image, there are two different ways it can be retrieved from memory, one way for each code. A stimulus term like "idea," on the other hand, probably has only a verbal code available for it, since it does not have an obvious imaginal representation. (This is not to say that people can't eventually create an image to help remember a word like "idea," but merely to say that the image is much more available and natural for concrete words.)

There is much more to be said about imagery and, in general, other nonverbal means of representing and remembering information (Kosslyn, 1978, 1981; Marschark & Cornoldi, 1990; Marschark, Yuille, Richman, & Hunt, 1987; Paivio, 1971). Some of this research is discussed in the next chapter, where we consider semantic memory and the role of imagery in general world knowledge. For now, consider an episodic memory study by Watkins, Peynircioglu, and Brems (1984). These investigators tested the idea that rehearsal, most commonly studied with verbal materials, might also have a pictorial or imaginal component. They presented picture–word pairs to two groups of subjects; one group was given verbal rehearsal instructions, the other group was given pictorial rehearsal instructions ("try to maintain an image of the picture in your mind's eye"). The pictures were displayed by slide projector, the words by tape recorder. Some of the picture–word items were followed by a 15-second interval of time, during which rehearsal could take place, and some were immediately followed by the next picture–word pair, thus preventing rehearsal. The top row of Figure 5-5 shows three sample pictures from the study.

After the list of pairs had been presented, subjects were given a cued recall task, in which either a fragment of the printed word or a fragment of the picture was presented as a cue; examples are shown in the middle and bottom rows of Figure 5-5. The most important results involved the match between study and test conditions. When subjects had been shown the pictures and had been given the 15-second rehearsal interval, their test performance was best on the picture fragment test. Likewise, subjects who had rehearsed verbally during the 15-second interval did best on the word fragment test. All other performance was relatively low, for example, on items that had received no rehearsal, and in conditions where the study and test formats did not match (e.g., word fragments during study but then picture fragments on the memory test). Stated a

FIGURE 5-5

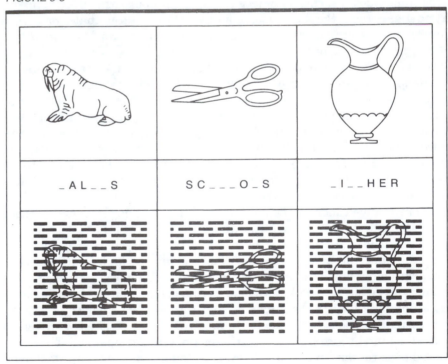

Three sample pictures used during input are shown in the top row. In the second row, three sample word fragment cues are shown; in the bottom row, corresponding picture fragment cues are shown. To make the picture fragment test more difficult, these cues were shown out of focus. (From Watkins, Peynircioglu, & Brems, 1984.)

different way, both types of rehearsal improved performance when the recall test was consistent with the subjects' type of rehearsal. But neither type improved performance if the retrieval cues were inconsistent with the type of rehearsal.

Storage Summary: Encoding Specificity

Storage is just one side of the coin, so to speak. The other side, retrieval, is obviously just as important. What good does it do to store something in memory if you can't retrieve it when you need it? Let's conclude this section on storage with a short summary that also previews several important ideas for the topic of retrieval. What generalizations can we draw from research on rehearsal, organization, and imagery? How are we to understand the phenomenon of storage into episodic memory? The best way to understand storage, it seems, is to consider it in light of retrieval, in terms of how the material will be retrieved from the memory system.

As a simple example of this principle, time yourself as you name the 12 months of the year—it takes only about 5 sec. Now time yourself as you name the 12 months of the year in alphabetical order. How long did that take? More like half a minute, right? It should be obvious that the way this information was acquired and stored—the way it's organized in memory—is based on chronological order. Thus retrieving the information in such a different, *incongruent* fashion mismatches the storage organization and therefore is quite difficult. A related example makes the underlying principle even clearer. I occasionally run into a former student "out in the world," that is, out of the school context in which I met the person. When this happens, I usually can't remember the person's name, even though I can often remember the name when the student comes to my office. The mismatch between storage and retrieval contexts turns me into an "absentminded professor," at least in that circumstance.

Compare this to the research you've just read about. What variables or conditions led to the best performance? There were certainly some experiments in which subjects were able to recall information *despite* their activity during learning; Hebb's subjects recalled the repeated digit list, for instance, and Glenberg et al.'s subjects recognized words they had originally been told were only part of a distractor task. And indeed, Ebbinghaus's results, with a very rapid presentation rate, attest to the ability to acquire information under adverse conditions (see Tulving, 1985), a kind of "brute force" memory effect.

But, for the most part, the research shows that memory performance is enhanced when there is a close correspondence between the study and test conditions, in other words, when the activities during testing *match* those of acquisition. This was the message of the Watkins et al. (1984)

experiment on word- and picture-fragments, and several other studies as well (e.g., Morris, Bransford, & Franks, 1977). Something that occurs during acquisition facilitates memory performance when retention is tested in a way that matches acquisition. Congruence—consistency between acquisition and retention conditions—improves our performance. Incongruence between acquisition and retention depresses our performance. Why?

In Tulving and Thompson's (1973) view, an important reason is captured by the phrase **encoding specificity.** By this phrase, Tulving and Thompson meant that information is encoded into memory *not* as a set of isolated, individual items. Instead, *each item is encoded into a richer memory representation, one that includes any extra information about the item that was present during encoding.* Thus, when you encounter "cat" in a list of words, you are likely to encode not only the word "cat" but also related information about that word. Importantly, this extra information would probably include "animal," in other words, easily retrievable concepts that are semantically related to "cat." In this situation, "animal" serves as your higher-order label or code for the clustered items "cat," "dog," and so on.

When your memory is tested, in a free recall task, for instance, you attempt to retrieve from memory the record or trace left by your original encoding. In this circumstance, if you encoded "animal" along with "cat," then the word "animal" should be an excellent **retrieval cue** for recalling "cat"—*a useful prompt or reminder for the information to be retrieved.* If you study pictures under a picture rehearsal condition, then picture cues will enhance your performance (e.g., Morris et al., 1977). If the prevailing conditions during the test are quite different, for example, if you are given word-fragment cues after pictorial rehearsal, then the likelihood of your retrieving the information decreases. The original context cues will provide you with the best access to the information during a recall attempt, whether those cues are based on verbal, visual, or other information (Schab, 1990, for instance, has found this effect with odors as the contextual cue; see Chapter 13 for references to memory enhancement depending on your emotional states during storage and retrieval).

In summary, storage of information into episodic long-term memory is affected by rehearsal, by organization, and by imagery. The presence of all three of these leads to a stronger memory trace. Furthermore, congruence between study and test conditions seems critical. Relevant rehearsal, including organizational and imaginal elements, improves performance, as does the provision of retrieval cues that were part of the original encoding of the material. Rehearsal that turns out to be *irrelevant* for the test conditions, however, is generally of little benefit.

Summary Points: clustering by category; chunking and organization; subjective organization; imagery and dual coding; encoding specificity

▼ Retrieval of Episodic Information

We turn now to the other side of the coin, the retrieval of information from episodic memory. And as we do, we reencounter the two theories of forgetting that have preoccupied cognitive psychology from the very beginning—decay and interference.

Decay

It's a bit unusual for the name of a theory to imply the content of the theory so clearly as the term *decay*. Nonetheless, that's what decay theory is all about: the older a memory trace is, the more likely that it has been forgotten, that it has *decayed* away, just as the print on an old newspaper fades into illegibility. Thorndike (1914) enunciated this principle in his *law of disuse:* habits, and by extension memories, that are used repeatedly are strengthened, and habits not used are weakened through *disuse*. Thorndike's proposal was a beautiful example of a theoretical hypothesis—easily understood and straightforward in its predictions. Unfortunately, it's wrong, at least as far as long-term memory is concerned.

A definitive attack on decay theory was provided by McGeoch (1932). In his influential paper, he argued from both theoretical and empirical grounds that decay theory was fundamentally wrong, that time per se is an inadequate basis for understanding or predicting loss of information. Instead, McGeoch claimed that the *activities* that occur during a period of time are responsible for forgetting. In short, intervening activities produce *interference* that disrupts retention. As Hall (1971) described it, McGeoch's central point was that "time should be thought of as a conceptual framework within which events take place. The iron bar that is tossed in the field does not rust because of time; rather, oxygen from the air combines with the iron to produce rust, and this process takes place within a time interval.... In short, environmental events themselves, rather than time intervals alone, must be considered in order to account for forgetting" (pp. 459–460).

Interference

Interference theory and tests of interference effects became a staple in the experimental diet of verbal learning psychologists, much to the current dismay of some cognitive psychologists. At least two reasons for this trend can be stated. First, the arguments against decay theory and for an interference approach were convincing, both on theoretical and empirical grounds. Demonstrations like the often-cited Jenkins and Dallenbach (1924) study made complete sense within an interference framework: after identical time delays, subjects who had slept after learning recalled more than those who had remained awake (Figure 5-6). The everyday activities encountered by the awake subjects seemed to interfere with their memory for the list. Fewer interfering activities intervened for the sleeping subjects, with the result of better performance.

A second reason for the popularity of interference studies, it seems, is that interference effects were easily obtained in the laboratory, especially with a task already in wide use, the paired-associate learning task. This task seemed "natural" for studying the components of interference. For one thing, it was almost infinitely adaptable—almost any variable

FIGURE 5-6

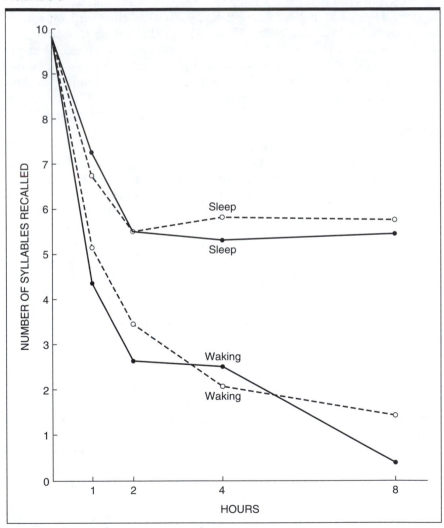

The classic Jenkins and Dallenbach (1924) result, showing higher recall of nonsense syllables for two subjects who slept after acquisition versus remaining awake after acquisition.

thought to influence interference could easily be incorporated. For another, it conformed in an obvious way to the theoretical *Zeitgeist* or "spirit of the times"; the stimulus–response (S-R) pairs of items, with a stimulus term coming to "elicit" the proper response, bore a direct and obvious relationship to the stimuli and responses of the animal learning laboratory, and to the dominant theoretical commitment to S-R behaviorism.

Paired-Associate Learning   Let's spend a few moments studying the paired-associate learning task (usually abbreviated as **P-A learning**), so you'll understand interference theory, and so you'll know one of our tried-and-true methods of testing memory. The basic elements of a P-A learning task are these (see also Table 5-5). *A list of stimulus terms is paired, item by item, with a list of response terms. After learning, the stimulus terms should prompt the recall of the proper response terms.* The items were usually C-V-Cs or words. In the "anticipation method," a subject would first see a stimulus term by itself, would try to name the correct response term that went with that stimulus, and then would see the stimulus–response pair together. Of course, subjects had to guess on the first trial, since they had not seen any of the pairs before. After that, however, the number of correct responses made to the stimulus terms would grow across repeated trials, showing that (in the terminology of behaviorism) the correct responses had become conditioned to the appropriate stimuli. A typical procedure was to bring a subject up to some predetermined accuracy criterion, say, one perfect trial, then ask the subject to learn another list of paired associates.

Table 5-7 presents several P-A learning lists to use as a demonstration. Let's deal only with list 1 for a moment. Cover this first list with another piece of paper, then slowly move the paper downward, one line at a time. Do this repeatedly, trying to learn the right responses to the stimuli. Keep track of how many trials it takes you to recall all ten of the response terms correctly.

You've now participated in the first half of a typical P-A learning study on interference. The second half of the study involves learning another list of paired associates; the nature or composition of the second list and its relationship to list 1 are of critical importance. Pick list 2, 3, or 4 from Table 5-7 and learn it to the same criterion, making sure to note how many trials it takes you to recall all response terms correctly.

If you picked list 2, you should have experienced little or no interference, since list 2 contains stimulus and response terms that are not similar to list 1's terms. In the terminology of interference theory, you were in the A-B–C-D condition, where the letters A through D refer to different lists of stimulus or response terms. This condition represents a kind of baseline condition in terms of interference, since there is no similarity between the A-B and the C-D terms (note, however, that you may have needed fewer trials on the second list because of "general transfer" effects from list 1, warm-up or learning to learn).

Table 5-7   LISTS OF PAIRED-ASSOCIATES

List 1 (A-B)	List 2 (C-D)
tall–bone	safe–fable
plan–leaf	bench–idea
nose–fight	pencil–owe
park–flea	wait–blouse
grew–cook	student–duck
rabbit–few	window–cat
pear–rain	house–news
mess–crowd	card–nest
print–kiss	color–just
smoke–hand	flower–jump

List 3 (A-B$_r$)	List 4 (A-B')
plan–bone	smoke–arm
mess–hand	mess–people
smoke–leaf	rabbit–several
pear–kiss	park–ant
rabbit–fight	plan–tree
tall–crowd	tall–skeleton
nose–cook	nose–battle
park–few	grew–chef
grew–flea	pear–storm
print–rain	print–lips

If you picked list 3, there should have been "massive" negative transfer; in other words, it would have taken you many more trials to reach criterion on the second learning list. The reason for this is that the same stimulus and response terms were used again, but in new pairings. Thus your experience on list 1, forming strong enough associations to reach criterion, interfered with the later activity of learning to re-pair the items. The standard term for this type of list was A-B–A-B$_r$, where the subscript r stood for "randomized" or "re-paired" items.

Finally, if you picked list 4 (the A-B–A-B' condition), there should have been considerable positive transfer, requiring many fewer trials to reach criterion on the second list. This is because the response terms in list 4 (designated B', read "B prime") are highly related to the earlier ones you learned (B). In list 1, for instance, you learned "plan–leaf"; in list 2, "plan" went with "tree."

These transfer and interference effects are all *proactive;* that is, they demonstrate the effects a prior task can have on a current learning task. Of course, we discussed proactive interference (PI) and release from PI at some length in the last chapter. Table 5-8 gives the general experimental design for a proactive interference study as well as for a retroactive interference (RI) study. To repeat, retroactive interference exists when some learning experience interferes with recall of an *earlier* experience—the newer memory interferes backward in time ("retro").

Table 5-8   DESIGNS TO STUDY TWO DIFFERENT KINDS OF INTERFERENCE

	Proactive Interference (PI)			
	Learn	Learn	Test	Interference Effect
PI group	A-B	A-C	A-C	A-B list interferes with A-C
Control group		A-C	A-C	

	Retroactive Interference (RI)			
	Learn	Learn	Test	Interference Effect
RI group	A-B	A-C	A-B	A-C list interferes with A-B
Control group	A-B		A-B	

Both proactive and retroactive interference were examined extensively (or excessively, depending on your viewpoint), with complex theories built on P-A learning results. Although a massive literature is available, no attempt will be made to cover it in depth here (but see standard works such as Postman & Underwood, 1973; Underwood, 1957; Underwood & Schultz, 1960; and Klatzky's very readable summary, 1980, Chapter 11). Instead, let's summarize a major difficulty encountered in this work, important because it was instrumental in the shift to a *cognitive,* rather than behaviorist, approach to memory.

Problems of Meaning   The behaviorist tradition had it that P-A learning was essentially a matter of association formation. In other words, the B terms in an A-B list became associated with—*conditioned to*—their A terms, so that presenting a stimulus from the A list should "elicit" the B response term. Likewise, if a *new* list were learned, say A-C, then the A-B associations had to be *unlearned* even as the new A-C connections were being conditioned (e.g., Kintsch, 1970; Underwood & Postman, 1960). The difficulties subjects experienced in learning A-C, of course, were due to proactive interference: there was competition from the old A-B associations when trying to learn the A-C pairings. As the A-C list was being mastered, it was believed that the A-B connections were being genuinely unlearned, basically similar to extinction in the animal laboratory.

The difficulties with such a proposal became very clear in a study by Slamecka (1966). He tested his subjects in the regular proactive interference design shown in Table 5-8, but with a twist. *Prior* to having the subjects learn list A-B and then list A-C, he had them generate their own "free associates" to the A list of words. For instance, if one of the A words was "cat," you might generate "dog" as an associate. You would then be asked to learn the A-B pair "cat–pin," and then later in the A-C list you'd have to learn "cat–desk." The traditional explanation, as noted above, was that the A-B connections would have to be unlearned when you were studying list A-C. But by the same token, in order to learn list A-B, you'd have to unlearn the free associates you gave during the generation task, the "cat–dog" connections.

Needless to say, this did not happen. The subjects experienced the normal interference effects between the arbitrary A-B and A-C lists, but none of that interfered with memory for their own free associates. What should have been altered by interference, the preexisting associations, was totally immune to it. In the face of existing associations in memory, laboratory-induced interference seemed downright puny.

Finding so major a difference between laboratory and real-world "items" suggested an unsettling conclusion: theories based on traditional learning tasks and paradigms were irrelevant, or at least inadequate, for an understanding of memory for words and language. It seemed entirely possible that the P-A learning laws weren't general, that they only applied fully to nonsense syllable learning in a P-A task. As Jenkins (1974) put it in the title of his article: "Remember that old theory of memory? Well, forget it!"

Retrieval Failure

Since the mid-1960s, a very different theory has come to dominate cognitive psychology's view of forgetting. Both the decay and interference theories suggested that information in long-term memory can truly be forgotten, that is, lost from memory. This more technical definition of the term **forgetting,** *loss from memory,* was implicit in the mechanisms thought to account for forgetting, for example, unlearning. The current view makes a radically different claim, that in essence there may be *no genuine forgetting* from long-term memory, save for possible loss due to organic or physical factors, for example, stroke (see Chapter 10). Instead, so-called forgetting is often a failure of retrieval.

An Everyday Example   Everyone is familiar with retrieval failure, although it often parades under a different name. Students claim that they knew the information, but that they "blocked" on it during the exam; if this isn't just a rationalization, then it would qualify as an example of retrieval failure. The more straightforward (believable) example is the classic **tip-of-the-tongue** phenomenon, the **TOT** state. People are in the TOT state when they are momentarily unable to recall some shred of information, often a person's name, that they know is stored in long-term memory.[9] Interestingly, even though you may be unable to retrieve a word or name during a TOT state, you usually have access to partial information about the target word, for instance, the sound it

---

[9]TOT is pronounced "tee-oh-tee," and *not* like the word "tot." Furthermore, in the "cognition *biz,*" we often use "TOT" as a verb: "The subject TOTed ("tee-oh-teed") seven times on the list of 20 names." For another regrettable example of "cognitive verbs," see Chapters 8 and 9, on "garden pathing."

starts with, its approximate length, and the stress or emphasis pattern in pronunciation. (Brown and McNeill [1966] is the classic TOT paper. Jones [1989] and Meyer and Bock [1992] report on words that sound like the unretrievable target as cues for successful retrieval. See Burke, MacKay, Worthley, and Wade [1991] for a state-of-the-art investigation of the TOT effect, including a list of questions that can be used to trigger the TOT state.)

But retrieval failure, like the TOT phenomenon, is not limited to occasional lapses in remembering names or unusual words. In fact, as Tulving and his associates found, it is a fundamental aspect of memory.

Research on Retrieval Failure   An early and powerful laboratory demonstration of retrieval failure was provided in a study by Tulving and Pearlstone (1966). In this study, two groups of subjects studied the same list of 48 items, four words from each of 12 different categories (animals, fruits, sports, etc.; other subjects learned shorter lists, or lists with fewer items per category, but we'll focus only on the two most dramatic groups here). The items were preceded by the appropriate name of the category, for example, "crimes–treason, theft; professions–engineer, lawyer," but subjects were told that they only had to remember the items themselves. Because both groups were treated identically until the beginning of the recall period, it can be assumed that both had acquired the same amount of information from the list, and both had retained equal amounts in memory. At recall, one group was asked for standard free recall. The other group was asked for free recall but was provided the names of the categories as retrieval cues, that is, a "cued recall" condition.

The results were both predictable and profound in their implications. The free recall group was able to recall 40% of the list items, while the cued recall group named 62% of the items. In short, the free recall group had only recalled a portion of the items that were actually learned. We know they learned more than they recalled because the cued group had been exposed to the same learning and retention conditions, yet had recalled more. As Tulving and Pearlstone put it, "Information about many words must be *available* in the storage . . . even when this information is not *accessible*" (p. 389; emphasis added) under free recall conditions.

One conclusion we can draw from these results confirms intuitions dating back to Ebbinghaus; the recall task often underestimates the amount of information that was learned. Recognition scores, not to mention savings scores, usually show much higher retention than recall scores.

A much more important implication is that unsuccessful retrieval, say, in the absence of cues, might prove to be a critical component of forgetting. In fact, retrieval failure might be the major (or even the only) cause of forgetting. On this view, *information stored in long-term memo-*

ry remains there permanently, so is **available,** just as a book on the library shelf is available. Successful performance, however, also depends on **accessibility,** *the degree to which information can be retrieved from memory.* Items that are not accessible are not immediately retrievable, just as the misshelved book in the library cannot be located or retrieved. This position suggests that information is not lost *from* memory, but instead is lost *in* memory, so to speak. This loss of access will persist until some effective retrieval cue is presented, some cue that "locates" the item that can't be retrieved.

Retrieval Cues and Encoding Specificity

You already know how access can be increased to an inaccessible memory trace. But you learned the principle under a different name, *encoding specificity.* The way to increase your access to information in memory is to reinstate the original learning context, to maximize the congruence between current test conditions and the conditions that prevailed during acquisition. In short, access is increased by effective retrieval cues. Any cue that was encoded along with the learned information should increase the accessibility of that information. This is why the category cues helped Tulving and Pearlstone's subjects to recall more than they otherwise would have. Similarly, this is why recognition memory tests usually reveal higher performance than recall tests. In a recognition test, you merely have to pick out which of several alternatives is the correct choice. What better retrieval cue for some piece of information could there be than the very information you're attempting to retrieve?

Subsequent research has demonstrated the power of the encoding specificity principle in quite dramatic fashion. (By far the most convincing demonstration I've ever seen is presented in Tables 5-9 and 5-10, taken from the Bransford and Stein [1984] book on problem solving; do that demonstration now, before reading further.)

Thomson and Tulving (1970) asked their subjects to learn a list of words for later recall. Some of the list words were accompanied by "cue words" printed in lowercase letters; subjects were told they need not recall the cue words, but that the cues might be helpful in learning the items. Some of the cue words were high associates of the list items, for instance, hot–COLD, and some were low associates, for instance, wind–COLD. During recall, subjects were tested for their memory of the list under one of three conditions, low- or high-associate cues, or no cues at all.

The results were exactly as predicted from the encoding specificity principle. High associates used as retrieval cues benefitted the subjects' recall both when the high associate had been presented during study and

Table 5-9

This demonstration experiment illustrates the importance of retrieval cues. You'll need a blank sheet of paper and a pencil. Please follow the instructions exactly.

Instructions: Spend 3 to 5 seconds reading each of the sentences below, and read through the list only once. As soon as you are finished, cover the list and write down as many of the sentences as you can remember (you need not write "can be used" each time). Please begin now.

A brick can be used as a doorstop.
A ladder can be used as a bookshelf.
A wine bottle can be used as a candleholder.
A pan can be used as a drum.
A record can be used to serve potato chips.
A guitar can be used as a canoe paddle.
A leaf can be used as a bookmark.
An orange can be used to play catch.
A newspaper can be used to swat flies.
A TV antenna can be used as a clothes rack.
A sheet can be used as a sail.
A boat can be used as a shelter.
A bathtub can be used as a punch bowl.
A flashlight can be used to hold water.
A rock can be used as a paperweight.
A knife can be used to stir paint.
A pen can be used as an arrow.
A barrel can be used as a chair.
A rug can be used as a bedspread.
A telephone can be used as an alarm clock.
A scissors can be used to cut grass.
A board can be used as a ruler.
A balloon can be used as a pillow.
A shoe can be used to pound nails.
A dime can be used as a screwdriver.
A lampshade can be used as a hat.

Now that you've recalled as many sentences as you can, turn to Table 5-10.

Sometimes the questions in Trivial Pursuit serve as successful retrieval cues—and sometimes not.

when no cue word had been presented. Presumably, when no cue word had been presented, subjects spontaneously retrieved the high associate during input and encoded it along with the list item. In contrast, when low associates had been presented during learning, *only* low associates functioned as effective retrieval cues. High associates used as retrieval cues were no better for these subjects than no cues at all. In other words, if you had studied wind–COLD, receiving "hot" as a cue word for COLD was of no value. Encoding specificity thus can even override existing associations during a recall attempt. (Note that encoded cues do not cause "unlearning" of the preexisting association; they simply function as more effective cues during the task.)

More surprising than this, encoding specificity can even override the usual advantage that recognition shows over recall. A series of influential papers by Tulving has demonstrated a paradoxical result, termed "recognition failure of recallable words" (e.g., Tulving & Thomson, 1973; Watkins & Tulving, 1975). In these studies, a weakly associated cue is presented along with the target word during original learning—say, "glue–CHAIR." When a recognition test is presented later, the target CHAIR is often not recognized if it appears in a very different context, for instance, in the set "desk, top, chair." In other words, subjects fail to identify CHAIR as a word they have seen previously in the experiment, since its current context is so different from the original encoding; this is recognition failure. Following this, however, subjects are given a cued

Table 5-10

Do not look back at the list of sentences in Table 5-9. Instead, use the following list as retrieval cues, and now write as many sentences as you can. Be sure to keep track of how many you can write down, so you can compare this to your earlier recall performance. Begin now.

flashlight	lampshade
sheet	shoe
rock	guitar
telephone	scissors
boat	leaf
dime	brick
wine bottle	knife
board	newspaper
pen	pan
balloon	barrel
ladder	rug
record	orange
TV antenna	bathtub

DEMONSTRATIONS

There are hundreds of projects you can do to examine episodic long-term memory. All you'll need for most of them is a set of stimuli to present for learning, and paper and pencil to record the subjects' recall or recognition. Here are just a few suggestions, to give you the idea.

1. Do the Bransford and Stein (1984) study in Tables 5-9 and 5-10. For some subjects, read only the two words per sentence (e.g., brick–doorstop, ladder–bookshelf), in a procedure similar to P-A learning. For others, read the sentences as suggested in the table. You'll definitely want to contrast free versus cued recall. Variations include using the second word in each pair (e.g., doorstop) as a kind of "backward cue" to the first word (brick), to compare cue effectiveness in both directions. Finally, compare the normal demonstration with one in which you read only the word pairs but suggest that the subjects try to make up their own sentences that relate the words together.

2. There is a reasonably large literature on the "generation effect," higher recall for words that have been generated than for words that subjects have merely read (e.g., Greene, 1988; Watkins & Sechler, 1988). Have one group of subjects generate words, for instance, "Name ten members in each of these categories: birds, weapons, beverages, vehicles." Have another group study the words generated by the first group. You can compare the second group's recall level to the number generated in the first group, and to the recall scores for group 1 (e.g., after the generation task is over, ask group 1 to "please recall exactly the words you just generated"). You might give a final recognition test to both groups, presenting words from each category that were and were not generated, for yes/no decisions.

3. Any number of interesting autobiographical memory projects can be conducted. Here are three examples you can easily adapt for a demonstration project.

   a. Brown, Rips, and Shevell (1985) asked subjects to estimate the dates of occurrence for various events, such as the attempt on President Reagan's life or the Three-Mile Island accident. They found that people's date-of-occurrence estimates depended on the amount of information accessible in memory about the event in question. In general, people dated the events as having occurred more recently when they knew more about them.

   b. Thompson (1982) asked his subjects to record two unique personal events per day in a diary-keeping procedure that lasted for one semester; subjects also rated the memorability of the events as they wrote them down. He then tested their memory for those events, as well as their roommates' memories for the same events, at the end of the semester.

   c. Hyman and Rubin (1990) gave subjects the titles and first lines of Beatles' songs and asked for recall; other subjects got the first lines as cues and had to recall the titles.

4. Do a naturalistic project on TOT effects, keeping a diary of your own retrieval failures. As mentioned in the text, the Burke et al. (1991) article has an extensive appendix, which lists questions used to induce a TOT state.

5. Roediger and Blaxton (1985) adapted the game Trivial Pursuit to the history of psychology. Consider writing such questions for a course you've taken, then giving the test to friends in the same course.

recall test. Here they routinely *do* recall CHAIR when presented with "glue" as a retrieval cue. While these experiments used rather arbitrary contexts (who would spontaneously think of "glue" as a cue for CHAIR?), the similarity of the result to the earlier point about congruous study and retrieval contexts is obvious. In short, even simple recognition depends on encoding specificity.

Tulving and Thomson (1973) explained the encoding specificity principle as follows: "Specific encoding operations performed on what is perceived determine what is stored, and what is stored determines what retrieval cues are effective in providing access to what is stored" (p. 369). Whatever information you encoded, target items as well as related information, determines what gets stored in your memory representation. That is, a retrieval cue will be effective if you thought of it and encoded it spontaneously during learning, or if it was presented (and you encoded it) during the learning sequence, that is, if the cue came either from conceptually driven or data-driven processes (Micco & Masson, 1991). Retrieval cues that are not effective simply don't match your encoded representation of the item, because they weren't explicitly presented or spontaneously generated during learning.

Are you ready for a final demonstration of this principle? We'll call it "failure to recall a recallable word." Think of all the words you've read in this chapter, and the lists you've learned. Limiting yourself to just these words, can you remember a word that goes with "parade"? If not, maybe it will be easier with a more appropriate cue, one you encoded specifically along with the target word. Can you fill in the blank if I give you the cue "two–shoe–_____"?

Summary Points: decay and interference theories; paired-associate learning and interference; retrieval failure; TOT phenomenon; retrieval cues and encoding specificity

▼ Autobiographical Memories

For the bulk of this chapter, we have discussed episodic memory from a single standpoint, that of laboratory studies on the principles of learning and memory. Episodic memory was defined at the beginning of the chapter as an autobiographical memory system, one in which personally experienced episodes and events are recorded. The laboratory analog of this definition is the memory experiment, in which memory for a personally experienced event—the list of words you were asked to learn, for instance—is tested by recognition, recall, or sometimes relearning. Since the laboratory analog has been the mainstay of memory research since the time of Ebbinghaus, this is what we have focused on so far.

In the past few years, however, there has been a huge increase in the number of studies about genuine autobiographical memory, real-world

Recognition memory for information acquired across an extended period is remarkably accurate across many years, whereas recall performance begins to decline within months.

investigations of memory for more natural experiences and information. A set of impressive investigations by Bahrick and his colleagues illustrates the nature of real-world memory for personal events.

The Bahrick Work Bahrick, Bahrick, and Wittlinger (1975) reported a fascinating study entitled "Fifty Years of Memory for Names and Faces." Nearly 400 subjects, ranging in age from 17 to 74, were tested for their retention of name and face information about members of their own high school graduating classes. For the youngest subjects, this represented a retention interval of only two weeks; for the oldest, the retention interval was 57 years. Pictures and names were taken from the subjects' high school yearbooks and were used in a variety of retention tests. In particular, subjects were asked for simple free recall of names and then were given five other tests: name recognition, picture recognition, picture-to-name matching, name-to-picture matching, and cued recall of names using pictures as cues.

Figure 5-7 shows the average performance on these six tests across the retention intervals, that is, time since graduation. The free recall curve (note that the *y*-axis on the right of the figure is to be used for free recall) shows an average of just under 50 names accessible for free recall a mere three months after graduation. Since the average size of graduating classes for all subjects was 294 (and no subjects had fewer than 90 in their classes), this level of free recall is actually quite low: it works out to

FIGURE 5-7

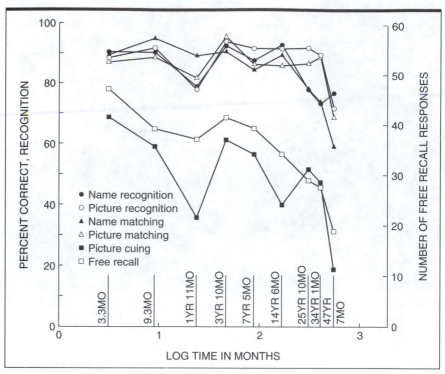

Results obtained by Bahrick et al. (1975) in their study of memory for faces and names across 50 years. The two curves that decline dramatically across intervals are recall curves, plotted against the right axis. The curves that depict recognition performance, plotted against the left axis, show remarkably high performance across a long span of time and begin to decline after about 35 years.

only about 15% of classmates' names. This number then dwindles further, so that the oldest group, having graduated an average 48 years earlier, recalled only about 18 names, something like 6% recall. Cued recall, with pictures as cues, was largely the same as free recall.

In obvious contrast, however, all four of the recognition tests showed impressive levels of retention. Simple recognition of names and faces was 90% at the three-month retention interval. Name recognition did not begin to decline noticeably until about 15 years later, and picture recognition remained in the 80–90% range until about 35 years later. And, as Bahrick et al. pointed out, the decline in the very oldest group may have been influenced by factors related to physical aging, possibly introducing a negative bias for the oldest group.

What leads to such impressive levels of retention, particularly when we compare them to the relatively lower performance of subjects in laboratory memory studies? As Bahrick et al. noted, in the typical situation, individuals have learned the names and faces of their classmates across a four-year (or longer) period. This situation is termed *prolonged acquisition*. According to the authors, this principle has two important components associated with it, *overlearning* and *distributed practice*. First, the information tested in the Bahrick et al. study was overlearned, in fact to a much higher degree than laboratory studies have examined (even Ebbinghaus didn't test the effects of a four-year-long learning phase). The result of such overlearning is much-improved retention. (Will you remember 80–90% of your Cognitive Psychology course material 35 years from now?)

Second, prolonged acquisition represents learning that was distributed across a very long period of time, in contrast to typical memory experiments in which learning opportunities are "massed" together over a short period. This neatly confirmed the standard laboratory finding that distributed practice leads to much better retention than massed practice (e.g., Underwood, Keppel, & Schulz, 1962). Bahrick's work, including memory for Spanish (1984) and math (Bahrick & Hall, 1991) learned in school, and for a city's streets and locations 50 years later (1983), shows this to be one of the soundest bits of advice that cognitive psychology gives to students. Distribute your practice and learning, rather than massing it together (better known as "cramming"). Indeed, the Bahrick results suggest that the laboratory-based effect is not only general to more naturalistic settings, but it is greatly magnified when naturalistic, everyday memories are tested (see also Hyman & Rubin, 1990; Smith & Rothkopf, 1984).

Psychologists as Subjects Finally, several modern-day Ebbinghauses have adopted the procedure of testing their *own* memories in carefully controlled, long-term studies. One major difference from Ebbinghaus's procedure was that Linton (1975, 1978), Wagenaar (1986), and Sehulster (1989) tested their memories for naturally occurring events, not artificial laboratory stimuli. For instance, Wagenaar recorded daily events in his own life for over six years, some 2400 separate events, and then tested his recall with combinations of four different cue types: *what* the event was, *who* was involved, and *where* and *when* it happened. Although he found that pleasant events were recalled better than unpleasant ones at shorter retention intervals, his evidence also showed that none of the events could truly be said to have been forgotten. Time-based cues, furthermore, were particularly useful in recalling events. Interestingly, the time lag since an event, while important, had a less powerful effect on recall than the salience or importance of the event, and the degree of emotional involvement. Sehulster's data, on memory for 25 years of performances at the Metropolitan Opera, showed very similar effects; that is, the importance or "intensity" of the performance was a predictor of superior recall.

The Relationship of Laboratory to "Real-World" Memory

The chapter ends on the lively—to say the least—debate on the value of laboratory experiments versus that of "real-world memory" research projects. The Neisser quotation you read at the beginning of the chapter, from 1978, represents one side of this debate, the side claiming that little if anything has been discovered about the "real" functioning of memory across 100 years of laboratory research (you read about another such paper, Haber's 1983 critique of iconic memory research, in Chapter 3). The argument is largely one of *ecological validity:* How can we discover how memory really works when we only test it with arbitrary tasks and arbitrary stimuli, in sterile, unrepresentative laboratory settings?

After only a few years, the opposite side of the debate was enunciated, with important papers by Mook (1983), G. R. Loftus (1983; also Utta, 1983), and others. The best known, by Banaji and Crowder (1989; also quoted in the introduction here), offers two basic criticisms of the "real-world research" movement. First, there is the undeniable fact that memory is a complex topic, influenced by a large number of variables in ways we only partly understand. In the face of this complexity, Banaji and Crowder argued, it makes no sense to abandon the laboratory setting, where extraneous variables and influences can be eliminated or held constant.

Distinctiveness or rated memorability is an important determinant of how accurately we remember an event, such as President Reagan's attempted assassination.

The second criticism was that the "promise" of everyday memory research was empty—the "bankruptcy of everyday memory" in Banaji and Crowder's words. Here the authors argued that no important insights or new discoveries had been made in the studies of everyday memory in the decade after Neisser's original remarks. Furthermore, they claimed that the results that had been obtained merely rediscovered what was already known from traditional laboratory research.

Cognitive psychology has yet to resolve this debate completely, although there has been some movement toward a more temperate position (e.g., Neisser, 1988; Conway, 1991; Neisser, 1991; Tulving, 1991). Many—no, most—agree with Banaji and Crowder that throwing out our laboratory methods and controls would be misguided. Some, however, might argue that the charge of "bankruptcy" was a bit premature. Whatever *your* position on this debate is, two fascinating outcomes were highlighted by this clash of opinions and the research that has ensued. It seems fitting to close this chapter on these outcomes, because they bring us back to our initial topics, metamemory and metacognition.

Is Human Memory So Awful?   We complain about how poor our memories are, how forgetful we are, how hard it is to learn and remember information. Are these accurate metacognitions?

Probably not. First, as Anderson and Schooler (1991) note, when we complain about memory failures, we neglect the "huge stockpile" of facts and information that we expect memory both to store and to provide access to. We underestimate the complexities, not to mention the sheer volume, of information stored in memory. Second, we fall into the trap of equating remembering with recall. When we say we've forgotten something, we probably mean we are unable to recall it right now. But as you've read repeatedly in this chapter, recall is only one way of testing memory. Recognition and relearning are far more "forgiving" in terms of showing that information has indeed been retained in memory. (And third, we focus on the failures of retrieval, without giving credit for the countless times we remember accurately; see also Chapter 11, on our tendency to search for confirming evidence.)

How much cognitive psychology will you remember in a dozen years? Your honest estimate is (probably) "not much at all." If so, then you've seriously underestimated your memory. A study by Conway, Cohen, and Stanhope (1991) examined *exactly* that, students' memory for the concepts, specific facts, names, and so on from a Cognitive Psychology course taken up to 12 years earlier. Figure 5-8 shows their results. *Recall* of material dwindled quite a bit across the 12 years, from 60% to 25% for concepts, for example. But *recognition* for the same material dropped only a bit, from 80% to around 65–70%; and recognition scores for all categories of information remained significantly above chance across all 12 years. Your honest estimate—your metacognitive awareness of having information in storage—can be quite inaccurate.

FIGURE 5-8

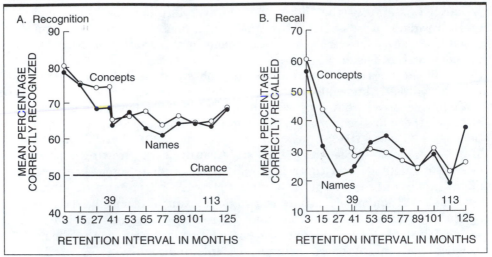

A. Mean percentages of correctly recognized names and concepts across retention intervals.
B. Mean percentages of correctly recalled names and concepts across retention intervals.
  (From Conway, Cohen, & Stanhope, 1991.)

Special "Flashbulb" Memories   On the other hand, we often seem to have—or believe we have—extremely accurate and very detailed memories for particular events, especially when the events were surprising or highly unusual. For example, Winograd and Killinger (1983) examined the "flashbulb memories" (Brown & Kulik, 1977) of college students for a significant event, the assassination of President Kennedy in 1963 (note that subjects were asked to recall their own particular circumstances when news of the event reached them, not whether they remembered the event itself). While the data showed an increase in the amount of recallable information as a function of the subject's age in 1963, the evidence also showed that the surprise or shock involved in such events may not be necessary for high levels of retention; subjects showed high recall for the Nixon resignation and the moon landing of the U.S. astronauts, neither of which was an unexpected, surprise occurrence.

Distinctiveness of the event, however, seems quite important (e.g., Schmidt, 1985). This is more than a little reminiscent of the old-fashioned **von Restorff effect,** *improved retention for a list item that is made distinct or different from the rest of the list,* say, by underlining it in red (e.g., Cooper & Pantle, 1967). And it's strikingly similar to the "surprise response" idea you encountered earlier, in connection with the effects of bizarre imagery on mnemonics (Hirshman et al., 1989).

Nonetheless, more recent studies suggest that "flashbulb memories" probably do not differ in kind from more ordinary types of memories (e.g., McCloskey, Wible, & Cohen, 1988). For instance, Christianson (1989) tested Swedish subjects' memories for the assassination of their

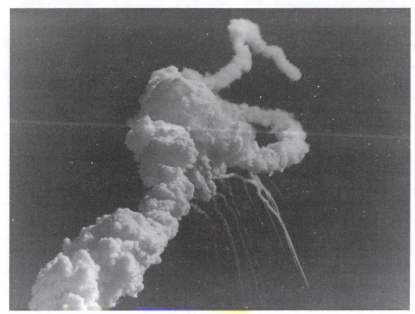

Most people recognize this distinctive photograph immediately, a picture of the explosion of the Space Shuttle Challenger. Do you remember when this disaster occurred? Do you remember what you were doing when you heard about the accident, or how you found out about it? (The Challenger exploded moments after take-off on January 22, 1986.)

prime minister in 1986, barely six weeks after the assassination and then again a year later. He found that only the general information was recalled with accuracy. Details that were recalled, in contrast, seemed to be a creative mixture of a few specifics plus more general knowledge. Despite our intuitions in such situations—"I remember *exactly* what happened" (see also Neisser, 1982) — the data indicate that no special accuracy attaches to "flashbulb memories," and therefore no special memory mechanisms need to be invented in order to account for such memories. Our metacognitive sense of *exact memory,* of a vivid, almost snapshot-like memory, is apparently often quite wrong. (Chapter 7 discusses a similar point and its relationship to the issue of eyewitness testimony.)

Summary Points: recall and recognition of autobiographical memories; overlearning, distributed practice; metacognitive awareness of remembering and forgetting; flashbulb memories

CHAPTER SUMMARY

1. The term metamemory refers to an awareness of how our memory system works and how to improve our learning and remembering. The classic method for improving such performance involves mnemonic

devices, specialized rehearsal strategies that (a) ensure adequate storage of the information and (b) provide a systematic method by which information can be retrieved. The classic mnemonic devices used a variety of techniques, especially visual imagery, to improve performance; familiarity with the mnemonic method provides a useful foundation for understanding both storage and retrieval effects in studies of memory performance.

2. Ebbinghaus was the first psychologist to conduct extensive investigations into the processes of learning and forgetting. Working on his own, Ebbinghaus invented methods of conducting such investigations; his use of the relearning task revealed a sensitivity to the demands of simple recall tasks, that such tasks tap consciously retrievable information, but may underestimate the amount of information actually learned and retained in memory. The classic forgetting curve he obtained, along with his results on practice effects, inspired the tradition of verbal learning and, later, cognitive psychology.

3. "Storage" in long-term memory is somewhat of a misnomer, since subjects are often asked to "learn" words they already know, so storage, or transfer to long-term memory, means tagging or noting in some fashion that a set of words was on the list to be learned. The important variables in storage are rehearsal and organization, whether these involve just verbal concepts or also include visual imagery and other nonverbal features.

4. Maintenance and elaborative rehearsal were generally viewed as having two distinctly different functions, the former for mere recycling of information without increasing its likelihood of retrieval, the latter for more semantically based elaboration and enrichment, where such rehearsal processed the information more deeply into the memory system and made it more memorable. Difficulties in this depth of processing framework involved definitions of the two types of rehearsal and specification of the notion of "depth." When memory performance is tested with a recognition task, the results often seem to disconfirm the hypothesis that maintenance rehearsal merely maintains information but does not make it more memorable.

5. Generally, the amount of rehearsal is positively related to recall accuracy for the primacy portion of a list. Organization, especially by category, but also by subjectively defined chunks or clusters, improves memory performance because it (a) stores the information securely and (b) provides a useful structure for successful retrieval. According to the encoding specificity principle, any related information that was encoded along with the studied information should serve as an effective retrieval cue. This is the case even if that related information is normally a lower-strength associate of the to-be-remembered material.

6. Interference was once thought to cause true forgetting from long-term memory. While interference is easily demonstrated in the laboratory using either proactive or retroactive interference tasks, the evidence

now suggests that interference may disrupt retrieval. On this view, retrieval failure is not an issue of true forgetting, since information stored in long-term memory remains available in memory. Instead, retrieval failure is often due to loss of access to the stored information. Effective retrieval cues provide access to otherwise unretrievable information.

7. Studies of autobiographical memory, or memory in real-world settings, show the same kinds of effects as laboratory studies, but sometimes more strongly. Recognition memory for information acquired across an extended period is remarkably accurate across many years, whereas recall performance begins to decline within months. Other autobiographical memory studies support the conclusions that long-term memory information is not truly forgotten, that distinctiveness or rated memorability is an important determinant of how accurately we can remember such events, and that our metacognitive awareness of how well we remember can often be quite faulty.

Glossary Terms: autobiographical memory; clustering; depth of processing; encoding specificity; episodic and semantic memory; flashbulb memories; interference versus decay; maintenance and elaborative rehearsal; metamemory; method of loci; mnemonic devices; nonsense syllables; paired-associate learning; peg-word mnemonic; primacy effect; recall, free and serial; recency effect; recognition; rehearsal; relearning; retrieval cue; savings score; serial position; subjective organization; TOT; visual imagery; von Restorff effect

SUGGESTED READINGS

Bower's 1970 paper on mnemonic devices is excellent, so your outside readings in this area should begin with this paper. Several books have dealt with mnemonics. An especially popular one by Lorayne and Lucas (1974), entitled *The Memory Book,* goes into great detail on a variety of mnemonic devices, including a system for remembering names and faces. I've always preferred Cermak's (1975) *Improving Your Memory,* however, since it contains almost all the same information in a much shorter and more useful fashion. Mendelson's (1993) book discusses memory improvement from the perspective of the normal aging process. Norman's (1976) book also contains a chapter on mnemonics. If you're more historically inclined, Yates's (1966) *The Art of Memory* is a fascinating review of the history of such devices, with quotations from the originals. And Luria's (1968) *The Mind of a Mnemonist* remains a classic study in the area of mnemonic devices.

The special issue of the *Journal of Experimental Psychology: Learning, Memory, and Cognition* that contains the 100th anniversary papers on Ebbinghaus is the July 1985 issue (Vol. 11, No. 3, pp. 413–500). Slamecka's delightful and informative introductory article is followed by 12 briefer articles commenting on various aspects of the Ebbinghaus tradition, and a final rejoinder by Slamecka; the 12 shorter pieces were written by a *Who's Who* list of researchers in the learning and memory field. A similar and also worthy collection is in Gorfein and Hoffman (1987).

The original book on autobiographical memory was Gruneberg, Morris, and Sykes (1978). Neisser (1982) has edited a book entitled *Memory Observed: Remembering in Natural Contexts,* which delves into both autobiographical memory and the topic of ecologically valid memory research. A fascinating study of John Dean's memory, also by Neisser (1981), appears in the book; in this paper, Neisser contrasts Dean's testimony before the Congressional committee with the transcripts of tape-recorded meetings between Dean and President Nixon. Neisser's conclusion was that Dean's memory was excellent for overall "gist," but no better than anyone else's on specific details. More recent sets of papers on autobiographical memory are found in Rubin (1986) and Cohen (1989). Consult the Banaji and Crowder (1989) paper and the entire "Science Watch" section of the *American Psychologist,* January 1991, for extensive discussion—and occasional "zingers"—in the debate between laboratory and real-world memory advocates.

Finally, Tulving's *Elements of Episodic Memory* (1983) is a substantive review of memory research accompanied by his personal reflections on various topics. Since Tulving is one of the true giants in the learning and memory field, his thoughtful comments and observations are often more important and provocative than others' carefully designed research and theories.

Chapter 6

SEMANTIC LONG-TERM MEMORY

▼ **Semantic Memory**

▼ **Categorization, Concepts, and Prototypes**

▼ **Priming in Semantic Memory**

▼ **The Generality of Semantic Networks**

[Memory is] a very complex representation, that of the fact to be recalled plus *its associates, the whole forming one "object" . . . known in one integral pulse of consciousness . . . and demanding probably a vastly more intricate brain-process than that on which any simple sensorial image depends. (James, 1890, pp. 650–651; 1983 edition, p. 612)*

Semantic memory is the memory necessary for the use of language. It is a mental thesaurus, organized knowledge a person possesses about words and other verbal symbols, their meaning and referents, about relations among them, and about rules, formulas, and algorithms for the manipulation of these symbols, concepts, and relations. (Tulving, 1972, p. 386)

Human concepts are probably . . . like hooks or nodes in a network from which many different properties hang. The properties hanging from a node are not likely to be all equally accessible; some properties are more important than others, and so may be reached more easily or quickly. . . . Thus, a concept would be a set of interrelationships among other concepts . . . everything is defined in terms of everything else . . . like a dictionary. (Collins & Quillian, 1972, pp. 313–314)

It is now known that human memory is associative in nature. (Wickelgren, 1973)

This chapter is concerned with a rather different kind of long-term memory than that discussed in Chapter 5. It concerns *semantic memory,* literally "memory for meaning," or to put it simply, "knowledge." **Semantic memory** is our *permanent memory store of general world knowledge,* variously described as a thesaurus, a dictionary, or an encyclopedia. Semantic memory is where your knowledge of language and other conceptual information is stored. It is the permanent repository of information you use to comprehend and produce language, to reason, to solve problems, and to make decisions. Whereas episodic memory is a personal, autobiographical store, semantic memory is a generic storehouse of knowledge.[1] That is, while your episodic memory differs substantially from mine, our semantic memories are thought to be largely similar—maybe not in exact content, depending on our cultural backgrounds, but certainly similar in terms of structure and processes. Thus you have no idea what *my* mother's maiden name is, but we all share a highly similar concept in semantic memory, the *concept* of a maiden

---

[1]Hintzman's (1978) term *generic memory* is a better one than *semantic memory* for at least two reasons. First, it implies the notion of "general world knowledge" more accurately, just as "generic green beans" implies regular, ordinary green beans. Second, the term *semantic memory* might be understood incorrectly to refer exclusively to language-based memories and thereby could exclude general world knowledge that is not word-based, for example, images (whether visual, kinesthetic, or otherwise) or knowledge of numbers and mathematics. Nonetheless, the term *semantic memory* was used first, it's the one we have gotten in the habit of using, and it's probably useless to try to change now.

name. Likewise, my specific memories of college are quite different from yours, but we all share a general kind of knowledge about being a college student.

As Tulving (1972) noted, the first usage of the term *semantic memory* appears to have been in M. Ross Quillian's doctoral dissertation in 1966. Quillian set himself the task of programming a computer to understand language, that is, to answer a variety of questions in a reasonably human-like fashion, and to be able to paraphrase English text. The inspiration for this work came not from psychology, but instead from computer science and artificial intelligence (AI). Machine translation, as it was known, had been a long-standing goal in computer science, yet progress toward this goal had been surprisingly slow. The overly confident predictions of the 1950s had failed to take into account a subtle yet important fact—even the simplest acts of human comprehension require vast amounts of knowledge, much more than the words to be comprehended would suggest. Thus for computers to understand, answer questions, or paraphrase, they needed to have this kind of knowledge base. It wasn't enough to have dictionary definitions of words: computers needed to have extensive knowledge of the world in order to understand even simple sentences. This is often referred to as *tacit knowledge,* the implied but not stated knowledge that is necessary to understand what *is* stated or mentioned.

A clear-cut illustration of the importance of tacit knowledge, with its implications both for machine translation and human comprehension, was contained in the Collins and Quillian (1972) chapter in *Organization of Memory.* Although lengthy, it expresses the scope of the issue quite well and demonstrates the need for a memory containing semantic information:

> At one time, I was trying to get a computer to be able to read sentences from pre-school children's books. My aim was to have the computer relate these sentences correctly to some body of information it had stored, its memory or "knowledge of the world." One such book, which described crossing a street, contained the sentences [sic], "The policeman held up his hand and the cars stopped." Now, suppose one asks what is the minimum amount of information a mechanism must have stored to relate this sentence to, if it is to comprehend it in a reasonably human-like way? In particular, consider whether the machine must have stored the fact that moving cars usually have drivers? One's first thought might well be no, since drivers aren't mentioned or directly involved in the sentence. But, suppose the sentences preceding this one in the book had said that there had just been an earthquake, and that two cars, parked on a hill, had started to roll down it. Then comes the sentence above, "The policeman held up his hand and the cars stopped." Virtually every adult reader of this will wonder: just how did the policeman manage that? In other words, in understanding the initial sentence, it seems that there indeed was some tacit use of the knowledge that cars ordinarily have drivers. If there were not, how can it be that, once a reader is led to believe that a moving car lacks a driver, he will then recognize that something is strange about a policeman being able to stop it just by holding up his hand? (pp. 327–328)

Semantic memory contains our long-term memory knowledge of the world, including our knowledge of words, concepts, and language.

Quillian's explicit point in this passage was that a computer must have a great deal of knowledge available in memory about the real world, even if it is only to comprehend a seemingly simple sentence. The implicit point in the quotation, and the point in the Collins and Quillian chapter as well, was that an adequate understanding of how *humans* comprehend language must take into account the same vast storehouse of knowledge that a computer would have to possess. The study of that vast storehouse is the study of semantic memory.

This chapter covers the basics of semantic memory, the fundamental structures and processes investigated in semantic memory research. We'll ask questions like "How is the meaning of a word represented in memory?" and "How are word meanings retrieved from memory?" We'll encounter the first wide-scale use of time as a measure of mental processes, *reaction time (RT)* to respond to simple sentences such as "A robin has wings." We'll consider two specific psychological models of semantic memory, theories that were advanced to explain what it is people know about words and word meanings, concepts, and their interrelationships. And finally, we'll return to two important ideas introduced earlier in the book, priming and automaticity.

This will set the stage for the following chapter, where the divisions of long-term memory are studied together. There, we'll delve into the question of *interactions* between the episodic and semantic systems. For instance, how does our general world knowledge influence our memory for specific events? We'll also deal with a new and important distinction in memory research, the difference between *implicit* and *explicit* memory tasks. Throughout both chapters—indeed, throughout the remainder of the book—the theme we will be most concerned with is the representation of knowledge, in Kintsch's (1974) terms, *The Representation of Meaning in Memory,* and retrieval of that knowledge.

▼ Semantic Memory

A study on "leading questions," also discussed in the next chapter, provides a convenient entry into the topic of semantic memory. Loftus and Palmer (1974) showed their subjects several short traffic safety films that involved car accidents. The subjects were asked to describe each accident after seeing the film and then were asked a series of questions. One of the questions asked for an estimate of the car's speed. As the authors pointed out, people are notoriously poor at estimating such factors, indicating that there might be some room for leading questions to have an effect. One group of subjects was asked "About how fast were the cars going when they hit each other?" The other four groups were asked virtually the same question, except that the verb "hit" was replaced with either "smashed," "collided," "bumped," or "contacted." As you might expect, subjects who got the stronger verbs like "smashed" in their questions gave higher estimates of speed: the question led them to a biased answer.

Hold it. *Why* would we expect this effect? Why are we not surprised that people estimated higher speeds when the question said "smashed" instead of "bumped" or "hit"? Our intuitive answer here is something like "Well, 'smashed' implies a more severe accident than 'bumped.'" But consider this intuitive answer again. *How* did Loftus and Palmer's subjects know that "smashed" implies a more severe accident? It's not enough merely to say that "smashed" *means* more severe. We're asking a more basic question than that. We want to know what is stored in memory that tells you what "smash" and "bump" mean. How is the difference between those two concepts *represented* in memory, and how do you *retrieve* those concepts when you encounter those words? How does memory represent the fact that "smashed" implies a severe accident, that robins have wings, that moving cars have drivers, or that bananas, canaries, and daisies are all yellow? In short, what is the structure and content of semantic memory *per se,* and how do we access the knowledge stored in it?

As you just learned, one of the earliest systematic attempts to answer such questions (aside from philosophical and strictly linguistic analyses) was Quillian's work in artificial intelligence (e.g., 1968, 1969). His model of semantic memory, *TLC* (for Teachable Language Comprehender), was not a genuine psychological model, but rather a computer program for understanding language.[2] Very shortly, however, Quillian began a collaboration with Allan Collins, and the psychological model they based on TLC became the first serious attempt in cognitive psychology to explain the structure and processes of semantic memory.

The Collins and Quillian (and Loftus) Model

The Collins and Quillian model of semantic memory (1972, also 1969, 1970; Collins & Loftus, 1975)[3] was an extensive theory of semantic memory, comprehension, and meaning. At the heart of the model were two fundamentally important assumptions—one about the *structure* of semantic memory and one about the *process* of retrieving information from that structure. Because these two assumptions have been typical of many models since the early Collins and Quillian work (e.g., Glass & Holyoak, 1975), including current connectionist models, you need a firm grasp on what they mean.

Nodes in a Network   As you read in the opening quotations, Collins and Quillian viewed the entries in semantic memory—the *concepts* in semantic memory—as being nodes in a network. In other words, the structure of semantic memory was said to be a **network,** *an interrelated set of concepts, or interrelated body of knowledge.* Each concept in the network is represented as a **node,** *a point or location* in the semantic space.

Furthermore, concept nodes are linked together by **pathways,** *labeled, directional associations between concepts.* This entire collection—nodes connected to other nodes by pathways—is the network. Note that in such a structure, every concept is related to every other concept, in the sense that some set of pathways, however indirect and long, can eventually be traced between any two nodes. (At one point, Collins and Quillian used the analogy of a large fishnet, where the knots correspond to nodes, and the strings that go from one knot to the next correspond to pathways.)

---

[2]Originally, there was a distinction between Artificial Intelligence and Computer Simulation; AI modeled human processes but was relatively unconcerned that the modeling stick to known facts about human mental processes, whereas Simulation modeled human processes to discover more about how humans did various mental operations. Quillian's research fell into the category of Artificial Intelligence. For a variety of reasons (see Chapter 13), the original distinction has largely been abandoned. Putting it simply, the AI approach doesn't work very well without a thorough knowledge of human mental processing.

[3]There were differences, of course, in the specifics of the models in these several papers, but for present purposes all are treated as roughly the same. Two issues about which the original model was vague did attract a great deal of experimental attention—the issue of cognitive economy and the representation of what was later referred to as typicality. Most debates over these issues, and whether or not the original model did or didn't account for the facts (e.g., Collins & Loftus, 1975; Smith, 1978), tended to degenerate into hair-splitting and so are not treated in any depth here (but see Chang's, 1986, thoughtful review).

Spreading Activation   The major process that operates on this structure is **spreading activation,** the *mental activity of accessing and retrieving information from this network.* Concepts are usually in a relatively quiet, unactivated state: they are at some resting, baseline level. For example, at this very instant in time, as you're reading this sentence, one of the many concepts in your semantic memory that is probably not activated is "machine." When you read that word, however, its mental representation receives a boost in activation; "machine" is no longer quiet and unactivated, it's active or primed, "awakened" so to speak. This activation, for Collins and Quillian, *was* the process of retrieval, the process of accessing the meaning of a concept.

A key feature of activation is that it spreads through the network. That is, once a concept becomes activated, it begins to spread that activation to all the other concepts to which it is linked. Thus activation begins at a concept node and then starts spreading throughout the network along the connecting pathways. The spread of activation corresponds to a search through memory. In Collins and Quillian's particularly apt description, the "search continually widens like a harmless spreading plague" (1972, p. 326).

Look at panel A in Figure 6-1, a simple diagram of a few concepts and the interconnecting pathways among them. Even such a simple network codes or represents a great deal of information. For instance, some of the facts coded in this network are that ROBIN is a member of the category BIRD, that a ROBIN has a RED BREAST, that a CANARY is YELLOW, and so on. Each of these simple connections records an elementary fact or **proposition,** a *relationship between two concepts.*

Note further that each of the pathways joining two concept nodes is a *labeled and directed* pathway. Each pathway specifies a certain relationship and the direction of that relationship. Thus ROBIN *isa* BIRD, *is a member of the category* BIRD, and BIRD has the *property* FEATHERS.[4] Moreover, the illustrations in Figure 6-1 show what would happen to this portion of your semantic network when the word "Robin" is presented. First, the concept corresponding to "Robin" becomes activated, illustrated by **boldface** in panel A. After this, the concept ROBIN will begin to spread activation to those concepts it is linked to, the **boldface** BIRD, RED BREAST, and BLUE EGGS concepts in panel B. *Those* concepts continue the spread of activation to *their* associated nodes, as depicted in panel C.

Collins and Quillian proposed that such a spread of activation is triggered each time a concept is activated in semantic memory. Thus when *two* concepts become activated, there are *two* simultaneous spreads of

---

[4]The *isa* relationship, indicating category membership, was a bit of cognitive jargon contributed by Rumelhart, Lindsay, and Norman (1972), in the same book as the 1972 paper by Collins and Quillian; it means "is a," as in "is a member of the category." The importance of the direction of the relationship is well illustrated by *isa,* since the reversed direction for *isa* is not true, that is, *All BIRDS are ROBINS. (Note: By convention, sentences that are intentionally wrong are prefaced by an asterisk.)

FIGURE 6-1

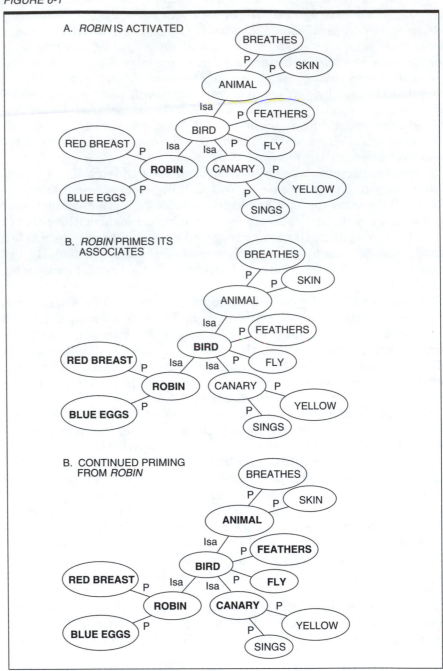

A portion of the semantic network is illustrated. In panel A, the concept ROBIN has been activated and is shown in boldface. In panel B, the spreading activation from ROBIN has now activated concepts linked to ROBIN, for example, the boldface BIRD, RED BREAST, and BLUE EGGS. In panel C, the continued spread of activation that originated from ROBIN is depicted.

activation, one from each concept node. As an exercise, study the top portion of Figure 6-1 and mark which concept nodes will become activated by a sentence like "A robin can breathe." To keep track of the original source of activation, write a 1 next to pathways and nodes that will be activated by ROBIN, and a 2 next to those activated by BREATHE. Take this demonstration through at least two cycles; first, the original node activates its connected nodes, then, second, those nodes activate *their* connected nodes. (In a sense, you are "hand simulating" the computerized memory search in TLC. This is a laborious process, which highlights one of the attractive features of computer simulation and artificial intelligence programming. Let the computer do all the dreary work of spreading the activation and keeping track of the sources, while you merely wait at your terminal for the program to tell you the final outcome of the search.)

Intersection Search What did you discover in that exercise? If you did it correctly, you should have discovered two important properties of spreading activation search. First, you found that the activation originating with ROBIN eventually primed a node that was *also* primed or activated by BREATHE. This is the *exact* process proposed by Collins and Quillian, and originally programmed into Quillian's TLC model, to explain how information is retrieved from semantic memory. The "harmless spreading plague" eventually encounters another "harmless spreading plague" that came from a different source. When that happens, then a connecting route or set of pathways has been retrieved from semantic memory. In the terminology of the model, *when the two spreads of activation encounter one another,* an **intersection** has been found between the two concepts, ROBIN and BREATHE.

Once an intersection has been found, a decision stage must operate to make sure that the retrieved pathway is valid, that is, it represents the relationship specified in the sentence. In other words, a similar pathway would be found between ANIMAL and RED BREAST as between ROBIN and BREATHE, but the decision stage would decide that it's not true that "all animals have red breasts." (Incidentally, this should sound somewhat familiar, a search stage followed by a decision stage; see Chapter 2 on a process model, or Chapter 4 on the Sternberg task.)

Related Concepts The second characteristic of intersection search that you should have discovered is that *other* concepts also become activated or primed during the search. That is, the intersection pathway was ROBIN *isa* BIRD *isa* ANIMAL *property* BREATHE. But many other concepts were also primed during the search; there should also be a 1 next to RED BREAST and BLUE EGGS from the first cycle, a 1 next to FLY, FEATHERS, and CANARY after the second cycle, and so on. Thus a spreading activation search not only retrieves the relevant pathway between two concepts, it also activates *related* concepts. These related concepts will not remain activated forever, of course, since activation is always presumed to decay after some amount of time. Nonetheless, for a short period, these related concepts have received a boost in their activation levels, making them temporarily more accessible. This *priming* of related concepts is absolutely key to an understanding of semantic processing; we'll return to it repeatedly throughout the chapter, and indeed throughout the entire book.

Smith's Feature Overlap Model

Given the excitement of studying meaning and how it is represented in memory, it is not surprising that other approaches to semantic memory soon appeared. We'll focus here on only one of those other approaches, the Smith Feature Overlap Model, since it offered a rather clear contrast to the Collins and Quillian model in some basic assumptions, and since it was the most successful challenger to that model. (See Chang, 1986, for a review of all the major models.)

Feature Lists   Smith's model (e.g., Smith, Rips, & Shoben, 1974) was considerably simpler than the Collins and Quillian network model in its assumptions about the structure of semantic memory, but as a consequence it was somewhat more elaborate in its assumptions about the process of retrieval. Its most basic structural element was the **feature list.** Rather than postulating extensive networks of concepts and pathways, Smith et al. suggested that we consider semantic memory to be a collection of lists. Each concept in semantic memory was represented as a list of **semantic features,** *simple, one-element characteristics or properties of the concept.* Thus the concept ROBIN would be represented as a list of ROBIN's features, like animate, red-breasted, smallish, winged, and feathered (see Figure 6-2).

Smith et al. suggested that these feature lists were ordered in terms of a factor they called *definingness.* That is, Smith et al. said that the feature lists stored in memory were ordered in a kind of priority ranking, with the most defining features for a concept toward the top of the list and the least defining features toward the bottom. Thus an absolutely *essential feature* was called a **defining feature,** like *animate* for BIRD, and would be stored near the top of the feature list. Conversely, features that are not particularly defining for the concept, say, that a ROBIN *perches in trees,* would be placed toward the bottom of the list. In fact, Smith et al. proposed that these lower features were more appropriately called **characteristic features** of the concept, *features that are merely common or frequent, but not essential to the meaning of the concept.* Thus characteristic features do not *define* what it is to be a ROBIN or BIRD: they may or may not perch in trees. But defining features are essential: to be a robin, it absolutely has to be animate.

FIGURE 6-2

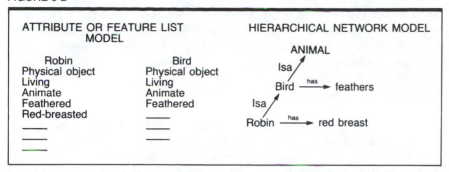

ATTRIBUTE OR FEATURE LIST MODEL | HIERARCHICAL NETWORK MODEL

Robin — Physical object, Living, Animate, Feathered, Red-breasted

Bird — Physical object, Living, Animate, Feathered

ANIMAL — Isa — Bird — has → feathers — Isa — Robin — has → red breast

Information in semantic memory is represented differently in feature list models and in hierarchical network models. In feature list models, a concept is represented as a list of simple semantic features; in hierarchical network models, concepts are represented as nodes that connect to other nodes via pathways. The Smith et al. (1974) model is a feature list model, and the Collins and Quillian (1972) model is a hierarchical network model. (Adapted from Smith, 1978.)

Feature Comparison The major process of information retrieval in the Smith model was a feature comparison process; follow along with the sequence of processes illustrated in Figure 6-3 as you read. Say you were given the sentence "A robin is a bird," and had to make a true/false judgment. According to the model, you would access the two concepts ROBIN and BIRD in semantic memory and then would proceed to compare the features on those two lists. This *Stage I* feature comparison process

FIGURE 6-3

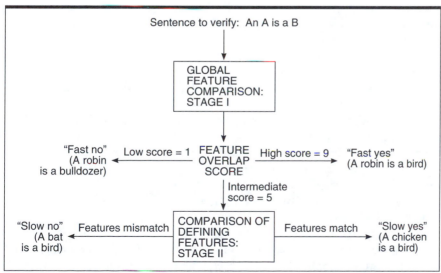

Sentence to verify: An A is a B

GLOBAL FEATURE COMPARISON: STAGE I

"Fast no" (A robin is a bulldozer) ← Low score = 1 — FEATURE OVERLAP SCORE — High score = 9 → "Fast yes" (A robin is a bird)

Intermediate score = 5

"Slow no" (A bat is a bird) ← Features mismatch — COMPARISON OF DEFINING FEATURES: STAGE II — Features match → "Slow yes" (A chicken is a bird)

The comparison and decision processes in the Smith et al. model, with sample sentences.

involved a global comparison of the features: some randomly selected subset of features on each of the two lists would be compared in order to "compute" the similarity between the two concepts. This comparison process yielded a *feature overlap score,* simply an index or measurement of the similarity of the two concepts; for illustration purposes here, assume that these scores range from 1 to 10.

Of course, for the concepts in "A robin is a bird," the feature lists should overlap a great deal: there are hardly any ROBIN features that aren't also BIRD features. The outcome of this feature comparison process then would be a very high overlap score (e.g., 8 or 9), so high that you could confidently respond "yes" immediately on the basis of this global comparison of features. Conversely, with a sentence like "A robin is a bulldozer," there should be so little feature overlap (e.g., 1 or 2) that you could respond "no" immediately without any further processing. These "fast yes" and "fast no" responses were called *Stage I responses* by Smith et al. When overlap scores are either very high or very low, there is no need to continue the search, so a response is made immediately.

Consider two other kinds of sentences, where the stated relationship isn't quite so obvious. First, consider "A chicken is a bird." As before, the process of retrieving information is the feature comparison process, now being performed on the CHICKEN and BIRD features. Most people's intuition is that chickens are a somewhat less "representative" example of the bird category. Compared to your "average" bird, chickens seem rather unusual—they don't perch or make nests in trees, they don't eat worms, they're larger, and so on. Isn't it clear then that the Stage I comparison process should find only an intermediate degree of overlap between CHICKEN and BIRD? Smith et al. claimed that when the overlap scores indicated only moderate similarity (say, between 4 and 6), a second comparison was necessary. The second comparison was referred to as a *Stage II comparison.*

Unlike the fast, global Stage I comparison, the Stage II comparison was a careful and rather slow one, and it used *only* the defining features to compute its evidence. Thus for the CHICKEN–BIRD sentence, only the defining features of the two concepts would be compared in Stage II. Since it is in fact true that chickens are birds, presumably there would be a match on all the tested features in this stage, yielding a "slow yes" response; the response would be "slow" because it involved Stage II comparison, and "yes" because all the defining features from CHICKEN would match those from BIRD.

Finally, consider the sentence "A bat is a bird." This sentence should also yield a moderate overlap score during Stage I, thus necessitating a Stage II comparison. During Stage II, however, there will be several important *mismatches.* It would seem that only the characteristic features of bats make them similar to birds. Their defining features (mammal, furry, teeth, etc.) give rather convincing evidence, however, that the sentence is false. This would be a "slow no" response, "slow" because it required Stage II processing, and "no" because of mismatches on the defining features.

Summary Points: network models; nodes, pathways, and spreading activation; priming; feature comparison; defining and characteristic features

Empirical Tests of Semantic Memory Models

Most of the early tests of semantic memory models adopted what was known as the **sentence verification task,** in which *simple sentences are presented for the subjects' yes/no decisions.* The stimuli often used the frame "An *S* is a *P*" (e.g., "A robin is a bird" or "A canary is green"), where *S* stood for Subject (robin, canary), and *P* stood for Predicate (bird, green). Accuracy scores for subjects' decisions about these simple sentences wouldn't tell us much, of course: people seldom are in doubt or make mistakes about such simple facts. Thus reaction time (RT) tests were the usual method of testing semantic memory models. Present subjects with simple sentences, some true and some false, and *time* the subjects as they make their yes/no decisions (the speed emphasis is clearly implied in the Smith et al. "fast" and "slow" responses). As is generally the case in the information processing framework, the assumption is that time provides a window into the unseen mental processes, here the processes of semantic memory search and decision.

Note, however, a distinguishing feature of semantic memory tasks, as opposed to virtually all the short-term and episodic long-term memory tasks we've discussed. In semantic memory tasks we are testing people on the *knowledge they already possess,* their conceptual, general world knowledge about robins, machines, and so on. The tasks for both short-term and episodic long-term memory provide a set of stimuli for the subject to master, to hold in short-term memory or to commit to long-term memory. Semantic memory tests, conversely, rely on subjects' existing conceptual knowledge. When subjects walk into the lab, they are not asked to learn a list, but instead are asked to demonstrate what they already know by saying "yes" or "no" to the stimulus sentences. Clearly, the tests rely on the assumption that people have the relevant knowledge in memory and, furthermore, that such semantic knowledge is largely similar among individuals (or at least is similar among the individuals within a language culture). Table 6-1 covers the basics of this kind of task.

Early Results Collins and Quillian's (1969) earliest report tested an obvious prediction from their model, that two concepts that are closer together in the network should require less time for verification than two that are farther apart. Refer again to Figure 6-1 and to the "hand simu-

Table 6-1   RECOGNITION TASKS IN SEMANTIC MEMORY

In Table 5-5, the recognition task consisted of two basic steps; the subject first learned a set of words on a list, and then made yes/no decisions on a test list, yes if the test word had been on the studied list, no if it had not been on the studied list. The two important features that make this a recognition test are:

1. Subjects make yes/no or forced choice decisions.
2. The decisions are based on information stored in memory.

For research in semantic memory, this task has been generalized to include information already stored in long-term memory prior to the beginning of the experiment.

Generalized Recognition Task (Semantic)

1. Information to be tested is already in long-term memory, for example, knowledge of categories ("A robin is a bird") or of words.

2. Make yes/no decisions to a sequence of test items, presented one at a time. Unlike episodic recognition tasks, here the "yes" response usually means the item is true. For example, in a sentence verification task, subjects say "yes" to "A robin is a bird," that is, to any sentence that is true. In a lexical decision task, subjects respond "yes" if the letter string is a word (e.g., MOTOR) and "no" if it is not (e.g., MANTY).

Dependent Variables: Typically, the major dependent variable is reaction time (RT), although accuracy is also important. Because the task usually involves yes/no decisions, guessing rate is usually 50%; if accuracy drops to 70% or 80%, then RT is somewhat questionable, often because subjects have traded accuracy for speed (i.e., they're faster than they would have been if they had maintained higher accuracy). Occasionally, subjects are given a response deadline; that is, they are given a signal after some brief interval, say, 300 msec, and must respond immediately after the signal. In such a task, error rate becomes the major dependent variable. Quite recently, different patterns of brain waves (ERPs) have been used instead of RT or errors (see the description of Kounios & Holcomb, 1992, in this chapter, and work described in Chapter 10).

Independent Variables: An enormous range of independent variables can be tested: for example, the semantic relatedness between concepts in a sentence like "An S is/has a P"; word length, frequency, concreteness, and the like in a lexical decision task; and the number of times a stimulus (word, picture) is repeated in the sequence of trials, and how recently it was repeated (referred to as "lag").

---

lation" you performed. If we assume that your conceptual knowledge about this portion of semantic memory is accurately represented in the figure, then several predictions can be made. For example, which sentence should be faster to verify, "A robin is a bird" or "A robin is an animal?" Right—"A robin is a bird," because it should take less time for the spread of activation to intersect for this sentence than for the "A robin is an animal" sentence. Likewise, if the figure is accurate, it should take less time to verify that canaries are yellow than that canaries can fly or that they breathe, again for the same reason.

Figure 6-4 shows the results of Collins and Quillian's (1969) test of these predictions. In the figure, Collins and Quillian used the symbol S to indicate a superordinate statement, what we've been calling *isa* sentences, and a P to indicate property statements. Tagged onto the S or P was a digit from 0 to 2, which indicated how many levels in the hierarchy the search had to proceed through in order to find the stated concept. As

FIGURE 6-4

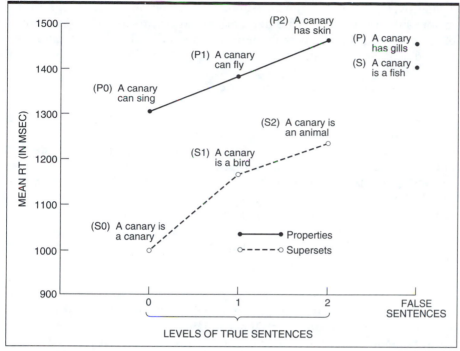

Reaction time to superordinate (S) sentences and property (P) sentences is shown as a function of levels within the hierarchy. An S2 sentence involves a superordinate connection two levels up the hierarchy; S1 means one level up in the hierarchy; a 0 level sentence had the predicate stored at the same hierarchical level. (From Collins & Quillian, 1969.)

you can see, reaction time increased as the semantic distance between the two concepts increased. For the superordinate sentences, searching for an S2 relationship (e.g., "A canary is an animal") required about 75 msec longer than searching for an S1 relationship ("A canary is a bird"). The same increase in time was also found for property sentences going up 1 versus 2 levels. (Note that a P0 sentence meant "up 0 levels": that is, the second term in the sentence, the predicate, was stored at the same level in the hierarchy as the subject of the sentence; for example, "A canary can sing.")

Collins and Quillian concluded that it takes longer to retrieve a relationship between two concepts when those concepts are stored farther apart in the semantic structure. Moreover, it appeared from these results that the *isa* pathways were stronger than the *property* pathways, since superordinate sentences were faster overall than property sentences (see Hampton, 1984, for confirmation).[5]

---

[5]Collins and Quillian, of course, tested many more concepts than just canaries and robins, although the tradition in this area of research is to illustrate the models using these words. In a depressing example of literal-mindedness, a student of mine once answered an essay question on semantic memory by saying "Collins and Quillian devised a psychological model to explain what people know about birds."

Clashing Models and Explanations   While this result sounds like strong evidence for the network model, it turns out that it was by no means a definitive test; it did not distinguish Collins and Quillian's model from the Smith et al. approach, for instance (although it might be argued that Smith et al. designed their model specifically to account for this kind of result).

Consider the feature overlap process in the Smith et al. model and how it would operate on these sentences. It should be clear that, on the average, there should be less feature overlap between any two concepts when those concepts are farther removed from one another in the hierarchy depicted in Figure 6-1 (note, however, that the Smith et al. model did *not* structure concepts into a hierarchy and that the rigid hierarchical scheme was later abandoned by Collins and Loftus [1975]). Sentences like "A robin is an animal," which Collins and Quillian called S2 sentences, would yield lower overlap scores than sentences like "A robin is a bird" (an S1 sentence) during a feature comparison process. Thus, on the average, more S2 sentences would need the extra comparison step of Smith et al.'s Stage II. This would of course tend to slow down the comparison process.

Let's discuss three specific issues that were debated in the literature as evidence for or against these two models: cognitive economy, property statements, and typicality. You'll get a flavor for how cognitive psychology tests models and theories, and in the process you'll encounter the evidence for the strongest generalization about semantic memory, a generalization known as the semantic distance or semantic relatedness effect. Although it was not necessarily clear at the time, all three of these issues are different expressions of the same underlying generalization: semantic memory's structure is based on semantic relatedness among concepts.

Cognitive Economy   A clear commitment of Quillian's (1969) TLC model was that redundant information is *not* stored in memory: "The sheer quantity of information involved . . . argues strongly that both the human subject's memory and our model thereof contain as little redundancy as possible and that it [should] contain stored facts only when these cannot otherwise be generated or inferred" (p. 228). This position has been given the name **cognitive economy**. To economize in the number of concepts that must be stored, *only nonredundant facts will be stored in memory.*

A rather straightforward example of this principle is that FLY appears only with BIRD in Figure 6-1, instead of also with ROBIN and CANARY. It seems very likely that Quillian adopted this principle because of his work with computer modeling. That is, storage space is at a premium in computer models (and certainly was in the late 1960s), so the principle of cognitive economy is a convenient principle to adopt for such work. Furthermore, the simple inference process, retrieving a property from a superordinate, could be invoked over and over and would yield the same outcome—knowledge that a robin does fly, for instance. Although the original statement of the psychological model (Collins & Quillian, 1969) indicated that an extreme stance on this principle was not being proposed, most early investigators realized that some degree of cognitive economy was intended.

There is clearly a grain or two of truth in the cognitive economy idea. After all, it strains the imagination to suppose that we fill our memories with such facts as "The philosopher Aristotle had two hands," that we would waste mental effort and space in such a colossal fashion. But where do we draw the line between information stored directly versus information relegated to the inference process? (Note that this is not an issue of insufficient space in memory; see Chapter 10.)

Another difficulty with the principle of cognitive economy involves more ordinary concepts and the issue of forgetting. For example, if as a child you learned that robins fly, you would store a connecting pathway between ROBIN and FLY in semantic memory. You might continue to do so for other birds as well, until you later found out that almost *all* birds fly. The principle of cognitive economy would seem to imply that when you learned the more general fact, and stored a pathway between BIRD and FLY, the redundant pathways to FLY from ROBIN and other birds would have to be *erased* or forgotten. This is a rather difficult position to swallow, given what we know about forgetting from long-term memory. To their credit, Collins and Quillian (1969) tested sentences in their experiment that *seemed* likely to require inferences—for instance, "A canary has skin." Nonetheless, the possibility existed that a different structure, one that was not cognitively economical, might be correct instead.

The best known of the studies that challenged the cognitive economy principle was done by Conrad (1972). In her study, Conrad first collected normative data from a sample of college students, asking them to write down properties of a variety of words (like "robin," "banjo," "onion," etc.). She tabulated the frequency with which different properties occurred in these written listings, then used the words in sentences for her verification task. Basically, Conrad found that there was little evidence for the economical scheme implied by cognitive economy: properties at various levels in the hierarchy seemed to be stored *repeatedly,* not in the overly tidy, nonredundant fashion implied by Quillian (see also Ashcraft, 1978b). Furthermore, the frequency with which properties were produced in the normative data was a much more powerful predictor of RT performance than the hierarchical scheme used by Collins and Quillian. High-frequency properties, like WINGS for the concept ROBIN, were verified more quickly than low-frequency properties, like FEET for ROBIN (see also Ashcraft, 1976; Glass, Holyoak, & O'Dell, 1974). It seemed very possible, in other words, that Collins and Quillian had obtained their result not because the properties or superordinates were more distant in a hierarchical structure, but instead because their "more distant" concepts were actually associated more weakly with the concepts. The cognitive economy effect, it seemed, was due to Collins and Quillian's failure to control for the effect of frequency or strength of association.

Property Statements   Another feature of Conrad's (1972) study took on added significance as more semantic memory experiments were conducted. Rather than limiting herself to category membership statements ("An S is a P"), Conrad tested statements of the form "An S *has* a P," that is, **property statements.** Essentially, a property statement is one that *asserts that some concept, S, has a certain property or characteristic, P;* for instance, "A robin has wings" or "A canary is yellow." As experiments using property statements began to appear, difficulties arose for the Smith feature comparison model.

Consider "A robin has wings." The normal Smith et al. comparison process, you'll recall, was to access the feature lists for both concepts, then do a global Stage I comparison on these lists. Sometimes, of course, this Stage I comparison was followed by a Stage II evaluation of just the defining features for the two concepts. For a property statement then, the model claimed that you access the feature lists for both concepts, your concept of ROBIN and your concept of THINGS WITH WINGS. You would then conduct the regular feature-overlap comparison process on these two feature lists.

Several aspects of this explanation were problematic, it turned out. One peculiarity involved categories like THINGS WITH WINGS, or to use a Smith et al. example, BROWN THINGS (as in "An ostrich is brown"). It seems a bit farfetched that we actually have concepts or categories in semantic memory corresponding to THINGS WITH WINGS or BROWN THINGS, each with its own feature list. A second puzzle involved the features that would be on such lists. Aside from *has wings* and possibly *can fly* for THINGS WITH WINGS, there would seem to be no other features on this list (what besides *brown* is on the BROWN THINGS list?). If so, this would make the Stage II comparison process quite implausible, since Stage II required the characteristic features to be separated from the defining ones. A third, more basic question can also be offered: If WINGS is already on the feature list for ROBIN, why is the feature comparison process between the ROBIN list and the THINGS WITH WINGS list even necessary?

In short, the Smith et al. model was extended to three different kinds of property statements; adjective (e.g., brown), relative adjective (e.g., small), and *has* properties (e.g., wings). Each type, however, required a distinctly different kind of comparison process to render it workable within the feature comparison approach (Ashcraft, 1978a). Furthermore, there was little or no evidence that subjects treated different kinds of properties differently, either in normative or RT studies (e.g., Ashcraft, 1976, 1978b; Glass et al., 1974).

As Collins and Loftus (1975) pointed out, their network approach contained both property and superordinate pathways and thus had no difficulty in explaining how people verify property statements: the same intersection search process applies to both. Furthermore, the troublesome distinction between defining and characteristic properties was not in the Collins and Quillian model, whereas Smith et al. had some difficulties in convincing researchers that such a distinction even existed, much less that it was as central to semantic memory processes as they had proposed (but see Malt, 1990, for the influence of subjects' *beliefs* that there are defining features for some categories).

Finally, Collins and Loftus made one additional telling criticism of the feature comparison model. They pointed out that the Smith et al. model stored any and all features about a concept *except* for that concept's superordinate, that is, the category to which it belongs. In their words, "While most people may not have learned some superordinate relations (e.g., that a beaver is a mammal, or a sled is a vehicle), there are many they have learned (e.g., that a wren is a bird, and a beaver is an animal). Why would they not use such information if it is stored? How in fact can they avoid using it? It is an unlikely model which postulates that people use information that is less relevant to make a decision, instead of information that is more relevant" (Collins & Loftus, 1975, pp. 425–426).

Typicality Effects   Earlier studies contrasted RTs to sentences like "Robin is a bird" and "Robin is an animal" and often interpreted the differences in terms of the size of the category being searched (e.g., Chang, 1986). But the important impact of the Smith model (e.g., Smith et al., 1974; also Rosch, 1973) was that it seemed to account for a somewhat different type of sentence, one in which the Subject terms sampled the entire category being tested.

Battig and Montague (1969) had collected an extensive set of norms, intended to be a source of stimuli for free recall and clustering studies. These norms showed clearly that there was a stable ranking or ordering of the members of a category. To use our familiar example, "robin" was the most frequently occurring member of the bird category: it was listed by 85% of the subjects. "Chicken," on the other hand, was listed by only 9% of the subjects. As you might suspect, such a range of occurrence says something important about people's representation of the semantic category BIRD (and other categories as well; see footnote 5) and, as a consequence, implies something important about their RT performance.

The important result in studies that used Subject terms from the whole range of frequencies was that frequently listed category members were verified more rapidly than others: you can decide "yes" to "Is a robin a bird?" more rapidly than to "Is a chicken a bird?" Under the standard assumption that time differences can reveal mental processes, this result suggested a new dimension to semantic memory. Unlike the equal-length pathways depicted in Figure 6-1, such a result suggested that

FIGURE 6-5

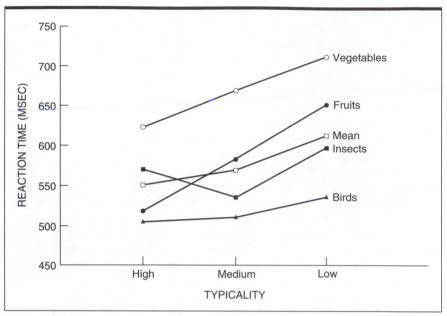

Mean RTs to members of categories that are high, medium, or low in typicality. The RTs are considerably faster than in comparable studies because the category names were given at the beginning of a block of trials and did not change within the block. Thus each trial consisted of only the target word, and subjects judged if it belonged to the given category name.

pathways to less-frequent category members were longer, making those members "farther" away in the semantic network. Under the Smith et al. scheme, less-frequent category members were said to have lower feature overlap with their superordinate than more-frequent members. In fact, it was exactly this kind of result (Rips, Shoben, & Smith, 1973; Rosch, 1973) that led Smith et al. (1974) to their feature comparison model. This important effect is now called the **typicality effect:** *typical members of a category can be judged more rapidly than atypical members.* Figure 6-5 illustrates the effect obtained in Smith et al.'s research. (We will return to typicality soon, since it is more important than this short discussion implies.)

Semantic Relatedness

Figure 6-6 illustrates a modified network representation of part of the bird category, one that incorporates the three issues we've been discussing. Note first that there is no rigid cognitive economy in the illustration; properties listed for a concept are linked directly to that concept, rather than indirectly via multiple pathways. Second, these pathways

FIGURE 6-6

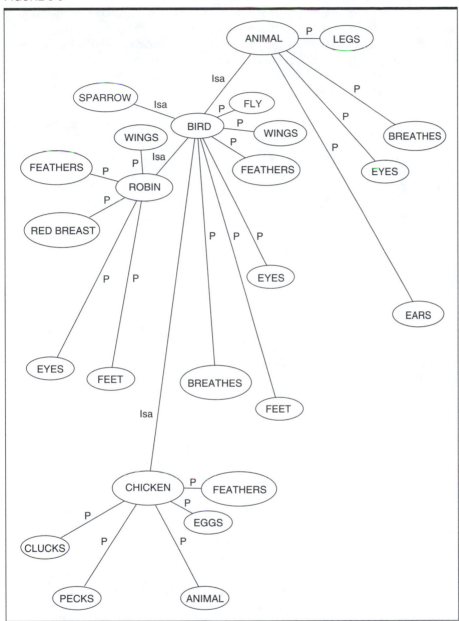

A portion of the semantic network is illustrated, taking into account three empirical effects: (1) there is no strict cognitive economy in the hierarchy, so redundant information is stored at several different concepts; (2) typical members of the category are stored more closely to the category name or prototype member; and (3) properties that are more important are stored more closely to the concept than those of lesser importance.

are of different lengths, reflecting the results that sentences with high-frequency properties are verified faster than those with low-frequency properties (this result was clearly anticipated by Collins and Quillian; see the introductory quotation). Finally, note how typicality effects are represented in the figure: typical or central members of the category are connected to the superordinate node by *shorter* pathways, whereas atypical or peripheral members are linked by *longer* pathways. In other words, the network structure of a category is illustrated in the figure, with the length of connecting pathways representing the degree to which two concepts are related. Shorter pathways denote concepts that are closer in semantic space or, to use a different terminology, denote concepts that are more strongly related to one another. Longer pathways denote lesser degrees of semantic relatedness.

Unfortunately, it is difficult in a two-dimensional figure to illustrate some other features of networks. For example, most researchers would agree that the *strict* hierarchical approach is incorrect. This conclusion is based on evidence that statements like "A beaver is an animal" tend to be verified more quickly than "A beaver is a mammal." Of course, in a strict hierarchy, the mammal sentence should be faster to verify or judge, since mammal is a subset of animal. Nonetheless, RTs to such sentences show a different effect than strict logic or hierarchies would imply (e.g., Rips et al., 1973). In the figure, this relaxation of the strictly hierarchical scheme would mean that there should be a connecting pathway from CHICKEN to ANIMAL, for instance, and that this pathway would be shorter than the CHICKEN *isa* BIRD pathway. Conceiving of such networks in three-dimensional space makes this easier to imagine, but harder to illustrate.

Regardless of how we diagram the illustrations, the empirical prediction from such a network is that performance, particularly RT performance, will vary directly as a function of the length of the connecting pathway. To state it slightly differently, the higher the semantic relatedness between concepts, the faster you are able to retrieve the connection between them. This is in fact the **semantic relatedness effect;** *concepts that are more highly interrelated can be judged "true" more rapidly than those with a lower degree of relatedness.* The important new ingredient here is that this semantic relatedness principle applies both to category statements ("An S *is* a P") *and* to property statements ("An S *has* a P"). To make a long story short, the prediction turns out to be true for both kinds of statements (e.g., Ashcraft, 1978a).

Results such as these suggested a great regularity in semantic memory structure. Concepts farther removed from one another in the hierarchy require more time for retrieval. Concepts closer together in the hierarchy require less time for retrieval and are more central to the meaning of the concepts or categories. This is the **semantic relatedness effect,** also called the **semantic distance effect,** which describes an important generalization: the closer two concepts are in semantic memory (distance), or the more related they are, the faster is the mental search process that retrieves information about the concepts. This idea is particularly easy to visualize for network models, where more activation accumulates at the closer concepts because a shorter distance has to be traveled (or alternately, that activation accumulates more rapidly at closer concepts due to shorter distances). A grander implication also follows from this effect as well; semantic relatedness is the basic dimension along which semantic memory, all our general world knowledge, is organized.

Additional Evidence   One form of additional evidence on the semantic relatedness effect has been reported quite recently, by Kounios and Holcomb (1992). In this experiment, pairs of words varied in their relatedness, either high (rubies–gems) or low (spruces–gems). Half of the time, the category member—the "Exemplar" in Kounios and Holcomb's term—came before the category (rubies–gems is an Exemplar–Category pair), and half the time the category came first (gems–rubies is a Category–Exemplar pair). Sentences were presented with one of three quantifiers, *all, some,* or *no,* thus altering the meaning and true/false nature of the sentences (e.g., "All rubies are gems" and "Some gems are rubies" are true, but "No rubies are gems" is false). The results of the experiment are shown in Figure 6-7. Look at the figure now; you'll see the same kind of increasing curve as before, for example, when typicality varied from high to low in Figure 6-5.

But look at the figure again. What is the label on the *y*-axis? This is *not at all* a standard RT effect for semantic relatedness. Instead, these scores are the amplitudes of brain wave patterns, recorded by electrodes placed on the subjects' scalps during the task. In other words, Kounios and Holcomb replicated the standard semantic relatedness effect using a radically different dependent measure, electrical activity in the brain!

The technical term for the data that Kounios and Holcomb collected is **event-related potentials,** always referred to by its abbreviation **ERPs.** The response being measured here is a (small) fluctuation in the electrical voltage—the electrical potential—in the functioning brain, recorded by means of an EEG (electroencephalogram). These potentials are *event-related* because they occur regularly, in time-lagged fashion, when a stimulus event is presented to the subject.

As Kounios and Holcomb explain, ERPs have become an increasingly useful measurement of cognitive processes in recent years. A major reason for this usefulness is the time-lagged nature just mentioned; present a stimulus, and a certain ERP component occurs within a narrow window of time, say, within 300–500 msec of the stimulus. By carefully controlling the subjects' muscle movements (including eye blinks), a researcher can be relatively sure that the observed change in electrical potential is a direct result of the stimulus that was presented.

Several different positive and negative ERPs have recently been stud-

FIGURE 6-7

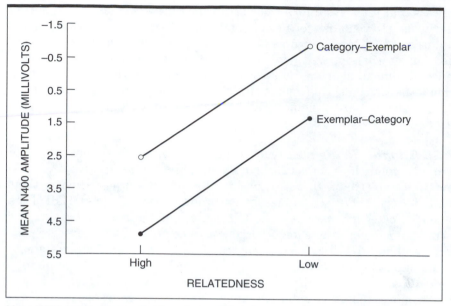

Mean N400 amplitude recorded from three midline sites, as a function of semantic related-ness and prime–target order.

ied in the intact, functioning brain. For example, an ERP known as *P300* is of interest in some studies; the *P* means it's a positive change in electrical potential, and the 300 means the change peaks 300 msec after the stimulus is presented (it is also called the *P3* component because it's the third positive component; Kounios & Holcomb, 1992). This ERP has been linked to activity in working memory (e.g., Donchin, 1981). In the Kounios and Holcomb study, the ERP of interest was the *N400* component, a *negative* change occurring roughly 400 msec after the stimulus, the sentence predicate in their study.

Figure 6-8 shows the actual pattern of recorded N400s, taken from one of the midline electrode sites (recordings were taken from a total of three midline sites, and five sites each on the left and right hemispheres). At the 400-msec point, the solid curve for "Exemplar–Category, Related" stimuli (e.g., "All rubies are gems") continued its drift downward. For all three other sentence types, however, there was a negative peak around 400 msec, especially when the subject and predicate were unrelated. In other words, the N400 component seemed to be particularly sensitive to the relatedness of the two concepts in the sentence or, more accurately, to their *un*relatedness.

Kounios and Holcomb's conclusion was that the N400 ERP component is especially affected by retrieval mechanisms in semantic memory.

FIGURE 6-8

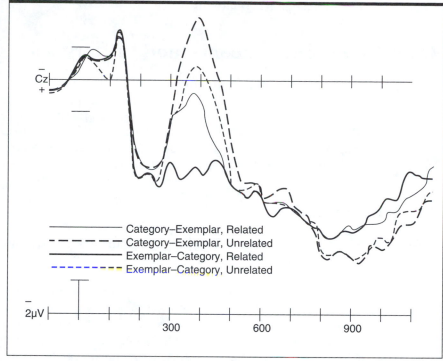

The event-related potentials at one midline site (Cz) for four types of trials; "Exemplar–Category" and "Category–Exemplar" refer to the order of the words. The onset of the target is shown by the vertical bar at the beginning of the time lines.

When the two words were related (or, in their Experiment 2, when the words had to be categorized as either abstract or concrete), there was a substantial difference in the ERP pattern compared to trials on which the words were semantically unrelated. Interestingly, because most semantic memory RTs are considerably longer than 400 msec, and because the N400 pattern was based on *amplitude* rather than time latency, these authors also suggested that normal RT measurements are probably reflecting decision-stage components of semantic processing more than retrieval-stage mechanisms.

It may be some time before this particular conclusion is checked and replicated; the claim that RTs reflect decision making more than retrieval certainly disagrees with the bulk of our common interpretations, not to mention the models of semantic memory (including connectionist approaches). But a more global conclusion seems quite certain even now. Electrophysiological data now being reported are supportive of several major factors thought to influence cognitive processing, including the factor of semantic relatedness.

Summary Points: sentence verification; cognitive economy; property statements; typicality; semantic relatedness; ERPs

▼ Categorization, Concepts, and Prototypes

A final series of important studies will nail down the principle of semantic relatedness and the structure of categories in semantic memory. This discussion will also set the stage for several important processes to be considered in later chapters, chief among them the comprehension of language. As preparation for this section, you might look up the words "bird" or "flower" in your dictionary, and note any illustration that accompanies the definition.

Concept Formation

Traditional research on *concept formation* (e.g., Bourne & Bunderson, 1963) showed subjects a series of arbitrary patterns and asked them to categorize each pattern as belonging or not belonging to the concept being tested. Oddly enough, subjects were not told what the target concept was ahead of time; they had to develop the concept by guessing and then paying attention to the feedback they received after making their decisions. Figure 6-9 shows a series of such patterns, along with the yes/no feedback you would receive in the task. Spend a few moments going through the patterns to see if you can figure out what the target concept is. (After you've worked on the task, check the end of the next paragraph to see if you were right.)

An extensive literature exists on this topic, and we know fairly well what factors influence performance (e.g., the number of different dimensions that are relevant, and the number that are redundant; see Kintsch, 1970, for a summary). What is not made clear by this literature, however, is how concepts formed by combining arbitrary features relate to concepts in the real world. That is, if "shaded circle" is the target concept being tested, how does such an arbitrary combination of dimensions relate to concepts like "game" or "vehicle"? These categories seem to have nothing comparable to the invariant, arbitrary features used in the laboratory. (The concept in Figure 6-9 is "shaded square on the left," a combination of the dimensions of shape, shading, and position.)

Natural Language Concepts

Beginning in the early 1970s, a very different approach to the topic of concept formation and classification appeared, largely due to Eleanor Rosch's important research. A central theme in Rosch's reports (e.g., 1973) was that traditional concept identification research "missed the

FIGURE 6-9

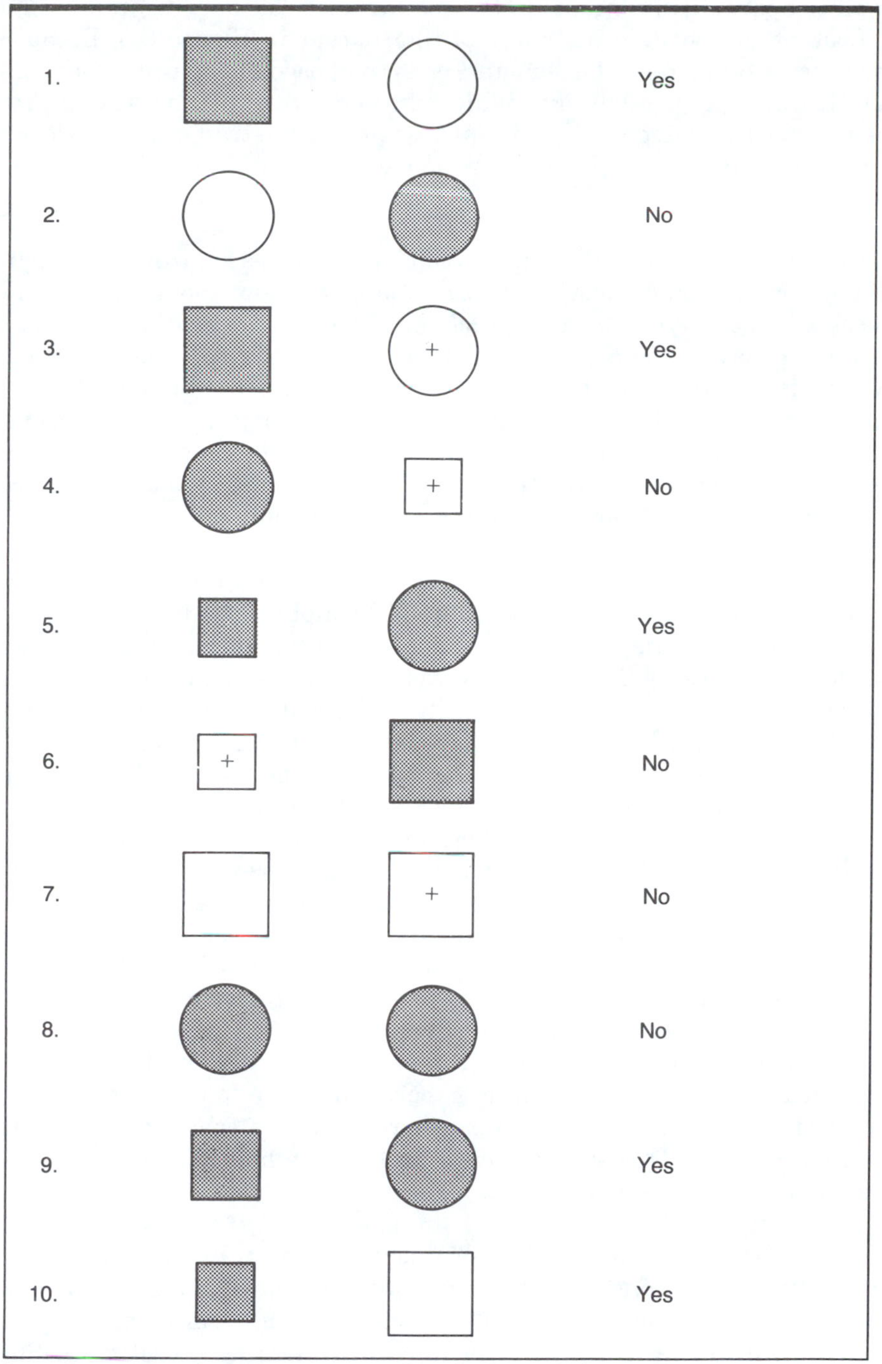

A set of ten concept formation patterns and feedback on which patterns are positive instances of the concept and which are negative. See text for the rule that expresses the concept.

boat" in the way implied above, that is, in testing stimuli that were not at all comparable to concepts in the real world.

Look at the positive instances of the concept in Figure 6-9. Because the concept defined by these instances is composed of separate, independent features, a question like "Which of the positive instances is a *better* member of the category or concept?" seems very strange: they are all equal, since they are all members. For example, patterns 3 and 5 are both positive instances, despite the fact that one is large and one is small.

But Rosch contended that such artificial categories bear little relationship to the natural categories we use in language and thought. **Natural categories,** *concepts and categories that occur in the real world of our experience,* have a complex internal structure, she argued. Questions like "Which is a better member of the dog category, collie or dachshund?" make perfectly good sense for natural categories, suggesting that the category "dog" has an internal structure in which some members are "better" or more representative than others. Given this obvious difference between natural categories and experimenter-defined concepts, Rosch argued that the concept formation literature may have given us "a quite distorted view of how *real* categories are learned and how they function in cognitive processes" (Rosch, 1973, p. 112, emphasis added).

Rosch was essentially saying that real-world category members do not belong to their categories in simple yes/no, all-or-none fashion; they are not bundles of independent features. Instead, real-world categories show the characteristic of *fuzzy boundaries,* with ill-defined or uncertain membership for many category instances. For example, is a sled a toy or a vehicle? Isn't a chicken a better member of the farm-animal category than of the bird category? Furthermore, as Collins and Loftus (1975) pointed out, no single feature seems absolutely necessary as a criterion of membership or classification. For example, having a skin or peel is certainly an important feature of the fruit category, yet a peeled orange is still a fruit. Contrast this with pattern 7 in Figure 6-9, in which violation of merely one feature makes the pattern a negative instance.

Rosch claimed, in short, that membership in categories is a matter of degree. Some members are highly representative or "good" instances, close in some sense to an "ideal" member. Others are "poor" instances, on the periphery, in that "grey" area where members seem to blend into another category. This should have a profound influence on how we represent and think about the world.

Perceptual Categories   To document her point, Rosch presented a fascinating study conducted with members of the Dani tribe in New Guinea (Rosch-Heider, 1972). Both short- and long-term memory tasks were administered, using chips of different colors as the stimuli. She found that the Dani learned and remembered more accurately when the chips were "focal" colors rather than "nonfocal" colors, or, putting it loosely, "a really red red" as opposed to "a sort of red red." The *central,* perceptually salient, "good" red, in other words, was a better aid to accuracy than the nonfocal "off-red." One compelling aspect of this study was that the language of the Dani contains only *two* color terms, one for "dark" and one for "light." Nothing in their language expresses meanings like "true red" or "off-red," and yet their performance was influenced by the centrality of focal versus nonfocal colors.[6]

Given the absence of separate color terms in their vocabulary, Rosch reasoned, it must be that there are structured, mental categories of colors in the subjects' semantic memories, categories that do not rely at all on the spoken language. Each category has a central tendency, a focal member that represents the "true" or "good" color, and also has noncentral, nonfocal members that are less representative. Thus the centrality or "goodness" of a color in its own category made a difference in the memory tasks, even without distinct words to name the different color shades. As you recall from the previous section on typicality, synonymous terms for *focal* are *central* or *typical,* and the words *peripheral* or *atypical* are synonyms for *nonfocal.*

Semantic Categories   Having demonstrated the structure of such perceptual categories, Rosch went on to demonstrate an analogous structure in natural, semantic categories. For example, in one set of studies (Rosch, 1973, 1975), subjects were asked to rate a list of category members on their "representativeness" or "typicality." She then found that categorization results—for instance, RT to verify that "An *S* is a *P*"—depended on the rated typicality of the instance (Rosch, 1973). This is a result you've already encountered, in Figure 6-5. Her later work extended this typicality effect even further. For example, she found that using the category name "prepared" people better for a judgment about a typical member than for a judgment about an atypical member (1975; more about this priming effect later). Members that are judged typical of a category, furthermore, tend to share more common features than those that are judged atypical. Typical members also tend to share *fewer* features with members of *other* categories (e.g., Rosch & Mervis, 1975; see Rosch, 1978).

Far from finding evidence that category members are "equal" in the traditional concept formation sense, Rosch's extensive program of research revealed repeatedly that natural concepts and categories have an internal structure. Real-world features do *not* occur independently of one another, although that is the way that shape, color, and so on are manipulated in the concept formation task. Instead, features or proper-

---

[6]Another feature of Rosch's study is interesting as well: she used a traditional paired-associate learning task with the Dani subjects, partly because its standard methodology would yield convincing results in this otherwise unusual and original experiment. Occasionally, it pays to use a thoroughly understood "shovel" when you're digging for something new.

ties of real objects come in correlated bundles. As a simple example, while shape and color may be independent in concept formation tasks, "wings" and "beak" are anything *but* independent in the real world: the things in the real world that have wings *often* have beaks too. We structure our mental representations of such categories in terms of these correlated features, with *typical* instances of the category stored centrally, at the "core" of the concept's meaning, and with *atypical* instances stored more peripherally.

Prototypes   The term that Rosch proposed for *the central, core instance of a category* is **prototype:** a "really red red" is a *prototypical* red, a "doggy dog" (1975, p. 198) is a prototypical dog. Rosch advanced the argument that our mental categories are represented in terms of a prototype, with typical members stored close to the prototype, and peripheral members stored farther away. When asked to think of or imagine a dog, for example, you generally think of your prototype; few of us would immediately think of a Chihuahua, but instead would think of a German shepherd, a terrier, or some other more "doggy dog." Think back now to our standard semantic memory category, BIRD. Did your dictionary have a picture of a rather ordinary looking, typical, yet nondescript bird next to the definition, and the same sort of generic picture of a flower? Such neutral, nondistinctive pictures are probably quite close to the mental representation of a prototype, the central, organizing representation in natural categories.

Besides the studies you read about earlier, what other kind of evidence is there that typicality and prototypes are important issues in the representation of word and category meanings? One of the cleverest studies on typicality was reported by Rips (1975). In his experiment, subjects read a story about an island inhabited by only eight species of animals: sparrows, robins, eagles, hawks, ducks, geese, ostriches, and bats. One group of subjects then read that a highly contagious disease had been discovered among all the sparrows; another group read that the robins had the disease, another that eagles were affected, and so on. Subjects were then asked to estimate the percentages of the *other* animals that would also contract the disease.

The subjects' estimates yielded strong evidence of a typicality or prototype effect. Species that are rated as quite typical or close to the prototype, such as sparrows, were judged very likely to infect virtually all the other species. Atypical instances, say, geese, were judged likely to infect only other atypical members—ducks, for instance—and this to a much lesser degree. The underlying issue of course was typicality, the representativeness of species within the overall category. Subjects assumed that if a typical instance had an important property, then that was sufficient to predict that *all* instances, typical and atypical, would share the property as well. If the property was only true of an atypical instance, however, subjects tended to doubt that the property would be shared throughout the category.

Internal Structure and Categorization

The generalization you should remember from Rosch's research is that categories and concepts in semantic memory are *internally structured* by semantic relatedness. Categories provide us with a way of classifying objects in our environment, and thereby predicting what the objects do, what properties they possess, and how they may be equated under certain circumstances but not under others. We have central, core meanings for each category and concept, and these can be represented as prototypes. Other instances of the concept are arrayed around the prototype, in a semantic distance sense, and can be thought of in terms of their similarities and dissimilarities to the prototype. Bruner, Goodnow, and Austin (1956), writing at the very beginning of modern cognitive psychology, claimed that "categorization is the *means by which the objects of the world about us are identified*" (p. 12). To this, we would add that the process of categorization, relying on existing general world knowledge, is guided or even determined by semantic relatedness and category structure.[7]

Summary Points: natural categories; fuzzy boundaries; prototypes; internal structure of categories

▼ Priming in Semantic Memory[8]

In Chapter 3 you read about automatic processing, in which mental processes occur without any intention or conscious effort. At that point, we introduced the notion of **priming**—a word is presented, for example, and because of automatic access to its meaning, priming boosts or *causes an activation of both that concept and other concepts that are related to it*. The effect of priming in that discussion was to influence subjects' performance in the shadowing task; hearing "While Bill was walking through the forest" was said to prime concepts in memory that are related to forests, so that "a tree fell across his path" intruded into the subject's spoken shadow (see Figure 3-15). In short, priming resulted in the activation of related concepts and thus influenced the subjects' selective attention.

Now we need to move beyond our general intuitions as to what words might be related to a priming word, as in the "forest–tree" example. The reason for this is straightforward: priming is very possibly the most fundamental process of retrieval from semantic memory. It has become one

---

[7]As a historical note, Bourne (1982) countered Rosch's criticism of the traditional concept formation research, by showing that subjects acquire prototype information even with arbitrary stimuli like those in Figure 6-9.

[8]I defer a treatment of Repetition Priming until the next chapter.

of the most frequently tested—and argued about—effects in the study of long-term memory, with dozens of articles appearing yearly. It appeared in the earliest semantic memory models and is the backbone of the most recent entries in the human cognition sweepstakes, connectionist or PDP models. Thus you need to understand priming, how it affects basic semantic memory processing, and how it has been studied in contexts ranging from word recognition to sentence comprehension.

Priming Tasks

Nuts and Bolts of a Priming Task   Let's introduce some precise vocabulary for the priming task, to facilitate the explanation that follows; Table 6-2 gives a concise description. *Any stimulus that is presented first,* in hopes that it will influence some later process, is called a **prime**—simple enough, you'll agree. The *stimulus that follows the prime* is the one we expect will be influenced in some way. This stimulus is called the **target,** since it is the presumed destination of the activation or priming process. Thus primes precede the targets, and targets are influenced by the primes.

Sometimes this influence is beneficial, as when a related prime makes the target easier or faster to process. This kind of *positive influence on processing* is referred to as **facilitation,** or sometimes simply **benefits.** Facilitation is almost always a speed-up of RTs, compared to the RTs in a baseline condition. Occasionally, the influence is negative, as when a prime is unrelated to the target and therefore is misleading or irrelevant. When the prime slows down RT performance to the target, the *negative influence on processing* is called **inhibition;** we also say, equivalently, that there were **costs** associated with the prime.

Finally, since priming produces a level of mental activation that will eventually dissipate, we often need to keep track of the period of time that intervenes between the prime and the target. In some studies, this period of time is filled with other stimuli or trials. In this case, the **lag** between prime and target, usually the *number of intervening stimuli,* is our index of the separation between prime and target; "lag 2" would simply mean that two trials came between the prime and the target.

In other studies, the period of time between the prime and the target is of interest. However nonintuitive, this period of time is often referred to as the **SOA,** the **stimulus onset asynchrony.** If you consider the prime and target to be the two halves of a complete stimulus, then the onset or beginning of the two halves occurs *asynchronously,* at different times. Thus we might present a prime, and then 500 msec later present the target. This would correspond to an SOA interval of 500 msec, where SOA is *the length of time between the onset of the prime and the onset of the target.*

SOA and Automaticity   The purpose of manipulating SOA (aside from making it more difficult for students to figure out the research) is to

Table 6-2   PRIMING TASKS

Essential Terminology

Prime: The stimulus or part of the stimulus expected to have some effect; the prime can either be Related to the target (e.g., bird–robin), Unrelated to the target (e.g., bird–truck), or Neutral (e.g., XXXXX–carrot).

Target: The stimulus or part of the stimulus expected to be affected by the prime.

Lag: The spacing between the prime and target in an "across trials" priming task; for example, lag 2 means two trials came between the prime and target.

SOA: Stimulus Onset Asynchrony, the time interval between the prime and the target in a "within trial" priming task, usually measured in milliseconds (msec).

A. Priming Across Trials

Virtually any generalized recognition task (see Table 6-1) can be adapted to a priming task.

Trials are arranged so that the Prime trial and the Target trial are separated by a fixed number of unrelated trials, for example, at lag 0, or at lag 2. Care must be taken so that an equal number of related targets are true and false, so subjects will not respond "yes" merely on the basis of trial-to-trial relatedness.

B. Priming Within Trials

Most studies of priming within trials use a lexical decision task or another format in which the complete stimulus can be separated into two parts (e.g., Kounios and Holcomb [1992] presented sentences like "Some gems are rubies" in two parts, "Some gems are" as the prime, and "rubies" as the target).

1. Each trial has both a prime and a target. The prime is presented briefly and is then followed by the target after some interval of time (SOA).

2. Three types of primes, Related, Unrelated, and Neutral, are usually presented at all SOAs. In some studies, the prime is followed by a blank or unfilled (short) interval, and in some the prime is masked before the target is shown.

For both types of priming tasks, we have the following:

Dependent Variables: The dependent variable is generally reaction time (RT), assuming that the error rates for the different conditions are approximately equal. If accuracy is the major dependent variable, then the *hit rate* and the *false alarm rate* are of particular interest. The hit rate is the percentage of true trials responded to correctly (saying "yes" to "yes trials") and the false alarm rate is the percentage of false trials responded to incorrectly (saying "yes" to "no trials").

Independent Variables: Aside from using different SOA intervals, the major independent variables are always the types and degrees of relationships between primes and targets. For instance, the prime could be a category name, and the targets would be either high or low typical members of the category; the prime could be a sentence, and the targets would be either high or low semantic associates of the final word in the sentence.

---

examine a particularly important aspect of priming. Is it an automatic process, a conscious process, or some combination of these? It is generally agreed that conscious processing will take some appreciable amount of time to get started, say at least $1/4$ second if not more. Thus if we present a prime and target separated by at least this 250 msec, then facilitation or inhibition due to the prime will reveal the influence of those conscious processes. Conversely, we can present the prime and target so that the

SOA interval is *less* than 250 msec. If there are priming effects with such short intervals, then we will conclude that the priming was automatic, that it happened too quickly to be attributed to conscious processes. This logic will reappear shortly, so make sure you understand the basics: conscious processes take more time to get started and to have their effects, so priming at very short SOAs can't realistically be attributed to conscious processing.

Two Examples of Priming

Let's illustrate priming with some early, fairly straightforward studies, first to examine priming across trials, then to examine it within a single trial.

Priming Across Trials; Word Naming   An early investigation of word naming and semantic priming was conducted by Freedman and Loftus (1971). These investigators asked subjects to name a member of a category that either began with a certain letter or was described by a certain adjective: for example, fruit–P or red–flower. Half of the trials showed the letter or adjective first, and then the name of the target category; in other words, the letter or adjective served as the prime on these trials, since it came first. In the other half of the trials, the reverse order was used: the category name was the prime, and the letter or adjective was the target.

Freedman and Loftus measured the subjects' RTs beginning with the target portion of the trial; for the "fruit–P" trial, the timer started when the letter P was presented and stopped when the subject named a word, for example, "plum." Freedman and Loftus found that performance was significantly faster when the category was used as a prime (fruit–P) than when the letter or adjective was the prime (D–mammal; red–fruit). This suggested that the category name activated its semantic representation and then primed the members of the category. When the letter or adjective targets were then presented, priming from the category name had made it easier to access a member of the category—the members had already been primed.

Conversely, receiving a letter or adjective as the prime had very little effect. No relevant activation of potential targets was possible with such primes, apparently, since no facilitation of word-naming latency (RT) was found. (If you believe that the subjects *can* rapidly activate words based on a letter prime, try the following demonstration. Check your watch, then give yourself 10 seconds to name as many words as you can that begin with D. You'll be surprised at how few you can name, particularly when you contrast that with naming members of a semantic category like fruits.)

In a related study, Loftus and Loftus (1974) again presented both "category–letter" and "letter–category" trials, but then tested the same category a second time. Part of the time, the second appearance of the category was on the next trial, at lag 0, and part of the time the prime and target were separated by two unrelated trials, a lag of 2. Furthermore, this procedure was combined with a "within trial" priming factor; half of the time the category and letter were presented simultaneously, and half of the time after a 2.5-sec interval (i.e., an SOA of 2.5 sec). The results of this study are presented in Figure 6-10.

Panel A shows RT to name a target when the category and letter were presented simultaneously (the advantage for the category–letter order here was presumably because the category name was read first, probably because of the physical arrangement of the stimulus terms; this is unspecified in the original report). As the figure shows, when a second retrieval from the category was required, subjects' responses were faster: it took almost 2.2 sec on the initial trial, but just under 1.9 sec on the target trial at a lag of 0. Furthermore, this benefit or facilitation of processing on the target trial was still apparent even when two unrelated trials intervened between the prime and target trials, that is, at lag 2.

Panel B displays the results from the other condition, when the prime preceded the target by 2.5 sec. While the same pattern of priming was obtained here, note also that processing was faster overall in this condition. The 2.5-sec interval shaved nearly 400 msec off the RTs, presumably because relevant concepts were activated during the SOA interval. Note that this study showed both kinds of priming effects: first, the priming of targets *within a single trial* was examined, comparing performance at the 0-msec versus 2.5-sec SOA; second, priming *across trials* was examined, looking at the speeding of performance at lag 0, then the somewhat lesser degree of facilitation at lag 2.

FIGURE 6-10

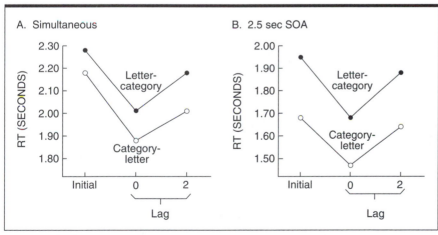

Reaction time in seconds is shown for simultaneous presentation of the prime and target (panel A) and an SOA of 2.5 seconds (panel B). In both panels, the curves show RT to the prime ("initial") and the targets at lags 0 and 2. (From Loftus & Loftus, 1974.)

Priming Across Trials; Sentence Verification   Similar outcomes were also reported in the sentence verification task we studied earlier. For example, Ashcraft (1976) found that a sentence such as "A sparrow has feathers" facilitated another sentence about the same category, for example, "A robin can fly," but only if the target sentence concerned a high-frequency or important property. As Figure 6-11 also shows, when the target sentence contained a low-frequency property (e.g., "robin has feet"), there was little if any facilitation due to priming.

In this study, the prime and target sentences were presented at lag 0; in Experiment 2, the facilitation for sentences with high-frequency properties was quite strong at lag 1 but was weak or nonexistent at lag 4. Unlike the Loftus and Loftus study, where prime and target trials included repetition of the category word, this study avoided repeating any words from primes to targets. This eliminated the possibility that the priming effect was due to some facet of repetition per se, a precaution that has turned out to be important (e.g., see Woltz, 1990, and Repetition Priming in Chapter 7).

Priming Within a Trial; the Matching Task   Rosch (1975) pursued her work on typicality and natural or *basic level categories* by testing for these effects in the context of semantic priming. For this work, she adapted the well-known letter matching task, devised by Posner and his colleagues (e.g., Posner, 1969; Posner & Snyder, 1975). In her study, subjects saw either pairs of words or simple pictures (line drawings) on each trial. They had to respond "same" if both words/pictures were from

FIGURE 6-11

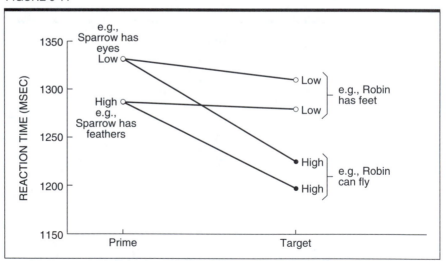

Mean RTs to prime and target sentences that contained either a high-frequency property or a low-frequency property. Primes and targets were presented at lag 0.

the same category (e.g., robin/sparrow), and "different" if the words/pictures were from different categories (e.g., robin/truck). Each trial was preceded by a prime, either the name of the category for relevant primes, or the word "blank" for neutral primes. Although several SOA intervals were tested, we'll focus on just one of her experiments, where the SOA interval between the prime and target was 2000 msec.

Figure 6-12 shows the results of this study. Look first at the middle panel of Figure 6-12, when two different members of the same category were presented in the target (e.g., robin, sparrow). For these "same" judgments, typicality had an obvious and strong effect; in all four conditions, high typical members were judged "same" more rapidly than medium (owl, eagle) or low typical (peacock, chicken) members. Note also that

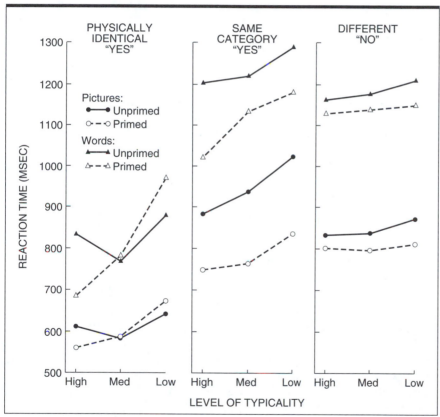

FIGURE 6-12

Reaction time in a "same/different" task, in which pairs of pictures or words were shown, and subjects said "same" or "yes" if both members of the pair were from the same category. Pair members were either physically identical (left panel), from the same category (middle panel), or from different categories (right panel). Pair members were either high, medium, or low in typicality and were preceded by either a neutral or relevant prime. The SOA was 2 seconds. (From Rosch, 1975.)

pictures were uniformly processed faster than words, suggesting that the simple line drawings Rosch used were somewhat closer to the subjects' mental representation of a prototype (this was even the case in Experiment 7, where picture and word trials were intermixed). But most importantly, the priming effect was quite strong in this condition. Pairs that were primed by the relevant category name (the dashed lines in the figure) were consistently faster than the unprimed pairs (solid lines).

Now look at the left panel, where the targets were physically identical pictures or words. Just as was found in earlier research (Posner & Snyder, 1975), the response is even faster when the two target stimuli are physically identical, because physical identity is a simple and fast basis for making "same" judgments. Despite that, typicality and priming effects were significant here too. Priming facilitated the judgments for high typical pairs; hearing "bird" as a prime made subjects faster to judge "robin robin" as belonging to the same category. There was no difference between primed and unprimed pairs at the medium level of typicality; that is, hearing "bird" before the word pair "owl owl" did not help subjects judge them to be members of the same category. And, interestingly, priming actually slowed down judgments on the low typical targets. For example, even though the target was "peacock peacock," a low typical, physical-identity pair, RT was 100 msec *slower* when that pair was primed by BIRD than when it was not primed at all.

Apparently, the category name activated the prototype of the category, and also the typical members that are highly similar to the prototype. This resulted in a benefit for those items that resemble the prototype; the category name "prepared" subjects for typical items, yielding facilitation. For items at the medium level of typicality, primes had neither positive nor negative effects. And for atypical items, it was almost as if the category name was misleading, as if the category name was barely related to the atypical members.

Priming, Automaticity, and Lexical Decisions

A large range of topics has been investigated with priming tasks, for example, visual perception and identification tests (e.g., Reinitz, Wright, & Loftus, 1989; Weldon, 1991), auditory perception and recognition of words (Goldinger, Luce, & Pisoni, 1989; Schacter & Church, 1992), word pronunciation (Balota, Boland, & Shields, 1989), and even the relatively neglected topic of how new information is added to semantic memory (Dagenbach, Horst, & Carr, 1990; Potts, St. John, & Kirson, 1989). We will focus just on two topics here, first priming and the mental lexicon, then priming and its effects on comprehending ambiguous words.

Priming and the Mental Lexicon We use the term **lexicon** or **mental lexicon** to refer to the *mental dictionary,* in other words our knowledge of words, their names, meanings, and possibly even their pronunciation.[9] The now classic *lexical decision task* has been used extensively to investigate the priming and semantic relatedness effects we're interested in now. It has also shown the intimate and unavoidable relationship between our semantic concepts and the words we use to name them—in other words, between the semantic and the *lexical* entries in memory.

You've already encountered this research, back in Chapter 2 when you read about the lexical decision task, in which subjects judge as rapidly as possible whether or not a string of letters forms a word (retrieval cues: OFFICE, MANTY, MOTOR). This task has been adapted to tests of semantic priming in a variety of ways. In the simplest version, we present two letter strings per trial, either of which may be a word or a pseudoword (a pseudoword looks like a real word and can be pronounced). The condition of greatest interest of course is the set of trials when both letter strings are words. In these trials, the investigator normally includes pairs of words that vary in their degree of semantic relatedness.

As Meyer and Schvaneveldt (1971; also Meyer, Schvaneveldt, & Ruddy, 1975) found, two related words such as BREAD BUTTER can be judged more quickly as "words" than two unrelated words, such as NURSE BUTTER. Table 6-3 displays the Meyer and Schvaneveldt (1971) results and shows this effect quite clearly. Related words were judged in 855 msec, compared to 940 msec for unassociated words.

One particularly interesting aspect of these results, and in fact all results with the lexical decision task, is worth pointing out here. It is not logically necessary for subjects to access the *meanings* of words in the lexical decision task. Technically, they need only "look up" the words in the *lexicon,* the mental dictionary, to determine if the word is there or not. Yet, the results repeatedly show the influence of the words' meanings: it is the meaningful connection between BREAD and BUTTER that facilitates this decision, rather than some lexical connection (you might think since both begin with B that there is a lexical basis for the facilitation, but the same benefits are found with word pairs that are quite dissimilar in spelling, for instance, NURSE and DOCTOR).

Apparently, even though the task only requires a judgment of word or nonword, we nonetheless access the words' meanings as part of our normal processing; the process is automatic, in the sense that you cannot avoid accessing the meanings. Therefore the relatedness of meanings influences performance. This should not be a surprise to you; it is exactly the same effect that Stroop found with his color words (see Chapter 1). In fact, the Stroop task is the conceptual "grandfather," so to speak, of all

---

[9]Conventionally, the term *mental lexicon* refers to word knowledge, that is, the mental dictionary, whereas *semantic memory* refers to general knowledge, for words as well as other concepts and ideas, that is, the mental encyclopedia. Some evidence (e.g., Allen, McNeal, & Kvak, 1992; Shelton & Martin, 1992; see also topics in Chapters 8 and 10) suggests that the two are at least partly separable.

Table 6-3   MEAN REACTION TIMES (RTs) OR CORRECT RESPONSES AND MEAN PERCENT ERRORS IN THE YES/NO TASK

Type of Stimulus Pair		Correct Response	Sample Stimuli	Mean RT (msec)	Mean Percent Errors
TOP STRING	*BOTTOM STRING*				
Word	Associated word	Yes	Nurse–doctor	855	6.3
Word	Unassociated word	Yes	Bread–doctor	940	8.7
Word	Nonword	No	Book–marb	1087	27.6
Nonword	Word	No	Valt–butter	904	7.8
Nonword	Nonword	No	Cabe–manty	884	2.6

From Meyer & Schvaneveldt, 1971.

such priming tasks and automaticity effects (though as mentioned in Chapter 1, there was no hint in Stroop's 1935 article that it would become so important many years later).

Priming Without Conscious Awareness   If accessing a word's meaning is automatic, can it occur even without conscious awareness of having seen the word? Marcel (1980, 1983) reported an impressive set of results that seem to answer "yes" to this question. Marcel examined word recognition in a lexical decision task with priming. He presented the primes in a rather different way than was typical, however: the prime was immediately followed by a scrambled visual pattern. The purpose of this scrambled pattern was to mask the prime, that is, to present the masking pattern so soon after the prime that subjects were not consciously aware of the prime word at all. You'll recall from the Visual Sensory Memory research in Chapter 3 that the circle marker cue in Averbach and Coriell's (1961) research acted as an "eraser" on round letters such as C. This effect was *backward masking,* when a stimulus prevents further processing of an earlier one by means of interference within the visual system.

This phenomenon was exactly the one Marcel used to prevent conscious awareness of the prime. By following the prime so rapidly with a masking pattern, he obtained complete backward masking. Subjects claimed they had seen no prime whatsoever. Nonetheless, relevant primes such as "child" facilitated lexical decisions about words such as "infant."

These results suggest that semantic priming, at least in the lexical decision task, can occur both automatically and without any conscious awareness; subjects did not realize consciously that they had seen a prime at all. Some degree of controversy has grown up around such findings (see also Carr & Dagenbach, 1986; Carr et al., 1982; Merikle, 1982), much of it focusing on methodological issues related to how long the prime is displayed, and whether it could have become partially conscious at even short durations. More recent evidence (e.g., Hirshman & Durante, 1992), however, indicates that the effect is genuine. Semantic priming, at least in the lexical decision task, can indeed occur automatically, without identification of the prime and without conscious awareness.

Priming and Conscious Processing An impressive set of demonstrations of priming and automatic word retrieval has been reported by Neely (1976, 1977; Neely, Keefe, & Ross, 1989). In one study (1976), Neely selected word pairs so that one of the members was the primary associate to the other at least 40% of the time (based on free association norms). These related pairs were contrasted with unrelated word pairs, and also with a condition in which the neutral letter X was paired with a word. For all trials in the experiment, subjects had to judge whether the target string, the second member of each pair, was an English word—the lexical decision task. As Figure 6-13 shows, the processes involved in making these lexical decisions were significantly facilitated when the

FIGURE 6-13

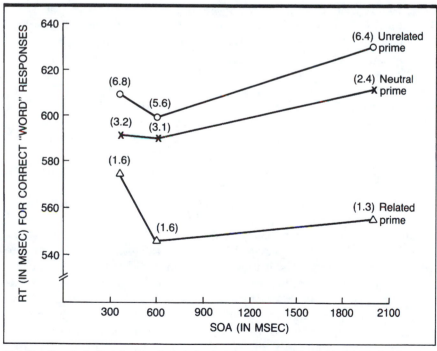

Reaction time to lexical decision targets is shown across SOA intervals for unrelated, neutral, and related prime conditions. The numbers in parentheses are the error rates in each condition. (From Neely, 1976.)

prime was a related, associated word. Facilitation grew from 17 msec at the shortest SOA to 56 msec with a 2000-msec (2-sec) SOA. Inhibition was observed for the unrelated word pairs; there was a relatively constant 16-msec cost of receiving an unrelated word as a prime.

In a more thorough examination of priming, Neely (1977) not only tested the effects of semantic relatedness on performance in the lexical decision task but also the possible effects of expectancy, that is, conscious or strategic factors. But rather than manipulate expectancy by altering the proportion of relevant and irrelevant primes, Neely decided merely to tell subjects what kind of targets would usually follow which primes. For some of the categories he tested, subjects were told to expect a target from the same category; seeing BIRD was a tip-off that a member of the bird category was very likely to be the target. For other categories, however, subjects were told to expect a switch; seeing BUILDING tipped the subjects off that a member of the body-part category was likely to appear in the target position, and vice versa.

The clever part of the study (although the subjects probably didn't think so) was that part of the time the tip-offs were correct and part of the time they were misleading. In other words, you were told that when you saw BIRD you'd then see a member of that category as the target. That usually happened. You were also told that when you saw BUILD-ING, you'd then probably see a body part as the target, and that when you saw BODY, you'd probably get a part of a building as a target. Most of the time this happened as you expected: BUILDING was followed by LEG, BODY was followed by DOOR or WINDOW. But part of the time it didn't happen as you expected: BUILDING would then be followed by WINDOW and BODY would be followed by HEART, even though you expected the other category. The cleverness here, of course, is that BUILDING would normally be a relevant prime for WINDOW, but because of the expectancies, subjects assumed they'd see a body part. Table 6-4 shows the various conditions Neely tested, along with examples of the stimuli.

Neely's results were fascinating (see Figure 6-14). For regular priming (BIRD–ROBIN), facilitation of word recognition was observed across the whole range of SOAs, a replication of the Posner and Snyder (1975) results with semantically related words instead of letters (and without repetition of the prime in the target). When BODY was the prime, there was facilitation for the expected BUILDING targets, but *only* at the longer SOAs. In other words, it took a while for the expectation of a category switch to take effect, but after it did there was observable facilitation. The truly impressive part of the results was that BODY yielded significant priming to HEART at the short SOAs, even though the subjects had been told to *expect* BODY to be followed by a part of a building. In other words, without enough time for the expectation of a category shift to affect processing, the prime facilitated its *own* related category members rather than those in the "expected" category. On the other hand, at

Table 6-4   CONDITIONS AND SAMPLE STIMULI IN NEELY'S
(1977) STUDY

Condition	Sample Stimulus[a]
No Category Shift Expected	
No shift	BIRD–robin
Shift	BIRD–arm
Category Shift Expected from Building to "Body Part"; from Body to "Part of a Building"	
No shift	BODY–heart, BUILDING–window
Shift to expected category	BODY–door, BUILDING–leg
Shift to unexpected category	BODY–sparrow

[a]PRIME is in capital letters.

FIGURE 6-14

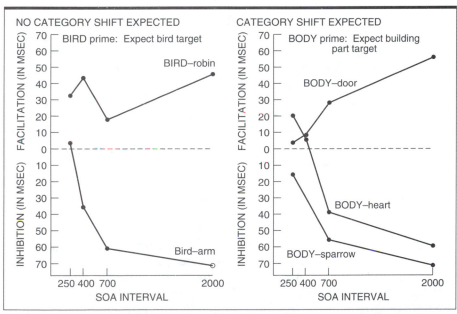

Reaction time to lexical decision targets. In the left half, subjects saw a prime and did not expect a shift in category; sample stimuli are BIRD–ROBIN for a relevant prime and BIRD–ARM for an irrelevant prime. In the right half, subjects expected the target to come from the building category if they saw BODY as a prime, and from the body part category if they saw BUILDING as a prime. When the shift in category occurred as expected, then RT was facilitated at longer SOAs. When the expected shift did not occur, there was facilitation at the short SOA when the prime was relevant (BODY–HEART). Inhibition occurred when the shift was completely unexpected (BODY–SPARROW). (From Neely, 1977.)

long SOAs, when the expectation did have time to affect performance, BODY yielded inhibition on its own category members when the expected shift to parts of a building *didn't* occur (BODY–HEART). This inhibition was similar to the BODY–SPARROW condition, a switch that the subjects *never* expected.

Neely's research provided a dramatic confirmation of the role of priming in semantic retrieval. Even with only the shortest of exposures, a relevant prime such as BIRD facilitates the processing of a related concept, ROBIN. This facilitation remains significant throughout a large range of SOAs. A relevant prime also facilitates the processing of related concepts even when subjects expect a switch in categories, but this facilitation only occurs immediately after the prime, before the conscious expectation of a category shift can have an effect. Finally, priming with an unrelated concept inhibits subjects' responses to the target, unless the unrelated target came from a category that the subject had been told to expect. This latter kind of facilitation only began to show up in the later SOA conditions, so was presumably due largely to conscious processing effects.

Priming and Ambiguous Words

The priming task has also "done duty" in the lexical ambiguity area of research. **Lexical ambiguity** refers to the fact that *many words,* such as bank, pen, will, or play, *have more than one meaning.* From the standpoint of semantic memory, it is interesting to ask, "How are ambiguous words retrieved from memory?" That is, when we access a concept in semantic memory, we retrieve the meaning of that concept. When the word name for the concept points to two or more distinct meanings, do we access all meanings? Do we access the most frequent meaning first? Or does the context of the word determine which meaning we access? From the standpoint of comprehension of language, ambiguous word studies provide a way of understanding the role of context, for instance, how a strong context can bias the interpretation of words as we read or hear.

The basic task here is to present the ambiguous word in a prime–target pairing, to see which aspects of meaning are facilitated. Just as BIRD primes related information, our ambiguous prime should activate the meanings and concepts to which it is related. The difference, of course, is that the ambiguous prime is related to two distinctly different meanings: BANK is related both to the concept MONEY and the concept RIVER. If both meanings are activated, even when the surrounding context of the prime is biased toward one meaning only, then this gives us one kind of evidence about context effects. If *only* the biased meaning is retrieved, that is, the meaning that fits the context, then this gives us rather different evidence about context. Thus the logic of the research is to examine which meaning or meanings of an ambiguous word become activated by

DEMONSTRATIONS

There are many experiments described in this chapter that you will not be able to replicate: the phenomenon of semantic retrieval is very fast and largely automatic. Some semantic retrieval tasks, however, tap into processes that occur more slowly or require decisions or judgments that can be measured with stop-watch or pencil-and-paper methods.

1. Category retrieval. To illustrate that semantic memory is organized according to the principle of semantic relatedness, time some subjects as they generate lists of words for you; or, alternatively, give the subjects a fixed amount of time, say, 15 sec, and tabulate how many words they generate in that period. You'll want to test several well-known semantic categories, for instance, trees, flowers, vegetables, fruits, insects, or mammals. Now contrast those results with some different categories, for example, red things, things that are soft, or things beginning with the letter m. You'll see some evidence of semantic relatedness even in the latter examples; for instance, in the red things "category," people are more likely to name "apple" and "tomato" together than "apple" and "fire engine."

2. As an added episodic memory twist, at the end of demonstration #1, have your subjects take a new sheet of paper, and have them list as many of the words they generated as they can remember, cautioning them to name only words they produced. Do you find more intrusions from the semantic categories?

3. The Rips (1975) demonstration, concerning the island with eight species of animals, is a nice way of looking at typicality effects; see how likely it is that eagles will infect the robins and sparrows, for instance, versus how likely it is that the robins and sparrows will infect the eagles, and so on. Try it with other categories too: A hard frost damaged the orange crop, but did it affect the kiwi fruit or papaya crops? The cost of shirts is going down, does that mean that gloves will be less expensive too?

4. Try constructing some sentences or very short stories that end in an ambiguous word. The sentences or stories should bias one or the other meaning of the ambiguous word quite strongly. After doing several of these, give your subjects a yes/no recognition task, asking "Which of the following words is related to the words you just read in the stories?" Use words that are related to both meanings, to see which ones they "recognize." Use the sentences in Table 6-5 as a guide. For example, one of your stories could include "The vampire was disguised as a handsome count. At the stroke of midnight, the vampire went out into the woods, searching for his first victim." With such a bias, you'd expect people to say "yes" on the recognition test to words like DUKE, TEETH, and maybe CLOCK; you would not expect them to say "yes" to NUMBER or BRAIN, although these are associated with words in the sentences.

5. To tap which sense of an ambiguous word people have comprehended, simply present the sentence with the ambiguous word, and have subjects write a continuation sentence or two. Score the continuations as related/unrelated to the meaning of the ambiguous word. Vary the degree of bias in the sentence, and compare to continuations written to a neutral context sentence.

looking at RTs to target words that are associated with the different meanings.

As a concrete example, consider Simpson's (1981) report in which lexical decisions were made on a variety of target words. In one experiment, ambiguous or nonambiguous primes preceded the targets (e.g., BANK–MONEY versus BOAT–MONEY). Some of the time, the ambiguous prime BANK was followed by RIVER, the "subordinate" or less frequent meaning of the word. Simpson found that under such circumstances, only the dominant meaning of the ambiguous word was activated by the prime; BANK primed MONEY, but BANK did not prime RIVER; see Figure 6-15.

In his second experiment, the prime was an entire sentence, sometimes related to the dominant meaning of the ambiguous word, sometimes to the subordinate meaning, and sometimes neutral; see Table 6-5 for examples. In contrast to the first experiment, Simpson found that the subordinate meaning of an ambiguous word *can* be primed, but only if the context of the priming sentence was strongly biased toward the subordinate meaning. That is, with a relatively neutral prime sentence like "We had trouble keeping track of the count," the ambiguous word COUNT seemed to prime only the NUMBER sense of the word. Priming of NUMBER was also strong when the prime sentence was biased toward that meaning, for example, "My dog wasn't included in the final count." But when the prime was biased toward the other meaning, "The vampire was disguised as a handsome count," then the word DUKE showed significant facilitation due to priming.

After reviewing many such experiments, Simpson (1984) concluded

FIGURE 6-15

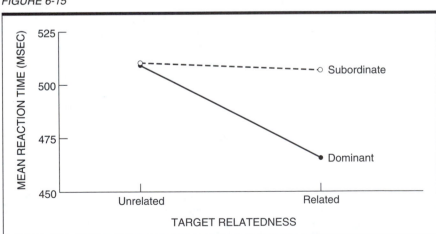

Mean RTs to targets in a lexical decision task using ambiguous words as primes. Targets were either related or unrelated and were associated with either the Dominant or Subordinate meaning of the ambiguous prime. (From Simpson, 1981.)

Table 6-5

Sentence Type	Example	Related Lexical Decision Targets	
		Dominant	Subordinate
(1) Ambiguous	We had trouble keeping track of the *count*.	NUMBER	DUKE
(2) Weak dominant	The musician kept losing track of the *count*.	NUMBER	DUKE
(3) Strong dominant	My dog wasn't included in the final *count*.	NUMBER	DUKE
(4) Weak subordinate	The king kept losing track of the *count*.	NUMBER	DUKE
(5) Strong subordinate	The vampire was disguised as a handsome *count*.	NUMBER	DUKE

Adapted from Simpson, 1981.

that while activation usually spreads to all the meanings of an ambiguous word, the amounts of activation depend on at least two factors—the dominance of the different meanings and the strength of the surrounding context. With no context, meanings are activated to a level that depends on their normal dominance. But with biased context, the biased meaning receives an extra boost in activation. A recent paper by Paul, Kellas, Martin, and Clark (1992) has advanced such conclusions several steps further, by showing how the different aspects of a word's meaning can be activated by different contexts; in a welcome procedural variation, these researchers returned to the "gold standard" task (MacLeod, 1992) of the area, the Stroop color naming task.

Findings such as these clearly suggest an important role for context in the more ordinary processes of accessing word meanings. That is, in routine processing of word meanings, context has a strong influence on activation and retrieval from semantic memory (e.g., Kintsch & Mross, 1985; Schwanenflugel & Shoben, 1985). As Simpson (1984) has noted, such a conclusion is strengthened by the "special case" provided by ambiguous words, since context effects cannot easily be separated from the normal process of meaning retrieval when the word being retrieved has only one meaning.

Summary Points: primes and targets; facilitation (benefits) and inhibition (costs); SOA; mental lexicon; lexical ambiguity

▼ The Generality of Semantic Networks

Let's conclude this chapter with a somewhat broader perspective on semantic memory and semantic networks than is suggested by the research you've been reading about. We claimed at the outset that semantic memory is your permanent knowledge store about concepts. Yet all the examples we've used, and all the research we've talked about, involved *nouns*. You might mistakenly conclude that networks are not useful for explaining the "smash" versus "bump" verb concepts with which we started. For that matter, you might also mistakenly conclude that semantic memory is only for *words*. The problem is that many of our concepts do not correspond to a simple, convenient one-word label (like that orange–purple–grey color of the sky at sunset). You'll recall that Rosch's subjects didn't have the vocabulary words for colors, yet showed that the differences among shades of color did have an effect on their memory performance. But we haven't talked about nonverbal concepts at all in this chapter.

Furthermore, we left at least one very important issue up in the air: the usefulness of networks versus feature lists as ways of representing semantic knowledge. We need to resolve the debate between Collins and Loftus (1975) and Smith et al. (1974). And finally, if semantic memory is truly the place where our general world knowledge is stored, then how is more complex knowledge retrieved and used? What does the priming of ROBIN by BIRD tell us about complex concepts and their retrieval, and about our memory for complex events?

Not for Nouns Only

What about concepts that are not nouns—does the network approach apply to them too? As it happens, the pervasiveness of network theories is nicely illustrated by work that addressed just such questions.

Consider Gentner's (1975) research on the semantic structure of verbs. By the time she began this work, it seemed quite natural to conceive of verb concepts as nodes in a network, with concept nodes connected to other nodes by pathways, activated by priming in a spreading activation sense, subject to the regular "laws" of semantic relatedness, and so on. In other words, the systematic relationships between members of verb "families," say, Gentner's verbs of possession (give, take, buy, sell, trade, etc.), seem to lend themselves to a "node and pathway" representation. In contrast, it certainly seemed difficult to dream up possible lists of features that would define the concepts and express their interrelationships as would be necessary for a feature list approach. Whereas feature list approaches seemed cumbersome, network approaches seemed tailor-made for such concepts.

Indeed, this is exactly the kind of representation that Gentner proposed. Her empirical data on accuracy of usage across childhood clearly demonstrated two results that were entirely compatible with network representations. First, the simpler verbs like GIVE and TAKE involve fewer nodes and pathways in their semantic representations and are mastered much earlier in a child's language use. Second, the more complex verbs such as BUY and SELL overlap considerably with some of the simpler concepts. SELL, for instance, can be decomposed into the simpler concepts GIVE and TAKE, which imply "possession" and "transfer of ownership," along with the extra notion of PAYMENT. Not surprisingly, children showed poor performance on the more complex verbs. At an early age, they treated "sell" as if it meant "give," then slowly added the semantic relationships and extra concepts necessary for a full expression of the meaning of SELL. These complexities were easily expressed within network notation systems; to my knowledge, no one ever tried expressing them in a feature list model that made empirical predictions. (See Gross, Fischer, & Miller, 1989, for work on the organization of adjectives in semantic memory.)

Moreover, semantic networks are not limited to concepts that can easily be labeled with a convenient, one-word name. Just as the research has done, we have simplified our study of semantic memory in this chapter by discussing only such simple concepts. This is not at all necessary, however. As an illustration, consider sensory concepts. A favorite example of mine was provided by Collins and Quillian (1972), the semantic concept of "the sound a rooster makes." To paraphrase their discussion, we have several semantic concepts that relate to this idea—the auditory concept of what a rooster actually sounds like, the verbal concept we call "cock-a-doodle-doo" in English, and, for that matter, the auditory concept of the *sound* that our verbal name has. Each of these is a distinct but related concept in semantic memory, and each is accessible by means of the normal retrieval process.

Networks Versus Feature Lists

Let's turn now to the network issue at a more general level. Which approach—the network model exemplified by Collins and Quillian's (1972; Collins & Loftus, 1975) work, or the Smith et al. (1974) feature comparison model—gives a more adequate explanation? Which model was "right," or at least closer to the truth?

In an interesting footnote to this debate, Hollan (1975) pointed out that feature-based and network-based models are not necessarily incompatible or contradictory, that in some sense the two approaches are merely superficially different ways of accounting for the same underlying knowledge (see also Collins & Loftus, 1975). While this theoretical point may be true, it is also true that the specific models we discussed differ at more than a superficial level.

In particular, consider how the models differed on the critical effects of priming, a topic you are surely expert on by now. At a general level, all the priming effects you have studied can easily be accommodated within network models of semantic memory, since every network model proposed in cognitive psychology has involved the principle of spreading activation (e.g., Anderson, 1976, 1983; Anderson & Pirolli, 1984; Glass & Holyoak, 1975). And priming, after all, was specifically predicted by the

Collins and Quillian network model. On the other hand, there were no mechanisms within the Smith et al. feature model to account for such priming, especially when the priming operates from one trial to another (e.g., Ashcraft, 1976; Loftus & Loftus, 1974). The Smith et al. model yielded RT predictions for processes occurring within a single trial, but was simply not equipped to handle priming effects from one trial to the next. As Eysenck (1984) put it, the Smith et al. model was "remarkably restricted" to the simple sentence verification task, especially to the verification of category statements. Given that priming has become a critically important factor in recent research, it was without a doubt a decided weakness that the Smith et al. model was so silent on this topic.

But are all feature comparison models equally silent on priming, in principle? The answer is "no." The history of this debate in cognitive psychology went something like this.

The original flush of success enjoyed by the Collins and Quillian model was cut short by empirical demonstrations of typicality and semantic relatedness, and by the evidence against strict hierarchical organization. While these factors did not genuinely violate any of Collins and Quillian's stated principles, their model was indeed quite vague on mechanisms to account for those variables. The Smith et al. model portrayed an alternate approach, one that seemed to do a very decent job of accounting for those results with testable, specific mechanisms. But then, more and more research began to look at priming effects, a difficulty for the premier feature model of the day. Furthermore, there was little effort on the part of feature list theorists to modify their models in order to account for such priming effects. From this perspective, the *purely* feature list approach to semantic memory died of inattention, rather than of some fatal empirical blow.

Just as important, more investigators in the mid- and late-1970s began to look at much more complex semantic relationships and representations than simple noun categories. Researchers began to explore comprehension of paragraphs, connected text, and spoken conversations. People became interested in large-scale semantic representations that involved distinctly episodic as well as semantic knowledge. In all these cases, serious attempts were made to model the obtained effects in computer simulation or AI models. The (often unspoken) consensus in most of this work was that network approaches provided a convenient, flexible, and powerful way of attacking these psychological processes.

A Connectionist Example

Networks had, in a sense, proved their usefulness in the research on basic semantic memory processes and were then expanded into more complex areas with great success. The most notable current example of this involves PDP or connectionist models. Recall from Chapter 3 that a connectionist model is, most fundamentally, a massive network of interconnected nodes. What's interesting is that the nodes in connectionist models can "be"—can represent— virtually anything. In particular, the nodes can represent simple features, like the line segments and patterns in Chapter 3. Other nodes can represent more complex features, for instance, the sort—"has wings," "red breast," "can fly"—that composed the Smith et al. model. Indeed, the flexibility of the connectionist approach is that, in principle, *any* type of knowledge can be represented by the nodes and their weighted, interconnecting pathways.

But how does this account for priming? In essence, the connectionist approach *blends* the network and the feature approaches; features represent the basic nodes in the connectionist structure, and the network pathways that connect the nodes are the instrument for priming effects. Martindale (1991) offers exactly the kind of example we need to illustrate this point; Figure 6-16 gives an informal depiction of the example. Pathways with highly positive weights connect a category name like FURNITURE with members of the category like CHAIR and SOFA. The pathways from FURNITURE to RUG, ASHTRAY, and the like will be fairly weak, however, because those members aren't particularly typical in that category. Now, if we present the category name FURNITURE, members like CHAIR and SOFA will be activated to a high level, thus making decisions about them relatively rapid. This is *exactly* the kind of effect found by Smith et al., shown in Figure 6-5. But RUG, in such a connectionist scheme, will actually be *slower* to verify, first because of the weak connection to FURNITURE, and second because the highly activated CHAIR will actually spread inhibition to RUG (when neighbor nodes at the same level inhibit one another, this is called *lateral inhibition*). This was precisely the priming effect found by Rosch, illustrated in

FIGURE 6-16

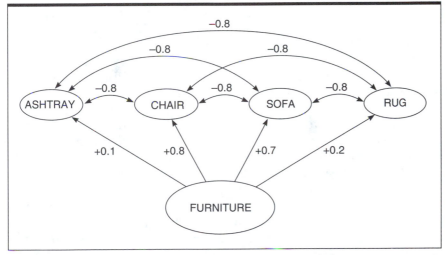

A small portion of a connectionist network. Note that the nodes at the same level exert an inhibitory influence on each other, and receive different amounts of facilitation from the category name. (Adapted from Martindale, 1991.)

Figure 6-12. The category name primed typical members, but actually inhibited responses to the atypical members.

Thus this simple extension of connectionist modeling to semantic memory combines *both* features *and* the advantages of networks. More generally, semantic relatedness is embedded in the structure of a PDP model, by the path weights that connect the nodes. As such, the entire notion of a concept's *internal structure* is coded by the patterns of weights and connections. And priming, both positive and negative activation, is the basic activity within the structured patterns in the network. Thus, in a very real sense, connectionist models of semantic memory and categorization (e.g., Rumelhart, Smolensky, McClelland, & Hinton, 1986; Shanks, 1991) show how networks, priming, and basic semantic features can be combined into a single framework.

Network approaches have also been proposed for describing the process of letter identification (McClelland & Rumelhart, 1981), as you read in Chapter 3, for explaining the effects of emotional state on learning (Bower, 1986), and for representing people's knowledge of simple arithmetic facts (Ashcraft, 1992; Campbell & Graham, 1985). As you'll discover throughout the rest of the book, cognitive psychology is completely "hooked" on the notion that permanent knowledge is represented as interconnected nodes in a network.

The Priming Argument

Cognitive science is also "hooked" on another idea, that priming is the same thing as spreading activation. That is, we usually assume that the priming effect is a direct result of spreading activation within the semantic network. When a related prime like "Sparrow has feathers" speeds up RT to a target like "Robin has wings," we interpret the speedup as being due to a spread of activation in the mental representation: nodes were primed, that is, activated or boosted above baseline, and therefore the subsequent response was faster than normal.

A recent argument (we have a never-ending supply in cognitive science) by Ratcliff and McKoon (1988; McKoon & Ratcliff, 1992; see also Dosher & Rosedale, 1989) has challenged this interpretation. Their argument, in essence, is that priming effects can be accommodated without the "overhead" of networks, spreading activation, and the like. In their position, known as *compound cue theory,* two things happen. First, the information presented in a trial is verified against the relevant concepts in semantic or lexical memory—this is very uncontroversial, since network-priming theories claim the same thing. But the second thing that happens is that a record of the stimulus is also stored in short-term memory, where it joins with whatever other short-term memory information is still there. This "joined" information forms the *compound cue* in this approach; if the stimulus on the last trial had been BREAD, and on this trial it's BUTTER, then BREAD–BUTTER would be the compound cue. Because that compound cue matches a pattern of information in semantic memory, it is said to be high in familiarity. This is another way of saying that the combination has occurred before and has been stored in memory. It is this higher familiarity that produces the priming effect, because it enables the subject to respond quickly.

Although Ratcliff and McKoon (1988) claimed that the bulk of the priming literature is consistent with their compound cue theory, more recent papers suggest that it is somewhat premature to bury spreading activation theories. McNamara (1992a,b), in particular, notes some difficulties that compound cue theory has with results from tasks other than lexical decisions, and with priming effects found across lags larger than 0 (e.g., Joordens & Besner, 1992).[10] McNamara also argues convincingly of the value of spreading activation theories from another standpoint, that they have inspired important work across the entire range of human cognitive processes. He concluded by saying that there is still "every reason to believe that spreading activation is a fundamental mechanism of memory retrieval" (1992a, p. 658). For now, in other words, spreading activation is still "alive."

Summary Points: networks for verbs; networks vs. feature lists; connectionist networks; priming vs. compound cues

CHAPTER SUMMARY

1. Semantic memory contains our long-term memory knowledge of the world, including our knowledge of words, concepts, and language. Early studies of the structure and processes of semantic memory generated two kinds of models, network approaches and feature list approaches.

2. The Collins and Quillian network model claimed that concepts are represented as nodes in a semantic network, with connecting pathways between concepts. Accessing a concept involved the process of spreading activation: activation spreads from the originating node to all those nodes connected to it by pathways. Several early studies, using the sentence verification task, supported an early version of this model, although the disconfirmation of the cognitive economy hypothesis was viewed as evidence against the model.

3. Smith et al. claimed that semantic concepts are lists of semantic features. Verification in their model consisted of accessing the feature lists and performing a comparison process on the features. While the Smith et al. model initially seemed more able to explain typicality effects, the model did not provide a particularly plausible account of how we verify property statements. More importantly, the phenomenon of semantic priming was not predicted by the model. When this phenome-

---

[10]Compound cue theory seems to rest quite heavily on lexical decision results, almost to the exclusion of other tests of semantic memory, and on rather arbitrary "learned" combinations of words in Dosher and Rosedale's (1989) report. It is not clear how the theory would explain either of the priming effects described in the "across trials" section you read earlier.

non became a central focus of semantic memory research, the feature list approach fell into relative neglect.

4. Concept formation research suggested that our concepts consist of the presence or absence of simple, independent features. Rosch challenged this notion and demonstrated that real-world concepts and categories involve "fuzzy boundaries"; that is, some members of categories are judged as more typical than others. Typical members are said to resemble the prototype of the category. Interestingly, typical members show greater effects of priming than do atypical members. Typicality effects support the generalization known as the semantic relatedness effect, that "yes" judgments will be speeded up if the concepts being judged are more highly related to each other.

5. A variety of tasks have been developed to examine the role of priming in the retrieval of information from semantic memory. In such research, a prime of some degree of relationship to a target is presented first, and then RT to the target is measured. When the prime is relevant, RT to the target is usually speeded up, even at very short time intervals (SOAs). This is generally taken as evidence that semantic priming is an automatic process. When the prime is irrelevant to the target, RT is generally slowed down at longer SOAs. This is usually interpreted as evidence that irrelevant primes generate a conscious expectation that slows down processing when the expectation is misleading. Among the tasks used to examine priming in semantic memory are word naming, sentence verification, and lexical decision tasks.

6. Because of the importance of priming, and because of the relative neglect of the feature list approach, cognitive psychology has now devoted considerable attention to the network approach to semantic memory. This approach is now found in a wide variety of topics and has been extended far beyond the simple noun concepts that were so heavily investigated in the 1970s. Priming and spreading activation appear to be central constructs in theories of semantic memory, especially in connectionist approaches, despite recent alternative approaches.

Glossary Terms: cognitive economy; defining and characteristic features; ERPs; facilitation/benefits; fuzzy boundaries; inhibition/costs; internal structure; lexical ambiguity; masking; mental lexicon; natural categories; networks; nodes; pathways; primes and priming; property statements; prototypes; semantic features; semantic relatedness; sentence verification; SOA; spreading activation; targets; typicality

SUGGESTED READINGS

I still have not found a more useful introduction to semantic memory than the 1972 Collins and Quillian paper. It's thought-provoking, insightful, clever, and delightful to read. I would strongly encourage you to read it, to see how these authors manage to discuss generalization and discrimination, basic memory retrieval, imagery, metaphoric language, language comprehension, and computer simulation while maintaining a lively, often humorous style. It's a classic.

Beyond that paper, several books and articles will fill in some gaps, or extend your understanding significantly. The entire second half of Tulving and Donaldson's 1972 book is devoted to papers on different aspects of semantic memory; this also includes Tulving's article on the episodic–semantic distinction. Somewhat later, Smith (1978) reviewed the field of semantic memory research and theory and elaborated considerably on models that represent hybrid approaches, as well as on related kinds of research that semantic models should account for; see also Chang's (1986) more recent review. And finally, there has recently been an attempt to integrate network and feature list approaches within one *hybrid model* (Kounios, Osman, & Meyer, 1987). In this model, both a network search and a feature list comparison process occur simultaneously; the one that finishes first is the one that governs RT to the stimulus. This approach suggests that at some deep level, network and feature list approaches are entirely compatible.

Research continues on the structure and processes of semantic memory. For the topic of categorization, see work by Dahlgren (1985) on social categories such as WORKER, EMPLOYER, and POLITICIAN; by Rifkin (1985) on "event categories" such as school activities and types of shopping; and by Adelson (1985) on abstract concepts in computer science. Recently, L. C. Smith (1984; no relation) has reported on the "semantic satiation" effect, that after continued repetition of the same concepts, the spread of activation can actually slow down due to excessive priming (see also Smith & Klein, 1990). Interestingly, semantic satiation affected word retrieval, but not lexical decision times. Smith and Osherson's (1984) paper discusses the concept of prototypes for "combined" concepts, for instance, *pet fish* or *brown apple*. The Suggested Readings section at the end of the next chapter lists additional papers that relate to semantic memory.

Chapter 7

INTERACTIONS IN LONG-TERM MEMORY

The first notion to get rid of is that memory is primarily or literally reduplicative, or reproductive. In a world of constantly changing environment, literal recall is extraordinarily unimportant. . . . Remembering is not the re-excitation of innumerable fixed, lifeless and fragmentary traces. It is an imaginative reconstruction, or construction, built out of . . . a whole active mass of organised past reactions or experience, and . . . a little outstanding detail which commonly appears in image or in language form. (Bartlett, 1932, pp. 204, 213)

Indeed, the primary reason for the widespread acceptance of the notion of schematic knowledge structures is that it is almost impossible to imagine how mental life could be managed without them. (Nisbett & Ross, 1980, p. 38)

It has been evident since the earliest clinical observations of the amnesic syndrome that patients possess implicit memory for recent experiences despite their inability to recollect those experiences consciously or explicitly. (Schacter, 1989, p. 700)

H aving studied episodic and semantic memory separately in the previous two chapters, we must now put them back together again. It's unreasonable, of course, to think that these two long-term memory systems are entirely separate, although cognitive psychology has studied them that way to gain an understanding of them in their "purest" forms. But there is just as much interest in the *interaction* of semantic and episodic memories in the research, so that's what we turn to now.

In the previous chapter, you read of a distinguishing feature of semantic memory research, that we test the subjects on the knowledge they bring to the laboratory. Episodic tasks, in contrast, present the to-be-learned material to the subjects, then test their memory for that material. While the research presented in this chapter also presents specific materials to the subjects, there are at least two major differences from standard episodic memory situations. First, the material to be learned is deliberately *meaningful.* This means more than simply presenting a list of words as opposed to nonsense syllables; in the present chapter, we're interested in how people remember a story, episode, or other real-world event. A second difference is in the typical results. Unlike the outcomes of many episodic memory tasks, the remembered information that we're focusing on in this chapter is significantly influenced by semantic knowledge—by knowledge of concepts and relationships, by general information about the world. The term for this, when already-known information influences our memory for new events, is *conceptually driven processing.* This is one of two overriding themes in this chapter—how remembering is affected by existing knowledge.

The second theme is implied by the above quotation from Schacter (1989), referred to as the distinction between *explicit and implicit memory.* More and more research is showing fascinating differences between performance on explicit memory tasks, when you consciously recall or remember information, and implicit memory tasks, when your performance need not involve any conscious recollection of the past event. There has been a tremendous surge of interest in this topic across the past several years, especially because of results obtained with brain-damaged individuals, and what those results tell us about the normal cognitive system. The use of such *neuropsychological* data for cognitive theorizing is a prime example of cognitive psychology's expansion into the multidisciplinary field of cognitive science.

We'll cover the explicit/implicit distinction in this chapter, and we'll talk about some of the results that suggest how important this distinction is to a complete understanding of human memory and cognition. This topic in particular is continued in Chapter 10, which focuses exclusively on neuropsychological studies of cognition. In both places, the emphasis will be on the extent to which unconscious processes affect our performance, and the various levels of analysis in cognitive science that measure those processes.

But first, let's put back together the two halves of long-term memory that were taken apart in the last two chapters. Putting it simply, how do our episodic and semantic memories work together?

▼ Reconstructive Memory and Semantic Integration

Table 7-1 contains a story called "The War of the Ghosts." The story is important not only because of the psychological points it raises, but also for historical reasons: Bartlett (1932) used it in one of the earliest research programs on remembering meaningful material. Please do the demonstration in the table now, before reading further.

Now that you have read and recalled the story, spend a moment jotting down some of the thoughts that occurred to you as you read and then tried to recall it. For example, if you remembered some specific details, comment on what made those details more memorable to you. Did you get most of the story line correct, or did you have to do some guessing? What was your sense of the story as you read it? You no doubt thought to yourself what a peculiar story it was, with unfamiliar names and characters, with vague and hard-to-understand twists of the story line, and with unexplainable events. The story is a North Pacific Indian (Eskimo) folktale, so it's not surprising that it differs so much from "normal" stories with which you are familiar.

Once you've exhausted your intuitions, turn to Table 7-2 and compare your recalled version with the retellings in the table. While your version may be closer to the original, because so little time passed between reading and recalling, you should be able to see points of similarity to the tabled retellings.

Table 7-1   BARTLETT'S (1932) "THE WAR OF THE GHOSTS"

===

Read the following, then attempt to reproduce the story by writing it down from memory.

One night two young men from Egulac went down to the river to hunt seals, and while they were there it became foggy and calm. Then they heard war-cries, and they thought: "Maybe this is a war-party." They escaped to the shore, and hid behind a log. Now canoes came up, and they heard the noise of paddles, and saw one canoe coming up to them. There were five men in the canoe, and they said:

"What do you think? We wish to take you along. We are going up the river to make war on the people."

One of the young men said: "I have no arrows."

"Arrows are in the canoe," they said.

"I will not go along. I might be killed. My relatives do not know where I have gone. But you," he said turning to the other, "may go with them."

So one of the young men went, but the other returned home.

And the warriors went on up the river to a town on the other side of Kalama. The people came down to the water, and they began to fight, and many were killed. But presently the young man heard one of the warriors say: "Quick, let us go home: that Indian has been hit." Now he thought: "Oh, they are ghosts." He did not feel sick, but they said he had been shot.

So the canoes went back to Egulac, and the young man went ashore to his house, and made a fire. And he told everybody and said: "Behold I accompanied the ghosts, and we went to fight. Many of our fellows were killed, and many of those who attacked us were killed. They said I was hit, and I did not feel sick."

He told it all, and then he became quiet. When the sun rose he fell down. Something black came out of his mouth. His face became contorted. The people jumped up and cried.

He was dead.

Bartlett's Research

Bartlett (1932), not unlike Ebbinghaus, wanted to study the processes of human memory with the methods of experimental psychology. Very much *unlike* Ebbinghaus, however, he wanted to study memory for *meaningful* material, so he used folktales, ordinary prose, and pictures in his investigations. His typical method had subjects study the material for a period of time, then recall it several times, once shortly after study and then again at later intervals. By comparing the subjects' successive recalls, Bartlett examined the progressive changes in what his subjects remembered. (Interestingly, if you test your memory several times, with only short periods between tests, your performance typically improves across tests, a phenomenon known as *hypermnesia* [e.g., Wheeler & Roediger, 1992]. If substantial time intervenes between tests, however, then we see the more customary effect, greater forgetting across time.)

Using these methods, Bartlett obtained evidence that human memory for such meaningful material is not especially reproductive—that is, it does not reproduce or recall the original passage in any strict sense of those terms. Instead, Bartlett characterized this sort of remembering as "an effort after meaning." The modern term for this is **reconstructive**

Table 7-2   TWO RETELLINGS OF BARTLETT'S (1932) "THE WAR OF THE GHOSTS"

First recall, attempted about 15 minutes after hearing the story:

Two young men from Egulac went out to hunt seals. They thought they heard war-cries, and a little later they heard the noise of the paddling of canoes. One of these canoes, in which there were five natives, came forward towards them. One of the natives shouted out: "Come with us: we are going to make war on some natives up the river." The two young men answered: "We have no arrows." "There are arrows in our canoes," came the reply. One of the young men then said: "My folk will not know where I have gone"; but, turning to the other, he said: "But you could go." So the one returned whilst the other joined the natives.

The party went up the river as far as a town opposite Kalama, where they got on land. The natives of that part came down to the river to meet them. There was some severe fighting, and many on both sides were slain. Then one of the natives that had made the expedition up the river shouted: "Let us return: the Indian has fallen." Then they endeavored to persuade the young man to return, telling him that he was sick, but he did not feel as if he were. Then he thought he saw ghosts all round him.

When they returned, the young man told all his friends of what had happened. He described how many had been slain on both sides.

It was nearly dawn when the young man became very ill; and at sunrise a black substance rushed out of his mouth, and the natives said one to another: "He is dead."

Second recall, attempted about 4 months later:

There were two men in a boat, sailing towards an island. When they approached the island, some natives came running towards them, and informed them that there was fighting going on on the island, and invited them to join. One said to the other: "You had better go. I cannot very well, because I have relatives expecting me, and they will not know what has become of me. But you have no one to expect you." So one accompanied the natives, but the other returned.

Here there is a part I can't remember. What I don't know is how the man got to the fight. However, anyhow the man was in the midst of the fighting, and was wounded. The natives endeavored to persuade the man to return, but he assured them that he had not been wounded.

I have an idea that his fighting won the admiration of the natives.

The wounded man ultimately fell unconscious. He was taken from the fighting by the natives.

Then, I think it is, the natives describe what happened, and they seem to have imagined seeing a ghost coming out of his mouth. Really it was a kind of materialisation of his breath. I know this phrase was not in the story, but that is the idea I have. Ultimately the man died at dawn the next day."

---

memory, in which *we construct a memory by combining elements from the original material together with existing knowledge.*

Two particularly notable aspects of Bartlett's results led him to this conclusion. The first aspect concerns *omissions,* information the subjects failed to recall. For the most part, people in Bartlett's studies did not recall many details of the story, either specific names (e.g., Egulac) or specific events in the narrative (e.g., the phrase "His face became contorted"). The level of recall for the main plot and sequence of events wasn't too bad, but minor events were often omitted. As a result, the retellings of the story are considerably shorter than the original. Of course, the subjects were not asked for *verbatim* (word-for-word) recall, so rephrasing and condensing are to be expected. Nonetheless, there were significant and widespread losses of information in the recall protocols.

The second aspect of Bartlett's results is more fascinating. There was a strong tendency for the successive recalls to *normalize* and *rationalize* the occurrences in the story. That is, subjects showed an overwhelming tendency to add to and alter the stories, to supply additional material that was not contained in the original. These changes often had the effect of making the story more "normal," conventional, or reasonable. It's likely that the story was quite strange to Bartlett's subjects, his friends and colleagues in Great Britain, so it is not especially surprising that their retellings modernized and demystified the original. For example, note how the ghost theme becomes progressively less prominent in the two retellings in Table 7-2, even though "ghosts" is part of the title of the story. What is fascinating about this result is the *source* of this additional material. Where did it come from, if not from the story itself? It came from the subjects' memories.

Schemata

Bartlett borrowed the idea of a **schema** to explain the source of these adjustments and additions.[1] In his use of the term, a schema was "an active organisation of past reactions or past experiences" (1932, p. 201), essentially what we've been calling general world knowledge. More generally, a schema is *a stored framework or body of knowledge about some topic.* Bartlett claimed that when we encounter new material, such as the "Ghosts" story, we try to relate the material to existing *schemata* (the plural of "schema"). If the material does not match an existing schema, then we tend to alter the material to make it fit (similar in spirit to Piaget's *assimilation*). As such, recall is not a true, exact recall or reproduction of the original material. Instead, it is a reconstruction based on elements from the original story and on our existing schemata.

Reconstruction Versus Episodic Recall   What do we have here? We have a seemingly simple task, "read this story then recall it," which we might expect to lead to a relatively pure episodic memory ("I remember reading the story about ghosts, and it goes like this . . ."). But when we turn to the results, we find that, unlike typical recall results in

---

[1]"I strongly dislike the term 'schema.' It is at once too definite and too sketchy . . . it does not indicate what is very essential to the whole notion. . . . I shall, however, continue to use the term 'schema' when it seems best to do so, but I will attempt to define its application more narrowly" (Bartlett, 1932, pp. 200–201). The widespread use and sketchiness of the term continued after Bartlett as well. Later in the chapter we will substitute the term *script,* which, at least currently, has a more definite connotation.

episodic tasks, subjects are remembering things that weren't there. The source of these remembered things must be the subjects' memories, their knowledge—however vague—of events such as "Indian warriors doing battle" and so on.

An unimaginative way of looking at these results would be to claim that information already stored in memory is exerting an interfering effect on current memory performance. We called it proactive interference in Chapter 5 (see also Dempster, 1985). A much more intriguing perspective is that normal comprehension takes place within the context of an individual's entire knowledge system. As such, efforts to understand and remember meaningful material involve one's own meaning system or general knowledge of the world. In short, what we already know exerts a strong influence on what we remember about new material.

Extensions of Reconstructive Effects   More recent research has fleshed out some of the details of this generalization and has added to our understanding of the importance of existing knowledge or schemata. For example, knowledge of the theme or topic of a passage improves people's memory for the passage (e.g., Bransford & Johnson, 1972; Dooling & Lachman, 1971). On the other hand, providing a theme, say, by attaching a title to a story, can also distort recall or recognition in the direction of the theme.

A clever demonstration of this distortion effect was provided by Sulin and Dooling (1974). One group of subjects read a paragraph about a fictitious character: "Gerald Martin's seizure of power. Gerald Martin strove to undermine the existing government to satisfy his political ambitions. Many of the people of his country supported his efforts..." (p. 256). A second group read the same paragraph, but the name Adolf Hitler was substituted for Gerald Martin. After a five-minute waiting period, subjects were shown a list of sentences and had to indicate whether each was exactly the same, nearly the same, or very different from one in the original story.

Preexperimental knowledge—that is, existing knowledge about Hitler—led to significant distortions in the subjects' recognition of sentences. Subjects who read the Hitler paragraph rated sentences as "the same" more frequently when the sentences matched their existing knowledge about Hitler, even though the original passage contained no such information (e.g., "Hitler was obsessed by the desire to conquer the world," p. 259). Furthermore, these *thematic effects,* as they were called, grew stronger in the group that was tested one week after reading the story.

This thematic effect was particularly striking in a second experiment that Sulin and Dooling conducted. One group read an account of Carol Harris ("Carol Harris was a problem child from birth. She was wild, stubborn, and violent..."). Only 5% of the subjects in this group said "yes" one week later when asked if the sentence, "She was deaf, dumb, and blind," had been part of the passage. In a contrasting group, the same paragraph was presented, but the name Helen Keller was used. Fully 50% of these subjects said "yes" one week later to the same critical question. The same pattern of results was also obtained by Dooling and Christiaansen (1977), in which subjects were told that the paragraph about Carol Harris that they had read a week before had in fact been about Helen Keller. Just as before, subjects responded "yes" to statements that referred to thematically consistent information, as if they were drawing inferences from their existing knowledge rather than remembering the passage on its own terms. Dooling and Christiaansen concluded that thematic effects are quite prominent during retrieval, at the time of test, since they were observed a full week after exposure to the passage.

Kintsch (1977) has pointed out that such results argue that recall for connected, meaningful passages is "neither reproductive nor constructive nor reconstructive, but all three" (p. 363). Immediately after reading, recall is fairly accurate—in other words, reproductive—especially for less exotic passages than "The War of the Ghosts." Note, however, that thematic inferences are still observed here, particularly when the title or topic of the passage "invites" the reader to draw such inferences. Later testing, especially when the topic or theme is already familiar to the subject, shows even more prominent reconstructive effects.

Finally, *constructive* effects, to use Kintsch's (1977) term, refer to drawing inferences from the passage *during* the original comprehension process. For instance, Sulin and Dooling's subjects no doubt inferred that it was the German government being undermined in the Hitler story. If they did so at the time of original reading, then the constructive memory effect should influence all later retrieval attempts. If the inference was only drawn at the time of retrieval, however, then the thematic effects would be part of reconstructive memory. In general, it can be quite difficult to disentangle inferences drawn during original comprehension from those drawn during retrieval (but see Frederiksen, 1975), unless performance is tested both immediately after comprehension and then again at a later time (and even this introduces another complexity, since recalling a passage once will influence a second recall attempt).

These are complex and important ideas, and we'll return to them again throughout this chapter and in Chapter 9, where the combination of semantic and linguistic knowledge is discussed. For now, just remember the most prominent feature of the results: existing knowledge can exert a tremendous influence on our memory for meaningful material. As a normal by-product of understanding, we relate new information to general knowledge already stored in memory. Subsequently, our performance in a memory task is based both on the new information and on general knowledge. It is probably impossible to find a more convincing example of conceptually driven processing than this—the effect that existing knowledge has on current comprehension. And, since a new *episode* is being influenced by existing *semantic* knowledge, this line of research demonstrates clearly a major topic of this chapter—the interaction of episodic and semantic memories.

Eyewitness Memory and Testimony

A famous program of research by Loftus and her colleagues has expanded this generalization and, in the process, has suggested some disturbing conclusions about the reliability of eyewitness testimony. To the generalization that "what we already know exerts a strong influence on what we remember" we can add "and what happens *after that* can also influence what we remember or recall." As if Bartlett's research weren't enough to call into question our ability to remember faithfully, Loftus's research demonstrates distortions in what is eventually recalled or recognized, depending on what has happened in the meantime.

Loftus's Initial Research   Loftus began this line of research by examining the effects of leading questions, that is, questions that tend to suggest to the individual what answer is appropriate.[2] This is the report we used to start our discussion of semantic memory in Chapter 6. Loftus and Palmer's (1974) subjects were shown films of car accidents and were asked to estimate the speeds of the cars when they "smashed," "collided," "bumped," "hit," or "contacted" each other. As you learned, the stronger verbs led subjects to estimate higher speeds; the results are in Table 7-3.

Loftus and Palmer pointed out that two interpretations were possible for this effect. One was simply a response bias interpretation, that subjects were uncertain of the exact speeds, so biased their estimates in the direction implied by the verb. This, of course, is the "leading question effect," that the phrasing of a question will bias the individual to respond in a certain way. While the effect is obviously important when issues of trial testimony are considered, it is a somewhat less interesting possibility here than the second interpretation.

The second possibility was the following. Rather than simply biasing the subjects' responses, it seemed possible that the question about speed had in some way *altered* the subjects' memory representation of the scene in the film. In other words, subjects might literally remember a more severe accident than they saw if they were later exposed to the implication that the cars had "smashed" together. This kind of effect is referred to as a *memory impairment*—a genuine change or alteration in

---

[2]An early set of questions was, "Do you get headaches frequently, and if so how often?" versus "if so, how occasionally?" The "often" group reported an average of 2.2 headaches per week, the "occasionally" group reported 0.7 per week (Loftus, 1980, p. 157). As I recall the anecdote, Loftus was interviewing potential candidates for an aspirin commercial with these questions and ended up starring in one of the commercials herself. If memory serves, her TV ad began with the line "I teach college." Readers are invited to draw the inference between aspirin and college teaching themselves.

Table 7-3   SPEED ESTIMATES FOR VERBS IN
             EXPERIMENT 1

Verb	Average Speed Estimate
Smashed	40.8
Collided	39.3
Bumped	38.1
Hit	34.0
Contacted	31.8

Adapted from Loftus & Palmer, 1974.

the subjects' memory for an experienced event as a function of some later event. (Note that the episodic memory literature also has a name for this kind of effect—retroactive interference.) For example, a week later, subjects were asked "Did you see any broken glass?" Many in the "smashed" group said yes, even though there had been no broken glass in the film.

The Misinformation Effect   As this sort of research became more common, investigators developed a standard task to test for the effects of misleading information. In the typical experiment, subjects see the original event in a film or set of slides. For purposes of illustration, say that the slides depict a car accident, and that one slide in particular shows a stop sign. Afterward, the subjects are exposed to some additional infor-

In eyewitness memory and testimony, any new information about an event is integrated with relevant existing knowledge. Thus, we are less then accurate when we attempt to retrieve such knowledge, since we are often unable to discriminate between new and original information.

mation, for instance, a narrative account of the car accident. Some subjects receive only neutral information, whereas others are given a specific bit of misinformation; for example, the narrative mentions "the yield sign." Finally, there is usually a two-choice recognition task, in which the subjects indicate what they remember from the original event, for example, whether it was a stop sign or a yield sign. (Sometimes, a recall test is given instead; see Zaragoza, McCloskey, & Jamis, 1987.)

The common result is that some subjects will incorrectly claim to remember the yield sign, the standard *misinformation effect*. Belli (1989), for instance, found that misled subjects showed more than a 20% reduction in accuracy, compared to control subjects who were not exposed to the misinformation. Loftus, Donders, Hoffman, and Schooler (1989) found, furthermore, that misled subjects were in fact faster in their incorrect judgments—picking the yield sign—than in their correct decisions, as shown in Figure 7-1. This suggests a rather surprising degree of misplaced confidence on the part of the misled subjects.

While these results implied that memory might truly be impaired or altered by the misinformation, several later studies called into question the original methods of testing, and hence the conclusion of memory impairment. The crux of the debate involves the nature of the recognition test, and the "different ways of arriving at the same memory report" (Loftus & Hoffman, 1989, p. 103). In particular, it's always possible that the subjects did not actually encode the original item (stop sign) when they saw the slides. If so, then the misinformation effect could either

FIGURE 7-1

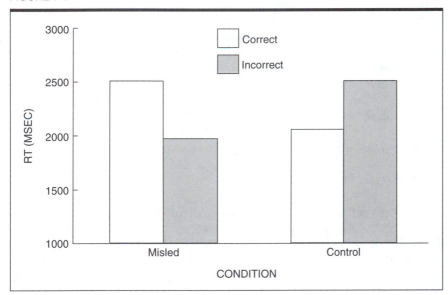

Mean reaction time to correct and incorrect targets (e.g., stop sign, yield sign) depending on whether the subject had been misled or not. Note that misled subjects were faster on "incorrect" responses, that is, saying "yes" to the yield sign.

reflect guessing or remembering the yield sign from the narrative (McCloskey & Zaragoza, 1985). In either case, the misinformation effect would not signify true memory impairment at all, but instead some other process. In fact, several studies (McCloskey & Zaragoza, 1985; Zaragoza & Koshmider, 1989) used a modified task that corrected for this problem; the results seemed to support the nonimpairment interpretation.

Loftus's (1991; Loftus & Hoffman, 1989) recent statements summarize the current view of these findings. Based on the accumulated evidence, she noted that genuine alteration of the original memory is at most only a small part of the overall misinformation effect. A larger component, she noted, is what's called *misinformation acceptance,* which is at least as disturbing as genuine memory impairment. In misinformation acceptance, the subject does not remember seeing the stop sign at all but is quite willing to "accept" the yield sign when the narrative mentions it; later on, the subject reports seeing the yield sign. In other words, subjects seem quite willing to accept information presented after the fact; they then become quite certain about these "second-hand" memories. These tendencies probably grow stronger as more and more time elapses since the original event, and the original memory becomes less accessible.

Zaragoza and Koshmider (1989) reported a similarly disturbing result; 15% of their *control* subjects selected the yield sign, even though those subjects had never seen or read the misinformation. In their words, "subjects may report misinformation even if they know they *do not remember seeing it*" (p. 246, emphasis added). Despite our sense that we remember episodes or events accurately ("I recall vividly that . . . ," or even better, "I saw it with my own eyes!"), we often misremember what we've experienced or form memories on the basis of suggestion from some other source besides the original event. And despite this, we are unjustifiably confident in our accuracy and surprisingly unaware of the unreliability of our own memories. As Loftus and Hoffman (1989) put it, both memory psychologists and the courts should find it interesting that such a memory can arise through the process of suggestion and then become "as real and as vivid as a memory that arose from the actual perception" (p. 103). How do you feel about the reliability of eyewitness testimony now?

Semantic Integration

Let's study a final research program within this general topic of reconstructive memory, a demonstration that related pieces of information become fused in memory. This third line of evidence is the well-known set of studies by Bransford and Franks (e.g., 1971, 1972). As before, this important set of results will be more sensible to you if you begin with the demonstration in Table 7-4.

Bransford and Franks (1971) were interested in the general topic of how people acquire and remember *ideas,* not merely individual sentences

Table 7-4 SAMPLE EXPERIMENT BY BRANSFORD AND FRANKS (1971)

Instructions: Read each sentence in the table individually. As soon as you have read each one, close your eyes and count to five. Then look at and answer the question that follows each sentence. Begin now.

The girl broke the window on the porch.	Broke what?
The tree in the front yard shaded the man who was smoking his pipe.	Where?
The hill was steep.	What was?
The sweet jelly was on the kitchen table.	On what?
The tree was tall.	Was what?
The old car climbed the hill.	What did?
The ants in the kitchen ate the jelly.	Where?
The girl who lives next door broke the window on the porch.	Lives where?
The car pulled the trailer.	Did what?
The ants ate the sweet jelly that was on the table.	What did?
The girl lives next door.	Who does?
The tree shaded the man who was smoking his pipe.	What did?
The sweet jelly was on the table.	Where?
The girl who lives next door broke the large window.	Broke what?
The man was smoking his pipe.	Who was?
The old car climbed the steep hill.	The what?
The large window was on the porch.	Where?
The tall tree was in the front yard.	What was?
The car pulling the trailer climbed the steep hill.	Did what?
The jelly was on the table.	What was?
The tall tree in the front yard shaded the man.	Did what?
The car pulling the trailer climbed the hill.	Which car?
The ants ate the jelly.	Ate what?
The window was large.	What was?

but integrated, semantic ideas. They asked their subjects to listen to sentences like those in Table 7-4 one by one, and then (after a short distractor task) answer a simple question about each sentence. After going through this procedure for all 24 sentences and taking a five-minute break, subjects were then given another test. During this second test, subjects had to indicate for each sentence whether it had been on the original list of 24 sentences or not, simply by deciding "yes" or "no." They also had to indicate, on a 10-point scale, how confident they were about their judgments: positive ratings (from 1 to 5) meant they were sure they had seen the sentence, negative ratings (from −1 to −5) meant they were sure they had not. *Without* looking back at the original sentences, take a moment now to make these judgments about the sentences in Table 7-5; OLD means "Yes, I've seen it before" and NEW means "No, I didn't see it before."

All 28 sentences in this recognition test were related to the original ideas in the first set of sentences. The clever aspect of the recognition test that Bransford and Franks devised, however, was that only four of the 28 sentences had in fact appeared on the original list; just as is true

Table 7-5   SAMPLE EXPERIMENT BY BRANSFORD AND FRANKS (1971)

Instructions: Check OLD or NEW for each sentence, then indicate how confident you are on a scale from 1 to 5 (5 is "very high confidence").

	OLD/ NEW	Confidence (−5 to +5)
1. The car climbed the hill.	_____	_____
2. The girl who lives next door broke the window.	_____	_____
3. The old man who was smoking his pipe climbed the steep hill.	_____	_____
4. The tree was in the front yard.	_____	_____
5. The ants ate the sweet jelly that was in the kitchen.	_____	_____
6. The window was on the porch.	_____	_____
7. The barking dog jumped on the old car in the front yard.	_____	_____
8. The tree in the front yard shaded the man.	_____	_____
9. The ants were in the kitchen.	_____	_____
10. The old car pulled the trailer.	_____	_____
11. The tree shaded the man who was smoking his pipe.	_____	_____
12. The tall tree shaded the man who was smoking his pipe.	_____	_____
13. The ants ate the jelly on the kitchen table.	_____	_____
14. The old car, pulling the trailer, climbed the hill.	_____	_____
15. The girl who lives next door broke the large window on the porch.	_____	_____
16. The tall tree shaded the man.	_____	_____
17. The ants in the kitchen ate the jelly.	_____	_____
18. The car was old.	_____	_____
19. The girl broke the large window.	_____	_____
20. The ants ate the sweet jelly that was on the kitchen table.	_____	_____
21. The ants were on the table in the kitchen.	_____	_____
22. The old car pulling the trailer climbed the steep hill.	_____	_____
23. The girl broke the window on the porch.	_____	_____
24. The scared cat that broke the window on the porch climbed the tree.	_____	_____
25. The tree shaded the man.	_____	_____
26. The old car climbed the steep hill.	_____	_____
27. The girl broke the window.	_____	_____
28. The man who lives next door broke the large window on the porch.	_____	_____

STOP. Count the number of sentences judged OLD.

of Table 7-5, the other 24 are NEW. As you no doubt noticed in Table 7-4, the separate sentences were all derived from four basic "idea groupings," for example, "The ants in the kitchen ate the sweet jelly that was on the table." Each of the complete idea groupings consisted of FOUR separate simple *propositions:* for example,

    (a) the ants were in the kitchen,
    (b) the ants ate the jelly,
    (c) the jelly was sweet,
    (d) the jelly was on the table.

The original set of sentences (Table 7-4) presented six sentences from each idea grouping. Two of the six were so-called ONES, simple, one-idea propositions like "The jelly was on the table." Another two sentences were TWOS, where two simple propositions were merged, as in "The ants in the kitchen ate the jelly." Finally, the last two were THREES, as in "The ants ate the sweet jelly that was on the table."

In Bransford and Franks's first two experiments, only ONES, TWOS, and THREES were presented on the original list; in the third experiment, a few FOURS also appeared during learning, but this made no difference in the results. In all three experiments, the final recognition test (Table 7-5) presented ONES, TWOS, THREES, *and* the overall FOUR for each idea grouping.

So what did they find? Just as your performance probably indicated, Bransford and Franks's subjects overwhelmingly judged THREES and FOURS as OLD; in other words, they judged that they *had* seen them on the study list (just as you probably judged question 20, the FOUR, as OLD). Furthermore, they were very confident in their ratings, as shown in Figure 7-2 (taken from Experiment 3). That is, people were recognizing the sentences that expressed the overall idea grouping most thoroughly, even when they had not seen exactly those sentences during study. Such responses are called *false alarms* or *false positives,* saying "OLD" when the correct response is "NEW."

FIGURE 7-2

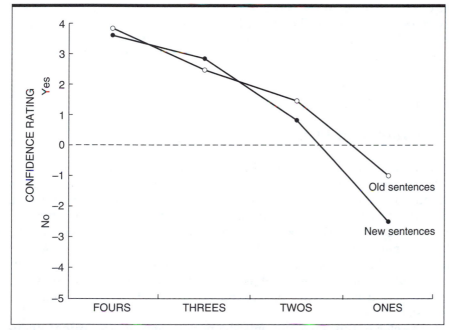

Confidence ratings for subjects' judgments about NEW and OLD sentences. (From Bransford & Franks, 1971.)

Moreover, subjects were not especially confident about having seen genuinely OLD sentences (e.g., #11, 17, 23, and 26 in Table 7-5); the only sentences they were sure about were NONCASE sentences (e.g., #3, 7, 24, and 28 in Table 7-5), in which ideas from *different* groupings had been combined. Furthermore, they were fairly confident that they had *not* seen ONES, as shown by the strong negative ratings in the figure (between −1 and −3), even though they had seen several sentences of that short length (e.g., #9 in Table 7-4). Apparently, since the shorter sentences didn't express the whole idea, subjects believed that they had not seen them before.

Semantic Integration What do these results suggest when considered in the light of Bartlett's and Loftus's demonstrations? Bransford and Franks (1971, 1972) concluded that subjects had acquired a more general idea than any of the individual study sentences had expressed, that subjects "integrated the information communicated by sets of individual sentences to *construct wholistic semantic ideas*" (1971, p. 348, emphasis added). Similar to what Loftus and Palmer's subjects had done, Bransford and Franks's subjects were reporting a *composite* memory, one in which related information was stored together in memory. All the related ideas expressed in the individual sentences seem to have been fused together into one semantic representation, one memory record of the whole idea. In such a circumstance, the subjects' later recognition performance was entirely reasonable: they were matching the combined ideas in the recognition sentences to their composite memory representations. Rather than finding verbatim memory, Bransford and Franks found "memory for meaning," memory based on the semantic integration of related material (see also Richardson, 1985; Radvansky & Zacks's, 1991, data indicate that subjects can structure the input sentences based on situation-specific "mental models"; also Radvansky, Spieler, & Zacks, 1993).

Technical and Content Accuracy

Note two general points here. First, recall or recognition of meaningful material seems quite unlike the recall and recognition we discussed in Chapter 5. That is, episodic memory tasks generally look for, and find, performance based solely on the items presented as stimuli. This is a very heavily data-driven kind of processing. Occasionally, say, in the clustering studies, subjects would recall information that hadn't been in the original list, for instance, "pear" intruding into recall of the fruit category. But for the most part, subjects involved in episodic tasks, in which nothing like a meaningful paragraph is presented, recalled what they were shown.

Let's refer to this aspect of episodic performance as **technical accuracy**—subjects recall or recognize with some degree of accuracy, where accuracy is defined as *recalling or recognizing exactly what was experienced.* In a more semantic task, however, we find very little emphasis on, or evidence for, remembering exactly what was presented. Instead, subjects are remembering the material in terms of its overall *meaning.* When scored according to strict, verbatim criteria, technical accuracy ranges from not especially impressive (Bartlett's and Loftus and Palmer's results) to dramatically inaccurate (Bransford and Franks's results)—"abysmally awful" in one researcher's words.

The second general point here is more important. Technical accuracy is an unsatisfactory way of evaluating memory for meaningful material, if you'll think about it for a moment. For one thing, it misses the important fact that subjects *are* remembering with a fairly high degree of accuracy—it's just a different kind of accuracy. Let's call this different kind of accuracy **content accuracy,** where accuracy here is defined as *recalling or recognizing the meaning or content of what was experienced.* The difference between these two terms is that technical accuracy stresses *verbatim memory,* while content accuracy stresses memory for concepts and ideas, the *meaningful, semantic content* of the material.

Which of these kinds of accuracy is more important? Well, it seems clear that each kind is important for different memory situations and demands. We should not dismiss technical accuracy too casually, I think. Bartlett's opinion notwithstanding ("literal recall is extraordinarily unimportant"), there are many situations in the real world in which technically accurate memory is important. It doesn't help me to remember the *concept* of "save" if I've forgotten how *my* word processor saves a manuscript, after all. And content accuracy isn't too helpful for other kinds of knowledge either, for instance, when I have to remember my social security number, the classroom I teach in, or my mother's birthday.

On the other hand, there are also countless situations in which technical accuracy is not called for, or even would be considered very inappropriate; for instance, you ask a friend "Hey, what did Dr. Wallace say in class yesterday?" and the friend responds with a verbatim retelling of the lecture. In such situations, instead, recalling the *gist* or overall meaning of an event is important. Your ability to paraphrase correctly, for example, is a demonstration of content accuracy. You will not be asked for verbatim recall of this text on your exams, although you may memorize verbatim definitions of certain key concepts and terms. Instead, you are usually tested on content accuracy, on how well you have retained the ideas and concepts, and on how well you can express these ideas in your own words.

Consider Bransford and Franks's subjects again, and the kind of memory system that produces false alarms to related sentences that have never been shown. Bransford and Franks's subjects made false alarms to FOURS such as "The ants in the kitchen ate the sweet jelly that was on the table." But isn't that the whole point of memory? Isn't this an instance of high—even perfect—content accuracy? In other words, what good would a memory system be to us if it *didn't* combine related information together into a unified, composite idea? It would be absolutely debilitating if our memories didn't pull related information together, if we didn't notice the semantic relationships among separate ideas, and if we didn't store them together. If our memories couldn't do this, then in a sense we could never understand—we could only record isolated fragments in memory, without drawing connections among them. To reduce it to concrete terms, think how useless your memory would be if you didn't realize that the jelly that the ants ate was the *same* jelly that was on the kitchen table!

Integrative Memory   By focusing on content accuracy, a different perspective on memory and cognitive processes emerges, one that emphasizes how the memory system deals with meaningful, related information. We store separate bits of information *together* to the extent that those separate bits are related to each other—the principle of semantic relatedness. We use what we already know, call it schemata, general world knowledge, or semantic memory, to understand new experiences in a conceptually driven fashion. Those new experiences then become part of our elaborated knowledge structures and continue to assist later cycles of conceptually driven processing.

Let's call this the *integrative memory tendency*. One negative consequence of this tendency is that the separate bits of information may not match our existing knowledge completely, leading to certain kinds of distortions when we attempt to remember (Bartlett, 1932). Moreover, later retrieval may be technically inaccurate, a definite problem in situations like eyewitness testimony where verbatim accuracy is the goal (Neisser, 1981). An overwhelmingly positive consequence of this tendency, however, is that content accuracy is enhanced, that we can understand and remember complex, meaningful events and episodes.

Summary Points: reconstructive memory; schema/schemata; thematic effects; memory impairment versus misinformation acceptance; semantic integration; technical and content accuracy

▼ Propositions

If you'll think for a moment about the kinds of experiments we've just been discussing, you'll notice an interesting fact: in most or all of the reconstructive memory studies, we intentionally "lure" subjects into making mistakes (at least in the sense of technical accuracy). That is, we present meaningful material like a story or a set of related sentences, then do something that "invites" mistakes of one sort or another. Bartlett gave his subjects a peculiar story, much too long to be remembered verbatim, and filled with unusual events; Loftus and Palmer lured subjects into remembering a more (or less) severe accident by the verbs they presented; and, however reasonable semantic integration is, it was clearly a "setup" for Bransford and Franks to present sentences that were so unmistakably related.

This is not to say that such research is unrepresentative, biased, or in some other way unfair or misleading; there are many situations in everyday affairs in which related information lures us into remembering something that wasn't in the original. Furthermore, it's obviously important to understand how human memory can be influenced by such factors. On the other hand, there is a more general kind of research in which semantic and episodic factors are combined, but the subjects are not deliberately misled or lured into mistakes. In this other kind of research, to which we now turn, we are merely interested in what subjects can recall when presented with ordinary connected prose. Putting it simply, aside from the occasionally distorting or misleading effects that existing knowledge can exert, what are the more ordinary effects of existing knowledge as we understand simple sentences, stories, and other forms of connected discourse?[3]

The Nature of Propositions

We're going to conclude in this section that what people remember from meaningful material is the *idea* or *gist,* the basic semantic relationships embedded in a sentence or paragraph. But to talk about remembering ideas, we need a way of representing those ideas, so we'll know what we mean by "meaning." We need some method of diagramming a sentence's meaning, to pin down what the vague term "meaning" means. And, in order to do research on content accuracy, we need some way of scoring subjects' recall to see if they remembered the meaning of a sentence or not.

By nearly unanimous agreement, the semantic unit that codes meaning is called a **proposition.** A proposition is a *representation of meaning that can be stored in and retrieved from memory.* Usually, a proposition represents—illustrates, in a sense—the meaning of a single simple sentence. In Anderson's (1985) terms, "A proposition is the smallest unit of knowledge that can stand as a separate assertion" (p. 114), that is, the smallest unit about which you can make true/false judgments. Let's begin with this basic unit of meaning by learning the terminology of propositions, and learning how they're structured.

---

[3]The dictionary definition of "discourse" is: "communication of ideas, information, etc., especially by talking; conversation." In cognitive psychology, we use the term to refer to any connected and meaningful sequence of words, from simple sentences up through paragraphs or, in principle, whole books. Completely interchangeable terms are *connected text* and *connected discourse;* understanding such discourse or text is referred to as *discourse processing* or *text processing.*

DEMONSTRATIONS

Countless demonstrations on general reconstructive memory effects are possible, all relatively easy to perform. An excellent source of ideas is Bransford's (1979) book, chock full of sample passages that can be tested.

1. Thematic effects. See Bransford's "washing clothes" paragraph, in which strangely neutral wordings are used to describe a procedure; some subjects are given the title "Washing Clothes," and some are not. See how recall differs between the two groups. (Bransford & Johnson, 1972, 1973, and Dooling & Lachman, 1971, report several other stories that can be used for the same purpose. Use also the Adolf Hitler/ Helen Keller examples from the chapter.)

2. Owens, Bower, and Black (1979) presented relatively ordinary stories; for example, a person makes a cup of coffee, goes to the doctor, goes to a lecture and then the grocery store. Some subjects read the story without context, but others read a preface: "Nancy woke up feeling sick again, and wondered if she might be pregnant." Their results showed what they called the "soap opera effect." For instance, subjects ascribed all sorts of motivations, intentions, and thoughts to Nancy—she's pregnant, having an affair with her college professor, and so on. Try writing a few such stories, presenting them to subjects, waiting several days for the "soap opera effect" to take hold, then testing the subjects' recall.

3. Capitalize on the unexpected. If an unusual event occurs during one of your classes—someone unusual or unexpected walks into the classroom, a disruption ensues—wait a week and then test "eyewitness memory" for the event. You may never know what *actually* happened, but you'll get a variety of reports on what people *think* happened. Loftus apparently staged such events in her classes for this purpose; check with your professor before staging one yourself.

The Basics   In Chapter 6, the term *proposition* was defined as a simple relationship between two concepts, one that can be expressed by a simple, declarative sentence: for example, "A robin has wings." Figure 7-3 diagrams this relationship in the familiar way, using network nodes and pathways. Next to that, the sentence is also diagrammed in terms of propositions. If you compare the two, you'll see that the propositional representation is only slightly different. First, we place a central node in the diagram; it stands for—represents—the overall sentence. Then each concept in the simple sentence is attached to the node by its own labeled pathway. Really, the only differences between the left and right diagrams are superficial.

But because sentences often express more than a relationship between *two* concepts, we are going to drop that limitation and redefine the proposition as the *set of semantic nodes connected by labeled pathways, where*

4. As a test of implicit/explicit memory, adapt the word stem completion task from the text. Have your subjects read a passage of text, occupy them with some distractor task for awhile, then have half of them attempt explicit recall of words in the passage, and half complete a number of word stems based on content words in the passage.

5. Administer the coin recognition test shown below to several people, to see how heavily we rely on reconstructive long-term memory. Be sure to have your subjects indicate how certain they are about their choice.

Which is a correct drawing of a U.S. penny?

FIGURE 7-3

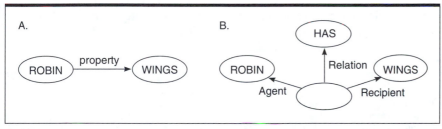

A simple network representation (A) and propositional representation (B) of "A robin has wings."

the entire collection of concepts and relationships expresses the meaning of a sentence.[4] And, as you'll soon see, we will no longer limit ourselves to diagramming relationships that are already stored in semantic memory. Instead, *any* set of meaningful relationships among concepts can be represented in propositional format. (Try sketching the propositions from the Bransford and Franks study, for example, "The ants ate the jelly." The propositional approach is exactly the one they used in constructing the ONES, TWOS, and so on.)

Semantic Cases as Pathway Labels   A genuine difference between simpler semantic networks and the propositional approach involves the labels on the pathways. In semantic memory, we limited ourselves to a small handful of types of relationships; in fact, we only used *isa* and *property* pathways. But a sentence can have many different kinds of relationships among the words, so we need a longer list of labels for the pathways in propositional notation.

Technically, the source of these relationships was a theory in psycholinguistics known as **case grammar,** an important approach advanced by Fillmore (1968) and others. In this theory, the sentence is analyzed in terms of the *semantic roles* played by each word—just as an actor or actress plays a certain *role* in a play, so each content word in a sentence plays a *role* in the meaning of the sentence. These different semantic roles are essentially the different labels we'll use in our propositional diagrams. The psycholinguistics of the theory will be covered at some length in Chapter 8. For now, we need only a basic understanding of the different semantic roles, to get going on the topic of propositions.

Consider a very simple sentence: "Laura eats spaghetti." To state the obvious here, "Laura" is the individual *doing* something in this sentence, "spaghetti" is the thing it is done to, and "eat" is the thing Laura does to the spaghetti. In propositional terminology, Laura is the *agent* or *actor* in this sentence, the individual (or sometimes the thing) performing the overall action in the sentence. What role is played by the spaghetti here? It is the *recipient* of the overall action, or alternatively, the *patient*.[5] And the overall action, the basic relationship being expressed in the sentence—eating—is called the *relation* in this approach, not a particularly memorable label, but useful because of its generality.

Consult Figure 7-4 to see a propositional diagram of "Laura eats spaghetti," along with a listing of the semantic cases used as labels in the propositional approach to meaning. A slight modification of the sentence,

---

[4]Note that the sentence is sometimes not a complete, grammatical sentence, yet is still a proposition; a phrase, for instance, or any meaningful fragment can also be represented in propositional format. For simplicity, however, we'll deal only with full sentences here. We will also postpone the more *linguistic* aspects of propositions until the next chapter.

[5]In more formal psycholinguistic terms, the *recipient* case is often called the *patient* case. Just as you are the *patient,* the one to whom things are done, when you visit the doctor's office, the patient case in a sentence identifies the person or thing to whom something is done.

FIGURE 7-4

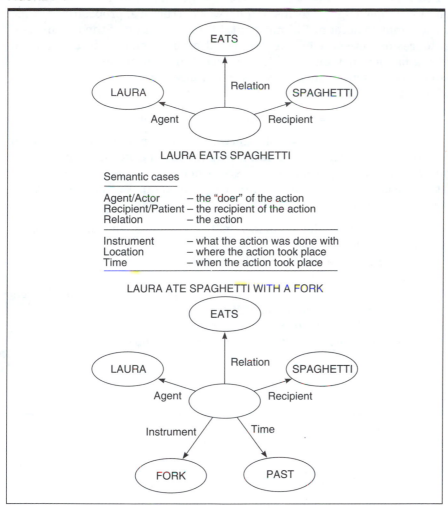

Propositional representations of two sentences, "Laura eats spaghetti" and "Laura ate spaghetti with a fork." The various semantic cases that appear in sentences are listed along with a brief explanation.

"Laura ate spaghetti with a fork," is also diagrammed, to show some of the other typical case roles in this approach. Bear in mind here that what we're doing is simply devising a way of diagramming or representing the *meaning* of a sentence (unlike what you did in seventh-grade English, when you diagrammed the *grammatical* roles played by the words). The more constituents there are in a sentence, the more concepts and pathways we'll need to represent the full meaning. Nonetheless, the entire meaning will still be shown by the proposition or set of propositions that represent the sentence.

Elaborated Propositions   Just as we attempted to account for semantic knowledge in terms of a network structure, propositional theories attempt to account for our mental representation of the meanings of sentences as networks of interconnected propositions. To illustrate, consider a particularly memorable sentence and its propositional representation, as presented in Figure 7-5 (sentence from Anderson & Bower, 1973, notational scheme based on Anderson, 1985). The sentence,

(1) The hippie touched the debutante in the park,

is represented here as a set of interrelated concepts, one for each main word in the sentence. Each relationship among the words is specified by the type of pathway that connects the nodes (e.g., agent, recipient or patient, location, etc.). Thus sentence (1) is composed of five relationships or connections of meaning:

- TOUCHing is the **relation** in the sentence, the *topic or major event* in the sentence.
- HIPPIE is the **agent** for this event, the *actor or individual* who did the TOUCHing.
- DEBUTANTE is the **patient or recipient** of the event, the *one who received the action* of TOUCHing.
- PARK is the **location** of the event, and the
- TOUCHing occurred at some unspecified **time** in the PAST.

FIGURE 7-5

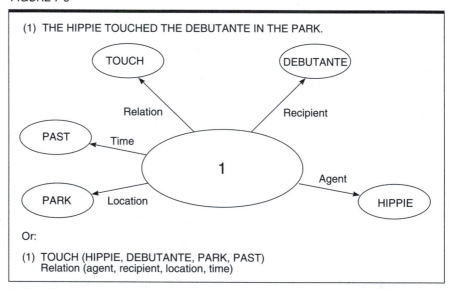

A propositional representation, in "node-plus-pathway" notation and in written form, of the sentence "The hippie touched the debutante in the park." Network notation after Anderson (1980) and Anderson & Bower (1973); written proposition after Kintsch (1974).

An alternate format for representing propositions involves a *relation,* usually the verb, followed by *an ordered list of concepts,* the **arguments** of the relation (e.g., Kintsch, 1974; see bottom of Figure 7-5).

Strengths of Propositional Theories What are the advantages of a proposition-based theory of long-term memory for meaning? First, note that the proposition accurately reflects the meaning of the sentence. While this may seem true just by definition, consider a more subtle point, that a propositional representation is relatively *unaffected* by superficial aspects of the sentence. For instance, look at Figure 7-5 and decide how the following sentences would be diagrammed:

> (1a) In the park, it was the debutante who was touched by the hippie.
> (1b) The hippie, who was in the park, touched the debutante.

If you concluded that Figure 7-5 represents *all* these sentences, you're right: each is just a superficially different way of saying the same thing (this glosses over rather subtle differences in active and passive sentences; see Chapters 8 and 9).

As it happens, people tend to be fairly *inaccurate* when it comes to remembering the actual surface form of sentences, whether they were active or passive, whether the prepositional phrase came first or last, and so on (e.g., Sachs, 1967). This is exactly what we would expect if people store and then remember the propositions specified by sentences rather than remember the verbatim sentences themselves. (Can you see the relationship to Bransford and Franks's results?)

Now consider a much more important advantage. We are interested in understanding what people store in memory when they comprehend complex meanings. This is a much more difficult task than representing the kind of relationship that stands between ROBIN and WINGS, you'll agree. One attractive feature of proposition-based theories is that the basic elements of nodes and pathways are flexible and powerful enough to represent the whole range of complexity in which we're interested. With propositions, we can represent simple semantic connections—ROBIN *has* WINGS—all the way up to complex, sentence-based connections—The hippie touched the debutante in the park.

Another demonstration of this power is that a second sentence that is related to the first can be incorporated into our representation, so that the relationship *between* the sentences is also coded. Consider an expanded set of sentences in the hippie story:

> (1) The hippie touched the debutante in the park.
> (2) So, (3) she slapped him.

Figure 7-6 diagrams both sentences in propositional format and connects them by means of a higher node, which represents the idea of **cau-**

FIGURE 7-6

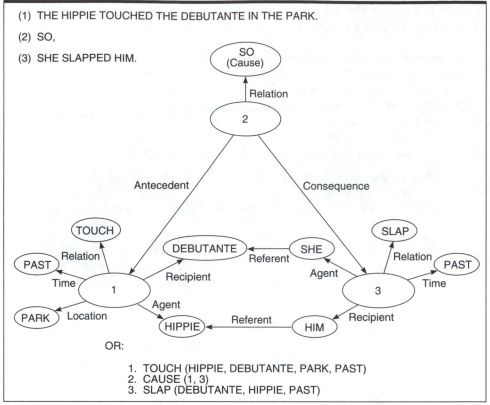

(1) THE HIPPIE TOUCHED THE DEBUTANTE IN THE PARK.

(2) SO,

(3) SHE SLAPPED HIM.

OR:

1. TOUCH (HIPPIE, DEBUTANTE, PARK, PAST)
2. CAUSE (1, 3)
3. SLAP (DEBUTANTE, HIPPIE, PAST)

A propositional representation, in network and written form, of "The hippie touched the debutante in the park. So she slapped him." Network notation after Anderson (1980) and Anderson and Bower (1973); written proposition after Kintsch (1974).

sation. That is, it should be clear from the figure that the two separate ideas or events are specified as nodes #1 and #3. Furthermore, because the meaning of #1 is the cause for the action in #3, another node (#2) must connect them with the idea of cause-and-effect. That is, because the idea of causation is a separate meaning from the TOUCHing and the SLAPping, we've given it its own separate node in the structure. (We'll ignore for now that some process must determine that "she" refers to the debutante and "him" to the hippie [e.g., O'Brien & Albrecht, 1991]. These forms of reference are discussed in Chapter 9.)

Try paraphrasing these sentences, rearranging phrases, substituting different words (e.g., "therefore" instead of "so"), and the like, and then see how your paraphrase compares to the meaning represented in Figure 7-6. Because the entire meaning of the story is completely specified as nodes #1, #2, and #3, any paraphrase will also be represented by the same set of propositions.

Equally important, several *different* ideas, expressed across more than one sentence, can all be related to one another in a single representation.

This ability to relate propositions to one another is crucial to the importance of propositional theories. Without this ability, such theories could never account for our understanding of a simple paragraph or story, in which one idea "leads" to the next, where one idea elaborates another, and so on. And you'll notice that the higher nodes that connect separate sentences serve a similar purpose as category nodes in semantic networks: they yield a *hierarchical* structure for the nodes, where higher nodes can be "decomposed" or broken down into separate elements or parts.

Rules for Deriving Propositions

Proposition-based theories, as mentioned, are almost universally accepted within cognitive psychology as the best way of representing complex meanings. Since meaning is so critical to an understanding of human cognition, and since you need to understand this important approach, we will spend some time dealing with propositions, learning how to derive them from connected discourse. Table 7-6 presents some sample sentences to use in practicing the rules; the rules themselves are somewhat modified from Anderson's (1980, pp. 106–107) listing. Spend a few minutes deriving a propositional representation based on those rules for the sentence,

(4) The hungry lion ate Max, who starved it.

Figure 7-7 contains corresponding steps to the rules that follow, illustrating the process of constructing a propositional representation of sentence (4). (Network diagrams, as opposed to list-format propositions, are

---

Table 7-6   SAMPLE SENTENCES FOR FORMING PROPOSITIONAL
REPRESENTATIONS

Begin with some very simple sentences, such as:
    (a) Mary bought a book.
    (b) John drives a Jeep.
Then progress to somewhat more complex sentences, such as:
    (c) Mary bought a German book.
    (d) John drives a Jeep that he bought in Texas.
    Note that (c) consists of a verb relation and an adjective relation, and (d) has two verb relations that involve both John and Jeep (but only one of them necessarily involves Texas).

    Think of some variations on these sentences, and how you'd alter the propositional structures to incorporate the changes. For instance, add to your structure for (d) to get:
    (e) After John went to Texas, he bought a Jeep. (It probably makes no difference if you diagram this using the relation AFTER or the relation THEN.)
    Finally, a challenging example from Anderson (1980) is the sentence:
    (f) "Nixon gave a beautiful Cadillac to Brezhnev, who is leader of the USSR."
    To get started on this one, note that Anderson identifies three propositions here, *give,* *beautiful,* and *leader of.* Be sensitive to implied concepts too, like the implied causation in the expanded "hippie" sentence, or the implied sequence in:
    (g) John went to Texas, and bought a Jeep.

FIGURE 7-7

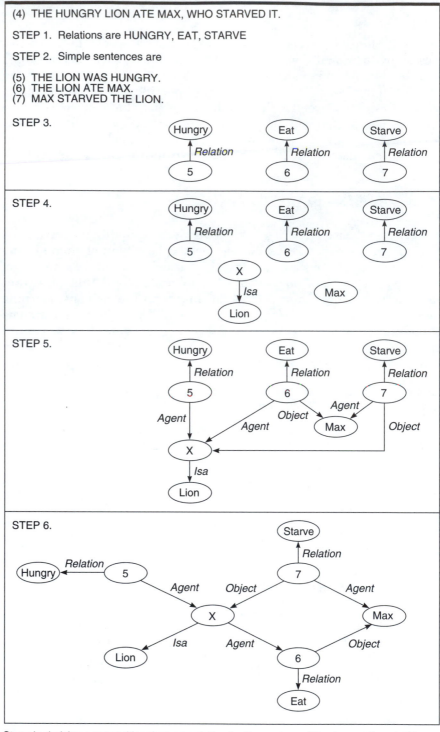

(4) THE HUNGRY LION ATE MAX, WHO STARVED IT.

STEP 1. Relations are HUNGRY, EAT, STARVE

STEP 2. Simple sentences are

(5) THE LION WAS HUNGRY.
(6) THE LION ATE MAX.
(7) MAX STARVED THE LION.

STEP 3.

STEP 4.

STEP 5.

STEP 6.

Steps in deriving a propositional representation for the sentence "The hungry lion ate Max, who starved it." (Adapted from Anderson, 1980.)

336

easier to understand, so I'd encourage you to stick with the "node and pathway" notation.) Any rule preceded by an * is an elaboration or modification to Anderson's scheme (but paraphrases are not starred). All rules should be applied to each sentence being analyzed.

1. Find all the relational terms in the sentence. These will usually be verbs, sometimes adjectives or relational expressions like *father of,* or occasionally prepositions like *above* or *on top of.* In sentence (4), the relations are *hungry, eat,* and *starve.*
2. Write a simple sentence or phrase for each relation, and give each one a number. Each sentence will contain only the one relation and its noun arguments. Each sentence will be one of the propositions from the original sentence. For sentence (4), you should get three separate simple sentences:

   (5) The lion was hungry.
   (6) The lion ate Max.
   (7) Max starved the lion.

3. Draw an oval to represent the overall node for each proposition, sentences (5) through (7), and number it to correspond to the simple sentence. Write the relation next to its oval, and connect the node to the relation by an arrow labeled *relation.*
4. Add a node to each proposition for each *argument,* each noun or "noun-like" word in the proposition (ignore function words like "the"). Two classes of nouns should be distinguished here. If a noun refers to a specific person or object, like Max, simply write the noun. If a noun refers only to an instance of a category, like lion, then create a new node and give it an arbitrary name like *X.* The *X* will stand for this particular instance of the category. Connect the *X* to its class noun with an *isa* arrow. Do not create different nodes for the same noun, but use the same node for both instances; *there should only be one *Max* node, even though Max occurs in both propositions (6) and (7).
5. Connect all the arguments to the numbered oval with arrows. Label the arrows with an appropriate semantic label, such as *agent, patient/recipient, or location.*
6. Rearrange the network to make it neat. *In other words, there is no significance at all to the position of the nodes. The meanings are coded in terms of nodes that are connected, and the nature of the pathway or arrow that connects them.

Are Propositions Real?

However theoretically elegant the propositional approach is in representing the meaning of connected discourse (and it *is* elegant), the ultimate test of the validity and usefulness of propositions is empirical (note that Artificial Intelligence, for example, would have a different opinion on what constitutes the ultimate test). It's all well and good to have an objective, systematic, and reasonable way of representing meaning, as is provided by propositional-based theories of meaning (e.g., Anderson, 1976; Kintsch, 1974). Yet, if this approach weren't supported by research results, it would be little more than an intellectual curiosity to cognitive psychology. Fortunately, a score of research reports have documented the psychological validity and utility of these hypothesized propositional structures. We'll discuss only a very few, to give you the flavor of this important kind of research.

The basic idea in all these tests is fairly straightforward. First, decide on the samples of connected text that are going to be presented, and derive their propositional structure. Having determined this structure, then determine which portions of the structure are more important to an understanding of the passage and which are less important; details of a minor episode, for instance, are relatively unimportant, but the overall outcome of a main episode is very important. Draw some predictions about recall, given what we know about the capacity of the memory system and the structure and importance of the elements in the passage. Finally, give the passages to subjects, and using the same rules as above, score their recall to see what is and isn't remembered, what is and isn't distorted, and what is and isn't invented.

Remembering Propositions   Let's begin with a classic study, one performed by Sachs (1967) before the advent of propositional theories. Sachs was testing a very general notion about memory—that people tend to remember meaning rather than superficial, verbatim information in the sentences they hear or read. Her subjects heard passages of connected text and were then tested on one critical sentence in the passage, either 0, 80, or 160 syllables after the critical sentence had been heard (see Table 7-7 for an example; why not read it now, and confirm Sachs's results for yourself?)

The test was a simple recognition test among four alternatives. One alternative was a verbatim repetition, one choice represented a change both in surface form and in meaning, and the other two represented changes only in surface form. When recognition was tested immediately, subjects were very good at recognizing the exact repetition; in other words, they rejected changes in superficial structure *and* changes in meaning. After comprehending the next 80 syllables' worth of the passage, however, performance was accurate only in rejecting the alternative that changed the meaning. In other words, subjects showed no preference for the repetition (d, the correct answer) over the paraphrases (a and c in the table) when the extra material intervened.

Sachs's conclusions were straightforward: we very quickly lose information concerning the actual, verbatim string of words that we hear (or read), but we do retain the meaning. Our memory for the input is then based largely on the propositions. We reconstruct what must have been

Table 7-7   SAMPLE PASSAGE FROM SACHS (1977) INCLUDING MULTIPLE
CHOICE RECOGNITION TEST FOR CRITICAL SENTENCE

Read the passage below at a comfortable pace, but without looking back. After you have finished reading, your memory for one of the sentences in the paragraph will be tested.

There is an interesting story about the telescope. In Holland, a man named Lippershey was an eye-glass maker. One day his children were playing with some lenses. They discovered that things seemed very close if two lenses were held about a foot apart. Lippershey began experimenting and his "spyglass" attracted much attention. He sent a letter about it to Galileo, the great Italian scientist. Galileo at once realized the importance of the discovery and set about to build an instrument of his own. He used an old organ pipe with one lens curved out and the other in. On the first clear night he pointed the glass toward the sky. He was amazed to find the empty dark spaces filled with brightly gleaming stars! Night after night Galileo climbed to a high tower, sweeping the sky with his telescope. One night he saw Jupiter, and to his great surprise discovered near it three bright stars, two to the east and one to the west. On the next night, however, all were to the west. A few nights later there were four little stars.

Now, without looking back, decide which of the following sentences occurred in the paragraph.
    a. He sent Galileo, the great Italian scientist, a letter about it.
    b. Galileo, the great Italian scientist, sent him a letter about it.
    c. A letter about it was sent to Galileo, the great Italian scientist.
    d. He sent a letter about it to Galileo, the great Italian scientist.
Check to see whether your answers were correct by referring back to the paragraph.

---

said based on the meaning that is stored in the propositional structure. Only in situations where there is something "special" about the verbatim string, say, in recalling a joke, do we appear to retain surface form as part of our ordinary memory for meaningful discourse (but see Masson, 1984).

Confirmation of this last point was offered by Kintsch and Bates (1977), who gave a surprise recognition test to students either two or five days after a classroom lecture. Some evidence of verbatim memory was present after two days, but very little persisted five days afterward. As expected, verbatim memory for details and extraneous comments was somewhat better than verbatim memory for general lecture statements. This was no doubt a von Restorff effect, as the authors noted; since there were very few detail and extraneous statements in comparison to lecture statements, memory for those infrequent (and therefore distinctive) statements was fairly good (see also Bates, Masling, & Kintsch, 1978). Even here, however, reconstructive memory seemed to play a role in remembering; students were better at rejecting items such as jokes that had *not* been presented than they were at recognizing jokes and announcements that *had* been heard (see also Brewer & Hay, 1984, on reconstruction of different linguistic styles).

Note that these results are consistent with the propositional approach to meaning: Sachs's subjects, as a current reinterpretation would say, were deriving the propositional structures of the passage they heard. They then retained only those structures, rather than the surface form of the sentences.

Gernsbacher (1985) has recently addressed the same phenomenon explicitly within the framework of propositional theories. In essence, she found the same results as Sachs did, both for verbal passages and picture stories (sequences of pictures that told a story nonverbally). Furthermore, Gernsbacher's research tested several explanations of why we lose the more superficial aspects of what we hear or see. Her conclusion, for both kinds of passages, was that people have poor memory for surface information because of *processing shifts* during comprehension. That is, as we comprehend the successive elements of a passage, we shift from building one propositional element to building the next one, then the next, and so on. Each time we shift in this manner, information from the previous *substructures* that were built becomes less and less available, so that eventually the only information that remains is the propositional structure that represents meaning. (This work is pursued more thoroughly in Chapter 9.)

Kintsch has reported several direct tests of propositional theory, in particular, the notion that a sentence with more underlying propositions is a more difficult sentence, hence harder to remember. In one set of studies (1974), short sentences were presented for simple free recall (five sentences were presented, followed by a two-minute recall interval, followed by another five sentences, etc.). The sentences had between two and four content words each, and from one to three propositions each; for instance, "The crowded passengers squirmed uncomfortably" and "The horse stumbled and broke a leg." Both sentences have four content words, but the first sentence has three propositions whereas the second sentence has only two. Kintsch's general predictions, based on propositional analysis, were upheld. Whereas subjects tended to recall about the same overall amount from all sentences, recall for the elements of any single proposition went down as the total number of propositions increased. Thus the more complex a sentence is, as indicated by the number of propositions it contains, the more there is to remember. Of course, with more to remember, less will be recalled.

Propositions and Priming   At a more detailed level, several experiments have both confirmed the psychological reality of propositions and tied them to a phenomenon you are quite familiar with—priming. Ratcliff and McKoon (1978, Experiment 2), for example, tested the possibility of priming effects within the propositions formed when we comprehend sentences. They presented sentences to their subjects and told them to learn the sentences for a later unspecified memory test. The test sentences were written so that each would contain two propositions, for example:

Geese crossed the horizon as wind shuffled the clouds.
The chauffeur jammed the clutch when he parked the truck.

After a 20-minute interval, filled with an unrelated task, subjects were shown single words in a recognition task and had to say "yes" if the word had been in one of the learned sentences and "no" otherwise.

The priming manipulation in the studies was in the sequencing of the trials during recognition. Sometimes the word on one trial (the prime) was immediately followed on the next trial by a word (the target) from a different sentence, and sometimes primes were followed by a target word from the same sentence. When the prime and target were from the same sentence, they either had occurred in the same proposition or in different propositions. For example, in the "geese" sentence above, the pair *geese–horizon* is from the same proposition, whereas the pair *geese–clouds* is from different propositions.

In the baseline condition, where primes and targets were from completely different sentences (e.g., *geese–clutch*), mean RT to targets was 847 msec (Experiment 2), as shown in Table 7-8. This is the *unprimed* condition, since the unrelated propositions from different sentences would not be stored together during learning. But when the prime and target words *did* come from the same sentence, the RT to the target was considerably shorter, 709 msec when they had been in the same proposition, and 752 msec when they were in different propositions within the same sentence; again, see Table 7-8 for examples. In other words, a prime–target pair like *geese–horizon* was 138 msec faster than baseline (847 msec – 709 msec), due to priming within the proposition. A pair like *geese–clouds* was 95 msec faster than baseline (847 msec – 752 msec), due to priming between the two propositions.

The support for propositional theories in these data should be clear. Words from the same sentence should be represented together in the propositions that are stored in memory; words from the same phrase or clause should be even more closely related in the stored propositions. Thus even though the words were not related in the strict sense of semantic memory—"horizon" is not a semantic property of "geese" after all—words stored together in a sentence's proposition still prime one

Table 7-8   PRIMING RESULTS FROM RATCLIFF AND McKOON (1978)

Condition	RT to Target	Priming Effect
Across sentences	847 msec	None; baseline
Between two propositions in the same sentence	752 msec	95 msec facilitation
Within a single proposition	709 msec	138 msec facilitation

Examples

Across sentences:	geese–clutch
Between two propositions in the same sentence:	geese–clouds
Within a single proposition:	geese–horizon

another. As such, these results are viewed as strong support for the psychological reality of propositions, the idea that we comprehend by constructing propositional representations of sentences, then remembering those propositions. As stored in memory, the words within a proposition are more closely related than words from different propositions, which in turn are more closely related than those from different sentences.

Summary Points: propositions; semantic cases—relation, actor, recipient, location, time; rules for propositions; remembering propositions; priming and propositions

▼ Propositions, Semantic Networks, and Scripts

Look back for a moment at Figure 7-7, the propositional representation of the "Max" sentence. Do you see anything that resembles a semantic memory "entry" or concept in this network? Not really—we have the elements of the sentence diagrammed as three basic idea units, with the relationship among the three clearly indicated, yet there is nothing in the figure that gives a clue as to what a lion is, what starving means, or for that matter what kind of creature Max is. We have claimed that when people read or hear connected discourse, they construct a propositional representation of the input, yet there seems to be something missing. How would you know that a lion is a ferocious enough animal that it just might eat someone who starved it, based on the diagram in Figure 7-7? And yet, knowing that lions are big and ferocious *must* have been part of your comprehension, because of your reaction to a slightly different sentence:

(8) The mouse ate Max, who starved it.

Clearly—and noncontroversially—when you comprehend a sentence, you do more than merely construct the correct propositional representation of the ideas in the sentence. The process must also include "looking up" the concepts mentioned in the sentence, retrieving them from semantic memory. This is of course a critical aspect of comprehension, since your semantic knowledge enables you to determine which semantic roles can be played by the different concepts.

Putting it simply, you access your semantic concepts for LION, EAT, and—presumably—MAN or HUMAN, the node with which "Max" will be associated. Having retrieved those concepts, you then can determine that a lion is big and ferocious enough to eat a man, that eating is something that lions do, and so on. Likewise, the semantic concepts you retrieved for "Laura ate spaghetti with a fork" guided your interpretation of that sentence, guided your analysis that SPAGHETTI is a food that can be eaten, and so on.

How do we know that this kind of semantic retrieval takes place during comprehension? We know because of your reaction—"this isn't quite right"—when we substitute concepts that *cannot* play those semantic roles, as in sentence (8) above, or something even more unacceptable (*"The textbook ate Max, who starved it"). We also know because of the reconstructive manner in which you recall sentences, stories, or other kinds of connected discourse; you often fill in your recall with details that were not mentioned in the original passage.

Scripts

To understand this point, we need to consider the much larger representations of knowledge that are stored in memory, representations of entire episodes or events that guide our comprehension and behavior. These are called **scripts,** *the large-scale semantic and episodic knowledge structures that accumulate in memory and guide our interpretation and comprehension of daily experience.* These structures must be considerably more detailed than the rather simple semantic memory concepts and propositions we've discussed, since people know considerably more about the world than just the bare meanings of words and how the words go together in sentences. As an example, consider the large amount of knowledge you have in memory that guides your comprehension of even a simple story:

> Billy was excited about the invitation to his friend's
> birthday party. But when he went to his room and shook
> his piggy bank, it didn't make a sound. "Hmm," he
> thought to himself, "maybe I can borrow some from
> Mom."

Scripts in Memory[6]   Think for a moment about the common meaning of the word "script," the dialogue and actions that are to be (literally) performed by the actors and actresses in a play. The script for a play details exactly what is supposed to happen in a stage production. In similar fashion, a mental **script** is a *general knowledge structure about ordinary events and situations.* In other words, a script is a mental representation of "what is supposed to happen" in a particular circumstance. Are you going to a restaurant? Your mental script tells you what to expect, what order the events will take, who the central characters are, and what you and they are supposed to do. Are you invited to a birthday party, taking an airplane flight, or sitting in a class on human memory and cognition? Your generalized knowledge of what happens in these settings guides your comprehension as the events unfold, and leads to certain expectations.

---

[6]*Schema* is an entirely synonymous term with *script* in this research. I prefer "script" because it has a clearer connotation to most people, and because "schema" has been used in many other cognitive contexts, for example, by Piaget. See footnote 1 for Bartlett's view on the term "schema."

The overall theory behind the notion of scripts is quite straightforward. People record in memory a generalized representation of events they have experienced, and this representation is *invoked,* that is, retrieved, when a new experience matches an old script.[7] One function of a script, in either a written or spoken story, is that it provides a kind of "shorthand" for the whole event; you need not describe each and every element of the experience, but can merely refer to the whole event by invoking the script. More importantly, the activated script provides a framework or context within which new experiences can be understood, and within which a variety of inferences can be drawn to complete your understanding (Abbot, Black, & Smith, 1985; Reiser, Black, & Abelson, 1985; Seifert, Robertson, & Black, 1985).

Let's develop this notion of scripts with a few examples. Consider the following abbreviated stories (taken or adapted from Schank & Abelson, 1977, pp. 38–40):

> (9) John went to a restaurant. He asked for a hamburger. He paid the check and left.
> (10) John went to a restaurant. He asked the waiter for a hamburger. He paid the check and left.
> (11) John went into the restaurant. He ordered a Big Mac. He paid for it and then ate it while driving to work.

According to Schank and Abelson (1977), our understanding of stories (9) and (10) is guided by our scripted knowledge of a particular situation, going to restaurants; story (11) is understood by a particular variant or track in the restaurant script, the "fast food" track. In memory, these authors claim, are recorded a tremendously large number of separate scripts, generalized knowledge structures pertaining to routine, frequently encountered situations or events such as going to restaurants. Thus the average adult, having experienced many different instances of "eating in restaurants," has a generalized script representation of this situation.[8]

Whenever we encounter a story like (9), elements of the story "trigger" or activate the appropriate script; in a real sense, the script is *primed.* As a consequence of this, all subsequent events in the story (or events in a real-world experience) are interpreted with reference to the script that is activated in memory. In Schank and Abelson's model, *phrases or words that activate a script* are called *headers,* which either name the script or

---

[7]We can also have scripts for situations we have only learned about indirectly, although they are probably rather impoverished or even biased compared to those learned through personal experience.

[8]Restaurants are to script theories as robins are to semantic memory theories. As before, don't develop a too-narrow understanding of the theory because of the examples. On the other hand, restaurants provide a particularly useful example of the overall nature of script theories, since the "restaurant experience" is a well-structured, highly ordered, and relatively common event.

refer to some semantically related concept that is part of the script. In a general sense, a header is nothing more than a *prime,* a concept that activates a related body of knowledge. Thus headers like HUNGRY (John was hungry) or WAITER will activate the restaurant script, providing access to the entire body of "restaurant knowledge."

In story (9) the explicit script name "restaurant" and the reference to a kind of food are sufficient to activate the script. Thus the explicit reference to "the waiter" in story (10) is in some sense unneeded: "restaurant" and "hamburger" are sufficient to activate the restaurant script. Schank and Abelson (1977) claim that, in general, two concepts are necessary to convince the reader that the restaurant script is indeed the focus of the story. In other words, it takes two headers to determine which script should be activated. Contrast (9) with "I met a bus driver in the restaurant," in which it is not at all clear that the remainder of the story will be about a restaurant experience (but note that "restaurant" information must be kept in mind, just in case that detail becomes important later on).

Furthermore, a story like (11) requires somewhat more specialized scripted knowledge than a general restaurant script. After all, a typical restaurant doesn't usually let you eat in your car. Clearly, the "Big Mac header" is instrumental here in activating a particular version or track in the overall script. If you have specific knowledge of that track, you won't be surprised that John ate his lunch on the way to work. If you've never heard of a Big Mac before, you'll have some difficulty in understanding why that event takes place.

Finally, consider a somewhat longer story (from Abelson, 1981):

> (12) John was feeling very hungry as he entered the restaurant. He settled himself at a table and noticed that the waiter was nearby. Suddenly, however, he realized that he'd forgotten his reading glasses.

While this story doesn't necessarily call up any particular track of the general restaurant script, it does illustrate some of the predictive and interpretive power that a script theory provides for explaining human comprehension. Virtually all readers (or listeners) will understand John's dilemma as "unable to read the menu." It makes little difference, actually, that "the menu" or even "a menu" was never mentioned. The restaurant script is activated by the headers HUNGRY and RESTAURANT, which in turn activate the whole set of **frames** (also called *slots*), *details about specific events within the script.* This prepares you to receive specific information about those frames. When the detail comes along, for instance, "the waiter," that particular detail is stored in the appropriate frame. If the detail does *not* come along, for instance, "the menu," it is simply inferred from the generalized script knowledge. Your comprehension then proceeds normally after "forgotten his reading glasses," since the unmentioned "thing you read in a restaurant" is supplied by the script.

In script terminology, the menu is a **default value** for the frame, the *common, typical value or concept that occupies the frame.* In the restaurant script, the default value MENU is the ordinary way that patrons find out what is available for dinner. Thus unmentioned details in the story are "filled in" by the default values. This means that a storyteller doesn't need to mention everything. We merely assume that the listener will supply any missing details from the stored script. In intuitive terms, the rule goes something like this: if no detail was mentioned, assume the normal, default values as specified by the script; if a detail was mentioned, replace the default value with the detail. Thus two plausible continuations of (12), one assuming the default value, and one not, might be:

(12a) Rather than go to his car to get his glasses, John asked the waiter to tell him what kinds of sandwiches they had.

(12b) But then the waiter told him that he wouldn't need his glasses, since tonight's dinner was a buffet.

Predictions   Figure 7-8 presents a generic "restaurant script," based on Schank and Abelson's (1977) work, as an indication of the generalized knowledge represented in scripts. If you have such a "conventional restaurant" script, this enables you to understand and predict the various events in the sequence. An individual with different experiences, however, may have some difficulties in understanding what's going on, for example, a small child who has only been to "fast food" restaurants. Thus comprehension should suffer to the degree that your current experience mismatches your script.

A well-known example of such difficulties in processing is presented in the story in Table 7-9 (Bransford, 1979); be sure to make an honest effort to understand the story before you read the explanation in the bottom portion of the table. As this passage shows, a story may activate a script but then *mismatch* the expected events in the script. Depending on the severity of the mismatch, we would predict difficulties in comprehension and/or recall. On the other hand, if a person lacks a specialized track within the script, we would then predict comprehension based on the more general script that *is* in memory.

A final prediction from script theory is important enough that it needs to be developed in greater detail. Note from the "shorthand" and default ideas above that everything need not be mentioned in a story for a person to understand. In fact, as Schank and Abelson (1977) put it, "when someone decides to tell a story that references a script, he recognizes that he need not (and because he would otherwise be considered rather boring, should not) mention every detail of his story. He can safely assume that his listener is familiar with the referenced script and will understand the

FIGURE 7-8

```
            Script: Restaurant    Roles: Customer
            Track: –                     Waiter
            Props: Tables                Cook
                   Menu                  Cashier
                   Food                  Owner
                   Check
                   Money

         Entry conditions:  Cust. is hungry, has money
          Exit conditions:  Cust. not hungry, has less money
                            Owner has more money

   SCENE 1:  Entering ──► Cust. into restaurant
                          To table
                          Sit down

   SCENE 2:  Ordering ──► Menu on table
                                 or
                          Asks for menu–waiter brings menu
                          Cust. reads menu
                          Cust. places order
                          Cust. waits for food ──► cook prepares food

   SCENE 3:  Eating ──── Waiter gets food from cook,
                            brings to Cust.
                          Cust. eats food ──► options
                                              Cust. returns food
                                              Cust. orders more

   SCENE 4:  Exiting ──── Waiter brings check
                          Cust. pays cashier, leaves tip for waiter
                          Cust. leaves restaurant
```

A depiction of a standard restaurant script. (Adapted from Schank & Abelson, 1977.)

Table 7-9   RESTAURANT EPISODE WITH EXPLANATION

Jim went to the restaurant and asked to be seated in the gallery. He was told that there would be a one-half hour wait. Forty minutes later, the applause for his song indicated that he could proceed with the preparation. Twenty guests had ordered his favorite, a cheese soufflé.

Jim enjoyed the customers in the main dining room. After two hours, he ordered the house specialty—roast pheasant under glass. It was incredible to enjoy such exquisite cuisine and yet still have fifteen dollars. He would surely come back soon.

Assume, therefore, that Jim went to a very special type of restaurant. The owner allows people who can cook at least one special meal to compete for the honor of preparing their specialty for other customers who desire it. Those who wish to compete sit in the gallery rather than the main dining room (although a central stage is accessible to both).

The competition centers on the competitor's entertaining the crowd, by singing, for example, or dancing or playing an instrument. The approval of the crowd is a prerequisite for allowing the person to announce his or her cooking specialty. The rest of the crowd then has the option of ordering it, and the person receives a certain amount of money for each meal prepared. After doing the cooking and serving the meal to the customers, the person can then order from the regular restaurant menu and pay for it out of the money received for cooking. In general, this arrangement benefits the manager as well as the person. The manager obtains relatively inexpensive entertainment, and the person is usually able to make more than enough money to pay for an excellent meal.

From Bransford, 1979.

story as long as certain crucial items are mentioned" (p. 38). In other words, the shorthand function of scripts relieves us of mentioning *all* the slots or frames in the script. We can assume that the reader/listener will *infer* those unmentioned details by means of the stored script.

A rather strong prediction from script theory then is that people's recall of a story will be influenced not merely by the details that *were* mentioned, but also by the events and details that were *inferred* based on scripted knowledge. As a simple example, if we developed a longer restaurant story, you might "recall" that the customer left a tip for the waiter, even though no tip was ever mentioned in the original passage. Where does the tip come from, so to speak? It comes from your script (the same place that the broken glass came from in Loftus and Palmer's "smashed" group). In short, these inferences come from long-term memory, from our semantic and scripted knowledge. And, importantly, they reflect *reconstructive memory* processes.

Evidence for Scripts

Rather convincing evidence for these predictions has been collected in the past several years, and we will spend a few moments discussing that evidence (just as was the case for propositions, a script theory unsupported by empirical results would be of interest only to nonpsychologists). In fact, we have already encountered some evidence of this nature, in the first section of the chapter on reconstructive memory. Why did Sulin and Dooling's subjects "remember" that they had read "She was deaf, dumb, and blind"? Because they were given the information that the story was about Helen Keller, and this triggered the subjects' memory for information on Helen Keller.

Evidence specific to the script theory approach has been reported by a variety of researchers (e.g., Bower, Black, & Turner, 1979; Graesser, 1981; Graesser & Nakamura, 1982; Long, Golding, Graesser, & Clark, 1990; Maki, 1989). The paper by Smith and Graesser (1981) is a good representative of such data. Smith and Graesser were investigating the role of typicality or relevance of specific events and actions in people's memory for script-based passages: Do we remember the predictable events and actions better than the unpredictable, or is it the other way around? They presented a total of ten passages to their subjects, each one related to a different scripted activity (taking the dog to the vet, washing a car, cleaning an apartment, etc.), and tested them with either a recall or recognition task. Tests were conducted 30 minutes after hearing the passages, then again after two days, one week, and three weeks.

What made the Smith and Graesser evidence so compelling was the care they took in constructing their passages. Stories mentioned both typical and atypical actions within each script situation; Smith and Graesser collected norms in order to know what's typical and what's not. In their standard analyses of recall and recognition performance, typical information was remembered better than atypical information. These scores, however, were then corrected for guessing, since the high accuracy on typical information probably included both events that were genuinely remembered as well as events that were merely reconstructed from the script knowledge.

When the scores were corrected for reconstructed guesses, recall and recognition were higher for *atypical* events than for typical events. In other words, in a story about taking the dog to the vet, subjects showed more accurate memory for the unusual, atypical events that occurred (e.g., "While waiting for the vet, Jack dropped his car keys"). Typical events, those anticipated by the script (e.g., "Jack led the dog into the waiting room"), were recalled more poorly once the scores had been corrected for guessing (note that correcting the scores for guessing makes this a technical accuracy score, since content accuracy would not distinguish the presented from the reconstructed information). Thus memory for the stories conformed to the *Schema Copy Plus Tag* hypothesis: you store a copy of the generic script as your main memory for the story and then tag onto that generic script the specific, atypical details that occurred (Graesser, 1981; Smith & Graesser, 1981).

This makes entirely good sense if you'll spend a moment thinking about it. When you hear a script-based story, the script leads you to expect certain events—the typical events—and provides default values for them. Such default values don't need to be stored in a memory trace for the story since they already are stored as part of the script. On the other hand, the script does not prepare you for unusual or atypical events, like dropping the car keys.[9] Thus when it is time to recall or recognize the story, the atypical events have an advantage over the typical ones: the atypical events *were* specifically stored during comprehension, since they were details that could not have been anticipated by the script (see Pezdek, Whetstone, Reynolds, Askari, & Dougherty, 1989, for the same effect in memory for real-world scenes).

Rounding out this sort of evidence, Nakamura, Graesser, Zimmerman, and Riha (1985) tested this hypothesis in a more naturalistic setting, using a classroom lecture as the input, and a later memory test as the evidence. As was found with the prose passages, memory was better for the atypical or irrelevant information (e.g., sipping a cup of coffee) than for more typical information (e.g., underlining a word on the blackboard). Part of the strength of the Nakamura et al. paper is that it extends the script approach to settings beyond written or spoken passages. Another strength is that the results were obtained in a natural, "nonmemory" setting. The students were unaware at the time of the lecture that their

---

[9]It should be clear that we are talking about atypical but still plausible events, like dropping the car keys in the vet's office. With highly implausible events, you get incoherence, something like the bizarre "Bransford Restaurant" in Table 7-9.

memory would be tested for events that happened during the lecture.[10] In other words, *incidental* memory in the Nakamura et al. study seemed largely the same as more *intentional* memory in the laboratory studies.

Summary Points: scripts; headers, frames, and default values; scripts and understanding, recall

▼ Divisions Within Long-Term Memory

We have nearly completed a three-chapter look at long-term memory, its functions, structures, and processes. We first dealt with episodic and semantic memory separately. And, in this chapter, we have considered how the two systems interact during the normal course of comprehension.

To bring this chapter to a close we'll consider two final issues—not to mention some of the most fascinating results on long-term memory that you'll ever encounter. The first concerns the integration of episodic and semantic memories. However much they interact during normal comprehension, there is growing evidence that they are distinctly *different* long-term memory systems.

Second, we come to an important distinction in long-term memory research, the distinction between *implicit and explicit* tests of long-term memory. This issue, especially, relates to the theme of Unconscious Processing that you read about in Chapter 2. And along with the evidence on episodic–semantic memory differences, the research on implicit and explicit memory suggests there are indeed some basic, functional—even *neural*—differences in the several varieties of long-term memory. Recent developments suggest that, in a very real sense, we do not have *one* unified long-term memory system. In Tulving's (1989) words, "The traditionally held views about the unity of memory are no longer tenable. A more appropriate view seems to be that of *multiple memory systems*" (p. 367, emphasis added).

The Semantic–Episodic Distinction

Let's return to the basic distinction between episodic and semantic memories that we've pursued in Chapters 5 and 6. Episodic memory is autobiographical, personally experienced memory, and semantic memory is generalized, world knowledge memory. It was obviously beneficial for cognitive psychology that Tulving (1972) enunciated this distinction: an avalanche of research was generated by his 1972 chapter, research that

---

[10]Lest this be misinterpreted, the students were tested on their memory for incidental events *during* the lecture, not on the content of the lecture. What a shame that Nakamura et al. didn't also test for some content information: it would have made an interesting comparison, whichever way the memory for content worked out.

established enormously productive pathways for the investigation of cognitive processes. Indeed, it's almost as if cognitive psychology had been waiting for one of its most respected practitioners to say "It's OK to study what people already know."

At several levels of analysis, it's clear that there is a distinction to be made between these two memory systems. We noted, for instance, that episodic tasks require the subjects to be exposed to some specific input during the experimental session, while a "pure" semantic task tests people on the knowledge they bring with them to the laboratory. Both tasks require retrieval, of course, although we tend to use words like "remembering" and "recollection" for episodic retrieval, and "knowing" for semantic retrieval; for instance, "I remember hearing that song yesterday" versus "I know who the president of France is." And in many respects, those two acts of retrieval are quite similar; for example, the priming effect occurs in both semantic and episodic memory studies. Even the dynamics of activation and priming appear to be very similar in the two memory systems (e.g., Yantis & Meyer, 1988).

Could two memory systems be so alike and yet still separate? As it happens, the answer to this question is very probably "yes." No one denies that these two memory systems are in constant and intimate interaction, of course: the fact that they *are* has been the dominant theme of this chapter so far. Such similarities have been interpreted as evidence that episodic and semantic memories are simply different aspects of the same long-term memory system (e.g., McKoon, Ratcliff, & Dell, 1986). But recent evidence has begun to show some rather different characteristics for semantic and episodic memory under certain testing situations.

***Neurological Evidence*[11]** Tulving's (1989) excellent paper summarizes two lines of evidence showing that episodic and semantic memories are in fact separate forms of long-term memory. The first kind of evidence is based on a case history, a detailed study of an individual—his initials are K.C.—who because of a serious brain injury shows rather complete separation of personal from more generic long-term memory. Read a portion of Tulving's description, to get the flavor of K.C.'s memory impairment.

K.C.'s case is remarkable in that he cannot remember, in the sense of bringing back to conscious awareness, a single thing that he has ever done or experienced in the past. . . . Those aspects of K.C.'s intellectual functioning that do not depend on remembering personal experiences are reasonably normal . . . he recognizes familiar objects . . . his understanding and use of language are unimpaired . . . and his thought processes are intact. . . . [But] K.C. does not remember any personally experienced events from either before or after his accident. (p. 362)

---

[11]Amnesia and other topics related to "brain and cognition" relationships are covered thoroughly in Chapter 10.

K.C. has a profound **amnesia**—*memory loss due to brain damage*—for events before *and* after his brain damage. And in particular, it is clear that his most serious memory deficit is one of "massive failure to retrieve . . . previously accessible personal experiences" (p. 363). That is, it seems as if his episodic memory system no longer works at all, although his semantic memory system does.

This pattern of impairment suggests that episodic and semantic memories are indeed separate, distinct long-term memory systems, distinct enough that one could be severely damaged while the other remains fairly intact. Interestingly, the distinction in long-term memory that was long supported by work on brain-damaged individuals is the distinction between *declarative knowledge* and *procedural knowledge*. For instance, Squire (1987) summarized a great deal of research on the memory deficits of amnesic patients and concluded that amnesia most frequently involves disruption of declarative knowledge, specific fact knowledge corresponding to episodic memories. Procedural knowledge, remembering *how* to do something, seemed preserved in amnesics, in Squire's view.

As Tulving (1989) acknowledged, there are some limitations on what can be learned about normal cognition from data on brain-damaged patients (but see Caramazza, 1986, and Caramazza & McCloskey, 1988, for a spirited defense of case studies). Patient K.C., Tulving noted, is unique: no other reports describe patients incapable of recalling *any* personal memories. Thus because we might worry about the generality of such results—an isolated case such as K.C. *could* have been atypical prior to his accident—Tulving presented further support for his conclusions, studies of brain functioning among normal individuals.

If you'll turn to the page of color illustrations in Chapter 10, you'll see an amazing set of photographs. In these pictures, the bloodflow to the brain is being measured (the techniques by which such photographs are taken are described in the Demonstrations section of Chapter 10). The logic behind such a procedure is that mental activity, say, retrieving some particular memory, involves an increase in neural activity—*activation,* quite literally. This increase should show up as an increase in bloodflow to whichever brain regions are being activated. Thus by injecting a small dose of radioactive material (irradiated gold in Tulving's report) into the bloodstream, the apparatus detects regions of the brain that have higher concentrations of radioactivity, on a very short time scale (e.g., 12 separate intervals of 0.2 sec each, across an 80-sec period).

What do the photographs show? In the bottom left picture, the subject was thinking about a fairly generic memory, the history of astronomy that he had read about many years before. In the bottom right picture, the subject was recalling personal memories from a summer nearly 50 years before, that is, a 50-year-old episodic memory. The red patterns in these pictures show regions where the bloodflow was above the baseline level, and the green regions show lower than average bloodflow.

Clearly—and dramatically—*different* brain activity resulted when these two memories were retrieved. If the memory for the history of astronomy is assumed to be a genuine semantic memory, then quite different regions of the brain seem to be active when retrieving semantic versus episodic memories. (The same kind of results were obtained when the subject retrieved recent semantic and episodic memories; see also Wood, Taylor, Penney, & Stump, 1980.) If anything, it appeared that episodic retrieval was accompanied by greater activation in the anterior (front) regions of the brain. This finding agrees with research on amnesia patients (reviewed by Schacter, 1987) showing that the frontal lobes are especially important for time-related aspects of memories. Semantic retrieval, conversely, seemed to activate more posterior (rear) regions of the brain.

Implicit and Explicit Memory

Consider finally a distinction only hinted at by the differences between episodic and semantic memory. When you retrieve an episodic memory, you are intentionally and explicitly accessing a memory record of some prior experience. If I ask you to learn and then recall a list of words, I am asking you to perform an **explicit memory** task: "Explicit memory is revealed when performance on a task requires conscious recollection of previous experiences" (Graf & Schacter, 1985, p. 501). On the other hand, I can test your memory for learned information in such a way that your performance can be facilitated *without any necessary involvement of conscious recollection*. This is an **implicit memory** test, in which your performance does not depend in any necessary way on conscious reflection or retrieval (Reber, 1989; Schacter, 1987).

The operative word in these definitions is "conscious." I can ask you to remember the list of words you studied back in Chapter 5, the list that accompanied the *peg-word mnemonic device*. If you can recall those words, you have deliberately and consciously remembered the experience of learning the list (here's a retrieval cue as a hint, if you're having difficulty: what's hanging out of your running *shoe?*)

In contrast, here's an implicit memory test for you to complete. Please fill in the blanks in the following word stems with whatever words come to mind:

GRE__ SH__ GO___ CRA__ TAB__

What words did you come up with to complete these stems? Did you generate common words like GREAT, SHOW, and GOOD? Or did you instead generate GREEN, SHOE, or even GOLD? Of course, completing the stem as SHOE was an obvious choice, since you had just read that word. But if you wrote down GREEN rather than GREAT, you just demonstrated a classic *implicit memory* effect. The word GREAT occurs nearly five times as frequently in English as GREEN. Under normal circumstances, you would be expected to retrieve the more frequent word

GREAT in this task, and likewise for GOLD, even though GOOD, for instance, occurs almost 16 times as frequently in English. And yet you just read the words GREEN and GOLD in the description of Tulving's research a few paragraphs ago. The important aspect of this demonstration is that you did not necessarily remember in conscious fashion that you had recently seen GREEN and GOLD. And yet, the fact that you read them recently makes you more likely to complete the stems with those words.[12]

Repetition Priming

The general term for this implicit memory result is **repetition priming.** In repetition priming, *a previous encounter with information facilitates later performance on the same information, even unconsciously.* Repetition priming effects have been established in any number of different research tasks, for example, in word identification and lexical decision tasks (e.g., Morton, 1979), in word and picture naming (e.g., Brown, Neblett, Jones, & Mitchell, 1991), and in rereading fluency (e.g., Masson, 1984). In all these, a previous encounter with the stimulus yields faster performance on a later task, even though you may not consciously remember having seen the stimulus before (see Logan, 1990, for the connection of repetition priming to automaticity).

In a classic demonstration of repetition priming, Jacoby and Dallas (1981) asked their subjects to study a list of familiar words, answering a question about each as they went through the list. Sometimes the question asked about the physical form of the word, for instance, "Does it contain the letter L?" Sometimes the question asked about the word's sound, "Does it rhyme with train?" And sometimes, the question asked about a semantic characteristic of the word, for example, "Is it the center of the nervous system?" This kind of manipulation ought to sound familiar to you—it was a direct manipulation of the *depth of processing* you studied in Chapter 5. Asking about the physical form of the word should induce only shallow processing, according to that framework, leading to relatively poor memory performance later on. Asking about rhymes demands somewhat deeper processing, and asking about semantic characteristics should demand full, elaborative processing on the list words.

At test, the subjects' *explicit memory* performance was assessed by a yes/no recognition task ("Did this word occur in the study phase?"). Here, their recognition accuracy was affected by the type of question they answered during study. When a question related to the physical form of the word had been asked during study, recognition performance was at chance, 51%; see Figure 7-9. When the question had asked about the

[12]To repeat, you are *more likely* to complete the stems as GOLD and GREEN, but not *certain* to, especially in uncontrolled situations. That is, there are many reasons why the demonstration may not work for you, including that you may not have read the Tulving section very carefully.

sound of the word, performance improved. And when truly semantic processing had been devoted to the word, recognition accuracy was quite high, 95%.

What made this a test of explicit memory was that subjects had to say yes/no based on whether they had seen the word earlier during the study phase. As we would expect, more elaborative processing led to better explicit memory performance.

The *other* test given to subjects, the *implicit memory test,* was a perceptual test. Here, words were shown one at a time for only 35 msec, followed by a row of asterisks as a mask. Subjects merely had to report the word they saw. In other words, the perceptual test did not require the subjects to remember which words they had seen earlier, or in fact to remember anything about the study phase. They just had to identify the briefly presented words.

In these perceptual recognition tests, identification of the words averaged about 80%, *regardless* of how the word had been studied. That is, a constant 80% of the previously presented words were identified in the perceptual test, versus identification of only 65% of control words that had not appeared earlier. Of special importance, it made no difference how the word had originally been processed, that is, with physical, rhyme, or semantic questions (see Figure 7-9).

This is the typical *implicit memory* result. Even with no conscious or necessary recollection of the original event, there is facilitation of performance when the stimulus is repeated. Measures of explicit memory, a recall or yes/no recognition task, generally show strong effects of how the information was studied. But measures of implicit memory, say, a perceptual or word stem completion task, usually show significant priming or facilitation regardless of how information was studied (see also Roediger, Stadler, Weldon, & Riegler, 1992).

Implicit Memory and Amnesia

Because Chapter 10 covers the topic of amnesia at some depth, only a brief mention of the results on implicit memory and amnesia will be given here. Basically, the general finding is that amnesia patients—almost by definition—have serious difficulties with explicit memory tasks. They have memory loss for information that was personally experienced: they are unable to recall their personal experiences in any conscious, explicit way. This deficit extends to laboratory tasks of episodic memory as well; in a study like Jacoby and Dallas's, amnesic patients likely would have performed at chance on the explicit test of recognition memory, regardless of the type of question they answered during study.

And yet, when tested with implicit memory tasks, amnesics often show perfectly normal levels of performance. That is, if amnesia patients had been tested in the Jacoby and Dallas study, their perceptual recognition scores would probably have been much like the normal subjects'

FIGURE 7-9

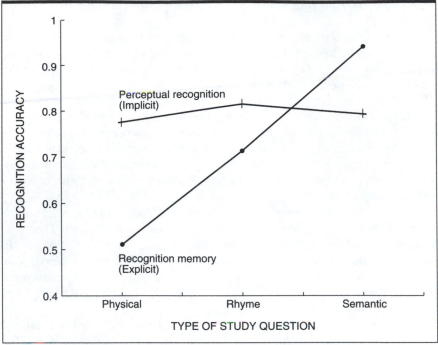

Recognition accuracy for words tested with an explicit or implicit memory task. Words were originally studied with questions asking about Physical, Rhyme, or Semantic characteristics of the words. The figure shows that implicit memory performance was unaffected by the original type of learning.

results, somewhere around 80% accuracy. Representative demonstrations of such implicit–explicit effects in amnesia have been reported by Graf, Squire, and Mandler (1984), Nissen and Bullemer (1987), and Warrington and Weiskrantz (1982), to name just a few.

Distinctions and Systems of Long-Term Memory

These are relatively new, and somewhat controversial, distinctions in the study of long-term memory. For example, some investigators (Greene, 1990; Neill, Beck, Bottalico, & Molloy, 1990; Srinivas & Roediger, 1990) have found that different kinds of encoding, rehearsal, or other processing strategies can influence implicit memory performance; the problem, of course, is that a deliberately chosen strategy should not influence unconscious, implicit performance. A specific model of encoding has been proposed to account for typical implicit/explicit differences (Nelson, Schreiber, & McEvoy, 1992); others (e.g., Rappold & Hashtroudi, 1991) suggest that the data-driven versus conceptually driven encoding processes are at the bottom of the effect. And quite recently, Challis and Brodbeck (1992) have found evidence for depth-of-processing effects on implicit performance, in direct contradiction to the Jacoby and Dallas (1981) results.

Roediger's (1990) review is probably the best summary at this point: this is an exciting, puzzling, and potentially fundamental topic in human memory research. Along with findings like the ERP data you read about in the last chapter (Kounios & Holcomb, 1992), one can only guess at the advances in understanding the varieties—or various disguises—of long-term memory, and the interactions and dissociations among those varieties.

Summary Points: semantic–episodic distinction; amnesia and episodic memory; activation of brain regions; implicit and explicit tests; repetition priming; preservation of implicit memory in amnesia

CHAPTER SUMMARY

1. Bartlett's (1932) early research demonstrated an important fact that motivates the topic "integrating semantic and episodic memory." When meaningful material is to be remembered, we tend to reconstruct the memory from two sources, the presented information and our existing knowledge. Bartlett used the term *schema* to refer to this existing knowledge base and found that the subjects' schemata led to various omissions, distortions, and alterations of the originally presented material.

2. Research on simulated eyewitness testimony, as well as more straightforward work on semantic integration, suggests that memory for meaningful material is not particularly accurate in a technical sense, because related information is either integrated in memory or accepted and then stored as having occurred originally. Content accuracy, however, is enhanced by such a tendency to integrate related information.

3. Comprehending a sentence involves constructing a propositional representation, in which the meaningful elements are represented as nodes connected by various pathways (e.g., agent, recipient). Considerable evidence has been reported in support of this notion; we tend to remember the gist or general meaning of a passage, rather than superficial aspects, and we routinely "recognize" a sentence as having occurred before even if the sentence is a paraphrase. Such technical inaccuracies are another kind of evidence for content accuracy, correct recognition or recall based on the meaningful content of the to-be-remembered material. Propositions form the base of several important lines of research, including studies of semantic memory performance, recall of connected prose, and comprehension and recall of stories.

4. Scripts are large-scale representations of complex events and

episodes, such as going to a restaurant or attending a birthday party. Script knowledge can be represented in the same kind of network structure as propositions and is assumed to be accessed by similar processes, for example, spreading activation. A story invokes a script by mentioning so-called headers, and these in turn activate the entire script. Script theories make a variety of predictions about comprehension and retrieval and provide a useful way of explaining how people understand and interact with the real world.

5. Along with the important organizing role provided by the distinction between episodic and semantic memory, recent research suggests a possible neurological difference between the two; it is important, nonetheless, to bear in mind that semantic and episodic memories are continually interacting systems of knowledge. Everyday experiences are understood by means of semantic concepts and connections, a confirmation of the pervasiveness of this kind of conceptually driven processing in normal cognition.

6. The distinction between explicit and implicit memory tests concerns whether an act of recollection does or does not involve conscious retrieval or awareness. Amnesic patients routinely show disrupted explicit memory performance, for instance, recalling personal experiences, and yet show relatively intact implicit performance, for instance, priming. Studies of the repetition priming effect in normal adults also show the implicit/explicit distinction; performance can be facilitated by a repeated stimulus even without conscious awareness of that influence.

Glossary Terms: amnesia; content versus technical accuracy; default values; explicit memory; eyewitness memory; frames; headers; implicit memory; memory impairment; misinformation acceptance; propositions; reconstructive memory; repetition priming; schema/schemata; scripts; semantic cases—agent, location, recipient, relation; semantic integration

SUGGESTED READINGS

As an interesting side issue to recent work on eyewitness testimony, a set of papers discusses the role cognitive psychologists might play in courtroom procedures, testifying to the unreliability of eyewitnesses; see papers by Loftus (1983a,b) McCloskey and Egeth (1983a,b), and the Science Watch section of the *American Psychologist,* May 1993.

Script and schema theories, along with propositional approaches to discourse processing, are the subjects of a good many research projects and are being applied to a large variety of comprehension situations. See Schank's (1972) basic paper on "conceptual dependency" as a challenging but essential introduction to his approach, Schank and Abelson (1977) as a very readable guide to the scope of the project, and Abelson's (1981) paper on the diversity of topics that can be accommodated within script/schema theory.

Several papers discuss the distinction between episodic and semantic memory: for example, McCloskey and Santee (1981); McKoon, Ratcliff, and Dell (1985, 1986); Neely and Durgunoglu (1985); and Tulving (1986, 1989). Of these, the Tulving (1989) paper is by far the most readable; start there. See Roediger (1990) for his useful commentary on the implicit/explicit distinction. A book edited by Lewandowsky, Dunn, and Kirsner (1989) contains rather high-level papers on implicit memory research and theory.

Chapter 8

LANGUAGE

▼ **Linguistic Universals and Functions**

▼ **Phonology: The Sounds of Language**

▼ **Syntax: The Ordering of Words and Phrases**

▼ **Lexical and Semantic Factors: The Meaning in Language**

The beginning of wisdom is learning the names of things. (Confucius)

Man is known ... as "the talking animal"; and language is assuredly a capital distinction between man and brute. . . . Language is a system of signs, *different from the things signified, but able to suggest them. (James, 1890, p. 980)*

I personally think we developed language because of our deep inner need to complain. (Lily Tomlin, "The Search for Signs of Intelligent Life in the Universe," TIME, *October 7, 1985)*

Language *is* the most common and universal feature of human society. More than any other aspect of human knowledge, language pervades every facet of our lives, from our most public behavior to our most private thoughts. We might imagine a society that has no interest in art, music, or biology, for example, or even one with no formal system of numbers and arithmetic. But it is simply inconceivable that a society would have no language, no means of communication among individuals. Every culture, no matter how primitive or isolated, has language, and every individual, unless deprived by nature or accident, develops skill in the use of language. The reasons are obvious: language gives us power.

This is a chapter on the basics of language, on its characteristics, functions, structure, and form. **Linguistics** is the academic discipline that takes language per se as its topic, and a good deal of what you'll read has come to us from that discipline. As you learned in Chapter 1, linguistics had a profound influence on cognitive psychology. Chomsky's rejection of behaviorism's explanation of language was a major turning point in the development of cognitive psychology; according to Wasow (1989), Chomsky's influence on the field of linguistics was equally dramatic. Since approaches such as Chomsky's seemed likely to yield new insights and understanding, psychology renewed its interest in language research in the late 1950s and early 1960s, borrowing heavily from linguistic theory in the process.

And yet, as psychologists began to apply and test linguistic theory, there dawned a realization of an important limitation in the purely linguistic approach. Language is a purposeful activity. It's there to *do* something—to communicate, to express thoughts and ideas, even to complain. Linguistics, however, focused on language itself as a formal, almost disembodied system, and regarded the human *use* of language as less interesting, tangential, or even irrelevant. Upon reflection, this view denied a fundamental interest in psychology—*behavior.* The notion that language *behavior* was somehow less interesting than language itself was unacceptable to psychology, even contradictory. Thus a new branch of cognitive psychology evolved, called **psycholinguistics,** *the study of language as it is used, and learned, by people.*

We will have time only for a brief survey of linguistics and psycholinguistics here. This chapter and the next focus on the nature and structure of language and cover two of the three traditional concerns in psycholinguistics—language comprehension and production. The third concern, language acquisition, is—most unfortunately—beyond the scope of this book, although several useful sources on that topic are cited in the Suggested Readings. Throughout this treatment, we will be especially concerned with the interrelationships between language and the human cognitive system responsible for its use and acquisition.

▼ Linguistic Universals and Functions

Defining Language

We need to begin with a definition of language, a statement that orients us toward critical issues that need to be explored. Webster's defines *language* as "the expression or communication of thoughts and feelings by means of sounds, and combinations of such sounds, to which meaning is attributed; human speech." That's not a bad start, to be sure. Note, for example, one particularly critical idea in the definition: meaning is *attributed* to the sounds, rather than residing in or being part of those sounds. As an illustration, the difference in sound between the words *car* and *cars* is the "s" sound, denoting plural in English. As often as not, this *is* the meaning of a final "s" sound—"more than one of something." But this meaning is not *inherent* in the "s" sound, any more than the word "chalk" *necessarily* refers to the white stuff used on blackboards. This is indeed an important idea in the study of language, that language is based on usually *arbitrary* connections between linguistic elements such as sounds and the meanings denoted by those sounds.

On the other hand, the definition is a bit confining. For instance, it restricts language to sounds, to human speech. By this rule, writing would be excluded from a consideration of language, as would sign language for the deaf. It is true, of course, that writing is a recent development in the history of language, dating back only about 5000 years, and it is equally true that the development of writing depended critically on the existence of a spoken language. Thus the spoken, auditory form of a language is more basic than the written version—is there any doubt that children would fail to acquire language if they were only exposed to books instead of speech? Nonetheless, we include written language in our definition for the indisputable reason that reading and writing are major forms of communication in modern society.

Going beyond the dictionary, let's offer a definition that is more suitable for our purposes. **Language** is defined as *a shared symbolic system* *for communication.*[1] First, language is symbolic. It consists of linguistic units, sounds that form words and other meaningful units that *symbolize* or stand for the referent of the word; the referent, the thing referred to by the final "s," is the meaning *plural.* Second, the symbol system is *shared* by all speakers of a language culture. Speakers and listeners all have the same set of arbitrary connections between sound and meaning, and they also share a common rule system that translates the sound-to-meaning connections in the appropriate direction. Third, the system enables *communication.* The speaker translates from the thought into a public message, according to the shared rule system. This enables the listener to retranslate the public, spoken message back into the underlying thought or meaning. (Except in situations that deal with sounds and speech exclusively, the terms speaker/ listener can also be interpreted to include writer/reader.)

Universals of Language

Hockett (1960a,b, 1966) proposed a list of 13 **linguistic universals,** *features or characteristics that are common to all known languages.* As distinct from various animal communication systems, Hockett proposed that only human language contains all 13 of these features. Several of the universals or "design features" he identified, such as the vocal–auditory requirement, are not now considered essential characteristics of language, although they may have been essential to the evolution of the language. Other features, however, are critically important to our analysis here. Hockett's full list of 13 linguistic universals is presented in Table 8-1, along with short explanations. We limit our discussion here to just four of these, plus two other features not mentioned by Hockett, since they are of greatest importance to our study.

Semanticity   As you already know, the term *semantic* means "meaning." It is an obvious yet important point that language exhibits semanticity, that language conveys meaning. Hockett's point here is that the sounds of human language carry meaning, whereas other sounds that we make, say, coughing or clearing our throats, are not part of our language because they do not usually convey meaning in the normal sense of the word. (I'm ignoring here the example of a roomful of students coughing in unison at, say, a professor's boastful remark, to indicate some collective editorial opinion or another. In this situation, the coughing sound is

---

[1]The *psycho*linguistic orientation of this chapter is particularly clear here, in the definition of language. A definition of language from the standpoint of linguistics is: the set of all acceptable, grammatical, "well-formed" sentences in the language. Note how there is no reference to or implication of a language *user* in this definition, or any hint that language is an *activity* engaged in by people for a purpose. Such a system, from a psychological point of view, misses practically all the really interesting action.

Table 8-1   HOCKETT'S LINGUISTIC UNIVERSALS

1. **Vocal–Auditory Channel.** The channel or means of transmission for all linguistic communication is vocal–auditory. Hockett excluded written language by this universal because it is a recent invention, and because it is not found in all language cultures.

2. **Broadcast Transmission and Directional Reception.** Linguistic transmissions are "broadcast," that is, transmitted in all directions from the source, and can be received by any hearer within range; the transmission is therefore public. By virtue of binaural hearing, the direction or location of the transmission is conveyed by the transmission itself.

3. **Transitoriness—Rapid Fading.** The linguistic transmission is of a transitory nature; it has to be received at exactly the right time, or else it will have faded (as contrasted with, say, a message transmitted to a recording device, which preserves the information). This implies that the hearer must perform the message preservation task by recording the message on paper or by storing information in memory.

4. **Interchangeability.** "Any speaker of a human language is capable, in theory, of saying anything he can understand when someone else says it. For language, humans are what engineers call 'tranceivers': units freely usable for either transmission or reception" (1960a). In other words, since I can understand a sentence you say to me, I can therefore say that sentence back to you: I can both receive and transmit *any* message. Contrast this with certain animal systems, in which males and females produce different calls or messages, and these cannot be interchanged.

5. **Total Feedback.** The human speaker has total auditory feedback for the transmitted message, simultaneous with the listener's reception of the message. This feedback is used for moment-to-moment adjustments to the production of sound.

6. **Specialization.** The sounds of language are specialized to convey meaning, that is, linguistic intent, as opposed to nonlanguage sounds. Consider a jogger saying "I'm exhausted," when the speech act conveys a specific meaning. Contrast this with a jogger panting loudly at the end of a run, when the sounds being produced have no necessary linguistic function (although a hearer might *infer* that the jogger is exhausted).

7. **Semanticity.** Linguistic utterances, whether simple phrases or complete sentences, convey meaning by means of the symbols we use to form the utterance.

8. **Arbitrariness.** There is no inherent connection between a symbol and the concept or object to which it refers; there is only an arbitrary connection between sound and meaning. Contrast this with iconic communication systems, such as the bee's waggle dance.

9. **Discreteness.** Although sound patterns can vary continuously across several dimensions (e.g., duration of sound, loudness of sound), language uses only a small number of discrete ranges on those dimensions to convey meaning. Thus languages do not rely on continuous variation of vowel duration, for instance, to signal changes in meaning.

10. **Displacement.** Linguistic messages are not tied in time or space to the topic of the communication; this implicates an elaborate memory system within the speaker/hearer in order to recall the past and anticipate the future.

11. **Productivity.** Language is novel, consisting of utterances that have never been uttered or comprehended before; new messages, including words, can be coined freely by means of rules and agreement among the members of the language culture.

12. **Duality of Patterning (Duality of Structure).** A small set of sounds, or phonemes, can be combined and recombined into an infinitely large set of sentences, or meanings. The sounds have no inherent meaning; the combinations do have meaning, by virtue of #7 and #8.

13. **Cultural or Traditional Transmission.** Language is acquired by exposure to the culture, to the language of the surrounding individuals. Contrast this with various courtship and mating communications of animals, in which the specific messages are genetically governed.

termed *paralinguistic* and functions much the way rising vocal pitch indicates anger. Then again, it could just be a roomful of coughing students.)

Arbitrariness   Hockett's feature of arbitrariness is one we just encountered in the dictionary definition of language. Arbitrariness means that there is no inherent connection between the units (sounds, words) employed in a language and the meanings referred to by those units. There are of course a limited number of exceptions to this, for instance, the onomatopoeia of *buzz, hum, zoom,* and the like, but these are few indeed. Far more commonly, the symbol we use to refer to something bears no relationship whatsoever to the thing itself. The word *dog,* in and of itself, bears no inherent resemblance or correspondence to the four-legged furry creature named by the word, just as the spoken symbol *silence* does not resemble its referent, true silence. Hockett's clever example drives the point home; *whale* is a small symbol for a very big thing, while *microorganism* is a big symbol for an extremely small thing.

Because there are no built-in connections between symbols and their referents, knowledge of language must involve learning and remembering the arbitrary connections. It is in this sense that we speak of language being a *shared* system. We all have essentially the same connections stored in memory, the same set of word-to-referent associations that constitute part of our knowledge of language. Thus by convention—by agreement with the language culture—we all know that *dog* refers to *that* particular kind of physical object rather than another. Obviously, we *have* to know what word goes with what referent, since there's no way to look at an object and decide what its name must be.[2]

Two important consequences of the arbitrariness of language deserve special attention, partly because they help to distinguish human language from several animal communication systems, and partly because they tell us about the human language user. These two consequences concern the *flexibility* of the symbol system and the principle of *naming.* Neither of these was listed by Hockett, although it is clear that they are derived from his point about arbitrariness.

Flexibility of Symbols   Note that it is the principle of arbitrariness that makes language entirely symbolic. *Desk* and *pupitre* are simply the

---

[2]Mark Twain captured the essence of naming and arbitrariness in a wonderful story called "Eve's Diary." On Wednesday of the second week after creation, Eve writes: "During the last day or two I have taken all the work of naming things off his [Adam's] hands, and this has been a great relief to him, for he has no gift in that line, and is evidently very grateful. He can't think of a rational name to save him, but I do not let him see that I am aware of his defect. Whenever a new creature comes along I name it before he has time to expose himself by an awkward silence. . . . The minute I set eyes on an animal I know what it is. I don't have to reflect a moment; the right name comes out instantly. . . . I seem to know just by the shape of the creature and the way it acts what animal it is. . . . When the dodo came along [Adam] thought it was a wild-cat—I saw it in his eye. But I saved him. . . . I just spoke up in a quite natural way of pleased surprise . . . and said, 'Well, I do declare, if there isn't the dodo!' "

English and French symbols for a particular object. Were it not for the history of our language, we might call it a *zoople* or a *manty*. Furthermore, a consequence of this symbolic aspect of language is that the system is tremendously flexible. That is, since the connection between symbol and meaning is arbitrary, it is also changeable and "inventable." We routinely shift our terms for the things around us, however slowly such change might take place; we used to call cars *automobiles,* whereas now that is a rather archaic term. People used to play records on their phonographs, then LPs on their hi-fis.

Contrast this degree of flexibility with the opposite of a symbolic system, which Hockett termed an "iconic" system. In an iconic system, each unit *does* have a physical resemblance to its referent, just as a map is physically similar to the terrain it depicts. In such a system, there is essentially no flexibility at all, because changing the symbol for a referent would make the connection arbitrary.

In fact, the human language that comes closest to being iconic is sign language, because it originally devised units, the sequences of hand movements, to resemble the thing being referred to. But even sign language now goes far beyond its original iconic scheme. True, some proportion of the ASL (American Sign Language) vocabulary remains physically similar to the referent (see Figure 8-1). But many more ASL words blend, simplify, and combine signs, or rely on rules that violate simple iconic connections. Howard (1983) notes, for example, that to intensify meaning, a sign is made more rapidly than usual. Thus to sign the concept VERY QUICKLY, you would sign QUICKLY in a rapid, tense fashion. This seemingly iconic relationship is undermined, however, with VERY SLOWLY; you would apply the normal rule for intensifying, making the sign for SLOWLY in a rapid, tense fashion.

FIGURE 8-1

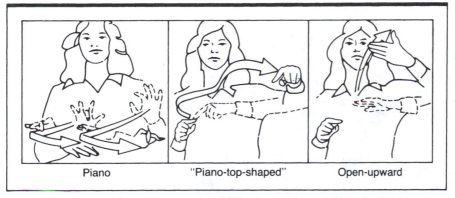

| Piano | "Piano-top-shaped" | Open-upward |

A signer creates an American Sign Language depiction of a grand piano. The sign is partially iconic because it resembles the physical object. (From Newport & Bellugi, 1978.)

Naming   A corollary point to arbitrariness and flexibility of symbols involves naming (e.g., see Glass & Holyoak, 1986). We assign names to all the objects in our environment, to all the feelings and emotions we experience, to all the ideas and concepts we conceive of. It's a trivially obvious point that, wherever it is you are sitting right now as you read this book, each object in the room has a name. Of course, in an unfamiliar or unusual place (an airport control tower or a car repair shop) you may not know the name of something, but it never occurs to you that the thing might therefore have no name.

Furthermore, we don't stop by naming just the physical objects around us. We have an elaborate vocabulary by which we refer to unseen characteristics, privately experienced feelings, and other intangibles and abstractions. Consider the vocabulary of this book, for instance: terms such as *perception, mental process, spreading activation, knowledge,* and *cognition* have no necessary physical referent. Words such as *justice, cause, frivolousness, likewise,* and *however* refer to no concrete object. Indeed, we even have words such as *abstractions* and *intangibles* that refer to the *idea* of being abstract.

A language does not have to be spoken to be a true language, as sign language for the deaf and symbolic computer languages show.

Another facet of this naming principle follows directly: we generate or invent names for the new objects and ideas about which we need to talk. For instance, someone once had the idea of putting a radio into an alarm clock, and *voila,* the uninspired but accurate term *clock radio* was introduced. For a better example, consider the following: at this very moment, I am "word processing" this chapter on my "personal computer," performing "block move," "block delete," and "global search" processes. Imagine how meaningless those phrases would have been 50 years ago (in fact, 50 years ago the term "computer" meant the person who computed values for printed mathematical tables). Because we want to talk about new things, new ideas, and new concepts, we invent new terms.[3]

Displacement   One of the most powerful devices our language gives us is the ability to talk about something other than the present moment, a feature Hockett called *displacement.* By conjugating verbs to form past tense, future tense, and so on, we can communicate about objects, events, and ideas that are not present but are remembered or anticipated. And when we use constructions such as "If I go to the library tomorrow, then I'll be able to . . . ," we demonstrate a particularly powerful aspect of displacement: we can communicate about something that has never happened, and indeed might never happen in the future, while clearly anticipating future consequences of that never-performed action. To illustrate the power and importance of displacement to yourself, try speaking *only* in the present tense for about five minutes. You'll discover how incredibly limiting it is to be "stuck in the present" by language.

Productivity   By most accounts, this final principle of **productivity** (also termed *generativity* by some authors) is the most important of all the linguistic universals, since it gives language its most notable characteristic, *novelty.* Although it is featured in Hockett's list of universals, he was by no means the first to appreciate its importance. Indeed, the novelty of language, and the productivity that novelty implies, formed the basis of Chomsky's (1959) critique of Skinner's book (see Chapter 1) and the foundation for Chomsky's own influential theory of language (e.g., 1957, 1965). It is an absolute article of faith in both linguistics and psycholinguistics that the key to understanding language and language behavior lies in an understanding of novelty, an understanding of the productive nature of language.

---

[3]Clearly, we don't merely name the new "things" around us: any new concept, whether object or emotion, gets named. An excellent example is the word *ambivalent,* composed of the prefix *ambi-* meaning "both or several," and *valent,* meaning "direction"; hence *ambivalent* means "tending toward two contradictory directions at once." According to *The American Heritage Dictionary of the English Language,* the word was coined by Freud. It's interesting how a relatively common feeling such as ambivalence went without a one-word name until so short a time ago. Note further that while Freud's naming of this emotion seems rule governed—that is, pick the Latin roots and put them together—the meanings of *ambi* and *valent* are of course arbitrary.

Consider the following: aside from trite phrases, customary greetings, and so on, *hardly any* of our routine language is standardized or repetitive. Instead, the bulk of what we say is novel. Our utterances are not memorized, are not repeated, but are *new*. This is the principle of productivity, that language is a productive and inherently novel activity, that we *generate* sentences rather than repeat them. When I teach the principle of productivity to my Memory and Cognition class, the *idea* I'm communicating is not new: I lecture about productivity every time. But the stream of sounds I produce during any one lecture, the sequence of words and sentences I use to talk about productivity, is *novel*. I'm sure that I have never said *exactly* "but the stream of sounds I produce during any one lecture. . . ." And even in somewhat stylized situations, as in telling a joke, the language is largely new. Only if the punchline requires a specific word, say, because of a double meaning or rhyme, do I try to remember the exact wording of a previously used sentence.

What does productivity mean for language? It means that language is a *creative* system as opposed to a repetitive system. We do not recycle sentences, so to speak. Instead, we create them on the spot, now in the active voice, now in the passive, with a prepositional phrase sometimes at the beginning, sometimes at the end, and so on. In a very real sense then, applying our productive rules of language to the words in our vocabulary permits us to generate an infinite number of utterances.

How can we understand any and all of the infinite set of sentences; what does it mean for a "theory of language" that speakers and listeners can generate and comprehend any one of this numberless set? In brief, it means that speakers of the language must have some flexible basis for *producing* or *generating* novel speech, for coming up with the different sequences of sounds and words that can be comprehended by listeners. And, likewise, hearers must have the same flexible basis in order to hear the sequence of words and recover from them what the intended meaning is. By most accounts, the basis for such productivity is a set of *rules*. To anticipate later sections of the chapter, rules form the basis for each level of language we will discuss, from our phonological system up through the highest level of analysis, the conceptual and belief systems we hold as we comprehend language.

Animal Communication Systems

The contrast between the flexible, productive human language system and the various animal communication systems is staggering. Consider the chimpanzee signaling system (Marler, 1967), for example. This system consists of several distress and warning calls, serving to alert an entire troupe of chimps to imminent danger. Chimpanzees produce a guttural "rraup" sound to warn others in the troupe of an eagle, one of the chimp's natural predators; they "chutter" to warn of snakes, and "chirp"

DEMONSTRATIONS

Most of the interesting demonstrations for this chapter will involve either your or your subjects' intuitions about the samples of language, rather than "hard data" like recall accuracy. The projects are worth doing, nonetheless.

1. A considerable amount of research investigates issues of ambiguity and our awareness of ambiguous sentences. Come up with sentences like the "Bill and Mary saw the mountains" one, or like the lexical ambiguity examples from Chapter 6 (see the Demonstrations section of that chapter too). Intermix some of these with nonambiguous sentences, then present the entire set to the subjects. When they recall the sentences later, do their rewordings preserve the ambiguity or do they resolve it?

2. Try prefacing the ambiguous sentences with a context that biases one or the other meaning, and then see if subjects' paraphrases are biased in the same direction or not.

3. Fascinating work by Fromkin (1971), Garrett (1975), and others has tabulated and made sense of speech errors, when we substitute or change sounds, syllables, words, and so on. Speech errors are not random but are quite lawful. For instance, when we make an exchange error, the exchange is between elements at the same linguistic level; initial sounds exchange places with other initial sounds, syllables with syllables, words with words (e.g., "to cake a bake"); if a prefix switches places, its new location will be in front of another word, not at the end. Collect a sample of speech errors, say, from your professors' lectures, then analyze them in terms of the linguistic level of the elements involved, and the types of errors such as (intended phrase in parentheses):

shift	she decide to hits it (decides to hit it)
exchange	your model renosed (your nose remodeled)
perseveration	He pulled a pantrum (tantrum)
blend	to explain clarefully (clearly/carefully)

to warn of leopards. The system thus exhibits semanticity, an important characteristic of human language. That is, each signal in chimpanzee has a different, specific referent—eagle, snake, and leopard. And furthermore, these seem to be arbitrary connections: "rraup" doesn't resemble eagles in any physical way, after all.

But, as Glass and Holyoak (1986) note, the troupe of chimpanzees cannot get together and decide to change the meaning of *rraup* from eagle to snake: the arbitrary connections to meaning are completely inflexible in these systems. (Moreover, this inflexibility is most probably due to at least partial genetic influence; compare this with Hockett's last universal, *cultural transmission*.) There is, furthermore, a vast difference between naming in human languages and in the animal systems. For

THE FAR SIDE   By GARY LARSON

THE FAR SIDE copyright 1985, 1986 & 1991 FARWORKS, INC. Distributed by UNIVERSAL PRESS SYNDICATE. Reprinted with permission. All rights reserved.

"Matthews ... we're getting another one of those strange 'aw blah es span yol' sounds."

instance, there seem to be no words in chimpanzee for other obviously important objects and concepts in their environment, "tree," for example (or presumably for more emotional or abstract concepts, given Harlow's famous demonstrations of the security and comfort needs of baby chimps; 1953). And as for displacement and productivity, consider the following delightful quotation from Glass and Holyoak (1986): "The monkey has no way of saying 'I don't see an eagle,' or 'Thank heavens that wasn't an eagle,' or 'That was some huge eagle I saw yesterday' " (p. 448).

In short, beyond the level of arbitrariness, no animal communication system seems to exhibit those characteristics that appear to be universally true of—and vitally important to—human language. In the wild, at any rate, there appear to be no genuine languages. In human cultures, genuine language is the rule, apparently with no exceptions.

Summary Points: linguistic and psycholinguistic definitions of language; linguistic universals; semanticity, arbitrariness, flexibility, naming, displacement, productivity; comparison to animal communication

Five Levels of Analysis, a Critical Distinction, and Whorf and a Favorite Myth

We conclude this introduction with three points. The first concerns the *five levels of analysis* necessary for a full exploration of language. The second is a traditional distinction between one's performance in language and one's internal competence. As it happens, this distinction has some important implications for the kinds of tasks we can use in psycholinguistic research. And finally, we will talk briefly about an enduring detail that, oddly enough, seems to be part of the "oral tradition" in courses on Language, the myth about the number of words for "snow" in the Eskimo language.

Five Levels of Analysis   The traditional view of language, a characteristically linguistic point of view, is that language is *the set of all acceptable, well-formed sentences in the language* (see footnote 1). In this scheme, sets of rules are said to *generate* the sentences, and the entire set of rules is called a **grammar.** In other words, the grammar of a language is *the complete set of rules that will generate or produce all the acceptable sentences and will not generate any unacceptable, ill-formed sentences.* According to most linguists (e.g., Chomsky, 1965), such a grammar operates at three levels: *phonology* of language deals with the sounds of language, *syntax* deals with word order and grammaticality, and *semantics* deals with accessing and combining the separate word meanings into a sensible, meaningful whole.

In his highly readable introduction to a book on psychology and language, Miller (1973; incidentally, the same Miller of "Magic Number Seven" fame) proposed that language is organized on *five* distinguishable levels, not just three. In addition to the three traditional levels of phonology, syntax, and lexical or semantic knowledge, Miller suggested that a psychological approach to language must include two higher levels as well. He called these the level of *conceptual knowledge* and the level of *beliefs.*[4] As he pointed out, "grammar, of course, deals with only the first three of these levels . . . and with the relations between them. A psychologist interested in language, however, must also remember that a person's concepts and beliefs play an essential role in his use and understanding of linguistic messages" (p. 8).

---

[4]Miller uses the term *lexical* for this third level, meaning "information about the meanings of words and combinations of words." His usage suggests a somewhat narrower connotation here than the one we have developed for *semantic,* and his "conceptual knowledge" level sounds more like the encyclopedic notion of semantic memory that we're familiar with in this book. We'll stick with the narrower connotation of *semantic/lexical* here, acknowledging at the same time that there is somewhat less of a distinction than the different terms would suggest.

Miller's example of these points is classic. Consider a hypothetical conversation, in which someone says:

(1) Mary and John saw the mountains while they were flying to California.

At the level of phonology, this sentence consists of a stream of sounds, a stream that the listener must somehow *decode* into words and phrases. At the syntactic level, the sentence is a string of words in a particular order, where the order helps to specify the intended relations among the words and ideas. So far, so good.

At a semantic or lexical level, however, the sentence is ambiguous: it has two distinctly different meanings. One meaning corresponds to the paraphrase "While Mary and John were flying to California, they saw the mountains," and the other to "While the mountains were flying to California, Mary and John saw them." Nothing at the levels of phonology or syntax can rescue us from this ambiguity. The sentence cannot be disambiguated at either of these levels, but instead must be attacked at a higher level.

Miller's discussion continues: "But that is ridiculous! Everyone knows that mountains do not fly. Anyone would know immediately that the sentence . . . means that Mary and John were flying, not the mountains. But how do we know this? Is it part of the lexical meaning of the word *mountain*? Certainly not. You can look up the meaning of *mountain* in any dictionary you like, and it will not tell you that mountains do not fly. Such knowledge is part of one's conceptual information about the world one lives in, not part of one's lexical knowledge about the meanings of words. So in order to understand how people understand language, we must recognize that they use their general conceptual information as well as their specific lexical information" (Miller, 1973, pp. 8–9). We have another name for conceptual knowledge, of course—*semantic memory*.

Miller discusses the final level, the level of one's *beliefs,* by suggesting a scenario in which the speaker of sentence (1) *did* intend to say that the mountains were flying. Miller suggests: "I don't know what you would say, but my response would be 'I don't believe you.' In the final analysis, I would appeal to my system of beliefs in order to evaluate what the speaker was saying" (p. 9). Note further that other cognitive evaluations are also possible here, such as "I don't believe you, but I do believe that *you* believe the mountains were flying" or "I don't believe you literally—are you being sarcastic, or maybe metaphorical?"

Finally, the most common response in a true conversation would probably be no unusual response at all. That is, imagine that the conversation that preceded the ambiguous remark was about Mary and John's first trip to the West; their flight was during the day, and they'd never seen the scenery before. In such a context, it seems likely that few listeners would even detect the ambiguity, at least at a conscious level. If they did, they might only make a mental note of it, while realizing at the same time what the intended, sensible meaning of the sentence was.

We'll have more to say about these last two levels of analysis, the conceptual knowledge and belief systems that speakers and listeners use while "doing" language, although most of that will be deferred until Chapter 9. For the most part, this chapter will focus on the more ordinary kinds of language, and on the first three levels of analysis that have been investigated much more thoroughly. Don't lose sight of the characteristics of the language user, however, with the conceptual knowledge and belief systems that invariably operate as we produce and comprehend language.

A Critical Distinction   Chomsky (1957, 1965) has long insisted that there is an important distinction to be drawn at the outset of any investigation into language, the distinction between **competence** and **performance.** Competence is *the internalized knowledge of language and its rules that fully fluent speakers of a language have.* It is an ideal knowledge, to an extent, in that it represents a person's complete knowledge of how to generate and comprehend language. Performance, on the other hand, is *the actual language behavior that a speaker might generate,* the string of sounds and words that the speaker utters.

Chomsky argued that competence was a purer basis for understanding linguistic knowledge, and that performance was a relatively less secure basis. The reasons for this should be obvious. When we produce language, not only are we revealing our knowledge of language, but we are also passing that knowledge through the human information processing system. As such, it is not surprising that performance reveals imperfections; after all, memory is fallible. A speaker may lose her train of thought as she proceeds through a sentence, and thus may be forced to stop and begin again; speakers may pause, repeat themselves, and so on. All these **dysfluencies,** these *irregularities or errors in otherwise fluent speech,* can be attributed to the *language user.* Lapses of memory, momentary distractions, intrusions of new thoughts—all these are imperfections in the language user, rather than in the user's basic knowledge of the language. Thus the discipline of linguistics, not particularly concerned with the psychology of memory limitations, imperfect attention, and the like, relies rather exclusively on the abstract *competence* that can be exhibited.

There's a subtle paradox here, of course. How are we to tap into a person's competence, to judge what is known about language, when by definition the person's competence can only be communicated to us through performance? Chomsky's strategy, not altogether misguided, was to rely on a speaker's *linguistic intuitions.* That is, a speaker might actually say "I was ... uh ... walking down the ... uh ... street when I saw, I mean *found....*" The minor dysfluencies are attributable to momentary distractions and so on. Nonetheless, the same speaker could hear or read that sentence and would undoubtedly judge it as somewhat unacceptable. In other words, Chomsky argued that we can come close to knowing about the competence that speakers possess by asking them to judge sentences according to their informed linguistic intuitions about what is and what is not acceptable. Only when we force the language user into an actual performance situation will we be misled or distracted by dysfluencies and mistakes.

As indicated earlier, *psycho*linguistics cannot afford to throw out performance; after all, we are in the business of investigating human behavior, not just an idealized, perfect speaker/hearer, but an actual person *doing* the behavior we're trying to understand. So psycholinguistics accepts competence as an important factor but also faces up to the task of understanding and explaining actual performance. As such, Miller's (1973) general point about conceptual knowledge and beliefs is important here too; if we exclude too much of the language user, then we miss many important characteristics of the very language we are trying to understand.

Whorf and a Favorite Myth   Whatever else you may or may not have heard about the topic of language, it's likely that you *have* heard the "folk wisdom" of our culture regarding, of all things, the large num-

ber of words for "snow" found in the Eskimo language. This "fact" is typically called upon to support one or another version of the *linguistic-relativity hypothesis,* by Whorf (e.g., 1956); the idea is also commonly referred to as "the Whorfian hypothesis."

Whorf's basic idea was that the language you know shapes the way you think about events in the world around you. In its strongest version, the hypothesis claims that language controls both thought and perception to a large degree; that is, you are unable to think about ideas or concepts that your language does not name. In its weaker version, the hypothesis claims that your language influences and shapes your thought, making it possibly more difficult to think about ideas without having a name for them.

Current thinking finds some merit in the weaker form of the Whorfian hypothesis, that language does indeed influence our thoughts to a degree. For example, "English speakers have no difficulty expressing the idea that, if there are 49 men and 37 pairs of shoes, some men will have to go without shoes. There are nonliterate societies where this would be a difficult situation to describe, because the language may have number terms only for 'one-two-many' (Greenberg, 1978)" (Hunt & Agnoli, 1991, p. 385). As another example, Hunt and Agnoli note the effect of language on working memory resources. If your language has a simple, one-word label for an idea, then expressing that idea in spoken language would not tax working memory very heavily. (Baddeley, 1992a, discusses a fascinating study by Ellis & Hennelly, 1980, in which Welsh subjects had shorter memory spans for Welsh number words than for English number words, this because the Welsh words take longer to say.)

On the other hand, a traditional example offered in support of the Whorfian hypothesis is the "well-known fact" that the Eskimo language has multiple terms for "snow," in contrast to the (impoverished) English language with only one. Writers routinely suggest one of several reasons for this, usually involving the idea that snow is more important to Eskimos, due to their northerly geographical location.

Martin (1986) has demonstrated that this line of reasoning is simply wrong, despite the persistence of the myth. Apparently, Boas (1911) wrote the original report. In passing, he listed four separate Eskimo words for snow. Whorf later referred to this idea (although he provided no data or citations to Boas) and rather carelessly suggested that there were five "snow words." Inflation set in in the late 1950s; early references to three or four such words turned into "Eskimo languages have many words for snow" (Eastman, 1975), which was then exaggerated even further by the popular press (Martin cites *The New York Times* editorial that mentioned the "one hundred types of snow" discussed by Whorf).

But even the original work is suspect, for important linguistic reasons. To paraphrase Martin (1986), consider two questions. First, "What is a word?" Would you consider the noun "snow" and the verb "snow" as one or two words in English; are "snowed," "snowing," and "snowy" different lexical entities in English, or just one lexical unit that has different grammatical markers attached? The original research on Eskimo apparently blurred over such distinctions in counting the words, failing to appreciate how Eskimo is a language "in which all word building is accomplished by multiple suffixation" (p. 419).

Second, "What is Eskimo?" If we collect language samples from across the Canadian North and Northwest, have we merely surveyed the minor variations of a single language, or have we in fact tabulated snow words across several *different* languages? Martin's conclusion is clear: there is no reason to believe that any single Eskimo language has more than two distinct roots or lexical bases that refer to snow, one for "snow in the air"—our "snowflake"—and one for "snow on the ground"—our "snow." She concludes that Eskimo is no more differentiated than English when it comes to snow words.

It would not be surprising, of course, for subtle distinctions to be more conveniently made in Eskimo "snow" words and terms than in English, simply because speakers of the two languages tend to talk about different things (e.g., Rosch, 1974). But the notion that non-Eskimos can't think about snow the way Eskimos can, because of the richness of Eskimo "snow terms," is based on a myth.

Summary Points: five levels of analysis; linguistic competence and performance; linguistic-relativity hypothesis and Whorf

▼ Phonology: The Sounds of Language

In any language interaction, the task of a speaker is to communicate an idea by translating that idea into spoken sounds. The hearer goes in the opposite direction, translating from sound to intended meaning. Among the many sources of information available in the spoken message, the most obvious and concrete one is the sound of the language itself, the stream of speech signals that must be decoded. Other sources of information, say, the gestures and facial expressions of the speaker, can be eliminated, as in a telephone conversation, with little or no disruption of the communication; in fact, gestures carry far less information than you might suspect (e.g., Krauss, Morrel-Samuels, & Colosante, 1991). But you can't do without the words and the sounds that form those words. Thus our study of the *grammar* of language begins at this basic level, the sounds and the rule system for combining them.

Sounds in Isolation

To state an obvious point, different languages sound different—they are composed of different sets of sounds. The basic sounds that compose a language are called **phonemes.** If we were to conduct a survey, we

Table 8-2   ENGLISH CONSONANTS AND VOWELS

English Consonants

Manner of Articulation		Bilabial	Labiodental	Dental	Alveolar	Palatal	Velar	Glottal
Stops	Voiceless	p (*p*at)			t (*t*ack)		k (*c*at)	
	Voiced	b (*b*at)			d (*d*ig)		g (*g*et)	
Fricatives	Voiceless		f (*f*at)	Θ (*th*in)	s (*s*at)	š (fi*sh*)		h (*h*at)
	Voiced		v (*v*at)	ð (*th*en)	z (*z*ap)	ž (a*z*ure)		
Affricatives	Voiceless					č (*ch*urch)		
	Voiced					ǰ (*j*udge)		
Nasals		m (*m*at)			n (*n*at)		ŋ (si*ng*)	
Liquids					l (*l*ate)	r (*r*ate)		
Glides		w (*w*in)				y (*y*et)		

English Vowels

	Front	Center	Back
High	i (b*ee*t)		u (b*oo*t)
			U (b*oo*k)
	I (b*i*t)		
		əl (b*ir*d)	o (b*o*de)
Middle	e (b*a*by)	ə (sof*a*)	
	ε (b*e*t)		ɔ (b*ou*ght)
	æ (b*a*t)	ʌ (b*u*t)	
Low			
		a (p*a*lm)	

From Glucksberg & Danks, 1975.

would find around 200 different phonemes present across all known spoken languages. No single language uses even half that many, however. English, for instance, contains about 46 phonemes (experts disagree on whether some sounds are separate phonemes or blends of two phonemes; the disagreement centers on diphthong vowel sounds, as in *few,* seemingly a combination of "ee" and "oo"). Hawaiian, on the other hand, uses only about 15 phonemes (Palermo, 1978). Note here that there is actually little significance to the total tally of phonemes in a language; no language is superior to another because it has more (or fewer) phonemes.[5]

Table 8-2 shows the Glucksberg and Danks (1975) typology of the phonemes of English, based on the characteristics of their pronunciation.

---

[5]Foss and Hakes (1978) diagnose such notions as *linguistic chauvinism,* "the belief that one's own language is the best of all possible languages . . . that one language is more 'complex' than another. Depending upon the mood of the chauvinist at the moment, this alleged fact may be used to condemn or to praise the language under discussion. (For example, the language is complex and therefore overly complicated, confused, and hard to learn. Or, the language is complex and therefore rich in expressive power and useful for communication.) . . . [In fact], every language so far studied by linguists appears to permit a range of expression as wide as any other. True, one language may have terms for concepts not named in another language (e.g., *electoral college, frisbee*). But this is a fact about the concepts that are of interest to the speakers of that language, it is not a fact about the complexity of the language itself" (pp. 6–7).

For consonants, three variables are relevant, *place of articulation, manner of articulation, and voicing. Place of articulation* simply refers to the place in the vocal tract where the disruption of airflow takes place; as shown in Figure 8-2, a bilabial consonant like /b/ disrupts the airflow at the lips, whereas /h/ disrupts the column of air at the very rear of the vocal tract, at the glottis. Second, *manner of articulation* refers to how the airflow coming up from the lungs is disrupted. If the column of air is completely stopped and then released, it's called a *stop consonant,* for example, the consonant sounds in "bat" and "tub." A *fricative* consonant, like the /f/ in "fine," only involves a partial blockage of airflow. Finally, *voicing* means whether the vocal cords begin to vibrate immediately with

FIGURE 8-2

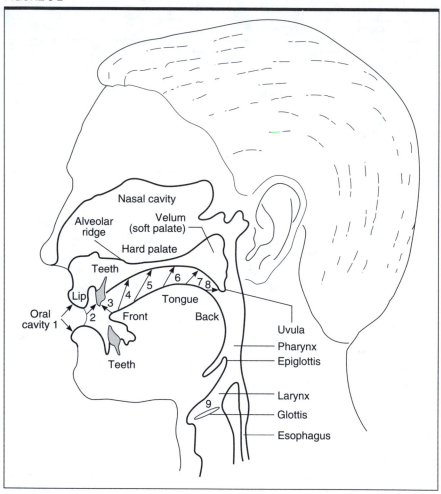

The vocal tract, illustrating places of articulation: 1, bilabial; 2, labiodental; 3, dental; 4, alveolar; 5, palatoalveolar; 6, palatal; 7, velar; 8, uvular; 9, glottal. (From Fromkin & Rodman, 1974.)

the obstruction of airflow—for example, the /b/ in "bat"—or if the vibration is delayed until after the release of air—the /p/ in "pat."

Vowels, by contrast, involve no disruption of the airflow. Instead, they differ on two dimensions; placement in the mouth, whether front, center, or back, and tongue position in the mouth, high, middle, or low. Scan the table, pronouncing the sample words, and try to be consciously aware of the characteristics that you (if you're a native or fluent English speaker) know so thoroughly at an unconscious, automatic level.

Let's develop a few more conscious intuitions about the basic sounds of language. Stop for a moment and put your hand in front of your mouth. Say the word *pot,* and then *spot.* Did you notice a difference between the two "p" sounds? Most speakers produce a puff of air with the "p" sound as they say "pot"; we "puff" very little (if at all) for the "p" in "spot" if it's spoken normally. Given this, you would have to agree that these two "p" sounds are different at a purely physical level. And yet, you *hear* them as the same sound in those two different words; you treat them as the same sound when you hear and comprehend those words. Figure 8-3 shows actual spectrograph patterns for two families of syllables, the /b/ family on the left, the /d/ family on the right. Note how remarkably different "the same" sound can look.

In the terminology of psycholinguistics, the two "p" sounds, despite their physical differences, are both instances of the same **phoneme,** the same basic sound group. That is, the fact that these two different sounds are treated *as if they were the same* in English means that they represent one phoneme. Thus a **phoneme** is a *category of language sounds that are treated as the same sound, despite any physical differences among the category members.* In other words, the English word "spot" does not change its meaning when pronounced with the "p" sound in "pot."

A classic illustration of phoneme boundaries is shown in Figure 8-4, from a study by Liberman, Harris, Hoffman, and Griffith (1957). When the presented sound crossed a boundary, that is, between stimulus values 3 and 5, between 9 and 10, subjects' identifications of the sound switched rapidly from /b/ to /d/, and then from /d/ to /g/. Variations within the boundaries, however, did not lead to different identifications: despite the variations, all the sounds from values 5 to 8 were identified as /d/.

There are two critical notions here. The first is that all the sounds falling within a set of boundaries are perceived as the same, despite physical differences among them. This is the phenomenon of **categorical perception.** Because English speakers discern no real difference between the *hard k* sounds in "cool" and "keep," they are "perceived categorically," that is, perceived as belonging to the same category, the /k/ phoneme.

The second notion is quite straightforward; *different* phonemes are the sounds that are *perceived* as being different by speakers of the language. The physical differences between /s/ and /z/ are important in English—changing from one to the other gives you different words, for example,

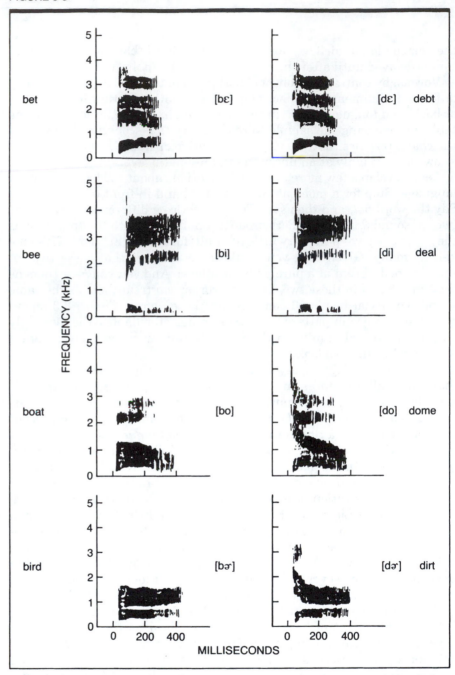

FIGURE 8-3

Spectrographic patterns of two families of syllables, showing the changes across time in the physical sound patterns. Depicted is "the problem of invariance" for consonants. There are dramatic changes in the initial portions of the patterns, induced by the following vowel, even though the consonant sounds from top to bottom are all classified as the same phoneme. For instance, the /b/ in *bet* and *bird* are physically very different, yet both are perceived as /b/. In contrast, the /b/ and /d/ sounds in *bet* and *debt* are very similar physically but are perceived as different phonemes. (From Jusczyk, Smith, & Murphy, 1981.)

FIGURE 8–4

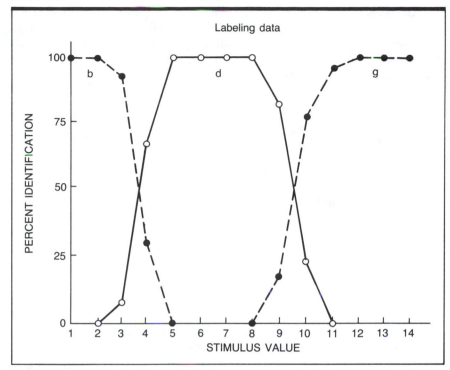

One subject's labeling data for synthesized consonants ranging from /b/ to /g/. Note that small changes in the stimulus value (e.g., from values 3 to 4) can result in a complete change in labeling, whereas larger changes (e.g., from values 4 to 8) that do not cross the phoneme boundary do not lead to a change in labeling. (From Liberman et al., 1957.)

"ice" and "eyes." This is no more—and no less—than saying that the /s/ and /z/ sounds in English are different phonemes. A most interesting side effect of such phonemic differences is that you can be quite insensitive to the phonemic differences of other languages if your own language doesn't use the distinguishing difference. Spanish does not use the /s/ versus /z/ contrast, so native speakers of Spanish have difficulty distinguishing "ice" and "eyes" in English. Conversely, the "hard k" sounds at the beginning of "cool" and "keep" are interchangeable in English: they are the same phoneme. But as Glucksberg and Danks (1975) note, this difference is phonemic in Arabic; the Arabic words for "heart" and "dog" differ *only* in their initial sounds, exactly the two different hard k sounds that we ignore in English.

Combining Phonemes into Words

From a stock of about 46 phonemes, English generates *all* its words, however many thousands that might be. This fact, that a small number of units can be combined so flexibly into so many words, is essentially the linguistic universal of *productivity,* at the level of phonology. Thus from a small set of units—phonemes—an essentially infinite number of combinations—words—can be generated. Recall further that the essential ingredient of productivity is *rules.* We turn now to the issue of combining phonemes into words, and to the rules by which this is accomplished.

Let's work with a simple example here. There are three phonemes in the word *bat,* the voiced stop consonant /b/, the short vowel sound /ae/, and the final voiceless /t/. Substitute the voiceless /p/ for /b/, and you get *pat.* Now rearrange the phonemes in these words, and you'll discover that some of the arrangements don't yield English words, for example, **abt, *tba,* and **atp.* Why? What makes **abt* or **atp* illegal pronunciation strings in English?

While it's tempting to say the reason is that syllables like **abt* cannot be pronounced, a moment's reflection suggests that this is false. After all, any number of such "unpronounceable" strings *are* pronounced in other languages, for example, the initial *pn-* in the French word for pneumonia is pronounced, while English just makes the "p" silent. Instead, the rule seems to be a bit more specific. English usually does not use a "voiced–voiceless" sequence of two consonants within the same pronounced syllable; in fact, it only seldom uses any two-consonant sequence when both are in the same "manner of articulation" category. (Of course, if the two consonants fall in different syllables, then the rule doesn't apply.)

Phonemic Competence and Rules Why does this seem to be an unusual explanation? The reason is that our knowledge of English phonology and pronunciation is not particularly verbalizable or expressible. You can look at the table, try to think of words that do combine consonants, and eventually come up with tentative pronunciation rules. But this is quite different from knowing the rules in an easily accessed and expressible fashion. And yet, you are a true expert at deciding what phoneme sequences can and cannot be used in English. Your implicit knowledge of how sounds are combined in English tells you that **abt* is illegal because it violates a rule of English pronunciation.

This *extensive knowledge of the rules of permissible English sound combinations* is your **phonemic competence.** These rules tell you what is and isn't permissible—*bat* is, but **abt* isn't. No one ever explicitly taught you these rules, of course; you abstracted them from your language environment as you acquired language. This competence tells you that a string of letters like "pnart" is only legal when the "p" is silent, but that "snart" is a legal string—not a word, of course, but a legal combination of sounds.

Because people are so certain about what is and isn't a permissible or legal string of sounds in English, and because they are so similar in their judgments, we must conclude that speakers of the language have this phonemic competence as part of their knowledge of language. The critical point here is that this extensive knowledge is *tacit;* it's implicit, even unconscious. While it's part of you, it is quite inaccessible to your deliberate attempts at retrieval.

Speech Perception and Context

We are now ready to approach the question of how people produce and perceive the speech signal. Do we merely hear a word and segment it in some fashion into its separate phonemes, or is this even a possibility given the nature of spoken speech? When we speak, do we merely string phonemes together, one after another, like stringing beads on a necklace?

Categorical Perception and the Problem of Invariance   The answer to both questions is "No." Even when the "same" sound is being pronounced, it is not physically identical to other examples of that "same" sound. The sounds—the phonemes—*change;* they change from speaker to speaker and from one time to the next within the same speaker. Most prominently, they change or vary from one word to another, depending on what sounds precede and follow.

This *variability in sounds* is referred to as the **problem of invariance.** This term is somewhat peculiar, because the problem in speech perception is that the sounds *are not* invariant—they change all the time. A simple illustration of this changeability is in Figure 8-5, where syllables ranging from /di/ to /du/ and /gi/ to /gu/ are shown in somewhat

FIGURE 8-5

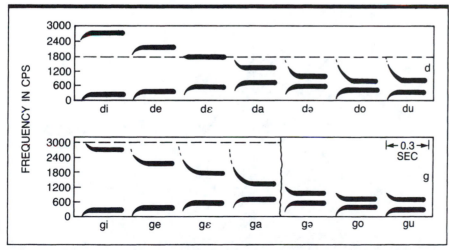

Idealized spectrographic patterns of the sounds /di/ through /du/ (and /gi/ through /gu/), showing only the two main formants. The initial phoneme changes physically across the range of vowel sounds, yet those different patterns are perceived as being the same consonant, either /d/ or /g/. (From Liberman, 1957.)

idealized form. Look at the pairs of dark patterns across the top. The /d/ sound in /di/ shows two *concentrations of energy,* called **formants,** one below 600 cps, one above 2400 cps. The patterns also show a slight rise at the beginning of the syllable. In /du/, however, the two /d/ formants are much closer together, and the initial sound is a falling, not rising, pattern.

A second illustration of the problem of invariance is in Figure 8-6, which shows the influence of each of the three phonemes in the word "bag." To pronounce "bag," do you simply articulate the /b/, then /ae/, then /g/? No! As the figure shows, the /ae/ sound influences both /b/ and /g/, the /g/ phoneme (dotted lines) exerts an influence well back into the /b/ sound, and so on. The technical term for these effects is **coarticulation:** *more than one sound is being articulated at the same time.* As you type the word "the," your right index finger starts moving toward "h"

FIGURE 8-6

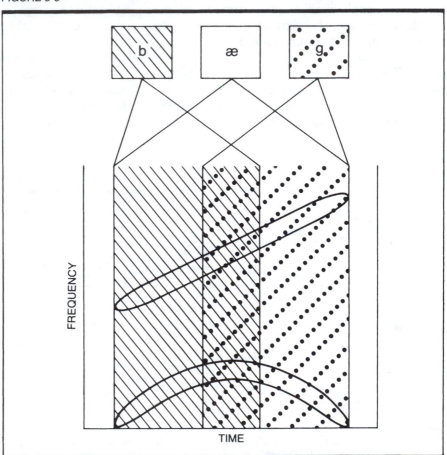

Coarticulation is illustrated for the three phonemes in the word *bag;* solid diagonals indicate the influence of the /b/ phoneme, dotted diagonals the influence of /g/. (From Liberman, 1970.)

before your left index finger has struck the "t." In like fashion, your vocal tract begins to move toward the /ae/ before you have articulated /b/, and toward /g/ before even finishing the /b/. This is yet another illustration of the problem of invariance: each phoneme changes the articulation of each other phoneme and does so differently depending on what the other phonemes are.

The simple fact is as follows. The sounds of language vary tremendously as we speak them. Yet we tolerate a fair degree of variability for the sounds within a phoneme category, both when listening and decoding from sound to meaning, and also when speaking, converting meaning into spoken sound. How do we do this; how do we tolerate this variability and still decipher the changeable, almost undependable spoken signal?

The answer is *context*. Putting it another way, the answer is *conceptually driven processing*. If we had to rely entirely on the spoken signal to figure out what was being said, then we would be processing speech in an entirely data-driven fashion, a bottom–up process. We would have to find some basis for figuring out what each and every sound in the word was, and then retrieve that word from memory based on the analysis of sound. This is virtually impossible, given the variability of phonemes. Instead, context—in this case the words, phrases, and ideas already identified— leads us to correct identification of new, incoming sounds.

A clever demonstration of this was performed by Pollack and Pickett (1964). They tape recorded several spontaneous conversations, spliced out single words from the tapes, then played the spliced words to subjects. When the words were presented in isolation, subjects identified them correctly only 47% of the time. Performance improved when longer and longer segments of speech were played, because more and more supportive syntactic and semantic context was then available. In a related study, Miller and Isard (1963) presented three kinds of sentences to subjects: fully grammatical sentences such as "Accidents kill motorists on the highways," semantically anomalous sentences such as "Accidents carry honey between the house," and ungrammatical strings such as "Around accidents country honey the shoot." Performance was uniformly worse as the presented strings dropped the semantic and syntactic factors that are normally present in well-formed sentences. (To make the task difficult, all three sentence types were embedded in white noise. Even in the "noisiest" condition, the words in grammatical sentences were recognized far more accurately.)

Specific applications of various bottom–up perceptual theories, for instance, template and feature-detection approaches, have generally failed to deal with the problem of invariance and the supportive role played by contextual factors of syntax and semantics. As a concrete means of testing such approaches, people have attempted to program computers to perceive speech. Importantly, the variability of the signal is what makes speech recognition by computer such a tough problem, one that apparently cannot be solved by a purely bottom–up mechanism.

Instead, the evidence points toward a combination of data-driven and conceptually driven processing. In such a combination, features of the speech signal are analyzed perceptually, and tentative identifications of different sounds are made. At the same time, the listener's *other* linguistic knowledge is being called into play—syntactic and semantic knowledge to be sure, as well as conceptual and belief systems. These higher levels of knowledge and analysis operate in parallel with the phonemic analysis and provide information to the perceptual mechanism that helps identify the sounds being analyzed. As a concrete example, imagine a sentence that begins "The grocery bag was. . . ." You are processing the "bag" segment of this speech signal. Having already processed the previous word to at least some level of semantic interpretation, you have developed a useful context for the sentence. To be simple about it, *grocery* limits the number of possibilities that can be mentioned in the sentence. (Recall in Chapter 3, where we considered the Warren and Warren [1970] "phoneme restoration" effect, how subjects "restored" the missing /p/, based on overall meaning, in the sentence "The *eel was on the orange"; see Table 3-2.)

Similar evidence for the role of context has been reported by Marslen-

A speaker communicates his or her idea by translating that idea into spoken sounds. Listeners must decode these speech signals back into meaning in order to understand the message. How would the context of a protest rally help you understand what this woman is saying?

Wilson and Welsh (1978) in a task that asked subjects to detect mispronunciations, and by Dell and Newman (1980) in a task that asked subjects to monitor spoken speech for the occurrence of a particular phoneme. And, of course, there were the powerful demonstrations of context effects in Treisman's (1960, 1964) shadowing experiments, also described in Chapter 3; when the sentence switched from the shadowed to the nonshadowed ear, the subjects' shadows followed the meaningful sentence rather than staying with the physical signal played in the shadowed ear. In short, context exerts a very strong influence on our perceptual processing of the physical speech signal.

Such results are so powerful that any reasonable theory of speech recognition must account for both aspects of performance, the data driven and the conceptually driven. A specific connectionist model that does exactly that was proposed by McClelland and Elman (1986). In their TRACE model, information is continually being passed among the several levels of linguistic analysis in a spreading activation fashion. Lexical or semantic knowledge, if activated, can thus alter the ongoing analysis at the perceptual level by "telling" it what words are likely to appear next; the model's predictions of what words are likely to appear are based on semantic knowledge. At the same time, phonemic information is being passed to higher levels, thus altering the patterns of activation there.

A particularly nice feature of the model, aside from the fact that it provides a reasonable account of the existing data, is its basic architecture, which includes networks of information that influence ongoing mental processes by means of spreading activation. In other words, we are inching toward a consensus in cognitive psychology: important topics such as speech recognition, semantic memory, and memory for complex events and experiences are all being approached from the same theoretical perspective, the "connectionism" of networks and spreading activation (see Chapter 13; also see Dell, 1986, for a spreading activation–network theory of sentence production).

A Final Puzzle

As if the preceding sections weren't enough to convince you of the need for conceptually driven processing, consider one final feature of the stream of spoken speech. Despite coarticulation, categorical perception, and the problem of invariance, we naively believe that *words* are somehow separate from each other in the spoken signal, that there is some physical pause or gap between spoken words just as there is a blank space between printed words.

This is not true. Our intuition is entirely wrong. Analysis of the speech signal shows there is virtually no consistent relationship between pauses and the ends of words. Indeed, if anything, the pauses we produce while speaking are longer *within* words than between words. As evidence of

FIGURE 8-7

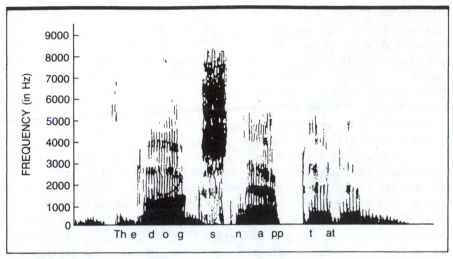

A spectrogram from the sentence "John said that the dog snapped at him," taken from fluent spoken speech. Note that the pauses or breaks do not occur regularly at the ends of words; if anything, they occur more frequently *within* the individual words (e.g., between the /s/ and /n/ sounds, between the /p/ and /t/ sounds; compare with the end of *the* and the beginning of *dog*). (From Foss & Hakes, 1978.)

this, see Figure 8-7, a spectrograph recording of a spoken sentence. Careful inspection of the patterns in correspondence to the words listed at the bottom illustrates the point: the pauses in the spectrograph bear no particular relationship to the ends of words. There must be other kinds of information that the human information processor uses to decode the spoken language signal.

How can our intuitions about our own language, that words are articulated as separate units, be so wrong? (Note that our intuitions about *foreign* languages—they sound like a continuous stream of babble—are much more accurate.) How do we segment the speech stream and come to know what the words and phrases are? Part of the answer to these questions is syntax, the second level of language analysis and the topic we will address next.

Summary Points: phonemes and phonemic competence; categorical perception, phonological rules; problem of invariance; coarticulation; conceptually driven processing

▼ Syntax: The Ordering of Words and Phrases

At the second level of analysis of language, we have **syntax,** *the arrangement of words as elements in a sentence to show their relationship to one another; sentence structure.* We've already studied how sounds are combined to form meaningful words. At this next level of analysis, we are interested in how the words are combined to form meaningful utterances, the study of syntax. Just as in phonology, where the rules for combining sounds might be termed a phonological grammar, our syntactic grammar is a set of rules for combining words into acceptable, well-formed sentences.

If you have a connotation associated with the word "syntax," it probably is not the psycholinguistic sense of "grammar," but the "school grammar" sense of the word instead. In school, if you said "He ain't my friend no more," your teacher might have responded "Watch your syntax" or "Your grammar is awful." To an extent, this kind of school grammar is irrelevant to the psycholinguistic study of syntax and grammar. Your teacher was being *prescriptive* by teaching you what is proper or prestigious according to some set of cultural values. At a global level, though, school grammar does relate to the psycholinguistic study of language; language is for expressing ideas, and anything that clarifies this expression, even arbitrary rules about "ain't" and double negatives, will, by definition, improve the communication of meaning. (And finally, of course, your teacher was sensitive to another level of language: people judge others on the quality of their speech.)

Unlike the school grammar idea, the psycholinguistic study of syntax is *descriptive;* that is, it takes as its goal a description of the rules by which words are arranged to form sentences. Let's take a simple example, one that taps into your syntactic competence. Which is better, sentence (2) or (3)?

(2) Beth asked the man about his headaches.
(3) *About the Beth headaches man asked his.

Your "school grammar" taught you that every sentence must have a subject and a verb. According to that rule then, sentence (3) is just as much a sentence as (2). Your syntactic competence, on the other hand, tells you that (3) is an ill-formed, unacceptable sentence (recall that a sentence preceded by an asterisk is intentionally wrong). You can even specify some of the rules that are being violated in (3); for example, (a) definite articles like "the" do not usually precede proper names, and (b) two nouns may not follow one another in the same phrase or clause.

An obvious point here is that the meaning of a sentence is far more than the meanings of the individual words in that sentence. The "far more," at this level, is the arrangement or sequencing of the words. We're speaking now of word-order rules, a critical part of English syntax. More than some languages (e.g., Latin), English relies heavily on word order to specify meaning. Consider "red fire engine" versus "fire engine red" (or even "red engine fire"). Despite the fact that "red" and "fire engine" can be nouns, a seeming violation of rule (b) above, our word-order knowledge of English tells us that the first word in these phrases is to be treated as an adjective, a word that modifies the following noun. Thus by varying word order alone, "red fire engine" is a fire engine of the usual color, and "fire engine red" is a particular shade of red.

There's more to it than just word order, however. We also rely on the ordering of larger units such as phrases or clauses to convey meaning. Consider the following sentences:

(4) Bill told the men to deliver the piano on Monday.
(5) Bill told the men on Monday to deliver the piano.

In these examples, of course, the positioning of the phrase "on Monday" helps us figure out what meaning was intended—whether the piano was to be delivered on Monday, or whether Bill had told the men something on Monday. Thus the sequencing of words and phrases contains clues to meaning—clues that speakers use to express meaning and clues that listeners use to decipher meaning. In general, we need to understand what these clues are and how they are used. We need to explore the various sets of syntactic rules that have been proposed in order to understand the influence of syntactic factors on comprehension.

Let's begin with Chomsky's important work, then progress to the more current psycholinguistic approach.

Chomsky's Transformational Grammar

Chomsky's overall theory of language (1957, 1965) is referred to as Transformational Grammar. Chomsky claimed that the grammar of the language consists of the rules used to generate its sentences. These rules involve transformations and changes from one internal, abstract form to another. Figure 8-8 depicts Chomsky's overall scheme.

One of Chomsky's critical insights was that sentences exist on at least two different levels, the internal, abstract **deep structure** level and the **surface structure** level. In this scheme, the deep structure version of a sentence is essentially what we mean when we say "the idea of the sentence"; it is *the meaning of the entire utterance, expressed in an abstract code or representation.* Surface structure, on the other hand, is *the external version of the sentence, (usually) the string of sounds and words in a spoken message.* A complicated set of rules is necessary to arrive at the deep structure, according to Chomsky, and a different, but equally important set is necessary to translate this deep structure into the surface structure of the sentence. Respectively, these are the *phrase structure rules* and the *transformational rules.*

Phrase Structure Grammar   The first set of rules to be discussed is the phrase structure grammar. This grammar generates the overall structure or form of the sentence, including the several phrase components and their individual subcomponents. The important point of the phrase structure grammar is that it accounts for the *constituents* of the sentence, the word groupings and phrases that make up the whole utter-

FIGURE 8-8

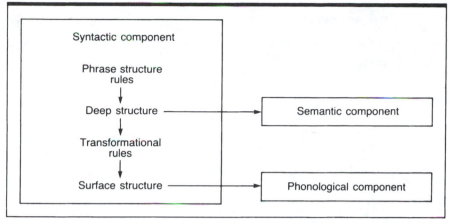

A depiction of the "Standard Transformational Grammar," showing the components responsible for sentence production. (From Carroll, 1986.)

ance, and the relationships among those constituents. A well-known example (Lachman et al., 1979), useful for illustrating the nature of a phrase structure grammar, is the sentence:

(6) The patio resembles a junkyard.

In a phrase structure grammar, the entire sentence is symbolized by an *S*. In this particular grammar, the sentence *S* can be decomposed into two major components, a noun phrase (*NP*) and a verb phrase (*VP*). Thus the first line of the grammar illustrated in Figure 8-9A shows *S* → *NP* + *VP*, to be read "The sentence can be rewritten as a noun phrase plus a verb phrase." Therefore the overall constituent structure of the sentence involves two phrases, the NP and the VP. In the second rule, the NP can be rewritten as a determiner (*D*), an article such as *the* or *a*, plus a noun (*N*): *NP* → *D* + *N*—in other words, "a noun phrase consists of a determiner and a noun." In rule #3 we see the structure of a verb phrase; a VP is rewritten as a verb (*V*) plus an NP: *VP* → *V* + *NP*.

As panel B of Figure 8-9 shows, six rewrite rules are necessary for generating the sentence "The patio resembles a junkyard." A different, but largely equivalent depiction of the grammar is shown in panel C, in which a tree diagram shows the most general components at the top and the specific word components at the bottom. An advantage of the tree diagram is that it reveals the *hierarchical* structure of the sentence very clearly, as well as the internal structure of the various parts as they relate to each other. Finally, a so-called bracket equivalent is shown in panel D.

The Inadequacy of Using Phrase Structure Grammar Alone
Chomsky's theory relied heavily on a phrase structure approach, because

FIGURE 8-9

A. REWRITE RULES

1. S(entence) → NP (Noun Phrase)   + VP (Verb Phrase)
2. NP   → D(eterminer)   + N(oun)
3. VP   → V(erb)   + NP
4. N   → patio, junkyard, ... etc.
5. V   → resembles, ... etc.
6. D   → the, a, ... etc.

B. SENTENCE GENERATION BY RULE (DERIVATIONAL HISTORY)

S → NP + VP	(by Rule 1)
S → D + N + VP	(by Rule 2)
S → D + N + V + NP	(by Rule 3)
S → D + N + V + D + N	(by Rule 2)
S → the + N + V + D + N	(by Rule 6)
S → the + patio + V + D + N	(by Rule 4)
S → the + patio + resembles + D + N	(by Rule 5)
S → the + patio + resembles + a + N	(by Rule 6)
S → the + patio + resembles + a + junkyard	(by Rule 4)

C. TREE DIAGRAM

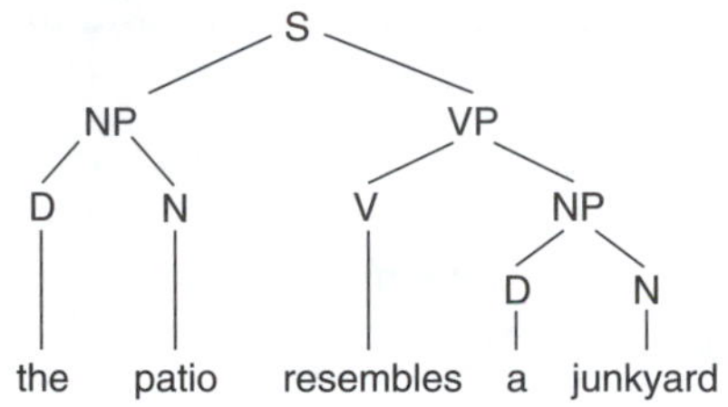

D. BRACKET EQUIVALENT OF TREE DIAGRAM

{(The patio) (resembles (a junkyard))}

A depiction of a phrase structure grammar: (A) the rewrite rules of the grammar, (B) sentence generation by the rules, (C) a tree diagram or hierarchical representation, and (D) a "bracket equivalent" diagram of the sentence. (From Lachman et al., 1979.)

it in fact captures an important aspect of language, its productivity. That is, this kind of grammar is *generative;* by means of such phrase structure rules, an entire family of sentences can be generated by the grammar. On the other hand, Chomsky also felt that this alone was insufficient. Consider, for example, two classic (overworked?) examples:

(7) Visiting relatives can be a nuisance.

(8) The shooting of the hunters was terrible.

A moment's reflection will reveal that these sentences are **ambiguous,** they have *more than one meaning*. The first sentence could mean "Going to visit one's relatives can be a nuisance," or "Having one's relatives come to visit can be a nuisance"; sentence (8) could be referring either to lousy hunters or to wounded hunters. These alternative meanings are revealed when we **parse** the sentences, when we *separate or* *divide the sentence into phrases and groupings,* much the way the phrase structure grammar does. The two meanings of sentence (7)—that is, the two deep structures—correspond to two different phrase structures. For sentence (7), the ambiguity boils down to the grammatical function of *visiting,* whether it is used as an adjective or as a verb. These two grammatical functions translate into two different phrase structures (*verb + noun* versus *adjective + noun*).

Sentence (8), however, has only one phrase structure; there is only one way to parse it.

{[*the shooting of the hunters*] [*was terrible*]}.

Thus sentence (8) is genuinely ambiguous at the level of surface structure: it has only one surface structure (one syntactic parsing), yet it is ambiguous. As such, it illustrates the limitation of the phrase structure approach that Chomsky noted: the phrase structure grammar generated a single string of words and a single surface structure, but that structure was ambiguous. There must still be something missing in the grammar: if it were complete, it wouldn't generate an ambiguous sentence.

A second difficulty Chomsky pointed out involves examples such as the following:

(9a) Patrick bought a fine French wine.
(9b) A fine French wine was bought by Patrick.

According to phrase structure rules, there is hardly any structural similarity at all between these two sentences; they differ radically in their surface structure. Yet, of course, they mean virtually the same thing, so at some level they *are* the same sentence, just different versions of it. People's intuitions—that active and passive paraphrases are more or less identical at the level of meaning—are not captured by the phrase structure approach. According to the phrase structure grammar, sentences (9a) and (9b) are *different.*[6]

Transformational Rules   Chomsky's solution to such problems was to postulate a second component to the grammar, a set of **transformational rules** that handle the many specific surface forms that can express an underlying idea. These transformational rules *convert the deep structure idea into a spoken sentence, into a surface structure.* By applying different transformations, we can form an active declarative sentence, a passive voice sentence, a question, a negative, a future or past tense, and so on. In this view, sentences (9a) and (9b) would differ only in their surface structures; one deep structure was merely transformed in two different fashions. Thus the sentences have different

---

[6]In Chapter 9 you'll read about the "advantage of first mention," how the first-mentioned topics in a sentence are understood as the focus of the sentence. Given these results, sentences (9a) and (9b) have slightly different meanings, roughly that (9a) is about Patrick and (9b) is about French wine.

transformational histories in that different transformational rules were applied to the deep structure, one set including the active voice, one the passive voice. Likewise, for a simple deep structure idea such as {(boy kisses girl)}, the transformational grammar could generate any of the following, depending on which particular grammatical transformations were selected:

(10a) The boy kissed the girl.
(10b) The girl was kissed by the boy.
(10c) Was the girl kissed by the boy?

More elaborate rules are also applied by this transformational component, for instance, rules that allow us to combine ideas. Consider two deep structures, such as {(boy kisses girl)} joined with {(girl is pretty)}:

(11a) The boy kissed the pretty girl.
(11b) The boy kissed the girl who was pretty.
(11c) The girl who the boy kissed was pretty.
(11d) Will the girl who is pretty be kissed by the boy?

Of these four paraphrases, sentence (11a) seems to be the simplest; after all, it's the shortest and manages to express the second idea as a simple adjective-plus-noun combination. Recall from the last chapter, however, that such a sentence would be analyzed as a combination of two *propositions,* the same two that are termed deep structures in linguistics. As you read in that chapter, sentences with more propositions are generally more difficult to comprehend, even when the overall length of the sentence is controlled. Thus one surface structure for the {(girl) (is) (pretty)} idea is merely "the pretty girl"; an equivalent structure, in terms of meaning, is "the girl who is pretty." On the other hand, sentences (11c) and (11d) are surely the most difficult to comprehend, largely because of the passive voice and the relative "who" clauses.

Limitations of the Transformational Grammar Approach

A great deal of research in the 1960s was devoted to the structural aspects of language we have been discussing. For example, some of the most serious work that tested linguistic theory in psychology involved the *derivational complexity* hypothesis. Much as we suggested for sentences (11a) through (11d), this hypothesis suggested that the difficulty of comprehending a sentence was directly related to the number of grammatical transformations that had been applied. In other words, if a deep structure had two transformations applied to it, it would be more difficult to comprehend than if only one transformation had been applied. As several authors note (e.g., Palermo, 1978), early results in this line of research tended to support the overall theory.

As the 1960s ended, however, psychology became increasingly dissatisfied with this linguistically motivated approach. Work by Fodor and Garrett (1966) was especially instrumental in dimming psychology's enthusiasm for the borrowed syntactic approach of linguistics. These researchers noted that much of the support for the derivational complexity hypothesis had failed to control potentially important factors in the stimuli. For instance, a derivationally more complex sentence generally has more words in it than a simpler one (contrast sentences (11a) and (11c)).

At least as persuasive as these criticisms, however, was a metatheoretical point of view. As more research was done, psychology became dissatisfied with the heavily syntactic focus of linguistic theory. To oversimplify just a bit, Figure 8-8 illustrates the kind of dissatisfaction that was felt. In that figure, the syntactic component yields a deep structure or meaning by means of phrase structure rules; this deep structure is then transformed grammatically by transformational rules. In a very real sense, this illustration depicts the difficulty that psychology had with linguistic theory: it would seem that *meaning* is a secondary factor in the syntactic component. It's almost as if the theory, as it was applied directly to language *use,* suggested that we first make up our minds what phrase constituents we're going to use in a sentence, and only *then* decide what it is we're going to talk about. This emphasis on syntax seemed to slight the important role of semantics: the idea to be expressed in a sentence was vaguely subordinate in importance to *how* it was going to be expressed syntactically. For psychologists concerned with how we use language to express meaning, this emphasis on syntax seemed to be a step backward.

Actually, this is somewhat of an oversimplified view, making it sound as if Chomsky inspired a generation of linguists to *avoid* meaning. It was not that extreme, of course. In fact, Chomsky repeatedly emphasized the joint importance of syntax *and* semantics. He pointed out that even a perfectly grammatical sentence may have no genuine meaning—a syntactically acceptable, but semantically *anomalous* sentence. By far the most famous example of such a sentence, invented by Chomsky, is: "Colorless green ideas sleep furiously." That the sentence is grammatically acceptable is clear; consider "Tired young children sleep soundly" as a syntactically parallel sentence. And yet, the "Colorless . . ." sentence has no meaning in the regular sense of that word. Chomsky's intent with this example was to illustrate that there are constraints imposed by meaning that are above and beyond syntactic factors, and that meaning is therefore also central to a complete grammar of the language. On the other hand, applying Chomsky's theory to the actual *doing* of language—turning his theory of competence into a performance theory of how we produce and comprehend sentences—only made it more apparent that a different approach was necessary.

We will turn to the major focus of this research, the semantic level of analysis, in a moment. But first, we must conclude this section on syntax with the current psychological view of syntactic processing.

The Cognitive Role of Syntax

From a psychological perspective, what is the purpose of syntax? Why do our sentences have to follow a set of syntactic rules? The answers are obvious, of course: we need syntax to help the listener figure out meaning, to minimize the processing demands of comprehension as much as possible. In a very real way, this purpose was neglected by linguists, which is not surprising given their relative lack of interest in performance. But from our perspective, it's useful to remind ourselves of this simple fact: if an infinite number of sentences are possible in a language, then the one sentence the speaker is saying to us right now could be about *anything*. Syntax helps listeners determine meaning and helps speakers convey it.

Bock's (1982) excellent paper on a "cognitive psychology of syntax" discusses several important issues that the cognitive approach to language must explain. To begin with, she notes that the syntactic burden falls somewhat more heavily on the speaker than the listener. After all, for comprehension, many of the syntactic aspects of a sentence are probably of lesser importance than semantic and conceptual factors. With only some difficulty, you can comprehend the meaning of

(12) *He told me not him hit.

On the other hand, when you have to *produce* a sentence rather than comprehend it, you must create a surface structure, a string of words and phrases that will communicate your idea as well as possible. In Bock's words, your sentence "requires the *paraphernalia* of the correct morphology, constituent structure and order, and clause structure and order, that is, the correct syntax" (p. 2, emphasis added). Thus syntax becomes a feature of language that is particularly related to the speaker's mental effort, the information processing involved in producing the sentence.

Two points that Bock raises should illustrate the current approach of psycholinguistics toward syntax. First, she considers the issues of automatic and conscious processes as they apply to language production. As we know, automatic processes are the product of a high degree of practice or overlearning. Bock notes that several aspects of syntactic structure are consistent with the notion of automaticity. For instance, children rely heavily on regular word orders, even if the native language they are learning has relatively irregular word order. The purpose for this is fairly obvious: by relying over and over on the same syntactic frames, those frames can be generated and used more automatically. Similarly, adults tend to use only a very few syntactic structures with any regularity, suggesting that these few can be called into service quite rapidly and automatically. Interestingly, the syntax you use can be strongly influenced by a previous sentence—quite literally, the priming of syntactic usage (e.g., Bock, 1986; West & Stanovich, 1986).

Planning In Bock's second point, she reviews evidence that shows an important interaction between syntax and meaning. In general, it seems that we tailor the syntax of our sentences to the accessibility of the lexical or semantic information being conveyed by the sentence. Phrases that contain more accessible information tend to occur earlier in a sentence. If a word is rare or difficult to retrieve, however, then the phrase it appears in tends to occur later in the spoken sentence.

These effects tell us something interesting about the mental mechanism that "plans" sentences. Earlier theories of sentence planning, for instance, Fromkin's (1971) theory (see Table 8-3), described planning as a sequential process; first you identify the meaning to be conveyed, then you select the syntactic frame, and so on. More recent research, however, shows how *interactive* the planning process is. Difficulties in one component, word retrieval, can prompt a return to an earlier planning component, say, to rework the syntax of the sentence. By selecting an alternate syntax, the speaker "buys" more time for retrieving the intended word (see also Kempen & Hoehkamp, 1987). Of course, such an interactive system contradicts the strictly hierarchical or sequential approaches to syntax, such as shown in Figure 8-9. In other words, recent data show that we begin our utterances when the first part of the sentence has been planned, but *before* the syntax and semantics of the final portion have been worked out or selected. Hesitations in our spoken speech are clues to the nature of planning, as are the effects of momentary changes in priming, lexical access, and working memory load (e.g., Bock & Miller, 1991; Lindsley, 1975).

Such work is an important reminder. That is, in its appropriate pursuit of semantic factors in language, psycholinguistics shunned syntax to a degree; "syntax is for linguistics, not psycholinguistics" approximates the attitude that existed for a while. This was an extreme reaction, of course, and is as incomplete an approach as one that ignores semantics. A considerable part of the next section and the next chapter will examine

Table 8-3   FROMKIN'S (1971) MODEL FOR THE PLANNING AND PRODUCTION OF SPEECH

Stage	Process
1	Identification of meaning; generate the meaning to be expressed
2	Selection of syntactic structure; construct a syntactic outline of the sentence, specifying word slots
3	Generation of intonation contour; assign stress values to different word slots
4	Insert content words; retrieve appropriate nouns, verbs, adjectives, and so on from the lexicon and insert into word slots
5	Add function words and affixes; fill out the syntax with function words (articles, prepositions, etc.), prefixes, suffixes
6	Specify phonetic segments; express the sentence in terms of phonetic segments, according to phonological (pronunciation) rules

how syntax and semantics *interact,* how syntactic devices that speakers use can influence the meaning being conveyed, and how semantic factors can sometimes override syntax.

Summary Points: grammar; syntax; Chomsky's Transformational Grammar; deep and surface structures; phrase structure; ambiguity; transformational rules; cognitive role of syntax; planning

▼ Lexical and Semantic Factors: The Meaning in Language

We turn finally to lexical and semantic factors, the third traditional level of linguistic analysis after phonology and syntax. This is the level of meaning in language, the level at which word and phrase meanings are "computed," to use the psycholinguistic jargon; in cognitive psychology, we call this *retrieval from memory.* Of course, there is more to this level than merely retrieving word meanings; after the lexical entry has been found in memory, the individual words and phrases must still be related to one another. To take a simple example, "Jill saw Bill" means something quite different from "Bill saw Jill," even though the individual words retain their meanings in both sentences. Even more dramatic, consider some reorderings and simple substitutions for the sentence we used earlier:

(6)   The patio resembles a junkyard.
(6b) The junkyard resembles a patio.
(6c) A patio resembles a junkyard.
(6d) The patio resembles the junkyard.
(6e) *A patio resembles the junkyard.

Clearly, we comprehend these sentences as having different meanings, some easier to compute (6b) than others (6c). The process of extracting meaning from the sentences is the concern of this third level of analysis. How do listeners accomplish this feat? How do speakers use the "paraphernalia" of syntax and existing knowledge to communicate meaning?

Interaction of Syntax and Semantics

In a way it seems peculiar to refer to semantics as merely one of the several levels of language analysis: language *is* meaning, at base, while phonology and syntax seem merely to be two necessary vehicles by which meaning is communicated. Note, however, that semantic factors do not stand alone in language, just as syntactic factors are not independent of semantics. Syntax is more than just word- and phrase-order rules. As you just read, syntax is sensitive to the accessibility of words: more accessible words tend to appear earlier in a sentence. Likewise, semantic factors refer to more than just word and phrase *meanings,* since different syntactic devices can be clues to meaning. To anticipate just a bit, note how syntactic differences in the following sentences influence the semantic interpretation:

(13a) I'm going downtown with my sister at four o'clock.
(13b) It's at four o'clock that I'm going downtown with my sister.
(13c) It's my sister I'm going downtown with at four o'clock.

Sentences (13b) and (13c) differ in a fairly subtle way from (13a) in what might be called the *focus* of the utterance. In a genuine sense, the focus of each sentence is different, so each *means* something slightly different. Imagine how inappropriate sentence (13c) would be, for instance, as a response to the question "Did you say you're going downtown at three o'clock?"

As proficient language users, we are sensitive to the focus or highlighted aspects of the sentences. We interpret these sentences as communicating somewhat different meanings; indeed, we organize our comprehension around the focus or highlight, and then remember those aspects better than ideas that were buried later in the sentence (e.g., Gernsbacher, 1991; Gernsbacher & Hargreaves, 1988). Clearly, our theories of language must include these sensitivities, since they have such a strong impact on our language performance. Because rearranging the clauses in sentences (13a) through (13c) changes our interpretations, our theory of language must reflect this in a psychologically relevant way.

Semantic Knowledge Can Overpower Syntax Semantic features can do more than merely alter the syntax of sentences; occasionally semantic characteristics will actually overpower the syntax of a sentence. Although many examples could be offered here, let's focus on just one study by Fillenbaum (1974); as you read, note how current terminology would label this an effect of top–down processing.

Fillenbaum presented "perverse" sentences to his subjects, sentences that were meaningful, but expressed an unusual or atypical meaning (of course, straightforward, sensible sentences were also presented). For instance, in "John dressed and had a bath," the normal order of events is backward, and "Don't print that or I won't sue you," is the opposite of a customary threat. After reading each of the sentences, the subjects had to write a paraphrase. Fillenbaum then scored their paraphrases against the originals.

Strikingly, over 60% of his subjects "normalized" the sentences, making them conform to the more typical state of affairs. For example, a representative paraphrase of the threatening sentence was "Don't print that, or I'll sue you." Fillenbaum then asked his subjects to reread their paraphrases to see if there was even a "shred of difference" from the originals. Over half the time, subjects saw no discrepancies at all. Apparently, the subjects' general knowledge was influential enough that it easily overpowered the syntactic and lexical aspects of the sentences. Sometimes we comprehend *not* what we hear or read, but what we *expect* to hear or read. (Try these: "Nice we're having weather, isn't it?" and "Ignorance is no excuse for the law.")

Don't make the mistake of thinking that syntax is irrelevant or unimportant simply because semantic factors can sometimes overpower syntax. Among the most powerful demonstrations of the importance of syntax is a recent paper on syntactic analysis by Osterhout and Holcomb (1992). These researchers used the ERP (event-related potential) technology you've been reading about, presenting sentences to subjects then recording the changes in their brain wave patterns. In this study, Osterhout and Holcomb contrasted the ERP patterns when sentences violated either syntactic or semantic expectations. When sentences end in a semantically anomalous fashion ("John buttered his bread with socks"), the N400 ERP pattern is typically observed, much as reported in Kounios and Holcomb's (1992) study of semantic relatedness (Chapter 6). But when the sentence ended in a syntactically anomalous fashion ("John hoped the man to leave"), a strong P600 pattern occurred (a positive electrical potential), 600 msec after seeing the anomalous word "to"; see Figure 8-10. This is rather dramatic confirmation of the important—

FIGURE 8-10

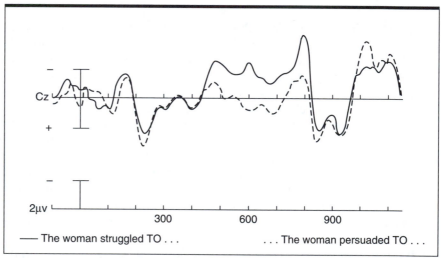

Mean ERPs to syntactically acceptable sentences (solid curve) and syntactically anomalous sentences (dotted curve). The P600 component, illustrated as a downward dip in the dotted curve, shows the effect of detecting the syntactic anomaly. Note that in this figure, positive changes go in the downward direction.

and seemingly *separate*—role of syntactic processing during language comprehension.

Semantic Factors in Language

Consider again the general conclusion of Fillenbaum's report, that we often hear what we expect to hear, not what is literally presented. This should sound familiar to you; our existing knowledge exerts an influence on our current mental processing. The previous two chapters dealt extensively with general world knowledge, exactly the kind of knowledge that Fillenbaum's subjects were consulting when they misinterpreted the perverse sentences. This is, of course, the same phenomenon that Bartlett (1932), Loftus and Palmer (1974), and others have identified too, though not in the context of experiments on language use per se. Given these similarities between semantic and psycholinguistic ideas, you won't be surprised to find out that the current psycholinguistic view on semantic analysis of language is already familiar to you as well: it's essentially the same semantic analysis you studied in the context of connected discourse. In short, the psycholinguistic approach to lexical and semantic factors in language relies heavily on two important notions, conceptually driven processing and mental representations called *propositions*. (Remember "The hippie touched the debutante in the park"?) Let's begin with a smattering of psycholinguistic jargon, then delve into the underpinnings of propositional theory.

Morphemes   We've been speaking throughout the chapter about "words" and "word meanings." These terms are technically inaccurate if we want to refer to the basic units of meaning in language. The correct term, instead, is **morpheme:** a morpheme is *the smallest unit of language that has meaning*. To return to the example we gave at the beginning of the chapter, the word *cars* is actually composed of two meaningful units, two morphemes: *car* refers to a semantic concept and a physical object, and *-s* is a meaningful suffix denoting "more than one of." In such an analysis, the word *unhappiness* is composed of three separate morphemes: *happy*, the base concept, the prefix *un-* meaning "not," and the suffix *-ness*, meaning "state or quality of being." At our current level, it makes little difference whether we speak of words or morphemes as they occur in sentences (although there is a debate over the issue of whether the meaning of a word such as "unhappiness" is literally stored in memory, or whether it is "computed" from the three individual morphemes; see Carroll, 1986). Later on, especially when we consider neurological impairments of language skill, we will need the distinction between words and morphemes, and between *free morphemes*, such as *happy, car*, and *legal*, and *bound morphemes*, such as *un-, -ness*, and *-s*.

Think about the verb "chase," as an example of how concepts might be represented in the mental *lexicon*, the mental dictionary of word meanings. The lexical representation of CHASE, which specifies the meaning of this morpheme in the lexicon, must indicate that *chase* is a verb meaning "to run after or pursue, in hopes of catching." As is always the case for such semantic memory concepts, CHASE is represented as a node in memory with pathways connecting it to related information, say RUN, PURSUE, CATCH, and the like. From our current perspective of psycholinguistics, however, you know a great deal more about *chase* than just its meaning. Your semantic competence, your extensive knowledge of the meaning of language, tells you that sentence (14) is a perfectly acceptable sentence based on semantic grounds:

> (14) The policeman chased the burglar through the park.

Sentence (15), on the other hand, is unusual based on the grounds of general world knowledge:

> (15) The mouse chased the cat through the house.

Sentence (16) violates the literal meaning of *chase:*

> (16) His insecurities chased him even in his sleep.

And finally, sentence (17) is not permissible at all:

> (17) *The book chased the flower.

Case Grammar

An important development in psycholinguistic treatments of semantics was a set of papers by Fillmore (e.g., 1968). Fillmore noted that syntactic aspects of sentences—which words and phrases served as the subject, direct object, and so on—are often quite irrelevant to the meaning of the sentence. As an example, Fillmore pointed out that traditional grammars would analyze sentence (18) and select *key* as the grammatical subject. The same kind of analysis would select *janitor* as the subject of sentence (19) and *key* as the object of the preposition:

> (18) The key will open the door.
> (19) The janitor will open the door with the key.

Fillmore observed that this purely syntactic analysis completely misses the critical issue, that the semantic relationship among *key, open,* and *door* is identical in the two sentences (p. 363). In short, the key is the thing that opens the door in both sentences, despite the fact that the word *key* plays a different grammatical role in the two sentences. In other words, the purely syntactic approach focuses on the grammatical roles played by the words in a sentence, but ignores the fact that a word may have the same semantic role *regardless* of its syntactic class. See Figure 8-11 for an illustration of this point, that syntax does not reveal the common thread of meaning that links the sentences, whereas a semantic case analysis does.

FIGURE 8-11

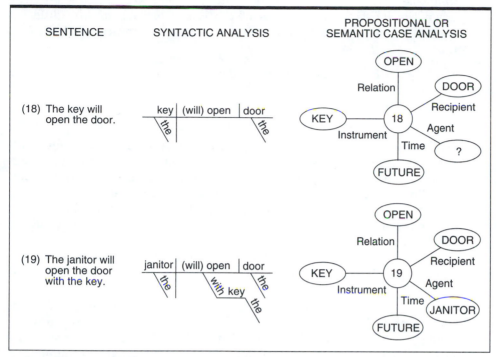

An illustration of a syntactic analysis and a semantic case analysis of two sentences. Note that the same word (e.g., *key* in (18) and (19)) serves different syntactic functions but plays the same semantic case role in both sentences.

Fillmore proposed that a sentence is better understood "as made up of a verb and a collection of nouns in various 'cases' in the deep structure sense" (p. 375). In other words, Fillmore proposed that language processing involves a *semantic* parsing, in which we focus on the *semantic roles played by the content words in the sentences.* These semantic roles are called **semantic cases,** or simply, **case roles.** As such, "door" is the *recipient* or *patient* of the action of OPEN in both sentences (18) and (19); "janitor" is the *agent* of OPEN, "key" is the *instrument,* and so on (this is the same as the semantic roles you studied in the last chapter, in connection with propositions).

Stated simply, each content word in the sentence plays a semantic role in the meaning of the sentence. That role is referred to as the word's *semantic case.* The significant—indeed, absolutely critical—point about such a semantic parsing is that it relies on people's existing semantic and lexical knowledge, their knowledge of what kinds of things will open, who can perform the opening, and so on.

As an exercise, and as a reminder of the material in Chapter 7, consider sentences (20) through (23) from the standpoint of semantic case. Just as we wrote labels next to the directed pathways in the propositional analysis of sentences such as "The hungry lion ate Max," we can write down the labels, or the names of the *case relations,* for the different semantic roles played by the content words in sentences (20) through (23).

(20) Bill hit the ball with the bat.
(21) The ball hit Mary in the leg.
(22) Bill hit Mary with the ball.
(23) Bill hit the ball in the park.

This analysis should reveal to you an obvious, yet important fact: syntactic roles such as subject and object are often of only secondary importance in understanding and interpreting sentences. Instead, your understanding of the entire set of sentences is greatly affected by *semantic case,* that Bill did the hitting, that he did it with a bat, that the ball was the object of the hitting, that the hitting of the ball caused a new object, Mary, to be hit, and so on.

Likewise, reconsider the "chase" sentences, (14) through (17). Your knowledge of CHASE, the overall *relation* in the sentence, is that some animate being does the chasing, a case we termed *agent.* Some other thing is the *recipient* of the chasing, but that thing need not be animate, just capable of being moved rapidly (e.g., you can chase a piece of paper being blown by the wind). On just this analysis, it is clear that sentence (14)—"The policeman chased the burglar through the park"—conforms to the normal situation stored in memory, so it is rather easy to comprehend. Sentence (15)—"The mouse chased the cat through the house"—*mismatches* the customary state of affairs between mice and cats. Nonetheless, either of these creatures can serve as the required animate *agent* of the relation CHASE, so sentence (15) is sensible. And finally, a semantic case analysis provides the reason why sentence (17)—*"The book chased the flower"—is unacceptable. A book is inanimate, so it mismatches the required animate *agent* role for CHASE; "book" cannot "play the role of agent" for CHASE. Likewise, "flower" seems to violate the moveable restriction on the recipient case.

Recent work by Bresnan (1978; Bresnan & Kaplan, 1982) has amplified and extended this important work on case grammars. In Bresnan's scheme, the mental lexicon does not merely contain simple word entries. Instead, each word entry includes a listing of the semantic cases (or arguments) that accompany that word. Thus the lexical entry CHASE would state that CHASE requires an animate agent, that some recipient (Bresnan uses the term *patient* to refer to this case) is required, and so on. Likewise, for the relation HIT, the case arguments would state that an animate agent is required for the relation, a recipient—either animate or not—is required, and some instrument must either be stated or implied.

According to this case grammar approach, when we perceive words in speech (or read them, presumably), we look up the concepts in the lexicon. This look-up process accesses not only the word's meaning, but also its syntactic *and* semantic case roles, and any case restrictions that apply as well. Thus after the word *hit* is processed, the semantic cases required for that relation are accessed. The remaining words in the sentence are processed similarly, with each content word being assigned to the proper syntactic and semantic role.

Evidence for the Case Grammar Approach

The major prediction of the case grammar approach can be stated in two parts. First, we assume that listeners (and readers) begin to analyze the sentence *immediately,* as soon as the words begin. Second, this analysis is a process of assigning each word to a particular semantic case role, with each assignment contributing its part to overall sentence comprehension.

As an example, read sentence (24).

> (24) After the musician had bowed the piano was quickly taken off the stage.

Your analysis of this sentence proceeds easily and without disruption: it's a fairly straightforward sentence. Now read sentence (25).

> (25) After the musician had played the piano was quickly taken off the stage.

What's different about sentence (25)? The verb "played" suggests that "the piano" is the semantic *recipient* of "play": when you read "played," your case role assignment for "piano" was *recipient*. But then you read "was quickly . . ." and realized you had made a mistake in interpretation. Sentences like (25) are called *garden-path sentences;* the early part of the sentence "sets you up" so that the later phrases in the sentence don't make sense given the way you assigned case roles in the first part. Figuratively speaking, the sentence leads you "down the garden path"; when you realize your mistake, you have to retrace your steps back up the path in order to *reassign* earlier words to different cases. Additional examples (from Singer, 1990) of this effect are shown in sentences (26) and (27).

> (26) The groundsman chased the girl waving a stick in her hand.
> (27) The old train the young.

Many research reports have studied how people comprehend such garden-path sentences, as a way of evaluating the case grammar approach to sentence comprehension (e.g., Frazier & Rayner, 1982; Mitchell & Holmes, 1985). For the most part, the results have been quite supportive of that explanation. For example, when subjects read such sentences, their eyes tend to fixate considerably longer on the later phrases that sig-

Calvin and Hobbes

by Bill Watterson

CALVIN AND HOBBES copyright Watterson. Distributed by UNIVERSAL PRESS SYNDICATE. Reprinted with permission. All rights reserved.

nal their error in comprehension (e.g., on "was quickly taken off" in sentence (25)). As shown in Figure 8-12, subjects spent from 40 to 50 msec longer when they encountered their error (at point D in the figure; D stands for the "disambiguating" part of the sentence that reveals the earlier misinterpretation).

This demonstrates quite clearly a kind of "recovery time" effect: the reader must recover from, or "undo," a mistake in interpretation. In the

FIGURE 8-12

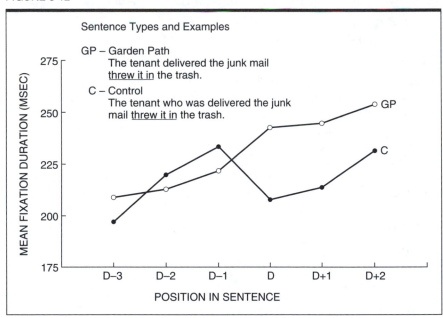

A depiction of the effect of garden-path sentences on reading time. The curves show eye fixations on phrases before and after D, the point in the sentence where the ambiguity is noticed and Disambiguated. The top curve shows the data from garden-path sentences; eye fixation time grows noticeably longer for these curves at D, when the ambiguity is noticed (the D phrase is underlined in the sample sentences). The bottom curve shows data from the control sentences, and no increase in reading time at point D. (Data from Rayner, Carlson, & Frazier, 1983.)

figure, this "undoing" happens at the point labeled D. These results, in fact, provide support for both parts of the case grammar prediction; first, that we parse the incoming sentence immediately rather than later, and second, that this parsing involves assigning words to semantic case roles as a way of comprehending.

A final point to note is that the case restrictions can sometimes be violated intentionally, although there are still constraints on that violation. For instance, consider sentence (16) again—"His insecurities chased him even in his sleep." Such a sentence is understood as a technical but permissible violation of the animate restriction for the agent role of CHASE. In a metaphorical sense, we can "compute" how insecurities might behave like an animate agent; thoughts can behave as if they were animate and can take on the properties of pursuing relentlessly, catching, and so on. A particularly fascinating aspect of language involves such figurative uses of words, and how case grammar accommodates such usage (see Gibbs & Nayak, 1991; Glucksberg & Keysar, 1990, Tourangeau & Rips, 1991).

Case Grammar, Propositions, and Comprehension

The case grammar approach was, in fact, the theoretical basis for the propositional approaches to semantics you studied in the last chapter. A relationship, generally a verb with a variety of cases or arguments, specifies the meaning of a sentence as an interrelated *proposition*. Each word in the utterance makes a connection with its semantic representation and is connected by one of several kinds of pathways to the other words in the sentence. Virtually the same scheme is characteristic of the case grammar approach: each word in the sentence fills a particular semantic case, plays a particular semantic role in the overall meaning of the sentence. The fact that propositions are usually represented as network diagrams, while case arguments are listed as the ordered arguments of a relation, is only a superficial difference. Beneath the surface, these are the same approaches.

According to these approaches, comprehension requires the listener to do three things. First, the basic word meanings must be retrieved from the mental lexicon, from semantic memory. Second, the words are assigned to the various case roles required by the relation expressed in the sentence; this is the same process as deriving a propositional structure for a sentence. Finally, the propositional structure or semantic case assignments must be related to the other structures within the sentence as well as across sentences in connected discourse.

Retrieval of word meanings and connotations is largely an issue of semantic memory retrieval. What properties are salient for the retrieved concept? Is the concept typical in its semantic category? Is the word itself ambiguous? Construction of the propositional structure, the *textbase* in Kintsch's (1974) terminology, is obviously aided by syntactic features of the utterance, as well as by general world knowledge. Included in this construction process, of course, is the accessing of semantic roles, and the assignment of words to these roles based on their meanings. Finally, relating the proposition to other propositional structures is guided by the structures already constructed (Gernsbacher, 1991) and by context-based expectations of what will follow in the next propositions.

Language production, likewise, involves largely the same issues and processes. An idea or set of ideas—a deep structure in other words—exists in the form of a propositional representation. This deep structure is manipulated syntactically to yield a string of words that conveys the deep structure meaning. Semantic retrieval must logically occur prior to the syntactic stage, at least to some degree, since we must know what we're going to talk about before we start casting the sentence into a particular syntactic form. On the other hand, the evidence summarized by Bock (1982) suggests that the *whole* syntactic structure of a sentence is not necessarily finalized as we start to utter the beginning of the sentence. And evidence reported in Chapter 10, on anomia, suggests that lexical retrieval, finding the word in memory, may indeed be a separate process from semantic retrieval, finding the relevant concept or idea.

Finally, if the sentence is but one of a series of connected, interrelated thoughts, then various syntactic and semantic signals must be included in the produced sentence to let the listener know that the topic has not changed, and to indicate that the present sentence is to be understood in the context of the previous ones. Material in the next chapter pursues these larger issues of comprehension.

Summary Points: lexical and semantic factors; focus; top–down processing; propositions and case grammar; semantic case roles; garden-path sentences

CHAPTER SUMMARY

1. Language is our shared system for symbolic communication, a system quite unlike naturally occurring animal communication systems. True language involves a set of characteristics, linguistic universals, that emphasize the arbitrary connections between symbols and referents, the meaningfulness of the symbols, and our reliance on rules for generating language. No known animal communication system contains these critical features.

2. Three traditional levels of analysis—phonology, syntax, and semantics—are joined by two others in psycholinguistics, the level of conceptual knowledge and the level of one's beliefs. Linguists focus on an idealized language competence as they study language, but psycholinguists are also concerned with language performance. As such, the final two levels of analysis take on greater importance as we investigate lan-

guage users and their behavior. To some degree, we can use people's linguistic intuitions to discover what is known about language; to the extent that language processes are automatic, however, our intuitions provide little insight into the processes behind our performance.

3. Phonology is the study of the sounds of language. Spoken words consist of phonemes, the smallest units of sound that speakers of a language can distinguish. Surprisingly, a range of physically different sounds will be classified as the same phoneme; we tolerate a fair degree of variation in the sounds we categorize as "the same." This is particularly important in the study of speech recognition, since the phonemes in a word exhibit a characteristic known as coarticulation. There is considerable overlap among successive phonemes, such that an initial sound is influenced by the sounds that follow, and the later sounds are influenced by what came before. As such, speech recognition relies heavily on conceptually driven processes.

4. Syntax involves the ordering of words and phrases in sentence structure, as well as features such as active versus passive voice. Chomsky's theory of language was a heavily syntactic scheme, with two sets of syntactic rules. Phrase structure rules were used to generate a deep structure representation of a sentence, and then transformational rules converted the deep structure into the surface structure, the string of words that makes up the sentence. There are a variety of syntactic clues to the meaning of a sentence, so an understanding of syntax is obviously necessary to psycholinguists. On the other hand, psycholinguistics has developed its own theories of language, at least in part because of linguists' relative neglect of semantic and performance characteristics.

5. Semantic factors in language are so powerful that they can sometimes override syntactic and phonological effects. The study of semantics breaks words down into morphemes, the smallest meaningful units in language; *cars* contains the free morpheme *car* and the bound morpheme *-s* signifying a "plural."

6. As the study of language comprehension has matured, the dominant approach to semantics claims that we perform a semantic parsing of sentences, assigning words to their appropriate semantic case roles as we hear or read. This case grammar approach is overwhelmingly similar to the propositional approach to meaning described in Chapter 7 and represents the current status of semantic theory in language.

Glossary Terms: arbitrariness; beliefs; case grammar; categorical perception; coarticulation; competence/performance; conceptual knowledge; deep/surface structure; displacement; flexibility of symbols; formants; garden-path sentences; grammar; linguistic intuitions; linguistic universals; morpheme; naming; phoneme; phonology; phrase structure; planning; problem of invariance; productivity; rewrite rules; semantic case roles; semanticity; syntax; Transformational Grammar; transformational rules; Whorf's linguistic relativity hypothesis

SUGGESTED READINGS

A variety of books provide excellent introductions to language and psycholinguistics. For instance, *Psycholinguistics* (2nd edition) by Slobin (1979) and Miller's *Language and Speech* (1981) are relatively short, approachable books. For full-length treatments, see Carroll (1986), Singer (1990), or especially Gernsbacher's forthcoming text (anticipated in 1993) *Fundamentals of Psycholinguistics*. McNeill (1987) devotes an entire chapter to the Whorfian position and its implications. Greene (1972) provides a good review of Chomsky's theory of language and considers its relationship to psychology. Chomsky's own *Language and Mind* (1968) explores many of the issues I've described briefly in this chapter and is more tractable reading than his earlier books on syntax (1957, 1965).

A variety of professional journals focus either heavily or exclusively on language and psycholinguistics: see the *Journal of Psycholinguistic Research, Journal of Speech and Hearing Disorders, Journal of the Acoustical Society of America* (especially for research in phonology), or more mainstream journals in cognitive psychology (especially *Journal of Memory and Language, Cognitive Psychology, Cognition,* and *Memory & Cognition*).

I used the example sentence "His insecurities chased him even in his sleep" to hint at the topic of figurative language, in which the literal meanings of the words are not intended. Some excellent sources on metaphor, simile, and other figurative language phenomena are Ortony's (1979) book *Metaphor and Thought,* Lakoff and Johnson's (1980) *Metaphors We Live By,* and papers by Glucksberg and Keysar (1990), Keysar (1989), and Nayak and Gibbs (1990). A memorable section of Collins and Quillian's (1972) "How to Make a Language User" discusses the role of context in figurative language and case relations. To give you the flavor of this discussion, the example they gave was: "You can 'grow' corn, but you cannot 'grow' children, except for the original Munchkins in the Oz books by Baum, where children grew on stalks like corn, and were 'picked' when they were old enough."

Finally, several good treatments of the fascinating process of language acquisition are available: see Reich (1986) or Lindfors (1987) for full-length treatments, Berko Gleason's (1985) edited book for original, noteworthy contributions, and a thorough anthology of important papers edited by Franklin and Barten (1988).

Chapter 9

COMPREHENSION: LANGUAGE AND SEMANTICS TOGETHER

Language simply does not work in isolation. It is a nice idea that one should in principle be able to fully describe and characterize language by itself as most linguists are trying to do, but in fact it is just not possible. The ability of linguists to ignore this ... has caused an unbelievable number of unrealistic studies to take place under the banner of linguistics. ... Understanding what one has heard is a complex process that ... cannot be reasonably isolated into linguistic and memory components but must be a combined effort of both. (Schank, 1972, pp. 626–628)

The advantage of distinguishing lexical from practical knowledge is that it helps to set manageable bounds on what phenomena a theory of linguistic communication can be expected to treat. ... But if we place practical knowledge outside the basic machinery of linguistic comprehension, we create the problem of explaining when and how it is invoked for interpretive purposes. ... The usual resolution of this problem consists of waving the hands vaguely toward a distant bridge that may someday need to be crossed. ... [But] a language machine that does not interact smoothly with a person's practical knowledge will say little or nothing of importance about the central problems of cognitive psychology. (Miller, 1977, p. 401)

There's more to language than just the words. (Jean Redpath, on A Prairie Home Companion, May 4, 1985)

Comprehension—even the title of this chapter needs to be explained a bit, if only because much of Chapter 8 dealt with language comprehension too. What does the word *comprehension* mean here that it didn't imply in Chapter 8? Basically, the expanded meaning here includes not only the fundamental language processes we studied in the last chapter, but also the additional processes we use when comprehending realistic samples of language, say, a passage in a book or a connected, coherent conversation. How do we comprehend? What is it that we *do* when we read and understand a sentence? What gets saved in memory as a function of comprehension? By taking a larger unit of analysis than simple, isolated sentences, we confront a host of intriguing questions and issues that are central to communication, and to cognitive psychology. And by confronting Miller's (1973) highest two levels of analysis, *conceptual knowledge* and *beliefs,* we address those important issues described above as the "distant bridge that may someday need to be crossed" (Miller, 1977). In other words, it's time to cross the bridge.

▼ An Introductory Overview

Comprehension is complex; *many* different processes and components work together to yield comprehension. Because it's easy to become swamped with detail, this chapter does not present the material in a "linear" fashion. Instead, we return over and over again to the basic issue of comprehension, each time digging deeper and deeper into the material. I hope at the end you'll have a better understanding of this material, and a greater appreciation of the amazing mental activities we take so much for granted. We'll start with some general principles and an illustrative model of the comprehension process.

Conceptual and Rule Knowledge

Let's start digging more deeply by returning to Miller's sentence.

(1) Mary and John saw the mountains while they were
    flying to California.

As we noted in the last chapter, straightforward *lexical knowledge* does not *disambiguate* the sentence, does not resolve the apparent ambiguity. As Miller put it, no dictionary is going to mention specifically that mountains don't fly. Instead, it is semantic memory—"conceptual knowledge" in Miller's description—that furnishes this knowledge. You retrieve information from semantic memory, that mountains can't fly but that people fly in airplanes all the time.[1] Obviously, the information stored in semantic memory and the processes used to retrieve that information are vital to an explanation of language comprehension.

Rules form yet another part of the knowledge that must be taken into account. In the last chapter, we discussed the tacit rule knowledge people have at the phonological and syntactic levels, as well as the distinctly semantic knowledge of *case rules*. These are all used to understand a sentence, of course. But additional levels of rules are operating when we deal with more complex passages of text or with connected conversation. Some rules have the flavor of strategies; for example, we tend to interpret sentence (2) as focusing on Tina, largely because she was mentioned first in the sentence (Gernsbacher, 1990).

(2) Tina gathered the kindling as Lisa set up the tent.

Other rules have to do with *reference,* building bridges between words referring to the same thing. For example, after reading sentence (2), how do you know that the phrase "After she got the fire started" refers to Tina? Still more rules parade under the name *pragmatics* and refer to a variety of "extralinguistic" factors in a sentence. As an example, indirect speech acts such as "Do you have the time?" or "Can you open the window?" mean something rather different than a literal reading would suggest. And finally, high-level rules operate in conversational interactions,

---

[1]I don't ever remember seeing an analysis of this sentence that discussed the other ambiguity, that Mary and John might have been flying without benefit of an airplane (as in that awful joke, "I just flew in from New York, and boy are my arms tired!"). But it's not all that difficult to imagine a fantasy context that makes this reasonable: Mary and John could be birds, for instance, in a Disney movie.

rules that specify how the participants in a conversation structure their remarks, and how they understand the remarks of others. As always, simply because you can't state the rule, or were never explicitly taught the rule, doesn't mean that the rule isn't there. Quite the contrary—it simply means that the rules are part of your implicit, tacit knowledge.

Investigating On-Line Language Comprehension

How can we investigate these comprehension processes? How do we determine that Tina is the focus of sentence (2), and that "she got the fire started" refers to Tina? Much of our evidence in Chapter 8 relied on people's linguistic intuitions, their (leisurely) judgments about the acceptability of sentences. But such evidence does not seem precise enough to address topics like reference. After all, you learned that much if not most of our retrieval from semantic memory is very automatic, hence not available to conscious introspection. Yet we need explicit evidence on such retrieval if we're going to offer concrete evidence on the workings of our language comprehension mechanisms. Critically, evidence based solely on introspections is simply not going to be persuasive enough to resolve the questions we're asking.

So how are we going to investigate these processes? The answer involves the standard cognitive approach you've read about in this book. In particular, psycholinguistics and cognitive psychology have devised an ingenious variety of tasks to tap **on-line comprehension** across the past 20 years.

What is an "on-line comprehension task"? It is a task that measures comprehension *as it occurs,* as the subject is in the very process of comprehending what is read or said. The tremendous recent advances in psycholinguistics have been made by using such tasks, specifically measuring *time and accuracy* performance during reading and listening. The term "on-line" here is of course borrowed from computer science, where a computer that is "on-line" is hooked up, connected, running, and in a global sense *doing* its task right now as we watch. In similar fashion, we are going to examine language processing *right now,* as the mental processes are "running and doing their tasks."

On-line tasks for reading comprehension almost always involve a time measurement, either examining how long a reader fixates the words being read, or how rapidly the reader can make simple "yes/no" judgments about words and ideas in the sentences. In the first task, a camera records eye movements so that the researcher has an exact determination of which word was being read, and an exact measurement of how long the reader's eyes stayed on the word. In an alternate method, the subject reads a sentence on a computer screen and is then immediately shown a word. Usually the subject must make a "yes" or "no" response to the word, indicating whether the word was or was not in the just-read sentence. Naturally, the apparatus measures the reaction time (RT) in milliseconds. And just as we inferred the structure of semantic memory from RT differences, we'll conclude something about comprehension based on how rapidly or slowly subjects make these yes/no decisions.

On-line tasks for comprehension of *spoken* language depend on rather different procedures but rely on the same kind of logic and reasoning. One approach uses an *interruption procedure,* in which we interrupt subjects during presentation of a sentence and ask for some sort of recall or memory performance based on what was just heard. Another uses the technique of *monitoring,* where subjects listen to a sentence and must detect a prespecified target; for instance, "listen for the sound /b/" or "listen for a word rhyming with 'bread.'" When the target is detected, the subject presses a key as rapidly as possible, and again an RT measurement is taken. In both approaches, the investigator determines the place of interruption or the location of the target. The trick, of course, is to pick that critical location as a function of lexical, syntactic, or semantic characteristics of the sentence being processed.

An Example A straightforward example may clarify this procedure, as well as introduce you to some of the substance of this research. In an early application of on-line methods, Jarvella (1970, 1971) had subjects listen to lengthy passages, but then interrupted them at various times. At an interruption, subjects were supposed to write down whatever they could remember from the "end of the passage just immediately preceding the interruption." Jarvella was testing the hypothesis that people hold information about a sentence in memory until that sentence or meaningful clause is completed; once the sentence is completed, however, they will essentially "file away" the overall meaning or gist of the sentence and turn their attention to the next, incoming sentence (very much in the same tradition as Sachs, 1967; see also Gernsbacher, 1985, 1990; Glanzer, Fisher, & Dorfman, 1984). To test this hypothesis, Jarvella constructed pairs of sentences that varied as to whether the middle clause did or did not complete a sentence. Consider sentences (3) and (4):

(3) The tone of the document was threatening. **Having failed to disprove the charges,** *Taylor was later fired by the President.*

(4) The document had also blamed him for **having failed to disprove the charges.** *Taylor was later fired by the President.*

While the first clauses in the sentence were different, note that the second clauses **(in boldface)** and the third clauses (*italicized*) were the same. Nonetheless, in sentence (3) the second clause is part of the final sentence, and under Jarvella's hypothesis should be retained in memory until the "Taylor" clause is completed and understood. Conversely, the second clause in sentence (4) is part of the first whole sentence and presumably would have been *purged* from working memory as a verbatim or active memory when that first sentence was completed. If subjects are interrupted at the end of the "Taylor" clause, the boldfaced clause should be remembered better in sentence (3), since it was part of the final sentence, than in sentence (4).

This is exactly what Jarvella found. As Figure 9-1 shows, recall accuracy for clause 2 was much higher when it was part of the second sentence than when it was part of the first sentence. Of course, the fact that verbatim recall of the first clause was low is not surprising: that clause happened "a while ago" during on-line processing. Likewise, the high recall of the last clause is predictable just on the basis of recency alone. Obviously, the compelling aspect of Jarvella's results was the very large difference in recall of the second clause, 54% when it was part of the second sentence, but only 21% when it belonged to an already completed and "purged" sentence.

Comprehension as Mental Structure Building

Jarvella's results seemed quite sensible, but in fact the demonstration was rather amazing. They seemed sensible in what we might reason, just from intuition, that when we test your memory for what was

FIGURE 9-1

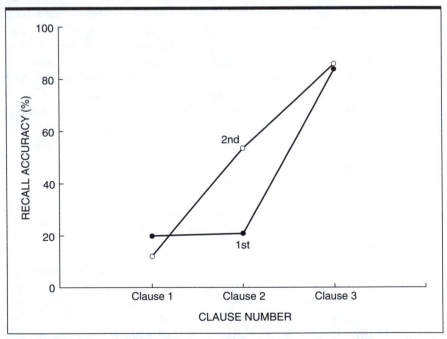

Recall accuracy for the first, second, and third clauses in pairs of sentences. The important effect is that the second clause was recalled very poorly when it was part of the first sentence, but rather well when it was part of the second sentence. (Data from Jarvella, 1970.)

just heard, you would remember the more recent sentence better than an earlier one. It almost sounds like a recency effect in short-term memory, doesn't it? But look at the sample sentences again. They have exactly the same number of words in them, and the last 13 words in each are *identical*. In other words, the critical clause 2 "having failed to disprove the charges" was equated for recency in both sentences; it was also the same length, thus equating simple memory load. And yet—this is the amazing part—it was recalled more than *twice* as accurately when it was part of the second sentence. Memory for sentences, or more generally for *discourse,* does *not* follow the standard serial position curve. The patterns of what we remember are affected by the groupings of the ideas in the sentences, by their placement in the sentence structure, and by the role the ideas play in the overall meaning of the sentence. What processes of comprehension can account for these patterns?

Gernsbacher's Structure Building Framework

Gernsbacher's recent program of research and her overall theory of sentence comprehension, called the *Structure Building Framework,* provide a concrete way of understanding these kinds of effects in language comprehension. The theory is summarized in Table 9-1; a full explanation is provided in Gernsbacher's book (1990; see also an overview chapter in 1991). Her basic theme is that language comprehension—indeed *any* comprehension of coherent material—is a process of building mental structures. *Laying a foundation, mapping information onto the structure,* and *shifting to new structures* are the three principal components of this structure building process.

Laying a Foundation and Mapping Information According to Gernsbacher, as we read sentences we begin to build a mental structure that stores the meaning of the sentence in memory. A foundation is initi-

Table 9-1   SUMMARY OF GERNSBACHER'S STRUCTURE BUILDING FRAMEWORK

Process	Explanation
1. Laying a foundation	Initiate a structure for representing clause or sentence meaning
2. Mapping information	Map or store congruent information into the current structure
3. Shifting	Initiate a new structure to represent a new or different idea

Control Mechanisms	Function
1. Enhancement	Increase the activation of coherent, related information
2. Suppression	Dampen the activation of information no longer relevant to current structure

ated as the sentence begins and most commonly is built around the first character or idea in the sentence. This is equivalent to saying that sentence (5),

(5) Dave was studying hard for his statistics midterm.

is *about* the character named Dave. More formally, we would say that the *discourse focus* (e.g., Rayner, Garrod, & Perfetti, 1992) of sentence (5) is "Dave and his exam."

Comprehension of this sentence, in Gernsbacher's scheme, involves initiating a new sentence structure, focused on the central character Dave. As the words "was studying" are read, their meanings are accessed in lexical and semantic memory, and *memory nodes* corresponding to those meanings are mapped onto the current "Dave structure." *Mapping* here simply means that these meanings are now attached to the concept DAVE, serving to elaborate the structure by specifying Dave's activities. Likewise, the prepositional phrase "for his statistics midterm" is processed. Because the concept MIDTERM is a coherent idea in the context of studying, these words or memory nodes are also added to the "Dave structure."

Shifting to a New Structure   We continue trying to map incoming words to the current structure, on the assumption that those words "belong to" the first idea unit, the structure under construction right now. But at some point, a *different* idea is encountered, an idea that does not fit well in the current structure. As an example, consider sentence (6) as a continuation of the "Dave story."

(6) Because the professor had a reputation for giving difficult exams, the students knew they'd have to be
well prepared.

In Gernsbacher's model, when you read "Because the professor," some *coherence* component detects the change in topic or focus. As you'll read in a moment, one clue to this change in focus is the chain of information you need to retrieve in order to figure out who "the professor" is; midterms are exams given in college classes that are taught by professors, therefore "the professor" must be the professor who teaches Dave's statistics class. Another clue, of course, is the word "because."

At such moments, you react by closing off the "Dave structure" and beginning a new structure, one about "the professor." While the "Dave structure" still retains its prominence in your overall memory of the story, you are now working on a new *current structure,* mapping the incoming ideas (reputation, difficult exams, etc.) onto that structure. And at the end of that phrase, you will have constructed two separate structures, one for each meaning (the phrase beginning "the students" will trigger yet another structure to be built, yielding three distinct substructures altogether).

Evidence for Structure Building   What evidence supports these claims about the comprehension process? In Gernsbacher's work, two major effects provide support for these mechanisms—the *advantage of first mention* and the *advantage of clause recency.* In the advantage of first mention, characters and ideas that were mentioned in the very first sentence, at the beginning of the entire episode, retain a special significance. The fact that Dave was the first-mentioned participant, and in fact was the first idea you encountered in sentence (5), means that Dave is the focus of the first structure you built. The advantage of first mention then is that you will remember Dave better, because Dave was the major element in the first foundation.

Consider the set of sentences in Table 9-2. In the first pair, the boldfaced name **Tina** shows that Tina was the semantic *agent* in these sentences. (Recall from Chapters 7 and 8 that the *agent* is the "doer" in a semantic case grammar. The *patient,* or *recipient,* is the one who receives the action, in these sentences Lisa.) In the first sentence, Tina is not only the agent but is also the first-mentioned character and so serves as the *focus* or *foundation* for comprehension. In the second pair of sentences, Tina is the *patient,* again either being mentioned first or second.

In this experiment (Gernsbacher & Hargreaves, 1988), as soon as the subject finished reading the last word in the sentence, a name appeared

Table 9-2   SAMPLE SENTENCES FOR GERNSBACHER STUDIES

Gernsbacher and Hargreaves (1988) Study

AGENT

A-1. **Tina** beat Lisa in the state tennis match.
A-2. Lisa was beaten by **Tina** in the state tennis match.

PATIENT

P-1. **Tina** was beaten by Lisa in the state tennis match.
P-2. Lisa beat **Tina** in the state tennis match.

Gernsbacher, Hargreaves, and Beeman (1989) Study

MAIN CLAUSES

M-1. **Tina** gathered the kindling as Lisa set up the tent.
M-2. As Lisa set up the tent, **Tina** gathered the kindling.

SUBORDINATE CLAUSES

S-1. As **Tina** gathered the kindling, Lisa set up the tent.
S-2. Lisa set up the tent as **Tina** gathered the kindling.

COORDINATE CLAUSES

C-1. **Tina** gathered the kindling, and Lisa set up the tent.
C-2. Lisa set up the tent, and **Tina** gathered the kindling.

From Gernsbacher, 1990, Tables 2.2 and 2.6.

on the screen. Subjects had to respond, as rapidly as possible, "yes" if the name had been in the sentence, and "no" if it had not (obviously, there were control conditions in which other names were shown during the test). Figure 9-2 shows the results of this experiment. The first bar in the graph shows RT for responding "yes" to the name Tina in sentence A-1, where Tina is the semantic agent *and* the first-mentioned character (of course, the Tina/Lisa sentences in the table were just one of 32 total sentence sets that were tested). It took subjects about 900 msec to say "yes" in this situation, compared to over 950 msec for responding to the second-mentioned agent, for example, Tina in sentence A-2. Thus there was a 50-msec advantage of first mention.

The second set of bars in the figure shows that this advantage of first mention also applied when the test name was the *patient* case in the sentence. In other words, we recognize the first-mentioned character more rapidly after sentence comprehension, presumably because the first-named character is central to the structure that was built during comprehension. It made no difference whether that first name was the agent or patient case in the sentence. Additional research ruled out the possibility that the effect was due to "Tina" being the syntactic subject of the sentence, that subjects might have rehearsed "Tina" more and so on.

Figure 9-3 shows a comparable set of results, but now including the *advantage of clause recency* (Gernsbacher, Hargreaves, & Beeman, 1989); see the bottom half of Table 9-2 for sample sentences in this exper-

FIGURE 9-2

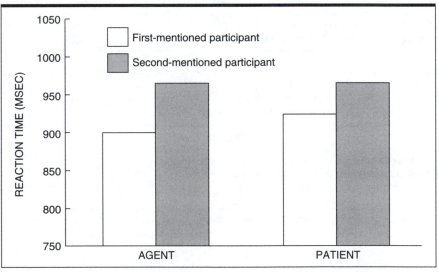

Mean reaction time to names that had appeared in the studied sentences, when the name was the first- or second-mentioned participant, and when the name played the Agent or Patient case role in the sentence. Data are from Gernsbacher and Hargreaves (1988). (From Gernsbacher, 1990.)

FIGURE 9-3

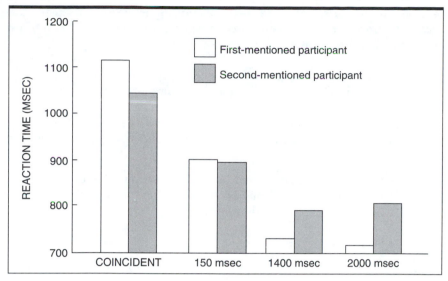

Mean reaction time to names that had appeared in the studied sentences, when the name was the first- or second-mentioned participant. Names were tested immediately at the end of the sentence (Coincident) or at varying delays after the end of the sentence (150, 1400, or 2000 msec later). Data are from Gernsbacher, Hargreaves, and Beeman (1989). (From Gernsbacher, 1990.)

iment. The subjects again read the sentences and, after reading the last word, were tested with a name. The difference in this experiment was that the yes/no test either came immediately after the last word—the "Coincident" condition—or after a variable delay, 150 msec, 1400 msec, or 2000 msec. The two longer delays led to the same result as before: the first participant showed the advantage of first mention on RT. But when the test was coincident with the last word of the sentence, there was an advantage of clause recency—faster responses to the most recently mentioned participant, for example, Lisa in sentence M-1. Gernsbacher et al.'s results suggested that this recency advantage was rather short-lived, however, because neither name was faster in the 150-msec delay condition.

An overall interpretation of these results involves two main points. First, the clause that is currently being processed has a brief advantage due to recency. This is not due so much to any short-term, working memory trace, however, as it is to the fact that the currently processed clause is in fact the one being built into a structure at that moment. Second, once the entire sentence has been processed, that is, once the structures that represent the entire sentence have been built, then the first-mentioned ideas maintain their advantage in accessibility. This advantage accrues because the first idea was the very foundation for all the structures built during comprehension. In other words, the first participant or idea is in the *discourse focus,* and later clauses are represented in *substructures*—important, of course, but subservient to the focus of the first clause, the most important idea in the sentence.

Enhancement and Suppression   Finally, we consider the two control mechanisms in Gernsbacher's model, to complete our understanding of the Structure Building Framework and to introduce the next major topic in comprehension, the problem of *reference.* Let's add just one more sentence to the "Dave story" to discuss full-blown comprehension in Gernsbacher's model.

(5) Dave was studying hard for his statistics midterm.

(6) Because the professor had a reputation for giving difficult exams, the students knew they'd have to be well prepared.

(7) Dave wanted an A on that test.

As noted above, when you encounter sentence (6), you initiate a new substructure, because there has been a change in focus. While the new substructure carries different information, it is still related to the first one. That is, two prominent ideas in sentence (6) map onto the ideas from sentence (5); EXAMS refers with a different name to the same concept as "midterms," and "the professor" maps onto the statistics course implied by sentence (5). According to Gernsbacher, such mappings reflect the activation of related memory nodes. That is, the PROFESSOR memory node becomes activated. This activation then combines with the activation from "midterm" and STATISTICS COURSE, because of their semantic relatedness. This is the process of *enhancement,* that the many related memory nodes are now being boosted or *enhanced* in their level of activation.

The *enhancement* process is largely the same as the important process of *spreading activation* in semantic memory that you studied in Chapter 6. Concepts that are semantically related to the words in the sentences become activated: their level of activation is *enhanced.* It is the *degree* of enhancement and activation among concepts that predicts which concepts will be remembered better or responded to more rapidly. And, the more frequently the same set of nodes is enhanced across the entire sentence, the more coherent the passage will be.

Note, however, that the enhancement of some memory nodes implies that other nodes will lose activation. That is, while sentence (6) enhances the activation of memory nodes related to PROFESSOR, EXAM, and so on, there is a simultaneous *suppression* of memory nodes that are now out of the main discourse focus. In other words, activated nodes that become unrelated to the focus will *decrease in activation* by the process of suppression. Figure 9-4 is an illustration of these competing tendencies. Note that as the professor clause is being processed

FIGURE 9-4

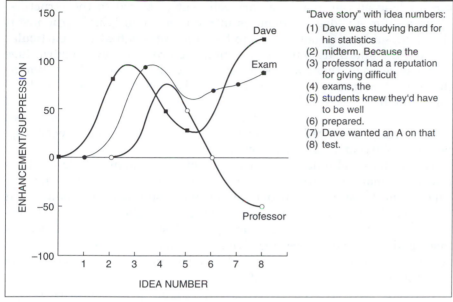

"Dave story" with idea numbers:
(1) Dave was studying hard for his statistics
(2) midterm. Because the
(3) professor had a reputation for giving difficult
(4) exams, the
(5) students knew they'd have to be well
(6) prepared.
(7) Dave wanted an A on that
(8) test.

Hypothetical activation curves for the concepts Dave, Exam, and Professor from the "Dave story" in the text. As concepts are introduced or mentioned again (Dave, Exam), their activation becomes enhanced. When the focus shifts, "old" concepts (Professor) become suppressed, that is, their activation dwindles.

(ideas #3 and #4), the activation level for DAVE drops: the Dave idea undergoes suppression. That is, although the memory nodes related to Dave remain important because they were in the first structure you built, they are momentarily "out of focus," so their activation is suppressed. Then, as the story unfolds further (ideas #5 to #7), the memory nodes for DAVE regain their enhancement, while the PROFESSOR nodes dwindle down. Thus the original Dave structure from sentence (5) receives renewed enhancement; in a sense, the comprehension process signals "Dave is back again, so expect more information on how he was studying for his midterm."

An Interim Conclusion: Interactive Language Processing

There's lots more to say about comprehension, of course, but an interim conclusion or summary might be helpful right now. Gernsbacher's model is one of the few current approaches to comprehension that attempts to deal with the entire range of processes necessary for discourse comprehension. The model claims that we lay a foundation for comprehension, revolving especially around the first-mentioned idea or character in the sentence, and continue mapping new ideas to that structure as long as the new ideas are coherently related to the structure. When a different idea or theme is introduced, the original structure is closed off, and a new one begins to be built. Although at any particular moment the information in the current structure will show an advantage of clause recency, there will be an overall advantage of first mention as the entire sentence or story is understood. The mapping of ideas to structures, finally, is controlled by two activation processes—enhancement and suppression. These account for the momentary focus of discourse: what's highly enhanced or activated is in the focus, what's been suppressed is currently out of the focus.

The model—and indeed most current comprehension models—tells us something more, however. At the more general level, consider what the experimental results and models tell us about on-line comprehension. It should be clear from this section that readers set about the task of comprehending *immediately* upon hearing the first words of a sentence. As more and more words are perceived, they too are processed and then related to ideas already encountered. You've run into this idea before, in Chapter 8, where the effects of ambiguity in a garden-path sentence were apparent in reading times (e.g., see Figure 8-12). Contrast this to the early approaches to comprehension (e.g., Fodor, Bever, & Garrett, 1974), which described comprehension in terms of an ordered series of discrete information processing stages. The "one after another" flavor of such models has now completely been abandoned. Instead, language comprehension is now viewed as a thoroughly *interactive* set of processes (e.g., Marslen-Wilson & Tyler, 1980). Each type of knowledge—phonological or orthographical, syntactic, lexical, semantic—is continually analyzed in the incoming sentences and continually adding its input to the ongoing processes of comprehension. Gernsbacher's model, heavily inspired by spreading activation theories, is representative of such current models. In other words, the relevant questions about comprehension these days are not "*Do* the components interact in processing sentences?" Instead, the questions are "*How* and *when* do the components interact?"

Summary Points: conceptual and rule knowledge; on-line comprehension and tasks; Structure Building Framework; enhancement and suppression; comprehension as an interactive process

▼ Reference, Inference, and Memory

Throughout the discussion of Gernsbacher's model, we avoided a specific discussion of two critically important ideas—the processes of *reference* and *inference*. We simply assumed that a reader can infer that "the professor" in sentence (6) referred back to Dave's statistics professor, that a midterm is an exam, and so on. But now the reference and inference steps need to be confronted, since they are critical to comprehending in a coherent fashion.

Reference involves finding the connections between separate elements in a sentence or passage of text. In sentence (5), "Dave was studying hard for his statistics midterm," the word *his* refers back to *Dave.* In this situation, *Dave* is called the *antecedent* of *his,* since it comes before the pronoun; the act of using "his" later on is called *anaphoric reference. Inference* is the process by which the listener or reader draws the connections and conclusions not specifically mentioned in the passage. Thus a reader or listener *infers* that "the professor" in sentence (6) is intended to refer back to the implied statistics class from sentence (5).

Reference is an issue for both written and spoken language, of course, although the mechanisms that permit a resolution of the reference question tend to be somewhat different in each, at least at a superficial level. In reading, you can always look back to the earlier sentence that contains the antecedent; if your memory fails for spoken language, on the other hand, your only recourse is to ask the speaker to repeat the sentence again. How do we comprehend a sentence that does not stand on its own, a sentence that requires reference to *another* sentence in order to be understood? Equally interesting is the topic of inference. What kinds of inferences are drawn during comprehension? How do we tailor our written and spoken language to the inferences that a listener or reader is likely to draw?

Simple Reference and Inference

To begin with, reference and inference are as common in language as any other feature we can identify. Part of the reason for this, no doubt, involves redundancy. Contrast a normal passage such as (8a) with (8b) to see how impossibly boring and repetitive language would be without the use of synonyms, pronouns, and so on:

(8a)   Mike went to the pool to swim some laps. After his workout, he went to his psychology class. The professor asked him to summarize the chapter that he'd assigned the class to read.

(8b*)   Mike went to the pool to swim some laps. After Mike swam some laps, Mike went to Mike's psychology class. The professor of Mike's psychology class asked Mike to summarize the chapter that Mike's psychology professor had assigned Mike's psychology class to read.

The sentences in (8b) also illustrate a second aspect of reference. It is virtually impossible to specify each component in a sentence; *no* sentence ever "stands on its own" completely. Sentence (8b) avoids pronouns of all sorts, referring to *Mike* instead of *he,* for instance. Yet even (8b) is incom-

We can *infer* what is happening in this scene from nonverbal behaviors like posture, gestures, and facial expressions, even though these are usually redundant with the spoken message.

plete, in that the full meaning of each term is not specified in the sentence itself. Instead of specifying everything, we rely on listeners to know the meanings of our words, to know about syntactic devices that structure our discourse, and to share our general conceptual knowledge of the world (e.g., to know that swimming laps can be "a workout," that professors assign chapters for their students to read). In fact, as you'll read in the last section of the chapter, if you *do* specify everything exactly, you're breaking an important conversational rule.

In naturally occurring discourse, there are several different kinds of reference that occur. Some reference is so direct that it seems to require no inference on the part of the listener whatsoever; for instance,

> (9) I saw a convertible yesterday. The convertible was
> red.

The reference here, of course, is that the convertible mentioned in the second sentence is the same one that was introduced with the indefinite article *a* in the first sentence. Clearly, the speaker of sentence (9) intended this implication, by using the definite article "the" in the second sentence. Just as clearly, someone who hears sentence (9) must *infer* this equivalence in order to comprehend the second sentence in a reasonable fashion. As Clark (1977) noted, it's conceivable that the concept in the second sentence refers to a different object, so the listener "is making a leap—perhaps only a millimetre leap—in drawing this implicature" (p. 414).

Pronoun reference requires the same reference and inference steps as sentence (9) but involves a slightly longer "leap." Consider:

> (10) Mike swims laps. He goes swimming three times a week.

In sentence (10), *he* can only refer to the word *Mike,* since the only concept introduced in the earlier phrase that can be equated with *he* is MIKE. That is, in English, the word *he* must refer to an individual, specifically a male. Contrast this with languages in which nouns have gender, and with the resultant need to make pronouns agree with the gender of the noun; translated literally from French, we get "Here is the Eiffel Tower. She is beautiful."[2]

Bridging

Clark (1977) used the term **bridging** to refer to the underlying mental processes that we're discussing. That is, Clark described all forms of reference, implication (he called it implicature, after Grice, 1975), and inference as *a process of constructing a connection between concepts.* Metaphorically, this is a process of building a *bridge* across which comprehension can pass. Bridging, clearly, is a two-party process; speakers and listeners must both build the same bridges if communication is to be successful. Consider the explicit bridge you need to draw to understand sentence (11), and how this kind of "reference by epithet" is altered dramatically with the substitution in sentence (12):

> (11) I saw Bob yesterday. The jerk criticized my tie.
> (12) I saw Bob yesterday. The psychologist criticized my tie.

Whereas the bridge between Bob and "the jerk" is clearly intended in sentence (11), most speakers would agree that the reference in sentence (12) is not nearly as strong: Is Bob the same person as "the psychologist" or not? One demonstration of this difference is to write a continuation of sentence (12), making it clear that a *different* person is intended by "the psychologist." Such a continuation—say, "But Bob said the guy was color blind"—generally will be unacceptable when appended to an epithet such as that in sentence (11).

In bridging, according to Clark, the speaker uses reference of one sort or another to indicate the kinds of implications that are intended by an

---

[2]Say what you will about rote memorization and drill; I remember the sentences *"Voici la tour Eiffel. Elle est belle."* perfectly from countless repetitions in ninth-grade French class. Then again, consistent with Bahrick et al.'s (1975) results, I've obviously retrieved and practiced those phrases many times since original learning. In any event, Madame Swearingen surely made a lasting impression!

FRANK & ERNEST reprinted by permission of NEA, Inc.

utterance. Definitionally, **reference** is the *linguistic process of alluding to a concept by using another name;* we use pronouns or synonyms to refer to the antecedent, for instance. **Implication** is *an intended reference in a sentence or utterance.* It is a connection of some sort that is not explicitly mentioned by the speaker but is intended nonetheless. In a sense, *implication* can be said to be "in the mind of the speaker," since the speaker truly intends to make the implication. As Harris and Monaco (1978) noted, there are at least two categories of implication, the kind that follows *logically* from a statement, and the kind that is *pragmatically* suggested. With the sentence "John forced Jim to rob the bank," it logically follows that "Jim robbed the bank." In contrast, it is only likely or probable—only pragmatically implied—from "She asked the student to call back later" that "He called back later." As such, there is always a *probabilistic* element to pragmatic implication: we are never entirely sure whether or not the implication was actually intended. The kinds of implications we're discussing here are pragmatic, for the most part.

Inference, finally, is "in the mind of the listener"; it is a process of *drawing connections between concepts, determining the referents of words and ideas in the passage, and deriving conclusions from a message.* Whereas *implication* refers to something that the speaker does, drawing inferences is something that the hearer does. Furthermore, it helps if we distinguish between *intended* implications and inferences and those that are *not intended.* We use the terms **authorized** and **unauthorized** for this purpose. An *authorized implication* is one intended by the speaker, and an *authorized inference* is an inference drawn by the listener that indeed was intended by the speaker. Similarly, an *unauthorized implica-*

tion is an accidental implication on the part of the speaker, and an *unauthorized inference* is a mistaken inference on the listener's part. In a very useful way, the term *authorized* refers to communication that is successful in conveying the intended meaning, and *unauthorized* refers to communication that fails to meet this goal. Authorized inferences are those pragmatic implications that indeed are true and intended, whereas unauthorized inferences may have been unintentionally suggested (see also McKoon & Ratcliff, 1986).

Complex Bridges

So far, we've examined only *direct reference,* which generally requires only a rather short inferential "leap" in order to draw the authorized connection. Clark discussed several other forms of referencing or bridging that involve *indirect reference* (see Table 9-3 for a list of Clark's typology with examples). These forms usually require much more work on the part of the listener in order to comprehend the utterances.

Consider sentences (13) and (14), examples of what Clark termed "indirect reference by association."

(13) Marge went into her office. The floor was very dirty.

(14) Bill was getting ready for the party. His suit had just come back from the cleaners.

Table 9-3   TYPES OF REFERENCE AND IMPLICATION

Direct Reference

a. *Identity.* Michelle bought a computer. The computer was on sale.
b. *Synonym.* Michelle bought a computer. The machine was on sale.
c. *Pronoun.* Michelle bought a computer. It was on sale for 20% off.
d. *Set membership.* I talked to two people today. Michelle said she had just bought a computer.
e. *Epithet.* Michelle bought a computer. The stupid thing doesn't work.

Indirect Reference by Association

f. *Necessary parts.* Eric bought a used car. The tires were badly worn.
g. *Probable parts.* Eric bought a used car. The radio doesn't work.
h. *Inducible parts.* Eric bought a used car. The salesperson gave him a good price.

Indirect Reference by Characterization

i. *Necessary roles.* I taught my class yesterday. The time I started was 1:30.
j. *Optional roles.* I taught my class yesterday. The chalk tray was empty.

Other

k. *Reasons.* Rick asked a question in class. He hoped to impress the professor.
l. *Causes.* Rick answered a question in class. The professor had called on him.
m. *Consequences.* Rick asked a question in class. The professor was impressed.
n. *Concurrences.* Rick asked a question in class. Vicki tried to impress the professor too.

Adapted from Clark, 1977.

In sentence (13), a reference back to *office* is made with the word *floor*. Since an office necessarily has a floor, it is clear that the implication in sentence (13) is that it was Marge's office floor that was dirty; in other words, Marge's office is indeed the antecedent. Conversely, the implication in sentence (14) must be *induced by the listener,* in Clark's terminology. That is, a person certainly *may* wear a suit to a party, but a suit is not a *necessary* part of such an event. In this situation, the speaker is authorizing the inference that Bill's party was somewhat formal, and that he was going to wear a suit. In Clark's words, "These 'associated' pieces of information vary in their predictability from the object, event, or situation mentioned—from absolutely necessary to quite unnecessary" (p. 415).

Think back to our discussion of semantic memory, and the typicality of instances in a category as well as the typicality of properties of those instances. Given that the "associated pieces of information" are associated in the speaker's and listener's semantic memories, it seems quite likely that the structure of concepts in semantic memory would at least partly determine what can and can't be inferred, how acceptable or understandable a referring sentence might be judged, and how quickly people would comprehend or verify a referring sentence. That is, a very predictable piece of information would be a very typical concept or property (e.g., McKoon & Ratcliff, 1989; O'Brien, Plewes, & Albrecht, 1990); Marge's office necessarily has a floor, but also probably has a desk, a chair, some shelves, and so on. It's conceivable that it has a potted plant, of course, but that is optional enough that sentence (15) seems less definite and would probably take more time to comprehend.

> (15) Marge went into her office. The African violet had bloomed.

Likewise, the degree to which a part can be induced or inferred by the listener probably depends on how accessible that part is in the structure of semantic memory; for instance, compare sentence (14) with (16):

> (16) Bill was getting ready for the party. The band had already begun to play.

The implication here, that the party featured a band as entertainment, may be a more difficult connection to infer than the one between Bill and "suit"; in Table 9-3 it would be *reference by indirect association—inducible parts (h),* a form of reference that probably needs considerable mental work to induce.

The Role of Semantic and Episodic Memory

We have nearly come full circle in this discussion. One implication of the above is that an unspecified, unexplained concept such as PARTY leads to a set of standard inferences on the part of a listener, something more or less like "ah, a generic party." But with more specification, with a more detailed context like "his suit" and "a band," something other than the normal, easy-to-retrieve attributes can be inferred.[3]

If you haven't realized it yet, we're discussing a phenomenon that you've already studied—*scripts*. Sentence (14) *instantiates*—that is, calls up from memory—a rather formal "party" script. Because people have considerable information stored about such situations, a variety of default values can be assumed for the several slots or frames in the script (e.g., there were guests at the party, probably some refreshments). In the typical party script, it's not surprising to find that there will be some form of entertainment, so "the band" fits that particular frame (although perhaps not as easily as something more inducible, such as "Bill was getting ready for the party. But his shirt was too wrinkled to wear."). Thus, if comprehension is to flow smoothly, more context will be needed to show where to expect deviations from the default values.

Finally, the specified context can even alter the way we comprehend the otherwise standard information that is presented, even if the standard information masks an otherwise ambiguous sentence. Think back to the "peculiar restaurant script" in Chapter 7. Hardly any of the details in that story fit easily into a regular restaurant script, but the added specification rendered the story comprehensible. Now reconsider the scene in sentence (8), with a different enough beginning that the antecedent of the final *he* is completely switched:

> (8c) Mike was apprehensive about class that day, since he had to give an oral presentation. He wondered if the students had read the chapter he had assigned them to read. Since he had some spare time, he decided to get his mind off the class. He went to the pool to swim some laps. After his workout, he went to his psychology class. The professor asked him to summarize the chapter that he'd assigned the class to read.

Supporting Evidence   Again you've read a section that describes comprehension in terms of the knowledge stored in memory. Retrieving information like *a midterm is an exam* and *wearing a suit to a party* allows you to understand the various forms of reference that are so common in language. But what research supports all these claims about reference and inference?

---

[3]A semantic hint for the context is "a celebration or victory party for someone named Bill." But the actual context for these sentences is episodic rather than semantic. I drafted this section the day before election day, 1992 (and, by coincidence, made final revisions on inauguration night the following January). Thus all the ideas about Bill, the suit, the band, and so on came from an anticipated "Democratic victory party" for President Clinton.

Quite literally, dozens of studies in the past 10 to 15 years have examined language comprehension from the standpoint of bridging or drawing inferences in written and spoken language. In general, the results of these studies confirm the broad outlines of models like Gernsbacher's (1990) Structure Building Framework, or in fact any model that includes drawing inferences in the list of on-line comprehension processes.

For example, many studies have shown that readers indeed draw elaborative inferences from text in an on-line fashion and then store those inferences as part of their long-term memory for the material that was read (e.g., Long, Golding, & Graesser, 1992; Noordman, Vonk, & Kempff, 1992; O'Brien, Shank, Myers, & Rayner, 1988). Interestingly, several of these studies have examined inferences as a function of the limited capacity of working memory (e.g., Fletcher & Bloom, 1988). One such study, by Singer, Andrusiak, Reisdorf, and Black (1992), went one step further than this, explaining individual differences in bridging as a function of working memory capacity and vocabulary knowledge. The gist of this work is that the greater your working memory capacity and vocabulary size, the greater is the likelihood that information necessary for an inference will still be in working memory and hence can be used for building the bridge between concepts. Recent work by Raney (1993) examined brain wave patterns (the ERP methodology) during reading, finding one distinct kind of pattern when a passage was read for the first time, and a different pattern, suggestive of higher-level comprehension, on second reading.

Enhancement and suppression effects, respectively higher and lower memory performance for ideas or characters in the discourse, have also been demonstrated. For example, Albrecht and O'Brien (1991) found that concepts rated as "central" to a passage are more interconnected in the memory representation and therefore are retrieved more rapidly than other, tangential concepts. Gernsbacher and Shroyer (1989) found that the indefinite *this* (e.g., "There was *this* guy in my class last semester") highlights the referent concept (e.g., "guy"), making it more accessible and more central to the focus of the discourse. Suppression, on the other hand, can occur merely because a concept was negated. For instance, if you read "There was *no* bread in the house," the concept BREAD is suppressed (MacDonald & Just, 1989). Concepts also undergo suppression if they are simply dropped from mention or reference in the discourse, thereby slowing down responses to those words. And in Gernsbacher (1990), suppression was isolated as one of the important differences between good and poor readers: poor readers are less adept at suppressing irrelevant information. This would mean that ideas unrelated to the discourse focus would remain activated during comprehension. Poor readers also shift from building one substructure to another too frequently, according to Gernsbacher's research (e.g., 1990, Chapter 5), making the end product of comprehension less coherent.

Summary Points: bridging as reference and inference; authorized and unauthorized implication, inference; complex bridges; retrieval from semantic, script memory

▼ Reading

A standard methodology in studying reading, still widely in use, seems quite straightforward: present subjects with a passage of text, have them read the passage in preparation for a test on the material in the passage, then administer a memory test, say, multiple choice, recall, or the like. Such a task certainly has face validity; it seems ecologically valid, since much of our reading is for the purpose of learning and remembering what we read. And, as you remember from standardized tests like the ACT or SAT, the task is easily instrumented in the laboratory.

But consider the weakness of this methodology: it reveals almost *none* of the details of mental processing that we want to understand. In the introductory section of this chapter, you saw a graph showing the hypothetical activation levels for concepts mentioned in a set of sentences (Figure 9-4) across time. We would very much like to know *directly* how concepts vary in their activation levels across a passage of text, since that should tell us a great deal about on-line comprehension. At the end of Chapter 8, you saw a figure of eye fixation times, where those times went up when the ambiguity of the sentence became apparent (see Figure 8-12). *This* is the methodology we need, a research procedure that reveals mental processing at the *microscopic* level of eye gazes, levels of activation, and so on. And this is the methodology you'll read about in this section, describing what cognitive psychology knows about *reading* based on on-line reading tasks.

Figure 9-5 shows a standard "eye fixation" or "gaze duration" laboratory setup. Most commonly, subjects are asked to read a passage silently as it appears on a computer monitor, and to prepare for some sort of comprehension test after they've finished reading. The computer monitor permits the investigator to control exactly what visual stimulus is presented, its duration, and so on. A critical second component to the apparatus is a camera of some sort, usually interfaced with the computer that controls the visual display. The camera is used to record the subjects' eye movements as the passage is read. Importantly, the computer–camera device allows the investigator to know exactly what word is being fixated at what time, and to record how long that fixation lasts.

Two Assumptions

Two central assumptions in all on-line research on reading are the immediacy assumption and the eye–mind assumption (Just & Carpen-

FIGURE 9-5   EYE-FIXATION LABORATORY

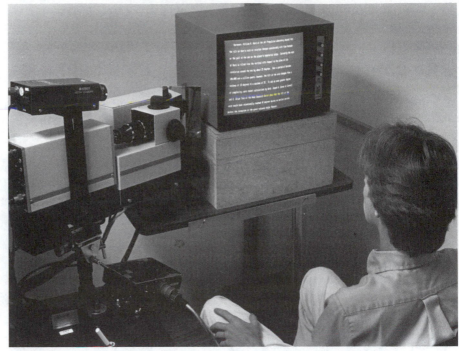

A student is reading from the computer-controlled display. The video camera on the left remotely registers the light reflections from the reader's eye. A computer uses this information to determine where the reader is fixating. (From Just & Carpenter, 1987.)

ter, 1980, 1987). The *immediacy assumption* states that readers try to interpret each content word of a text as that word is encountered in the passage. This is normally a good strategy for reading, even though it occasionally leads to mistakes that need to be "repaired." For example, consider the sentence fragment "Mary loves Jonathan . . . ," which then concludes with "apples." According to the immediacy assumption, the word *Jonathan* would most likely be misinterpreted when it is encountered, and this error would have to be corrected in order for the sentence to be understood. A similar, though somewhat more subtle example is found in sentence (17), also from Just and Carpenter (1980):

(17) Although he spoke softly, yesterday's speaker could
      hear the little boy's question.

Obviously, as you reach "hear the little boy's question," you realize that you've misinterpreted the early part of the sentence; in the jargon of this research, you've been "garden pathed." You no doubt assigned *he* to *speaker* initially; you then had to repair or recover from this mistake by *re*assigning *he* to *boy* (refer back to the section in Chapter 8 entitled "Evidence for the Case Grammar Approach"). Note also that this is not a straightforward instance of direct reference, because the pronoun occurs before the antecedent is mentioned. In such circumstances, the general strategy for determining an antecedent—connecting the pronoun to the nearest element in the passage that can serve as an antecedent—yields a mistake. Note finally that the immediacy assumption explicitly contradicts the notion that each level of analysis in language must complete itself before the next level begins to operate. In other words, the immediacy assumption is an *interactive processing* assumption.

The second central assumption is the *eye–mind assumption*. This assumption states that the eye remains fixated on a word as long as that word is being actively processed during reading. This is contrasted with the notion that information from several consecutive fixations is held in some sort of buffer or memory and is analyzed only *after* several fixations have been collected. If this were the case, there should be relatively short gaze durations across several positions in a sentence, followed by a much longer one during which the semantic processing of the buffered information takes place. Yet the data we consider next explicitly disconfirm this possibility.

Basic On-Line Reading Effects

A clear demonstration of the exquisite detail afforded by this task and apparatus is presented in Figure 9-6, taken from Just and Carpenter's (1987) important theory of reading (see also Just & Carpenter, 1980). In the figure, you see two sentences taken from a scientific passage that

FIGURE 9-6

1	2	3	4	5	6	7	8	9
1566	267	400	83	267	617	767	450	450

Flywheels are one of the oldest mechanical devices known to man.

1	2	3	4	5	6	7
400	616	517	684	250	317	617

Every internal- combustion engine   contains a small

8	9	10	11	12	13
1116	367	467	483	450	383

flywheel that converts the jerky motion of the pistons into the

14	15	16	17	18	19	20	21
284	383	317	283	533	50	366	566

smooth flow of energy that powers the drive shaft.

Eye fixations of a college student reading a scientific passage. Gazes within each sentence are sequentially numbered above the fixated words with the durations (in msec) indicated below the sequence number. (From Just & Carpenter, 1980.)

Just and Carpenter's college subjects were asked to read. Above the words in the sentence are two numbers. The top number indicates the order in which subjects fixated or gazed at the elements in the sentence; 1–9 in the first sentence, and 1–21 in the second. The number below this is the *gaze duration,* measured in milliseconds. That is, Just and Carpenter's technique permitted them to measure precisely how long each fixated element in the sentences was looked at *as the subjects read the passage.* So, as an example, the initial word in sentence 1, "Flywheels," was fixated for 1566 msec, slightly over a second and a half. The next word gazed at, *are,* was only fixated 267 msec. The fourth word, *of,* wasn't fixated at all by this subject, so neither a gaze number nor time is presented there.

A few words of explanation are in order before we turn to the theory of reading built on such results. Just and Carpenter's (1980) data were for scientific passages, read by college subjects who were asked to read naturally, without memorizing, and then be ready to recall each passage. The passages were representative of technical writing, in which a new concept, such as a flywheel, is introduced, defined, and then explained. Subjects rated their prior familiarity with the topics as "entirely unfamiliar." The average reading rate of Just and Carpenter's subjects was about 225 words per minute, somewhat slower than reading rates for simpler material (say, newspaper stories or novels).

A few general characteristics of the data afforded by this technique deserve preliminary mention as well. To begin with, note that every content word in Figure 9-6 was fixated by the subject (and by all the other subjects as well). According to Just and Carpenter, this is the norm for all kinds of text that have been studied. "There is a common misconception that readers do not fixate every word, but only some small proportion of the text. . . . However, the data . . . show that during ordinary reading, almost all content words are fixated" (pp. 329–330). Short function words, however, like *the, of,* and *a* tend not to be fixated. Also, readers tend to skip some content words if the passage is very simple for them (say, a children's story given to an adult), or if they are skimming or speed-reading.

Another obvious feature of the gaze durations is their variability. Recall in Chapter 3 that the duration of a single fixation was estimated at around 200–250 msec, each fixation followed by a saccade of nearly 100 msec. These estimates come from situations in which the viewer is merely gazing out upon some scene, for instance. In the reading studies, however, subjects are reading for comprehension. Their successive fixations on the *same* word are summed together here, giving a duration for the total time that a particular word was fixated during on-line reading (subjects were explicitly told not to reread earlier parts of the passage).

This is a critical part of Just and Carpenter's approach, since the total gaze duration on words and larger segments of text provided the basic empirical ingredient of the model: "Unlike a listener, a reader can control the rate of input. . . . A reader can take in information at a pace that matches the internal comprehension processes. By examining where a reader pauses, it is possible to learn about the comprehension processes themselves" (p. 329). Thus the differences in gaze duration for different words, and for different sections of the entire passage, gave Just and Carpenter a window on the process of comprehension.

The Just and Carpenter Model

A real strength of the on-line reading task is that it provides evidence at *two* levels of comprehension. First, the figure shows the durations of rather microscopic, word level processes. But gaze durations also allowed Just and Carpenter to examine larger, *macroscopic* processes, for example, comprehension time at the level of ideas and propositions. The word-by-word gaze durations presented in Figure 9-6 addressed the microscopic level and were analyzed by Just and Carpenter in terms of various word level variables (e.g., length, frequency in the language, position in the sentence, whether the word was repeated or not). Just and Carpenter then combined gaze durations *across* the words in a clause, phrase, or sentence, quite literally adding together the gaze durations of the individual words. By this method, Just and Carpenter examined the overall time to process larger units of text.

Table 9-4 presents the "Flywheel" passage in a "sector by sector" fashion—roughly speaking, an idea unit. To the left of each line there is a "category" label; each sector was categorized as to its role in the overall paragraph structure. To the right are two columns of numbers—observed gaze durations for a group of subjects and estimated durations—based on the READER model's predictions. So, as an example, the 1921 msec observed for sector #1 is the total of the separate gaze durations for that sector, simply the sum of the durations for the words in that sector (averaged across subjects). Note also that different kinds of sectors take different amounts of time; for instance, definition sectors tend to have more difficult words in them and are a bit longer than other sector types, so they show longer gaze durations. Even a casual examination of the observed and predicted scores shows that the model does a commendably good job of predicting gaze durations (in fact, for the numbers in Table 9-4, the correlation between observed and expected is +.985).

Model Architecture and Processes   Figure 9-7 illustrates the overall architecture and processes of the Just and Carpenter (1980, 1987) model. Note first that several elements of this model are already familiar to you. For instance, the major "combining" place in the model is working memory, the location at which visual, lexical, syntactic, and other kinds of information are "active." Long-term memory contains a wide variety of knowledge types, semantic or conceptual knowledge, and also knowledge

Table 9-4

Category	Sector	Gaze Duration (msec)	
		Observed	Estimated
Topic	Flywheels are one of the oldest mechanical devices	1921	1999
Topic	known to man.	478	680
Expansion	Every internal-combustion engine contains a small flywheel	2316	2398
Expansion	that converts the jerky motion of the pistons into the smooth flow of energy	2477	2807
Expansion	that powers the drive shaft.	1056	1264
Cause	The greater the mass of a flywheel and the faster it spins,	2143	2304
Consequence	the more energy can be stored in it.	1270	1536
Subtopic	But its maximum spinning speed is limited by the strength of the material	2440	2553
Subtopic	it is made from.	615	780
Expansion	If it spins too fast for its mass,	1414	1502
Expansion	any flywheel will fly apart.	1200	1304
Definition	One type of flywheel consists of round sandwiches of fiberglass and rubber	2746	3064
Expansion	providing the maximum possible storage of energy	1799	1870
Expansion	when the wheel is confined in a small space	1522	1448
Detail	as in an automobile.	769	718
Definition	Another type, the "superflywheel," consists of a series of rimless spokes.	2938	2830
Expansion	This flywheel stores the maximum energy	1416	1596
Detail	when space is unlimited.	1289	1252

From Just & Carpenter, 1980.

of "discourse structure," essentially the kind of information that tells us how passages of text are structured. Additionally, "scheme of domain" information, which we've termed *scripts,* as well as the episodic information an individual might have, is also included. Each of these types of knowledge can "match" the current contents of working memory and update or alter those contents. In simple terms, what you know combines with what you've already read and understood, and together these permit comprehension of what you are reading now.

As a concrete example, reconsider the fragment "Mary loves. . . ." Because of the immediacy and eye–mind assumptions, we assume that the reader has fixated *Mary* and then *loves,* processing them from the visual feature level up to the lexical level. The reader has also derived syntactic and semantic information from long-term memory, so that these words can be assigned to their proper case roles; *loves* is assigned as the *relation* being expressed, *Mary* is assigned to the *agent* case. Because of syntactic and case role expectations, the reader will now expect a particular case to occur, most likely the *recipient* or *patient* case

FIGURE 9-7

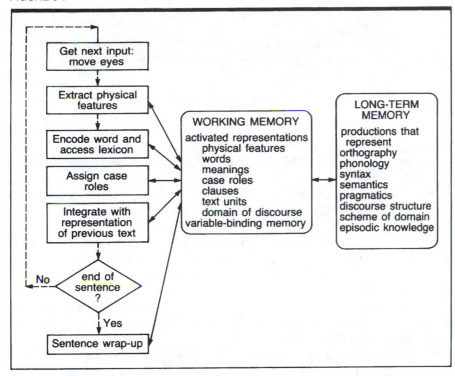

The Just and Carpenter (1980) model, showing the major structures and processes that operate during reading. Solid lines represent the pathways of information flow; the dashed line
shows the typical sequence of processing.

(e.g., Clifton, Frazier, & Connine, 1984). Essentially, the reader is
searching for a word to fill the role of "who or what Mary loves." Along
comes *Jonathan*. The word is looked up in memory, is found to satisfy the
case restrictions for a recipient, and is at least tentatively assigned to the
recipient role. Then, of course, this assignment must be undone when
apples is read; the word *apples* doesn't match any remaining case roles
that can accompany the relation LOVE, so a reassignment of *Jonathan*
must take place.

Eye Movements and Integration The initial assignment of a word
to a case role is made immediately, upon encountering it in the passage.
If that initial assignment is wrong, and the word needs to be reassigned,
then we might observe this reassignment process as a *regressive eye
movement*. Indeed, in earlier research, Just and Carpenter were specifically interested in these regressive movements (e.g., Just, 1976). Subjects read sentences such as (18) and (19), and the camera apparatus
monitored their eye movements.

(18) The tenant complained to his landlord about the leaky roof. The next day, he went to the attic to get his luggage.

(19) The tenant complained to his landlord about the leaky roof. The next day, he went to the attic to repair the damage.

Film of the subjects' eye movements provided spectacular evidence about comprehension during reading. In sentence (18), the blotch of light on the film that represented the subject's fixation point moved along until *luggage* was encountered, then "bounced" up immediately to the word *tenant*. In sentence (19), the blotch of light came to "repair the damage" and "bounced" up to *landlord*. These eye movements, according to the eye–mind assumption, illustrated the underlying mental processes of finding antecedents and determining case roles.

In Just and Carpenter's (1980) later data, subjects were under instructions to avoid rereading; regressive eye movements occurred only about 12% of the time with those instructions. Thus in the fragment example "Mary loves Jonathan . . . ," we would expect a word like *apples* to receive additional fixation time, a longer gaze duration, because it triggers extra mental processing related to the mistaken original case assignment and the need for reassignment. This is precisely the kind of effect that Just and Carpenter observed.

Finally, in more lengthy passages such as the "Flywheel" text, two additional processes are observed. *Sentence wrap-up* refers to an integrative process that occurs at the end of a sentence. During sentence wrap-up, readers tie up any remaining "loose ends"; for instance, any remaining inconsistencies or uncertainties about reference are resolved here, and any final bridging inferences that may be necessary are drawn here. Note that sentence wrap-up occurs at the *ends* of sentences. *Interclause integration* seems to be a similar component, but one that operates on the separate clauses *within* a sentence.

An Overview   Table 9-5 summarizes both the local and global processing effects that Just and Carpenter (1980) found. It also illustrates the claim that the cognitive approach, in the form of on-line examination of reading and comprehension, has made significant headway in understanding the complex processes of reading.[4] Careful inspection of the table, and the gaze duration values in Figure 9-6 and Table 9-4, will show several correspondences between textual characteristics and gaze

---

[4]One factor left out of the table is phonological effects in reading. Even though silent reading is not normally thought of as containing any necessary sound-based component, such effects have been found; see Hanson, Goodell, and Perfetti (1991; also Perfetti, Bell, & Delaney, 1988), on "tongue twister" effects in silent reading. As a small demonstration, do you remember in Chapter 3, in the section on attention, when you read "And Hunter was blunter"? Even though you were reading silently, didn't you notice the rhyme?

Table 9-5   VARIABLES AND EFFECTS THAT INFLUENCE GAZE
             DURATIONS

Gaze Duration Affected by:	Effect on Gaze Duration
Sweep of eyes to start new line	Increase
Number of syllables in word	Increase
Word frequency in English	Decrease
Beginning of line	Increase
Novel word	Increase
Repetition of infrequent word	Decrease
Topic or content word	Increase
Semantic-based expectation (if confirmed)	Decrease
Case role assignment	Varies by case role
Reassignment of case role	Increase
Other error recovery	Increase
Integration of information (after each word, after clauses, at the end of a sentence, a sector, and a paragraph)	Increase
Retrieval difficulty of scripted knowledge	Increase
Sentence wrap-up	Increase
Reference and inference processes	Increase

Adapted from Just & Carpenter, 1980, 1987.

durations. For instance, the word "flywheels," at the beginning of the passage, commands a lengthy gaze for several reasons; it is at the beginning of a line, it is a rare word, and it is a "topic" word in the discourse structure. Note that the second occurrence of "flywheel" commands a shorter duration, partly because it is a repetition of a word currently held in working memory. In Table 9-4, contrast sector #9, "it is made from" with sector #18, "when space is unlimited." Though each has four words, sector #9 receives an observed gaze duration of only 615 msec, compared with the 1289 msec on sector #18. Part of this is due to the frequency of the words in sector #9, and the fact that this sector conveys less information. Sector #18, conversely, contains a word with four syllables, contains the last word in a sentence, *and* contains the last word in a paragraph.

   As a final note here, Just and Carpenter's comments on top–down and bottom–up processing are worth considering. They note that some models of reading, especially those concerned with the initial encoding phase of reading, focused rather exclusively on bottom–up, or data-driven, processing—the kinds of visual features that are extracted from print, how those features are combined into patterns that then permit word encoding and recognition, and so on. Other models have focused primarily on top–down, conceptually driven processes, explaining how contextual effects influence reading comprehension. Just and Carpenter's model is "between the extremes. It allows for contextual influences and for the interaction among comprehension processes. Knowledge about a topic, syntactic constraints, and semantic associates can all play a role in activating and selecting the appropriate concepts. However, the printed words themselves are usually the best information source that the reader has, and they can seldom be entirely replaced by guesses from the preceding context. Thus the top–down processes can influence the bottom–up ones, but the role is to participate in selecting interpretations rather than to dominate the bottom–up processes" (p. 353).

A Summary

An in-depth description of the experiments that support the general relationships of Just and Carpenter's model is not possible here, if for no other reason than lack of space. Reading comprehension research has become one of the most active areas of investigation; an adequate review would not only be quite lengthy, it would be out of date almost as soon as it was written. Suffice it to say that every level of language analysis has been examined in terms of reading comprehension effects, and the general outline provided by the Just and Carpenter model seems flexible enough that most, if not all, of the results can fit comfortably within it. Here is just a brief listing of some recent work attesting to the importance of factors listed in Table 9-5:

- The effects of *word frequency, syntactic structure, and context* (Altmann, Garnham, & Dennis, 1992; Inhoff, 1984; O'Seaghdha, 1989)
- The effects of *sentence context on word identification* (Paul et al., 1992; Schustack, Ehrlich, & Rayner, 1987; Simpson, Casteel, Peterson, & Burgess, 1989)
- The effects of *ambiguity* (Frazier & Rayner, 1990; Rayner & Frazier, 1989)
- The effects of *topic and thematic structure on reading* (O'Brien & Myers, 1987; Taraban & McClelland, 1988), especially the *relatedness of successive paragraphs* and the presence of an *informative introductory paragraph* (Lorch, Lorch, & Matthews, 1985)
- The effects of *scripted knowledge on word recognition and comprehension* (Sharkey & Mitchell, 1985)
- The effects of *discourse structure on the understanding of reference* (Malt, 1985; Murphy, 1985)

When we examine these studies in detail, we find that each uses a somewhat different methodology, focuses on different aspects of reading, and examines different kinds of hypotheses. When viewed at arm's length, however, they all converge on the same overall position: reading and reading comprehension are affected by linguistic effects in the text, to be sure, but they are also dramatically influenced by cognitive effects. These cognitive factors, including the structure of the mental lexicon, the nature of semantic and scripted knowledge, and the effects of expectations or top–down processes, exert a tremendous *interactive influence* on how we read.

The usual effect of such cognitive influences is to smooth and facilitate our reading. Words and ideas are more predictable in one context than in another, and the cognitive system capitalizes on its immense store of knowledge to develop and use an elaborate context. Embedding the new information into an existing contextual framework should, of course, lead to better comprehension and a stronger, more durable memory record of the information. Sentences such as (20) and (21),

> (20) How many animals of each kind did Moses take
>   onto the ark?
> (21) What is the nationality of Thomas Edison, inventor
>   of the telephone?

on the other hand, or the "garden-path" sentences mentioned previously, show the less-than-desirable context and cognitive effects that occasionally crop up. Read sentences (20) and (21) again, if you didn't notice the "semantic illusion" (Erickson & Mattson, 1981; Reder & Kusbit, 1991). The reason we "fall for" the illusion, that we do not immediately notice what is wrong with the sentence, should be clear: it's merely another illustration of the power of conceptually driven processing. Just and Carpenter's remarks notwithstanding, semantic and contextual effects can exert a remarkably strong effect, even on the reading of simple statements.

Summary Points: eye gaze durations; immediacy and eye–mind assumptions; micro- and macroscopic processes

▼ Conversation

We turn now to the last major section of the chapter, comprehension of spoken language, and specifically the comprehension of conversation. By *conversation* we mean normal, everyday language interactions, say, an ordinary talk among friends, which is the major focus of this section. But the issues we will consider are not restricted to this kind of conversation. Many of them apply to *all* spoken language interactions—how professors lecture and students comprehend, how people converse on the telephone, how an interviewer and a job applicant talk, and so on.

As important as an understanding of conversational interaction is, let's admit at the outset that we seem to know far less about this topic than we do about reading. There are many fewer experimental tests of hypotheses in this section than in the earlier sections; the hypotheses and theories here rest much more heavily on intuition and speculation. As noted in the previous chapter, "language by ear" is far more common than "language by eye"; we acquire language almost exclusively by exposure to the spoken form. And yet, ironically, it is very difficult to investigate spoken language comprehension with the same rigor as can be achieved for written language.

On the other hand, much of what we've learned about reading and writing has to apply to conversation and spoken language comprehension to a fair degree. It is the same comprehension system doing the understanding in both formats, after all. So, for example, the Structure Building Framework you read about at the outset can be applied in a general way to conversations (most or all of Just and Carpenter's model of reading should apply too). And furthermore, much of the higher-level processing in a conversation occurs at a relatively conscious level. As such, our intuitions are worth more in these settings than in understanding the fast, automatic components of reading.

The Structure of Conversations

Let's examine two very general characteristics of conversations, to set the stage for the rest of our discussion, and to begin developing a standard vocabulary with which to talk about conversational phenomena. Much of our understanding of these characteristics has come not from psychological research, but instead from related fields such as linguistics and sociolinguistics. The two categories we'll focus on are conversational turn taking and the effects of social role and setting.

Taking Turns   Although a conversation might open in any number of ways, Schegloff (1972) has pointed out that in fact we actually use a fairly limited number of conversational "openers." Most commonly, we merely address the other person, request or offer some information, or fall back on a standard, stereotyped expression or topic—respectively, "Hi, Larry," "Do you have the time?" "May I help you?" or "How's it

During a conversation, speakers develop a rhythm as each person takes successive turns speaking. Nonverbal interaction can occur during a turn, such as when a listener nods to indicate attention or agreement.

going?" (Extensive studies are needed, of course, to examine the openings of more serious conversations, icebreakers such as "Excuse me, but I couldn't help noticing your perfume" or "Haven't we met before?") Similar conversational "closers" are also required for a well-structured conversation; note how stereotyped the last two or three exchanges are in a phone conversation.

Once a conversation has been opened, somewhat of a rhythm develops as the participants take successive turns. First, there is actually very little overlap between participants' utterances. Generally, two people will speak simultaneously only at the change of turns, when one speaker is finishing and the other is beginning. On the other hand, there tends to be a fair amount of nonverbal interaction during a turn, for example, when a listener nods to indicate attention or agreement (or instead offers the neutral "um-hmm" kind of utterance, showing that he or she is following the speaker's meaning; Duncan, 1972). Second, participants' total number of turns and the duration of those turns are quite variable among individuals, although there is some evidence that the length of any one speaker's turn is a fairly stable individual characteristic (Jaffe & Feldstein, 1970). The pauses during speaker's turns, however, tend to be about the same length for all participants.

Finally, it seems that there is a fairly fixed set of rules for turn taking, that is, for indicating to other participants that your turn is over, and for determining who the next speaker will be. According to Sacks, Schegloff, and Jefferson (1974), three rules characterize turn taking and turn relinquishing. First, the current speaker is in charge of selecting the next speaker. This is often accomplished by directing a comment or question toward another participant. The second rule is that if the first rule isn't used—if the current speaker doesn't select the next one—then self-selection applies, and any participant can jump in. The third rule is that the current speaker may continue to speak if no one else takes a turn, but is not obliged to.

Speakers use a variety of signals, both linguistic and pragmatic, to indicate what the next move in the conversation will be. A common "turn-yielding" signal is a long pause. So if a speaker does not intend to relinquish the conversational turn, this kind of "turn-yielding" signal is withheld. Other "failure to yield" signals include trailing off in midsentence without completing the grammatical clause or the thought, withholding such endings as "you know," or even looking away from other participants during a pause (Cook, 1977). On the other hand, if a speaker *does* intend to yield to someone else, he or she may apply the first rule, drop the pitch or loudness of the utterance, stop gesturing, or merely stop talking *and* make eye contact with another participant. All these signals indicate a willingness to yield the role of speaker.

Social Roles and Settings While conversations are in general quite loosely structured, there is still a range of conversation *types,* where each type exerts an influence on the contributions made by the participants (for simplicity's sake, we will only discuss two-person conversations here). For instance, a conversation between two peers differs from a conversation between two individuals of different status or position in many ways: the social roles and relationships of the participants will influence factors such as topic, length of turns in the conversation, and even the nature of the utterances (see Kemper & Thissen, 1981, for research on social roles and the "politeness" ethic).

In a similar vein, the setting or purpose of the conversation also influences its character. As an example, Blom and Gumperz (1972) investigated conversations in a Norwegian town, where a standard or formal language, taught in school, coexists with a local dialect, an informal language. People in this town routinely switch from one language to another (a process called *code-switching*) depending on the social setting. For instance, a lecturer will speak in the formal language but will switch to dialect in order to encourage class discussion. A business transaction between two people will be conducted in the formal language; at the end of the transaction, the two people might switch to dialect to discuss more personal topics. We do similar things in English, in terms of tone, word and topic choice, and the like. (See Carroll, 1986, for a more thorough discussion of the social factors in conversation. I attempted such a switch with the "icebreaker" comment mentioned earlier.[5]

Cognitive Conversational Characteristics

We now turn to a consideration of the more cognitive and language-related aspects of conversations. We're still most interested in ordinary conversations, since these are the least formalized, the least regulated by rules and expectations, and the least predetermined; compare the usual flow of topics in an ordinary conversation to the highly structured interactions in a formal debate, for example. Thus ordinary conversation is a more interesting topic of investigation, at least for cognitive psychology, since there are so many more decision points, and since the structure and events during conversation reveal more clearly the underlying mental processing on the part of the participants.

The Linguistic Setting   Participants in a conversation must juggle many kinds of information simultaneously, in order for the conversation to be successful. To begin with the obvious, we must handle several levels of language—phonetic, syntactic, lexical, and semantic or conceptual factors. Contextual information also guides and influences our under-

---

[5]Perhaps we shift conversational tone automatically, without any metacognitive awareness of the shift. On the other hand, conversational style can certainly be under conscious control; don't you "watch your language" in front of your parents or your boss?

DEMONSTRATIONS

1. Momentary pauses, uhs, and other dysfluencies often indicate some mental planning is taking place before the speaker utters the next phrase or sentence, or some retrieval is taking more time than usual. Keep a record of such dysfluencies in a sample of spontaneous speech, and try to determine what characteristics of the next phrase required the extra planning time; for example, a rare or difficult word or a complex syntactical structure.

2. The focus of discourse, whether a phrase, sentence, or paragraph, is difficult to specify; Gernsbacher's model, however, would predict that the focus will maintain an overall higher level of enhancement at the end of the passage. Try writing sentences like the "Tina/Louise" sentences in Table 9-2, or short episodes like the "Dave and his statistics exam" one. Have your subjects listen to the sentences, and then have them write one or two sentences to continue the story and/or bring it to a close. Score the continuation for focus to see if it matches the focus you intended for the stimulus sentences.

3. After an interval of time, you might ask the subjects who did Demonstration 2 to recall the sentences, both your stimuli and their own continuations. See whether the ideas they recall were usually the ideas that were "in focus."

4. One of the best student projects I ever graded was a test of the politeness ethic in conversational requests. On five randomly selected days, the student sat next to a stranger on the bus, turned, and asked "Excuse me, but do you have the correct time?" All five strangers answered her. On five other randomly selected days, she said to the stranger "Tell me what time it is," not in an unpleasant tone, but merely in a direct fashion; none of the strangers answered. Devise other situations in which you violate the politeness ethic or other conversational rules, and note people's reactions. If done properly (*don't* go overboard!) you'll learn about the rules of conversation; if done improperly, it'll turn into a demonstration project on aggression.

---

standing; to use Carroll's (1986) example, the sentence "I like the way your hair looks" means one thing by itself, but quite another if someone has just commented on your out-of-style clothes. And, of course, context will influence word recognition, reference, and inference processes, and other aspects of comprehension, as you just read a moment ago.

Pragmatics: The Conceptual and Belief Settings Beyond these linguistic kinds of information, we reencounter Miller's (1973) highest levels of analysis, the conceptual level and the level of beliefs. At the risk of putting words into Miller's mouth, let's consider these two levels from the perspective of **pragmatics,** *knowledge of the social rules of language* (this treatment is inspired, at least in part, by the analysis of conversational rules you'll read about in a moment).

At the *conceptual level* of analysis and comprehension, a conversational participant attempts to understand an entire utterance on a straightforward, nearly literal level. At this level, the listener deals with the spoken utterance as it is customarily understood. It is necessary to make several assumptions here, illustrating part of the pragmatics of normal conversation. For instance, the listener assumes that the speaker is conveying information sincerely, and that the utterance is intended by the speaker to be taken at face value. Note that the phrase "nearly literal" permits us to include figures of speech at this regular conceptual level. That is, we are not limited to a completely concrete or literal interpretation of the words, but can judge expressions of one sort or another as having a straightforward, although metaphorical or figurative, meaning (e.g., "putting words into Miller's mouth"; see e.g., Gibbs, 1989, 1990).

These things that the listener assumes can be referred to as *default conversational assumptions* (Edwards & Potter, 1993, discuss the social psychological aspects of such assumptions). And, of course, when the original listener takes a turn in the conversation, the original speaker becomes the listener and must make the same default assumptions. Operating under these default assumptions means that the speaker's utterance was sensible, that the listener must construct a sensible interpretation of it, and that the constructed interpretation must be the one intended by the speaker. As an example, imagine studying in the library, when your friend says:

(22) Can I borrow a pencil?

This is a perfectly straightforward speech act, a request with no unusual elements. The default assumptions seem to apply completely, and there is no misunderstanding of the utterance. Consider now a variation:

(23#) May I borrow a pencil with lead in it?

For reasons to be made explicit later, this question seems to violate a rule of conversation. (Such sentences, which are peculiar under normal circumstances but acceptable under an appropriate context, will be noted with the symbol #; sentences that are unacceptable under any context will still be starred.) Why would someone say "a pencil with lead in it" when all pencils have lead in them? But by the same default assumptions, any strange, contradictory, or otherwise unusual "pieces" of the utterance must be assumed to have a sensible and reasonable meaning too. Now the listener must attempt to find the sensible meaning that the speaker surely had in mind. A reasonable interpretation on the part of the listener here is that the friend's pencil lead broke. On the other hand, if you had just loaned a pencil to your friend, and then the friend asked question (23#), the question takes on a rather pointed quality (so to speak), as an expanded paraphrase suggests:

(23a) Thanks for loaning me the pencil. Now may I borrow a pencil with lead in it?

Finally, there is the highest level of conversational comprehension, the *belief* level. At this level (again, at the risk of reading more into Miller's scheme than was originally intended), the listener goes beyond a conceptual analysis of the utterance. Here, the listener evaluates both the utterance *and* the speaker. This is considerably more complex than the puzzlement generated by a question such as (23#), which the listener attempts to interpret by virtue of the normal default assumptions. At the belief level, the listener essentially questions the speaker's knowledge, motivation, and even the speaker's opinion of the listener. Putting it colloquially, the listener tries to figure out where the speaker is "coming from."

For example, you mention to your friend Frank that you're going to take Psychology of Personality next term. Think for a moment about your reaction if Frank were to say any of the following to you:

(24) Why would you want to take Dr. Wilson's Personality class? It's just a bunch of experiments with rats,
isn't it?
(25) Yeah, I'm taking Wilson's class next term too. John
told me he's going to assign some books he thinks
I'll really like.
(26) Maybe you shouldn't take Wilson's class next term.
Don't you have to be pretty smart to do all that
reading?

In (24), you assume that Frank has made the remark in all sincerity, that it was intended to mean just what it says. Since you know that research on laboratory animals has had rather little to do with the field of personality, your evaluation of Frank is that he knows considerably less about personality theory than you do. Frank's utterance prompted you to evaluate both the statement *and* Frank. Since he presumably uttered a sincere statement, one you know to be based on misinformation, you revise your "theory of Frank" to include this new information: "Frank's a good guy, but he sure doesn't know much about personality theory."

In sentence (25), a likely interpretation is that Frank is boasting a bit about being on a first-name basis with the professor. Indeed, he's authorizing this inference by using a more familiar term of address than is customary for professors (for an analysis of usage of proper names, see Brown & Ford, 1961). And in sentence (26), you no doubt get the distinct impression that Frank believes you to be less than capable of doing the required work for the course and has expressed this belief in a rather ham-fisted way.

On-Line Theories During Conversation   Let's invent some terms to refer to each participant's thoughts and understanding. It is obvious, yet important, that each participant in a conversation has an idea of what the other participant knows, what that person is familiar with, interested in, and so on. A classic illustration of this involves adult–child conversations (e.g., DePaulo & Bonvillian, 1978; Snow, 1972; Snow & Ferguson, 1977), in which the adult's awareness of the child's lack of sophistication and knowledge prompts the adult to simplify and adjust what is said.[6] This is, of course, a completely normal and necessary sensitivity, making the adult's speech understandable for the child.

This sensitivity to the participants' knowledge is displayed to some degree in *all* conversations. In a conversation, each participant develops at least two informal theories or models of the other participant. One of these is quite straightforward, *a theory of what the other participant knows, believes, feels, and so on.* We'll call it the person's **direct theory** of the other participant. When your friend Frank commented that the Personality class was about research with rats, your *direct theory* of Frank was something like "Frank knows virtually nothing about the psychology of personality." Thus the *direct theory* is simply one participant's idea or model of the other person.

The second informal theory is more indirect and relates somewhat more to issues of social psychology. This second theory is *an evaluation of the other participant's direct theory—what you think the other participant believes about you.* For lack of a better term, let's call this a **second-order theory.** Obviously, when Frank suggested that you possibly weren't smart enough to take the class, *his* direct theory (of you) was that you weren't smart enough. *Your* second-order theory is—roughly speaking—"Frank must think that I'm pretty dumb." (See Table 9-6 for intuitive examples of the direct and second-order theories in the three short conversations with Frank.) Because participants in conversations develop and continually revise these informal theories during the conversational interaction, the theories are perfect examples of on-line language processing, however difficult they are to investigate.

Discourse Structure in Conversations

While ordinary conversation may be the least regulated and structured of all verbal interactions, it is nonetheless far from a random phenomenon. Whether you're having a conversation merely to "pass the time of day" or for a specific purpose, a pattern of topic maintenance and topic shift becomes apparent. What is involved in maintaining topic and mak-

---

[6]In fact, even *children* modify the complexity of their speech when talking to children younger than themselves; see Tomasello and Mannle (1985).

Table 9-6   EXAMPLES OF DIRECT AND SECOND-ORDER THEORIES

For all three conversations, Chris's first sentence and direct theory are the same.
Chris: "I think I'll take Personality with Dr. Wilson next term."
Chris's Direct Theory: Frank is interested in what courses I'm taking.

CONVERSATION #1

Frank replies: "Personality? Ah, that's just a bunch of experiments with rats, isn't it?"
Chris's Direct Theory: Frank doesn't know much about Personality research.

CONVERSATION #2

Frank replies: "Yeah, I am too. John told me he's going to assign some books he thinks I'll really like."
Chris's Direct Theory: Frank knows the professor on a first-name basis, and he's bragging about it by calling him John.
Chris's Second-Order Theory: Frank thinks I'll be impressed that he calls the professor John, and that the professor is concerned that he'll like the books.

CONVERSATION #3

Frank replies: "Hmm, maybe you shouldn't take that class. Don't you have to be pretty smart to do all that reading?"
Chris's Direct Theory: Frank is a jerk, he just insulted me.
Chris's Second-Order Theory: Frank thinks I'm not smart.

ing acceptable or "legal" contributions to the conversation? The answers here include both cognitive factors, related to comprehension, and interpersonal and social factors. Because all such factors have an impact on comprehension, we need to consider them all.

Cognitive Factors in Topic Maintenance   Initial topic selection is rather irrelevant to our purposes here. The initial topic can be virtually anything, of course, depending on current events, shared experiences among the participants, immediate circumstances, and so on. These factors are beyond the scope of this treatment, except for one point: there is always the assumption that the speaker selects a topic that is of interest to the listener (see Table 9-7, later in this section).

Once the topic has been selected, however, we become interested in the cognitive factors that operate to maintain that topic, and how people discern topic from other participants' contributions. There are two parts to this process, *comprehension* and *expansion*. The first simply involves comprehending the speaker's topic or focus, essentially a process of drawing inferences. The second involves contributing some new information to the topic.

Comprehension   Schank (1977; see also Litman & Allen, 1987) has provided a provocative analysis of topic maintenance and topic shift, including a consideration of what is and is not *a permissible response,* called simply a *move,* after one speaker's turn is over. Let's adapt

Schank's example as a starting point for this analysis. Consider sentence (27), an opener in a conversation between two friends, Ben and Ed, about their mutual acquaintance Tony. For simplicity and clarity, Ben and Ed will be the speakers/listeners in this conversation for this entire section.

> (27) Ben: "Tony bought a red car in Baltimore yester-
> day."

According to Schank, Ed's reply is constrained in several ways. The major constraint is that Ed must infer what Ben considers the most important information in his remark and must then respond in some fashion to that. In fact, it is Ben's responsibility to make this inference process easy for Ed, by highlighting his intended topic one way or another.

Assume that Ben has done this by referring to the central idea, the *discourse focus,* in the normal fashion, for example, by mentioning it first. This is of course a direct application of Gernsbacher's (1990) comprehension model to the topic of spoken discourse. If the following is the complete propositional representation for Ben's remark,

BUY (Tony, car, yesterday, Baltimore) & RED (car)

then the discourse focus might simply be the most important concepts in the representation, TONY, BUY, and CAR. Let's assume that this is indeed what Ben intended to communicate in his remark, and for clarity, let's call it Ben's *Intended Topic.*

Ed's responsibility now is to infer what the Intended Topic is. We'll refer to Ed's understanding as the *Inferred Topic,* in similar fashion to the earlier discussion of reference and inference. If Ed's Inferred Topic is correct, then he has figured out Ben's Intended Topic successfully, in which case he might reply

> (28) "Great, he's needed a new car for a long time."

Contrast this with a case in which Ed has clearly *mis*understood Ben's point; that is to say, Ed's Inferred Topic is wrong:

> (29#) Ed: "I bought a new shirt last week."

Why is (29#) an inappropriate move? There is, after all, a shred of connection between the two. But most of us would agree that (29#) is at best a peculiar response. Why? Because it was based on an incorrect Inferred Topic, it was *not* close enough to Ben's Intended Topic. It seems to suggest that Ben's Intended Topic was BUYING, that Ben was authorizing the inference that BUYING was his discourse focus. Instead, it seems safe to conclude that Ben's Intended Topic involved the combination or intersection of at least two or three major concepts in the sentence, and that for some reason, Ed failed to infer that focus correctly.

Thus Schank suggests the following for the comprehension phase. Many Inferred Topics are possible at each turn in a conversation, where each involves some meaningful intersection of two or three concepts in the sentence. The speaker's job is to simplify the listener's task, by highlighting what the Intended Topic is. The listener's job is to figure out the correct Inferred Topic. Presumably, if Ed's Inferred Topic is correct, and he then contributes a remark like (28), the conversation will proceed smoothly. But if his remark resembles (29#), then Ben will judge Ed's remark as an *illegal move*.

Expansion Schank points out that the listener—Ed, here—can select among several different possibilities when taking a turn in the conversation. Each possibility represents a different way to expand upon Ben's original remark, to convey some new information to Ben. These *Potential Topics* consist of two parts, the Inferred Topic and the New Information Ed wants to convey. Having already inferred the topic of Ben's remark, Ed must now select the New Information he wants to add to it. Of course, many possibilities exist here: for instance, (a) the problems Ed is having in finding a new car to buy, (b) why Tony bought the car he did, (c) why Tony shouldn't have bought a car, (d) how Tony broke a deal he had made to buy Ed's car, and so on (examples adapted from Schank, 1977, p. 423). The important point is that these specific possibilities differ in their level of generality, either at the *Same Level* or at a *Higher Level* (Schank suggested three levels of generality here; two should be sufficient for this discussion).[7]

Say Ed comments directly on the Inferred Topic, by saying

(30) Ed: I thought he was going to buy *my* car!

This conversational move combines the correct Inferred Topic with New Information at the same level of generality; Ed's New Information is at the *Same Level* of generality as the original remark. Alternatively, Ed may comment at a *Higher Level* of generality, still based on the same Inferred Topic of TONY, BUY, CAR, as in sentence (31).

(31) Ed: "Well, this isn't the first time Tony has broken his word to me."

Figure 9-8 diagrams several different pathways in Ben and Ed's conversation, showing different Intended and Inferred Topics and different kinds of New Information. Think of these pathways in exactly the same way we considered *bridges* earlier in this chapter: they convey an implied connection of meaning that the listener must infer. Importantly, Ed's comments require different amounts of cognitive work on Ben's part for comprehension to be successful. A conversational move at the Same Level maintains high coherence with the original comment and thereby

---

[7]I have altered Schank's terminology in these sections, to highlight the central ideas being considered.

FIGURE 9-8

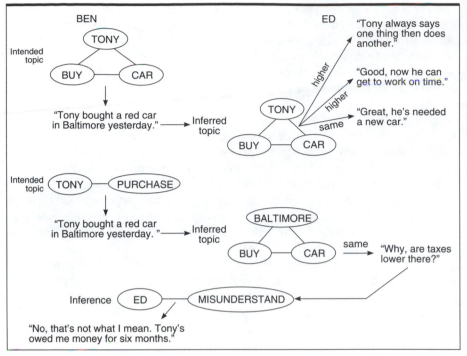

A diagram of the Intended and Inferred Topics in short conversations between Ben and Ed, and the actual contributions the characters make to the conversation.

reduces the memory and comprehension load placed on Ben. A comment at any Higher Level, however, will require Ben to do considerably more work in deriving the Inferred Topic; Ed has in a sense disguised his Intended Topic by not mentioning intermediate links in the inferential bridge.

Conversational Rules

Note in the above analysis of topic maintenance and shift that there is an implicit assumption governing conversational responses at each change of turn: a response must be relevant to the topic that prompted it. In other words, while some of the responses listed for Ben's original statement were peculiar, that peculiarity had to do with Ed's failure to derive the authorized focus in one way or another. On the other hand, none of those responses were completely irrelevant, as sentence (32#) would be:

(32#) Ed: I feel like eating some lunch.

Such a response, under the normal default conversational assumptions, is illegal: there is no obvious way to relate Ed's statement to what went before it in the conversation, at least in the conventional sense of being "relevant." The apparent irrelevance of (32#) seems to have completely disrupted the normal conversational process.

Grice's Conversational Postulates   A very useful consideration of the rules of conversations, the "terms" of the unspoken contract in a sense, was provided by Grice (1975; see also Norman & Rumelhart, 1975, for an expansion of some of Grice's ideas). Grice began his essay by noting that there is one overriding principle that governs participants in a conversation. He termed this the **cooperative principle.** According to this principle, both (all) participants enter into an unspoken contract with each other. The terms of this contract are such that each participant will contribute to the conversation in an appropriate manner, continuing until a mutually agreeable stopping point is reached. During the conversational exchange, any lawful response on the part of a participant is permissible and can shift the topic this way or that. The contract would generally also be considered to specify, however vaguely, the mutually agreed upon purpose for the conversation, for example, small talk, sharing or obtaining information, and the like.

Beyond this cooperative principle, Grice listed several other *rules that govern contributions or moves in a conversation,* called **conversational postulates.** Grice argued that each of these postulates or rules is a law of conversation, and that each is part of the unspoken contract that governs an exchange. Generally speaking, all the rules are followed by all the participants. As such, the exchange among participants is sensible, coherent, and mutually enjoyable. Table 9-7 lists the conversational postulates, with a few additions beyond the work of Grice (1975) and Norman and Rumelhart (1975).

Violating the Conversational Rules   While the conversational flow is generally sensible and uninterrupted, a participant may occasionally violate one of the conversational rules. A clear example would be when one participant lies about something, for whatever reason. In such a case, if the lie was intentional and goes undetected, an agreed-upon purpose for the conversation has been violated: the sharing of information is undermined by the lie. If the lie *is* detected, of course, then other processes intervene, no doubt influenced by social roles, settings, degree of acquaintance of the participants, and so on.

A second possibility here is that a bending of the rules has occurred, not an outright lie perhaps, but an exaggeration, for example. Grice pointed out that there is a ranking or priority among the rules, such that the later ones, for example, those concerning manner and tone, can be violated with greater impunity than the earlier ones. Furthermore, the listener's evaluation of a speaker who violates a later rule will be less

---

Table 9-7   CONVERSATIONAL POSTULATES AND RULES

---

1. **Cooperative Principle:** Be sincere; make your contributions reasonable, given the agreed-upon purpose of the conversation.
2. **Be Relevant**
   a. Don't say what others already know; don't state the obvious.
   b. Don't be superfluous; don't say too much, don't be too informative.
   c. *Don't wander; stick to the topic.
   d. *Don't say what others aren't interested in.
3. **Be Informative:** Make your contributions as informative as possible or as necessary.
   a. Don't mislead; don't say something you believe is false, or something you don't have the evidence for; don't overspecify.
   b. Don't say more than you know.
   c. Don't say less than you know.
4. **Manner and Tone**
   a. Be clear, easily understood.
   b. Avoid obscurity, ambiguity.
   c. *Don't boast.
   d. Be brief, orderly.
   e. Be polite.
5. ***Relations with Conversational Partner**
   a. Infer and respond to partner's knowledge and beliefs.
   b. Correct partner's misunderstandings.
6. ***Mark Intentional Violations of Rules**
   a. Use linguistic or pragmatic (stress, gestures) markers.
   b. Use blatant violation as a marker.
   c. Invite partner's inference as to your reasons for the violation.

Adapted from Grice, 1975, and Norman & Rumelhart, 1975; additions are starred.

---

harsh—something like "Well, I certainly doubt that, but I can see how you might believe it anyway."

More interesting for our purposes, however, are situations in which a rule violation occurs not for the purpose of getting away with a lie, but for some more subtle or complex reasons. Reconsider Ben's original utterance (27), "Tony bought a red car in Baltimore yesterday," followed by Ed's seemingly irrelevant remark (32#), "I feel like eating some lunch."

One possibility here, as already mentioned, is that Ed has illegally shifted the topic of the conversation. The shift is truly illegal according to the first and most important of Grice's postulates, *Be relevant.* If Ben decides that Ed's remark was truly a violation of this rule, and if Ed does not further justify his comment, then the "politeness" ethic of conversation has also been violated. As noted, this may prompt Ben to reexamine his opinion of Ed—his direct theory—along the lines of the belief level discussed earlier.

Short of that, a variety of sensible reasons might exist for Ed's comment. All of them acknowledge his apparent failure to be relevant, of course, but at the same time they point out reasonable reasons for this failure. By far the simplest one is that Ed didn't hear what Ben said; Ben might try repeating himself here, prefaced by something like "Ed, didn't you hear what I said? I said that Tony bought. . . ." A related, though somewhat less likely possibility, is that Ed mistakenly thought that Ben had signaled the end of his turn, and that the topic had been mutually exhausted. Of course, a more normal way for Ed to switch the topic in such a situation would be to use a phrase like "Not to change the subject, but" or "Oh, by the way." These phrases *mark* a deviation from normal conversational response, showing that the deviation was intentional (i.e., Postulate 6 in Table 9-7).

It's even possible that the violation was intended to convey sarcasm, irony, or some other "editorial comment." In these instances, of course, the literal meaning is to be ignored, because a secondary meaning is the one authorized by the speaker. In (32#), Ed is violating the "relevance" rule so blatantly that he invites the inference "I'm too disgusted to comment on Tony." Such conversational moves depend a great deal on the shared experiences and opinions of the two participants, not to mention the context that has developed within the conversation (e.g., Wilkes-Gibbs & Clark, 1992). Indeed, in many situations, we can intend exactly the opposite meaning of what our literal words mean; for example, Ed: "Oh, I'm so happy for Tony," uttered with heavy inflectional stress to highlight the sarcasm. (See Gibbs, 1986a, for an analysis of sarcasm. Keenan, MacWhinney, & Mayhew, 1977, found that recognition memory for naturally occurring conversational statements was better when the statements were of "high interactional content," that is, involved sarcasm, humor, or personal criticism.)

Empirical Effects in Conversation

Let's conclude with some evidence about the conversational effects we've been discussing. As mentioned, conversation is a particularly difficult phenomenon to investigate. Staging a conversation in a controlled laboratory setting could easily alter the very behavior and mental processes we're hoping to study. Aside from the fact that it's eavesdropping (in violation of a *social* rule of conversation), investigating naturally occurring conversation without alerting the participants violates any number of ethical guidelines for conducting research. As such, investigators have often had to rely either on the commonalities between reading and conversational comprehension, or on people's "conversational intuitions" or judgments. Nonetheless, a few studies have used more precise empirical methods. Let's focus on just one, which involves a stereotyped conversational interaction and what's known as *indirect requests*.

Indirect Requests   One of Grice's conversational postulates involves the manner in which we speak—*be polite*. As it turns out, this politeness rule often translates into an interesting way of expressing requests, commands, and so on; we use a sentence that is *not* intended to be understood literally, but instead is to be understood as an *indirect* and hence polite way of expressing the authorized meaning. That is, when you want to make a request of someone, you often make your request in an indirect form. Indirect requests such as "Do you happen to know what time it is?" are very common, and considerably more "legal," according to the rules of conversation, than a direct statement to a stranger might be (e.g., "Tell me what time it is"). Thus we *mark* our requests, commands, and so on to conform to the politeness rule, certain that our authorized meaning will be inferred. (Of course, the classic examples here involve our parents' remarks such as "Don't you think we ought to mow the grass?" or "I'll bet the car needs washing.")

One of the most impressive investigations of such indirect requests was reported by Clark (1979). The study involved telephone calls to some 950 merchants in the San Francisco area, in which the caller asked a question that the merchant would normally be expected to deal with on the phone (e.g., what time do you close, do you take credit cards, how much does something cost). The caller would immediately write down a verbatim record of the call as soon as she hung up.[8] Two typical conversational interactions might be:

(33) Merchant: "Green's Pharmacy."
     Caller: "Hi. Do you close before seven tonight?"
     Merchant: "Uh, no. We're open until nine o'clock."
     Caller: "Thank you very much. Goodbye."

(34) Merchant: "Hello, Scoma's Restaurant."
     Caller: "Hello. Do you accept any credit cards?"
     Merchant: "Yes we do—we even accept Carte Blanche."

Of course, the caller's questions here are indirect; if they were direct, the caller would expect a simple yes or no answer. Instead, the caller is actually authorizing a somewhat different interpretation. Roughly, the Intended Topic is "When do you close tonight?" and "Which credit cards do you accept?"

Merchants' responses were classified according to a variety of groupings, including their extensiveness or completeness, whether they responded to the question or to the indirect request, and so on. Not surprisingly, Clark found that the merchants responded to the Intended Topic, the authorized request, rather than merely to the literal question posed by the caller.

Of greater interest was the level of inference that was apparent in the merchants' responses. Consider two different kinds of restaurants, one

---

[8]Clark's research assistant was a woman whom Clark described in a footnote as having sacrificed her left ear and right index finger to conduct those 950 "experimental trials," all for the advancement of science. What a shame there's no "Ebbinghaus Award" for the dogged, long hours of work that often go into research.

that only accepts Visa and MasterCard, and one that accepts virtually all credit cards. Given the merchant's need to be informative while not saying more than is necessary, we would expect the merchant in the first restaurant to respond "We *only* accept Visa and MasterCard." Such a specific response is both informative and brief.

Why doesn't the merchant at the second kind of restaurant, the one that accepts all major credit cards, do the same thing, that is, list all the cards they take? Because to do so would be too informative. Instead, such merchants either replied "Yes we take all major credit cards," or invited that inference by saying "we *even* take Carte Blanche." (If you were the caller, which cards would *you* infer you could use at Scoma's?) And finally, for reasons too obvious to mention, no one would expect the merchant simply to respond "Yes we do." Needless to say, Clark (1979) found no such uninformative responses in his results.

A Conversational Conclusion

Reflect for a moment on the difference between the research results you read about in the Reading section, and those you just studied about conversations. The differences in the two areas are almost embarrassingly large: the minute detail and precision of on-line reading research techniques can barely be compared to the intuitive hypotheses and the often crude categorization of spoken responses in the conversational research studies. While we've claimed that intuition and introspection are somewhat more reliable in settings where the mental processes are more conscious, this begins to smack of rationalization after a point. Furthermore, such reasoning eventually runs the risk of overjustifying the introspective approach (and remember what trouble *that* got us into about 80 years ago, and how long it took us to overcome "the solution to the introspection problem"). It is a rather safe prediction, consequently, that future developments in research on conversation will have to grapple seriously with issues of methodological precision. The "prize" will go to whomever can devise an analogue to the on-line reading paradigm, an "on-line conversational task."

The task we need must do two things. First, it must satisfy cognitive psychology's need for reliable, objective, and precise data. While conversation may be inherently a more difficult process to investigate carefully than reading is, this should not dissuade us from trying to improve our methods. After all, the very fact of cognitive psychology's existence attests to the ingenuity of researchers who believed that unseen mental processes *could* be investigated scientifically.

Second, the task must not sacrifice the richness and complexity of conversational interaction. In many ways, conversation is the highest and most complete expression of our cognitive processes. Normal, everyday conversation involves nearly every memory subsystem and set of processes we've discussed so far in this book, from auditory perception and pattern recognition up through the scripts stored in long-term memory. As an example, consider the role of working memory in conversation. The limited resources of working memory clearly influence our utterances in conversations. For instance, these limitations may force a speaker to reintroduce a topic if its most recent mention was too long ago, or may force a listener to ask "What are you talking about?" if the topic has been lost in the meantime. These are quite obviously the kinds of mechanisms Gernsbacher (1990) was talking about with the terms *enhancement* and *suppression,* now considered from the standpoint of the activity of working memory. If you've let your discourse focus wander away from a central concept, you've let it become suppressed. To assist the listener, you enhance that concept—you reintroduce it as the topic of a new structure that the listener should begin to build. The transitory nature of the conversational input is such that memory is more critical here than in reading.

For reasons such as these, conversation may well be the ultimate example of human cognitive processing. However difficult it may be to investigate conversation carefully, and however imprecise our theories are, we mustn't exclude conversation from our science of cognition.

Summary Points: turn taking, social roles; Intended and Inferred Topics; direct and second-order theories; conversational rules and postulates; indirect requests

CHAPTER SUMMARY

1. A variety of on-line tasks have been devised to investigate comprehension of language, for instance, tasks involving interruption during reading or hearing, and tasks requiring the subject to monitor a spoken passage for a particular target sound or word. These on-line tasks have generally supported the view that comprehension is an interactive process, in which phonetic, syntactic, lexical, and semantic or conceptual factors are in continual operation, each assisting the others during the comprehension process.

2. Sentence comprehension has been described as a process of Structure Building, in which you map incoming concepts onto the structure under construction until a new concept switches the discourse focus. Concepts enjoy an advantage of first mention in later tests of memory and for a brief time enjoy a recency advantage.

3. Reference and inference in language involve the notion of bridging, where a speaker intends a certain meaning that must be inferred by the listener. A variety of reference types exist, some requiring fairly complex bridges on the part of the listener for comprehension to succeed. The source of knowledge that permits speakers to include reference in their

messages, and listeners to infer the basis for those bridges, is not just our knowledge of syntax and word meanings, but involves the entirety of semantic memory.

4. Tremendous progress has been made in understanding the mental processes of reading, largely by using the on-line method of recording the durations and locations of eye fixations during reading. Just and Carpenter's (1987) model of reading is built on this kind of data and makes predictions concerning gaze durations and comprehension based on a variety of local and global factors; for instance, word frequency and recency in the passage influence local processing, whereas the difficulty of retrieving semantic and scripted knowledge influences global processing factors. The technology that enables this kind of investigation promises to provide a wealth of information about reading and comprehension.

5. Conversations are rather highly constrained interactions and follow an extensive, but largely implicit, set of rules. Some of these govern the selection of the speaker when a participant finishes a turn, but many more govern the nature or topic of participants' contributions. Conversational topic shifts involve selecting some part of a participant's utterance to form the basis for a new contribution, but then adding some new information. Schank's work on topic shift is a particularly important analysis of this process of topic shifting.

6. Participants in a conversation develop theories of the other speakers, called direct theories, as well as theories of what the other speakers think of them, called second-order theories. When we engage in conversation, we not only tailor our contributions to these theories, but we also follow a set of rules called conversational postulates. These postulates make up the unspoken "contract" between conversational partners. When a rule is being violated intentionally, usually to make some other point (e.g., sarcasm), we mark our violation so that its apparent illegality as a conversational move will be noticed and understood.

7. Conversation is a rich and complex topic and demonstrates the complete range of mental processing that cognitive psychology investigates. Empirical work on conversational interaction often tests general notions about direct theories, the politeness rule, or indirect requests. While such work is useful, it lacks the degree of precision that is present in reading research, for example. To further the study of conversation, on-line comprehension tasks will need to be developed.

Glossary Terms: advantage of clause recency, first mention; authorized/unauthorized; bridging; conversational postulates; cooperative principle; direct/second-order theory; enhancement; expansion; gaze duration; implication; indirect request; inference; inferred/intended topic; mapping; on-line tasks; pragmatics; reference; structure building; suppression

SUGGESTED READINGS

One of the more interesting psycholinguistic topics that was too far afield to consider here involves speech errors, errors in producing the sounds of words, say, by switching sounds among words, and more complex errors, such as substituting one word or phrase for another (see Chapter 8 Demonstrations). At the phonological level, see a thorough paper by Harley (1984). For word errors, the classic papers are by Fromkin (1971, 1973) and Garrett (1975, 1980); Dell (1986) has recently proposed a spreading activation theory of speech errors. It might be interesting to contrast what is known about such errors today with Freud's psychodynamic explanation (1901/1966), to see if the presumably ego-related "slips of the tongue" he noticed are lawfully related to the phonological and semantic explanations proposed today. Books on the psychology of language (e.g., Carroll, 1986; Gernsbacher, 1993) will contain enough references and ideas to get you going.

An interesting focus in reading comprehension research involves the "illusion of knowing," the illusion that you *do* understand a passage, even though testing reveals that you have not understood. See papers by Epstein, Glenberg, and Bradley (1984) and Glenberg, Wilkinson, and Epstein (1982). Maki and Berry (1984) have reported an interesting study on metacomprehension of textual material; in the naturalistic setting of the university classroom, they had students predict what would be remembered. And in terms of reading skill in children, see the Aaronson and Ferres (1986) paper. Several recent books provide up-to-date information on reading research; see especially *The Psychology of Reading and Language Comprehension* by Just and Carpenter (1987).

Indirect speech acts such as requests and commands still provide fertile ground for research on conversation. An interesting direction, related to our direct and second-order theories, involves a situation in which the speaker anticipates some obstacle to getting the needed information; for instance, you need to know what time it is, and your conversational partner clearly is not wearing a watch. Analyses of how we tailor our speech to overcome or take into account such obstacles are contained in Francik and Clark (1985) and Gibbs (1986b). For work on the pragmatic and non-linguistic contexts of conversations, see McNeill's (1985) review, entitled "So you think gestures are nonverbal?"; see Giles and Coupland (1991) for a treatment from sociological perspectives. And finally, consult any recent paper by Clark, the acknowledged leader in the field of conversational research, for further work on the processes of reference (e.g., Clark & Marshall, 1981; Clark & Wilkes-Gibbs, 1986; Isaacs & Clark, 1987; Wilkes-Gibbs & Clark, 1992).

NEUROCOGNITION

Of fundamental importance, the nervous system is the product of a long evolution. The original functions of some parts have been altered by layer upon layer of modifications. . . . We cannot expect the design of the brain to resemble anything that a human would consider optimal. (Sejnowski & Churchland, 1989, p. 341)

Just where memory is localized in the brain is a beguilingly simple question. (Squire, 1987, p. 56)

One cannot have an adequate theory about anything the brain does unless one also has an adequate theory about that activity itself. . . . To paraphrase Wittgenstein, one can know every brain connection involved in concept formation, but that won't help one bit in understanding what a concept is. (Gardner, 1985, pp. 286–287)

Two Stories In Chapter 7, you read about patient K.C., whose accident left him with a profound amnesia. Despite his brain damage, he is perfectly competent at language, his intelligence is normal, and he is able to converse on any number of topics. But when asked about an experience from his past, he cannot truly remember; often he manages to reconstruct a plausible "memory" based on general knowledge. K.C.'s brain damage seemed to destroy his ability to access episodic memory, while leaving his semantic memory system intact. This pattern, *a disruption in one component of memory but no impairment of another,* is termed a **dissociation.** Can episodic and semantic memories be one and the same, given K.C.'s dissociation between the two? Probably not.

Patient P.S. was a 38-year-old financial analyst when a malformation of blood arteries and vessels in her brain hemorrhaged, causing appreciable damage in the temporal lobe of her left hemisphere. Extensive testing (Sokol, McCloskey, Cohen, & Aliminosa, 1991) revealed a startling dissociation in her ability to perform simple mathematics. She made a substantial number of errors to simple multiplication facts. For instance, to 7×7 and 9×4, she made 78% and 83% errors, respectively. To *any* single digit problem with a zero, she was *always* wrong (e.g., she'd say $0 \times 2 = 2$). But she only made two *rule* errors in the 66 "long multiplication problems" she worked, problems like 193×17. Both errors were forgetting to carry to the next column. Is our knowledge of arithmetic and math one single, indivisible collection of information? P.S.'s disruption suggests not: she seemed to demonstrate a dissociation between simple fact retrieval and the calculation procedures of multiplication.

How must the cognitive system be organized for disruptions like these to take place?

You've now studied a great deal about human memory and cognitive processes, and you've read the highlights about human language. With this background, you are now ready to digest some of the newest and most fascinating evidence in the field of cognitive science, evidence on the relationships between the brain and human cognition. Because the terminology necessary for talking about the brain can be daunting, it seemed reasonable to postpone a complete treatment of this topic until you were solidly grounded in the basics of memory and language. But now that you have this foundation, you can launch into a study of the brain. We'll cover some basics of neurology and brain anatomy, then deal with two primary topics, brain-related deficits first in language and then in memory.

This area of investigation is sometimes referred to as *cognitive neuropsychology,* a "hybrid term . . . applied to the analysis of those handicaps in human cognitive function which result from brain injury" (McCarthy & Warrington, 1990, p. 1). One such handicap that you may know about is a language disruption, often caused by stroke, called *aphasia.* But as important as the evidence from brain damage is, we also need other kinds of evidence too, for instance, about the neurochemical and neurobiological activities that support normal learning and thought processes, changes in the brain that accompany aging, and so on. We are therefore interested in contributions from all the various neurosciences—neurochemistry, neurobiology, neuroanatomy, all the "neuro-somethings"—as they relate to human cognition. Because existing terms often have different or even controversial connotations, I have elected to call this field the study of *neurocognition,* the neuroscience of cognition.

Understanding cognitive handicaps is an obvious goal; no one can dispute the importance of rehabilitation and retraining for victims of brain damage. But our interest in cognitive science goes a step further. We want to understand *normal* cognition from the standpoint of the human brain. That is, we wish to learn about normal cognition through whatever means are available to us. Toward this goal, more and more investigators are beginning to examine the behavioral and cognitive effects of brain damage (e.g., McCloskey, 1992). As you'll see throughout the chapter, sometimes the great misfortune of brain damage leads to a clearer understanding of normal processes.

It has always been important to cognitive psychology that its theories and models not contradict known neurological and physiological effects—this goes without saying, of course. But more than this, cognitive theorists have often been quick to point out the plausibility of their theoretical constructs in terms of brain structures and processes; for instance, spreading activation resembles the spreading patterns of neuronal interaction, and the basic data structure in connectionist models is decidedly brain-like (hence the alternate name *neural net modeling*). Recently, however, this interdisciplinary approach has seen cognitive psychology informing the neurosciences, providing new outlooks, tasks, and conceptual tools with which to address significant questions about neurological functioning (e.g., Kounios & Holcomb, 1992). In the opinions of several researchers (e.g., Moscovitch, 1979; Seron, 1982), the cognitive influence on the neurosciences has been a rejuvenating one, though also one that has posed new and often more difficult questions. As is becoming even clearer now, the "cross-fertilization" between the neurosciences and cognition is beneficial, even crucial, for both areas.

Needless to say, the treatment here can only focus on a few highlights of the topic of neurocognition; as Crick and Asanuma (1986, p. 333) said of their chapter, "It is clearly impossible to describe most of what is known, even though this represents [only] a tiny fraction of what one would like to know." To ensure that you understand both the nature of the evidence and its significance for cognitive science, I've introduced several simplifications, especially in terminology and in the scope of topics to be considered. Clearly, this chapter is only an introduction to the topic, barely scratching the surface of a genuinely complex area. Consider the material here as (possibly) your *first* systematic exposure to the topic of brain and cognitive processes. And throughout the chapter, bear in mind that the cognitive psychology of the future will be even *more* neurocognitive in its interests and scope.

Let me repeat the point from above, to make sure our purpose is clear. Why should you be interested in these topics, the anatomy of the brain, the effects of brain damage, and the like? Because studying how cognitive processes can be impaired, destroyed, preserved, or splintered apart by brain damage may give us new insights about the normal mind and how it works. The stories are fascinating, to be sure. But for cognitive science, the *implications* of the stories are even more so.

▼ Basic Neurology

At birth, the human brain weighs approximately 400 grams (about 14 oz). It grows to an average of 1450 grams in adults, slightly over 3 pounds, and is roughly the size of a ripe grapefruit. The basic building block of the brain, indeed of the entire nervous system, is the **neuron,** *the cell that is specialized for receiving and transmitting a neural impulse.* Neurons are the components that form nerve tracts throughout the body as well as all the structures of the brain. How many neurons are there in the brain? Unfortunately, the available estimates vary tremendously. Kolb and Whishaw (1990) suggest a grand total of 180 *billion* cells of all types in the brain, including not only neurons but nonneural cells too (e.g., connective and circulatory tissue). An estimated 50 billion of these cells are, in Kolb and Whishaw's estimate, neurons that are "directly engaged in information processing" and cognition (p. 4). To put that figure in perspective, consider that the Milky Way galaxy has on the order of 100 billion stars.[1]

---

[1]Intuitively, it would seem a rather straightforward job of getting an accurate estimate of the number of neurons in the brain. Yet as several authors point out (e.g., Squire, 1987), estimation techniques rely on counting neurons in some small portion of the brain and then extrapolating to the whole brain. This procedure is suspect because the density of neurons varies widely in different brain regions, as does the density and thickness of different structures.

Neurons

Figure 10-1A illustrates an idealized or prototypical neuron. While the details of structure vary, each neuron within the nervous system shows the same general principles. At one end of the neuron, many small branch-like fingers called *dendrites* serve to "gather" a neural impulse into the neuron itself. In somewhat more familiar terms, the dendrites are the *input* structures of the neuron, taking in the message that is being passed along in a particular neural tract.

The central portion of each neuron is the cell body or *soma* and is the place where the biological activity of the cell is regulated. Extending from the cell body is a longish extension or tube, the *axon,* that ends in another set of branch-like structures called *axon terminals* or sometimes *terminal arborizations;* the latter term obviously derives from the tree-like form that these structures have. The axon terminals represent the *output* end of the neuron, the place where the neural impulse ends *within* the neuron itself. Obviously, this is the location where an influence on the *next* neuron in the pathway must take place.

Figure 10-1B gives a schematic diagram of the basic elements of the nervous system that are activated during a simple reflex, for example, jerking your arm away when you accidentally touch a hot stove. *Receptor cells* react to the physical stimulus and trigger a pattern of firing down a sequence of *sensory neurons.* The tracts of sensory neurons pass the message along into the spinal cord, which normally routes the message in two directions. For the simple reflex action, the message loops quickly through the spinal cord and then goes back out to the arm muscles through a tract of *motor neurons.* These terminate at the *effector cells,* which connect directly to the muscle fibers and cause the muscles to pull your arm away from the hot stove.

As the reflex triggers the quick return of a message out to the muscles, it simultaneously routes a message up the spinal cord and into the brain. Thus the second route involves only the central nervous system, the spinal cord and brain. There is only one kind of neuron in the central nervous system, called an *interneuron* or *association neuron.* Because we are concerned only with the brain here, we are interested only in the interneurons of the central nervous system. Thus, for the rest of the chapter, we'll simply refer to "neurons" rather than "interneurons."

Synapses There may be relatively few or many axon terminals emanating from a single neuron. In either case, these terminals will be adjacent to dendrites from other neurons. Thus an impulse within a neuron terminates at the axon terminals and is "taken up" by the dendrites of the next neurons in the pathway, the neurons whose dendrites are adjacent to the axon terminals. This *region where the axon terminals of one neuron and the dendrites of another come together* is known as the **synapse.** For the most part, the neurons do not actually touch one another (some regions of the brain contradict this rule). Instead, the

FIGURE 10-1

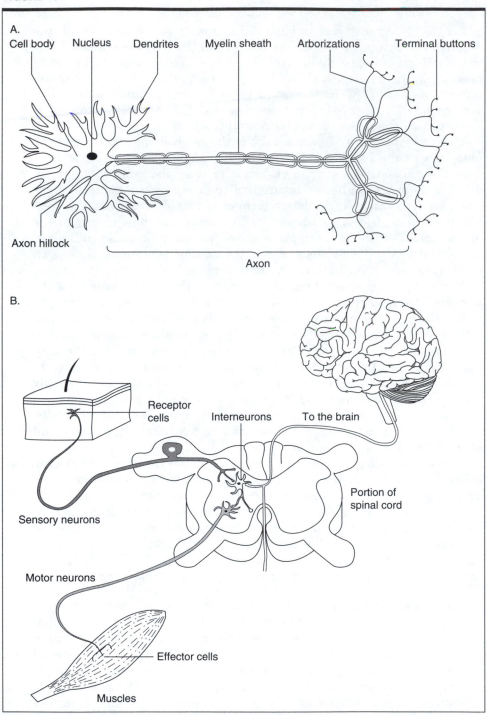

A.

Cell body   Nucleus   Dendrites   Myelin sheath   Arborizations   Terminal buttons

Axon hillock

Axon

B.

Receptor cells

Interneurons   To the brain

Sensory neurons

Portion of spinal cord

Motor neurons

Effector cells

Muscles

An illustration of the various structures of a neuron. Note that the lower diagram illustrates a sensory-motor reflex arc.

FIGURE 10-2

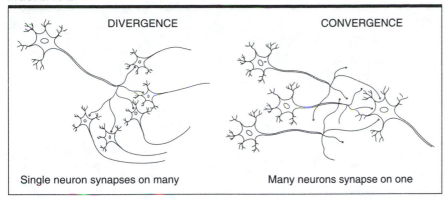

DIVERGENCE   CONVERGENCE

Single neuron synapses on many   Many neurons synapse on one

The patterns of divergence and convergence in the nervous system.

synapses in the human nervous system are extremely small physical gaps or clefts between the neurons. Note also that the word *synapse* is used as a verb: a neuron is said to *synapse* on another, meaning that it passes its message on to that other neuron.

A general law of the nervous system, especially in the brain, is that any single neuron will synapse on a large number of other neurons. The evidence for this *divergence* is that a typical neuron synapses on anywhere from 100 to 1000 other neurons (e.g., Squire, 1987). Likewise, many different neurons will synapse on a single "destination" neuron, known as *convergence*. Figure 10-2 shows a schematic diagram of neurons, as a visual summary of these basic laws and principles.

For the bulk of the nervous system, the "bridge" across the synaptic cleft involves chemical activity within the synaptic cleft itself. A neuron releases a chemical *transmitter substance,* or simply a *neurotransmitter,* from small *buttons* or *sacs* in the axon terminals. This chemical "fits into" specific receptor sites on the dendrites of the next neuron and thereby causes some effect on that next neuron. There are two general effects possible, *excitation and inhibition.* A *Type I* neuron contains a neurotransmitter that has an excitatory effect; it tends to activate or fire the neuron on which it synapses. *Type II* neurons, conversely, release a different kind of neurotransmitter, one that has an inhibitory effect; it tends to prevent the firing of the neuron on which it synapses. As Crick and Asanuma (1986) point out, this "working assumption" about Type I and II neurons is important for several reasons, including the important observation that "no axon makes Type I synapses at some sites while making Type II at others" (p. 339). In other words, if neuron *a* makes an excitatory synapse on neuron *b,* then *a* will not also inhibit neuron *c* (but of course some *other* neuron could inhibit either or both of *b and c*). Figure 10-3 illustrates the physical differences between Type I and II synapses.

FIGURE 10-3

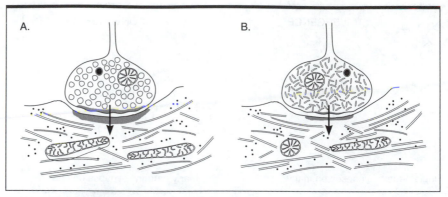

Idealized diagrams of a Type I (A) and Type II (B) synapse. See text for explanation. (From Crick & Asanuma, 1986.)

Neurotransmitters   Some 30 different neurotransmitters have been identified and studied[2] (Iversen, 1979). Many seem to have rather ordinary functions, maintaining the physical integrity of the living organism, for instance. Others, especially *acetylcholine* and possibly norepinephrine, seem to have major influences on cognitive processes like learning and memory (Drachman, 1978; Sitaran, Weingartner, Caine, & Gillin, 1978; Squire, 1987). Interestingly, decreased levels of acetylcholine have been found in the brains of people with Alzheimer's disease. It's tantalizing to suggest this as part of the explanation for the learning and memory deficits observed among such patients, although it could instead be a side effect of the disease (e.g., Riley, 1989). In either case, the result suggests that acetylcholine plays some kind of essential role in normal learning and memory processes.

Before leaving the neuronal level of the nervous system, note that significant research is being done on various psychobiochemical properties of the neural system, for instance, the direct influence that different chemical agents have on neurotransmitters, and the resulting behavioral changes. As an example, Thompson (1986) describes progress in identifying neuronal changes believed to underlie memory storage and retrieval. Just as various psychoactive drugs affect the functioning of the nervous system in a physical sense, current research is now identifying the effects of drugs and other treatments on the functioning of the nervous system in a psychological or cognitive sense. At a more global level, related work by Nelson, McSpadden, Fromme, and Marlatt (1986), for example, has examined the influence of alcohol intoxication on metamemory and long-term memory retrieval. In general, Nelson et al. found that alcohol depressed recall from long-term memory but did not lead to a

[2]Kolb and Whishaw (1990) count 10 "classical" neurotransmitters and about 25 peptides that seem to exert similar effects.

generalized overconfidence effect in the subjects' estimates of their ability to recall. This is quite unlike the overconfidence that intoxicated persons show when they estimate their abilities to drive while intoxicated, for example.

Summary Points: neuronal structure—dendrites, soma, axon, axon terminals, synapse; neurotransmitters; excitatory and inhibitory action; acetylcholine

Brain Anatomy

Ignoring many levels of intermediate neural functioning and complexity, we now take a tremendous leap from the level of single neurons to the level of the entire brain, the awesomely complex "biological computer." To account for all human behavior, including bodily functions that occur involuntarily (e.g., digestion), would require an extensive discussion of both the central and the peripheral nervous systems. But to explore neurocognition, we can essentially limit ourselves to just the central nervous system, the brain and spinal cord. In fact, our discussion even omits much of the central nervous system too, save for the **neocortex** (or **cerebral cortex**) that sits at the top of the human brain, and a few other nearby structures.

In Figure 10-4, the physically lower brain structures are referred to

FIGURE 10-4

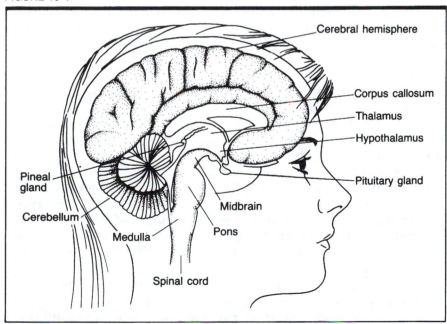

Some of the major components of the human brain. The lower components ("old brain") are visible in the figure because the outer layer of the neocortex has been cut away.

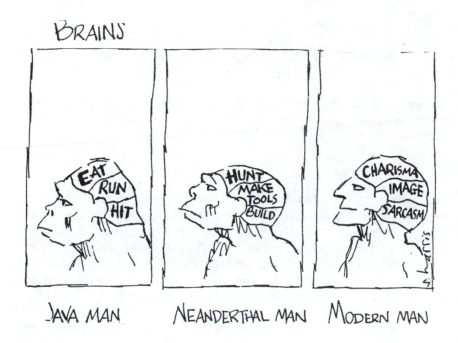

BRAINS

JAVA MAN   NEANDERTHAL MAN   MODERN MAN

collectively as the "old brain" or "brain stem." This portion of the brain is older in terms of evolution, for the most part governing basic, primitive functions (digestion, heartbeat, breathing). The various old brain structures are present in all mammals.

Figure 10-5 shows the **neocortex,** *the top layer of the brain, responsible for higher-level mental processes.* The neocortex is a wrinkled, convoluted structure that virtually surrounds the old brain. Laid out flat, each of the two halves or hemispheres would cover about a square meter, and be the thickness of the cover of a hardback book. The wrinkling is "nature's solution to the problem of confining the huge neocortical surface area within a shell that is still small enough to pass through the birth canal" (Kolb & Whishaw, 1990, p. 15). It is the most recent structure to have evolved in the human brain and is considerably larger in humans than in lower animals; compare the average weight in humans, 1450 grams, to that of the great apes, 400 grams.

Because it is primarily responsible for higher mental processes such as language and thought, it is not surprising that the human neocortex is so large, relative to the rest of the brain. About three-fourths of the neurons in the human brain are in the neocortex. The number of neurons in the neocortex has been estimated at anywhere from 5 to 100 billion; from 10 to 20 billion is a safe, if possibly conservative, figure.

A side view, as in Figure 10-5, reveals the four general regions or *lobes* of the neocortex; clockwise from the front, these are the *frontal lobe, parietal lobe, occipital lobe, and temporal lobe,* named after the skull bones on top of them (e.g., the temporal lobes lie beneath your temples). Note

FIGURE 10-5

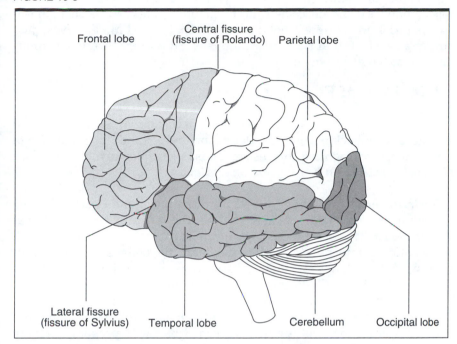

The major components of the cortex.

that these lobes are not separate from one another in the brain. Instead, each hemisphere of the neocortex is a single sheet of neural matter. The lobes are formed by the larger folds and convolutions of the cortex, with the names used as convenient reference terms for the regions. As an example, the central fissure, or fissure of Rolando, shown in the figure is merely one of the deeper folds in the brain, serving as a convenient land-mark between the frontal and parietal lobes.

Three other subcortical (below the neocortex) structures are especially important to neurocognition. Deep inside the lower brain structures is the **thalamus,** meaning "inner room" or "chamber." It is often referred to as the gateway to the cortex, since virtually all messages entering the cortex come through the thalamus (a portion of the sense of smell is one of the very few exceptions). In other words, the thalamus is the major relay station from the sensory systems of the body into the neocortex.

Just above the thalamus is a broad band of nerve fibers called the **corpus callosum.** As described later, the corpus callosum ("callous body") is the primary bridge across which messages pass between the left and right halves of the neocortex.

The third structure is the **hippocampus,** from the Latin for "sea horse," referring to its curved shape. The hippocampus lies immediately interior to the temporal lobes, that is, underneath the temporal lobes but in the same horizontal plane. Research on the effects of damage to the hippocampus will be described later, including one of the best known case histories in neuropsychology, that of patient H.M. For now, just learn one new fact, that the hippocampus is critical for storing new information into long-term memory.

Principles of Functioning

Two important principles of functioning in the neocortex are described here, necessary background knowledge for understanding the effects of brain damage on cognitive processes. These principles involve the ideas of *contralaterality* and *hemispheric specialization*.

Contralaterality   When viewed from the top, the neocortex is seen to be divided into two mirror-image halves, the **left and right cerebral hemispheres.** This of course follows a general law of anatomy, that with the exception of internal organs like the heart, the body is basically bilaterally symmetrical, has symmetrical structure on both sides (*lateral* simply means "to the side"). What is somewhat surprising, however, is that the control centers for one side of the body are in the *opposite* hemisphere of the brain. This is *contralaterality* (*contra* means against or opposite). In other words, for evolutionary reasons that will probably remain obscure forever, the right hemisphere of the brain receives its input from the left side of the body, and also controls the left side. Likewise, the left hemisphere receives input from and controls output to the right side of the body.[3]

Figure 10-6 shows the principle of contralaterality in the context of visual input, where the principle is a bit trickier to understand. The contralaterality in vision goes from the visual field to the hemispheres of the brain. That is, a visual stimulus that appears out in front and to your left is in your left visual field. This image is "projected to" the contralateral hemisphere—to the right hemisphere—for initial processing. Likewise, if a visual stimulus appears off to your right, in your right visual field, then it is initially projected to the left hemisphere. As the figure shows, the reason for this pattern relates to the structure of the retina; the left *half* of each retina projects its inputs to the left hemisphere, the right *half* of each retina projects to the right hemisphere. Of course, contralateral projection from visual field—or any other sense modality—to brain does not yield segregation of the information in the normal brain. That is, because information in one hemisphere is readily transmitted to the oth-

---

[3]Coghill's (1929) speculation on the original cause for contralaterality is sensible, though admittedly not verifiable. Imagine a simple creature, wiggling through the "primordial ooze" millions of years ago, being attacked from the left by a predator. A motor reflex *to the right* would be highly adaptive for the organism, evolutionarily speaking. Thus the contralaterality of sensory–motor connections may have originally been due to the "survival value" of contralateral reflexive actions.

FIGURE 10-6

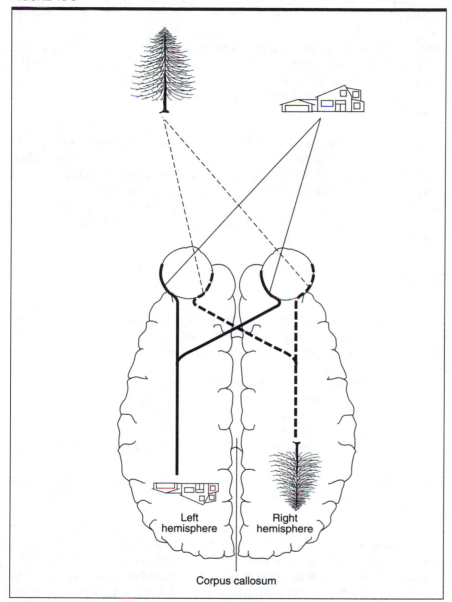

Left
hemisphere

Right
hemisphere

Corpus callosum

The figure depicts the binocular pathways of information flow from the eyes into the visual cortex of the brain. The patterns of stimulus-to-brain pathways demonstrate the contralaterality of the visual system. Note that the pine tree is shown entirely in the left visual field, so it is projected onto the visual cortex of the right hemisphere; the house is presented to the right visual field and hence is projected onto the left hemisphere.

er hemisphere via the corpus callosum, the information passes freely back and forth.

Hemispheric Specialization   The second surprise concerning lateralization in the neocortex involves different specializations within the two cerebral hemispheres. Despite their mirror-image appearance, the two hemispheres *do not* mirror one another's abilities. Instead, each hemisphere tends to specialize in different abilities and tends to process different kinds of information. This is the full principle of **cerebral lateralization and specialization,** that *different functions or actions within the brain tend to rely more heavily on one hemisphere or the other, or tend to be performed differently in the two hemispheres.* This is *not* to say that some process or function can *only* happen in one particular hemisphere. It merely says that there is often a tendency, sometimes strong, for one or the other hemisphere to be especially dominant in different processes or functions.

The most obvious evidence of lateralization in humans is the overwhelming incidence of right-handedness, across all cultures and apparently throughout the known history of human evolution (e.g., Corballis, 1989). Accompanying this tendency toward right-handedness is a particularly strong left-hemispheric specialization in humans for language. That is, for the majority of people, language ability is especially lateralized in the left hemisphere of the neocortex: countless studies have demonstrated this general tendency.

In contrast, the right cerebral hemisphere seems to be somewhat more specialized than the left hemisphere for nonverbal, spatial, and more perceptual information processing (see Moscovitch, 1979, for a review of the range of such left–right hemisphere characterizations). The evidence suggests, for instance, that face recognition (Ellis, 1983) and mental rotation (Deutsch, Bourbon, Papanicolaou, & Eisenberg, 1988), both requiring spatial and perceptual processing, are especially dependent on the right cerebral hemisphere. Table 10-1 provides a summary of data on cerebral lateralization.

Most people have heard of these "left brain/right brain" issues, often from the popular press. Such treatments are notorious for exaggerating and oversimplifying what's known about laterality and specialization. For instance, in these descriptions the left hemisphere ends up with the rational, logical, and symbolic abilities—the boring ones—while the right hemisphere gets the holistic, creative, and intuitive processes—the sexy ones. Corballis (1989) notes that the right hemisphere achieves "a certain cult status" in some such treatments.

But even ignoring that, it's far too easy to misunderstand the principle of hemispheric lateralization and specialization, too easy to say "process X happens in *this* hemisphere, process Y in *that* one." Consider a rather ordinary act, the naming of a picture. What are the mental processes necessary for this act, and where are those processes performed in the

Table 10-1   SUMMARY OF DATA ON CEREBRAL LATERALIZATION

Function	Left Hemisphere	Right Hemisphere
Visual system	Letters, words	Complex geometric patterns, faces
Auditory system	Language-related sounds	Nonlanguage environmental sounds, music
Somatosensory system	?	Tactile recognition of complex patterns, Braille
Movement	Complex voluntary movement	Movements in spatial patterns
Memory	Verbal memory	Nonverbal memory
Language	Speech, reading, writing, arithmetic	Prosody?
Spatial processes		Geometry, sense of direction, mental rotation of shapes

Functions of the respective hemispheres that are predominantly mediated by one hemisphere in right-handed people. (From Kolb & Whishaw, 1990.)

neocortex? At a minimum, picture naming involves some visual analysis and encoding of the picture itself, along with perceptual organization to segregate the figure from the background. After encoding the picture as a memory trace, it would then have to be matched to information in semantic memory, followed by a lexical access process to retrieve the name. Finally, some set of motor responses must be set into motion, in order to say the name out loud.

Disruption of any one of these processes could lead to an inability to name the picture, of course. The more important point here is that "simple" picture naming has tapped mental processes and procedures from a variety of brain regions in both hemispheres and requires a complex coordination of those processes. Thus several different patients, each with dramatically different localized brain damage, could show an inability to name the pictures, each for a different reason relating to different lateralized processes.

Nonetheless, there is rather striking division of labor in the neocortex, in which the left cerebral hemisphere is specialized for language. This is almost always true: it characterizes up to 85% or 90% of the population. The percentages are this high, however, *only if* you are a right-handed male, with no family history of left-handedness, and if you write with your hand in a normal rather than inverted position (e.g., Friedman & Polson, 1981). If you are female, if you are left-handed, if you write with an inverted hand position, and so on, then the "left hemisphere/language rule" is not quite as strong. In such groups, the majority will have the customary pattern, but the percentages will not be as high as 85–90%. Thus directing language input to the left cerebral hemisphere will be optimal and efficient for many people, but not for all. (For simplicity, however, we will rely on the convenient fiction of "language in the left hemisphere" for the rest of the chapter.)

Split Brain Research

Despite the exaggerated claims you often read, there is in fact a good deal of careful empirical work on the topic of lateralization and specialization of different regions in the two hemispheres. Among the best known is the research on *split brain patients*.

Prior to about 1960, evidence for hemispheric specialization had been rather indirect; neurologists and researchers would simply note the location and kind of head injury that was sustained, and the kind of behavioral or cognitive deficit that was observed after the injury. Sperry (e.g., 1964), however, put the facts of anatomy together with a surgical procedure for severe epilepsy. In this operation, the corpus callosum is completely severed in order to restrict the epileptic seizure to just one of the cerebral hemispheres. For patients who required this radical surgery, a remarkably informative test could be administered, one that could reveal the different abilities and actions of the two cerebral hemispheres. That is, from the standpoint of brain functioning, when a patient's corpus callosum is surgically cut, the two hemispheres are unable to communicate with each other. Sperry's technique was to test such people by directing sensory information to one side or the other of the body—for instance, placing a pencil in the left or right hand of such a patient, or presenting a visual stimulus to the left or right visual field.

The effect of the surgery, of course, was to prevent the neural activation that arrived in one hemisphere from crossing over to the other hemisphere. Thus if a patient had a pencil placed in the left hand (the patients were prevented from seeing the objects and their hands, of course), the neural impulse would be directed to the right hemisphere, but then would be unable to cross over into the left hemisphere. The patients were usually able to demonstrate the *use* for the object when the sensation was "sent" to the right hemisphere, by making the appropriate hand movements, as if they were writing with the pencil. Nonetheless, they were usually *not* able to name the object unless it was placed in their right hands. This is exactly what would be expected from someone whose knowledge of language is localized in the left hemisphere, but whose perceptual, nonverbal knowledge is localized in the right hemisphere. Similar effects were obtained with purely visual stimuli as well, that is, when the left half of a picture was projected to the right hemisphere, and vice versa. (Incidentally, Sperry earned the Nobel Prize for medicine in 1981 for his research; the award was made jointly to him and to Hubel and Wiesel, whose research on specialized feature detectors in the visual cortex was described in Chapter 3.)

While the principle of contralaterality has been a mainstay of neurological research for a long period of time, recent evidence suggests that lateralization of skills is usually not as absolute as was previously believed. For instance, split brain patients sometimes showed some limited language abilities in the right hemisphere. For such reasons, current researchers usually subscribe to the less extreme version of this principle given earlier. For instance, we say that different functions tend to occur more or less *efficiently* in one hemisphere or the other, or tend to occur somewhat *differently* in one side or the other (e.g., Friedman & Polson, 1981; Moscovitch, 1979; see Gardner, 1985, for a particularly lucid discussion of such differences and their consequences).

One danger in the too-simple principle of lateralization is that it overlooks the *plasticity* of the human brain, for instance, the ability of one part of the brain to take over the functions of a region that has sustained some sort of damage, say, through stroke or accident. Some evidence suggests that the younger an individual is, the more plasticity will be apparent in recuperation from such damage (plasticity is also higher for left-handed persons). On the other hand, there is at least some evidence to suggest that the area that takes over in the event of damage may forfeit its own "normal" function (e.g., Woods, 1980) or may perform the new function in less than an optimal fashion; see Aram and Eisele (1992) for a review of evidence that challenges the traditional view of plasticity. (Note that plasticity, in the sense that neurons may "grow" new synaptic pathways, may also be implicated in normal learning and memory; see Gallagher, 1985, and Thompson, 1986.)

Summary Points: neocortex, left and right hemispheres, lobes; contralaterality; hemispheric specialization; plasticity

▼ Methods of Investigation

The methods for investigating the structure and functioning of the brain fall into two broad categories, those involving medically based techniques and those based on behavioral assessments.

Medically Based Techniques

Lesions   Needless to say, the investigation techniques used by Sperry, deliberate lesioning of the brain, are limited in their usefulness for revealing the secrets of cognitive processing. Only two kinds of subjects, laboratory animals and patients with medical conditions requiring brain surgery, can be used. A long-standing tradition, however, reports case studies of people who by disease or accident have experienced damage—lesions—to the brain. Much of the evidence described below on language and memory disruptions comes from such cases, victims of strokes, aneurysms, head injuries, and other accidental circumstances. In all cases, the site of the brain lesion is an important guide to the kind of disruption in behavior that is observed, and vice versa (e.g., neurologists attempt to determine the location of a lesion based on how the behavior has been altered).

FIGURE 10-7

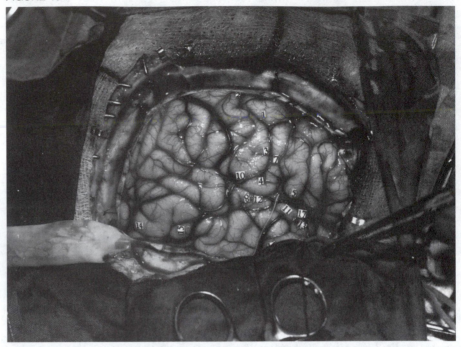

The exposed cortex of one of Penfield's patients. Numbers indicate the areas of the brain Penfield stimulated with the electric probe. When the area numbered 13 was stimulated, the patient recalled a circus scene. Stimulation of other areas also evoked specific memories.

Direct Stimulation   A variety of other techniques have also been used to study localization and specialization of function in the brain. In particular, consider the method of direct stimulation, pioneered by Penfield, the famous Canadian neurosurgeon. In Penfield's technique, the patient in brain surgery remains conscious during the surgery, having only a local anesthetic in order to prevent pain in the scalp. The surgeon then applies minute electrical charges to the exposed brain, thus triggering very small regions. The patient is then asked to answer questions or report out loud on the thoughts and memories that enter awareness. By comparing the patient's reports to the different regions that are stimulated, a kind of map of cerebral functioning can be developed; see Figure 10-7.

Generally, the patients in Penfield's procedure reported ideas or episodes that had a dream-like quality to them. Although they often reported seemingly distinct memories, it was seldom possible to check on the accuracy of these reports. Their dream-like nature suggests that they were heavily influenced by reconstructive processes; that is, they may not have been genuine, recalled memories. On the other hand, by stimulating different regions of the exposed brain, a great deal has been discovered about the localization of different functions, kinds of knowledge, and so on, in different parts of the neocortex (e.g., Ojemann, 1982; Ojemann & Creutzfeldt, 1987; Penfield & Jasper, 1954; Penfield & Milner, 1958).

While such research often yields fascinating evidence, it has some clear-cut difficulties. For one thing, it is necessarily restricted to clinical settings, that is, patients requiring brain surgery. Second, there is at least some evidence that the organization of a patient's brain function may differ from the normal pattern quite substantially, for instance, in epileptic patients (Kolb & Whishaw, 1990), thus questioning the generality of such results.

Imaging Technology   Considerable work is now being done with the amazing recent developments in the medical technology of brain imaging. Imaging techniques such as the *CT scan* (computerized tomography) and *MRI* (magnetic resonance imaging) can give surprisingly clear pictures of the structure of the brain, as shown in the Demonstrations section. More exciting still are techniques that yield images of the *functioning* of the brain, for instance, the *PET scan* (positron emission tomography) or *functional MRI* techniques (see the color illustrations). In this technique, the image shows regions of the brain with heightened neural activity, with different colors reflecting high or low levels of blood flow, oxygen uptake, and the like. An obvious advantage to these techniques is that they show the brain in action, rather than just showing the physical structures in the brain. A second advantage is that they can be applied with (apparently) minimal risk to normal subjects.

The set of color pictures from Tulving's (1989) paper on the dissociation between episodic and semantic memory relied on a similar procedure, computer-assisted detection of blood flow patterns in a patient injected with an irradiated substance that binds to oxygen in the blood.

EEGs and ERPs   You've already read of two studies that represent an important contemporary research method. Traditionally, brain wave patterns were studied rather crudely with *EEG* recordings, *electroencephalograms*. In this technique, electrodes are attached to the subject's scalp, and the device records the patterns of brain waves. More recently, researchers have focused in particular on *event-related potentials, ERPs,* the momentary changes in electrical activity of the brain when a particular stimulus is presented to the subject (e.g., Donchin, 1981).

Figures 6-8 and 8-10 both depicted the results of this exciting ERP technology. By carefully controlling surrounding conditions, and measuring the elapsed time since a stimulus was presented, we can begin to see how the electrical activity of the brain changes *moment by moment* when the subject is processing a stimulus. As you'll recall from Chapter 6, there was a noticeable negative swing in electrical potential, approxi-

DEMONSTRATIONS

Most people are fascinated with the various imaging and brain investigation techniques that are used in empirical and clinical settings. Because of that fascination, and because few if any projects on brain–cognition relationships will be feasible without specialized equipment and populations of subjects, this Demonstrations section presents brief descriptions of some of these techniques.

Noninvasive Procedures

In addition to the type of research discussed in the text about testing normal individuals, the other major noninvasive procedure involves **EEG** (electroencephalogram) recordings, the brain wave technique that forms the basis for the **ERP** technique.

Electrodes are attached to the subject's scalp, and the electrodes transmit records of the changes in electrical activity of the brain to the recording machine. The traditional paper-and-pen system is rapidly being replaced by computer-assisted storage and analysis of the brain wave patterns.

In the **ERP** technique, brain waves are recorded in conjunction with specific stimuli presented to the subject, such that the ERP record can be analyzed as a function of the precise onset of the experimental stimulus. ERPs are analyzed in terms of positive or negative changes, relative to baseline, in "chunks" of time; for example, a negative change within the period of 300–500 msec after the stimulus would be a N400 ERP, a negative change centered around the 400-msec time interval.

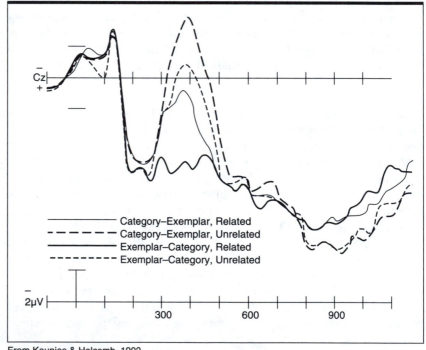

From Kounios & Holcomb, 1992.

Imaging Techniques

Full descriptions of the more technical aspects of these techniques are presented in Kolb and Whishaw (1990).

MRI and Functional MRI   MRI, which stands for magnetic resonance imaging, is a technique that produces picture-like images of the brain (or of any anatomical structure). Functional MRI uses the MRI technology to provide images of the dynamic changes in brain activity as it processes information. In either case, the subject is placed in a strong magnetic field, and through a complicated process involving radio waves, the variations in the magnetic field are processed into pictures of the brain tissue by computer.

The test is somewhat unpleasant, especially for people who are claustrophobic; the subject must lie motionless in a small space, surrounded by an extremely noisy machine, for upward of 20–30 minutes. The test is also rather costly. On the other hand, the test is considered to be quite safe, since the magnetic fields and radio waves are not dangerous. And recent applications (see the color illustration on page 493 from Schneider, Noll, & Cohen, 1993) have achieved mapping of brain activity with 1-mm^2 (1 square millimeter) resolution.

A. Overall procedure for obtaining brain scans with a video display.

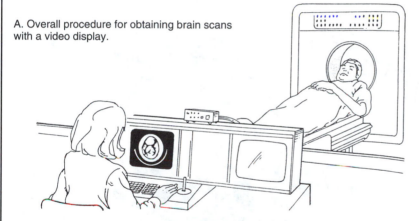

Brain scanning techniques. All cognitive activities—from reading this text, to feeling anxious over a test, to listening to a lecture on modern architecture—are accompanied by an increased demand for energy within localized areas of the brain. These demands are met by increased blood flow and glucose supply. By monitoring oxygen, glucose, and blood flow, it is possible to identify the areas of increased metabolism and hence determine which areas of the brain are most active. (From Solso, 1992.)

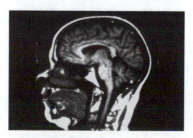

MRI scan.

CT Scan   Whereas a simple x-ray picture is two-dimensional, CT scans provide approximations to three-dimensional pictures of the brain. Basically, a beam of x-rays is passed through the brain. The amount of radiation not absorbed by the brain is detected on the opposite side, and this pattern is recorded in a computer's memory. This process repeats, in 1° steps, going around the head. The computer then reconstructs cross-sectional images of the brain, where each cross-section shows a different plane or "slice" of x-ray pictures through the brain.

The technique is especially useful for locating tumors and damage due to vascular (e.g., hemorrhage) or physical injury; because it shows only the physical structure, it cannot detect dynamic conditions such as epilepsy. Exposure to x-rays and cost are the major drawbacks to the technique.

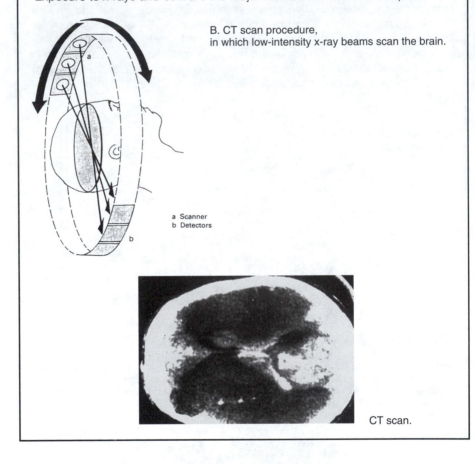

B. CT scan procedure, in which low-intensity x-ray beams scan the brain.

a Scanner
b Detectors

CT scan.

mately 400 msec after the target stimulus was presented, when the target was semantically unrelated to the prime (the N400 ERP; Kounios & Holcomb, 1992). In Chapter 8, a P600 ERP—a positive swing approximately 600 msec after the stimulus—was observed when subjects encountered a syntactically anomalous word or phrase in a sentence.

PET Scan   In a PET scan, the subject is given a substance, often glucose or oxygen, that has been tagged radioactively. Because bloodflow will increase to areas of the brain that are active, radioactivity should be higher in those areas that are most active. Thus the PET scan measures the concentrations of radioactivity across the brain. These concentrations are recorded by a special detector, saved in a computer's memory, and then used to recon-struct pictures of the brain. In the images output by the computer, color codes are used to indicate degrees of activity or inactivity.

The value of the technique is that, like functional MRI, it responds to *activity* in the brain, not just structure or anatomy. Drawbacks would include cost and possible risks associated with exposure to radioactive substances. A disadvantage from the research standpoint is that PET scans give a rela-tively coarse-grained image (e.g., compare the resolution of the PET scans to the 1-mm^2 resolution of functional MRI).

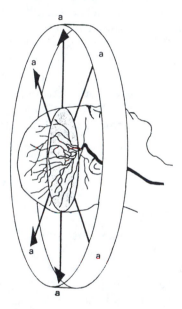

C. PET scan procedure, in which radioactive tracers are detected by peripheral sensors. These techniques have been useful in medical diagnosis and in studies of neurocognition.

Behavioral Methods of Investigation

Two general behavioral methods for investigating brain–cognition effects are in use. In the first, we adapt standard laboratory tasks to search for laterality and specialization of functions. Often, this involves the dual task procedure you've read about throughout the book; normal, intact subjects perform two tasks that either depend on the same or on different hemispheres for performance. In the second, we search for dissociations in the performance of brain-damaged individuals, patterns of preserved and damaged functions that tell us about the architecture of mental processes.

Testing Intact Subjects   Hemispheric specialization, laterality, localization, and the like can be studied in the intact, undamaged brain, although testing techniques require considerably more care and precision than ordinary laboratory methodologies. For instance, if we make sure that our subjects are fixating their visual gaze straight ahead, we can show a visual stimulus to either the right or left visual field. By doing this, we can then ensure that the neural message transmitted by the eyes is being *initially* projected into the left or right hemisphere, although of course the message can then be passed across the corpus callosum to get it from one hemisphere to the other. As an example, Klatzky and Atkinson (1971) presented a visual stimulus to the "wrong" hemisphere and managed to measure the extra time required for processing (see also Koenig, Wetzel, & Caramazza, 1992, for "wrong hemisphere" effects in the lexical decision task).

Dual Task Methods   An important application of cognitive analysis to the topic of lateralization involves using the standard dual task method. Recall that this method enables us to tax the attentional, mental resource system by having subjects perform two tasks at once, each task varying in difficulty. In their important review paper, Friedman and Polson (1981) proposed using this method to examine lateralization and hemispheric specialization. Their logic was as follows. If two tasks depend critically on the mental resources of *just one* hemisphere, then performing them together may well overburden that one hemisphere. In this situation, one or both of the tasks will be performed poorly, since that hemisphere's resources are inadequate to support both kinds of performance at their optimal levels. Alternatively, if the two tasks do not overtax the one relevant hemisphere, or if one of the tasks can be "shift-

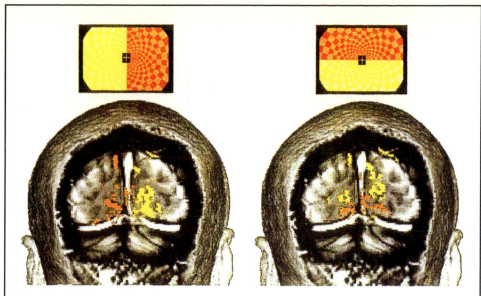

Functional MRI scan. From Schneider et al., 1993.

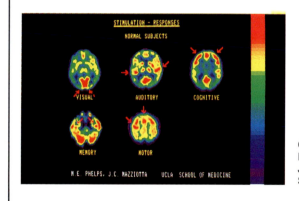

Color PET scans. Courtesy of Drs. Michael E. Phelps and John C. Mazziotta, UCLA School of Medicine.

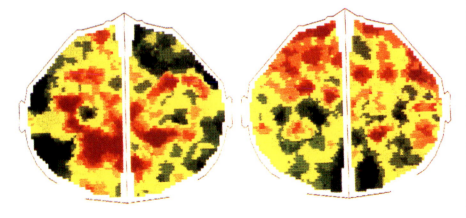

Color PET scan results showing activity during semantic (left) and episodic (right) retrieval. From Tulving, 1989.

ed" to the *other* hemisphere, then dual task performance may show very different patterns.

A rather simple example should clarify these notions (see Kinsbourne & Cook, 1971). If you try to balance a short stick on the finger of one hand, this motor activity depends almost exclusively on the resources of the contralateral hemisphere; if you balance it with your right hand, your left hemisphere is largely responsible for how long you can keep the stick balanced. Such lateralized motor control *cannot* be shifted to the other hemisphere.

Now to this single task we add a *second* task, repeating a short sentence out loud while still balancing the stick. Since the mental processing required for repeating the sentence should require the left hemisphere's resources for most (male, right-handed, etc.) people, the left hemisphere is being called upon to maintain both of the tasks, stick balancing *and* sentence repetition. Performance on either of these tasks should be worse than in the comparison condition, when the stick is being balanced with the left hand. This is indeed what Kinsbourne and Cook (1971) found. What these investigators also found, however, was that left-handed balancing actually *improved* when subjects also had to repeat the sentences.

As Friedman and Polson argue, this result contradicts the simple notion that there is one common pool of mental resources that can be allocated freely to any and all tasks. Instead, the result makes sense only if we assume that the two cerebral hemispheres have *separate* pools of resources, and that the subjects' level of arousal (hence available resources) will increase when two tasks, as opposed to just one, are required. This view takes into account the different specializations of the two cerebral hemispheres, of course, but makes a more refined point about hemispheric specialization as well. For some tasks, the supposedly "wrong" hemisphere may in fact be able to perform many functions that had previously been thought to be completely lateralized.

More recent work suggests some complexities in applying this technique in a meaningful way. Sussman (1989), Steiner, Green, and White (1992), and others have proposed ways of avoiding or taking into account the methodological difficulties and complications inherent in such attempts. For example, Steiner et al. note that handedness, a subject's base rate of performing a manual task (e.g., finger tapping), and other statistical complexities require caution when conducting such research. Nonetheless, research is continuing to show new ways in which the modularity and lateralization of mental operations can be teased apart in normal subjects.

Dissociations   We want to understand the different functions of the brain, including their possible localizations, and how they relate to one another. One way to do this is by testing brain-damaged subjects using the *method of dissociations*. This is a *logical* rather than a technological technique, in which we search for *behavioral evidence for the independence of processes or functions*. This terminology, briefly mentioned at the beginning of the chapter, deserves a bit of expansion here, since the technique is one of the foundations of neurocognition.

Consider two mental abilities or functions, a and b. If damage to a particular region of the neocortex disrupts both a and b, this is evidence that these two abilities rely—at least in part—on the same damaged region. Alternately, if abilities a and b are completely separate, damage to the a region would not alter performance on ability b; likewise, damage to a different region b would not change ability a. An obvious and common example here is the independence of vision and hearing—different regions, different abilities.

When such independence is demonstrated, the reciprocal pattern of impairment is called a *double dissociation*. That is, a double dissociation exists when one patient shows normal ability a, like hearing, but disrupted ability b, vision, while a *different* patient shows just the opposite pattern, disruption of a but preserved ability b.

The significance of this is that the double dissociation implies that the two abilities are separate and distinct, both anatomically and psychologically; if they were not separate, then brain damage affecting one ability would necessarily affect the other one as well. When evidence of a double dissociation exists, particularly when data from normal subjects also suggest that the abilities are independent, we have a powerful demonstration of separate components or *modules* of processing (Fodor, 1983). Because the study of aphasia provides classic examples of a double dissociation, we now turn to that topic.

Summary Points: lesion; direct stimulation; imaging; ERP; testing normal subjects; method of dissociations

▼ Aphasia

A particularly large literature exists on brain-related disorders of language, based on individuals who through the misfortune of illness or brain injury have lost the ability to use language. Formal studies of such disorders date back to the mid-1800s, although records dating back to 3500 B.C. mention language loss due to brain injury (see McCarthy & Warrington, 1990). Other disorders in cognitive and symbolic processes can be manifested as a result of brain injury or damage, of course, such as disruptions of the ability to recognize faces, recall specific words, or perform mathematical calculations; Table 10-2 provides a list and short explanation of several of these disruptions. Even so, none of these impairments cuts to the heart of our humanness as does the loss of language, the loss of our very ability to communicate with others.

The disruption of language due to a brain-related disorder is known as

Table 10-2   BRAIN-RELATED DISRUPTIONS OF LANGUAGE AND COGNITION

Disorder	Disruption of
Language Related	
Broca's aphasia	Speech production, syntactic features
Wernicke's aphasia	Comprehension, semantic features
Conduction aphasia	Repetition of words and sentences
Anomia (anomic aphasia)	Word finding, either lexical or semantic
Pure word deafness	Perceptual or semantic processing of auditory word comprehension
Alexia	Reading, recognition of printed letters or words
Agraphia	Writing
Other Symbolic Related	
Acalculia	Mathematical abilities, retrieval or rule-based procedures
Perception, Movement Related	
Agnosia	Visual object recognition
Prosopagnosia	(Visual) face recognition
Apraxia	Voluntary action or skilled motor movement

an **aphasia.** Aphasia is always the product of some sort of physical injury to the brain, either brain damage sustained in an accident or a blow to the head, or diseases and medical syndromes such as stroke. A major goal in neurology is to understand the aphasic syndromes more completely, so that individuals who suffer aphasia may be helped more effectively. From the standpoint of neurocognition, the disruptions of language that are observed in aphasic patients can also help us understand language and its neurological basis.

Although there are many different kinds of aphasic disorders, with great variety in their effects and severity, three basic forms are the most common. These are *Broca's aphasia, Wernicke's aphasia, and conduction aphasia.*

Broca's Aphasia

As described by Kertesz (1982), **Broca's aphasia** is characterized by *severe difficulties in producing speech;* it is also called *expressive* or *production aphasia.* Patients with Broca's aphasia show speech that is hesitant, effortful, and phonemically distorted. Aside from relatively "automatic" sequences such as "I don't know," such patients generally respond to questions with only one-word answers. If words are strung together, there are few if any grammatical markers present in the utterance. Interestingly, such patients typically show less impairment of comprehension, both for spoken and written language.

This syndrome was first described by the French neurosurgeon Pierre

FIGURE 10-8

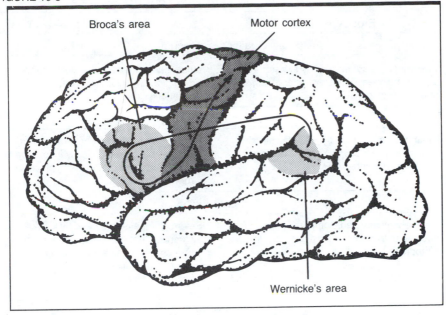

Broca's area and Wernicke's area are shown in the cerebral cortex.

Broca in the 1860s, who was also able to identify the damaged area responsible for the disorder. The site of the brain damage, an area toward the rear of the left frontal lobe, is therefore called *Broca's area.* As shown in Figure 10-8, Broca's area lies adjacent to a major motor control center in the brain. This no doubt accounts for the motor difficulties typical of the aphasia, the inability to produce fluent spoken speech.

Wernicke's Aphasia

Loosely speaking, the impairments in **Wernicke's aphasia** are the opposite of those in Broca's aphasia; see Table 10-3 for a listing of the typical impairments in both aphasias, including speech samples. In patients affected by Wernicke's aphasia, *comprehension is impaired, as are repetition, naming, reading, and writing, but the syntactic aspects of speech are preserved;* it is sometimes referred to as *receptive* or *comprehension aphasia.* In this syndrome, "copious unintelligible jargon is produced" (Kertesz, 1982, p. 30), either with unrecognizable content words, recognizable but often inappropriate semantic substitutions, or *neologisms,* invented nonsense words. In Kertesz's description of a woman with Wernicke's aphasia, the nature of the disorder is very apparent:

She speaks in sentences and uses appropriate pauses and inflectional markers separating lexical items. One can distinguish between words even when they are

Table 10-3   CLASSIC IMPAIRMENTS IN BROCA'S AND WERNICKE'S APHASIAS

Broca's Aphasia	Wernicke's Aphasia
Quality of Speech	
Severely impaired; marked by extreme effort to generate speech, hesitant utterances, short (one-word) responses	Little, if any, impairment; fluent speech productions, clear articulation, no hesitations
Nature of Speech	
Agrammatical; marked by loss of syntactic markers and inflections, and use of simple noun and verb categories	Neologistic; marked by "invented" words (neologisms) or semantically inappropriate substitutions; long strings of neologistic jargon
Comprehension	
Relatively unimpaired, compared to speech production. Word-finding difficulty may be due to production difficulties	Severely impaired; marked by lack of awareness that speech is incomprehensible; comprehension impaired also in nonverbal tasks (e.g., pointing)
Speech Samples	

Broca's Aphasia. Experimenter asks the patient's address.
"Oh dear. Um. Aah. Oh! Oh dear. very-there-were-ave. avedeversher avenyer." (Correct address was Devonshire.)
Wernicke's Aphasia. Experimenter asks about the patient's work prior to hospitalization. "I wanna tell you this happened when happened when he rent. His- his kell come down here and is—he got ren something. It happened. In these ropiers were with him for hi-is friend—like was. And he roden all o these arranjen from the pedis on from iss pescid."

Adapted from Kertesz, 1982.

neologistic. . . . She speaks without articulatory errors or hesitations. . . . She does not appear to have any word-finding difficulty, but in an extraordinary fashion, neologisms of variable length and phonemic complexity replace substantive words, mostly nouns and verbs. She talks as if she spoke without mistakes. . . . There is a rather curious cool and calm manner about her speech as if she did not realize her deficit . . . a very characteristic feature of this disturbance. (pp. 41–42)

The German investigator, Carl Wernicke, identified this disorder in 1874, as well as the left-hemisphere region that is damaged. This region is thus known as *Wernicke's area,* also illustrated in Figure 10-8. Note that the area, toward the rear of the left temporal lobe, is adjacent to the auditory center of the brain, in the left temporal lobe.

If you'll think about these two aphasias for a moment, you'll notice that several rough distinctions can be drawn between them in terms of linguistic characteristics you studied in Chapter 8. A Broca's aphasic, with neurological damage near the motor control area, demonstrates disorders in the motor aspects of language—fluent, coordinated speech—but relatively normal comprehension at a semantic level. Syntactic markers are especially absent here, as if *bound morphemes* such as *-er* and *-ing* had become unavailable. Indeed, this aphasia is sometimes called *agrammatic aphasia*, referring to the lack (prefix *a-*) of grammatical form that is evidenced. In contrast, *free morphemes*, word stems and content words, seem relatively unaffected.

On the other hand, a Wernicke's aphasic can generate speech fluently and grammatically, but the *semantic* aspects of the speech are severely impaired: invented nonsense words substitute for genuinely semantic words. As a product of brain damage in different locations, in other words, quite opposite aspects or components of linguistic ability seem to be lost and preserved. This is a classic demonstration of double dissociation.

Conduction Aphasia

Considerably less common than Broca's and Wernicke's aphasias, *conduction aphasia* is a more narrow disruption of language ability. Both Broca's and Wernicke's areas seem to be intact in conduction aphasia, and indeed individuals with conduction aphasia can both understand and produce speech quite well. Their language impairment, however, is that they are *unable to repeat what they have just heard.* In intuitive terms, the intact comprehension and production systems seem to have lost their normal connection or linkage. And indeed, the site of the brain lesion in conduction aphasia appears to be the primary pathway between Broca's and Wernicke's areas, called the *arcuate fasciculus* (Geschwind, 1970); quite literally, the pathway between the comprehension and production areas is no longer able to *conduct* the linguistic message.

Other Aphasias

As Table 10-2 shows, a variety of highly specific aphasias are also possible. Though most of these are quite rare, they nonetheless give evidence of the separability of several aspects of language performance. For instance, in *alexia* (or dyslexia), there is a disruption of reading without any necessary disruption of spoken language or aural comprehension. Some alexias/dyslexias are categorized as *visual word form dyslexias,* when the visual processing system seems to be disrupted; for instance, disruption of letter or word recognition. *Central dyslexias,* on the other hand, affect "the ability to derive sound or meaning from print" (McCarthy & Warrington, 1990, p. 215), including so-called deep dyslexia, in which the disorder can be as specific as disruption of the reading of abstract, but not concrete, words.

In *agraphia,* conversely, the patient is unable to write. Amazingly, a few reports describe patients with alexia *but without* agraphia—in other words, patients who can write but then cannot read what they have just written (Benson & Geschwind, 1969). In *pure word deafness,* a patient cannot comprehend spoken language, although he or she is still able to read and produce written and spoken language. In short, the picture we now are beginning to see shows that language skills and abilities consist of many different components, some quite independent or dissociated from others. Often, the only way to observe this independence is to test a brain-damaged patient whose particular injury has led to a breakdown of the normally coordinated system.

Anomia

One final type of aphasia deserves brief mention here, because it relates to the separation of the semantic and lexical systems discussed in Chapters 6 and 8. **Anomia** or **anomic aphasia** is a disruption of word finding, an *impairment in the normal ability to retrieve a semantic concept and say its name.* In other words, some aspect of the normally automatic semantic or lexical components of retrieval has been damaged in anomia. Although moderate word-finding difficulty can result from damage virtually anywhere in the left hemisphere, full-fledged anomia seems to involve damage to the left temporal lobe (e.g., Coughlan & Warrington, 1978; see McCarthy & Warrington, 1990, for details).

On the surface, anomia resembles the normal tip-of-the-tongue (TOT) phenomenon; patients seem to "know the word" yet be unable to name it. Several researchers (e.g., Geschwind, 1967; Goodglass, Kaplan, Weintraub, & Ackerman, 1976), however, have noted some differences. For example, in a normal TOT state, subjects usually have partial knowledge of the target word, for instance, the sound it begins with or the number of syllables. Anomics in the Goodglass et al. (1976) study, however, showed no evidence for this partial knowledge.

More recent work, however, suggests that anomia can involve retrieval blockage *only* for the lexical component of retrieval; that is, semantic and lexical retrieval may be separate processes. For instance, Kay and Ellis (1987) tested an anomic patient who seemed to know the meaning of the concept he was unable to name, and also knew when he had come up with the wrong word to name it. His difficulty seemed to involve finding the *lexical* representation that corresponded to the already retrieved semantic concept (see also Ashcraft, 1993). That is, at a superficial level his difficulty resembled total blockage of retrieval. Careful questioning, however, indicated no problems with semantic retrieval, but instead an occasional disruption of the normal lexical access process. If this inference is correct, then it may truly be that the lexical representations of words and the retrieval of those lexical entries are rather separate from the corresponding semantic concepts and their retrieval.

Generalizing from Aphasia

While it is a mistake to believe that our eventual understanding of language will be reducible to a catalog of biological and neurological

processes (e.g., Mehler, Morton, & Jusczyk, 1984), knowledge of the neurological aspects of language should nonetheless be useful for something
beyond the rehabilitation and treatment of aphasia. What do studies of
such abnormal brain processes tell us about normal cerebral functioning
and language?

Well for one, the very different patterns of behavioral impairments in
Broca's and Wernicke's aphasias, stemming from different physical
structures in the brain, certainly imply that these two physical structures are responsible for different aspects of linguistic skill. Furthermore, these selective impairments and different brain locations also rein-
force the notion that syntax and semantics are two separable aspects of
normal language (e.g., Osterhout & Holcomb, 1992). That is, the double
dissociations indicate that different, independent modules govern comprehension and speech production. Other dissociations, of course, indicate yet more independent modules of processing, for example, separate
modules corresponding to reading and writing.

An intriguing inference from such studies is that the specialized cerebral regions signal an innate, biological basis for language; that is, the
human nervous system is rather specifically adapted to learn and use
language, as opposed to simply being *generally* able to do so. Several theorists have gone a significant step further in this issue, discussing the
possible evolutionary mechanisms responsible for lateralization, hemispheric specialization, the dissociation of syntax and semantics revealed
by Broca's and Wernicke's aphasias, and even cognition in general (Corballis, 1989; Geary, 1992; Lewontin, 1990). These are fascinating lines of
reasoning on the nature of language and cognition as represented in the
brain.

Summary Points: aphasias—Broca's, Wernicke's, conduction; alexia,
agraphia, anomia; left hemisphere regions for language; implications for
normal language

▼ Amnesia

Amnesia is *the loss of memory or memory abilities.* Amnesia is one of the
oldest and most thoroughly investigated mental disruptions due to brain
disorders, as well as one of the more common results of brain injury and
damage. While some amnesias are quite temporary, due, for example, to
a strong blow to the head, the amnesias we are interested in here are relatively permanent, due to enduring changes in the brain.[4]

Many different kinds of amnesias have been studied, and we have
space only to discuss a few of these; as always, additional readings are

---

[4]Note that we do not pursue psychodynamic, "functional" amnesias here, that is, amnesias presumably induced by anxieties and other factors related to personality dysfunction.

suggested at the end of the chapter. A few bits of terminology will help you understand the material and will alert you to the distinctions in memory that are particularly relevant for neurocognition.

First, the loss of memory in amnesia is always considered in relation to the date of the brain injury or damage. If a person suffers loss of memory for the events *prior to brain injury,* this is called a **retrograde amnesia.** Note that *retro-* here has the same connotation as in the Chapter 5 discussion of retroactive interference—the loss is *backward in time.* The other form of amnesia is **anterograde amnesia,** *loss of memory for events occurring after brain injury.* An individual will often show both forms of amnesia, although the extent of the memory loss is usually different for events prior to and after the damage. For instance, someone with severe head injury from a car accident might show retrograde amnesia for the two weeks preceding the accident. The same individual's anterograde amnesia, loss of memory for events since the accident, could easily last months or years, depending on the severity of the damage.

Second, both the kind of memory system being tested and the kind of task being administered are critically important, because so many kinds of memory disruptions are possible. There are amnesias that reflect disruption of only short-term memory, amnesias that interfere with declarative long-term memories while leaving procedural long-term memories intact, and several "material-specific amnesias" (McCarthy & Warrington, 1990), for instance, disrupted recognition memory for faces, or for routes and buildings in "mental maps." And evidence is now accumulating that amnesia interferes with *explicit* memory performance, remembering deliberately learned and normally recallable facts, while often preserving *implicit* memory, information retrieved without conscious intent or awareness.

We begin the story of amnesia with a classic, extremely well known case history, that of a patient known in the literature as H.M. In preparation, try to remember what you read early in the chapter about the *hippocampus.* If you remember the one fact you were asked to learn, that the hippocampus is critical for storing new information in long-term memory, you have done *exactly* what H.M. is unable to do, learn.

Patient H.M.[5]

Kolb and Whishaw (1990) tell an interesting history of modern neuropsychology's work on memory. Beginning about 1915, the famous researcher Karl Lashley began investigating the question of where learned habits and behaviors are stored neurally, by selectively lesioning

---

[5]I have relied heavily in this section on two summaries of H.M.'s deficits, Kolb and Whishaw's (1990, pp. 539–543) account, and the 14-year follow-up study by Milner, H.M.'s primary investigator, and her colleagues (Milner, Corkin, & Teuber, 1968).

or removing portions of the neocortex in animal subjects. But after hundreds of experiments, Lashley still had no evidence showing that specific lesions destroyed specific memories. He concluded, in his famous 1950 paper, that the *engram*—the specific memory encoded into the brain—was represented throughout the neocortex, rather than in one particular structure or region.

A mere three years later, an accidental discovery by a neurosurgeon named William Scoville "revolutionized the study of the memory process" (Kolb & Whishaw, 1990, p. 525). Scoville performed radical surgery on a patient known as H.M., sectioning H.M.'s hippocampus in both the left and right hemispheres, in an attempt to gain control over his severe epileptic seizures. To Scoville's surprise, the outcome of this surgery was a pervasive anterograde amnesia: H.M. became completely unable to learn and recall anything new. While his memory for events prior to the surgery remained intact, as did his overall IQ (in fact, his IQ is 118, well above average), he completely lost the ability to store new information in long-term memory.

In Kolb and Whishaw's (1990) view, the report of H.M.'s condition (Scoville & Milner, 1957) was the second most important paper in neuropsychology, second only to Broca's original report on aphasia. In particular, they note that no one could have predicted, based on Lashley's work, that damage to a *single* structure could have yielded such a result, and certainly not a structure largely thought to influence only the sense of smell. But there was the evidence: "Surgery had interfered with the process of storing or retrieving new memories but had not touched stored memories themselves. The case of H.M. . . . shifted the emphasis from a search for the location of memory to an analysis of the process of storing memories" (pp. 525–526).

Across the intervening years, H.M. has served as a subject for Milner's research team on hundreds of tasks, documenting the many facets of his pervasive anterograde amnesia. His memory for events prior to surgery, including his childhood and school days, is quite good. His language comprehension is normal, and his vocabulary is above average. Yet any task that requires him to retain information across a delay shows severe impairment, especially if the delay is filled with an interfering task. For instance, after a 2-minute interference task of repeating digits, he was unable to recognize photographs of various faces. He is unable to learn sequences of digits that go beyond the typical short-term memory span of seven items. The impairments apply equally to nonverbal and verbal materials, a result apparently related to the bilateral (both sides) lesions from his surgery (left hemisphere lesions in the hippocampus tend to yield amnesia for only verbal memories).

Interestingly, there is evidence that H.M. is normal when it comes to motor learning. That is, he was able to learn a rather difficult motor skill, mirror-drawing; this task required that H.M. trace between the lines of a double-star pattern while looking at the pattern and his pencil

FIGURE 10-9

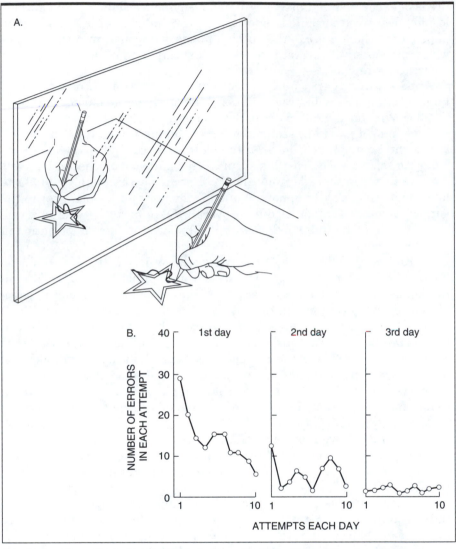

A. In this test the subject's task is to trace between the two outlines of the star while viewing his or her hand in a mirror. The reversing effect of the mirror makes this a difficult task initially. Crossing a line constitutes an error. *B.* H.M. shows clear improvement in motor tasks on the star test, which is a procedural memory. (After Blakemore, 1977.)

only in a mirror (see Figure 10-9). His performance showed a completely normal learning curve, with very few errors on the third day of practice, although on days 2 and 3 he did not remember ever having done the mirror-drawing task before. Likewise, H.M. has also shown systematic learning and improvement on a procedural task, the Tower of Hanoi problem you'll read about in Chapter 12. Although he could not remember particular moves in the problem and spoke of not remembering the task itself, his performance nonetheless improved across repeated days of practice (reported in Kolb & Whishaw, 1990).

Implications for Memory

What do we know about human memory now as a function of H.M.'s disrupted and preserved mental capacities? How much has this person's misfortune told us about memory and cognition?

The most apparent source of H.M.'s amnesia is a disruption in the process of transferring information to long-term memory. That is, H.M.'s retrieval of presurgical information is intact, indicating that his long-term memory per se, including retrieval, was unaffected by the surgery. Likewise, his ability to attend to questions and answer them, and to perform other simple short-term memory tasks, indicates that simpler attentional and awareness functions are also intact. But he has a widespread disability in transferring new information into long-term memory, a function possibly corresponding to *elaborative rehearsal* or the role of the central executive component of working memory.

Note that this disability seems to affect most or all of H.M.'s "deliberate" or explicit storage of information in long-term memory. That is, he is unable to learn a list of words for later recall and does not respond accurately when tested on recognition for episodic information. In the description given in Milner et al. (1968), this deficit extends almost completely to even "real-world" episodic material, save for a very few circumstances that remain constant in his life. For example, although he had been taken to visit his hospitalized mother three times in one week, he "seemed not to remember any of these visits . . . he kept saying that he felt a little uneasy and wondered if something might be wrong with one of his parents. . . . Gradually this uneasiness wore off, and although he was told repeatedly that he could telephone home any time he wished, he no longer seemed to know why he should do so. . . . [Eighteen months later], H.M.'s father died suddenly. . . . When questioned two months later, he seemed to be dimly aware of his father's death" (pp. 216–217). At the time the report was written, H.M. was unable to describe anything about the job he had held for six months.

As noted above, H.M. showed quite normal acquisition on a skilled motor task, despite the obviously damaged process of acquiring verbal-based memories. Thus it seems that material requiring deliberate transfer to long-term memory, including laboratory and real-world episodic information, was disrupted by the lesions to the hippocampus. Note that this finding does not necessarily mean that the disrupted process—say, rehearsal—takes place in the hippocampus. Instead, it might simply be that the hippocampus is a critical pathway for successful transfer to long-term memory, a route through which the process takes place rather than the actual location of that process. In Squire's (1987) view, this "route" or "pathway" idea is central to understanding how "amnesia appears to reflect neither direct injury to, nor loss of, those brain regions in which information is processed and stored. Instead, amnesia seems best explained by hypothesizing a neural system, which is damaged in amnesia, that ordinarily *participates* in memory storage without being itself a *site* of storage" (p. 180, emphasis in original).

Other research on patients with similar lesions (e.g., Penfield & Milner, 1958; Zola-Morgan, Squire, & Amalral, 1986) have confirmed the importance of the hippocampus to this process of storing new information in long-term, explicit memory. In some sense then, the hippocampus is a gateway into long-term memory; in Squire's (1992) view, the hippocampus is absolutely essential for declarative or explicit, that is, verbal or verbalizable, memory.

Disruption Within Working Memory

According to Schacter (1989), it is generally true that "global" amnesics perform fairly normally on tests of intelligence, language, and perception, but quite poorly on laboratory tasks that "require recall and recognition of study-list materials across retention intervals of as little as a few minutes" (p. 699). On the other hand, this is not uniformly the case. For instance, Cermak (1982) discusses evidence for a form of amnesia in which short-term, but not long-term, memory has been disrupted, that is, seriously impaired short-term memory spans yet unimpaired long-term retention of verbal material (Shallice & Warrington, 1970). Such cases generally involve different anatomical regions of damage, in particular, the left parietal lobe.

Schacter (1989) notes two important conclusions from such data. First, they describe a double dissociation between short-term and long-term memory. This of course indicates that separate processes or cognitive systems are used for the two kinds of memory functioning. Even by itself, this is a profoundly important conclusion: the distinction between brief retention of recent information and permanent retention of the past, noted even by James in 1890, is supported by the finding of a double dissociation.

The second conclusion, in Schacter's view, is that the results pose a difficulty for traditional information processing models like that of Atkinson and Shiffrin (1968). That is, if an amnesic patient shows seriously impaired short-term memory span, yet is still able to store new information in long-term memory, we are forced to reexamine the notion that previous storage in short-term memory is *required* for eventual long-term memory formation.

But of course, you've learned something more recent and sophisticated about short-term memory than the ideas summarized in the original information processing model. In particular, you learned about Baddeley's (1986) model of working memory, with the executive control system and its separate "slave systems" for articulatory rehearsal and visual–spatial processing. In several researchers' views, Baddeley's proposed system provides a useful account for these varieties of amnesia. That is, a damaged articulatory loop component would lead to the observed short-term memory deficit in some patients, while leaving the storage of long-term memories intact; this is exactly the pattern observed by Vallar and Baddeley (1984). Presumably, the opposite pattern of disruption, damage to the executive controller but not the articulatory loop, might account for performance among other patients (e.g., Van der Linden, Coyette, & Seron, 1992).[6] More generally, the neurocognitive research suggests that the components of working memory can be dissociated; that is, they are isolable, separate components of memory processing.

Implicit and Explicit Memory

As discussed in Chapter 7, a distinction in long-term memory research that is gaining in importance is the one between implicit and explicit memory. To refresh your memory, an *explicit* memory reflects a memory that is deliberately stored and recalled from memory and—by definition—one that is verbalizable; I remember that $5 \times 3 = 15$, that my car is blue, and so on. An *implicit memory,* however, is one that does not "demand conscious recollection of a specific previous experience. In this type of test, memory for a recent experience is inferred from facilitations of performance, generally known as *repetition* or *direct priming* (emphasis mine) effects, that need not and frequently do not involve any conscious recollection of the prior experience" (Schacter, 1989, p. 695).

We mentioned this division of implicit versus explicit memory in Chapter 2, in the theme "Unconscious Processing," and rediscovered it in Chapter 7 as well. Recall a typical result, that a subject will be more likely to complete a word fragment like TAB____ with TABLET if given prior exposure to the word TABLET. This will happen even if the subject is not able to recall TABLET on the list of words studied previously (e.g., Tulving, Schacter, & Stark, 1982).

This is an important distinction in understanding the topic of amnesia. As Schacter (1989) noted, clinical assessments of amnesia as far back as 1845 have realized that patients have an implicit kind of memory for recent experiences despite being unable to recall those experiences deliberately. Direct evidence for this effect is now common. For instance, Warrington and Weiskrantz (1968) reported the word completion effect noted above, that amnesics and control subjects will complete the word stem with a word presented earlier on a study list. But on an explicit yes/no

---

[6]For recent work on the involvement of the frontal lobes in executive control functions, see especially Case (1992) and Stuss (1992), both in an entire issue of *Brain and Cognition* devoted to the frontal lobes.

recognition task, the amnesic subjects were seriously inaccurate: they had no explicit memory of having seen the original word. Similar results were obtained by Graf, Squire, and Mandler (1984), where merely giving amnesics explicit memory instructions ("remember the words you just saw") resulted in impaired performance compared to those who received the implicit instructions ("complete the word stem with the first word that comes to mind"; see Schacter, 1989, 1992, for reviews of such studies).

Schacter's distinction between implicit and explicit memory seems to overlap considerably with one that Squire (1987) has recently discussed as the primary symptom of amnesia. That is, Squire notes that amnesic patients generally perform quite poorly on tests of *declarative knowledge,* knowledge that is verbalizable, often episodic, and open to conscious recollection. An amnesic's *procedural knowledge,* however—knowledge of *how* to do something—is usually preserved, according to Squire. Of course, procedural knowledge in this sense would include the motor learning skills that H.M. was able to master, despite his inability to explicitly remember previous experiences with the mirror-writing task.

The implications of these studies are fascinating. They imply rather separate memory systems in the brain, one for explicitly, consciously, deliberately acquired and recalled information, and a separate one for implicitly acquired information not open to conscious recollection; alternatively, the results imply separate routes into (or out of) a common mental representation. The veritable explosion of recent research on this topic attests to the importance of the topic, especially because of its implications for an understanding of normal cognition.

For instance, Shimamura and Squire (1989) found that amnesics did not differ from normal control subjects when the priming of preexisting memory representations was tested, that is, a repetition priming task. But amnesics showed no implicit memory effect when they were tested on associations that had been shown during the experiment. In other words, their "normal" implicit memory effect was limited to knowledge that had already been stored in memory; the amnesia prevented new information from being stored.

Conversely, Paller et al. (1992) tested amnesic subjects who had an impaired ability to recognize faces. In the task, pairs of pictures were presented, and subjects made same/different judgments about the two faces. When a pair of pictures was repeated, the subjects showed faster RTs. That is, with the face recognition task, they *did* show a significant repetition priming effect on new information, despite their amnesic impairment in recognizing faces explicitly.

Summary Points: retrograde and anterograde amnesias; H.M.'s impaired storage of new information but preserved motor learning; implicit versus explicit memory; dissociations within working memory; declarative and procedural knowledge in amnesia; repetition priming

▼ Concluding Remarks

The chapter concludes with a few remarks on the scope of neurocognition and a theoretical note on neurocognition and connectionism.

Other Cognitive Disruptions

By far the best-known disruptions of cognitive processing due to brain damage are the aphasias and amnesias you just read about. But it is a mistake to assume that other cognitive processes might escape from possible disruption when injuries or illnesses affect the brain.

For example, Table 10-2 lists *apraxia* and *agnosia* as two forms of cognitive impairment; apraxia is a disruption in the voluntary motor movement system, and agnosia is a disruption in visual recognition. How is apraxia a disruption of cognitive processing, you may ask. *Apraxia* ("without action") is defined as disruption of voluntary movement due to something other than conditions like paralysis; for instance, an individual with apraxia may be unable to imitate a sequence of hand movements. There are data showing, for example, that apraxic patients have great difficulties learning the pursuit rotor motor task (following a moving point of light on a rotating disk; e.g., Heilman, Schwartz, & Geschwind, 1975). This is noteworthy in part because of cases like H.M., who shows preserved motor learning despite pervasive amnesia.

Agnosia[7] ("without knowledge") is the disruption of visual object recognition, even without any disruption in the normal visual processing of stimuli. For instance, Rubens and Benson (1971) described a patient who could not identify objects or demonstrate their use when they were shown to him. When allowed to touch the objects, however, he could identify them immediately.

A fascinating disorder—certainly to researchers interested in mathematical cognition—is *acalculia,* a disruption of the normal ability to use numbers and mathematical operations. McCloskey and his colleagues (e.g., McCloskey, Caramazza, & Basili, 1985; Sokol et al., 1991) describe the performance of several patients with brain damage that resulted in acalculia. An example of one of their patients was described at the beginning of this chapter (Sokol et al., 1991). Patient P.S. made frequent errors to simple multiplication problems like 7×9, was always wrong when she multiplied by 0 (e.g., she said $0 \times 2 = 2$), yet showed no disruption in her ability to perform "long multiplication" on paper. Her brain lesion was in the left temporal lobe, suggesting that symbolic mental activity, language as well as math, relies heavily on left hemisphere processing. Other work, for example, a paper by Temple (1991), has shown a

---

[7]This disorder was originally called *seelenblindheit,* a German term translated as "mindblindness." Freud introduced the term *agnosia* in 1891, to distinguish the memory disorder from simpler impairments of perceptual processes; see McCarthy and Warrington (1990, pp. 22–23).

double dissociation between math fact retrieval and rule-based performance and also attests to the importance of the left hemisphere for numerical and mathematical operations (see also Ashcraft, Yamashita, & Aram, 1992; Geary, 1993).

Connectionism and Neurocognition

We return, in closing, to connectionism, the up-and-coming (some would say it's already arrived; some would say it shouldn't have) computer simulation and theorizing framework in cognitive science. We need to mention some general issues in neurocognitive research, and comment on the compatibility of those issues with the assumptions in connectionism. We then cover one specific combination of connectionism and neurocognition that illustrates the potential usefulness of these approaches.

A Brief Review   First, you need a quick review of the basics of connectionism. Recall that the central feature of connectionist models is that a large number of very simple units can act in concert to simulate even very complex activities. Briefly, the methods by which this scheme works involve the following (reread the relevant sections of Chapter 3 for the introductory treatment of connectionism):

1. Input units, output units, and usually "hidden units" too are massively interconnected in the model's architecture.
2. Weights between units are assigned, and then adjusted or updated as a function of feedback into the system.
3. A unit has both positively and negatively weighted connections to other units, such that each can selectively excite and inhibit other units in the network.
4. Complex mental operations are the combined effects of the "massively parallel processing" that characterizes the network.

Advantages of Connectionism   Two important advantages of the connectionist approach are frequently mentioned (e.g., McClelland, Rumelhart, & Hinton, 1986; Rumelhart, 1989). First, there is the overwhelming structural similarity of connectionist models to the network of neurons in the brain. That is, the brain is a massive set of interconnected neurons, just as a connectionist network is a massive set of interconnected nodes. Moreover, there is a strong similarity even at the level of individual units, neurons or nodes. That is, in the nervous system, a neuron either fires or it doesn't, and when it does fire, that affects the next neuron in the sequence. This yes/no, binary aspect of neural firing is exactly parallel to the fire/no fire nature of the units in a connectionist model. Finally, the weights between units in the connectionist approach are either positive or negative, corresponding to excitatory and inhibitory neural synapses. It is clearly no accident that one of the alternative terms for connectionism is *neural net modeling*.

The second advantage is that from such simple elements arises truly complex behavior, both for the neurons in the brain and the units in a connectionist model. In other words, a point of pride among connectionists is that one need not postulate enormously complex, specialized processing components to generate complex behavior. Instead, complexity in the behavior of a connectionist model arises from the (massively parallel) interactions of countless simple units, just as is the case in the brain.

Potential Difficulties While these advantages sound beneficial, there are some potential difficulties and points of disagreement. Recall the entire motivation behind the connectionist approach; in essence, the rationale is that connectionist models parallel the way the cognitive system works and therefore can shed light on that cognitive system.

But is the relationship between a connectionist structure and the brain really that parallel? From one perspective, the answer to this question is "no." That is, in at least two ways, the connectionist approach seems somewhat contradictory with what you've just studied about neurocognition; whether the contradictions are real or only superficial awaits further developments in both fields.

One of the dominant themes in this chapter is that double dissociations in neurocognitive studies suggest that separate, independent modules of processing account for the overall complexity of language and cognition. For example, there seem to be separate syntactic and semantic modules for language, separate retrieval and rule-based modules for mathematics, and so on. These modules even differ on an anatomical basis sometimes; often, different physical regions of the brain are damaged in double dissociations. And yet, an apparent strength of connectionism is that it treats all mental operations, and all stored knowledge entering into those operations, as homogenous, as due to the varied outcomes of parallel processing through the neural net. At least in spirit then, the neurocognitive and neural net approaches appear to be pointing in opposite directions, one toward modularity, the other toward homogeneity. Maybe future neural net models will need separate modules, or maybe the modularity of human cognition does not require modularity at the level of the neural net.

Other reasons for worry exist as well, although it is too early in the development of connectionism to determine how serious some sources of concern are. Some researchers argue that connectionist models should not be considered as true scientific *theories,* but instead should be considered literally as *models,* "working miniature replicas" in a sense, much as biology or medicine uses an "animal model" to study drug and treatment effects (e.g., McCloskey, 1991; see also Massaro, 1988, for other objections and recommendations).

Possibly more damaging is an observation made by Crick and Asanuma (1986; Crick, by the way, is the Nobel laureate of the Watson and Crick team, who discovered the double helix structure of DNA). They note a troublesome difference between the nervous system and connectionist networks. In connectionism, each unit has both positively and negatively weighted connections to other units, enabling each unit to activate some connected units while simultaneously inhibiting others. This is a central feature of the network's processing. And yet, in the nervous system, a single neuron will make only one of the two types of synapses on other neurons, either the Type I excitatory synapse or the Type II inhibitory synapse.

Again, the differences between the neural net structures in the brain and connectionist models may turn out to be trivial or fundamental— only time will tell. But compelling demonstrations, like the Farah and McClelland (1991) model below, suggest that it's too early to dismiss the potential of connectionism out of hand.

A Connectionist Model of Semantic Memory Impairment   Farah and McClelland (1991) have offered a tantalizing glimpse of how connectionism and neurocognition can join forces in explaining a genuine puzzle in the field of memory impairments. The puzzle involves a strange dissociation in semantic knowledge, reported by Warrington and McCarthy (1983; also Warrington & Shallice, 1984). These researchers reported on four brain-damaged patients who showed dissociations in semantic memory. In particular, the patients they described had serious difficulties in identifying *living things,* but little or no difficulty in identifying *nonliving things.* For instance, patient J.B.R. could only identify 6% of a set of pictures of living things and could only define 8% of the words that named those living things ("parrot," "daffodil"). When shown pictures of nonliving things, however, J.B.R. was successful at naming 90% of them. And fully 79% of the words that named those nonliving things ("tent," "briefcase") could be defined.

How could semantic memory be splintered and fractionated to the extent that a person's access to categories of living things would be disrupted, while access to nonliving things would be preserved? A possible explanation is that semantic memory is organized into just these two very broad categories, living and nonliving things. But this is a bit too convenient; we might wonder "Why living versus nonliving things? Why not concrete versus abstract, high versus low frequency, or some other distinction?"

Warrington and Shallice (1984) suggested a more plausible explanation. Suppose that the bulk of your knowledge about living things is coded in semantic memory in terms of *sensory* properties—a parrot is a brightly colored animal that makes a distinctive sound. Likewise, suppose that most of what you know about nonliving things involves their *functional* properties—a briefcase is for carrying around papers and books. Warrington and Shallice suggested that a possible reason for the dissociation in their patients could be a selective loss or blocking of sensory knowledge. If so, that might explain the patient's impairments in naming and defining living things.

FIGURE 10-10

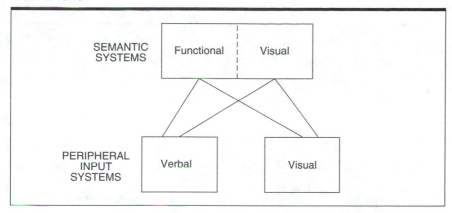

Schematic diagram of the parallel distributed processing model of semantic memory.

Quite recently, Farah and McClelland (1991) decided to build a connectionist model in order to evaluate the Warrington and Shallice hypothesis; a schematic diagram is shown in Figure 10-10. In their model, semantic memory contains two basic types of knowledge, visual (sensory) and functional, and input to the semantic system can be either verbal or visual. After constructing the model, Farah and McClelland then "lesioned" it, that is, "damaged" the visual units in the semantic memory network by either altering the connection weights or literally disconnecting the visual units from the rest of the network.

The outcome of this procedure was strikingly similar to the patients' dissociations. That is, when the visual units were lesioned, the network then showed extremely poor accuracy on associating names and pictures of living things; this is shown in the left panel of Figure 10-11, as is the quite modest decline in accuracy for the nonliving thing category. Conversely, when the network's functional units were lesioned rather than the visual units, it was the nonliving category that suffered (right panel, Figure 10-11).

Does this demonstration prove that impairment of patient J.B.R.'s visual semantic knowledge accounts for the dissociation? No, of course not; the model makes the correct prediction, certainly a big point in its favor, but such evidence is *never* taken as proof that the model is correct. Instead, think of the Farah and McClelland demonstration in this way. Warrington and Shallice asked, in essence: "Is it possible that impairment of sensory knowledge could produce the dissociation between living and nonliving things?" An appropriate answer to this question is: "Yes, it's entirely possible, because just such a dissociation was produced in a connectionist model." In other words, the connectionist model provides a degree of assurance—probably a large degree at that—that the Warrington and Shallice hypothesis is reasonable and

FIGURE 10-11

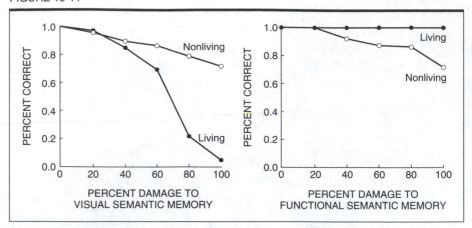

Performance of the basic model, as measured by probability of correctly associating names and pictures for living and nonliving things, after different amounts of damage to visual and functional semantics units.

should be pursued further both with the impaired patients and connectionist modeling.

Summary Points: cognitive disruptions of apraxia, agnosia, acalculia; differences in connectionist and neurocognitive approaches; connectionist approach to semantic memory impairment

CHAPTER SUMMARY

1. The study of the relationships between the functioning brain and its cognitive processes is termed *neurocognition,* a field that relies heavily on tests of patients who have experienced brain damage and thus have impaired mental functioning of some sort. The combination of neurological and cognitive approaches represents one of the most important future directions for cognitive science.

2. Neurons transmit messages through the nervous system by taking in a message through the dendrites, passing it along the axon to the axon terminals, then releasing a neurotransmitter into the synapse between neurons. The action from one neuron to the next can be either excitatory or inhibitory, but not both.

3. The human neocortex, plus a few subcortical structures, is the site of our higher order mental processes. The four regions or *lobes* in the neocortex are the frontal, parietal, occipital, and temporal lobes. The neocortex is divided into a left and a right cerebral hemisphere, with the corpus callosum connecting the two.

4. A variety of methods have been used to investigate the different abilities and specializations of the two hemispheres, including studying the effects of lesions and direct stimulation, new imaging techniques, and the logical method of searching for dissociations among processes and operations. In general, language and other symbolic activities are lateralized in the left hemisphere for most people, and visual–spatial abilities in the right hemisphere.

5. An *aphasia* is a disruption of language ability due to brain damage, usually in the left hemisphere. Broca's and Wernicke's aphasias, respectively, show disruptions of syntactic, fluent speech and disruptions of comprehension. Other less common aphasias include conduction aphasia, alexia and agraphia, and anomia. The research indicates many of these language functions are compartmentalized, represented as separate modules, as evidenced by double dissociations in performance.

6. *Amnesia* is the loss of memory due to brain damage, either for memories prior to (retrograde) or after (anterograde) the damage. Patients like H.M. display severe impairments in the ability to learn new information, associated with lesions of the hippocampus. Lesions in other regions yield different kinds of amnesias, for instance, severely disrupted short-term memory span.

7. Amnesia often, if not always, shows a disruption of explicit or declarative memories, while leaving implicit memory or procedural knowledge intact. Evidence for this conclusion includes the repetition priming effects found in amnesics and normal subjects.

8. Connectionism and neurocognitive approaches are being combined to yield new insights into brain–cognition relationships. Despite the promise of such combinations, it is not yet clear how some discrepancies in the two approaches might be resolved.

Glossary Terms: agraphia, alexia; amnesia—anterograde and retrograde; anomia; aphasia; axon, axon terminals; contralaterality; corpus callosum; dendrites; dissociations; hemispheric specialization; hippocampus; lesions; neocortex; neurons; neurotransmitter; plasticity; repetition priming; soma; split brain; synapse; thalamus

SUGGESTED READINGS

A variety of texts and chapters can be consulted for accounts of neurocognition. If you're new to the area, start with the stunning case histories presented in Sack's *The Man Who Mistook His Wife for a Hat* (1970) or *Toscanini's Fumble* by Klawans (1988); these are not carefully "scientific" case histories, but are intriguing and informative nonetheless. Ornstein and Thompson's (1984) *The Amazing Brain* is a superb newcomer's introduction to the structure and functioning of the brain; start there to begin learning the basics. Good treatments at a higher level are Ellis and Young (1988) and Shallice (1988). Kolb and Whishaw's (1990) book is a veritable bible of neuropsychology; see also Bridgeman's (1988) text. McCarthy and Warrington (1990) have written a highly readable, thorough book on the entire range of impaired cognitive processes; each chapter discusses historical papers, current work, and anatomical and theoretical considerations.

Chapters by Schacter and by Sejnowski and Churchland in Posner's (1989) *Foundations of Cognitive Science* provide excellent, high-level reviews of memory and cognition from a neurocognitive standpoint. Schacter's (1992) paper focuses on the neurocognition of implicit memory. Antrobus (1991) suggests a neurocognitive explanation of dreaming and proposes a connectionist model to simulate dreaming. And finally, Corballis's (1989) review article on the possible evolutionary influences for laterality is fascinating reading, as is Lewontin's (1990) chapter on the evolution of cognition.

Chapter 11

DECISIONS, JUDGMENTS, AND REASONING

It does not trouble people much that their heads are full of incomplete, inconsistent, and uncertain information. With little trepidation they go about drawing rather doubtful conclusions from their tangled mass of knowledge, for the most part unaware of the tenuousness of their reasoning. The very tenuousness of the enterprise is bound up with the power it gives people to deal with a language and a world full of ambiguity and uncertainty. (Collins, Warnock, Aiello, & Miller, 1975, p. 383)

From the psychologist's point of view, thinking must not be confused with logic because human thinking frequently is not rigorous or correct, does not follow the path of step-by-step deduction—in short, is not usually "logical." (Newell & Simon, 1972, p. 876)

This chapter and the next one on problem solving probably come closer to everyday conceptions of "human thought" than any of the material presented so far in this book. It's important, obviously, that you appreciate the material you've already studied as a crucial part of cognitive psychology. As you read in the first chapter, simply because you are relatively unaware of mental processes doesn't mean that they aren't important to a complete understanding of cognition. Nonetheless, it's time now to delve into the topics of decision making, reasoning, and problem solving, the rather slow and very deliberate kinds of thinking that will round out our study of cognitive psychology.

A general thread that runs through much of the decision-making and reasoning research is that we are often overly influenced by the general world knowledge that is stored in our memories. The influence of stored information is quite pervasive; it affects how we perform in the classic forms of reasoning as well as in less well-defined judgment and decision-making situations. A second thread is just as pervasive, and just as important in decision making; far more than is logical, we tend to search for evidence that confirms our decisions, beliefs, and hypotheses, and as such are considerably less skeptical than we ought to be.

We'll begin by examining two classic kinds of reasoning problems and then switch to a seemingly very simple kind of decision making and reasoning—mental comparisons between concepts or objects. We'll then proceed to the study of a somewhat different kind of situation, reasoning about the likelihood of events where relevant information in memory is generally lacking or insufficient. The strategies people use to make these judgments are of particular interest, since they reveal a variety of "rules of thumb" or short-cut methods on which people rely. These methods work well sometimes, but sometimes they lead to distortions and biases in reasoning. Overall, this research provides convincing examples of the uncertainty of human reasoning and of the often surprising inaccuracies in our stored knowledge.

▼ Formal Logic and Reasoning

At some point during their college careers, most students are exposed to the classic forms of reasoning, often in a course on logic. For our purposes, two of these forms, *syllogisms* and *conditional reasoning problems,* are important to understand. A general finding in the research on such reasoning tasks is that people are not particularly good at solving such problems correctly when the problems are presented in an abstract form. Our solutions are often better when the problems are presented in terms of concrete, real-world concepts. If we generate our own examples, however, the accuracy of our solutions depends on how critically or skeptically we generated the examples. In some situations, our general world knowledge almost prevents us from seeing the "pure" (i.e., logical) answer to logic problems.

Syllogisms

A **syllogism,** or **categorical syllogism,** is a *three-statement logical form, with the first two parts stating the premises or statements taken to be true, and the third part stating a conclusion based on those premises.* The goal of syllogistic reasoning is to understand how different premises can be combined to yield logically true conclusions, and to understand what combinations of premises lead to invalid or incorrect conclusions.

Often, syllogisms are presented in an abstract form, such as:

(1a) All A are B
All B are C
Therefore, all A are C

In this example, the two premises state a certain relation between the abstract elements A, B, and C, basically a class inclusion or subset–superset relation. *All A are B* says that the set A is a subset of the group B, that A is included in the set B. The third statement, "Therefore . . . ," is the conclusion. By applying the rules of syllogistic reasoning, it can be determined that the conclusion *All A are C* is true in this example; that is, the conclusion follows logically from the premises. Inserting words into the syllogism will verify the truth of the conclusion: for instance,

(1b) All poodles are dogs
All dogs are animals
Therefore, all poodles are animals

One difficulty or confusion that people have, however, is illustrated by the following example:

(1c) All poodles are animals
All animals are wild
Therefore, all poodles are wild

The difficulty here is that the conclusion is *logically* true; since the conclusion follows from the premises, the syllogism is valid. Of course, it's easy to think of counterexamples, situations in which the conclusion is not true in the real world of poodles—hardly any poodles are wild, after all (Feldman, 1992). Yet the rules of syllogistic reasoning are that the truth of the premises is *irrelevant* to the validity of the syllogistic argument. What matters, instead, is that the conclusion does or does not follow from the premises. In the case of example (1c), the conclusion is valid even though the second premise is empirically false. Thus applying syllogistic reasoning to real-world problems is at least a two-step process: first, determine if the syllogism itself is valid; second, if the syllogism is valid, determine the empirical truth of the premises.

Now consider another example:

> (2a*) All A are B
> Some B are C
> Therefore, some A are C

(In formal logic, *some* means "at least one, and possibly all.") Try inserting words into this example, to see if the conclusion is correct. For example,

> (2b*) All polar bears are animals
> Some animals are white
> Therefore, some polar bears are white

Despite the fact that words can be substituted that lead to a correct statement of fact, this second syllogism is *false*. Because the two premises do *not* invariably lead to a correct conclusion, the entire form of the syllogism is invalid (the reason for the asterisk). The incorrectness of the conclusion in (2a) stems from the qualifier *some*. While it may be that the conclusion is empirically true when you use one or another concrete example, this isn't necessarily the case for *all* examples. Thus the second conclusion is false, as shown by the following:

> (2c*) All polar bears are animals
> Some animals are brown
> Therefore, some polar bears are brown

As shown in Figure 11-1, a Venn diagram illustration can often help in determining whether a syllogism is true or not. For instance, in the first illustration, the "All–All" form shows that it is necessarily true that "All A are C." The circles, which represent the class of things known as A, B, and C, are nested such that A is a subset of B, and B is a subset of C. There is simply no other way to represent the premises in Venn diagrams except by concentric circles (when A and B are identical, their boundaries overlap completely, and the diagram merely shows one circle labeled both A and B).

In the second entry in the figure, the *incorrectness* of syllogism 2 is

FIGURE 11-1

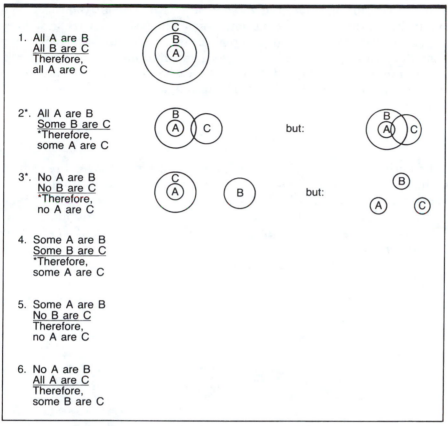

1. All A are B
   All B are C
   Therefore,
   all A are C

2*. All A are B
    Some B are C
    *Therefore,
    some A are C

    but:

3*. No A are B
    No B are C
    *Therefore,
    no A are C

    but:

4. Some A are B
   Some B are C
   *Therefore,
   some A are C

5. Some A are B
   No B are C
   Therefore,
   no A are C

6. No A are B
   All A are C
   Therefore,
   some B are C

Venn diagram illustrations for three categorical syllogisms. If a diagram can be constructed that shows the conclusion doesn't hold for all cases, then the conclusion is false. The first diagram in (2*) shows why (2*) is incorrect, since it is not necessarily true that some A are C. The second diagram in (2*) shows that an arrangement can be found that seems to support the argument. Likewise, the first diagram in (3*) shows why (3*) is incorrect, since it is not necessarily true that no A are C. The second diagram in (3*) shows an arrangement that does seem to support the conclusion.

illustrated by the first Venn diagram. In that illustration, a portion of B that does not contain A is exactly the portion that overlaps with C. Thus it isn't necessarily true that some A are C. The second Venn diagram for this problem, however, illustrates the "Some polar bears are white" conclusion, one that is true of the real world even though the syllogism is not true. (The third syllogism is similar to the second; that is, it's false, but the second Venn diagram seems to show that it's true.)

In general, although people's performance on syllogisms improves when they are shown how to use Venn diagrams or how to generate specific examples (Helsabeck, 1975), this procedure will only work if you try to find ways of showing the syllogism to be false. That is, it is all too easy to come up with examples or Venn diagrams that mistakenly confirm an incorrect conclusion. Adopting a skeptical attitude about the conclusion and trying to diagram the situation to show how the conclusion is false are more likely to be helpful strategies. As an exercise, try generating Venn diagrams for the final three syllogisms in the figure. As you work, bear in mind that the best strategy is to search for negative evidence. In other words, try to diagram the problem so that the syllogism is shown to be false.

Conditional Reasoning

Conditional reasoning is a second important kind of logical reasoning to understand. Conditional reasoning problems always contain two major parts, a *conditional clause* or statement that expresses some relationship, followed by some *evidence* pertaining to the conditional clause. **Conditional reasoning** involves a *logical determination of whether the evidence supports, refutes, or is irrelevant to the stated relationship.*

In conditional reasoning, you are given two statements. The first statement, the *conditional,* actually consists of two subclauses, which follow an *if–then* format. Respectively, the *if* clause and the *then* clause are

"This CD player costs less than players selling for twice as much."

Drawing by Weber (c) 1989; The New Yorker Magazine, Inc.

known as the **antecedent** and the **consequent** of the conditional clause (for clarity, we'll drop the word *clause,* and simply refer to "the *if*" or "the antecedent," and "the *then*" or "the consequent"). The *if* states the possible cause, and the *then* states the *effect* of that possible cause. After the *if–then,* you are given a second statement, some evidence about the truth or falsity of one of the propositions in the *if–then* relationship. The goal of such reasoning is to take the evidence and decide what follows from the evidence and the *if–then* statement. In other words, is the conditional *if–then* statement true or false given this observed evidence, or is the evidence irrelevant to the *if–then*?

The most general form of the conditional statement is:

> If *p,* then *q.*

The conditional statement is then followed by the evidence, any one of the following four possibilities:

A. *p* (that is, *p* is true), *therefore q*
B. *not p* (that is, *p* is not true) no conclusion
C. *q* (that is, *q* is true) no conclusion
D. *not q* (that is, *q* is not true), *therefore not p*

According to the conditional *if–then* statement above, if some antecedent condition *p* is true, then its consequence (the *consequent*) *q* is true. Now if there is evidence showing that *p* is indeed true (possibility A), it follows logically that *q* must be true. As a simple example of such conditional reasoning, consider the following example (adapted from Matlin, 1983):

> If I am a freshman, then I must register for next semester's classes today.

When given the evidence that *p* is true, *I am a freshman,* then the consequent *q* must be true, *I do have to register today;* this is possibility A from above. Likewise, on evidence that *q* is not true, *I do not have to register today,* it must therefore be that *p* is not true, *I am not a freshman;* this is possibility D from above.

In a conditional reasoning problem, one may use the evidence either to *affirm* or to *deny* a proposition in the *if–then* statement; the affirming or denying can be applied to either the *if* or the *then*. This yields four possibilities, which are called (A) *affirming the antecedent,* (B) *denying the antecedent,* (C) *affirming the consequent,* and (D) *denying the consequent.* All four of these possibilities are illustrated in Table 11-1.

Valid Arguments   As the table shows, only two of these four possibilities (A and D) lead to a true conclusion according to the rules of logic. In the first possibility, you may affirm the antecedent (A); this is the same as saying that the evidence shows that *p* is true. Affirming the antecedent, also known as the *modus ponens,* then permits the conclu-

Table 11-1   CONDITIONAL REASONING

Form	Name	Example
A. If p, then q Evidence: p Therefore, q	Modus ponens: affirming the antecedent (valid inference)	If I am a freshman, I have to register today Evidence: I am a freshman Therefore, I have to register today
B. If p, then q Evidence: not p *Therefore, not q	Denying the antecedent (invalid inference)	If I am a freshman, I have to register today Evidence: I am not a freshman *Therefore, I do not have to register today
C. If p, then q Evidence: q *Therefore, p	Affirming the consequent (invalid inference)	If I am a freshman, I have to register today Evidence: I have to register today *Therefore, I am a freshman
D. If p, then q Evidence: not q Therefore, not p	Modus tollens: denying the consequent (valid inference)	If I am a freshman, I have to register today Evidence: I do not have to register today Therefore, I am not a freshman

sion that the consequent is also true. In the other valid form of conditional reasoning (D), you may deny the consequent, a method also known as the *modus tollens*. This means that the evidence *not q* is true (in other words, that *q* is not true). The valid conclusion here is that *p* is not true. Because of the evidence *not q*, we conclude *not p*.

Invalid Arguments   While both of these arguments lead to a correct conclusion, the other two possibilities are not valid. That is, denying the antecedent (B) does not permit the conclusion that the consequent is false; likewise, affirming the consequent (C) does not permit the conclusion that the antecedent is true. Let's continue with the college registration example from above, where the conditional statement is "If I am a freshman, then I must register today." If we deny the antecedent by offering the evidence "I am not a freshman," this does not lead to the conclusion that "I do not have to register today." It could be that two groups of students must register today, all freshmen as well as all sophomores in the first half of the alphabet. Thus just because you're not a freshman doesn't necessarily mean you don't have to register today. Likewise, if we affirm the consequent, we assert that "I must register today." This does not permit the conclusion that "I'm a freshman," however; you might be one of those sophomores in the first half of the alphabet, after all.

Evidence on Conditional Reasoning   Generally, the research shows that people are relatively good at inferring the truth of the consequent given evidence that the antecedent is true (affirming the antecedent, the *modus ponens*). When given the conditional *if p, then q*

Table 11-2   CONCRETE AND ABSTRACT CONDITIONAL REASONING PROBLEMS

Concrete

Rembrandt's work is known to every artist. Everyone who knows Rembrandt's work appreciates its beauty. John does not know Rembrandt's work. Is it true, therefore, that John is not an artist? Is it true, therefore, that John does not appreciate the beauty of Rembrandt's work?
Conditional A:
If a person is an artist, then that person knows Rembrandt's work.
Evidence: John does not know Rembrandt's work.
Correct Conclusion: John is not an artist.
The Evidence here is *not q,* denying the consequent. Therefore, we conclude correctly *not p.*
Conditional B:
If one knows Rembrandt's work, then one appreciates its beauty.
Evidence: John does not know Rembrandt's work.
Incorrect Conclusion: John does not appreciate its beauty.
The Evidence here is *not p,* denying the antecedent. Therefore we *cannot* conclude *not q.*

Abstract

If the object is square, then it is blue.
1. Evidence: The object is square.
Is the object blue? *Yes: affirming the antecedent.*
2. Evidence: The object is not square.
Is the object blue? *No conclusion possible: denying the antecedent.*
3. Evidence: The object is blue.
Is the object square? *No conclusion possible: affirming the consequent.*
4. Evidence: The object is not blue.
Is the object square? *No: denying the consequent.*

From Wason & Johnson-Laird, 1972.

and the evidence that p is true, people usually infer correctly that q is true. For instance, Rips and Marcus (1977) found that 100% of their sample drew this correct conclusion. Much more difficult, apparently, is denying the consequent (the *modus tollens*), in which the evidence *not q* leads to the valid conclusion *therefore, not p.* Only 57% of Rips and Marcus's subjects drew this conclusion correctly (in a simpler version of the problem, 77% concluded correctly that p could never be true given the evidence *not q*). Wason and Johnson-Laird (1972) found similar results in their investigation of conditional reasoning, in which problems were stated in either concrete or relatively abstract form (see Table 11-2 for examples of each kind of problem, as well as the conclusions that can be drawn).

Errors in Conditional Reasoning   People's errors in conditional reasoning seem to fall into three categories. First, people sometimes draw incorrect conclusions by means of the two invalid forms, denying the antecedent (B) and affirming the consequent (C). A second, more subtle error is often found as well. People have a tendency to *reverse* the propositions in the *if* and *then.* They then proceed to evaluate the given evidence against the now-reversed conditional. This kind of error is

FIGURE 11-2

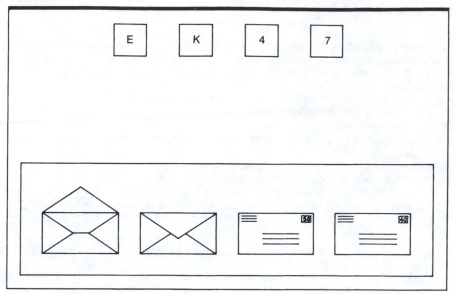

At the top of the illustration are the four cards in the Wason card problem. Which card or cards would you turn over to obtain conclusive evidence about the following rule: A card with a vowel on it will have an even number on the other side? At the bottom of the illustration are four envelopes. Which envelopes would you turn over to detect postal cheaters, under the rule that "an unsealed envelope can be stamped with the less expensive stamp"?

termed an *illicit conversion*. As an example, with a conditional of *If p, then q,* and evidence *q,* people tend to switch the conditional to **If q, then p.* They then proceed, incorrectly, to decide that the evidence *q* implies that *p* is true. Clearly, this is incorrect, since the order of *p* and *q* in the conditional is meaningful: the *if* often specifies some possible *cause,* and the *then* specifies a possible *effect.* Obviously, we cannot draw correct *cause–effect* conclusions if we reverse the roles of the cause (*p*) for some outcome and the result (*q*) of some cause.

The third kind of error that is found can be termed *searching for positive evidence,* also called the *confirmation bias.* As a demonstration, consider the now-classic study of conditional reasoning (reported in Wason & Johnson-Laird, 1972) illustrated in Figure 11-2, the "Wason card trick" problem. Four cards are visible to you, as shown in the figure, and each card has a letter on one side and a number on the other. The task is to pick the card or cards you would turn over to gather conclusive evidence on the following rule:

> If a card has a vowel on one side, then it has an even number on the other side.

Give this question some thought before you continue reading.

Of the subjects that Wason tested on this problem, 33% turned over only the E card, a correct choice conforming to the *modus ponens* method of affirming the antecedent. A thorough test of the rule's validity, however, requires that another card be turned over (in other words, the rule might be rephrased "Only if a card has a vowel on one side will it have an even number on the other side"). Only 4% of the subjects turned over the correct combination to check on this possibility, the E card (*modus ponens*) and the 7 card (the *modus tollens*). That is, turning over the 7, which would serve as negative evidence (*not q*), was rarely considered by the subjects. Instead, they much preferred turning over the E and the 4 card—46% of the subjects did this, where turning over the 4 is an instance of the invalid process of affirming the consequent (in other words, the rule doesn't say anything about what will be on the other side of a consonant; it could be an odd or an even number).

In short, turning over the E represents a search for positive evidence about the rule, evidence that *p* is true. The general tendency in such situations, however, is to stop the search for evidence there, or to continue searching for additional positive evidence (turning over the 4). Searching for *negative* evidence, that is, evidence that might show *p* to be false, was seldom done. Apparently, in this rather abstract problem, people have a general tendency to search only for information that would confirm the rule or hypothesis.

In a rather different situation, however, Johnson-Laird, Legrenzi, and Legrenzi (1972) found that 21 of 24 subjects made both of the correct choices. The difference between the two studies had to do with the concreteness of the situation. In the Johnson-Laird et al. study, subjects were trying to find cheaters on the postal regulations, where unsealed envelopes could be stamped with a less expensive stamp than sealed envelopes.

Think about this situation. What *if–then* rule is being tested? Since either a sealed or an unsealed envelope could be mailed with a more expensive stamp, the rule must be:

> If the envelope is sealed, then it must carry the expensive stamp.

When asked to detect cheaters, subjects not only turned over the sealed envelope, but also the envelope stamped with the less expensive stamp, that is, the *modus tollens* choice corresponding to the 7 card above. Since the subjects were not postal workers, it seems clear that it was the concreteness of the situation that oriented the subjects toward the "skeptical" attitude mentioned earlier. Their skepticism led them to search actively for negative evidence; in the process, they demonstrated logical conditional reasoning. (There is an unmistakable similarity here to the stages of concrete and formal operations in Piaget's theory of cognitive development, in which children around 12 years of age begin to reason formally, that is, abstractly; see Piaget, 1967, or Flavell, 1963. Interestingly, the present evidence would suggest that *adults* often fail to demonstrate formal or abstract reasoning processes, even though they can reason correctly in more concrete situations.)

Hypothesis Testing

Part of the importance of conditional reasoning derives from its connection to scientific hypothesis testing. Consider a typical experimental hypothesis:

> If theory A is true, then data resembling X should be obtained in the experiment.

Now if data resembling X are indeed obtained, there is a strong tendency to conclude that theory A must be true. That is, if the evidence is that data resembling X were obtained, this affirms the consequent. We then feel as if this evidence lets us conclude that *p* is true, that theory A is correct. What's wrong with this? It's a simple error of affirming the consequent, and concluding mistakenly that this is evidence that the antecedent is true. Note how seductive this error is. Of course it just might be true that theory A is correct. But then, it's also possible that theory A is incorrect and that some other (correct) theory would also predict data X.

Because of the illogic of affirming the consequent, and because we want to test hypotheses, our experiments test a *different* hypothesis than "Theory A is correct." As you learned (or will learn) in statistics, we test the *null* hypothesis in hopes that our evidence will be inconsistent with the predicted null outcome. Note the form of such a test:

> If the null hypothesis is true (*if p*), then there will be no effect of the variable (*then q*).

If we obtain evidence that there *is* an effect of the variable, that is, that the consequent is not true, we can then conclude that the antecedent is not true; we conclude that the null hypothesis is false, in other words. This is the essence of hypothesis testing, to conclude that the *if* portion of the null hypothesis is false based on an outcome that denies the consequent of the null hypothesis. Although subjects make a variety of errors in such situations, especially when the *if–then* relationship becomes more complex (Cummins, Lubart, Alksnis, & Rist, 1991), the typical mistake is simply to search for positive, confirming evidence (e.g., Klayman & Ha, 1989).

Summary Points: syllogisms; validity of the syllogism versus empirical truth of premises; Venn diagrams and searching for confirming evidence; conditional reasoning; affirming the antecedent/modus ponens; denying the consequent/modus tollens; confirmation bias; hypothesis testing

▼ Decisions

How do we make decisions? How do we choose among several alternatives, say, on a multiple-choice test, or decide which of several options is the best under some set of circumstances? What role does the information stored in memory play in decision making, and how certain are the decisions we make based on that information?

In a sense, we've been studying decision making all along in this book, although the decisions were often fairly simple, for example, deciding "yes" or "no" in semantic or lexical decision tasks. While performance in such tasks is usually interpreted in terms of search and retrieval processes, the Collins and Loftus (1975) model of semantic memory actually proposed a decision-based explanation for performance differences. Imagine that each semantic node that is activated during a search is then evaluated in a decision mechanism. If so, then each node might be thought to contribute evidence for or against a decision, in almost a democratic, voting-like process. That is, some retrieved connections will be very positive evidence *for* a decision; if the statement is "A robin has feet," then the *isa* pathways to BIRD and ANIMAL would be persuasive evidence for a "yes" decision. Alternatively, for a sentence like "A bat is a bird," both positive and negative evidence would accumulate, until eventually some criterion is reached for a "no" decision.

This is a useful notion, one we will encounter several times in this chapter. At base, it is that decision making can be viewed as a search for evidence, where the ultimate decision depends on some criterion or rule for evaluating the evidence. A search may turn up either positive or negative evidence or may uncover *both* positive and negative evidence. How we make decisions as a function of such evidence, and how the evidence itself is evaluated, is at the heart of the decision-making and reasoning process.

Let's turn to a very simple setting, in which we compare two objects or symbols, to see how the information stored in memory can influence comparison processes. We'll then turn to more complex decision-making and reasoning situations, again looking for the influence of stored knowledge and the evaluation of that information.

Decisions About Physical Differences

One of the very earliest areas of research in psychology was the area of **psychophysics;** indeed, a great deal of research on psychophysics was conducted well before psychology per se came into existence (e.g., Fechner, 1860). The topic of interest in psychophysics was the *psychological experience of physical stimulation, that is, how perceptual experience differs from the physical stimulation that is being perceived.* In particular, research on psychophysics investigated the relationships between the physical dimensions of stimuli and the subjective, psychological experience of perceiving those stimuli.

In general, what was discovered by these early researchers was that the subjective experience of magnitude, regardless of the particular dimension involved (brightness, loudness, etc.), was *not* identical to the physical magnitude of the display. Instead, there is a *psychological dimension* of magnitude that forms the basis of our perceptions. The psychological dimension is different from the physical dimension such that our perceptual experience is not a direct and perfect function of the physical stimulus.

For instance, the perceived brightness of a light is not a direct function of the light's physical brightness. Instead, perceived brightness depends on several factors, such as the absolute level of brightness, the brightness of the background, and the duration of the stimulus. Likewise, the amount by which brightness must be *changed* in order to perceive the change depends on more than just the amount of physical change in brightness. Perceived change depends critically on the initial level of the light's brightness. A dim light needs only a small boost in brightness for subjects to detect a difference, whereas a very bright light will require a much larger boost for the change to be noticed. The amount of change required for people to detect the change is called a **jnd,** a *just noticeable difference* (as in Weber's Law; see Haber & Hershenson, 1973, for example). The point now is that the size of the jnd increases as the physical stimulus becomes more intense. If only one jnd separates two

Decisions about size differences are psychophysical judgments, which are speeded up when stimuli differ by a great amount.

dim lights, the same physical difference in brightness between two *bright* lights may not be detectable. Our perceptual mechanism is affected by the psychological dimension of brightness, a *different* dimension than physical brightness. Thus psychological processing of a stimulus does not accurately mirror the physical stimulus properties. Instead, distortions and alterations of the stimulus are introduced during perception, and these distortions and alterations can be attributed to the human perceiver.

Of particular relevance to our discussion is a phenomenon we may call the **distance** or the **discriminability effect**—*the greater the distance or difference between the two stimuli being compared, the faster the decision that they differ* (Woodworth & Schlosberg, 1954). In other words, it's easier to discriminate between two physical stimuli that are very different (a finger snap versus a gunshot) than between two stimuli that are very similar (shots from two different guns). This is not at all a new finding in psychology; Moyer and Bayer (1976) cite four separate sources for this effect that were published before 1940.

Decisions About Symbolic Differences

Much more recently, investigators have found that a variety of similar effects are obtained in tasks involving **symbolic comparisons,** that is, comparisons not between two physical objects or stimuli but *between two symbols,* two objects represented by written or spoken symbols. The connection with the earlier work is that the distance effect still holds for mental comparisons of symbols. But because the effect is now based on symbolic rather than physical differences, the effect is called the *symbolic distance effect.* Just as in psychophysical judgments, the source of the symbolic distance effect is the person, the individual making the mental comparison and forming the judgment. The big difference here is that semantic and other long-term memory knowledge, rather than perceptual information, is influencing the decision-making process.

Consider the stimuli in panels A and B of Figure 11-3. Which dot is higher? Now despite the obviously simple nature of this decision, it is true that it takes some amount of time to make the decision. To begin with, the time to decide which dot is higher depends on the separation of the dots: the greater the separation, the faster the decision. This is the simple physical distance effect again—two stimuli can be discriminated more quickly when they differ more (Moyer & Bayer, 1976).

Now consider the bottom two illustrations. For panel C in Figure 11-3, which balloon is higher? For panel D, which yo-yo is lower? It is probably not obvious to you at a conscious level, but when subjects are asked "Which balloon is higher?" their judgments are affected not only by the discriminability of the two heights, but also by the *semantic* dimension required for the judgments (Banks, Clark, & Lucy, 1975). In other words, the semantic knowledge that balloons are held at the bottom by strings,

FIGURE 11-3

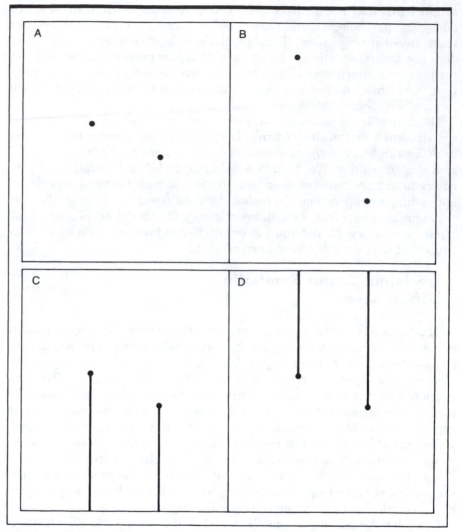

Stimuli used by Banks et al. (1975) in a study of physical and symbolic comparisons. In the top two panels, subjects were asked which dot is higher or lower. In the bottom two panels, subjects were asked which balloon is higher/lower and which yo-yo is higher/lower.

float up in the air, and are therefore oriented in terms of "high-ness" was a significant influence on the subjects' decision times; describing the illustrations as "balloons" led subjects to treat the pictures symbolically, rather than as mere physically different stimuli. When the same pictured display was accompanied by the question "Which balloon is *lower*?" judgments were much slower. And as you would expect, the situation was reversed when subjects judged stimuli like those in panel D, the yo-yos. "Which yo-yo is lower?" yielded faster decisions than "Which yo-yo is higher?" since semantic knowledge about yo-yos is that they hang *down* from their strings.

The name for this second effect is the *semantic congruity effect* (e.g., Banks, 1977; Banks et al., 1975). It states that the subject's decision will be faster when the dimension being judged *matches* or is *congruent* with the implied semantic dimension in the figure. In other words, the implied dimension in the balloon illustration is height, since balloons float up. When asked to judge "how high" some "high" object is, the judgment is speeded up since "height" is semantically congruent with "high." Likewise, "low-ness" is implied in the yo-yo display, so judging which of two "low things" is lower is also a congruent decision. Figure 11-4 displays the general form of both the symbolic distance effect and the semantic congruity effect (Banks, 1977).

Number Magnitude   Some of the clearest research supporting these idealized curves comes from Banks's work on judgments of numerical magnitude. In this research, subjects are shown a pair of digits, say, 1, 2, or 7, 8. In one condition, the instructions are to pick the smaller of the two values; in another, subjects are asked to pick the larger value. Of course, in all conditions, the RT to make the judgments is the dependent variable of major interest.

Can you predict what the results of such comparisons are, based on the distance and congruity effects? First, the larger the difference between the digits, the faster the judgments are made. In other words, picking the smaller of the pair 1, 3 will be faster than picking the smaller of 2, 3 since 1 and 3 differ from each other more than 2 and 3 do. This is the *symbolic distance effect,* similar to the physical distance effect, but now based purely on the symbolic meanings of the digits and the magnitudes to which they refer. Second, judgment time is affected by semantic congruity. Picking the *smaller* of two *small* digits is faster than picking the *larger* of two small digits, and vice versa. When the instructions ask for a judgment of smallness, symbols referring to small quantities are faster. When the instructions ask for a judgment of largeness, symbols referring to large quantities are faster to judge. To repeat, this latter result is the semantic congruity effect.

A variety of fascinating conclusions are supported by results such as these. First, when people make mental comparisons and judge magnitudes of purely symbolic quantities, there is a pronounced semantic distance effect. Just as in psychophysics, the psychological difference is not the same as the physical difference. In this case, the psychological differences between pairs of digits do not perfectly mirror the actual numerical differences between digits. Banks's research (e.g., Banks, Fujii, & Kayra-Stuart, 1976) suggests strongly that our mental representation of number and numerical magnitude is a nonlinear one. That is, it is a representation in which the psychological distances between larger numbers are *compressed,* relative to the distances between smaller numbers. Thus just as two bright lights are perceived as being more similar than two

FIGURE 11-4

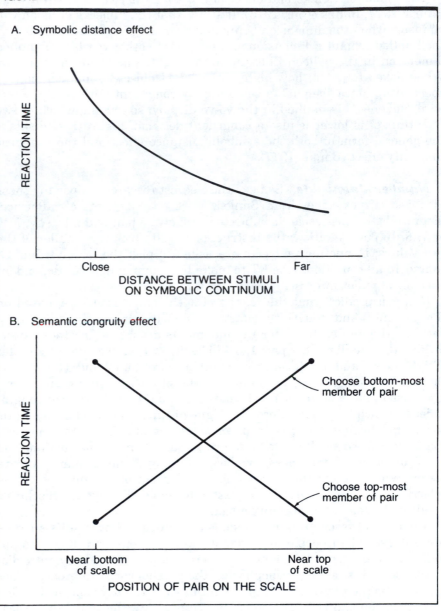

Idealized curves showing (A) the symbolic distance effect and (B) the semantic congruity effect. (From Banks, 1977.)

dim lights, two large numbers are psychologically closer together than two small numbers. In short, 1 and 2 are more different psychologically than 8 and 9 are, even though the numerical differences between the pairs are the same. This psychological distance between mental symbols is a strong determiner of performance.

Second, when we are asked to judge magnitudes, the dimension of judgment must match the implied semantic dimension in order for the comparison to be made quickly. A mismatch between the psychological dimension and the one specified by instructions (e.g., "choose the larger one" when the two things are small) slows down the comparison, even when the same quantities are being compared (see also Marschark & Paivio, 1979; Shoben, Sailor, & Wang, 1989).

At a more global level, the research also attests to another important idea as well: the particular *form* of a concept's representation in memory exerts an influence on the judgments we make. This is not a new idea, of course—after all, the network distances among concepts in semantic memory were said to be responsible for RT differences in semantic memory research. What is new, however, is the generality of this effect. We are asking subjects to compare two concepts stored in memory on some dimension of magnitude. By timing their judgments, we can come to understand *how* those concepts are represented in memory. This kind of task, timed mental comparisons, can be applied widely to all sorts of symbolic concepts.

Imagery Which is larger, a squirrel or a rabbit? Which is smaller, a mouse or a dog? Several investigators, notably Moyer (1973), have documented the symbolic distance and semantic congruity effects when people make judgments of this sort. What is fascinating is that the judgments are being made on the basis of the *visual image* of the object. That is, the evidence suggests that when people make these *larger/smaller* judgments about real-world objects, they retrieve mental images of the objects, then mentally scan the images to decide which one is larger or smaller. Moyer had his subjects estimate the absolute sizes of animals and then make timed comparisons between different pairs. His results, depicted in Figure 11-5, showed that RT decreased as the differences in size between the animals increased—the symbolic distance effect, of course. Furthermore, the relationship between image size and RT was logarithmic, as shown on the logarithmic scale of the *x*-axis. In other words, the size differences are compressed at the larger end of the scale relative to the smaller end, exactly what Banks (1977) found about the mental number line.

A final important aspect of these results relates to the mental imagery basis for the judgments. As Moyer (1973) and others (e.g., Kosslyn & Pomerantz, 1977) have argued, results such as these imply strongly that the semantic information being retrieved from memory is *imaginal*. That is, the retrieved information is in the form of visual images that have

FIGURE 11-5

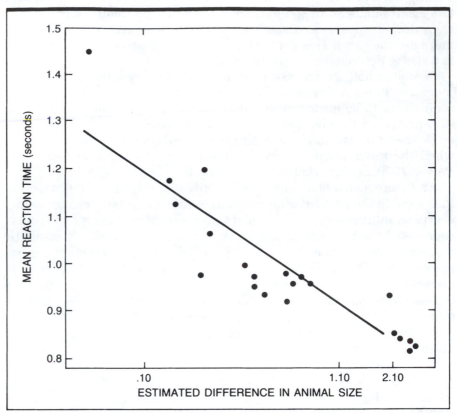

Moyer's (1973) reaction time results for judgments of which two animals is larger, plotted as a function of the estimated difference in size of the two animals. Note that the x-axis is plotted on a logarithmic scale.

been stored in long-term memory, not simply verbal-based propositions (see also Anderson, 1983).

Semantic Orderings   Consider some results by Holyoak and Walker (1976). These investigators had subjects make comparisons of pairs of concepts along the semantic orderings of time, quality, and temperature; for example, compare "minute versus hour," "average versus poor," "cool versus cold." The instructions given to subjects said either to choose the *longer/better/warmer* or the *shorter/worse/colder* of the two concepts in the pair. Just as was found in the numerical judgment task, subjects' performance demonstrated both the symbolic distance and the semantic congruity effects. Judgments were faster when the pair of terms differed a great deal (e.g., perfect versus poor) than when they differed by less (perfect versus excellent). And judgments were faster if the dimension of judgment was congruent with the stimulus values; for example, choosing the longer of "century versus decade" was easier than choosing the shorter of those two. And, in a study by Friedman (1978), the same kind of symbolic distance and semantic congruity effects were found when the concepts being compared had no physical or quantitative dimension at all; for example, choose the better or worse of pairs such as "lose versus peace," "hate versus pressure," and "allow versus young."

The important extension that these results provide is that the distance and congruity effects were found to influence decisions even when the underlying representation of the compared concepts was *not* quantitative. The strong implication here is that more abstract orderings must be mentally represented in a very similar fashion to number and other quantity-based orderings since they all "behave" in a similar way. Our mental representations of such semantic terms, and in particular the way those terms are ordered, influence our judgments in very much the same way as more quantitative representations do. The nature of the mental representation, furthermore, can introduce distortions that are analogous to those found in perceptual tasks. We make simple comparisons and decisions based on our stored knowledge. The form of that knowledge can distort our judgments to a surprising degree.

Judgments of Geographical Distance Perhaps not surprisingly, people's judgments of geographical distance seem to follow the same principles (e.g., Baum & Jonides, 1979; Holyoak & Mah, 1982). The point in this research is to have subjects make distance or location comparisons, then examine those comparisons to determine what the subjects' "mental maps" are like. In one such study, Holyoak and Mah (1982) tested subjects at the University of Michigan, asking them to rate the distances between American cities on a 1 to 9 scale. When no particular geographical reference point was given—the Neutral condition—subjects based their judgments on their own local viewpoint. As Figure 11-6 shows, they overestimated distances for nearby, Midwestern cities: they rated Kansas City, a fairly nearby city, as much further away than it really is, but Denver and Salt Lake City, more distant cities from Ann Arbor, as much closer together. Thus Holyoak and Mah demonstrated the familiar symbolic distance effect—the further away the cities were, the closer together they were in the mental representation. They also confirmed a certain "egocentrism" in adult thought; in a sense, the distorted "New Yorker's view of the world" can be transplanted *anywhere*.

Summary Points: psychophysics; jnd and discrimination; symbolic comparisons; symbolic distance effect; semantic congruity effect

▼ Decisions and Reasoning Under Uncertainty

Needless to say, some of the decisions we've been discussing, for instance, judging which of two numbers is smaller, are quite rapid and fairly automatic. We are not consciously aware of the differences in time

FIGURE 11-6

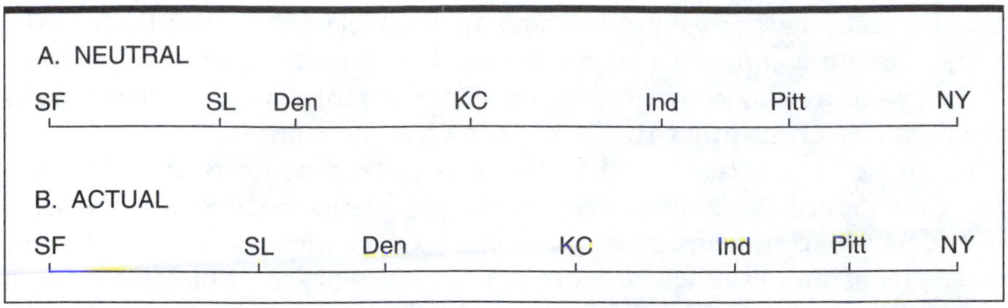

A. NEUTRAL

SF   SL   Den   KC   Ind   Pitt   NY

B. ACTUAL

SF   SL   Den   KC   Ind   Pitt   NY

Results of Holyoak and Mah's (1982) study of the relative locations of cities along an east-west line. Estimates in the Neutral perspective were made from the subjects' current location, Ann Arbor, Michigan, roughly halfway between Indianapolis and Pittsburgh on the east-west line. Subjects overestimated the distances to Denver, Kansas City, and Indianapolis, as shown by the Actual distances at the bottom.

necessary to make the digit judgments, nor can we introspect accurately on the basis of those decisions. We are typically only consciously aware of the *outcome* of those automatic processes: we know consciously that we responded "7" to the question "Which is larger, 4 or 7?" If asked to indicate why we responded that way, however, we tend to give rather intellectualized answers that probably have little if anything to do with the actual mental basis for the decision that was made (e.g., Ericsson & Simon, 1980). Furthermore, we are unaware of the exact nature of the mental representation that leads us to the judgment; to be blunt, nobody has conscious awareness of the compressed mental number line, although the research indicates that this is how numerical magnitude is mentally represented, from early grade-school ages up through adults (e.g., Banks, 1977; Duncan & McFarland, 1980).

In contrast to such relatively automatic decision making, the bulk of the cognitive research on decisions involves very deliberate and slow reasoning and decision-making situations. In fact, in many ways the research on such decisions is very similar to the area of problem solving, in which there is a clear connotation of slow, deliberate processing. One aspect of this similarity relates to familiarity: the domains of reasoning and problem solving that we investigate are usually not well known or understood by the subject, or they involve material that is not highly familiar to most people. Another similarity involves the notion of uncertainty: there is often no certain answer to the problems, or at least no good way of deciding if a particular type of solution is the correct approach or not.

And finally, the major conclusions of this kind of research are highly similar to the conclusions you'll read about in the next chapter on problem solving. People make decisions and base their reasoning on a variety of strategies, some good and some not so good. This is also a characteristic of much problem solving. Because of these similarities, investigations of such strategies are often impossible to categorize clearly as "reasoning" on the one hand or "problem solving" on the other. Thus, to an extent, putting a topic in a chapter on reasoning versus in a chapter on problem solving is quite arbitrary and suggests a neater division than is truly possible.

Algorithms and Heuristics

By far and away the most influential work done in this area of decision making has been that of Tversky and Kahneman (e.g., 1973, 1974, 1980; Kahneman & Tversky, 1972, 1973; Kahneman, Slovic, & Tversky, 1982; Shafir & Tversky, 1992). It is quite rare that research in cognitive psychology influences other fields as well, and yet Tversky and Kahneman's work has had an impact in such diverse areas as law, medicine, and business (e.g., Libbey, 1981; Parker, Porter, & Finley, 1983). Indeed, any situation involving human reasoning and decision making would probably be an appropriate area to study within the framework these authors have provided.

A basic distinction is necessary here at the outset in order to understand the nature of this important research. In many reasoning and problem-solving settings there are two general approaches that can be taken in order to achieve a problem solution or reason out an appropriate answer. One approach is termed an **algorithmic approach,** and the other is a **heuristic approach.**

An **algorithm** is a *specific rule or solution procedure, often quite detailed and complex, that is guaranteed to furnish the correct answer if it is followed correctly.* We are familiar with algorithms largely through our schoolwork in arithmetic and mathematics. For example, we all learned an algorithmic approach to complex multiplication, a set of rules for applying operations in certain orders to arrive at the correct answer. If the rules are applied correctly, the algorithm provides the correct answer.

In the contrasting approach, the solution method involves what is known as a **heuristic.** A heuristic is *a "rule of thumb,"* as opposed to a formal, specified rule. It's an informal, "seat of the pants" strategy or approach that works under some circumstances, for some of the time, but *is not guaranteed to yield the correct answer.*[1]

The Eight-Letter Problem   As an example, consider a question like the following: How many four- and five-letter words can be formed from the set of letters A, B, M, N, O, R, S, and T? There is, of course, a perfectly appropriate and accurate algorithm that will provide the answer to this question; take *all* possible four- and five-letter combinations, write

---

[1]The word *heuristic* comes from the Greek stem meaning "to invent or discover." The same word stem leads to the word *eureka,* the classic exclamation, supposedly uttered by Archimedes in his bathtub, meaning roughly "Aha, I've found it!"

DEMONSTRATIONS

1. The professional stereotypes research indicates that subjects ignore base rates (prior odds) when personality descriptions match the stereotypes ("likes mathematical puzzles" for engineers), or even when the description is deliberately neutral ("of high ability and high motivation" for engineers or lawyers). It would be interesting to investigate professional stereotypes themselves in such a task. Take a situation like "there are 30 professors and 70 plumbers in a room." If the characteristic you pick seems to match a stereotype (e.g., "reads historical novels as a hobby"), it should alter the probabilities estimated by your subjects. You might see whether mismatching characteristics have an opposite effect. Try descriptions with characteristics that vary in plausibility to see how this affects the judgments; for example, a professor who plays golf, one who swims, one who scuba dives, one who competes in surfing competitions.

2. Test the "Wason card trick" situation in a variety of ways, with a drawing of the cards on paper versus real note cards, under instructions that emphasize "make a guess as to which two cards" versus "think very carefully about which two cards" should be turned over. Try it again with the sealed envelope/postage stamp scenario, or other similar situations. For instance, Griggs and Cox (1982) tested conditional reasoning on a familiar conditional rule: if the person is drinking alcohol, then that person must be at least 21 years old. Set up the four cards, Drinking Alcohol, Drinking a Coke, 16 years old, 21 years old, and see which cards your subjects turn over to check for violations of the drinking laws.

3. Develop other stories to be tested in the "If only . . ." situation of the simulation heuristic, and see if the subjects' personal knowledge of the situation influences the number or kind of changes, or if it prompts them to focus on the true cause of the incident. For example:

Although Gary usually kept up in his coursework, he fell behind that semester because of his heavy course load and his outside job. He had done the library work, but was going to have to write and type the entire term paper the night before the due date. As luck would have it, in the middle of typing, the power went out and his word processor lost the entire document. The next day, as he walked to his professor's office to ask for an Incomplete, he thought to himself "If only. . . ."

4. Having people complete the diagrams on the naive physics beliefs is a virtually failsafe project. Be sure you interview your subjects on their reasons for drawing the pathways they drew (be sure you understand the correct pathways before you try explaining the principles behind them). It would be interesting to know how other groups of subjects respond; in Donley and Ashcraft's (1992) paper, the professors in the physics department performed essentially perfectly, while professors—all of them PhDs—in other departments were no more accurate than students in the undergraduate physics sequence.

them down, then check each combination against a dictionary to see if it is a word or not (for reasons to become clear later on, spend a moment right now simply estimating the *total* number of four- and five-letter combinations that are possible, regardless of whether the combination spells a word). Such a procedure is likely to be similar to the way we might program a computer to solve the problem: follow some very systematic and orderly procedure that is guaranteed to yield the result, however long it might take to get there.

A heuristic approach to this problem, in stark contrast, seems very human indeed: it is not particularly systematic or orderly, it relies fairly heavily on "educated guessing," and it is especially prone to distortions, inaccuracies, and, in the present example, to omissions. One heuristic for this problem might be "Assume that most of the words start with a consonant." Another might be to attempt to find words beginning with familiar spelling patterns such as *st* and *sm* (e.g., *star, smart*). Note that neither of these heuristics will generate all the candidate words. For instance, if you rely on the first heuristic, you'll miss such words as *abort*. The second heuristic will steer you away from relatively unusual spelling combinations such as the "oa" in *boat* and *moat*. And neither heuristic reminds you to form plurals, for example, *boats, bars*. Indeed, these characteristics are the very hallmarks of the heuristic approach: it will work part of the time, or for part of the answer, but it is very unlikely to furnish the complete, accurate answer.

Table 11-3 shows the correct algorithmic approach for the first part of this problem, the formula that specifies the number of possible combinations. It also illustrates an important point, one reason why people rely so heavily on heuristic rather than algorithmic approaches. The algorithm here, with a total of eight letters to be arranged, will generate 8400 four- and five-letter combinations. This is a staggering number of combinations, far more than people can realistically be expected to generate on their own (this is another reason we use computers to do such algorithmic work—they don't get bored by such repetitive tasks as taking all combinations). It's almost as if people realize at the outset that the algorithmic approach is too lengthy for either a mental or pencil-and-paper solution, so they opt instead for the passable heuristic approach. It won't supply all the answers, but it'll be good enough (see "satisficing" in Chapter 12).

As an exercise, see how many four- and five-letter words you can generate from the list of letters, trying to keep track of the different heuristics you used. Having done this, work the problem again, this time writing the letters down on scraps of paper that can be rearranged on your desk. Most people are surprised at how many more words are immediately apparent when the letters can be physically manipulated in front of them. Clearly, using scraps of paper is a better heuristic than trying to rearrange the letters mentally, which requires maintaining in memory all the combinations you've tried.

Table 11-3   COMPUTING THE NUMBER OF COMBINATIONS

Let's use the example of the eight letters A, B, M, N, O, R, S, and T. The first part of the question involves computing the number of different four-letter combinations possible among these eight letters, then the number of different five-letter combinations, then adding these two together. The second part, scanning the resulting list of combinations to see which are words, has a different solution, so we'll focus here on just the first part.

The rule for computing combinations is as follows. Let N be the number of elements that can be combined, here the eight letters. Let r be the number of elements that should appear in the combinations; here we are interested first in four-element combinations, then five-element combinations. The rule for computing the number of combinations is:

$$N!/(N - r)!$$

where the symbol "!" means factorial (e.g., 4!, is $4 \times 3 \times 2 \times 1$). Thus for the four-letter combinations, we have $8!/(8 - 4)!$ which reduces to $8!/4!$, or $40,320/24 = 1680$ letter combinations of length four. Likewise, for the five-letter combinations, we have $8!/(8 - 5)!$, which reduces to $8!/3!$, or $40,320/6 = 6720$ letter combinations of length five. Thus for the total number of four- and five-letter combinations, we have $1680 + 6720 = 8400$ unique combinations.

Compare these values to the following: in a demonstration study, subjects estimated the total number of four- and five-letter combinations to be 300, well short of 8400.

Heuristic Reasoning and Judgments

Kahneman and Tversky's research has focused extensively on a set of reasoning heuristics that appear to characterize much of people's everyday reasoning about uncertain events. That is, their interest has been in how people predict the likelihood of future events, how people categorize events or occurrences, and how various biases and errors in such judgments can be accounted for by an understanding of the reasoning process.

In some of the situations they have studied, there is an appropriate algorithm that can be applied to arrive at the correct answer. Many of these kinds of situations involve *probabilistic reasoning,* the sort of judgments and likelihood estimations that students are often asked to make in the probability chapter of an undergraduate statistics book. Knowledge of the algorithms, of course, doesn't necessarily mean that the individual understands them, can use them spontaneously, or can recognize all the situations when they should be applied. Indeed, Kahneman and Tversky found that a sample of graduate students in psychology, all of whom had been exposed to the relevant statistical algorithms, did well on very simple problems but still relied on the heuristic, rather than algorithmic, method when given more complex situations. On the other hand, several studies have shown more positive effects—good transfer and improved reasoning—when some relevant training is given (e.g., Agnoli, 1991; Agnoli & Krantz, 1989; Fong & Nisbett, 1991; Lehman, Lempert, & Nisbett, 1988). Incidentally, reading Tversky and Kahneman's papers, for instance, the 1973 article, is often very helpful to students as they *study* probability in a statistics class. See Nisbett, Krantz, Jepson, and Kunda (1983) on statistical heuristics that people use in everyday reasoning.

Other situations that have been studied involve peoples' estimates of likelihood when precise probabilities cannot be assigned or have not been supplied, although elements of statistical and probabilistic reasoning are still appropriate to a correct reasoning solution. And finally, some of the settings that have been studied involve very uncertain, or even impossible situations, for example, asking people to predict the outcome of some hypothetical event. For instance, how would the outcome of World War II have changed if Germany had developed the atomic bomb before the United States?

We'll begin with the most heavily researched of Kahneman and Tversky's heuristics, the representativeness and availability heuristics, then devote some attention to other kinds of judgment processes. As you read, try to develop your own examples of reasoning situations that are similar to the stated examples. You'll be surprised at how frequently we use such heuristics in everyday decision making and reasoning, even though we may feel that we seldom if ever use probability in the "real world."

The Representativeness Heuristic

If you toss a coin six times in a row, which of the following two outcomes is more likely: HHHTTT or HHTHTT? Most of us would agree, and quite rapidly at that, that the second alternative, the one with the alternations between heads and tails, is a more likely outcome than the run of three heads followed by three tails. But if you'll stop and think about it for a moment, you'll realize that each of these alternatives is *exactly* as likely as the other, since each is *just one* of the possible ways six coin tosses can occur (the total number of distinct outcomes is 2^6, i.e., 64 distinct sequences of heads and tails).

Part of what fools us, no doubt, is that we think of the alternating pattern HHTHTT as a *representative* of a whole class of outcomes, the class where most of the outcomes are random-looking alternations between heads and tails. This is incorrect, of course, since the problem asked about the likelihood of exactly the two given sequences, not the general class of sequences with alternations. But the mistake we make is an important indicator of how we often reason in similar situations (see problem 1 in the Appendix at the end of this chapter).

According to Kahneman and Tversky (1972), when we judge the likelihood or probability of uncertain events, we do so on the basis of the event's representativeness. The *representativeness heuristic* is a judgment rule in which your estimate of the probability of an event is determined by one of two features: (1) how similar the event is to the population of events it came from, or (2) whether the event seems similar to the process that produced it. In other words, we judge whether event A

One of the richest sources of evidence about human reasoning is gambling.

belongs to class B based on the extent to which A is representative of B, the degree to which it resembles B, or the degree to which it resembles the kind of process that B is known to be.

Random Processes   In our coin-toss example, we all know that getting heads or tails is a chance, or random, process. Given that event B, tossing coins, is random, we then judge the sequence HHTHTT as much more likely or probable than HHHTTT, because the alternating sequence HHTHTT *resembles* the outcome of a random process more than HHHTTT. The thinking here, rather illogical but nonetheless understandable, is that a random process ought to look random; it ought to generate a random-looking outcome. Accordingly, the sequence of three heads then three tails looks *nonrandom,* and hence seems to be much less likely. Likewise, since the likelihood for six tosses is three heads and three tails (in the long run), virtually *any* sequence with three of each will appear more representative than sequences with more of one outcome than the other. (See Pollatsek, Konold, Well, & Lima, 1984, for evidence on people's beliefs about random sampling processes.)[2]

---

[2]Gilovich, Vallone, and Tversky (1985) explored people's beliefs in "shooting streaks" in basketball, where the likelihood of a second "hit" is judged to be higher after a "hit" has already happened. Their analysis of shooting accuracy of the Philadelphia 76ers, and of Cornell players' predictions and performance, indicates no objective basis for the belief, but indicates strong subjective beliefs nonetheless. This is, of course, a situation in which the "parent population" of events is presumed to be nonrandom, in other words, is believed to be a relatively long sequence of "hits" during a shooting streak; the presumption, however, is incorrect. In short, people perceive patterns in genuinely random sequences.

Representativeness of the Parent Population Consider now a situation more like Kahneman and Tversky's first criterion, where the event is similar in essential characteristics to its parent population (i.e., to the population of events from which the event of interest is drawn). These authors' example of this situation goes as follows:

In a certain town there are two hospitals. In one, about 45 babies are born each day, in the other only about 15. As you know, about 50% of all babies are boys, although on any day, of course, this percentage may be higher or lower. Across one year, the hospitals recorded the number of days on which 60% or more of the babies were male. Which hospital do you think had more such days? (After Kahneman & Tversky, 1972, p. 443. Decide on your own answer before reading further.)

The majority of Kahneman and Tversky's subjects claimed that the number of days with 60% or more male babies would be about the same for the two hospitals; 28 of the 50 subjects drew this conclusion. Twelve of the 50 subjects said the larger hospital would have more such days, and only 10 subjects said the smaller hospital would have more days with 60% or more male babies. Another group of subjects was tested with a slightly different question, which asked about days on which "less than 60%" of the babies were male. These results were largely comparable. Thus with either question, most subjects believed that both hospitals would have about the same number of days on which 60% or more (or fewer) of the babies would be male.

Let's explain this. Consider the conclusion that subjects drew, that both the small and large hospital have about the same number of "extreme" days. People know that there will be variations around the expected percentage of 50%, and that 60% is somewhat extreme. Since events that are "somewhat extreme" do occasionally happen, a small and a large hospital both having 60% or more male babies is viewed as representative of a larger population, that being the population of all hospitals having a few days, just by chance, where 60% or more of the babies are male. Note that there is an implicit—and incorrect—assumption here that "extreme" means the same thing for the two hospitals.

In fact, the correct answer here is that the smaller hospital will probably have more days on which 60% or more of the babies were male. The reason for this is an elementary notion in statistics and sampling. Extreme or unlikely outcomes are *more* likely to be seen as the sample size gets *smaller*. That is, with fewer events, the likelihood is *greater* that the events will vary from the expected proportion. Thus, in reality, it is more likely that the small hospital will have more extreme days, days on which 60% or more babies are male, than the large hospital. The reason is that the 60% proportion is being computed on an average of 15 births, instead of 45. Another way of saying this is that, given the fifty–fifty odds, 60% is not as extreme an occurrence out of 15 opportunities as is 60% out of 45 opportunities; 60% or more male babies is not as extreme for the small hospital as it is for the large one.

Table 11-4   BIASES IN THE REPRESENTATIVENESS HEURISTIC

1. *Ignoring Base Rates (Ignoring Prior Odds)* (Adapted from Johnson & Finke, 1985)
Questions:
(a) Why are more graduate students first-born than second-born children?
(b) Why do more hotel fires start on the first ten floors than the second ten floors?
(c) In baseball, are more runners thrown out by pitchers on first base or on second base?
The bias: In all three questions, people tend to ignore base rates. To answer the questions correctly, we should consider:
(a) How many first-born versus second-born people are there?
(b) How many hotels even *have* a second ten floors?
(c) How many runners on first base versus second base are there?

2. *Base Rates and Stereotypes*
Question:
Frank is a rather meek and quiet individual, whose only hobby is playing chess. He was near the top of his college class and majored in philosophy. Is Frank a librarian or a businessman?
The bias: The personality description seems to match a librarian stereotype, whether the stereotype is true or not. Second, we fail to consider base rates, that is, the relative frequencies of the two professions. In other words, there are far more businessmen than librarians, a base rate that tends to be ignored because of the stereotype "match."

3. *Gambler's Fallacy*
Question:
You've watched a (fair) coin toss come up heads five times in a row. If you bet $10 on the next toss, would you choose heads or tails?
The bias: The Gambler's Fallacy is that the next toss is more likely to be tails, because "it's time for tails to show up." Of course, the five previous tosses have no bearing at all on the sixth toss, assuming a fair coin. The bias is related to the law of small numbers, in particular, that we expect randomness even on the "local" or short-run outcomes. Thus getting tails after five heads seems more representative of the random process that produces the outcomes, so we mistakenly prefer to bet $10 on tails.

On statistical grounds, this is precisely the same reasoning as the fact that "all heads" is a more likely outcome for two coin tosses than it is for six coin tosses. "All heads" for two coin tosses has a probability of .25, whereas "all heads" for six coin tosses has a probability of .0156. The Appendix explains the algorithmic, statistical basis for both the six-flip coin toss and the hospital examples; Table 11-4 summarizes the representativeness heuristic and several of the biases that stem from its use.

This particular bias in the representativeness heuristic is termed *insensitivity to sample size.* It means, in brief, that when people reason about such events, they fail to take into account the size of the sample or group on which the event is based. Few are fooled, probably, with the "all heads" example for two versus six coin tosses, partly because the extreme event ("all heads") is easier to conceptualize than the "more than 60% male" occurrence (it would be interesting to know which way subjects would respond if the hospital example were changed from "greater than 60%" to "all male babies"). But with the more abstract example, people often fail to understand how a smaller group is more likely to show more "extreme" outcomes than a larger group.

Another way of expressing this insensitivity is that people believe in *the law of small numbers*. Now the *law of large numbers*—that a *large* sample will be more representative of its population—is true. But people erroneously believe that the law of small numbers is true as well. People incorrectly assume that a small sample will be just as representative of its parent population as a large sample will (see also Bar-Hillel, 1980).

Stereotypes   Another bias, also due to the representativeness heuristic, is of particular importance since it probably affects our every-day reasoning about other people more than the statistical or probabilistic situations (Table 11-4 provides additional examples and explanations of the representativeness effects and biases). Kahneman and Tversky (1973) reported some fascinating evidence on estimations of likelihood based on personality descriptions. They read various personality descriptions to subjects, then had them estimate the likelihood or probability that the described individual was a member of one versus another profession. To a surprising degree, people's estimations can be influenced by the similarity of a description to a widely held stereotype.

Consider first the situation; 100 people are in a room, 70 of them lawyers, 30 of them engineers. Given this situation, answer the following question:

1. An individual named Bill was randomly selected from this roomful of 100 people. What is the likelihood that Bill is a lawyer?

Simple probability tells us that the chances of selecting a lawyer are .70, given the situation described. People generally reason correctly in such situations, according to Kahneman and Tversky, that is, in a "bare bones" situation. The technical term for these "bare bones," the 70:30 proportion, is *prior odds* or, simply, *base rates*. Prior to any other information, the probability of sampling a lawyer is .70, and the probability of sampling an engineer is .30.

Consider now two slightly different situations. There are still the same 70 lawyers and 30 engineers. But now, you are given a description of two randomly selected individuals and are asked "What is the likelihood that this individual is an engineer?" (adapted from Kahneman & Tversky, 1973, pp. 241–242):

2. "Dick is a 30-year-old man. He is married with no children. A man of high ability and high motivation, he promises to be quite successful in his field. He is well liked by his colleagues."

3. "Jack is a 45-year-old man. He is married and has four children. He is generally conservative, careful, and ambitious. He shows no interest in political and

social issues and spends most of his free time on his many hobbies, which include home carpentry, sailing, and mathematical puzzles."

Kahneman and Tversky's subjects did *not* judge the probabilities for these two descriptions to be the same as the prior odds, that is, .70 for lawyers, .30 for engineers. Instead, they assumed that the personality descriptions contained relevant information and adjusted their estimates accordingly. In particular, for both descriptions 2 and 3, subjects responded that the probability was close to .50, that is, about a fifty–fifty chance that Dick and Jack were engineers.

Note that description 3 was intended to resemble the stereotype many people have of engineers. It mentions such factors as "careful" and "mathematical puzzles," which presumably are representative of engineers—at least they are representative of our *stereotypes* of engineers. Here, subjects essentially ignored the prior odds and based their judgments on the description itself. The same thing happened with description 2, even though it was intentionally written to be totally uninformative with regard to Dick's profession.

It's illogical, but probably understandable, that description 3 led to distorted estimates. People viewed the personality description as representative of the engineering profession, so adjusted their estimates upward from the .30 level. The stereotype may be wrong, or at least biased or inaccurate in some details, but people still based their judgments on the description and stereotype more than on the prior odds. Of course, the appropriate strategy is to weight the new evidence, taking into account its predictive accuracy along with the prior odds (there's an algorithm for this too, but it requires knowledge of the predictive accuracy of the new evidence). Instead, people tend to view *any such evidence* as a basis for accurate prediction, and in the process they lose sight of prior odds (see also Fischhoff & Bar-Hillel, 1984).

All things considered, however, it's hardly understandable at all that subjects would do the same thing with description 2, that is, take that evidence as even remotely relevant. And yet this is what they do, even when the evidence is intentionally neutral. In fact, Fischhoff and Bar-Hillel (1984) found that very few of their subjects regarded intentionally neutral descriptions as truly neutral. Instead, they categorized the personality descriptions as belonging to one of the two professions, *despite* the description's neutrality, and were surprisingly confident in their categorizations as well. It may be, in such situations, that subjects believe that the evidence is *meant* to be taken as relevant (e.g., see the "be relevant" conversational postulate in Chapter 9). In any event, the distortions evident in the subjects' answers are intriguing. Apparently, as Kahneman and Tversky put it, "people respond differently when given no specific evidence and when given worthless evidence. When no specific evidence is given, the prior probabilities are properly utilized; when worthless specific evidence is given, prior probabilities are ignored" (1973, p. 242).

The Usefulness of the Representativeness Heuristic   We've focused on the biases and errors that crop up when people rely on the representativeness heuristic. Basically, people tend to ignore the relevant information available in a situation and base their reasoning instead on how much an outcome resembles or seems representative of the population or process being considered. On the other hand, heuristics were defined as strategies that sometimes *do* provide a correct answer. In other words, heuristics are not invariably misleading: if they were, then we presumably would never use them. As Nisbett and Ross (1980) point out, heuristics are generally useful but lead to errors when they are over- or misapplied, or when they substitute for use of a more complex, but appropriate strategy.

What *is* useful about the representativeness heuristic is that it often provides a very good basis for judging likelihoods of *general* classes of outcomes. Imagine that the original six coin toss example is changed slightly. Instead of being asked which of these two outcomes is more likely, imagine being asked which of these two *kinds* of outcomes is more likely. In such a rewording, it is now obvious that the specific sequences are of less interest than the *general* classes they represent, one being an alternating pattern in the fifty–fifty situation, and one being a pair of straight runs with length of three. Of course, the *kind* of pattern represented by HHTHTT is *much* more likely than the kind represented by HHHTTT (see the Appendix). Thus if you had bet money on the coin, and

Safety

安全
安全
안전

Sicherheit
Sécurité
Seguridad

If you are sitting in an exit row and you can not read this card or can not see well enough to follow these instructions, please tell a crew member.

非常口の隣にご着席で、英語がおわかりにならない方は、乗務員にお申し出ください。

您若坐在走道位子並且不懂英文,請告知本機服務員。

출구쪽 줄에 앉으시고 영어를 못읽어드시면 승무원에게 말씀하십시오.

Wenn sie neben einem ausgang sitzen und sie verstehen kein Englisch, bitte verständigen sie die flugzeugbesatzung.

Si vous êtes assis dans une rangée de sièges à côté d'une sortie, et vous ne comprenez pas la langue anglaise, veuillez le dire à un membre de l'équipage.

Si usted se encuentra sentado/a en una fila de asientos a la par de una salida u usted no entiende el idioma inglés, favor de avisarle a un tripulante.

then saw a sequence *like* HHHTTT, you'd be much more suspicious that the coin was rigged than if you saw a sequence *like* HHTHTT.

Likewise, we have to imagine that professional stereotypes have at least *some* relationship to the individuals who engage in that profession, even though we would admit that the stereotype is only a loose description, that it isn't *necessary* that each person in that profession have this or that characteristic, and that stereotypes are often related to deplorable practices such as discrimination. For example, it is not surprising that one stereotype about engineers is that they are more interested in quantitative topics than "the average person." After all, much of engineering involves highly quantitative information. Hearing that some individual, either a lawyer or engineer, *enjoys* mathematical puzzles, then, matches an engineering stereotype, and therefore seems representative of the *kind* of individual in that profession.

Summary Points: algorithms; heuristics; probabilistic reasoning; representativeness heuristic; random processes, parent populations; insensitivity to sample size; the law of small numbers; stereotypes

The Availability Heuristic

What proportion of all medical doctors are women? What proportion of U.S. households own a microwave oven, a color TV, or a VCR? How much safer are you in a commercial airliner than in a private car, or vice versa? Questions such as these ask you to estimate the frequency or probability of real-world events, even though you are unlikely to have the evidence or knowledge stored in memory. Each of the questions is answerable in the sense that the precise answer is a matter of public record (although it may not be easy to obtain). And yet, since we do not know the precise answer, we must *estimate* the answer based on the shreds of information we do have in memory. How do we perform this estimation process?

The simplest basis for making these estimates is to try to recall relevant information or examples from memory. The *frequency* with which events occur is a kind of information that is coded in memory (e.g., Hasher & Zacks, 1984), perhaps automatically (see Chapter 5). So when we attempt to retrieve examples of the events from memory, the way their frequency has been coded in memory is an important factor. If the retrieval of examples is easy, we infer that the event must be fairly frequent or common. If retrieval is difficult, then we estimate that the event must *not* be frequent.

This is the second important strategy that Tversky and Kahneman (1973) have discussed, the **availability heuristic.** In this heuristic, we evaluate "the frequency of classes or the probability of events . . . by the ease with which relevant instances come to mind" (p. 207). "Ease of retrieval" is what the term *availability* means here.[3] In short, when people have to make estimates of likelihood or frequency, their estimates are influenced by the ease with which relevant examples can be remembered.

The Usefulness of the Availability Heuristic   The availability heuristic often provides a very good strategy for responding. That is, the ease of remembering examples is reasonably well correlated with objective frequency; in general, frequent events are indeed more easily remembered than infrequent events, simply because events of all sorts are noticed and then coded in memory as they occur. As an example, answer the following: Are there more red cars or yellow cars? Most people would estimate that red cars are more numerous, based on casual observation. Here we would expect no particular bias in the mental coding of frequency of car colors, so our estimates based on availability in memory should be fairly good.

Biases Within the Availability Heuristic   While the availability heuristic is often a reliable way of making estimates (indeed, it is often the *only* way we have of making estimates in many situations), there are nonetheless some distortions and biases that may stem from it. Basically, any factor that leads to storage of information or events in memory can influence our reasoning here, since our judgments are based on what can be remembered easily. If reasonably accurate and undistorted information is in memory, then the availability heuristic probably does a reasonable job. But to the extent that our memory contains information that is inaccurate, incomplete, or influenced by factors other than objective frequency, there may be biases and distortions in our reasoning.

In particular, any factor besides frequency that calls attention to the event may make the event more memorable, make it stand out more in memory. In the terms we used in Chapter 5, such events may be more *accessible* for retrieval. This will bias our estimates, since the ease of retrieval would be influenced not simply by frequency but also by those other memorability factors.

Some of the biases that occur are no doubt due to personal reasons—preferences, dislikes, or other idiosyncratic factors. As a simple example, if your friend's Volvo needs repeated trips to the mechanic, you may develop an inflated view of how unreliable Volvos are; if your *only* source of knowledge is the friend's opinion, the availability heuristic has biased your judgment.

More generally, there are biases not due to personal factors, but instead to other kinds of knowledge stored in memory. These other fac-

---

[3]Note that this differs from our use of the term in long-term memory research, in which *availability* connotes the *presence of information in memory,* whether or not the information is *accessible.* See Chapter 5 on "Encoding Specificity" and "Retrieval Failure."

tors, sometimes obvious and sometimes subtle, will also influence how easily we can remember examples and hence will introduce errors in our estimates.

General World Knowledge   As an illustration of the availability heuristic, estimate the ratio of the number of Chevrolet cars sold to the number of Cadillacs sold. According to the availability heuristic, you base your estimate on whatever frequency-based knowledge you may have in memory. If you have no personal reason to notice one kind of car more than another, your estimate may be a reasonably fair guess about the relative frequency of different makes of cars. Apart from personal biases, however, your general world knowledge tells you that Cadillacs are rather expensive, whereas Chevrolets are considerably less expensive. Given such economic factors, you might estimate that relatively few Cadillacs are sold compared to Chevrolets.

Alternatively, the cost factor might cause you to adjust your initial guess upward, in a sense correcting your frequency estimate by the additional information that Cadillacs are possibly *less* frequent than your initial guess due to their cost; this is called the *anchoring and adjusting heuristic,* by the way (e.g., Carlson, 1990). Most people estimate that Chevrolets are about 10 or 15 times more numerous than Cadillacs. According to recent General Motors data (1991 and 1992 combined), however, the ratio is almost exactly 5:1 for all models of Chevrolets versus all models of Cadillacs. Subjects almost uniformly report that the cost factor led them to their high estimates; most are quite surprised at the actual ratio. (Here's another surprise, especially for city dwellers; the GM truck division sells almost exactly the same number of vehicles per year as the car division, a 1:1 ratio.)

Familiarity Biases   Another example, studied directly by Tversky and Kahneman, shows very clearly how the bias in availability is related to "ease of recall." The authors constructed lists of names, 39 names per list, with 19 women's and 20 men's names per list. One group of subjects heard the lists, and then had to recall as many names as they could remember. Another group heard the lists, then estimated whether the list contained more names of men or women. In two of the four lists that were tested, the women's names were famous (e.g., Elizabeth Taylor) and the men's names were not; in the other two lists, the men's names were famous (e.g., Richard Nixon) and the women's names were not. In the recall groups, subjects remembered an average of 12 of the 19 famous names, but only 8 of the 20 less famous names. This, of course, shows that familiar or famous names were more easily recalled.

The important connection between ease of recall and estimation bias came from the groups that had to estimate the proportion of male versus female names. Here too, the fame of the names influenced the judgments. Subjects who heard the "famous female" lists estimated that there had been more women's names, and those who heard the "famous male" lists said there had been more men's names. Thus in this study, there was clear evidence, first, that the famous names were indeed more easily recalled, and second, that this greater availability for recall influenced the estimates of frequency.

Salience and Vividness Biases   Examples of the availability heuristic in the everyday world are not difficult to imagine. For instance, consider people's feelings about traveling by airplane. Many people do not know that, statistically, one is far safer traveling by commercial airliner than traveling by private car; the National Transportation Safety Board and National Highway Transportation Safety Council statistics state that air travel is many times safer, based on normalized passenger-miles traveled. People who have no particularly relevant information stored in memory, that is, those whose only information comes from casual attention to news media and the like, presumably would judge that one is much safer when traveling by car than by airliner.

This bias can be attributed to the factor of *salience* or *vividness*. The news accounts of an airline accident are far more vivid, and given far more attention, than accounts of passenger car accidents. And even though airplane crashes are rare, the number of victims involved is often dramatic enough that the event makes a much stronger impression than is objectively called for. But when you estimate air versus car safety factors, of course, the vividness of the recalled information tends to bias your judgment. For those who *do* know intellectually that air travel is safer, we might look for other evidence of the bias; for instance, people are surely more nervous when traveling in an airliner, on the average, than when traveling in a private car.

The Simulation Heuristic

The final heuristic to be discussed is called the *simulation heuristic*. In this heuristic, we are asked to make some prediction of future events; alternatively, we are asked to imagine some different outcome of an event or action. The use of the term *simulation* here comes from the area of computer simulation. In a computer simulation, certain "starting" values are entered, and the simulation then proceeds to forecast or predict some set of outcomes based on the processes written into the program. In similar fashion, the **simulation heuristic** involves *a mental construction or imagining of outcomes, a forecasting of how some event will turn out or how it might have turned out under another set of circumstances.*

The ease with which these plausible scenarios or outcomes can be imagined is the basis for the simulation heuristic. To the extent that a hypothetical sequence of events can easily be imagined, the events are *available* in the sense of Tversky and Kahneman's term. Alternatively, if it is difficult to construct a plausible scenario, the hypothetical event or

outcome would be viewed as unlikely, or possibly would not be constructed or imagined at all. In short, the "ease of construction" or "ease of imagining" the outcomes is the operative factor in the simulation heuristic.[4]

An example of this heuristic was given earlier, when you were asked
to imagine possible outcomes if Germany had developed the atomic bomb
before the United States. Given the role the atomic bomb played in ending World War II, people presumably would give far more weight to this
in answering the question than if they were asked about the development of some other device, say, a long-range bomber or submarine.

On the other hand, imagining an outcome different from the actual
one may be quite difficult, especially in less dramatic examples. This
should also affect the way the simulation heuristic guides our thinking.

Consider an example discussed by Kahneman and Tversky (1982, p.
203):

*Mr. Crane and Mr. Tees were scheduled to leave the airport on different flights, at
the same time. They traveled from town in the same limousine, were caught in a
traffic jam, and arrived at the airport 30 minutes after the scheduled departure
time of their flights. Mr. Crane is told that his flight left on time. Mr. Tees is told
that his flight was delayed, and just left five minutes ago. Who is more upset, Mr.
Crane or Mr. Tees?*

As you would expect, almost everyone decides that Mr. Tees is more
upset; in Kahneman and Tversky's study, 96% of the subjects made this
judgment. The unusual aspect of this, as the authors note, is that from
an objective standpoint, Mr. Crane and Mr. Tees are in *identical* positions—both missed their planes, and because of the traffic jam, both
expected to miss their planes. Kahneman and Tversky continue by
explaining that the only reason Mr. Tees might be more upset is that it
was more "possible," in some sense, for him to have caught his flight.
That is, people can imagine a variety of scenarios in which the limousine
could have arrived at the airport a mere five minutes earlier than it did;
for example, the traffic jam could have cleared or the driver could have
taken an alternate route. All these scenarios involve the simulation
heuristic, in which the initial values (e.g., traffic jam, departure time)
are entered into the subject's mental simulation of "getting to the airport
as quickly as possible." Because it's easier to imagine an outcome in
which the limousine arrives a few minutes earlier than it is to imagine
one in which it arrives a half-hour earlier, we feel that the traveler who
"nearly caught his flight" will be more upset.

---

[4]The term *simulation heuristic* comes from Kahneman and Tversky (1982). The basic notion, "ease of
construction" from memory, however, was included in their original statement of the availability heuristic (1973). Note that the two heuristics rely on somewhat different mental processes—actual retrieval of
information for the availability heuristic, but active imagining of plausible outcomes for the simulation
heuristic. The recent (1982) elaboration of the simulation heuristic makes it clear that something rather
different from the straightforward availability heuristic is intended, so the two are treated separately
here. But since the mental simulation process relies on construction from memory, and hence at least
some retrieval, this final heuristic can also be viewed as a version of the availability heuristic focused on
the "predicted future."

The Undoing Heuristic   A much more complete example of the simulation heuristic, including the data reported by Kahneman and Tversky (1982), is contained in Table 11-5. This example illustrates a particular version of the simulation heuristic, the *undoing* of some outcome by changes in the events that led up to it. This is essentially the process of judging that an event "was close to happening," "nearly occurred," "could have happened if only," and so on (p. 203). Read the story now, and decide how you would complete the "If only . . ." phrase before continuing.

Kahneman and Tversky characterize the changes that people make in the sequence of events, that is, possible changes that lead to different outcomes, as belonging to one of three types. *Downhill changes* are those that remove a surprising or otherwise unusual event from a story or scenario, thereby making the story more coherent or "typical." In the sample story, the majority of subjects who heard the "route" version of the story made a downhill change by suggesting, for instance, that "if he had taken his usual route rather than a different one, the accident could have been avoided."

An *uphill change* is one that brings some new and unlikely event into the story, one that might change the outcome, but would be rather unusual or unanticipated in such a scenario; this is the category labeled "Other" in Table 11-5. An uphill change might have been something like "Shortly after he left work, Mr. Jones had a flat tire that delayed him, and thus he avoided the accident."

Horizontal changes, finally, are those in which one detail or event in the story is replaced by another of comparable likelihood. Such a change in this story could have Mr. Jones arriving at the intersection two or three seconds earlier or later than he did. Given the realities of driving, such a difference would be easy to imagine, presumably, although the focus of the story apparently led the subjects to think about other possible events instead.[5]

Kahneman and Tversky's results for this story suggested that people confine themselves largely to downhill changes when they "undo" or imagine alternate outcomes. Uphill changes were rarely introduced by the subjects, and horizontal changes were, in the authors' term, "nonexistent." Note the biases operating here. A downhill change "normalizes" the story by substituting a regular for an unusual event or detail. We seem to have a bias to make such downhill changes, for two apparent reasons. First, downhill changes can be more easily imagined—there's ease of retrieval again. Second, downhill changes seem more "plausi-

---

[5]Kahneman and Tversky's terms *downhill* and *uphill* changes are metaphorically related to cross-country skiing, where the distance between two points is *not* the same in both directions, at least from the skier's perspective: going downhill from a peak to a valley is far easier than going uphill from the valley to the peak. Likewise, in the simulation heuristic, downhill changes are far easier to imagine than uphill ones. Unfortunately, the metaphor is misleading for the term *horizontal changes,* since these form the bulk of cross-country skiing, but apparently are extremely unusual in the simulation heuristic.

Table 11-5   STORIES FOR THE SIMULATION HEURISTIC

Route Version

1. Mr. Jones was 47 years old, the father of three, and a successful banking executive. His wife has been ill at home for several months.

2a. On the day of the accident, Mr. Jones left his office at the regular time. He sometimes left early to take care of home chores at his wife's request, but this was not necessary on that day. Mr. Jones did not drive home by his regular route. The day was exceptionally clear and Mr. Jones told his friends at the office that he would drive along the shore to enjoy the view.

3. The accident occurred at a major intersection. The light turned amber as Mr. Jones approached. Witnesses noted that he braked hard to stop at the crossing, although he could easily have gone through. His family recognized this as a common occurrence in Mr. Jones' driving. As he began to cross after the light changed, a light truck charged into the intersection at top speed and rammed Mr. Jones' car from the left. Mr. Jones was killed instantly.

4a. It was later ascertained that the truck was driven by a teenage boy, who was under the influence of drugs.

5. As commonly happens in such situations, the Jones family and their friends often thought and often said, "If only . . . ," during the days that followed the accident. How did they continue this thought? Please write one or more likely completions.

Time Version

(substitute 2b)   2b. On the day of the accident, Mr. Jones left the office earlier than usual to attend to some household chores at his wife's request. He drove home along his regular route. Mr. Jones occasionally chose to drive along the shore, to enjoy the view on exceptionally clear days, but that day was just average.

"Boy" Focus Version

(substitute 4b)   4b. It was later ascertained that the truck was driven by a teenage boy named Tom Searler. Tom's father had just found him at home under the influence of drugs. This was a common occurrence, as Tom used drugs heavily. There had been a quarrel, during which Tom grabbed the keys that were lying on the living room table and drove off blindly. He was severely injured in the accident.

Number of Subjects Responding to the "If Only" Stem in the Five Different Categories of Responses

Response Category	Story Version	
"IF ONLY" COMPLETION FOCUSES ON:	*ROUTE VERSION*	*TIME VERSION*
Route	33	8
Time	2	16
Crossing	14	19
Boy	13	18
Other	3	1
	65 respondents	62 respondents

From Kahneman & Tversky, 1982.

ble"—it's more plausible that Mr. Jones left on time than it is that he left early and then had a flat tire.

Uphill changes, where an unusual event is introduced, might objectively be just as likely as any detail in the original story and could just as easily alter the outcome of the story. And yet, people apparently do not make uphill changes very frequently. The bias, of course, is that unusual or atypical events are difficult to imagine or construct. As such, they are not usually generated by the mental simulation; it's as if the simulation "goes for" the default, typical values. Finally, it's quite odd that a simple substitution of one detail for another is never made: Mr. Jones could have left work three seconds earlier or later, the truck could have been going slower, and so on.

Strangest of all, subjects seldom focused on the actual *cause* of the accident, the teenage boy. That is, they seldom altered anything concerning the boy's behavior, even though it was his actions, not Mr. Jones's, that caused the accident. Kahneman and Tversky speculate that this is due to a *focus rule,* that we tend to maintain properties of the main object or focus of the story unless a different focus is provided. In support of this speculation, the alternate version of the story shown at the bottom of the table ("Boy Focus") was substituted, in which the boy becomes the principal focus. In this version, subjects were much more likely to complete the "if only" sentences by removing the *cause* of the accident, the boy himself. In the original version, only 28% of the subjects mentioned the boy in their constructed versions, but 68% mentioned him in the revised focus version.

Hindsight Note, finally, that the simulation heuristic provides a compelling explanation of the *hindsight effect,* the after-the-fact feeling that some event was very likely to happen or was very predictable, even though it wasn't predicted to happen *beforehand.* In thinking about the now-completed event, the scenario under which that event could have happened is, obviously, very easy to imagine—after all, *just* that scenario happened. The connection between the initial situation and the final outcome is very available, after the fact, and this availability makes *other* possible connections seem less plausible than they otherwise would seem. In terms of the simulation heuristic, the hindsight effect may be nothing more than a bias in which otherwise plausible outcomes are now less easy to imagine than the outcome that actually happened (for recent evidence on hindsight bias, see Hell, Gigerenzer, Gauggel, Mall, & Muller, 1988, and Hoch & Loewenstein, 1989).

Applications of the Simulation Heuristic In many ways, it seems that the simulation heuristic may come closer to what people mean by such terms as *thinking* and *considering* than anything else we've covered so far. That is, it is easy to recognize less dramatic examples of undoing and other kinds of forecasting or simulating in our everyday thinking, and the influence of factors like salience, hindsight bias, and so on. For example:

> If I stop for a cup of coffee, I might miss my bus.
> If I hadn't been so busy yesterday, I would have remembered to cash a check.
> In looking back, I guess I could have predicted that waiting until senior year to take statistics was a bad idea.

Presumably, such thinking is often the reason we decide to do one thing versus another; we think through the possible outcomes of different actions, then base our decision on the most favorable of the forecasted outcomes. As such, the mental simulation process, taking certain input conditions then forecasting possible outcomes, could be an important way of understanding general cognitive processes related to planning.

A general warning is important to bear in mind here, based on studies of how people generate possible outcomes of future events. Hoch (1984), for instance, asked one group of subjects to think of favorable outcomes when predicting some future event, and asked another group to think of unfavorable outcomes. Subjects who generated favorable outcomes were then less able to imagine unfavorable outcomes when asked to consider the "other side of the question." Initial predictions also influenced the estimates of how likely one or the other outcome might be; subjects who began by generating favorable outcomes were much more "certain" that a favorable outcome would actually happen. On the other hand, if subjects generate reasons that some outcome might *not* happen, their confidence in their predictions tends to be much more realistic (Hoch, 1985). The warning should be clear: overly optimistic predictions at the outset will then bias our ability to imagine negative outcomes and will inflate our view of the likelihood of a positive outcome. (Aw, come on, what could go wrong if I wait until next week to start my term paper?)

Summary Points: availability heuristic, ease of recalling instances; biases due to general world knowledge, familiarity, salience, and vividness; simulation heuristic; undoing; downhill and uphill changes; hindsight

▼ Issues in Everyday Reasoning

These are not the only heuristics that are used, of course, although no comprehensive catalog of reasoning heuristics has been offered (but see Kahneman, Slovic, & Tversky, 1982, for a thorough treatment of heuristics from a variety of disciplinary perspectives, and Collins & Michalski, 1989, for a theory of plausible reasoning). Such a catalog, if it existed, would include many other procedures besides the ones we've covered here. For instance, people often develop analogies based on known events and situations in order to reason about unknown or poorly understood domains. While this strategy works well in some cases, it leads to misconceptions and errors in others, just as any heuristic does. As an example, Kempton (1986) has investigated people's understanding of home heat control, in particular, their understanding of a furnace thermostat. According to some people's (incorrect) understanding, it seems, thermostats work in an analogous fashion to water faucets—turn it up higher to get a higher flow of heat/water.[6]

Another useful heuristic has been called the "prototypicality heuristic," a strategy in which we generate examples to reason out an answer rather than follow the correct, logical procedures of deductive reasoning in, say, solving syllogisms. Cherniak (1984), who has studied this heuristic (see also Tversky & Kahneman, 1983), describes it as "a kind of local and temporary Piagetian regression from abstract to concrete" (p. 625). Using it is truly illogical, in the sense that a correct, alternative procedure exists that will yield the correct answer—the algorithms of syllogistic reasoning. However illogical the use of this heuristic might be, it nonetheless reduces subjects' errors when they are working under time constraints (see also Cherniak's thoughtful discussion of the conversational postulates and application of the heuristic). In any event, given the current state of research on decision making and reasoning, it seems safe to conclude that heuristic reasoning strategies such as these hold the promise of accounting for much of what we're calling *everyday reasoning*.

Mental Models

In all the reasoning situations we've discussed, there is the implicit assumption that only *some* relevant information is stored in long-term memory on which to base a judgment or decision. And yet, we haven't dealt explicitly with this idea, or with the consequences of various states of knowledge for a person's accuracy in reasoning. Surely it makes a difference in our reasoning if we know a great deal, just a little, or absolutely nothing about the domain of reasoning, or if our knowledge contains distortions or inaccuracies.

Let's refer to your knowledge of a domain—whether a simple device like a water faucet or something complex like a computer—as a **mental model.** The completeness of this model, whether you are a novice or an expert, will clearly affect your reasoning in this domain. But mental

---

[6]As another example, people often treat the elevator call button like a doorbell: if the elevator takes too long in coming, people push the button again, as if the elevator "hadn't heard" the call button/doorbell. There is probably an element of superstitious reinforcement here as well, when someone pushes the already-pushed button and the elevator arrives shortly thereafter, purely by coincidence; maybe it's quasi-magical thinking (Shafir & Tversky, 1992), in which we do something even though we know it does not cause some event to happen.

models are not restricted to physical devices, of course. Any body of information you have stored in memory about a situation, an event, a procedure, and so on can be termed a mental model in this sense. For instance, your scripted knowledge (see Chapter 7) of a restaurant can be used as a mental model in reasoning about restaurant events. As we discussed for heuristics, the knowledge and procedures people use in evaluating and forecasting outcomes would themselves be called *mental models* in those domains. In other words, you have a mental model of "coin toss outcomes" and of "airport limousine travel," not to mention a very general mental model of "affluence and the American economy" that influences your estimates of Chevrolet and Cadillac sales.

It should be obvious then that our mental models in different domains can vary from true and complete knowledge (expertise, in other words) all the way down to no knowledge or information at all, ignorance. (People's awareness that they *do not know* something is actually quite interesting itself; see Gentner & Collins, 1981, and Glucksberg & McCloskey, 1981.) The most interesting situation to study is when knowledge is incomplete and/or inaccurate; indeed, the fact that we are so concerned with how people *estimate under uncertainty,* and with their errors in reasoning, implies that complete and certain knowledge is usually not available to people. This focus on errors in the reasoning and decision literature is quite reminiscent of the Piagetian tradition of studying cognitive development by analyzing children's *errors* in logical thought problems. It also represents the general tendency in cognitive psychology to study accuracy or inaccuracy in performance as a way of understanding mental processing.

A Mental Model of the Physical World: McCloskey's "Naive Physics" Some of the most intriguing (and entertaining) research on mental models and reasoning has been reported by McCloskey and his colleagues. McCloskey has investigated people's conceptions of the physical world, in particular, their understanding of the principles of motion. Figure 11-7 presents several of the problems McCloskey has studied; the remaining section will be more meaningful to you if you spend a few moments working through the problems before reading further.

By asking subjects to complete such diagrams, and then explain their answers, McCloskey (e.g., 1983) has provided a very convincing example of the *misconceptions* or *faulty mental models* that people often have. For instance, in one of his studies (McCloskey, Caramazza, & Green, 1980), 51% of the subjects believed that a marble would follow a curved path after leaving the tube depicted in Figure 11-7A. Likewise, some 30% responded that the ball in Figure 11-7B would continue on a curved path after the string broke, often adding that this curved path would eventually straighten out. In the airplane–ball question (Figure 11-7C), only 40% gave the correct answer; the most common incorrect answer (36% of the subjects) was that the ball would fall straight down. Figure 11-8

FIGURE 11-7

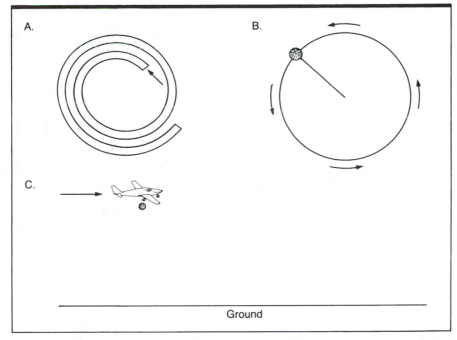

Ground

Stimuli used by McCloskey. For (A), imagine that the curved tube is on a table top, and a ball or marble is tossed in (see arrow). Draw the path of the ball when it exits the tube. For (B), imagine that the ball is being twirled around and that the string breaks. Draw the path the ball will take once the string breaks. For (C), imagine an airplane is traveling at a constant speed, and a ball is dropped from the airplane. Draw the path of the ball as it falls to the ground.

shows both the correct and incorrect answers that people gave to these problems, along with the percentage of people who gave the answers.

One rather compelling aspect of McCloskey's results involves the domain of knowledge that was being tested—the motion of physical objects. This is not a rarefied, unusual kind of knowledge that is foreign to people. As McCloskey notes, we have *countless* opportunities in our everyday experience to witness the behavior of objects in motion, and to derive an understanding of the principles of motion from that experience. Anyone who has ever thrown a ball has had such opportunities. And yet, the mental model that we derive from that experience is flawed.

A second compelling aspect to the research concerns the nature of the mental model itself. As analyzed by McCloskey, people's erroneous understanding of bodies in motion is amazingly similar to the so-called *impetus* theory of motion, which states that setting an object in motion puts some *impetus* or "movement force" into the object, with the impetus then slowly dissipating across time. For instance, in the tube problem in Figure 11-7A, one subject said: "The momentum from the curve [of the tube] gives it [the ball] the arc. . . . The force that the ball picks up from

FIGURE 11-8

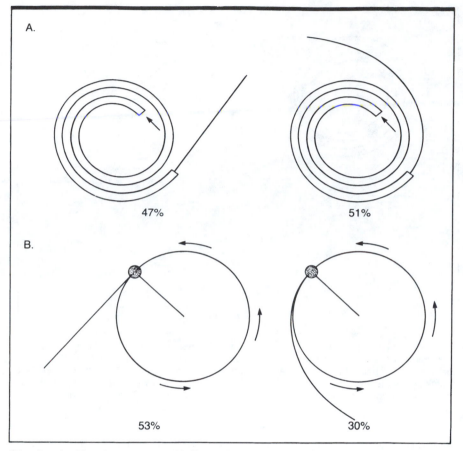

Stimuli and subjects' responses to McCloskey's problems in Figure 11-7, along with the percentages of subjects making that response.

the curve eventually dissipates and it will follow a normal straight line" (McCloskey, 1983, p. 309).

The punchline here is that the impetus theory was the accepted explanation of motion during the 13th and 14th centuries, a view that was finally abandoned by physics when Newton's laws of gravity and motion were advanced some *300 years ago*. The correct mental model, basically, is that a body in motion will continue in a straight line unless some other force, for instance, gravity, is applied. If some other force is applied, then that force will combine with the continuing straight line movement. Thus when the ball leaves the tube, or when the string breaks, the ball will move in a straight line: no "curved force" continues to act on it since no such thing as "impetus" has been given to it. Likewise, the horizontal movement of the ball dropped from the airplane continues until the ball hits the ground. This movement is augmented by a downward movement

FIGURE 11-8 *(Continued)*

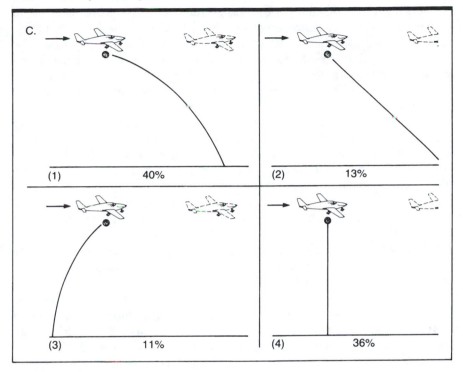

caused by gravity; the ball accelerates vertically as it continues its previous horizontal motion. (If you demonstrated a naive belief in impetus, you might take some consolation in the fact that, across recorded history, people have believed in impetus theory *longer* than they have in Newton's laws.)

Issue #1: The Source of Our Mental Models

Where do our mental models come from? What is the source of our knowledge about bodies in motion, furnace thermostats, or "affluence in the United States"? We can only offer a simple, undifferentiated answer—experience. That is, we obviously derive information about the world around us from our everyday experience, acquiring and storing knowledge, then using it and modifying it as a function of further experience. This answer, while obviously true, is also just as obviously unsatisfactory and incomplete. What is it about our experience with water faucets that leads to a reasonably accurate mental model, as distinct from our experience with furnace thermostats? How can we derive relatively accurate notions about the frequency of red and yellow cars, on the one hand, but such inaccurate notions about the paths of moving objects, on the other?

Only a little research addresses this kind of issue, the nature of our experience and the kind of information that we derive from it. Some of the difficulty we experience involves the difficulty of the problems (e.g., Proffitt, Kaiser, & Whelan, 1990), and other such factors. For example, Medin and Edelson (1988) found that, depending on the structure and complexity of the problem, subjects may use base rate information appropriately, may use it inappropriately, or may ignore it entirely. We do know that instruction and training influence reasoning. Taking a physics class improves your knowledge of the rules of motion, though doesn't completely eliminate the misbeliefs (Donley & Ashcraft, 1992). Likewise, instruction in statistics, probability, and hypothesis testing improves your ability to reason accurately in those domains (e.g., Agnoli & Krantz, 1989; Fong & Nisbett, 1991; Lehman et al., 1988).

On the other hand, consider again the professional stereotypes we dealt with earlier, and the degree to which a match on the stereotype will alter people's estimations of likelihood. Where do we learn these stereotypes? Why is it that we will agree that stereotypes such as "quiet" for librarians or "wears a tweed coat" for professors are often wrong, but then turn around and rely on them in other situations as if they were true? To some degree, we may already have an explanation of this phenomenon: just as we abstract the central, typical members of categories from our experiences (e.g., Rosch, 1978; see Chapter 6), we also may abstract or distill stereotypes from our everyday experiences. Indeed, one way of defining the term *stereotype* is that it represents a *prototypical* member of a category, the prototypical librarian, doctor, or college professor. A difficulty with this explanation, of course, is that stereotypes may often diverge considerably from the frequency of characteristics in our experience; I find it difficult to imagine that college professors truly wear tweed coats more frequently than members of other professions (but maybe that's my bias due to the availability heuristic).

In short, given that our mental models in different domains can be incomplete or inaccurate, cognitive psychology needs to investigate the *acquisition* of those mental models very thoroughly. Part of this need is simply the need to know the source of the information. An even more important part, in some situations, involves our need to correct people's mental models when they are wrong. Likewise, people's misconceptions about probabilities, for instance, the erroneous belief in the law of small numbers, seems to persist regardless of advanced training (e.g., Tversky & Kahneman, 1971). If we understood the original source of the incorrect models, we might have a better idea of how to change them, how to correct people's misconceptions through education.

Issue #2: The Metacognitive Paradox

A second issue that needs some empirical attention might be termed the *metacognitive paradox*. Putting it simply, why is it that we don't notice how wrong our mental models are? For instance, how can we catch and throw balls when our mental model of the ball in motion is so dramatically incorrect? Note that this is a somewhat different question from the one addressed earlier, that of how we acquire incorrect information in the first place. From the standpoints of personal bias, vividness, and so on, it's easy to imagine how people might store faulty information in memory and make incorrect predictions and estimations based on that information. But now we're asking a different question—when an incorrect prediction is made, why isn't the incorrectness noted and incorporated into memory? If our mental models are based on experience, shouldn't they be "self-correcting" in that we are afforded many later experiences that reveal the basic errors in the models? Why doesn't our general metacognitive awareness guide us away from incorrect mental models?

In the absence of a cogent, complete answer to these questions on the part of either the metacognition theorists or the reasoning and decision-making theorists, we can only speculate. Perhaps we fail to notice when our mental models lead us to erroneous conclusions because the feedback we get is weak or easy to ignore. That is, maybe there are relatively few situations that reveal our incorrect predictions to us in a graphic, dramatic way. If so, there would be few situations that would call for revising our stored knowledge. Another possibility is that our models are sometimes close enough to "correct" that the error in our predictions and estimations is small. Given that most people are not particularly skilled at throwing a ball, for instance, maybe the difference in aim under the impetus versus the correct mental model of motion is so insignificant that we literally don't notice the incorrect prediction at all.

Finally, maybe we fail to notice the incorrectness of our predictions because the *cost* of being wrong is usually small. As an example, please estimate the answer to the following problem:

$$1 \times 2 \times 3 \times 4 \times 5 \times 6 \times 7 \times 8$$

Tversky and Kahneman (1983) found that people's estimates for this problem averaged 512, substantially lower than the mean estimate for the same problem in a different order,

$$8 \times 7 \times 6 \times 5 \times 4 \times 3 \times 2 \times 1$$

Here the average estimate was 2250. The point here is that no particular consequence attaches to your estimates—dramatically wrong though they may be (the answer to the 8!—8 factorial—problem is 40,320). Likewise, it "costs" very little to press the elevator button repeatedly, to believe that Cadillac sales are extremely infrequent, or to imagine that some behavioral ritual might influence the roll of a die (e.g., Shafir & Tversky's "quasi-magical" thinking; 1992). On the other hand, the cost might be great in other situations, for example, if you mismatch your professor's stereotype of a "good student," or a potential employer's stereotype of a "good employee."

In short, our mental models sometimes reflect an incorrect understanding of the world, just as our heuristic reasoning strategies sometimes lead us to inaccurate predictions and estimations. If the theme of metacognition is to be taken seriously, the inconsistencies between its implications and the results on reasoning must be addressed. We need to know the limitations of metacognitive awareness, and these must be coherently related to our reliance on heuristic processes in reasoning and decision making.

Summary Points: mental models; expertise versus uncertainty; "naive physics"; the source of mental models; metacognition and biases in reasoning

CHAPTER SUMMARY

1. Human reasoning is not especially logical, as shown in formal syllogistic and conditional reasoning problems. People often look for positive evidence for a suggested conclusion and are often swayed by knowledge stored in memory. When a more skeptical attitude is adopted, and when the reasoning involves more concrete concepts, reasoning accuracy tends to improve.

2. Deciding which of two physical stimuli is louder, brighter, and so on is a psychophysical judgment. These decisions are speeded up when the two stimuli differ by a great amount. When symbolic stimuli are compared, the same effect is obtained, termed the *symbolic distance effect*. Additionally, judgments are speeded up when the evaluated dimension (e.g., choose the larger) matches the stimuli being compared (e.g., two "large" digits); this is called the *semantic congruity effect*. Both of these results are obtained in simple comparisons of numbers, as well as in comparisons of qualities such as hot/cold. In all symbolic situations, our mental representation of quantity influences our judgments.

3. Algorithms are systematic rules and procedures that generate correct answers to problems, whereas heuristics are quick rules of thumb that are often useful but are not guaranteed to yield the correct solution. Three important heuristics have been investigated in circumstances when people reason about uncertain events.

4. The *representativeness heuristic* guides people to judge outcomes as likely if they seem representative of the type of event being evaluated; for instance, a random-looking sequence of coin tosses is judged more representative of coin toss outcomes almost regardless of the true probabilities involved. Included among the reasoning effects predicted by this heuristic are various stereotyping results.

5. In the *availability heuristic,* people judge the likelihood of events by how easily they can remember examples or instances. These judgments can therefore be biased by any other factor, such as salience or vividness, that affects the storing of examples in memory.

6. In the *simulation heuristic,* people forecast or predict how some outcome could have been different. These forecasts are influenced by how easily the alternative outcomes can be imagined. Interestingly, when people complete "if only" statements, the changes they include tend to normalize the original situation by removing an unusual event and substituting a more common one. Such normalizations can be affected by the *focus* of the situation.

7. In everyday reasoning, we rely on *mental models* of the device or event to make our judgments. These mental models are sometimes quite inaccurate. In the best-known research, people's mental models of physical motion lead them to incorrect predictions (e.g., the trajectory of a ball dropped from an airplane). Ongoing research hopes to determine both the original sources of such incorrect models and methods of instruction that help people overcome their misconceptions.

Glossary Terms: algorithm; availability; conditional reasoning; confirmation bias; familiarity bias; heuristic; hindsight bias; mental models; naive physics; representativeness; salience and vividness; semantic congruity; simulation; stereotypes; syllogisms; symbolic distance; undoing

SUGGESTED READINGS

Some areas of research on reasoning that were not covered here include linear series problems and reasoning by analogy. See Potts (1974) for research on linear series problems; for example, "Sue is taller than Jan, Jan is taller than Betty, who is the shortest?" This research reveals the symbolic distance and congruity effects that were described earlier, but now for information acquired within the experimental context (i.e., for episodic memory information). Rumelhart and Abrahamson (1973) proposed an interesting account of reasoning by analogy, and R. J. Sternberg (1977) has advanced a large theory of analogical reasoning; see also Holyoak (1985) for a paper on analogical transfer.

Research on decision making in relatively applied situations is becoming very common. For applications to medical decision making, see papers by Medin, Altom, Edelson, and Freko (1982), and Patel and Groen (1986). Keren and Wagenaar (1985) have discussed decisions and heuristic strategies in blackjack. And Nisbett and Ross (1980; also Kunda & Nisbett, 1986) have discussed heuristic reasoning and judgments with reference to script theory and to social judgments of behavioral consistency. Kahneman et al. (1982) is an excellent collection of relevant papers; Tversky and Kahneman (1983) is an integrative review of this area. Recent work on the training of statistical and deductive reasoning processes is presented in Fong, Krantz, and Nisbett (1986), and Cheng, Holyoak, Nisbett, and Oliver (1986).

Finally, more specific evidence on the sources of erroneous mental models has been discussed by McCloskey and Kohl (1983) for "curvilinear impetus" and McCloskey, Washburn, and Felch (1983) for the "straight down belief." Kaiser, Proffitt, and Anderson (1985) have extended this kind of work to children, discovering that errors on the curved tube problems, for instance, are reduced when subjects see a display that actually depicts motion. On the other hand, Kaiser, Jonides, and Alexander (1986) have found that correct solutions and reasoning strategies did not generalize from familiar to unfamiliar, abstract problems.

APPENDIX 11A: ALGORITHMS FOR COIN TOSSES AND HOSPITAL BIRTHS

1. *Coin Tosses.* To begin with the obvious, the probability of a head on one coin toss is .50. Flipping a coin twice, and keeping track of the possible sequences, yields a .25 probability for each of the four possibilities HH, HT, TH, TT. In general, when the simple event has a probability of .50, the number of possibilities for a sequence of n events is 2 raised to the nth power. Thus the number of distinct sequences for six coin tosses is 2^6, a total of 64 possibilities.

Two of the 64 possibilities are "pure sequences," HHHHHH and TTTTTT. Two more involve "double sequences," HHHTTT and TTTHHH. All the remaining 60 possibilities involve either or both of the following characteristics: (1) more of one outcome (e.g., heads) than the other; and (2) at least one alternation between the two outcomes at a position *other than* halfway through the sequence. Thus the probability of a "pure sequence" is 2/64, as is the probability of a "double sequence." Getting any *one* of the other 60 possibilities of course has a likelihood of 1/64. But getting a "random-like" outcome, that is, any outcome other than "straight" or "double," has a probability of 60/64.

2. *Hospital Births.* Many statistics texts contain tables of the binomial distribution, the best way to understand the hospital births example. Since most of these tables only go up to a sample size of 20, we'll use a revised hospital example, comparing hospitals with three versus nine births per day (note that the 1:3 ratio is the same as the original example, 15:45). The probabilities for the original example will be more extreme than these, but they'll be in the same direction.

We are again dealing with an event whose basic probability is .50, the likelihood that a newborn infant is male (ignoring the fact that male births are actually slightly more common than 50%). What is the probability that, in three births, not a single one will be female, that is, that all three will be boys? According to the binomial tables (see Table 11-A), this probability is .1250. This is the probability that on any randomly select-

Table 11-A   BINOMIAL PROBABILITIES FOR EXACT NUMBER OF RELEVANT
OUTCOMES, WHERE THE SIMPLE PROBABILITY OF THE OUTCOME
IS .50

$N = 3$	$N = 9$	$N = 15$	$N = 45$
Exact # of relevant outcomes:			
0.1250	0.0020	9.1527	27.0488
1.3750	1.0176	10.0916	28.0314
2.3750	2.0703	11.0417	29.0184
3.1250	3.1641	12.0139	30.0098
	4.2461	13.0032	31.0047
	5.2461	14.0005	32.0021
	6.1641	15.0000	33.0008
	7.0703		34.0003
	8.0176		35.0001
	9.0020		36.0000

ed day, the three-birth hospital will have all boys, $p = .1250$. Across the 365 days in a year, we expect an average of 45.655 such days (365 × .1250).

The temptation now is to consider the likelihood of exactly three boys in the nine-birth hospital. But this is not the relevant comparison. The relevant comparison to the "all boys" probability in the three-birth hospital would be "all boys" in the nine-birth hospital. This puts the comparison on the same footing as the original problem, 60% or more as the "extreme" cutoff.

The probability of exactly nine boys out of nine births is .0020, two chances in a thousand. For a whole year, we expect only 0.73 such days (365 × .0020). Now it should be clear: the criterion of "extreme," all boys, is considerably more likely in the smaller sample than in the larger one, $p = .1250$ versus .0020. Multiplied out, the prediction is 45 days for the small hospital, versus .70 days for the large one. For a closer approximation to the original example, work out the probabilities that two-thirds or more of the newborns are male. For the three-birth hospital, this can happen two ways—either two boys are born, or three are born. The two probabilities here are .3750 and .1250, respectively. By adding these, we get the probability that the three-birth hospital, on any randomly selected day, will have either two or three boys born out of the three births (obviously, the only other outcomes are 0 or 1 boy, which also has a .50 probability).

But "two-thirds boys" as a criterion for the larger hospital means six or more boys out of nine births, that is, either six, seven, eight, or nine boys. These probabilities, respectively, are .1641, .0703, .0176, and .0020. The sum of these is the probability of two-thirds or more boys out of nine, $p = .1540$. In short, the probability of two-thirds or more boys in the three-birth hospital is .50; for the nine-birth hospital, the "same" event, two-thirds or more boys, has a probability of .1540. Multiply these probabilities by 365 days/year to see which hospital will have more days on which two-thirds or more of the births are male, the three- or the nine-birth hospital. By extension, which hospital will have more days on which 60% or more of the babies were male, the 15-birth hospital or the 45-birth hospital?

The answer: the 15-birth hospital should have about 111 days with 60% or more boys, contrasted with 42 such days for the 45-birth hospital.

PROBLEM SOLVING

Rate of acquisition and rate of extinction in learning have occupied us for a generation. Perhaps in the coming generation we can concern ourselves more directly with the utility of learning: whether, one thing having been learned, other things can be solved with no further learning required. When we have achieved this leap, we will have passed from the psychology of learning to the psychology of problem solving. (Bruner, 1957, reprinted in Bruner, 1973, p. 237)

It seems that all cognitive activities are fundamentally problem solving in nature. The basic argument . . . is that human cognition is always purposeful, directed to achieving goals and to removing obstacles to those goals. (Anderson, 1985, pp. 199–200)

The Newell and Simon approach to problem-solving did not produce a flurry of related experiments by other cognitive psychologists, and problem solving never became a central research area in information-processing cognition. . . . Newell and Simon's conceptual work, however, formed a cornerstone of the information-processing approach. (Lachman et al., 1979, p. 99)

My favorite example of "problem solving in action" is the following true story. When I was a graduate student, I attended a departmental colloquium at which a candidate for a faculty position was to present his research. As he started his talk, he realized that his first slide was projected too low on the screen. A flurry of activity around the projector ensued, one professor asking out loud, "Does anyone have a book or something?" Someone volunteered a book, the professor tried it, but it was too thick—the slide image was now too high. "No, this one's too big. Anyone got a thinner one?" he continued. After several more seconds of hurried searching for something thinner, another professor finally exclaimed, "Well, for Pete's sake, I don't believe this!" He marched over to the projector, grabbed the book, opened it halfway, and then put it under the projector. He looked around the lecture hall and shook his head, saying, "I can't believe it. A roomful of PhDs, and no one knows how to *open a book*!"

This chapter examines the rather slow and deliberate cognitive processing called problem solving. Just as in the area of decision making and reasoning, problem solving studies an individual who is confronted with a difficult, time-consuming task: a problem has been presented to the individual, the solution to the problem is not immediately obvious, and the individual is often uncertain what to do next. We are interested in all aspects of the person's activities, from initial understanding of the problem, the steps that lead to a final solution, and, in some cases, the way a person decides that a problem has finally been solved. Our interest in these questions needs no further justification or explanation than this: we confront countless problems in our daily lives, problems that are important for us to figure out and solve. We "rely on our wits" in these situations; we attempt to solve the problem by mentally analyzing the situation, devising a plan of action, then carrying out that plan. As such, the mental processing involved in problem solving is, by definition, part of cognitive psychology.

Let's start with a simple "recreational" or "toy problem" (Anderson, 1993). It will take you a minute or two at most to solve the problem, even if you're one of those people who loses patience with "brain teasers" very quickly (VanLehn's [1989] 9-year-old subject seemed to understand it completely in about 20 seconds, and solved it out loud in about 2 minutes).

1. *Three Men and a Rowboat.* Three men want to cross a river. They find a boat, but it is a very small boat. It will only hold 200 pounds. The men are named Large, Medium, and Small. Large weighs 200 pounds, Medium weighs 120 pounds, and Small weighs 80 pounds. How can they all get across? They might have to make several trips in the boat. (VanLehn, 1989, p. 532)

Why should we be interested in such recreational problems? The answer is very straightforward; as is typical of *all* scientific disciplines, cognitive science studies the simple before the complex, searches simpler settings to find basic principles that generalize to more difficult settings. After all, not all of the everyday problems we confront are tremendously complex: figuring out how to prop up a slide projector is not of earthshaking significance (well, it probably was to the fellow interviewing for the job). In either case, the reasoning is that we can often see large-scale issues and important processes more clearly when they are embedded in simple situations. Indeed, one aspect of problem solving you'll read about, functional fixedness, provides an *exact* account of why a roomful of PhDs didn't think about opening the book to make it thinner. Needless to say, functional fixedness was discovered with a simple, recreational problem.

The Status of the Problem-Solving Area   As the introductory quotations illustrate, problem solving is somewhat of an odd topic in cognitive psychology. In Bruner's view, problem solving was an obviously important goal to be pursued by psychology, one of the many that had been excluded by the behaviorist tradition. Because the overriding concern during the "birth" of cognitive psychology in the 1950s was to *re*-introduce those significant mental activities that had been ignored by behaviorism, Bruner's remarks about problem solving fell on receptive ears.

And yet, in the view of Lachman et al., the early research in problem solving, exemplified by Newell and Simon's work on chess, cryptarithmetic problems, and logic theorems, did not spawn the same kind of research tradition in cognitive psychology as, say, Tulving's work on retrieval cues or Collins and Quillian's work on semantic memory. A major reason—possibly *the* reason—for this was methodological. That is, Newell and Simon (1972) pointed out that studying significant problem solving requires us to examine a lengthy sample of behavior, often up to 20 or 30 minutes worth of activity. This means that the typical measures of RT and accuracy are quite irrelevant to experiments on problem solving. Instead, the major kind of data in problem solving is the **verbal protocol,** the *transcription and analysis of the subjects' verbalizations as they solve the problem.*

Without a doubt, it was the use of verbal protocols that influenced many researchers' opinions about problem solving, especially given the similarities between verbal protocols and the discredited method of introspectionism. In fact, the status of verbal reports as data is still a topic of some debate; see Ericsson and Simon (1980) and Russo, Johnson, and Stephens (1989) for contrasting views. This aspect of problem-solving research, along with issues of experimental design, control of variables, and so on, placed problem solving outside the *strict* information-processing tradition of stage models, flowcharts, and the like. The irony here, of course, is that Newell and Simon's *conceptual* approach—that humans can be conceived of as processors of information—was the very foundation of the information-processing approach. (See Lachman et al., 1979, Chapter 4, for a full account of these influences.)

There are still lingering signs of the division between "the information processors" and the "problem solvers" in contemporary cognitive psychology, to be sure. But in most respects, the division has either broken down or become irrelevant.[1] Each group has made discoveries that have been important for the other tradition. For instance, the notion of heuristics, originally derived from problem solving, is applicable and important to a thorough understanding of reasoning, as you read in Chapter 11. Likewise, theories of language comprehension are critical to an understanding of some important problem-solving activities (e.g., Kintsch & Greeno, 1985). Thus problem solving deserves as prominent a place in mainstream cognitive psychology as any topic you've studied so far.

Let's begin with a description of the classic problem-solving research of the Gestalt psychologists, during the period 1920–1950. As you read in Chapter 1, the Gestalt movement coexisted with behaviorism early in this century but never achieved the central status that behaviorism did. In retrospect, however, it was an important influence on cognitive psychology, particularly with respect to problem solving.

Possibly more than in any material you've read so far, it's important for you to spend time working through the examples and problems that

---

[1]Whereas graduate students are trained in more traditional modes of cognitive research in many places, there is usually a "Pittsburgh connection" in the background of a problem-solving researcher. There seem to be three categories of problem solvers: those who have been affiliated with Carnegie Mellon University, such as Newell, Simon, Chase, Hayes, and Anderson; those affiliated with the University of Pittsburgh, where Greeno, Glaser, Chi, and others pursued this area; and those who are "second generation," working on problem solving with researchers who have "done time" in Pittsburgh. Then again, maybe the "Pittsburgh connection" is nothing more than my availability heuristic at work, since only one or two exceptions spring to mind.

Professor Herbert A. Simon

are provided. Hints usually accompany the problems, and the solutions to all problems are presented either in the text or, for numbered problems, at the end of the chapter. Many of the insights of the problem-solving literature pertain to conscious, strategic activities that you'll discover on your own as you work through the sample problems. Furthermore, simply by working the examples you'll probably improve your own problem-solving skills; to paraphrase Bruner (1973), no one ever gets better at problem solving without solving problems.

▼ Gestalt Psychology and Problem Solving

Gestalt is a German word that translates *very* poorly into English: the one-word translations of "whole" or "field" fail miserably at indicating what the term actually means. Roughly speaking, a **gestalt** refers to a *whole pattern, a form, or a configuration.* It is a cohesive grouping, a perspective from which the entire "field" can be seen. A variety of translations have been used at one point or another (*holism* is probably the best of them; note, however, that holistic psychology, whatever that is, is certainly *not* the same as Gestalt psychology). No single translation of the word ever caught on, however, which prompted Boring (1950) to remark that Gestalt psychology "suffered from its name." Consequently, we use the German term *gestalt* itself, rather than some inadequate translation.

Figure 12-1 shows several patterns that demonstrate various Gestalt principles (e.g., closure, good continuation). They demonstrated (to the *Gestalters,* anyway) that humans tend to perceive and therefore deal with integrated, cohesive wholes. As Boring (1950) described it: "The most concise way to characterize *Gestalt* psychology is to say that it deals with *wholes.* . . . In perceiving a melody you get the melodic form, not a string of notes, a unitary whole that is something more than the total list of its parts or even the serial pattern of them. That is the way experience comes

FIGURE 12-1

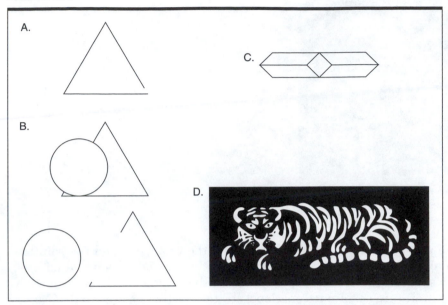

Several figures that illustrate various Gestalt principles of perception. In A, we perceive the figure as a triangle, despite the missing segment. In B, we tend to "see" a triangle partially blocked by a sphere; as the second version shows, the two parts can be separated to show how the lines may not continue. In C, we generally do not see a two-dimensional pattern; instead, we tend to see an optical illusion, a three-dimensional figure that switches orientation. In D, we "see" a complete pattern, due to the Gestalt principle of "closure." (Part D from Matlin, 1983.)

to man, put up in significant structured forms, *Gestalten*" (p. 588). Thus it was the *Gestalt* psychology movement that advanced the notion that "the whole is different from or greater than the sum of its individual parts."

Early Gestalt Research

The connection between the term *gestalt* and interest in problem solving is best explained by anecdote (see Boring, 1950, pp. 595–597). In 1913, Wolfgang Köhler, a German psychologist, went to the Spanish island of Teneriffe to study "the psychology of anthropoid apes" (p. 596). Trapped there by the outbreak of World War I, Kohler experimented with visual discrimination among several animal species. In the course of this research, he began to apply Gestalt principles to animal perception. His ultimate conclusion, in essence, was that animals do not perceive individual elements in a stimulus, but that they perceive *relations* among stimuli. Furthermore, "Kohler also observed that the perception of relations is a mark of intelligence, and he called the sudden perception of useful or proper relations *insight*" (Boring, p. 596).

Still stranded on the island, Kohler continued to examine "insight learning." He presented problems to his subjects and searched for evi-

Grande builds a three-box structure to reach the bananas, while Sultan watches from the ground. *Insight,* sometimes referred to as an "Ah-ha" experience, was the term Kohler used for the sudden perception of useful relations among objects during problem solving.

dence of genuine problem solving in their behavior. By far the most famous of his subjects was a chimpanzee named Sultan (Kohler, 1927). In a simple demonstration, Sultan was able to use a long pole to reach through the bars of his cage and get a bunch of bananas. Kohler made the situation more difficult, by giving Sultan two shorter poles, neither of which was long enough to reach the bananas. After failing to get the bananas, and sulking in his cage for a while, Sultan (as the story goes) suddenly went over to the poles and put one inside the end of the other, thus creating *one* pole that was long enough to reach the bananas.

Kohler found this to be an apt demonstration of insight, a sudden solution to a problem by means of an insightful discovery. In another situation, Sultan discovered how to stand on a box to reach a banana that was otherwise too high to reach. In yet another, he discovered how to get a banana that was just out of reach through the cage bars—he walked *away* from the banana, out a distant door, and around the cage. All these problem solutions seemed to illustrate Sultan's perception of *relations* and the importance of insight in problem solving.

Difficulties in Problem Solving

Other Gestalt psychologists, most notably Duncker and Luchins, pursued the research tradition with human subjects. Two major contributions of this later work are generally acknowledged, essentially the two sides of the problem-solving coin. One involved a set of *negative* effects related to rigidity or difficulty in problem solving, the other insight and creativity during problem solving.

Functional Fixedness   Two papers on functional fixedness, one by Maier (1931) and one by Duncker (1945), serve to identify and define this particular difficulty that arises during problem solving. **Functional fixedness** refers to *a tendency to use objects and concepts in the problem environment in only their customary and usual way.* Maier (1931), for instance, had subjects work on the Two String problem. Two strings are suspended from the ceiling, and the goal is to tie them together. The problem is that the strings are too far apart for a person merely to hold one, reach the other, then tie them together. Available to the subject are several other objects, including a chair, some paper, and a pair of pliers. Even standing on the chair does not get the subject close enough to the two strings.

In Maier's results, only 39% of the subjects came up with the correct solution during a 10-minute period. The solution (if you haven't tried solving the problem, do so now) involves using an object in the room in a *novel* fashion. The correct solution is to tie the pliers to one string, swing it like a pendulum, then catch it while holding the other string. Thus the functional fixedness in this situation was failing to conceive of the pliers in any but their customary function; subjects were *fixed* on the normal use for pliers and failed to appreciate how they could be used as a weight for a pendulum.

A similar demonstration is illustrated in Figure 12-2, the Candle problem from Duncker (1945). The task is to find a way of mounting the candle on a door or wall, using just the objects illustrated. Can you solve the problem? If you haven't come up with a solution after a minute or two, here's a hint: can you think of another use for a box besides using it as a container? In other words, the notion of functional fixedness is that we generally think of only the customary uses for objects, whereas successful problem solving often involves finding *novel* uses for objects. By conceiving of the box as a platform or means of support, you can then solve the problem (empty the box, thumbtack it to the door or wall, then mount the candle in it).

Of course, it's not surprising that problem solvers experience functional fixedness. After all, we comprehend the problem situation by means of our general world knowledge, along with whatever *procedural knowledge* we have that might be relevant to the situation. When you find PLIERS in semantic memory, surely the most accessible properties involve the normal use for pliers. Far down on your "list" would be characteristics

FIGURE 12-2

The Candle problem used by Duncker. Using only the pictured objects, figure out how to mount the candle to the wall or door.

related to the *weight* of the pliers, or aspects of their *shape* that would enable you to tie a string to them. Likewise, BOX is probably stored in semantic memory in terms of "container" meanings—that a box can hold things, that you put things into a box—and not in terms of "platform/support" meanings (see Greenspan, 1986, for evidence on retrieval of central versus peripheral properties). Simply from the standpoint of routine retrieval from memory, then, we can understand why people often experience functional fixedness.

Negative Set   A related difficulty in problem solving is termed **negative set** (or simply *set effects*). This refers to *a bias or tendency to solve problems in one particular way, using a single specific approach, even when a different approach might be more productive.* The term *set* is a rough translation of the original German term *Einstellung,* which means something like "approach" or "orientation"; the (awful) phrase "mind set" is probably the closest expression we have to the term in English.

The classic demonstration of set effects comes from the Water Jug problems, studied by Luchins (1942). In these problems, you are given three jugs, each of a different capacity, and are asked to measure out a desired quantity of water using just the three jugs. As a simple illustration, consider the first problem in Table 12-1. You need to measure out

Table 12-1

Problems	Capacity of Jug A	Capacity of Jug B	Capacity of Jug C	Desired Quantity
1	5 cups	40 cups	18 cups	28 cups
2	21 cups	127 cups	3 cups	100 cups

Luchins's Water Jug Problems

Problems	Capacity of Jug A	Capacity of Jug B	Capacity of Jug C	Desired Quantity
1	21	127	3	100
2	14	163	25	99
3	18	43	10	5
4	9	42	6	21
5	20	59	4	31
6	23	49	3	20
7	15	39	3	18
8	28	76	3	25
9	18	48	4	22
10	14	36	8	6

Note: All volumes are in cups.

28 cups of water and can use containers that hold 5, 40, and 18 cups (jugs A, B, and C). The solution is to fill A twice, then fill C once, each time pouring the contents into the destination jug. This approach is an *addition solution,* since you add the quantities together. For the second problem, a *subtraction solution* is appropriate, fill B (127), subtract jug C from it twice (–3, –3), then subtract jug A (–21), yielding 100.

Luchins's (1942) demonstration of negative set involved sequencing the problems so that subjects developed a particular set or approach for measuring out the quantities. The second group of problems in Table 12-1 illustrates such a sequence. Go ahead and work the problems now before you read any further.

If you were like most subjects, your experience on problems 1 through 7 led you to develop a particular approach or set: specifically, B – 2C – A—fill jug B, subtract C twice from it, then subtract A from it to yield the necessary amount (subtracting A can be done before subtracting 2C, of course). Subjects with such a set or *Einstellung* generally failed to notice the far simpler solution possible for problems 6 and 10, simply A – C. That is, about 80% of the subjects who saw all 10 problems used the lengthy B – 2C – A method for these problems. Compare this to the control subjects, who saw only problems 6 through 10; only 1% of these subjects used the longer method. Clearly, the control subjects had not developed a set for using the lengthy method, so they were much more able to find the simpler solution.

Consider problem 8 now. Only 5% of Luchins's control subjects failed to solve problem 8. This was a remarkable result since 64% of the "negative set" subjects, those who saw all 10 problems, failed to solve it correctly. These subjects had such an orientation toward the method they had already developed that they were surprisingly unable to generate a method that would work on problem 8 (note that B – 2C – A does *not* work on this problem). Greeno's (1978) description here is very useful— by repeatedly solving the first seven problems with the same formula, subjects learned an "integrated algorithm." This algorithm was strong enough to bias their later solution attempts and prevent them from seeing the simple solution, $28 - 3 = 25$.

Several problems that often yield such negative set effects are presented in Table 12-2; hints to help overcome negative set, if you experi-

---

Table 12-2

---

2. One morning, exactly at sunrise, a Buddhist monk began to climb a tall mountain. The narrow path, no more than a foot or two wide, spiraled around the mountain to a glittering temple at the summit. The monk ascended the path at varying rates of speed, stopping many times along the way to rest and to eat the dried fruit he carried with him. He reached the temple shortly before sunset. After several days of fasting and meditation, he began his journey back along the same path, starting at sunrise and again walking at variable speeds with many pauses along the way. His average speed descending was, of course, greater than his average climbing speed.

Show that there is a spot along the path that the monk will occupy on both trips at precisely the same time of day.

3. A woman has four pieces of chain. Each piece is made up of three links. She wants to join the pieces into a single closed ring of chain. To open a link costs 2 cents and to close a link costs 3 cents. She has only 15 cents. How does she do it?

4. Show how to move only two pennies in the left diagram to yield the pattern at the right.

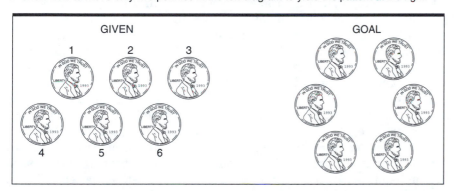

5. Six drinking glasses are lined up in a row. The first three are full of water, the last three are empty. By handling and moving only one glass, change the arrangement so that no full glass is next to another full one, and no empty glass is next to another empty one.

HINTS

---

2. Although the problem seems to call for a quantitative, numerical solution, think of a way to represent the problem using visual imagery.
3. You do not have to open a link on *each* piece of chain.
4. Try rotating the left pattern, as a way of determining which pennies are already in position.
5. How else can you handle a glass of water besides moving it to another location?

Answers to all numbered problems are provided at the end of this chapter.

ence it, are at the bottom of the table. These problems lack the precision of Luchins's demonstration, of course: we cannot point to the exact equation or method that *is* the negative set in these problems, but only to the general approach or incorrect representation that people often adopt. On the other hand, the problems are useful in that they seem to resemble real-world problems much more closely than the rather arbitrary water jugs do.

As the slide projector problem in the introduction suggests, functional fixedness and negative set are probably very common everyday occurrences. Possibly because we eventually find an adequate solution to our everyday problems *despite* the negative set, or without overcoming our functional fixedness (e.g., eventually locating a thinner book), we are less aware of these set and functional fixedness difficulties in our problem-solving behavior. The classic demonstrations, however, illustrate rather dramatically how rigid such behavior can be, and how barriers to successful problem solving can arise.

Summary Points: status of problem solving in cognitive psychology; verbal protocols; Gestalt psychology; functional fixedness; negative set

▼ Insight and Analogy

On the more positive side of problem solving, several of the problems reported in this early literature attested to insight in problem solving. As Wickelgren (1974) notes, problems requiring insight for their solution often require the problem solver to draw some critical inference from the statement of the problem. For instance, if a problem states that some number is an even integer, then solution of the problem might depend on inferring from this information that the number is a multiple of 2; that is, the number n might be represented alternatively as $n = 2m$, where other information in the problem might give details about m. Depending on circumstances, this can be the sort of inference that suggests insight.

For instance, in a programming class I took once, part of the program needed a random number for its computations. For some reason, the random number had to be even. The professor stressed that we "try to solve the problem with the simplest programming steps possible." One method, not notably insightful, was merely to make the computer supply a random number, and then go through the laborious programming steps of dividing it by 2, checking to see if there was a remainder or not, then repeating the process if the number had been odd. A better solution, we discovered, was to have the computer pick a random number, and then double it. Obviously, the number will be even under this operation regardless of whether the original number was odd or even.

Sometimes, the necessary insight for solving a problem comes from an analogy: an already-solved problem is similar to a current one, so the old solution can be adapted to the new situation. The standard historical example of this is the story of Archimedes, the Greek scientist who had to determine if the king's crown was solid gold, or if some silver had been mixed with the gold. Archimedes knew the weights of both gold and silver per unit of volume, but could not imagine how to measure the volume of the crown. As the anecdote goes, he stepped into his bath one day, and noticed how the water level rose as he sank into the water. He then realized the solution to his problem. The volume of the crown could be determined by immersing it in water and measuring how much water it displaced. (So excited by his insight, he then jumped from the bath, and ran naked through the streets, shouting "Eureka! I have found it!" See footnote 1, Chapter 11, for the connection between the words *eureka* and *heuristic*.)

Greeno's (1978) influential review proposed that analogies, as well as linear-series problems, could be characterized more generally as *problems of inducing structure,* one of the three major types of problems in Greeno's typology. In such problems, the subjects' task is to take the givens in the problem and induce or figure out the embedded structure and relations among the elements. Once this structure has been induced, then the problem is solved. For example, in the analogy MERCHANT : SELL :: CUSTOMER : _____, you must induce the relation between MERCHANT and SELL, and then apply that relation to CUSTOMER. Although the analogical relation is different in BIRD : WORM :: HORSE : _____, the underlying process is the same—identify the relation between the A : B pair, then project it onto C, yielding D. Graphically, we have A → B and C → D, where the arrows denote the same relationship. Likewise, in series problems, like 1 2 8 3 4 7 5 6 . . . , the embedded structure of the problem must be induced in order to decide what the next number in the sequence must be. Considerable research has examined how people accomplish these processes (see Novick, 1988; Novick & Holyoak, 1991; Rumelhart & Abrahamson, 1973; and Sternberg, 1977).

A difficulty, however, is that the situations we face in more complex problems often seem to mask or disguise the critical relation that must be induced, or present us with so many potential relations that we can't decide which to pursue in order to develop a useful analogy. When the induction of relations and structure is more complex, we are probably more likely to call a solution to the problem "insightful"—the connection is remote enough that we judge the solution to be creative and insightful.

Analogy Problems

To gain some feeling for analogies, read the Parade story in Table 12-3, a story used by Gick and Holyoak (1980) in an important study of problem solving. Try to solve the problem now, before reading the solution at the bottom of the table.

Table 12-3

THE PROBLEM
Parade–Dispersion Story

A small country was controlled by a dictator. The dictator ruled the country from a strong fortress. The fortress was situated in the middle of the country, surrounded by farms and villages. Many roads radiated outward from the fortress like spokes on a wheel. To celebrate the anniversary of his rise to power, the dictator ordered his general to conduct a full-scale military parade. On the morning of the anniversary, the general's troops were gathered at the head of one of the roads leading to the fortress, ready to march. However, a lieutenant brought the general a disturbing report. The dictator was demanding that this parade had to be more impressive than any previous parade. He wanted his army to be seen and heard at the same time in every region of the country. Furthermore, the dictator was threatening that if the parade was not sufficiently impressive he was going to strip the general of his medals and reduce him to the rank of private. But it seemed impossible to have a parade that could be seen throughout the whole country.

THE SOLUTION

The general, however, knew just what to do. He divided his army up into small groups and dispatched each group to the head of a different road. When all was ready he gave the signal, and each group marched down a different road. Each group continued down its road to the fortress, so that the entire army finally arrived together at the fortress at the same time. In this way, the general was able to have the parade seen and heard through the entire country at once, and thus please the dictator.

Gick and Holyoak had their subjects read this Parade–Dispersion problem, a somewhat different army fortress story (the Attack–Dispersion story), or no story at all. They then asked them to read and solve another problem, the classic Duncker (1945) Radiation problem presented in Table 12-4. Read and solve this problem now; plan on spending a good five or ten minutes before you read any further.

The Radiation problem is interesting to study for a variety of reasons, including the fact that it is rather ill-defined, and thus comparable to many problem-solving situations in the real world. Duncker's subjects produced three general approaches to the problem: avoiding contact between the ray and the nearby tissue; changing the sensitivity of the surrounding tissue to the effects of the ray; and reducing the intensity of the rays as they pass through healthy tissue.

For the first, some unobstructed pathway to the tumor, say, the esophagus, might be used; subjects eventually gave up on this solution pathway. For the second, some chemical injection might desensitize the surrounding tissue, or heighten the tumor's sensitivity; the lack of such a chemical substance makes this a dead end as well. Correct solutions, on the other hand, used the third approach, often by developing an analogy to some other, better understood situation.

Gick and Holyoak (1980) adapted this problem to an in-depth study of

Table 12-4   RADIATION PROBLEM

Suppose you are a doctor faced with a patient who has a malignant tumor in his stomach. It is impossible to operate on the patient, but unless the tumor is destroyed the patient will die. There is a kind of ray that can be used to destroy the tumor. If the rays reach the tumor all at once at a sufficiently high intensity, the tumor will be destroyed. Unfortunately, at this intensity the healthy tissue that the rays pass through on the way to the tumor will also be destroyed. At lower intensities the rays are harmless to healthy tissue, but they will not affect the tumor either. What type of procedure might be used to destroy the tumor with the rays, and at the same time avoid destroying the healthy tissue?

Attack–Dispersion Story

A small country was controlled by a dictator. The dictator ruled the country from a strong fortress. The fortress was situated in the middle of the country, surrounded by farms and villages. Many roads radiated outward from the fortress like spokes on a wheel. A general arose who raised a large army and vowed to capture the fortress and free the country of the dictator. The general knew that if his entire army could attack the fortress at once it could be captured. The general's troops were gathered at the head of one of the roads leading to the fortress, ready to attack. However, a spy brought the general a disturbing report. The ruthless dictator had planted mines on each of the roads. The mines were set so that small bodies of men could pass over them safely, since the dictator needed to be able to move troops and workers to and from the fortress. However, any large force would detonate the mines. Not only would this blow up the road and render it impassable, but the dictator would then destroy many villages in retaliation. It therefore seemed impossible to mount a full-scale direct attack on the fortress.

Solution to the Radiation Problem

The ray may be divided into several low-intensity rays, no one of which will destroy the healthy tissue. By positioning these several rays at different locations around the body, and focusing them all on the tumor, their effect will combine, thus being strong enough to destroy the tumor.

Solution to the Attack–Dispersion Story

The general, however, knew just what to do. He divided his army up into small groups and dispatched each group to the head of a different road. When all was ready he gave the signal, and each group marched down a different road. Each group continued down its road to the fortress, so that the entire army finally arrived together at the fortress at the same time. In this way, the general was able to capture the fortress, and thus overthrow the dictator.

problem solving by analogy. In one of their experiments (which we have just simulated here), subjects read the Parade story, then solved the Radiation problem. In case you didn't notice, there are strong similarities between the problems: the Parade story can serve as an analogy in helping you solve the Radiation problem. Yet Gick and Holyoak found that only 49% of the subjects who first solved the Parade problem realized it could be used as an analogy for the Radiation problem. A different initial story, the Attack–Dispersion problem (see bottom of Table 12-4), provided a stronger "hint" about the radiation problem; fully 76% of these subjects used the analogy in solving the Radiation problem. In contrast, only 8% of the control group, which merely attempted to solve the Radiation problem, came up with the "dispersion" solution (i.e., multiple pathways) described at the bottom of the table.

In another experiment, Gick and Holyoak provided an explicit hint to their subjects, telling them that the "attack" solution might be helpful as they worked on the Radiation problem. Fully 92% of the "hint condition" subjects used the analogy in solving the Radiation problem, and most found it "very helpful." In dramatic contrast, only 20% of the "no hint" subjects produced the dispersion solution, even though they too had read the Attack–Dispersion story. In short, only 20% *spontaneously* noticed and used the analogous relationship between the problems. Table 12-5 summarizes the results obtained by Gick and Holyoak.

What makes these two stories different in their usefulness for discovering the analogy to the Radiation problem? One of the very interesting aspects of Gick and Holyoak's report is that they analyzed the stories in terms of their *propositional* structure (see Chapters 7 and 9). Figure 12-3 reproduces their analysis and shows how close the two stories are in their underlying structure (the numbers refer to propositions in the original stories, from a paragraph structure analysis similar to the ones presented in Chapter 7 for story grammars and scripts). In Greeno's terms, this similarity should make the relation ARMY : FORTRESS :: RAYS : TUMOR easier to induce.

Recent evidence by Gentner and Toupin (1986) supports this idea. In

Table 12-5   SUMMARY OF GICK AND HOLYOAK'S (1980) RESULTS

Study 1 (Experiment II originally; after Gick & Holyoak, Table 10)

Subjects in groups A and B are given a general hint that their solution to one of the earlier stories may be useful in solving the Radiation Problem.

Group	Order of Stories	Percentage of Subjects Who Used the Analogy on the Radiation Problem
Group A	Parade, Radiation	49%
Group B	Attack–Dispersion, Radiation	76%
Group C	No story, Radiation	8%

Study 2 (Experiment IV originally)

Subjects in group A are given the general hint (as above). Subjects in group B are given no hint whatsoever.

Group	Order of Stories	Percentage of Subjects Who Used the Analogy on the Radiation Problem
Group A (Hint)	Attack–Dispersion, Radiation	92%
Group B (No hint)	Attack–Dispersion, Radiation	20%

FIGURE 12-3

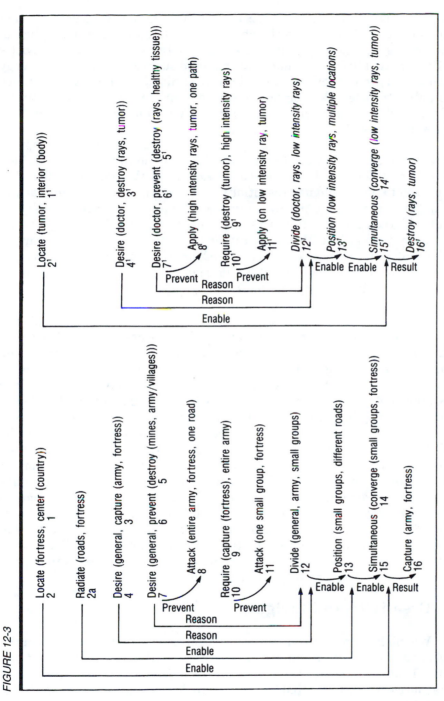

A side-by-side propositional analysis of the Attack–Dispersion and Radiation stories, as analyzed by Gick and Holyoak (1980). The strong parallels between the stories are clear in the illustration. (From Gick & Holyoak, 1980.)

their study, analogies from one problem to another were detected and used more readily if the initial story was "systematic," that is, explicit in describing the cause–effect connections in the story. And in Novick's (1988) work, structural similarity prompted successful use of the analogy more for a group of experts than for novices; novices tended to experience negative transfer when problems were similar only at a surface or superficial level (see also Gentner, 1983; Holyoak & Koh, 1987; Ross, 1989).

And yet, as Gick and Holyoak noted, the situations are not perfectly related. In the army fortress problem, for instance, the many roads radiate *out* from the fortress like spokes. There is nothing in the radiation problem statement that corresponds exactly to this detail; in fact, the solution to the problem is essentially achieved when you realize that you can "invent" multiple pathways *in* toward the tumor. Nonetheless, the "attack" theme seems to have been semantically similar enough to the "destroy tumor" idea that this, rather than "troops on parade," carried the analogy (Spellman & Holyoak, 1992, analyzed analogical mapping in people's reasoning about the 1991 Persian Gulf War, i.e., "If Saddam is Hitler then who is George Bush?").

Analogies and Heuristics   Of course, there are many analogies that we might attempt to draw that would *not* be useful for solving a particular problem. Thus we can refer to a strategy of solving problems by analogy as a *heuristic*—it might work if a useful analogy is found, but it is not at all guaranteed to work. For instance, the army fortress analogy is completely irrelevant to the problems in Table 12-2; although *different* analogies may be appropriate, there is often little in the problem to suggest exactly *which* analogy might be the most useful. In research by Reed, Ernst, and Banerji (1974), an almost perfectly analogous solution to one problem failed to improve performance on a second problem. As these authors point out, problem solving by analogy may be more difficult than it would appear, especially if the analogy is difficult to remember. For instance, the availability of useful phrases like "divide and conquer" for the army fortress problem might be all that's needed to help subjects draw the analogy. For the difficult problem that Reed et al. studied, no such simple phrase or mnemonic was possible, so there was little transfer from one problem to the other.

Creativity and Insight

We might argue that a subject who solves the Radiation problem by using an army fortress analogy has come up with an insightful solution. A difficulty, however, is that the term *insight* is not a scientific one; it has no clear definition that we can use to decide what is and what is not insightful. This is also the case for the term *creativity*. In some ways, we might say that the analogy solution to the Radiation problem is creative.

Does this mean something different than calling it insightful? Are the terms *insight* and *creativity* interchangeable?[2]

Wallas (1926) proposed that insight was just one of four steps in the creative process. In particular, his analysis suggested that creativity involves:

1. Preparation—formulating the problem and making some preliminary attempts to solve it.
2. Incubation—setting the problem aside and working on other things.
3. Illumination—achieving some important insight into the problem or the solution.
4. Verification—checking to make sure that the solution actually solves the problem.

One implication of this four-step process is that *creativity* is only an appropriate term when the problem being solved is very lengthy; in other words, any problem solved by the preliminary attempts in step 1 might, by definition, be excluded from the term *creativity*. On the other hand, Wallas's formulation, while sensible, is hardly scientific or testable. How would we judge the "importance" of some insight, for instance, in order to test someone's performance in the illumination stage? Wouldn't our judgments and evaluations make this a highly subjective, that is, nonscientific, assessment?

There has been some work done on the steps that Wallas included in his scheme. For instance, Fulgosi and Guilford (1968) found that problem solving did in fact improve if subjects were given a break during the session; while the break could have provided an opportunity for *incubation,* its function was probably to allow recovery from fatigue (or possibly release from PI). Adamson and Taylor (1954) found that functional fixedness declined when they interpolated a delay between problems; in their study, an object used to solve the first problem had to be used in a novel way to solve the second problem.

And yet, the heart of the proposal—the illumination stage, during which insight is achieved—seems almost impossibly difficult to investigate in any other than anecdotal fashion. That is, using hints and suggestions, as Gick and Holyoak did, would be one way of affecting the illumination stage. In essence, if we highlight some useful analogy, does this help the subject achieve the "important insight"? On the other hand, we

---

[2]Greeno (1978) considers other uses of the term *creativity* as well, including our sense that creativity reflects some special process, as in artistic creativity. Design and invention, or creativity in composition (as in writing or musical composition), require deep knowledge of the objects and structure of the problem space, as well as some "mechanism" that permits the individual to judge whether the achieved solution is good or not. In general, this kind of creativity is very poorly understood in psychology (see also Weisberg, 1993).

could argue that *giving* subjects the analogy turns our investigation into merely a study of ordinary problem solving, that providing the analogy robbed the situation of its potential for "creative insight."

Summary Points: analogies; inducing structure; creativity and insight; incubation

▼ Basics of Problem Solving

What the Gestalt psychologists lacked, as many critics pointed out, was a careful and scientifically precise way of defining their concepts and explanatory variables. Their fundamental assumption, concerning the futility of studying a phenomenon by reducing it to components, also made their research difficult to accept at face value. For instance, a subject might spend considerable time on the Radiation problem, musing over different possibilities, trying different plans, and then finally arrive at a useful solution. And yet, the Gestalt preference was to consider the final solution, but *not* break the lengthy solution process into components. From our modern perspective, this preference was ill-advised. If you tried three plans to solve a problem, found each of them deficient, then finally found a fourth that worked, wouldn't we learn a considerable amount about your problem-solving processes by analyzing the unworkable as well as the workable plans? In fact, Gick and McGarry (1992) have gone one step beyond that, showing that initial solution failures on one problem can often *improve* your solutions on a second problem—literally showing that people can "learn from their mistakes."

For reasons such as these, modern cognitive psychology adopted a more reductionistic approach to the study of problem solving. For instance, Newell and Simon's analysis of a cryptarithmetic problem (1972, Chapter 6), consists of a *microscopic* analysis and interpretation of *every* statement made by a single subject as he solved a problem, all 2186 words and twenty or so minutes of problem-solving activity. When we compare the influence of Newell and Simon's work to the much more modest and general influence of Gestalt psychology, we must conclude that the modern approach is better suited to the task of investigating human problem solving.

We cycle back here to an elementary question, in order to profit from the greater degree of precision offered by modern cognitive psychology's examination of problem solving. The question, simply enough, is "What is a problem?"

In Newell and Simon's (1972) thumbnail description, "A person is confronted with a *problem* when he wants something and does not know immediately what series of actions he can perform to get it" (p. 72). The "something" in this definition can be renamed for more general use as a **goal,** *the desired end-point or solution of the problem-solving activity.*

Problem solving, then, consists of goal-directed activity, moving from some initial configuration or state through a series of intermediate steps, until finally the overall goal has been reached—an adequate or correct solution. The difficulty, of course, is in determining *which* intermediate states are indeed on a (the) correct pathway—"Will step A get me to step B or not?"—as well as in devising operations or "moves" that achieve those intermediate states—"How do I get to step B from here?"

Characteristics of Problem Solving

Let's start by listing several characteristics that define what is and what is not a genuine instance of problem solving. Anderson (1980, 1985), for example, lists the following:

1. *Goal Directedness.* The overall behavior or activity we're examining is directed toward achieving some goal or purpose. By such a characteristic, we would exclude daydreaming, for instance; it's mental, but it's not goal directed. Alternatively, if you've locked your keys in your car, there is considerable physical as well as mental activity going on. The goal-directed nature of those activities, your repeated attempts at getting into the locked car, make this an instance of true problem solving.

2. *Sequence of Operations.* An activity must involve a sequence of operations or steps in order to qualify as problem solving. In other words, a simple retrieval from memory, say, recalling your address or phone number, is not an instance of problem solving, since it does not require a discernible sequence of separate operations or stages. Doing a long division problem or solving the "locked car" problem, on the other hand, definitely involves a sequence of mental operations, so these are instances of problem solving.

3. *Cognitive Operations.* Solving the problem, that is, achieving a solution to the overall goal, involves the application of various cognitive operations. Various *operators* can be applied to different problems, where each operator is a distinct cognitive act in the sequence, a permissible step or move in the problem space. For long division, retrieving an answer would be an operator, as would be subtracting or multiplying two numbers at some other stage in problem solution. Often, the cognitive operations will have some behavioral counterpart, some physical act that completes the mental operation, such as writing down a number during long division.

4. *Subgoal Decomposition.* As implied by the third characteristic, each step in the sequence of operations is itself a kind of goal, a **subgoal.** A subgoal is *an intermediate goal along the route to eventual solution of the problem.* Subgoals represent the decomposition, or breaking apart, of the overall goal into separate components. In many instances, subgoals themselves must be further decomposed into smaller subgoals. Thus solving a problem involves breaking the overall goal into subgoals, then pursuing the subgoals—and *their* subgoals—one after another until the

final solution is achieved. This yields a hierarchical or "nested" structure to the problem-solving attempt.

An intuitive illustration of such a nested solution structure is presented in Figure 12-4, a possible solution route to the Locked Car problem. Note that during the solution, the first two plans led to barriers or blocks, thus requiring that another plan be devised. The problem solver finally decided on another plan, breaking a window in order to get into the locked car. This decision is followed by a sequence of related acts, the search for some heavy object that will break a window, the decision as to which window to break, and so forth. Each of these decisions is a subgoal

FIGURE 12-4

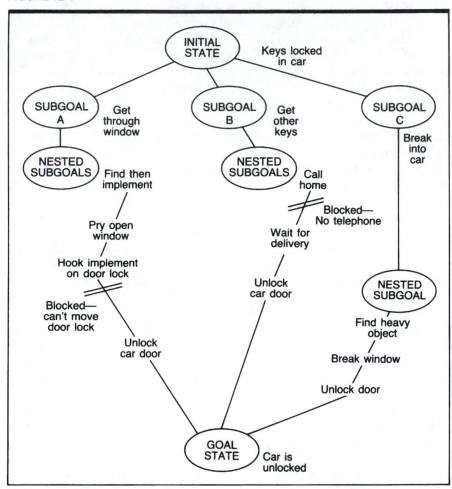

A representation of part of the problem space for "getting into a locked car." Note the barriers that are encountered under plans A and B.

nested within the larger subgoal of breaking into the car, itself a subgoal in the overall solution structure.

A Vocabulary of Problem Solving

These four characteristics define what qualifies as an instance of problem solving. Many important ideas beyond just these characteristics are embedded in these four points, however. Let's reexamine some of these points, looking now toward an expanded *vocabulary* of problem solving, a set of terms we will use to describe and understand how people solve problems.

The Problem Space   The term *problem space* is critical in analyzing problem solving. Anderson (1985) defines it as simply the various states or conditions that are possible in the problem. More concretely, the **problem space** includes *the initial, intermediate, and goal states of the problem. It also includes the problem solver's knowledge at each of these steps,* both knowledge that is currently being applied as well as knowledge that *could be* retrieved from memory and applied. Any external devices, objects, or resources that are available can also be included in the description of the problem space. Thus a difficult arithmetic problem that must be completed mentally has a somewhat different problem space than the same problem as completed with pencil and paper.

To illustrate, VanLehn (1989) describes a 60-year-old man's initial error in the "Three Men and a Rowboat" problem. The man focused only on the arithmetic of the problem and said essentially "400 pounds of people, 200 pounds per trip, it'll take two trips of the boat." When he was reminded that the rowboat couldn't row itself back to the original side, he adopted a completely different problem space.

In some problem contexts, we can speak of problem solving as a *search of the problem space,* or metaphorically, a *search of the solution tree,* in which each branch and twig represents a possible pathway from the initial state of the problem. For problems that are "wide open," that is, those that have many possibilities that need to be checked, there may be no alternative but to start searching the problem space, node by node, until some barrier or block is reached. As often as not, there will be information in the problem, however, that permits us to *restrict* the search space, that is, information that reduces the relevant search space to a manageable size. Metaphorically, this information permits us to *prune the search tree.*

A general depiction of this situation is in Figure 12-5. The initial state of the problem is the top node, and the goal state is some terminal node at the bottom. For "wide open" problems, each branch may need to be searched until a dead end is encountered. For other problems, information may be inferred that permits a restriction in the branches that are

FIGURE 12-5

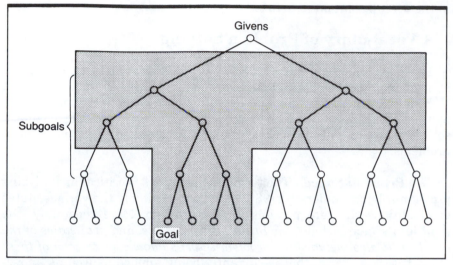

A general diagram of a problem space, with various branches of the space illustrated. Often a hint or an inference can prune the search tree, restricting the search to just one portion; this idea is represented by the shaded area of the figure. Note that in most problems, the problem-space tree is much larger, so the beneficial effect of pruning is far greater. (Adapted from Wickelgren, 1974.)

searched (the shaded area of the figure). Clearly, if the search space can be restricted, if the solution tree can be "pruned" of its dead-end branches, then problem-solving efficiency will be increased.

The Operators   The term **operators** refers to *the set of legal operations or "moves" that can be performed during problem solution.* The term *legal* means permissible in the rules of the problem. For example, an *illegal* operator in the six-penny problem of Table 12-2 would be to move *more* than two pennies; in Three Men and a Rowboat, an illegal operator is having the men swim across the river or loading the boat with too heavy a load.

For so-called *transformation problems* (Greeno, 1978), applying an operator will *transform* the problem into a new or revised state from which further work can be done. In general, applying a legal transformation operator moves you from one node to the next, along some connecting pathway in the search space. This general notion can be seen in Figure 12-5, in which the connecting pathways denote application of an operator. For instance, in solving algebraic equations, one transformation operator is "move the unknowns to the left." Thus for the equation $2X + 7 = X + 10$, application of the operator would move the single X to the left of the equal sign, by subtracting X from both sides of the equation.

Often, there are constraints within the problem that prevent us from applying certain operators. In a vague way, the "destruction of healthy tissue" was such a constraint in the Radiation problem. That constraint prevented the simple solution of applying the ray directly, where direct application would be a simple operator. In algebra, by contrast, constraints are imposed by the "rules of algebra"; for example, you can't subtract X from one side of the equation without subtracting it from the other side too.

The Goal   The goal is, of course, the ultimate destination, goal state, or solution to the problem. For recreational problems in particular, the goal is nearly always stated explicitly in the problem. Hence, given that recreational problems usually present *an explicit and complete specification of the initial and goal states,* we can describe such problems as **well-defined.** Solutions to such problems involve progressing through the legal intermediate states, by means of known operators, until the goal is reached. In contrast, in **ill-defined** problems, *the states, operators, or both may be only vaguely specified.* For instance, the Buddhist Monk problem in Table 12-2 states a rather vague goal, "Show that there is a spot. . . ." Likewise, problems with more real-world character are often distressingly vague in their specification of the goal: write a term paper that will earn you an A, write a computer program that does X in as economical and elegant a fashion as possible, and so on.

An Example: DONALD + GERALD   Let's consider a well-known recreational problem now, to pin down some of these terms and ideas. The problem is a *cryptarithmetic* problem, in which letters of the alphabet have been substituted for the digits in an addition problem. Your task is to reverse the substitutions, to figure out which digits go with which letters in order to yield a correct addition problem. The obvious restriction is that the digits and letters must be in one-to-one correspondence—only one digit per letter, and vice versa. Plan on spending 15 minutes or so on the problem; this is about the average amount of time it takes people on their first attempt. Make notes on paper as you work, so you can go back later to retrace and analyze your attempt to solve the problem. (Incidentally, this is the cryptarithmetic problem that Newell and Simon's single subject worked on.)

```
  DONALD      (Hint: D = 5)
+ GERALD
  ROBERT
```

Now that you've worked on the problem and have found (or come close to) the solution, we can use the insights you developed to fill in our definitions of terms. To begin with, the initial state of the problem consists of the statement of the problem, including the rules, restrictions, and hint you are given. These, along with your own knowledge of arithmetic (and pencil and paper), are your problem-solving tools for this problem. Each conceivable assignment of letters to digits makes up the entire problem space, and each *substitution operator* you might apply constitutes a branch or pathway on the search tree (a *substitution operator* here is an operator that substitutes a digit for a letter). Note, in correspondence to the shaded area of Figure 12-5, that the hint D = 5 serves to prune the search tree by a tremendous amount. Without the hint, you can only start working on the problem by trying some arbitrary assignments, then working through until an error shows up, followed by returning "up" to an earlier node and reassigning the letters to different digits. (Even without the hint, however, there is only one solution to this problem.)

You no doubt started working on the problem by replacing the Ds in the ones column with 5s, then immediately replacing the T with a 0. You also probably wrote a 1 above the tens column, for the carry operation from 5 + 5. A quick scan of the problem revealed one more D that could be rewritten. Note that the position you were in at this point, with three Ds and a T converted to digits, is a distinct step in the solution, an intermediate state in the problem, a node in the problem space. Furthermore, each substitution you made reflected the application of an operator, a cognitive operation that transforms the problem to a different intermediate state.

As you continued to work the problem, you were forced to infer information as a way of making progress. For instance, in working on the tens column, L + L + the carried 1, you can infer that R is an odd number—any number added to itself then augmented by 1 will yield an odd number. Likewise, you can infer from the D + G column that R must be in the range 5 to 9, and that 5 + G can't produce a carried 1. Putting these together, R must be a large, odd number, and G must be 4 or less. Each of these separate inferences, each mental conclusion you draw, is also an instance of a cognitive operation, a simple mental process or operator that composes a step in the problem-solving sequence. Each of these, furthermore, accomplishes some progress toward the immediate subgoal, *find out about L.*

Greeno (1978) refers to this process as one of *constructive search.* Rather than blindly assigning digits and trying them out, people usually draw inferences from the other columns and use those to limit the possible values the letters can take. This approach is typical in *arrangement problems,* the third of Greeno's (1978) categories, in which some combination of the given components must be found that satisfies the constraints in the problem. In other kinds of arrangement problems, say, anagrams, a constructive search heuristic would be to look for spelling patterns and form candidate words from those familiar units. The opposite approach, sometimes known as *generate and test,* merely uses some scheme to generate *all* possible arrangements, then tests those one by one to determine if the problem solution has been found (recall the algorithmic solution to the eight-letter example in Chapter 11).

A related aspect of problem solving here (it can be postponed, but your solution will be more organized if it's done now) is quite general and

Table 12-6

Intermediate State	Known Values	Reasons/Statements from Protocol
1 5ONAL5 <u>GERAL5</u> ROBER∅	∅123456789 T D R is odd	Since D is 5, then T = ∅, and carry a 1 to the next column. So the first column is 5 + something = odd, because L + L + 1 = R will make R odd.
	G is less than 5 R is odd, and greater than 5	R must be bigger than 5, since less than 5 would yield a two-digit sum in the D + G column, and there would be an extra column in the answer. G is less than 5.
1 1 5ONAL5 <u>G9RA15</u> ROB9R∅	∅123456789 T D E G is less than 5 R is odd, greater than 5	O + E is next. If E were ∅, it would be fine, but T is already ∅. So this column must have a carry brought to it. This means that E must be 9, so that the O + 9 + the carried 1 = o
1 11 5ONAL5 <u>G9RAL5</u> ROB9R∅		If E = 9, then A + A must have a carry brought to it, so then the A + A + the carried 1 = 9. Now, 4 would work for A, and so would 9, but 9 is already taken.
1 11 5ON4L5 <u>G9R4L5</u> ROB9R∅	∅123456789 T AD E R is odd, greater than 5 G is less than 5 L is greater than 5	So A has to be 4. So L + L + the carried 1 has to produce a carry, thus, L is greater than 5. 5 and 9 are taken.
1 11 5ON4L5 <u>G974L5</u> 7OB97∅	∅123456789 T AD R E G is less than 5, L is greater than 5	So the odd R must be 7. Since L + L yields a carry, L isn't 3.
11 11 5ON485 <u>G97485</u> 7OB97∅	∅123456789 T AD RLE N is greater than or equal to 3 G is less than 5	L must be 8, since 8 + 8 + 1 = 17. That only leaves O, N, G, and B. Since O + 9 needs a carry, then N + 7 has to yield a carry. So N has to be at least 3.
11 11 5ON485 <u>197485</u> 7OB97∅	∅123456789 TG AD RLE N is greater than or equal to 3	So G looks like 1. That leaves O, N, and B, for 2, 3, and 6. N can't be 3, because B can't be the ∅ in 3 + 7 = 1∅. And it can't be 2, because 2 + 7 = 9 and the 9 is taken.
11 11 5O6485 <u>197485</u> 7O397∅	∅ 12 34 56789 TGBADNRLE	That leaves N to be 6, so that makes B = 3.
11 11 526485 <u>197485</u> 723970	∅ 123456789 TGOBADNRLE	So O has to be 2. Check the addition.

A sample solution of the DONALD problem, showing intermediate states, known values, and an edited protocol. (Zero is drawn with the slash, ∅, to distinguish it from the letter O.)

Table 12-7   ADDITIONAL CRYPTARITHMETIC PROBLEMS

6.	CROSS	7.	LETS	8.	SEND
+	ROADS	+	WAVE	+	MORE
	DANGER		LATER		MONEY

Hint: R = 6.

almost constitutes "good advice" rather than an essential feature of subjects' performance. Some mechanism or system for keeping track of the information you know about the letters is needed, if only to prevent you from forgetting inferences you've already drawn. Indeed, such an external memory aid can go a long way toward making your problem solving more efficient. In some instances, it may even help you generalize from one problem variant to another (as in the next example, the Tower of Hanoi problem). Table 12-6 presents a rather compressed verbal protocol of the solution to the DONALD problem, which you might want to compare to your own solution pathway. The table also shows intermediate steps and a notational system for keeping track of known values. Table 12-7 presents several more cryptarithmetic problems that you might want to solve.

Summary Points: four characteristics of problem solving; problem space; search; legal operators; goal; well- and ill-defined problems; inferences and constructive search

▼ Means–End Analysis: A Fundamental Heuristic

Several heuristics for problem solving have been discovered and investigated in problem-solving research. You've already read about the analogy approach, and the final section in the chapter, on Improving your Problem Solving, describes and illustrates several others. But in terms of overall significance, as well as importance to the field of research, no other heuristic comes even close to the heuristic known as **means–end analysis.** This heuristic formed the basis for Newell and Simon's groundbreaking work (e.g., 1972), including their very first presentation of the information processing framework in 1956. Because it shaped the entire area, and the theories devised to account for problem solving, it deserves our special, focused attention here.

The Basics of Means–End Analysis

Means–end analysis is the best known of the heuristics of problem solving. In this approach, *the problem is solved by repeatedly determining*

the difference between the current state and the goal or subgoal state, then finding and applying an operator that reduces this difference. Means–end analysis nearly always implies the use of subgoals, since achieving the goal state usually involves the intermediate steps of achieving several subgoals along the way.

The basic notions of a means–end analysis can be summarized in a sequence of five steps.

1. Set up a goal or subgoal.
2. Look for a difference between the current state and the goal/subgoal state.
3. Look for an operator that will reduce or eliminate this difference. One such operator is the setting of a new subgoal.
4. Apply the operator.
5. Apply steps 2–4 repeatedly until all subgoals and the final goal are achieved.

At an intuitive level, means–end analysis and subgoals are very familiar to us and represent "normal" problem solving. The often-quoted example of means–end analysis in real-world problem solving comes from Newell and Simon (1972, p. 416):

I want to take my son to nursery school. What's the difference between what I have and what I want? One of distance. What changes distance? My automobile. My automobile won't work. What is needed to make it work? A new battery. What has new batteries? An auto repair shop. I want the repair shop to put in a new battery. . . .

Clearly, we've been considering means–end solutions all along in this chapter. The Locked Car problem, for instance, is a clear-cut example of means–end analysis; the goal is decomposed into subgoals, subgoals are further decomposed into more subgoals, actions at each step are taken in order to satisfy the subgoals and, eventually, the overall goal.

Means–End Analysis and the Tower of Hanoi

The most thoroughly investigated recreational problems are the Tower of Hanoi problem and the Missionary–Cannibals problem (also known as the Hobbits–Orcs problem). These famous problems, not coincidentally, show very clearly both the strengths and limitations of the means–end approach. We'll leave the Missionary–Cannibal problem, presented in Table 12-8, as an exercise for you to learn from, and then return to it later when we discuss Newell and Simon's computer simulation of means–end analysis. After you've worked on the problem for a while, look at the hint at the bottom of the table. To get you started, note that only three moves are possible at the beginning, and one of these is illegal because it leaves more cannibals than missionaries on the start side. Either of the other two moves, however, works fine.

Table 12-8

The Missionary–Cannibal Problem

Three missionaries and three cannibals are on one side of a river and need to cross to the other side. The only means of crossing is a boat, and the boat can only hold two people at a time. Devise a set of moves that will transport all six people across the river, bearing in mind the following constraint: the number of cannibals can never exceed the number of missionaries in any location, for the obvious reason. Remember that someone will have to row the boat back across each time.

Hint: At one point in your solution, you will have to send more people back to the original side than you just sent over to the destination.

The Tower of Hanoi problem is shown in Figure 12-6. Work on it very carefully, using the three-disk version in the figure. Try to keep track of your solution, so you'll understand how the problem demonstrates the usefulness of a means–end analysis. So that you'll be familiar with the problem and be able to reflect on your solution, work it several times again after you've solved it. See if you can't become very skilled at solving the three-disk problem by remembering your solution and being able to generate it repeatedly.

By the way, an excellent strategy (heuristic) for this problem is to solve it *physically,* using a set of physical objects that you can move around. Use a dime, nickel, and quarter for disks A, B, and C, and move these around on a sheet of paper on which you've drawn the three pegs 1, 2, and 3. Lining the coins up vertically will represent stacking them on the pegs. You'll find that this physical method, along with your notes, will give you a much better understanding of the problem, a particularly useful "hint" about solving the larger versions of the problem, and much clearer insight into the means–end approach (according to Ahlum-Heath & DiVesta, 1986, verbalizing your thinking also helps to solve the problem at the beginning).

FIGURE 12-6

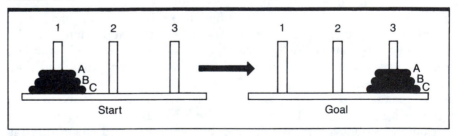

The goal of the problem is to move all three disks from peg 1 to peg 3, so that C is on the bottom, B is in the middle, and A is on top. The restrictions are: you may move only one disk at a time, and only to another peg; you may not place a larger disk on top of a smaller one.

Now that you've worked the problem several times, consider your solution in terms of subgoals and means–end analysis. Your goal, as stated in the problem, is to move the stack of disks A, B, and C from peg 1 to peg 3. Applying the means–end analysis, your first step sets up this goal. The second step in the analysis reveals a difficulty: there is a difference between your current state and the goal, simply the difference between the starting and ending configurations. You then look for a method or operator that will reduce this difference, and then apply that operator. As you no doubt learned from your solution, your first subgoal is "Clear off C." This then generates two more subgoals, "Move B so that C is free to move" and "Move A so that B is free to move."

The next step involves a simple operator that satisfies the most recent subgoal, "Move A to 3." This, of course, does not accomplish the overall goal, since B is still on C. But it does permit satisfying the *next* subgoal, "Move B so that C is free." So the next operator is "Move B to 2": B can't go on top of A, since that violates a restriction, and it can't stay on top of C since that prevents getting C to the bottom on peg 3. Now, there is still one barrier before the subgoal "C at the bottom of peg 3" can be satisfied: you have to remove A from peg 3. Thus the next operator is "Move A to 2," which allows "Move C to 3." This intermediate state still doesn't satisfy the goal, of course, but it clearly satisfies an important part of the solution—make C the bottom-most disk on peg 3.

From this state, AB on 2 and C on 3, it should be easy to see the final route to solution. Merely "unpack" A from 2, putting it temporarily on 1, move B to 3, then move A to 3. The seven moves that solve the problem are shown in Figure 12-7.

The Four-Disk Version

After you've worked the problem several times, solving it again becomes rather easy. You come to see how each disk needs to move in order to get C on 3, then B, and finally A. Spend some time now on the same problem, but use four disks instead of three. Don't work on this larger version blindly, however. Think of it, instead, as a *variation* on the three-disk problem. In other words, see if you can't determine which part of the four-disk problem is "old," already understood from your experience with three disks. The part that is old has exactly the same subgoals as it did in the simpler three-disk version, and virtually the same moves. As a hint, try renaming the pegs as the *source* peg, the *stack* peg, and the *destination* peg.

Did you solve the four-disk problem? If you did, compare your notes to those you took for the three-disk problem. In particular, compare the first set of moves for the four-disk problem to those you made for three disks. You'll notice several interesting relationships. The first seven moves in the larger problem serve to prepare the pegs so that D can go to peg 3 on the eighth move. Of course, you already knew from the simpler

FIGURE 12-7

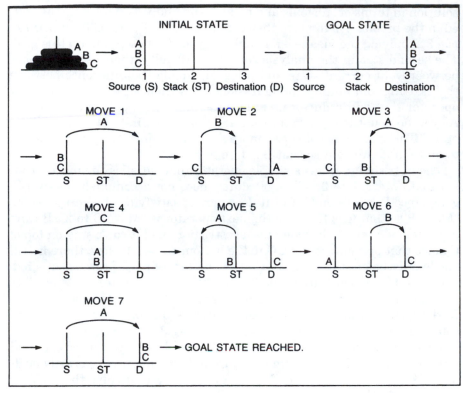

A representation of the solution to the Tower of Hanoi problem. Note that the pegs have been renamed as "Source," "Stack," and "Destination." Moving the three disks requires seven moves. Consider these seven moves as one unit, called "moving a pyramid of three disks."

problem that it takes seven moves to relocate three disks (a strong hint). Thus the eighth move gets that new, fourth disk to its destination.

If your notes are good, you'll also notice that you moved the top three disks in exactly the same order as you did in the simpler problem—not surprising, since the four-disk problem is really just the three-disk problem plus an extra disk on the bottom. The only differences are that pegs 2 and 3 switch roles for your first seven moves, and for the last seven moves, pegs 1 and 2 switch roles. (See Figure 12-8 for the four-disk version of the problem. Based on this pattern, can you determine how to solve the five-disk version? Here's a hint: the pegs switched roles twice in the "one-more-than-three disk" version, so adding yet another disk should cause *another* cycle of role switching in the "one-more-than-four-disk" version.) In Simon's (1975) analysis, if you can begin to think of a *larger* operation, "move a *pyramid* of three disks," then the relationships among the different tower problems become clear.

FIGURE 12-8

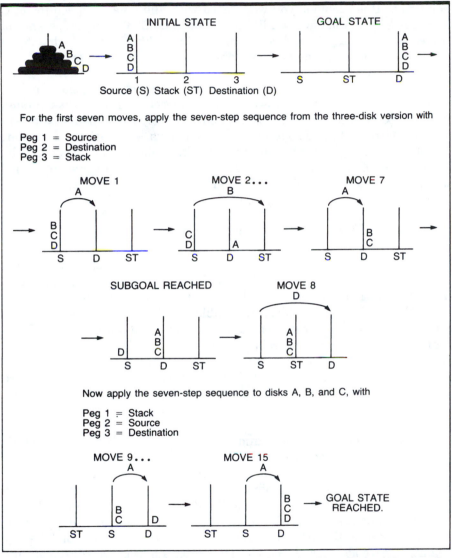

A representation of the solution to the four-disk Tower of Hanoi problem. The variation from the three-disk version is that the pegs must switch roles. In the beginning, the subgoal is to "move a pyramid of three disks" so that D can move to peg 3. After that, the subgoal is again to "move a three-disk pyramid." In both the first and second halves, the pegs must switch roles in order for the problem to be solved.

By now, you've surely gained considerable insight into not only the Tower of Hanoi problem but also the general idea of means–end analysis and subgoals as applied to transformation problems. Throughout your solution to this problem, you were faced with dilemmas—I need to get C to 3, but B is on top of C, so I'll have to move B off. This is the essence of a means–end analysis and solution—solving subgoals, in which achieving one subgoal often means developing and solving another set of subgoals first. Another important idea revealed by these problems is the notion that larger versions of the problem are merely extensions of simpler versions (e.g., the four-disk version is merely the three-disk version with an extra disk; the five-disk version is merely the four-disk problem with an extra disk, and so on). When problems are variations on earlier, simpler versions, and when essentially the same set of moves can be repeated, we call the problem **recursive:** our solution involves recursive or *repeated application of an embedded set of moves to the new, more complex configurations in the larger problem.*[3]

General Problem Solver (GPS)

We've spent considerable time on the Tower of Hanoi problem to illustrate the importance of subgoals and the means–end solution strategy. This strategy is important to understand for at least two reasons. First, it is a heuristic that is widely applicable to all sorts of problem-solving situations, from the Tower of Hanoi to your own Locked Car. We've learned a great deal about problem solving by studying this heuristic, for instance, the difficulties in problem solving because of memory limitations (e.g., losing track of your subgoals). In your own notes, were there places where you lost sight of the overall subgoal you were working on, and consequently moved disks at random until you remembered or regenerated that subgoal?

A second reason for understanding means–end analysis is its historical importance to cognitive psychology and problem solving. *General Problem Solver*—known as *GPS*—was the name of a computer simulation by Newell, Shaw, and Simon (1958), described in great detail in their later work (e.g., Ernst & Newell, 1969; Newell & Simon, 1972; see footnote 9, Chapter 1, for reference to Newell and Simon's 1956 presentation of their logic theorem program, an early version of GPS, on "the day cognitive psychology was born"). This program was the first genuine computer simulation of problem-solving behavior. It was a general-purpose, problem-solving program, not limited to just one kind of problem, but widely applicable to a large class of problems in which means–end

---

[3]According to legend, a group of Buddhist monks is working on the 64-disk version of the Tower of Hanoi problem, and when they solve it, the world will come to an end. This implies a "conspiracy of silence" on our part, since by recursive extension, "the 64-disk problem is really just the 63-disk version with an extra disk at the bottom, and the 63-disk problem is really just . . ."

analysis and solution by means of subgoals was appropriate. Newell and Simon ran their simulation on various logical proofs, on the Missionary–Cannibal problem, on the Tower of Hanoi, and on many other problems, to demonstrate its generality.

Why was this so impressive a demonstration, so noteworthy that the new cognitive psychology took Newell and Simon's insights and made them centerpieces in this new discipline? What was new and impressive, it seems, was their realization that human mental processes could be modeled or simulated by a computer program. That is, Newell and Simon's critical insight was that human mental processes were of a symbolic nature, and that the computer's manipulation of symbols was a fruitful *analogy* to such processes.

In a very real sense, and highly appropriate to their topic of investigation, Newell and Simon had hit upon a solution to a *very* difficult problem: How do we investigate human mental processes? Their solution was essentially an analogy between human thinking and the operation of a computer program. Conceive of human thought as internal symbol manipulation. How can we be sure that such a conceptualization is even reasonable? Run the hypothesized symbolic manipulations in a computer program. If the program generates output similar to that generated by humans, then we have to conclude two things—first, that the computer has done something remarkably close to what we defined as *thought,* and second, that the similarity of the program's and the human's output suggests that the program is a decent theory or model of how humans behave in that kind of situation.

The GPS System   Newell et al. (1958; also Ernst & Newell, 1969) attempted to create a computer simulation that would solve problems in much the same way that people do. To this end, their simulation included several mechanisms or characteristics believed to be true of humans. Three of these were quite straightforward; GPS was a serial-processing system, had a limited short-term memory, and was able to retrieve relevant information from long-term memory.

The fourth characteristic represented the belief that human problem solving was largely a matter of heuristic processing, that people solve problems not by some systematic, large-scale algorithmic approach, but instead by a set of heuristic strategies. The Newell et al. evidence for heuristic processing, as you will recall, came largely from *verbal protocol analysis,* the careful poring over transcripts of subjects' verbalizations as they solved lengthy problems. The particular heuristic that interested these researchers the most, and the one featured in GPS, was the means–end analysis. GPS's problem solving, in other words, could be described as setting and achieving goals and subgoals within the relevant problem space.

The most remarkable characteristic of GPS, when it was proposed, was that it worked; in fact, it seemed to work quite well on a rather large range of problems. This in and of itself was quite impressive, since no other theory of problem solving had ever demonstrated that level of generality and success before. Newell et al. had made no unreasonable assumptions, it seemed, so the theory itself seemed plausible as well. This was rather compelling evidence for the usefulness of heuristics as explanations of human problem solving, as well as the usefulness of computer simulation as a way of theorizing about human mental operations.

An important characteristic of GPS was its formulation as a *production system* model, essentially the first such model proposed in psychology. A **production** is a pair of statements, called either a *condition–action* pair or an *IF–THEN* pair. In such a scheme, if the production's conditions are satisfied, the action part of the pair takes place. In the GPS application to the Tower of Hanoi, three sample productions might be:

- IF the destination peg is clear *and* the largest disk is free, THEN move the largest disk to the destination peg.
- IF the largest disk is not free, THEN set up a subgoal to free it.
- IF a subgoal to free the largest disk is set up *and* a smaller disk is on it, THEN move the smaller disk to the stack peg.

The close correspondence between a production system and the subgoal structure of the problem is very straightforward (e.g., see Anderson, 1993; you'll read more about such production systems in Chapter 13).

Such an analysis suggests a very "planful" solution on the part of GPS: setting up a goal and then subgoals that will achieve the goal sounds exactly like what we would call *planning*. And indeed, such planning characterizes both people's *and* GPS's solutions to problems, not just the Tower of Hanoi, but all kinds of transformation problems. GPS had what amounted to a "planning mechanism," a mechanism that abstracted the essential features of situations and goals, then devised a plan that would produce a problem-solving sequence of moves. Provided with such a mechanism, and the particular representational system necessary to encode the problem and the legal operators, GPS yielded an output that resembles the solution pathways taken by human problem solvers.

Limitations of GPS   Later investigators working with the general principles of GPS found some instances when the model did not do a particularly good job of characterizing or stimulating human problem solving. Consider now the Missionary–Cannibal problem that you have already worked; the solution pathway is presented in Figure 12-9. The problem is especially difficult, most people find, because of one critical move. At step 6, the *only* legal move is to return one missionary and one cannibal back to the original side of the river. Having just brought two missionaries over, this return trip seems to be moving *away* from the overall goal. That is, the return of one missionary and one cannibal seems to be incorrect, because it appears to *increase* the distance to the

FIGURE 12-9

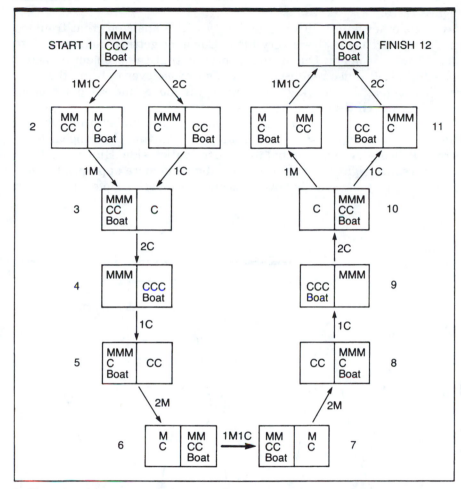

An illustration of the steps required to solve the Missionary–Cannibal problem. The left half of each box is the "start side" of the river, and the right half is the "destination side." The numbers and letters next to the arrows represent who is traveling on the boat. (From Glass & Holyoak, 1986.)

goal: it's the only return trip that moves *two* characters back to the original side. Despite the fact that this is the only available move (other than returning the same two missionaries who just came over), subjects have difficulty in selecting this move (Thomas, 1974).

To put it bluntly, GPS does *not* have this difficulty. Greeno (1974) conducted a series of studies on solutions to the Missionary–Cannibal problem and compared his subjects' solutions to the "behavior" of GPS. He found several steps in the solution pathway on which the subjects and GPS diverged. For instance, at step 6, where human subjects resist taking two characters back across, GPS had considerably less difficulty; see Figure 12-10.

On the other hand, GPS had difficulty with some steps that troubled the human problem solvers very little. Consider getting from step 10 to step 11 for a moment. Our intuition here is that the problem is nearly solved, that all that's required is sending *anyone* over to bring that last cannibal across. We quickly accomplish this move, and solve the problem. Yet from GPS's perspective, the subgoal that is being attempted is "move the last cannibal to the destination." To accomplish this subgoal, the boat is sent to the start side, thereby permitting the subgoal to be accomplished—move a cannibal to the destination side. Human problem solvers realize right away that a *new* subgoal is more appropriate—forget getting just *one* cannibal over, because now *both* people on the start

FIGURE 12-10

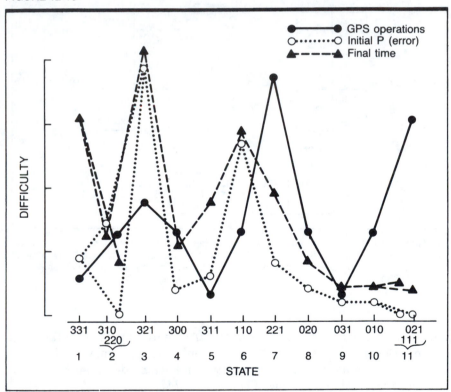

The difficulties experienced by GPS and by human problem solvers on the Missionary–Cannibal problem. Along the x-axis, the three-digit numbers refer to the "start side" of the river. The first digit is the number of missionaries, the second digit is the number of cannibals, and the third digit represents the boat (1 means the boat is on the start side). Step numbers 1–11 have been added, to correspond to Figure 12-9. (From Greeno, 1974.)

side can cross and attain the final goal. But GPS doggedly works to satisfy its nested subgoals and fails to appreciate how a new subgoal is more appropriate.

Beyond GPS   Greeno's demonstration of some of the inaccuracies in GPS may make you think, "Well why study GPS if it's wrong?" While this is an understandable sentiment, it misses a critically important point about progress in science and the role of models in achieving that progress. In a sense, we always "know" that a model or theory is wrong, that it is at least somewhat inaccurate or incomplete in some respects. From this standpoint, the purpose of a model or theory then is one of highlighting where our knowledge is incomplete and of guiding new research. Newell and Simon claimed that problem solving is a process of setting and achieving goals and subgoals, moving in a planful way from state to state by means of legal operators. This set of assumptions captured a fair amount of truth, it would seem: GPS and models based on it often provided a very good description of human problem-solving performance (e.g., Atwood & Polson, 1976). Thus at a general level, the model provided a demonstration of means–end analysis in *human* problem solving: humans and GPS often generated the same behavior. GPS also highlighted areas of ignorance in cognitive psychology's knowledge and provided a precise set of predictions against which new experimental results could be compared. Greeno's study, for instance, was able to compare people's performance to a known standard, a means–end analysis as performed by GPS, to find out when this heuristic did and did not explain problem-solving activity.

No one still takes GPS as the ultimate criterion against which performance should be compared. For example, Hayes and Simon (1974) acknowledged a serious shortcoming in GPS with their program called UNDERSTAND: GPS needed a precise description of the problem, a thorough specification of the problem representation, before it could begin to solve the problem. This reflected an incomplete aspect of GPS—it couldn't understand language—now remedied by the UNDERSTAND system. Briefly, UNDERSTAND takes as its input the usual sequence of English sentences that describe a problem and builds a problem representation based on its comprehension of the input sentences. On the other hand, it seems entirely accurate to say that *all* current research on problem solving has been influenced by one or another aspect of the GPS system, its analysis of heuristics and their application, its precise predictions that could be tested empirically, or even its underlying formalism as a production system (e.g., Anderson, 1983, 1993). Stated simply, GPS got us started.

Summary Points: means–end analysis; goals and subgoals; recursive solutions; GPS, a production system model

▼ Improving Your Problem Solving

Sprinkled liberally throughout this chapter have been hints and suggestions about how to improve your problem solving. Some of these were based on empirical research, and some on intuitions that various people have had about the problem-solving process. In this final section, we pull together these hints and suggestions and present a few more that haven't yet been discussed. For reference, Table 12-9 lists the suggestions found in this section. The goal of the section is to help you improve your own problem solving, to promote an active and informed problem-solving approach. Problem solving is, after all, a very conscious and deliberate activity. To the extent that you can approach new problems in a planful and informed way, your own problem-solving performance should benefit.

General Factors

1. Increase Your Domain Knowledge   Simon has explicitly considered the question "What makes problems difficult?" in many of his studies of problem solving. Probably the most important factor that determines how easy or difficult a problem will be for someone is the person's *domain knowledge.* Not surprisingly, a person who has only limited knowledge or familiarity with a topic is far less able to solve problems efficiently in that domain.

Much of the research supporting this generalization comes from Simon's work on the game of chess (e.g., Chase & Simon, 1973). In several studies of chess masters, an important, although not surprising, result was obtained: chess masters can get a glimpse of the arrangement of pieces on a chess board and are then able to remember or reconstruct the arrangement far better than novices or individuals of moderate skill. This advantage only holds, however, when the arrangement is legal, that is, when the locations of the pieces are sensible within the context of a

Table 12-9   SUGGESTIONS FOR IMPROVING PROBLEM SOLVING

1. Increase your domain knowledge.
2. Automate some components of the problem-solving solution.
3. Follow a definite scheme or plan.
4. Draw inferences.
5. Develop subgoals.
6. Work backward.
7. Search for contradictions.
8. Search for relations and analogies among problems.
9. Reformulate the problem representation.
10. Represent the problem physically, with objects or verbalization.
11. If all else fails, try practice.

Becoming an effective problem solver requires practice to strengthen a certain knowledge, as these chess players exhibit.

real game of chess. When the locations of the pieces are random, then there is no advantage for the skilled players.

In short, *rich knowledge of the domain* allows the chess masters to perceive arrangements and patterns more rapidly and more accurately. The similarity of this advantage to the advantages of top–down processing in other situations is not coincidental (e.g., go back and look at Figure 2-5). Domain knowledge also permits the expert to plan ahead, to "think forward" several moves at a time. Such planning is only possible with good knowledge of the domain.

Related research in the domain of physics problems has been reported by Larkin, McDermott, Simon, and Simon (1980). In their work, expert physicists, college professors, were compared with "novices," students who had completed one college physics course. The problems that were presented for solutions were sufficiently challenging that neither group knew immediately what the answer was or how the problem ought to be solved. The experts, on the one hand, spent considerable time "playing" with the problem, almost like "mental doodling" with the givens and goals, then solved the problem in a rather straightforward, purposeful fashion. The novices, on the other hand, spent much less time investigat-

DEMONSTRATIONS

The problems you're solving throughout the chapter can be used without change to demonstrate the principles of problem solving. Here are some interesting contrasts and effects you might want to make.

1. Compare either the time or number of moves that subjects make in learning and mastering the Tower of Hanoi problem when you label the pegs 1, 2, and 3 versus labeling them Source, Stack, and Destination. Try giving some subjects a "reduced" problem, by first showing them a partially solved Tower of Hanoi. Does this hint influence the number of moves they make in solving the full problem? The four-disk version?

2. Try rearranging the Luchins Water Jug problems, so that in the first three or four problems the subjects see both the regular B − 2C − A type as well as the simpler ones. Does the rearrangement prevent the negative set effect? Try using the original order but providing a hint that "not all problems can be solved with the same method."

3. Some people complain that they are "terrible" at recreational problems because of social or emotional factors—they get embarrassed, frustrated, and so on. Within the limits of ethical practice, try having pairs of subjects work either competitively or cooperatively on a small set of problems, to see which leads to faster or more successful problem solving.

ing the givens of the problem and demonstrated much more "aimless" application of equations in their solution attempts.

Larkin et al. suggest that because the experts have rich knowledge of the domain, they are able to classify problems more readily (i.e., "work" problems, "inclined plane" problems), thereby knowing which group of formulas is appropriate to use. The rich domain knowledge, or *domain schema,* thus guides their solution in an efficient, skilled way. Because the novices lacked such a developed schema, they were more likely to search in a rather undirected fashion for a solution that worked, trying first one and then another equation or approach in the hopes that "something would turn up."

2. Automate Some Components of the Problem-Solving Solution

A second connection also exists between the question "What makes problems difficult?" and the topics you've already studied. Kotovsky, Hayes, and Simon (1985) tested subjects on various forms of the Tower of Hanoi problem and also on problem *isomorphs,* problems with the *same form* although different details. (For instance, in their "Monster" story, three sizes of monsters must pass around globes of different sizes, with the goal of having the large monster holding the large globe, the small monster holding the small globe, and so on. The additional rules and constraints in the problem make it merely a transformation of the Tower of Hanoi problem.) In their results, Kotovsky et al. noted that a serious impediment to successful solutions was the transient memory load at various intermediate states. That is, at some intermediate state a person may have to hold three or four nested subgoals in working memory, then solve them in the appropriate order to achieve some more general sub-goal. If this load on memory was too great, however, subjects' performance deteriorated.

The solution to this memory load problem, they suggested, was to automate the rules that govern moves in the problems. To illustrate, by becoming familiar with the moves that transfer three disks to another peg, the subject can then make those moves automatically. This enables the subject now to hold *other,* higher-level subgoals in working memory, with less chance of losing them due to interference (see also Carlson, Khoo, Yaure, & Schneider, 1990).

This should sound familiar to you—it is the general argument for the performance advantages due to automaticity. When components of a task become automatic, they now require little or no conscious effort for their performance and consume few, if any, conscious resources for their execution. The mental resources that are freed by this automaticity can now be devoted to other aspects of the task, for example, maintenance of higher-level subgoals in working memory (this is why I urged you to work the three-disk problem repeatedly, until you had the sequence of moves firmly in mind). In the opinion of Kotovsky et al. (1985), memory load and limitations in working memory are very general and pervasive sources of difficulty in problem solving, thus recommending automaticity—not to mention pencil-and-paper notes—as a way of improving performance.

3. Follow a Systematic Plan   Aside from improving your domain knowledge and working toward more automatic components of problem solving, we can make one more general suggestion. It is *follow a systematic plan* (e.g., Polya, 1957).

As a good example, Bransford and Stein (1984, 1993) have proposed a system they call *The IDEAL Problem Solver,* where the word *IDEAL* is a mnemonic for the five steps of problem solving they propose. Their first step, *identifying problems,* suggests that there are many problems in need of solution and that attention devoted to identifying problems is a critical preliminary component of an adequate problem-solving strategy. Next, *defining problems* is essentially what Polya intended with his advice to understand the problem. Defining the problem means understanding and representing the problem in such a way that the solution can be worked on. It also includes devising a keeping-track mechanism and figuring out a general plan for working on the problem. *Exploring alternative approaches,* in the Bransford and Stein scheme, involves an

Table 12-10

9. *Landscape Gardening.* How do you plant four shrubs so that each shrub is exactly the same distance from each other shrub?

10. *Bowling Pins.* The 10 bowling pins below are pointing toward the top of the page. Move any three of them to make the arrangement point down toward the bottom of the page.

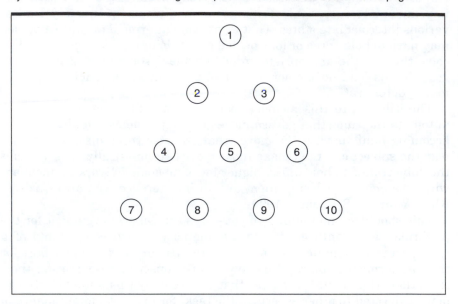

11. *Bookworm.* A set of encyclopedias is on the shelf, arranged in the usual left-to-right alphabetical order. A bookworm begins eating his way from page one of the A volume, and stops at the last page of the B volume. Each book cover is one-quarter-inch thick, and each volume is one-inch thick. How far does the bookworm have to chew?

12. *Ten Pennies.* Show how you can arrange 10 pennies so that you have five rows (straight lines) of four pennies in each row.

13. *Jars of Beads.* There are two large jars. One is filled with a large number of red beads and the other is filled with the same number of blue beads. Five beads from the red bead jar are scooped out and dumped into the blue bead jar. Someone then reaches into the blue bead jar and scoops out five beads without knowing what color they are, and dumps them into the red bead jar. Are there the same number of red beads in the red bead jar as there are blue beads in the blue bead jar?

14. *Vinegar and Oil.* Two small bowls are side by side, one containing oil, one containing vinegar. You take a spoonful of the oil and stir it into the vinegar. You then take a spoonful of the mixture and put it back into the bowl of oil. Which of the two bowls is more contaminated, or are they equally contaminated?

HINTS

9. We don't always plant shrubs on flat lawns.

10. Pins 1, 2, 3, and 5 form a diamond at the top of the drawing. Consider where the diamond might be for the arrangement that points down.

11. Visualize a shelf full of encyclopedias, or draw a few volumes. Which page of volume A is closest to volume B?

12. You need not space the coins equally, and several coins must do double or even triple duty, participating in as many lines as possible. What geometric figures involve fives?

13. Try assigning some numbers and working it out for those values.

14. Think about problem 13.

assessment of your current approach or plan and a consideration of other approaches that might also be fruitful. *Acting on the plan* is obviously the actual solution attempt, when you apply the plan you've devised. This is followed by *looking at the effects,* a reconsideration of the solution to determine if it is adequate, or if a better one should be attempted.

Heuristics of Problem Solving

While this undoubtedly sounds like good advice, a natural reaction is "Yes, but when I'm stuck on a problem, advice to explore alternative approaches doesn't help much. I can't *think* of alternative approaches when I'm stuck." To help with this difficulty, we conclude the chapter now with a collection of problem-solving heuristics. Although not all of them can be applied to all problems, they still constitute our best advice to you for improving your problem-solving performance. (Table 12-10 presents several more recreational problems for you to work on as you read this section; hints are at the bottom of the table.)

4. Draw Inferences   Wickelgren's (1974) influential book on how to solve problems began its discussion of heuristics with *inference.* Wickelgren's advice here is: "Draw inferences from explicitly and implicitly presented information that satisfy one or both of the following two criteria: (a) the inferences have frequently been made in the past from the same type of information; (b) the inferences are concerned with properties (variables, terms, expressions, and so on) that appear in the goal, the givens, or inferences from the goal and the givens" (p. 23).

Try drawing as many inferences as you can before you actually try to figure out the answer to the following problem (from Posner, 1973, pp. 150–151; the solution is at the end of this chapter).

15. *Two train stations are fifty miles apart. At 2 P.M. one Saturday afternoon two trains start toward each other, one from each station. Just as the trains pull out of the stations, a bird springs into the air in front of the first train and flies ahead to the front of the second train. When the bird reaches the second train it turns back and flies toward the first train. The bird continues to do this until the trains meet.*

If both trains travel at the rate of twenty-five miles per hour and the bird flies at a hundred miles per hour, how many miles will the bird have flown before the trains meet?

You've encountered the idea of drawing inferences already, both for problem solving (the cryptarithmetic problem earlier), as well as for language comprehension (e.g., Whitney, Ritchie, & Crane, 1992). For this problem, did you start thinking about how far the bird would fly before meeting the second train, then how far it would fly on the return trip before meeting the first one? If so, you have chosen a rather misleading representation for the problem. Instead, draw some inferences about the

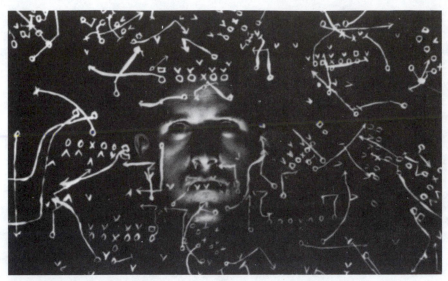

Drawing a diagram to represent a problem helps to improve problem-solving abilities.

trains and their traveled distance, not about the bird. How far will each train travel, and how long will that take?

Drawing such inferences should help you abandon your original representation. Realizing that the trains will be traveling for a total of one hour before they meet, you can then put this inference together with the bird's speed, 100 mph; now the problem is trivially easy. Another advantage of drawing inferences, possibly, is that it guides your search of the problem for relevant information. By focusing this search, you may overcome the distractions in the first paragraph of the story—this may be an instance of overcoming negative set.

A second aspect of inference might be mentioned as well. When you get stuck on a problem, it's often a good idea to return to the initial statement of the problem and see if you have drawn inferences that are unnecessary or unwarranted. For example, the Nine-Dot problem in Figure 12-11 stumps many people (work on it now) until they go back and realize they've made an unwarranted assumption: the problem does *not* require you to stay within the boundaries of the nine dots as you draw the lines. (It's of interest here that this unnecessary assumption is "predicted" by the *gestalt* of the problem—we "see" the *square* of dots, and this configuration somehow limits us to staying within the square.) The unwarranted restrictions we place on ourselves seem, at least globally, to be the same as the negative set effects we studied earlier; it can be very difficult to "step back" from your assumptions and discard an approach that isn't working.

Try applying the inference heuristic to a final example, Wickelgren's

FIGURE 12-11   PROBLEM 16: NINE-DOT PROBLEM

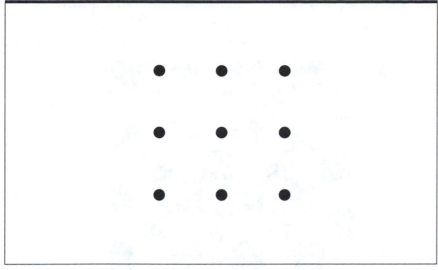

Without lifting your pencil, connect all nine dots with four straight lines. The solution to this problem is presented at the end of the chapter.

Notched Checkerboard in Figure 12-12. Be sure to work on the problem for a while before reading the hint at the bottom of the figure. And bear in mind the general advice of drawing inferences: ask yourself "What *else* do I know about the problem?"

5. *Develop Subgoals* Wickelgren also recommended a *subgoal heuristic* for problem solving, that is, breaking a large problem into separate subgoals. This, of course, is the heart of the means–end approach, which we discussed extensively. There is a slightly different slant to the subgoal approach, however, that bears mention here. Sometimes in our real-world problem solving, there is only a vaguely specified goal and, as often as not, even more vaguely specified subgoals. How do you know when you've achieved a subgoal, say, when the subgoal is "find enough articles on a particular topic to write a term paper that will earn an A"?

Simon's (1979) term **satisficing** is important to bear in mind here; it means *finding a solution to a goal or subgoal that is satisfactory although not as good as some other solution that might be achieved.* At least for some problems, the term-paper problem included, an initial *satisfactory* solution to subgoals may provide you with additional insight into the problem. For instance, as you begin to write your rough draft, you realize there are gaps in your information. Your originally satisfactory solution to the subgoal of finding references turned out to be insufficient, so you can recycle back to that subgoal to improve your solution. You might only

FIGURE 12-12   PROBLEM 17: CHECKERBOARD PROBLEM

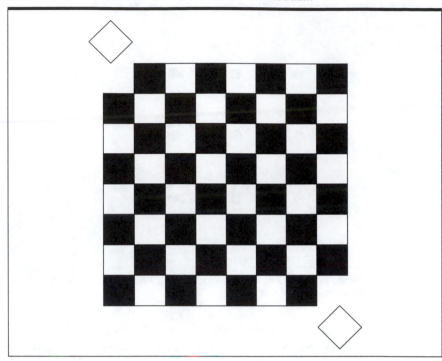

You have a regular checkerboard and 32 dominoes. Each domino covers exactly two adjacent squares on the checkerboard. Therefore 32 dominoes will cover the 64 squares on the checkerboard. If two squares were cut off the checkerboard at opposite corners, could you place 31 dominoes on the checkerboard so that all the remaining 62 squares are covered? If you can, show how; if you cannot, say why. (From Wickelgren, 1974.)

discover this deficiency by going ahead and working on your next subgoal, the rough draft.

6. Work Backward   Another heuristic that Wickelgren discussed was *working backward,* in which a well-specified goal may permit a tracing of the solution pathway in reverse order, thus working back to the givens. The standard illustration of the working backward heuristic is the following game. Working backward is essentially the only way to solve the problem, and it solves it perfectly (after Wickelgren, 1974, p. 142):

Fifteen pennies are placed on a table in front of two players. Players must remove at least one, but not more than five pennies on their turns. The players alternate turns of removing pennies, until the last penny is removed. The player who removes the last penny from the table is the winner. Is there a method of play that will guarantee victory?

In case you haven't figured it out, here's the solution, given by the working backward heuristic. Think of the goal, in which *you* remove the final penny or pennies. There must be from one to five pennies on the table for you to be the winner. This means, by working backward from this goal, that on your next to last turn, you must force your opponent to leave you at least one penny on the table. You can do this, obviously, by leaving your opponent *six* pennies when you finish your next-to-last turn. Thus to guarantee victory, make sure that your opponent leaves you a winning move; remove only as many pennies as you must in order to leave your opponent with six pennies on the table.

7. Search for Contradictions   In problems that ask "Is it possible to . . ." or "Is there a way that . . . ," *searching for contradictions* in the givens or goal state is often a useful strategy. For example, Wickelgren uses the following illustration: Is there an integer x that satisfies the equation $x^2 + 1 = 0$? A simple algebraic operation, subtracting 1 from both sides, yields $x^2 = -1$. This, of course, contradicts the known property that any squared number will be positive. This heuristic can also be helpful in multiple-choice exams. That is, maybe some of the alternatives contradict some idea or fact in the question, or some fact you learned in the course. Either will enable you to rule out those choices immediately.

8. Search for Relations Among Problems   In searching for relations among problems, you actively consider how the current problem may resemble one you've already solved, or one you already know about. We had a clear-cut example of this strategy in our discussion of the four- and five-disk Tower of Hanoi problem, in which knowledge of the simpler three-disk version can be applied to the more complex versions.

At a more general level, searching for relations among problems is another way of saying that an analogy from a problem you've already solved may be a good strategy for working on your current problem (Bassok & Holyoak, 1989; Ross, 1987). Don't become impatient, by the way. Bowden (1985) found that subjects often found and used information from related problems, but only if sufficient time was allowed for them to do so. Try it on the problem in Figure 12-13.

9. Reformulate the Problem Representation   Another heuristic, not specifically mentioned by Wickelgren, involves the more general issue of the problem representation, how you choose to represent and think about the problem. Often, when you get stuck on a problem, it will be useful to go back to the beginning and reformulate or reconceptualize the problem in some way. For instance, as you discovered in the Buddhist Monk problem, a quantitative representation of the monk's speed, distance traveled, and so on is an unproductive way of conceptualizing the problem. After running into a dead end, return to the beginning and

FIGURE 12-3   PROBLEM 18: SIXTEEN-DOT PROBLEM

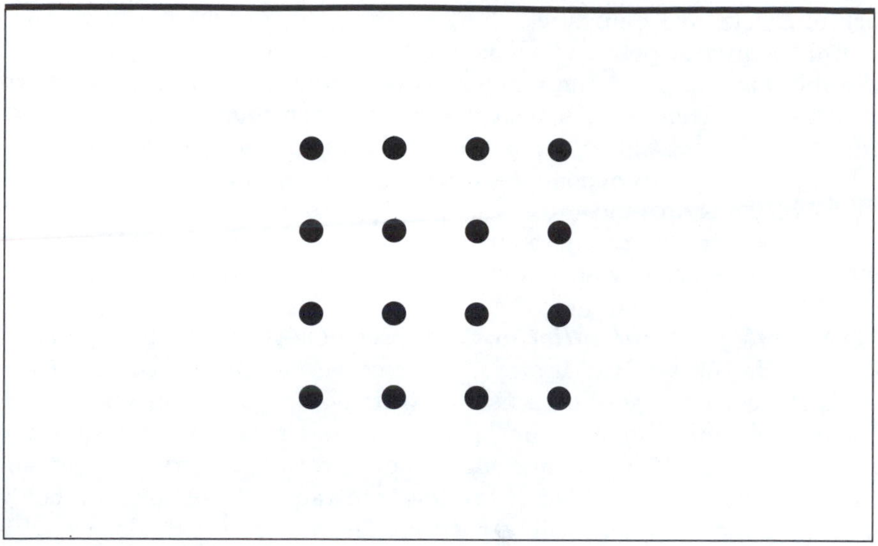

Without lifting your pencil, show how you can join all 16 dots with six straight lines.

try to think of *other* ways of conceptualizing the situation. Try a visual imagery approach, especially a "mental movie" that includes action. In the Buddhist Monk problem, "superimposing" two such mental movies will permit you to see him walking up and down at the same time, thus yielding the solution.

For other kinds of problems, try a numerical representation, including working the problem out with some examples. This may give you a feel for the problem, or may turn up a contradiction or inference that will advance your solution. Another kind of reformulation involves restating the givens. Even a simple reordering of the givens in the Bird–Train problem might have juxtaposed the critical elements, making it more likely that you'd draw a useful inference at the outset.

10. Represent the Problem Physically   The next-to-last heuristic (or "bit of advice") involves a *physical representation of the problem*. It's almost always a mistake to attempt to solve problems using only the "mental scratch pad." Instead, draw a diagram, scribble on some slips of paper, move some real coins around, verbalize the problem, and so on. It may simply be that a physical representation makes your search more systematic. That is, a physical model or version of the problem may help you avoid random trial-and-error moves and may promote a more systematic trial-and-error approach.

Another advantage of a physical model or representation is that you can minimize the time you spend on writing. To keep track of your solutions, you'll of course want to write your moves down on paper, as you did for the Tower of Hanoi. But if you also have to draw an illustration of the Tower problem for each successive state, you'll waste a lot of time and possibly make it more difficult to maintain your subgoals and goals in memory.

11. If All Else Fails, Try Practice Finally, for problems we encounter in classroom settings, from algebra or physics problems up through such vague problems as writing a term paper and studying effectively for an exam, there is a final heuristic that should help your problem solving. It's a well-known effect in psychology—even Ebbinghaus recommended it. If you want to be good at problem solving, *practice* problem solving. Practice within a particular knowledge domain will strengthen that knowledge, push the problem-solving components closer to an automatic basis, and will furnish you with a deeper understanding of the domain. While it isn't a flashy heuristic, practice is, without a doubt, a *major* component of skilled problem solving and of gaining expertise in any area.

Summary Points: domain knowledge, automaticity, and a systematic plan; the IDEAL problem solver; problem-solving heuristics; satisficing

CHAPTER SUMMARY

1. Newell and Simon's insights on the role of computer simulation in an understanding of human information processing were central to the development of cognitive psychology in the late 1950s. Their research methods, however, were rather different from those developed in verbal learning, so the area of problem solving has only recently become a mainstream topic within cognitive psychology.

2. The early Gestalt psychologists studied problem solving and discovered two major barriers to successful performance—functional fixedness and negative set. Problem solving, according to these researchers, required insight and creativity. Unfortunately, these latter terms have never been adequately defined for scientific purposes.

3. Problem solving can be viewed as achieving a goal by progressing from an initial state through several intermediate states, until the goal state is reached. Operators are the mental acts that achieve this progress. While some problems lend themselves to algorithmic solutions, the bulk of human problem solving can best be understood as involving heuristic processing.

4. Means–end analysis is the best understood of the problem-solving heuristics. In it, we determine the difference between our current state and the goal state, determine what subgoals are necessary to reduce this difference, and apply simple operators to move from subgoal to subgoal. While this is a valuable heuristic, Newell and Simon's GPS system, based on means–end analysis, did not match the characteristics of human performance in several situations. Nonetheless, this heuristic is one of the most useful problem-solving strategies we know about.

5. A variety of other heuristics have been suggested as ways of

improving your own problem solving. Among them are increasing your knowledge of the problem domain, automating some of the necessary components of the solution, searching for contradictions and for analogical relations to other problems, reformulating the problem representation, representing the problem in some physical form, and practicing your problem-solving skills.

Glossary Terms: analogy; domain knowledge; functional fixedness; gestalt; goal and subgoal; GPS; insight and illumination; means–end analysis; negative set; operator; problem space; production; satisficing; search tree; verbal protocol

SUGGESTED READINGS

Four books on how to solve problems (Bransford & Stein, 1993; Hayes, 1989; Levine, 1988; Wickelgren, 1974) provide extensive practice in the different heuristics and approaches. See Mayer (1992) as well, particularly for his discussion of creativity, and the contrasting view on creativity in Weisberg (1993). To relate problem solving to the theme of metacognition, see Metcalfe (1986); she found that adults had virtually no useful metacognitions on their abilities to solve problems, and she interprets this as supporting the ideas of insight and illumination in problem solving.

Spellman and Holyoak's (1992) excellent paper shows the role of analogies in truly real-world problem solving. Part of the justification for U.S. involvement in the Persian Gulf War was the analogy between Saddam Hussein and Hitler. In Spellman and Holyoak's study, subjects developed the remaining relationships in this analogy. For example, was George Bush analogous to Winston Churchill or Franklin Roosevelt, Kuwait to Poland, and so on? Inadvertently, the study also demonstrated the importance of domain knowledge for such reasoning; so small a proportion of their college students knew enough World War II history that follow-up studies had to supply brief histories for them to work with. Interestingly, the authors suggested that analogical reasoning has implications for the everyday understanding of social cognition; an added benefit was the success of their connectionist model of analogical reasoning in predicting the nature of subjects' analogies.

ANSWERS TO CHAPTER 12 PROBLEMS

1. *Three Men and a Rowboat.* Medium and Small row themselves across the river, then either one of them rows back to the start side. Large rows himself across to the destination side. The man who stayed on the destination side now rows back to the start side, and both of the lighter men row to the destination.

2. *Buddhist Monk.* Rather than thinking in terms of one monk, let a *different* monk walk down from the top on the same day as the other walks up. Looking at it this way, isn't it obvious that the two will meet during their journey? Thus walking on separate days is irrelevant to the goal, "Show that there is a spot. . . ."

3. *Chains and Links.* Open all three links on one chain—that's 6 cents. Put one opened link at the end of each other piece, then join the pieces by looping a closed link into an opened one. Closing the three links costs 9 cents, for a total of 15 cents.

4. *Six Pennies.* Hold the diagram sideways, so coin 1 is at the top right. Coins 1, 2, 4, and 6 are already in place, so move coins 3 and 5.

5. *Six Glasses.* Numbering the glasses left to right, pour the contents of glass 2 into glass 5.

6. *Cross + Roads*	7. *Lets + Wave*	8. *Send + More*
96233	1567	9567
62513	9085	1085
158746	10652	10652

9. *Landscape Gardening.* Dead-end approaches try to arrange the shrubs on a flat, two-dimensional lawn. Instead, think in three dimensions. Put three shrubs at the base of a hill, and the fourth one at the top of the hill. The arrangement is that of an equilateral, three-sided pyramid.

10. *Ten Bowling Pins*

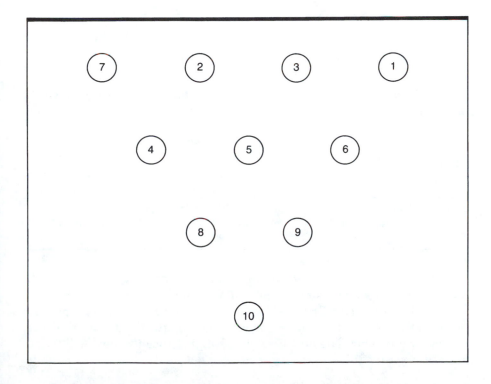

11. *Bookworm.* The bookworm eats one-half inch, the front cover on volume A and the back cover on volume B. As arranged alphabetically, left to right on the shelf, the front cover of A is next to the back cover of B, so the bookworm need only eat through these two covers.

12. *Ten Pennies.* (One of at least two solutions)

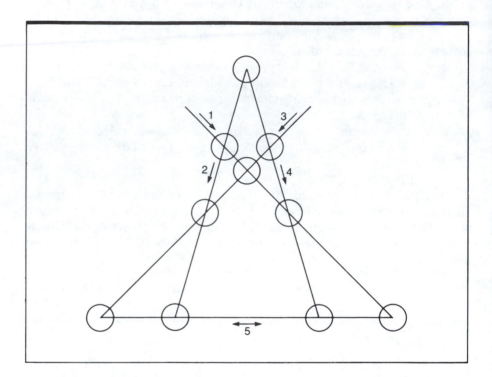

13. *Beads and Jars.* Assign numerical values in order to solve the problem. Test two or three different values to verify that the answer is "yes."

Table 12-11

	Red Bead Jar	Blue Bead Jar
Assume 50 beads in jar	50R − 5R = 45R	50B + 5R
Assume 1 red bead is moved back	45R + (1R + 4B)	(50B + 5R) − (1R + 4B)
Result	46R + 4B	46B + 4R

14. *Oil and Vinegar.* Solve this problem in the same way as the blue/red jars problem, using values and fractions of units.

15. *Bird and Two Trains.* The trains are 50 miles apart, and each travels at 25 mph. Thus the trains will meet midway between the cities in exactly one hour. The bird flies at 100 mph. Since the bird will fly one hour, it must fly 100 miles.

16. *Nine-Dot Problem*

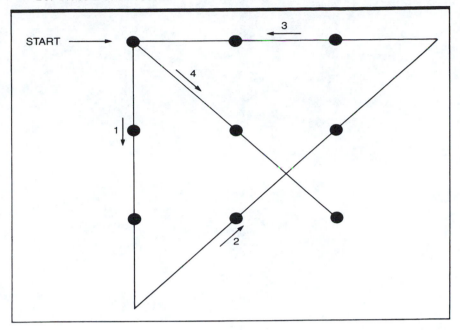

17. *Checkerboard.* No matter where you place a domino, it will cover a black and a white square. By removing two white squares, however, you have prevented the 31 dominoes from covering the notched board, since the board is missing two squares of the same color.

18. *Sixteen-Dot Problem*

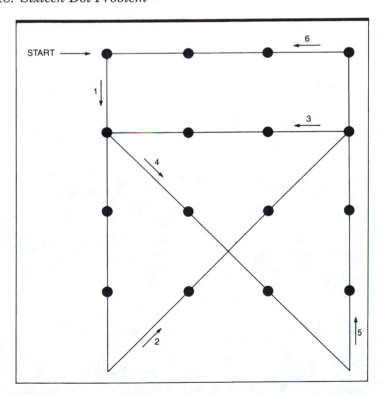

CURRENT DIRECTIONS

Most people who know much about AI [Artificial Intelligence] are very impressed—and rightly so, for it epitomizes the most powerful and successful approach to psychology ever known. . . . Moreover, there is a "wave of the future" air about it: the AI bandwagon carries farsighted progressives, bold and unfettered. Yet, in some sense, Artificial Intelligence has not kept its "promise." There are today no arguably intelligent machines (discounting "micro-experts"); no plausible fraction of common sense has ever been programmed; no current system has the linguistic competence of a three-year-old child—and none is in sight. (Haugeland, 1985, p. 250)

The result of all this flux is that the merely descriptive literature of the emotions is one of the most tedious parts of psychology. . . . I should as lief read verbal descriptions of the shapes of the rocks on a New Hampshire farm as toil through them again. (James, 1890, p. 1064)

A psychology that cannot interpret ordinary experience is ignoring almost the whole range of its natural subject matter. (Neisser, 1976, p. 4)

Two rhetorical questions appeared in the opening paragraphs of this book. The first posed the overall question that cognitive psychology asks: "How do people think?" At this concluding point in the book, you may feel as if you only have partial answers to this question. You can state with some precision how sensory information enters into the human information processing system, how that information makes contact with its long-term memory representation, how information held in working memory is combined into new patterns, and how those new patterns are stored within memory. You can discuss linguistic processes, the interactions of syntax and semantics, and the pragmatics of conversational interaction. You can explain the heuristics of reasoning and problem solving. Yet none of these "pieces" seems to embody the answer to the question.

The fault here lies within the question, I think, not within cognitive psychology. Consider a different question: "How do people live?" Your answer to that can only be another question: "What do you mean, 'live'? Do you mean from a biological standpoint, or from the perspectives of anthropology, psychology, sociology, economics . . . ?" The list continues, obviously, since there are countless perspectives from which a meaningful answer can be offered.

Likewise, "How do people think?" can be answered from many perspectives, each just as valid, each depending on a different sense of the word *think*. *Think* is really a cover term or category name; for example, Webster's dictionary lists 14 different meanings for the word. As such, it's not surprising that there is no *single* way to answer the question. Try rephrasing the question, substituting any of Webster's 14 definitions (e.g., call to mind, recognize, reason, expect, plan, draw inferences). You'll find you can offer a specific and fairly satisfying answer to the question now.

The second rhetorical question implied that cognitive psychology is relevant to many other disciplines outside psychology proper: "After all, what human endeavor doesn't involve thought?" The answer to this one is that *thought,* broadly defined, enters into virtually every human activity worth considering. Yet you've studied very little in this book that addresses areas outside mainstream cognitive psychology. Eyewitness testimony, interpersonal effects in conversations, and the impact of coursework on misconceptions about the physical world and probability are among the very few "applications" of cognitive psychology you've read about. Was the original claim empty? Does cognitive psychology really have significance and relevance outside the laboratory?

No, the original claim was not empty, and yes, cognitive psychology *is* relevant. One of the main purposes of this concluding chapter is to demonstrate this, to illustrate the impact of cognitive psychology on different areas of human endeavor, and the reciprocal impact of these other areas on research activity in cognitive psychology.

We're going to examine three such areas here. One of them is *computerized cognition.* We will consider artificial intelligence and computer-based theories in cognitive science, to see where the computer—this *universal machine*—is getting us. Second, we'll discuss a newly resurrected topic in human experimental psychology, the impact of *emotion on cognitive processing.* Enough research now exists on topics like "mood and memory" and "anxiety and performance" that we can offer a few brief generalizations about this growing area. Finally, we'll discuss *applied cognition.* Out of the enormous array of real-world topics that are being addressed by cognitive science, we'll focus especially on educational applications.

The first 12 chapters of this book covered what cognitive psychology has learned in the 30–40 years of its current incarnation. Without this material, from the initial sensory memories up through complex reasoning and problem solving, there would literally be no cognitive psychology, to say nothing of "current directions." But what's *really* going to be interesting is what we will learn in the *next* 30–40 years.

▼ Computerized Cognition and Cognitive Science

We think psychology can profit from trying to build a language-using machine, just as the theory of flying has profited from trying to build a flying machine (Collins & Quillian, 1972, p. 348).

Terminology

The term *computerized cognition* is deliberately vague. It does not specify who is doing the cognition: Is it humans, whose mental operations are being simulated on a computer system, or is it computers,

The ultimate in computerized cognition—R2D2 and C3P0 even had personality.

whose internal processes fit at least some definitions of *thought* and *cognition?* This vagueness is quite intentional. In the beginning, there was a sharp distinction between computer simulation and artificial intelligence. **Computer simulation** was *the mimicking of human processes by means of computer program,* an alternative and often preferable way of theorizing about human cognitive processes. By programming one's theory of this or that cognitive operation, one could determine how carefully thought out the theory was, and how successful it was in explaining the phenomenon under investigation. Computer simulation was the domain of cognitive psychology—it was what psychologists did with the computer analogy, and often still do. For computer simulation then, it was clearly the *humans* that were doing the thinking. The computer program was intended to simulate cognitive processes and thereby serve as a psychological theory or model of those processes.

Artificial intelligence (AI), on the other hand, was what researchers in computer science did. **Artificial intelligence** was characterized by *an attempt to program computers to do human-like things, especially to reason and to understand language, but with no necessary connection to how these processes are accomplished by humans.* The goal in AI, stated simply, was to program intelligence, to devise computer systems that could behave in an intelligent fashion. This was not a "mimic the humans" exercise; AI wanted to program a computer so that it was truly doing the thinking.

In a real sense, the field of artificial intelligence imagined that much of the human "paraphernalia" was irrelevant to intelligent behavior. The awkward and inefficient aspects of human intelligence—limited attention, heuristic processing, and the like—could be improved upon in the artificial variety, or so it was thought. Now, a good 30 years after some rather extravagant claims about what artificial intelligence research was on the verge of accomplishing (see Haugeland, 1985, especially Chapter 6), we find no systems or programs that have achieved even the language skills of a three-year-old. No one, neither computer scientists nor cognitive psychologists, realized just how complex such ordinary activities as language comprehension were.

For this reason, among others, the rigid distinction between computer simulation and artificial intelligence has largely been abandoned. Since AI cannot be accomplished without a thorough understanding of how people manage to be intelligent, research in AI is now more attentive to issues in cognitive psychology. And as you've read throughout, we use the term **cognitive science** now to describe the joint interests of psychology, artificial intelligence, and linguistics. The cognitive science approach takes all these groups' interests in intelligent behavior and addresses those interests from the multidisciplinary perspectives of the separate fields.

Gardner (1985, p. 6) defines cognitive science as an empirically based approach to questions about the nature of knowledge, its components, sources, development, and deployment. He further lists two absolutely central characteristics associated with cognitive science.

First, cognitive science is concerned with mental representations of knowledge. A strong belief is that these representations exist at a level different from biological or neurological levels at one end of the continuum, and sociological or cultural levels at the other end. In short, there is a true *cognitive* level of analysis in the study of knowledge, and this is the level with which cognitive science is concerned.

A second characteristic of cognitive science mentioned by Gardner is the faith that the computer will be central to our understanding of the human mind. In other words, computers will not merely provide us with an excellent empirical tool with which to do research. They will also provide us with an excellent proving ground for our theories, and an excellent source of ideas about knowledge and mental representation. In some circles, the distinction between human cognition and intelligent processing by computer has become so blurred as to be of little use. In such a situation, the vagueness of a term such as *computerized cognition* is exactly what's needed (just as "information processing" is a better description of computers' activities than "data processing").

The Computer as a Tool in Cognitive Science

Several reasons prompted cognitive psychology, and now cognitive science, to consider computer simulation as a desirable way of theorizing about mental processes. To begin with, a computer program must be a completely specified set of instructions telling the computer what to do and when to do it: if it's not completely specified, the program simply won't run. A verbal theory, on the other hand, may seem definite and clear but, on close inspection, often turns out to contain vague or ill-defined terms and processes. Thus a principal advantage of theorizing by means of computer programs is that it forces the theorist to think through all the elements of the theory. A related advantage is that this process of crafting a computerized theory can reveal pockets of ignorance, gaps in our knowledge that need to be addressed by further research. Programming a computer to spread activation through long-term memory, for example, forces the theorist to consider exactly what concepts are in long-term memory, how they are structured and interconnected, how the notion of activation is to be realized, how "far" the activation spreads, and how long the activation remains. The degree of precision required for a successful computer simulation is thus far greater than that usually achieved by purely verbal theories (but see Cherniak, 1988).

Another advantage is particularly relevant to cognitive psychology, since many of the topics we study are so richly complex. The computer, programmed to perform some set of operations on some base of information, will continue tirelessly to perform those operations, however tedious, difficult, time-consuming, and complex they might be. This gives the theorist tremendous power in modeling cognitive processes. A process such as spreading activation can be implemented on a rather large and realistic base of knowledge, as in contemporary connectionist models. The number of distinct computations or manipulations of the knowledge may be extremely large, far larger than any human theorist (or research assistant) could be expected to compute by hand. Yet the computer will do as it is told and report back the outcome of even the most complex of processing sequences. (Note, however, that a traditional goal of science is the construction of parsimonious theories, theories that are as simple and unburdened with excess baggage as the data will permit. A distinct worry, therefore, is that the power of the computer seduces the theorist into ever more complex, rather than ever more parsimonious, theories; see Loftus, 1985, for a superb discussion of this point.)

Computerized Theories in Cognitive Science

We have encountered several examples of "computerized theories," that is, computer simulations of human mental processes, in the course of studying cognitive psychology. McClelland and Rumelhart (1981, 1986; Rumelhart & McClelland, 1982, 1986), for example, have proposed a computer-based, connectionist theory of pattern recognition, which you encountered at some depth in Chapter 3. In their model, pattern recognition is implemented as a spreading activation process, in which simple feature detectors, more complex pattern nodes, letters, and words represent different levels of knowledge representation. Activation is passed in parallel among and within these levels, influenced by the stimulus being presented and the priming effects of prior context, and eventually yields what we would term "perception and recognition" of visual patterns. Because of the number of separate activations, and the number of different informational nodes at the several levels, the model requires computations far too numerous and complex to be done by hand. And yet, the model is a perfectly reasonable approach to pattern recognition, incorporating effects such as top–down priming and context that we know to be true of perception. (Whether it is or is not a genuine psychological theory of pattern recognition, however, is a matter of some debate; see McCloskey, 1991, and Seidenberg & McClelland, 1989.)

Another important computerized theory that deserves mention is Schank and Abelson's (1977) important work on scripts; you studied scripts in Chapter 7 (retrieval cue—restaurants). In their theory, events, and stories based on them, are comprehended by a program called **SAM,** which stands for *Script Applier Mechanism.*[1] SAM encodes a story, accesses knowledge stored as real-world scripts, and then "comprehends" the event being described.

How do we know that SAM comprehends? A variety of results demonstrate this; for instance, SAM can paraphrase the stories, can answer questions based on the events, and can even translate the story into another language. In all three cases, the yardstick used to measure SAM's understanding is a kind of *Turing test.*[2] Read SAM's output; if the output indicates that SAM understood the story correctly, has given reasonable answers to the questions, has translated the story adequately— in short, has dealt with the tasks in a reasonably human-like way—then SAM has passed the Turing test. Table 13-1 presents some sample input and output from SAM; you be the judge.

ACT*

More ambitious models of human cognition have also been proposed. Notable among these is the **ACT*** (pronounced "Act-star") model by John

---

[1] **SAM** is actually just one of a family of related programs in the Schank and Abelson system. Another one, PAM, is a general system that understands *plan*-based stories; a third, TALESPIN, produces stories based on scripted knowledge. See Schank and Riesbeck (1981) for descriptions, including miniature versions of the programs.

[2] The Turing test was devised by Alan Turing, the British mathematician and early computer scientist (e.g., 1950). In the classic description of the Turing test, you deliver a question to two rooms—say, via teletype; one room has a computer in it, the other has a person in it. When the answers to the question are communicated back to you, again by teletype, you try to decide which room has the person in it, and which has the computer, based on the nature or quality of the answers. If you are unable to decide, then the computer has "passed" the Turing test—the computer simulation is successful. In general, of course, we apply this logic without going through the rigamarole of having two rooms, communicating by teletype, and so on. We simply examine the output, and decide how adequate it is compared to the way a person would have responded to the question.

Table 13-1

---

1. *Input:* John went to a restaurant. He sat down. He got mad. He left.
   Output (Long paraphrase): JOHN WAS HUNGRY. HE DECIDED TO GO TO A
   RESTAURANT. HE WENT TO ONE. HE SAT DOWN IN A CHAIR. A WAITER
   DID NOT GO TO THE TABLE. JOHN BECAME UPSET. HE DECIDED HE WAS
   GOING TO LEAVE THE RESTAURANT. HE LEFT IT.
2. *Input:* John went to New York by bus. On the bus he talked to an old lady. When
   he left the bus, he thanked the driver. He took the subway to Leone's. On the
   subway his pocket was picked. He got off the train and entered Leone's. He had
   some lasagna. When the check came, he discovered he couldn't pay. The man-
   agement told him he would have to wash dishes. When he left, he caught a bus
   to New Haven.
   Output: JOHN WENT TO A BUS STOP. HE WAITED AT IT A FEW MINUTES.
   HE ENTERED A BUS. THE DRIVER GOT THE TICKET FROM JOHN. . . . THE
   CHEF PREPARED THE LASAGNA. THE WAITER GOT IT FROM THE CHEF. . . .
   THE DRIVER TOOK JOHN TO NEW HAVEN. HE GOT OFF THE BUS.
   Question 1 (input to SAM): Why did John go to New York?
   Answer 1: BECAUSE JOHN WANTED TO GO TO LEONE'S.
   Question 4: Did anything unusual happen on the subway?
   Answer 4: A THIEF PICKED JOHN'S POCKET.
   Question 10: How was John able to take the bus to New Haven?
   Answer 10: PROBABLY JOHN HAD A TICKET.
   (SAM also generates a Chinese translation of the story here.)

Sample input and output, Schank & Abelson's SAM (pp. 178–180).

Anderson (1983, 1990); the acronym **ACT** stands for "Adaptive Control of
Thought." We will not be concerned here with the modifications and
amendments that have been necessary across the several versions of the
model. Instead, we want to describe the ACT* model and its explanation
of cognitive processes at a level that will illustrate its generality, some of
its principal mechanisms, and some of its theoretical ideas.

The Structure of ACT* Let's begin with familiar notions, seeing
how they are embedded within ACT*, before we progress to the new
ideas in the model. Figure 13-1 shows an overall representation of the
ACT* architecture, the overall structure of the memory system according
to Anderson.

First, you'll notice a familiar term, *working memory.* For now, understand this component in its usual sense, the mental "scratch pad" that
keeps track, holds intermediate outcomes, and so on (we'll revise this
concept later on). In the model, various encoding processes serve to bring
information from the outside world into working memory. These include
the sensory memory processes we discussed in Chapter 3, along with the
attentional mechanisms that transfer sensory memory information into
working memory. And, as was characteristic of even the first serious
information processing model (Atkinson & Shiffrin, 1968), overt behavior
that results from cognitive processing is also controlled most directly by
working memory.

FIGURE 13-1

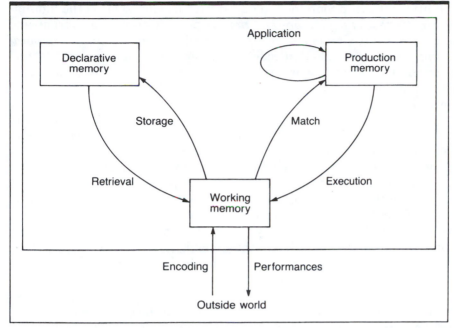

The architecture of Anderson's (1983) ACT* model, showing the major components and the processes that occur within the system.

The next major component is **declarative memory,** a term introduced in Chapter 2 in the discussion of the "representation of knowledge" theme. In Anderson's usage, declarative memory is the long-term memory system for factual knowledge, which includes both semantic and episodic information. It is the explicit, usually verbalizable, knowledge stored in long-term memory, whether of a general nature or specific to the individual. As in most models of long-term memory knowledge, facts stored in Anderson's declarative memory are encoded as a function of strength. That is, the accessibility of information in long-term memory is determined by the strength of encoding, from weak and relatively inaccessible up to strong and highly accessible information. As Anderson (1993) notes, strength grows as a function of practice; the similarities to models of word recognition, semantic memory, and episodic storage and retrieval are unmistakable.

Note the further similarities as well. We concluded in Chapter 6, for example, that semantic knowledge is stored as an interrelated network of nodes, connected by linking pathways, and accessed by means of spreading activation. All these aspects are also true of Anderson's declarative memory. ACT* stores a broader range of information than just abstract, semantic nodes, however. Anderson (1983) claims that, in fact, there are three distinct kinds of knowledge codes, three types of representations that are contained in declarative memory. One is the familiar *abstract propositional representation,* especially useful for verbal and other symbolic concepts and relationships. The second type is a *temporal string,* a representation that codes the order of a set of items, events, and so on. And the third type is a *spatial image,* which codes the spatial configuration of a stimulus pattern or event (including visual images, of course).

As the arrows in Figure 13-1 indicate, new information is stored in declarative memory by the actions of the working memory component. Likewise, when knowledge is retrieved from declarative memory, a copy of the representation is placed into working memory; in other words, that information is now activated and ready to be processed.

Production memory is the third and most important component of the ACT* architecture. This third memory component is the one that distinguishes ACT* as a genuinely different theory from, say, the Collins and Quillian network model or the Schank and Abelson script theory. Production memory is closely related to the term **procedural knowledge** (Anderson, 1976, 1982), which means *knowledge of how to do things.* For example, knowledge of how to ride a bicycle is procedural knowledge, as is knowledge of how to drive a car, how to bake a cake, and how to carry in addition and borrow in subtraction. All these kinds of knowledge are part of production memory, along with other "how to" kinds of information. According to Anderson, the difference between procedural and declarative knowledge is the difference between "knowing how" and "knowing that." Thus production memory is *the long-term memory store for procedures, for procedural knowledge,* for "knowing how."

In ACT*, the distinction between procedural and declarative knowledge is of fundamental importance. One illustration that proves they are indeed different is the ease with which we can verbalize our declarative knowledge (a robin has wings), in contrast to the awkwardness with which we describe our procedural knowledge. Try to give an accurate verbal description of tying shoelaces or a necktie, to illustrate how fluent procedural knowledge often fails to translate into clear, precise verbal expression. In this sense, of course, procedural knowledge is very similar to implicit memory (recall from Chapter 10 that both of these are usually preserved in amnesia, despite loss of declarative, explicit memory). Another example involves language, in particular, our easily verbalized word knowledge, but difficult-to-verbalize knowledge of the rules for putting words together into coherent sentences.

The reason this component is called production memory is because of a basic assumption embedded into ACT* about how things happen in cognition. ACT* is a group of interrelated computer simulations and artificial intelligence programs, all designed around the notion of **production systems.** A production system is *a set or system of productions,* to be circular about it. Well, what's a production, then? A **production,** in Anderson's view, is the basic building block of dynamic cognition, the units out of which thought is composed. You encountered productions in the last chapter, although only briefly, when you read about the Newell et al. (1958) GPS system. There, you read that a production is an *IF–THEN pair of statements, where the IF part specifies a certain condition, and the THEN part specifies a certain action.* Schematically, a production says *IF Condition X is true, THEN take Action Y;*

> IF a glass of liquid is raised to your lips,
> THEN tilt the glass and drink.

The actions in these IF–THEN productions do *not* need to be physical movements, however. They can also be—and in cognitive models, usually *are*—mental actions, or even relationships among concepts. For instance, a simple production that states a semantic, propositional relationship is:

> IF person 1 is the father of person 2,
> THEN person 2 is the son of person 1.

Likewise, a slightly more complex production would be:

> "IF person 1 is the father of person 2, and IF person 2 is
> the father of person 3,
> THEN person 1 is the grandfather of person 3."
> (Anderson, 1983, p. 6)

In Anderson's words, "Underlying human cognition is a set of condition–action pairs called productions. The condition specifies some data patterns, and if elements matching these patterns are in working memory, then the production can apply" (1983, p. 5). When the production applies, then the action part is executed. Sometimes this results in observable behavior, such as drinking the liquid in a glass. Sometimes it results in some internal mental activity, such as searching for some new fact in declarative memory. It *always* results in adding a new element to working memory, essentially the record that the action has been taken. This addition to working memory is the way that the system keeps track of what it's already done, and what remains to be completed in some task or mental operation. Thus when a production is applied (or, in the jargon of production systems, "when a production *fires*"), a record of its action is placed in working memory to update the "state" or current condition of the system.

Productions can be very simple, as the above examples were, or more complex: more than one condition can be specified in the IF clause, and more than one action can be specified in the THEN clause. Regardless of their complexity, however, they are all stored in production memory. Note that even for relatively simple cognitive acts, there would be *many* relevant productions. In his sample production system for performing addition, Anderson (1982) listed 12 separate productions, and even this set required that the simple addition facts such as 2 + 3 and 4 + 9 be retrieved from declarative memory.

When viewed in this light, the cognitive theorist's job is to specify all the productions that are necessary to accomplish some mental activity or behavior. Given the size of this task, even for simple mental acts, it becomes clear how modern computer technology has infiltrated, and become indispensable to, the world of cognitive theory. As mentioned, Anderson's ACT* is programmed as a computer simulation. Thus Anderson is theorizing about mental activity by programming a computer with productions, then testing the program to see if it performs the way people do, errors and all.

Processing in ACT*   As illustrated in Figure 13-1, working memory accesses production memory through a *matching* process. Consider a situation in which conditions A, B, C, and D are true—all four of those conditions or states are currently in working memory. First, production memory will have, among its myriad productions, some group of productions that are relevant to the task being performed; in other words, production memory will have a group of productions whose IF clauses mention some of the relevant conditions A through D. Imagine that production #25 (the numbers are arbitrary, of course) says "IF A and B and C, THEN do X"; also imagine another production, #28, which says, "IF A and B and C and D, THEN do Y." It should be clear from this simple example that production #28 will be the production to "fire" or act next, since the overall state or situation in working memory matches #28's conditions more closely than #25's (or any other production's conditions). As a consequence, when #28 fires, its action clause—do Y—is *executed* or performed. The result of this execution is that a physical or mental action may be taken, and a record of Y will be deposited in working memory (see Anderson, 1983, 1989, for details).

Second, the additional loop in Figure 13-1, labeled *application,* is a mechanism by which new productions are learned and existing productions are modified. The system monitors its own performance and acquires, modifies, and strengthens productions as a consequence of its successes and failures. If firing a production in a particular circumstance leads to errors, then feedback on those errors can be incorporated as modifications to the production. For example, a second grader might give the answer 12 to the problem 42 – 3, showing evidence that one or more productions in the child's subtraction knowledge are faulty (e.g., since you can't take 3 from 2, write down the 2, then take 3 from 4; see the description of this research by Brown & Burton, 1978, later in the chapter). Via feedback, the error in the child's procedural knowledge will be corrected, in this case by elaborating procedural knowledge to include the procedure of borrowing. In a very real sense, ACT* learns productions by "doing," and then by correcting and doing again.

Finally, when sets of productions are used repeatedly to perform the same actions, they can be grouped or "chunked" together in a general process called *composition*. Through this mechanism, what was once a sequence of separate productions becomes a single, unitized production. A straightforward example of this would be tying your shoes. What began as a series of discrete steps (in sequence, the THEN clauses would be something like "hold a lace in each hand, cross them and switch hands, loop one lace through the opening," etc.) eventually becomes a *composed production,* a single production with the THEN clause, "tie the laces."

Empirical Support for ACT*   The empirical tests of ACT* principles have, for the most part, been quite supportive of the model and the general approach. Anderson (1983, 1989) provides treatments of these tests. For present purposes, consider the following brief summary. ACT* predicts virtually the entire range of episodic and semantic effects discussed in Chapters 5 and 6. The model predicts practice effects, encoding specificity effects, and even traditional paired-associate learning effects; it predicts semantic relatedness, typicality, and general priming effects as well.

More impressive, though, are the applications to problem solving, where ACT* truly comes into its own. As Anderson (1993) notes, ACT* assumes a means–end approach to problem solving. By adopting this approach, presumably a great deal of human problem-solving performance—including the errors people make—can be understood. In fact, this is exactly the approach being taken in the development of computer-based tutors. For example, Anderson (1992; also Anderson, Boyle, Corbett, & Lewis, 1990) reports on tutoring programs, derived from the ACT* framework, that are now being used to help students in high school mathematics. As the student interacts with the tutor, the tutor tries to interpret the student's problem-solving attempt, by consulting its stored productions. In a sense, the computerized tutor asks itself "Which rules of mathematics does this student still not understand?" Based on this analysis of rules yet to be mastered, the tutor then selects new problems for the student to work on.

By tailoring the questions it asks in this fashion, the program literally tutors the student who is learning mathematics. Early results of this work are impressive: "Typical evaluations have students performing approximately one standard deviation better than control classrooms (if given [the] same amount of time on task) or taking one half to one third the time to reach the same achievement levels as control students" (Anderson, 1993, p. 42). Impressive evidence indeed.

Summary Points: computer simulation and artificial intelligence; Turing test; ACT* and production systems; procedural knowledge

▼ Cognition and Emotion

In the past 15–20 years, a number of studies have appeared concerning the general relationships between cognitive processes and emotion. Indeed, a new journal—*Cognition and Emotion*—is devoted to exactly this topic, the various ways that emotional states, anxiety, moods, and so on may affect the ongoing stream of cognitive processes. Obviously, the topic of emotion is one of psychology's oldest interests. James (1890) not only commented on it, as illustrated at the beginning of the chapter, but also contributed one of the major theories to explain emotion and emotional arousal. Our interest here, of course, is not in the theories of emotion per se—those are topics in personality and clinical psychology. Instead, cognitive psychology is interested in the *effects* that our emotions have on everyday memory and cognition. This brief section summarizes some of the basic findings to date and shows how the cognitive approach, broadly defined, is being applied to the topic of emotion.

Emotion and Memory

Ellis and Hunt (1993) note that we all have a general idea of the effect of emotion or mood on memory: "Most of us are personally aware that under certain emotional states, such as feeling sad or depressed, we are less attentive to our environment and are less likely to process information in an effective fashion" (p. 332). This introspective awareness is important to cognition for the obvious reason—it suggests a testable hypothesis and a fairly specific cognitive effect.

In particular, the intuition is that negative emotional states result in decreased attention to the task at hand. We might draw several predictions from this; for example, depression might yield an inadequate encoding of stimulus material, insufficient or inefficient mental processing, or some other type of general interference with normal mental processing. Given the tools of cognitive psychology, we should be able to investigate these possibilities.

Ellis and his colleagues have done precisely that. For example, in an early study on mood and memory, Leight and Ellis (1981, Experiment 2) tested subjects who were in either a sad or neutral mood. The manipulation of a subject's emotional state was accomplished by one of the standard "mood induction" procedures, the Velten (1968) technique. In this procedure, subjects read a set of self-referring statements, either the set that contains neutral statements, or the set that contains negative, sad statements (see Table 13-2 for sample statements from the Velten procedure, including statements that induce a happy, elated mood). After the statements were read, the effectiveness of the mood induction was checked, to make sure that subjects had truly been "placed" in the intended mood state. Then, subjects were given a simple five-trial learn-

Table 13-2   SAMPLE OF VELTEN (1968) MOOD INDUCTION STATEMENTS

Sad Mood

1. Today is neither better nor worse than any other day.
2. However, I feel a little low today.
3. Sometimes I wonder whether school is all that worthwhile.
4. Every now and then I feel so tired and gloomy that I'd rather just sit than do anything.
5. Too often I have found myself staring listlessly into the distance, my mind a blank, when I definitely should have been studying.

Happy Mood

1. Today is neither better nor worse than any other day.
2. I do feel pretty good today, though.
3. This might turn out to have been one of my good days.
4. If your attitude is good, then things are good, and my attitude is good.
5. I feel cheerful and lively.

Neutral Mood

1. Oklahoma City is the largest city in the world in area, with 631.66 square miles.
2. Japan was elected to the United Nations almost 14 years after Pearl Harbor.
3. At the end appears a section entitled "Bibliography notes."
4. We have two kinds of nouns denoting physical things: individual and mass nouns.
5. This book or any part thereof must not be reproduced in any form.

ing experiment; the lists to be learned were composed of six-letter non-sense words (e.g., BONKID, NATVIM, MUTLEN).

Figure 13-2 shows the results of this experiment. The graph clearly shows that subjects in the neutral mood state performed better, in terms of mean number of items recalled, than those in the sad emotional state. Interestingly, when the subjects returned 24 hours later, for the second learning session, their performance still depended on the initial learning session. That is, subjects who had been in a neutral mood on day 1, and were again in the neutral mood on day 2, outperformed all other groups. Subjects originally tested in the sad mood did poorly on day 2, even if they were in the neutral mood on day 2. Leight and Ellis suggested that subjects used the first day's test to develop various encoding and rehearsal strategies for the nonsense words. Neutral subjects' performance indicated that they had developed reasonably successful strategies. And, if they were again in the neutral mood on day 2, they continued to use those strategies. Subjects who had been sad on day 1, however, had not devised particularly effective learning strategies. On day 2, then, they seem to have continued with those poor strategies, thereby showing a continued low level of performance.

What about being in a happy, upbeat mood? Note that our intuition for the effects of a positive emotional state tends to differ somewhat from the earlier intuition. Introspectively, wouldn't you expect that being in a happy mood might actually enhance your performance? As it happens,

FIGURE 13-2

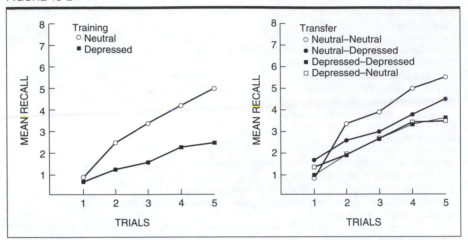

Recall in training and transfer as a function of mood state conditions. (From Leight & Ellis, 1981.)

according to several studies (e.g., Leight & Ellis, 1981, Experiment 1; Seibert & Ellis, 1991), this second introspection is very probably incorrect. That is, subjects who are in a happy or elated mood do just as poorly as those in a sad mood. To paraphrase Seibert and Ellis, either happy or sad thoughts may distract your focus from those thoughts necessary for good task performance, and thus would produce interference. Seibert and Ellis's (1991) data supported this hypothesis completely. Both the happy and sad subjects reported far more irrelevant, extraneous thoughts during the learning task, and both groups recalled significantly fewer items than did the neutral mood group.

The basic consequence of an emotional state, then, appears to be one of general interference. *Any* strong emotional state tends to disrupt your focus or attention to the demands of the task. Ellis and Ashbrook (1988) suggested a *resource allocation* hypothesis as an explanation; the mood state affects cognitive processing so that mental resources—working memory, attention, effort, and the like—are not allocated efficiently to the task at hand. The consequence is interference with some aspect of performance, whether initial encoding of the stimulus, rehearsal or storage strategies, or, presumably, retrieval processes. In support of this explanation, Hertel and Rude (1991) have shown how instructions to focus attention during the task can counteract the effects of depression.

Mood Congruence   We turn now to a topic that has received considerable attention in the literature, the **mood congruence effect.** This effect is simply that *memory performance is enhanced for material that matches the learner's mood.* If you are in a particular mood, you tend to

What does the elation over a victory predict for later memory?

show better memory for information that matches your mood; you remember material better if it is *congruent* with your own mood or emotional state.

A widely known and cited series of studies by Bower, Gilligan, and Monteiro (1981) illustrates the mood congruence effect very nicely. In their first experiment, Bower et al. induced either a happy or sad mood in subjects by means of a posthypnotic suggestion. While experiencing the induced mood, subjects read a story about two characters—one who is happy (Andre), and one who is sad (Jack). Subjects returned a day later and recalled the story under a neutral mood. Recall was scored by converting the written retellings of the story into their underlying propositions (see Chapter 7).

Overall, the two groups of subjects recalled the same number of ideas from the story, regardless of whether they had been happy or sad when they read it. But the *proportion* of happy and sad ideas recalled depend-

THE FAR SIDE   By GARY LARSON

© 1991 FarWorks, Inc./Dist. by Universal Press Syndicate

THE FAR SIDE copyright 1985, 1986 & 1991 FARWORKS, INC. Distributed by UNIVERSAL PRESS SYNDICATE. Reprinted with permission. All rights reserved.

"Well, it's a delicate situation, sir. ... Sophisticated firing system, hair-trigger mechanisms, and Bob's wife just left him last night, so you *know* his mind's not into this."

ed heavily on the subjects' mood. Sad subjects—that is, subjects who had been in the sad mood when they read the story—overwhelmingly recalled facts about the sad character in the story; in fact, 80% of the facts they recalled were about "sad Jack." Subjects who had read the story in a happy mood, likewise, recalled more about the happy character; some 55% of their recalled facts were about Andre.

In later experiments, Bower et al. tested to see if the effect would also be obtained when the mood was induced *only* during recall. That is, subjects read the story in a neutral mood, then later recalled it while either happy or sad. The evidence here was negative—no mood congruence effect was obtained when mood was manipulated only at retrieval. This suggested to Bower et al. that the mood congruence effect is a genuine learning effect, that is, one that influences what subjects selectively learn during reading. More recent work, however, has called this interpretation into question (e.g., Blaney, 1986). For example, a few studies

FIGURE 13-3

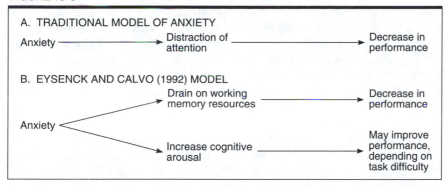

A. TRADITIONAL MODEL OF ANXIETY

Anxiety → Distraction of attention → Decrease in performance

B. EYSENCK AND CALVO (1992) MODEL

Anxiety →
- Drain on working memory resources → Decrease in performance
- Increase cognitive arousal → May improve performance, depending on task difficulty

Traditional model of anxiety (A) and the Eysenck and Calvo (B) model.

have shown the effect at retrieval; a few have failed to replicate the original Bower et al. results. In Blaney's view, the issue—Does the mood congruence effect happen at encoding, retrieval, or both?—remains unresolved at present.[3]

Anxiety and Performance

On the surface, the effects of anxiety on cognitive processing might seem to be quite similar to those of mood or emotional state. After all, anxiety should have some of the same properties as emotions, in terms of distracting the learner from the requirements of the task, diverting necessary attention, and producing irrelevant thoughts during the memory task. Such an effect of anxiety is diagrammed at the top of Figure 13-3.

But there seems to be more to anxiety than just this. Eysenck and Calvo (1992; see also Humphreys & Revelle, 1984) argued that anxiety actually has two effects—worry and cognitive arousal. That is, anxiety produces a tendency toward worrisome thoughts, which will decrease the available working memory resources that can be devoted to a task. But anxiety also produces a kind of cognitive arousal, which affects one's alertness and, sometimes, the effort devoted to a task; see the bottom of Figure 13-3. In the Eysenck and Calvo (1992) theory, these effects combine to yield what they call *processing efficiency*. That is, the quality of cognitive performance, say, the accuracy of a subject's recall, is only part of the equation. Quality must be viewed in terms of the *mental effort* required to achieve that quality; loosely speaking, quality of performance divided by mental effort equals processing efficiency.

---

[3]State-dependent learning is demonstrated when the learner's physical state influences later memory performance. For example, if the subject is intoxicated during learning, then later recall, tested without being under the influence of alcohol, generally shows poorer performance. Blaney (1986) indicates, however, that research has shown either weak or inconsistent evidence for "mood state dependent learning."

The most appealing feature of Eysenck and Calvo's (1992) theory of anxiety and performance, from our perspective, is that it is embedded solidly into a memory system that has been extensively investigated, Baddeley's (1986) working memory. In their view, one of the two major effects of worry is to consume some of working memory's limited resources, in particular, the resources used by the central executive component. Accordingly, any task that requires a heavy involvement of the central executive should be especially prone to disruption when the subjects are highly anxious.

The second effect of worry, however, is in the opposite direction. Worry can serve as a motivational force, in which additional working memory resources may be devoted to the task. This is basically the well-known effect of arousal on performance: some intermediate amount of arousal is often optimal for performance, whereas too little or too much arousal will degrade performance. As the authors note, these kinds of effects can be examined within a dual task procedure. That is, if an anxious subject must devote more effort in order to perform well on a task, then the extra effort must be consuming mental resources that were momentarily free. Depending on the difficulty of the task, such effects may show up in the subjects' secondary task performance as an overall decline in processing efficiency—for example, high quality of performance but at a steep price in effort.

One other kind of anxiety effect can be mentioned in passing, *mathematics anxiety*. Math anxiety is a very situation-specific effect: only when they are doing math is there a decline in the performance of highly math anxious subjects, unlike other more general types of anxiety. Hembree (1990) has catalogued the characteristics of subjects who score high on tests of mathematics anxiety; they tend to do poorly on math achievement tests, take fewer elective courses in math, and earn lower grades on those courses they do take.[4] Research on the cognitive consequences of math anxiety, however, is just beginning (e.g., Faust, 1992; Ashcraft & Faust, 1994). Note, however, that one of the more devastating consequences has already been mentioned: if highly math anxious individuals take fewer math courses and earn lower grades, this surely has a negative effect on their expertise in math, on the "domain knowledge" we deemed so relevant to problem solving in Chapter 12.

Summary Points: emotional effects on memory; resource allocation and rehearsal; mood congruence; anxiety effects and processing efficiency; math anxiety and expertise

---

[4]Interestingly, the tendency for women to score higher in mathematics anxiety is much weaker than conventional wisdom suggests and is only apparent when rather select samples, rather than the general population, are tested (e.g., Hyde, Fennema, Ryan, Frost, & Hopp, 1990).

▼ Applied Cognition

We turn to the last of our three "current directions," that portion of cognitive psychology concerned with application of research and theoretical knowledge to practical, real-world problems and issues. As you might suspect, given the breadth of our interests in cognitive psychology, any number of examples could be given in a section on applied cognition.

To illustrate this breadth, we start with a brief overview of some of the more noteworthy applications in law and medicine. Then we'll turn to one particularly important instance of applied cognition—classroom learning of arithmetic and math. In addition to illustrating the usefulness of a cognitive approach to education, and the desirability of applying our cognitive theories to the task of education, this topic also provides somewhat of a unification of several topics that we've covered—learning, memory representation, the acquisition of rules, and the modeling of complex thought by means of computer simulation.

Law

A variety of topics in cognitive psychology can be applied to the law, usually from the standpoints of memory functioning and recall of past experiences.

Consider eyewitness testimony again. There is no doubt, based on research discussed in Chapter 7, that the accuracy of eyewitness testimony can be seriously compromised. Several factors, including leading questions, misinformation after the fact, and the emotional impact of violent events (see Burke, Heuer, & Reisberg, 1992; Loftus, 1979; Loftus & Burns, 1982), have been shown to influence subjects' recall of episodes. Given that juries often rely heavily on eyewitness accounts of a crime or accident, it is clearly important to understand as much as possible about these effects. Other legal applications of cognitive science—and psychology in general—are gaining in importance as well; Loftus (1991) discusses an entire range of such issues.

One of the most fascinating recent applications of the cognitive science approach concerns the issue of "simulated amnesia." It is apparently fairly common that someone—often a defendant charged with committing a violent crime—claims to be suffering from amnesia for the crime. In fact, Kopelman (1987; also Schacter, 1986) indicates that up to 70% of murder suspects make such claims. The legal issue, of course, is whether the amnesia is real or simulated—whether the defendant is truly suffering amnesia or merely inventing this as a ploy.

Horton, Smith, Barghout, and Connolly (1992) designed an especially clever way of investigating this question. In their work, subjects were first given a list of 16 words to be learned for a later memory test. After the study trial, control subjects were then given an implicit memory test, one of two word fragment completion tests, and then an explicit memory test, free recall of the study list.

Two other groups got a special set of instructions prior to the memory tests. The "uninformed amnesia" group was simply asked to simulate amnesia, with no further detail provided; for example, "During the rest of this experiment, please perform any tasks that you are given the way you think a person with amnesia would do them" and "Based on what you write down on the word completion test and the recall test, I want you to try to convince me that you suffer from amnesia for the list of words you have just studied" (p. 351). The second group was also asked to simulate amnesia, but these subjects were told how amnesics usually perform. That is, this "informed amnesia" group was told that amnesics perform normally on the implicit memory test, word completion, but quite poorly on the explicit test, free recall (see Chapter 10).

The Horton et al. results were quite clear. Both of the "amnesia" groups recalled 0% of the words in the free recall task, compared with 60% accuracy by the control subjects. In other words, both "amnesia" groups accurately faked the typical amnesic effect on free recall. But the results in the word completion task were dramatically different. Here, the uninformed group completed fewer than 10% of the target word fragments, fewer even than on baseline words that had not appeared in the study list. The control and informed subjects, however, completed about 70% of the word fragments correctly; see Figure 13-4. Of course, the informed subjects had been told that amnesics do as well as normals on word completion, so they did not artificially lower their performance here. The critical result, therefore, was that uninformed subjects showed a pattern on word completion that is completely *uncharacteristic* of amnesia. They mistakenly assumed that amnesia affects *all* memory performance; thus they did poorly on the implicit test that even true amnesics would have performed successfully.

Within limits, Horton et al. note, such patterns might be expected of a criminal defendant who decides to simulate amnesia. Thus, in a very important sense, the implicit memory test served somewhat as a lie detector: someone who is faking amnesia is unlikely to know how well a true amnesic performs on implicit memory tasks.

Medicine

Medical diagnosis, in many important ways, involves virtually every aspect of cognitive psychology that you've studied. Imagine a doctor who is attempting to diagnose an illness. At one point, the doctor may need to examine the patient's x-rays. As any physician will tell you, however, reading an x-ray is somewhat of an art—the x-ray patterns made by various illnesses are often distressingly vague, difficult to discern, and hard to differentiate. Performance in such situations can be referred to as

FIGURE 13-4

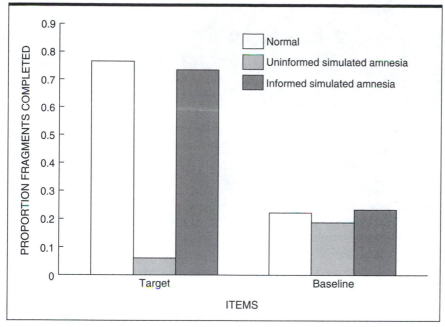

Fragment completion data as a function of instructions (normal, uninformed simulated amnesia, or informed simulated amnesia) and type of item (target or baseline). (From Horton et al., 1992.)

data-limited, since there are *limitations in the quality of the "data," or stimuli, being processed.* Reading the x-ray is a data-limited task for the physician, because of limitations in the x-ray pattern itself. This is in contrast to performance that is **resource-limited,** that is, *insufficient mental resources to sustain optimal processing.*

Studies of expert diagnosticians have approached this issue from multiple standpoints. One of these involves visual pattern recognition and the role of top–down processes. That is, maybe an expert diagnostician has developed an extensive mental representation of both the prototypical "pneumonia configuration" and the degree of variation from the prototype that can often be expected. How are such prototypes acquired, given the data-limited nature of the x-ray? How is related knowledge about this and other illnesses stored in memory, and are there better ways of teaching this information to yield a stronger, more reliable memory representation? Recent evidence shows that expert diagnosticians show very accurate memory for abnormal x-ray patterns (Myles-Worsley, Johnston, & Simons, 1988). Interestingly, they tended *not* to remember much from the normal x-rays they saw; their recognition memory for normal x-rays was relatively poor.

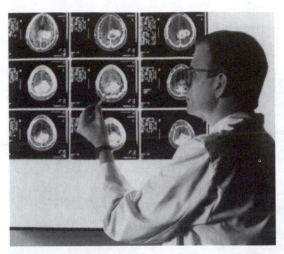

Interpreting the information in these CT scans is a data-limited task for the diagnostician, due to the limitations in the quality of the data.

Equally interesting, but from a very different standpoint, is the decision-making process a physician exhibits. Say a patient presents three symptoms that are typical of several rather different diseases. What kind of reasoning strategies does the expert diagnostician use, in contrast to a doctor just learning diagnosis? Research by Patel and Groen (1986) showed that expert cardiologists relied primarily on a forward reasoning method, whereas novices often attempted to reason backward, from a presumed illness back toward the symptoms (also Patel, Groen, & Arocha, 1990).

Does the physician make a decision based on the representativeness heuristic; for example, are these three symptoms more typical or representative of one of the diseases? If the decision is made to administer more laboratory tests, we might wonder if the tests were ordered to support a diagnosis or to rule out alternatives (e.g., Eddy, 1982). Recall from Chapter 11 that people seem to seek evidence that *confirms* their hypotheses, whereas a better reasoning strategy would be to seek potentially *disconfirming* evidence. (On the other hand, many diagnostic tests are designed to detect a true disease pattern, so seeking disconfirming evidence may be less critical here than in conditional reasoning.)

Finally, is the physician unduly influenced by the availability heuristic—does the presence of these three symptoms *usually* signal a certain disease, and if so does the physician overlook other symptoms that may signal a far less common disorder, one that is less available for recall by the physician? (The list of possibilities could go further; are physicians unduly influenced by recency of similar symptoms, by the vividness or salience of certain symptoms?)

Table 13-3

1. 16	2. 472	3. 29	4. 43	5. 42	6. 831
+ 12	− 326	− 6	+ 79	− 3	− 158
28	156	23	23	12	583

Sample arithmetic problems with answers. See if you can determine the incorrect procedures or bugs that generated the wrong answers.

Education

It should go without saying that a thorough understanding of learning, memory, and cognitive processing will allow a more empirical theory of education, and more effective teaching and learning in the classroom. There is, of course, a very long history of mutual influence between psychology and educational theory and practice. Elements of behaviorism, particularly in classroom management and discipline, are still apparent in many preschools and elementary schools. Similarly, other psychological influences, especially that of Piaget's school of thought, have had an influence on educational practice, inspiring quite different kinds of teaching practices and curricular decisions.

What kinds of educational applications from cognitive psychology are both possible and relevant? Let's consider just one here, the acquisition of knowledge and skill in mathematics. One desirable aspect of this topic is that careful cognitive research has provided a fresh and useful way of approaching students' difficulties in math. Just as important, this application also provides teachers with more effective ways of assessing and understanding their students' knowledge and performance.

Problem Solving, Math, and Cognition   You are a third-grade teacher, grading math homework. One of your students, who seems to be having particular difficulty with multicolumn addition and subtraction, submits a paper with the problems and answers in Table 13-3. Look carefully at the problems and the answers. While a few of them are done correctly, others show very strange errors, answers that are "off" by strange amounts. What would you conclude about this student's knowledge of arithmetic, based on this homework? Isn't it pretty clear that this child is seriously "lost," that he or she has failed to learn some fundamental facts about addition and subtraction, or at a minimum that the child was paying so little attention that the homework is full of careless mistakes?[5]

If you answered "yes" to any of these questions, then you have missed the same aspect to the incorrect answers that many teachers would miss.

---

[5]It would actually be quite unusual for any *single* child to demonstrate this variety of bugs; I have combined these bugs into one table here merely for purposes of illustration.

The aspect that you missed relates to the different kinds of knowledge that a child acquires about math, and the ways in which that knowledge is stored and used. From the first and third problems, you might infer that the student does indeed know some "facts" of addition and subtraction, maybe just the simpler combinations. But the other problems seem to show something quite different, possibly no knowledge of the larger facts, or at least inconsistent or undependable mastery of them.

An impressive program of research (e.g., Brown & Burton, 1978; Brown & VanLehn, 1980; VanLehn, 1990) has analyzed thousands of such errors in children's arithmetic, from the standpoint of *procedural knowledge*. That is, in ways exactly parallel with Anderson's ACT* production system, these researchers have analyzed arithmetic in terms of the *rules* or *procedures* that must be applied to solve problems successfully. Of course, basic knowledge of the simple facts is important to performance: a child must know that 3 + 3 = 6, for example, and be able to retrieve this knowledge fluently and automatically (e.g., Ashcraft, 1992). But if we look only at the "facts" of arithmetic, we are ignoring the rich and sometimes complex procedural knowledge of "*how* to add and subtract," knowledge that includes the procedures of carrying and borrowing.

In Brown and VanLehn's work, such "how-to" knowledge is the procedural knowledge that the child acquires as part of the normal process of instruction. Often, of course, this knowledge will be acquired correctly—though with some difficulty—and the child will be able to solve problems correctly. Sometimes, however, children will learn a procedure, or possibly just one part of a procedure, *incorrectly*. When this happens, the incorrect procedure functions just as any other bit of procedural knowledge: when a certain problem calls for a particular operation, that operation will be performed. In the case of faulty learning, the child will make a mistake when a particular problem "calls up" a particular incorrect procedure.

In computer programming and simulation, *a mistake in the program* is called a **bug.** Bugs in a program will cause systematic errors in the answers supplied by the program, since an incorrect procedure is being applied. In just this spirit, Brown and VanLehn refer to children's incorrect procedures in arithmetic as *bugs*. In this approach, there is an error or mistake in one part of the child's procedural knowledge, an error that produces a particular error in performance. The incorrect procedure is systematic in that it causes the same kind of error each time.

Note further, in exactly parallel fashion to the production system, that certain problems will "satisfy" or match the condition (IF) part of a production, and will consequently cause the action (THEN) part of the production to occur. Thus some incorrect answers will, upon careful analysis, reveal the underlying bug that generated them. The teacher's task then becomes one of determining which procedures a child has learned incorrectly. In almost a literal sense, the teacher must *debug* the child's procedural knowledge, just the way a computer programmer debugs a program that contains an error.

What does cognitive science tell us about how children learn mathematics?

Consider a rather simple bug, as illustrated by the second problem in the table. Here, the "facts" of subtraction are performed accurately, but the child has failed to decrement the 7 in the top row after borrowing from it (*decrement* means to reduce by one, just as *increment* means to increase by one). Thus 1 has been borrowed from the 7 in order to perform 12 − 6 = 6, but then the 2 is subtracted from the 7, rather than the decremented 6. Here, the bug is relatively simple. BORROW is a three-part procedure, (a) getting 10 ones from the column to the left, (b) adding the 10 ones to the column on the right, and (c) decrementing the number in the column from which you borrowed. The particular bug that produces the error in the second problem involves only action (c), decrementing the number that was borrowed from. A comparable bug in addition would be to fail to add the carried 1.

On the other hand, some bugs may be quite subtle, or may appear so infrequently—because of the particular problems being worked—that no one notices the systematic error. For instance, problem 5 does not reveal the bug that causes the error in problem 6, since the incorrect answers to these problems come from different bugs. Finally, bugs often occur in combinations, making it even more difficult to determine which aspects of the child's knowledge are faulty.[6]

<hr />

[6]VanLehn (1990) has recently suggested that children's bugs are not as systematic or stable as had previously been thought. It may be, however, that the general nature of a child's errors is stable, in that a specific feature in a problem, say, a pair of 0s in the top number of a subtraction problem, will yield one of several related errors; see Ashcraft, Yamashita, and Aram (1992) for a possible categorization of errors by problem features.

Table 13-4

Problem Number	Bug
1	No bug
2	Forget to decrement (the 7) after borrowing
3	No bug
4	Add all: each number is treated as a single digit, so 23 is the sum of 4 + 3 + 7 + 9
5	Instead of borrowing, bring down the 2 and subtract the 3 from the 4
6	Subtract all borrows from the leftmost column

In principle, of course, any of the rules or procedures in math could be learned incorrectly. The consequences, however, can often be rather difficult to detect; a math problem must call on that procedure in order for us to observe the child's bug. Thus to diagnose a child's bugs requires a set of problems that will "call" or "fire" the incorrect rule.

Note also one other necessary factor for diagnosing a child's bugs: the teacher must realize that errors in the homework may reflect something systematically wrong with the child's knowledge, instead of merely assuming that the child is careless or inconsistent. Indeed, one reason that Brown and VanLehn's work is so important is just this: it has made educators aware of the possibly systematic and lawful basis of some errors. This realization, obviously, is a necessary precondition for the instruction a child needs to perform arithmetic accurately. If teachers realize this possibility, then they can target their teaching efforts much more precisely. See if you can profit from this realization now, by diagnosing the remaining bugs in Table 13-3; descriptions of each bug are presented in Table 13-4. If you can determine which arithmetic rules are faulty in these problems, can you now tailor your teaching to this child's needs more effectively?

Other research on the general topic of math and problem solving (e.g., Reed, 1984; Reed, Dempster, & Ettinger, 1985; Reed & Saavedra, 1986) is examining people's algebraic knowledge and, in particular, their often faulty problem solving when confronted with word problems. One particularly fascinating aspect of their results involves subjects' use of a procedure, say, simple averaging, when the problem calls for a very different procedure. As an example, consider the following word problem (from Reed, 1984):

> If one pipe can fill a tank in two hours, and another can fill it in ten hours, how long will it take to fill the tank with both pipes working together?

One-third of Reed's college student sample merely averaged the two numbers, and estimated that it would take six hours for both pipes to fill the tank. If this sounds reasonable to you, stop for a moment, and consider this: How could it take six hours for *both* pipes to fill the tank when just *one* of the pipes can do it alone in two hours?

It's difficult to summarize the research on applied cognition because such research is so widespread, is influenced by so many related disciplines and approaches, and is so thoroughly integrated into the everyday "practice" of cognitive psychology. Perhaps it will suffice merely to say the following: the science of memory and thought not only addresses the basic, fundamental questions of memory and cognitive processes but is also eager to apply its talents and skills to questions of everyday and practical concern. To date, such applications have provided important insights and discoveries in fields as diverse as medicine, education, business, and law. But, of course, this is not surprising. After all, what human endeavor doesn't involve thought?

Summary Points: legal applications—eyewitness testimony, implicit memory and simulated amnesia; medical applications—expertise, reasoning, decision making; educational applications—bugs in math procedures

CHAPTER SUMMARY

1. The term *computerized cognition* refers to work in artificial intelligence and cognitive science on the programming of intelligent computer systems. While models of human mental processing have been constructed by means of computer simulation for many years, computerized cognition goes beyond this work by trying to create a system that can behave intelligently.

2. Anderson's ACT* model, for instance, is a large-scale computer model of human memory and mental processes. This model addresses a large range of psychological processes and is particularly suited to an analysis of problem solving. Schank and Abelson's theory of language comprehension, likewise, is programmed as an artificial intelligence system that understands stories by means of scripted knowledge. Such models illustrate, among other things, the importance of top–down processing and network representations of knowledge.

3. Research on the cognitive consequences of emotion and anxiety is beginning to show a standard pattern of effects. Emotion, whether positive or negative, tends to impair performance because it distracts attention from task demands. Interestingly, learners tend to show better memory for emotional material that is consistent with their own mood during a memory test, the mood congruence effect.

4. Anxiety is now thought to have two rather opposite effects on performance, an impairment due to the draining of working memory resources, and a possible improvement due to the increased effort and arousal that anxiety can produce. This account neglects long-term influ-

ences that can arise, for instance, when math anxious individuals avoid math classes and thus achieve lower expertise in math.

5. A wealth of examples can be given to show the impact of cognitive psychology on various applied areas, among them law, medicine, and education. A particularly important application to education has been the notion of procedural knowledge, as applied to children's knowledge of arithmetic. In this work, children's errors often show *bugs,* inaccurate knowledge of a particular rule or procedure in arithmetic; for example, in subtraction, a child may always borrow from the leftmost digit. By considering errors in arithmetic as due to inaccurate knowledge of the procedures for borrowing, carrying, and so on, a teacher can diagnose a child's misunderstanding more accurately and can therefore target the necessary corrective instruction more precisely.

Glossary Terms: ACT*; artificial intelligence; bugs; computer simulation; data-limited and resource-limited; declarative and procedural memory; mood congruence; processing efficiency; production system; Turing test

SUGGESTED READINGS

A variety of excellent books describe artificial intelligence and the intersection of cognitive psychology and AI; see, for instance, Haugeland's *Mind Design: Philosophy, Psychology, Artificial Intelligence* (1981), his *Artificial Intelligence: The Very Idea* (1985), and Winston's *Artificial Intelligence* (1984); Raphael's *The Thinking Computer: Mind Inside Matter* (1976) is good, though somewhat dated. An advanced undergraduate text, *Cognitive Science: An Introduction* by Stillings, Feinstein, Garfield, Rissland, Rosenbaum, Weisler, and Baker-Ward (1987), covers the new field of cognitive science in great depth. The journal *Cognitive Science* publishes current, though difficult, original articles on topics at the intersection of cognitive psychology, computer science, and linguistics; *Artificial Intelligence Magazine* contains articles about current AI projects written for the informed reader. Finally, the two-volume set *Parallel Distributed Processing* (McClelland & Rumelhart, 1986; Rumelhart & McClelland, 1986) provides an extensive (but difficult) discussion of the connectionist approach to cognitive modeling; try Martindale (1991) for an introduction to cognitive psychology from the neural network standpoint.

General books and articles on the cognitive psychology of emotion, anxiety, and stress include Mandler (1984, 1989) and Eysenck (1992). See also Chapter 12 of Ellis and Hunt (1993).

A variety of books describe applications of cognitive psychology to education. See Gagne's (1985) *The Cognitive Psychology of School Learning* for a general overview, Berger, Pezdek, and Banks (1986) for a collection of papers on applications of cognitive psychology, and the journals *Cognition and Instruction* and *Applied Cognitive Psychology* for papers on specific issues such as mathematics and reading.

Finally, Gardner's (1985) book, *The Mind's New Science: A History of the Cognitive Revolution,* is a superb account of the origins, current state, and future directions of cognitive science. If you want to pursue modern cognitive psychology at a deeper level, I can't think of a better place to start than Gardner's literate, captivating, and informative analysis.

Accessibility: the degree to which information can be retrieved from memory. A memory is said to be accessible if it is retrievable; memories that are not currently retrievable are said to have become inaccessible (Ch. 5).

Acoustic–Articulatory Code: the form of mental representation using sound- (acoustic) or pronunciation-related (articulatory) information (e.g., as distinct from the visual code) (Ch. 4).

ACT*: Anderson's (e.g., 1983) model of human cognitive processes. The acronym stands for Adaptive Control of Thought. ACT* is a computer-based production system model, composed of declarative, production, and working memory components (Ch. 13).

Actor: see **Agent.**

Advantage of Clause Recency/First Mention: the speed-up of RT to information in the most recently processed clause/information mentioned first in the sentence (Ch. 9).

Agent (also Actor): In the case grammar approach, the individual that performs some action in a sentence is the *agent;* for example, Bill in "Bill hit the ball with the bat." See also **Case Grammar** (Ch. 7, 8).

Agraphia: a disruption in the ability to write, due to some brain disorder or injury (Ch. 10).

AI: see **Artificial Intelligence**.

Alexia: a disruption in the ability to read or recognize printed letters or words, due to some brain disorder or injury (Ch. 10).

Algorithm: a specific rule or solution procedure that is guaranteed to yield the correct answer if followed correctly (contrast with **Heuristic**) (Ch. 11).

Ambiguous: having more than one meaning, said both of words (e.g., "bank") as well as sentences (e.g., "They are eating apples") (Ch. 8).

Amnesia: memory loss due to brain damage, injury, and so on. *Retrograde* amnesia is loss of memory for information prior to the damage, *anterograde* amnesia is loss of memory for information after the damage (Ch. 2, 7, 10).

Analogy: a relationship between two similar systems, problems, and so on; a heuristic in which a problem is solved by finding an analogy to a similar problem (Ch. 12).

Analysis-by-Synthesis: a term in Neisser's (1967) book referring to the combination of two types of mental processing; today referred to as the combination of data-driven and conceptually driven processing (Ch. 2).

Anomia: a disruption of word finding or retrieval, due to some brain disorder or injury (Ch. 10).

Antecedent (in conditional reasoning): the IF clause in standard conditional reasoning (IF–THEN) tasks. In the statement "If it rains, then the picnic will be canceled," the antecedent is "If it rains" (Ch. 11).

Antecedent (in language): the concept to which a later word refers; for example, "he" refers to the antecedent Bill in "Bill said he was tired" (Ch. 8, 9).

Aphasia: a loss of some or all of previously intact language skills, due to brain disorder or damage (Ch. 10).

Applied Cognition: a term denoting various applications and extensions of cognitive research and findings to real-world issues and problems, for instance, in education and medicine (Ch. 13).

Arbitrariness: one of Hockett's (1960) linguistic universals, that the connections between linguistic units (sounds, words) and the concepts or meanings referred to by those units are entirely arbitrary; for example, it is arbitrary that we refer to a table by the linguistic unit "table" (Ch. 8).

Arguments: in a proposition, the arguments are the ordered concepts that specify the meaning of the proposition. The *arguments* of the *relation* HIT in the sentence "Bill hit the ball yesterday" are BILL as the *agent,* BALL as the *object,* and YESTERDAY as the *time.* See also **Case Grammar** (Ch. 7).

Articulatory (Rehearsal) Loop: in Baddeley and Hitch's (1974) working memory system, the articulatory loop is the component responsible for recycling verbal material via rehearsal (Ch. 4).

Artificial Intelligence (AI): the branch of computer science in which computer systems are programmed to behave intelligently, for example, programmed to understand spoken speech (Ch. 13).

Association: a general term referring to a connection or link between two elements. In classical behaviorism, an association was formed between a stimulus and a response. In various models of long-term memory, associations are the links or pathways between concept nodes; for example, the *isa* pathway between ROBIN and BIRD (Ch. 1, 6).

Attend: the verb form of "attention," meaning "to pay attention to" (Ch. 2, 3).

Attention: the mental energy or resource necessary for the completion of mental processes, believed to be limited in quantity and under the control of some executive control mechanism (Ch. 2, 3).

Audition: the sense of hearing (Ch. 3).

Auditory Sensory Memory (also Echoic Memory): the sensory memory system that encodes incoming auditory information and holds it briefly for further mental processing (Ch. 2, 3).

Authorized: intended or correct. An implication of a speaker's statement is said to be authorized if the speaker intended the implication to be drawn; if the listener draws the intended inference, the inference is said to be authorized (contrast with **Unauthorized**) (Ch. 9).

Autobiographical Memory: memories of specific, personally experienced "real-world" information, for example, of one's activities upon learning of the *Challenger* space shuttle disaster; the study of those memories (Ch. 5).

Automatic, Automaticity: occurring without conscious awareness or intention, and consuming little if any of the available mental resources (Ch. 2, 3).

Availability: (in decision-making research) ease of retrieval (Ch. 11).

Availability: (in memory research) the presence of information in the memory system. Information is said to be available if it is currently stored in memory (contrast with **Accessibility**) (Ch. 5).

Availability Heuristic: a decision-making heuristic in which we judge the frequency or probability of some event on the basis of how easily examples or instances can be recalled or remembered; thus the basis of this heuristic is "ease of retrieval" (Ch. 11).

Axon: the long, extended portion of a neuron (Ch. 10).

Axon Terminals: the branch-like ending of the axon in the neuron, containing neurotransmitters (Ch. 10).

Backward Masking: see **Masking**.

Behaviorism: the movement or school of psychology in which the organism's observable behavior was the primary topic of interest, and the learning of new stimulus–response associations, whether by classical conditioning or by reinforcement principles, was deemed the most important kind of behavior to study (Ch. 1).

Beliefs: the fifth level of analysis of language, according to Miller, in which the listener's attitudes and beliefs about the speaker influence what is comprehended and remembered (Ch. 8).

Benefits: see **Facilitation**.

Bottleneck: intuitive description of the limitation of short-term memory (Ch. 1, 4).

Bottom–Up Processing: see **Data-Driven Processing**.

Bridging: Clark's (1977) term for the mental processes of reference, implication, and inference during language comprehension. Metaphorically, a bridge must be drawn from "he" back to "Gary" to comprehend the sentence "Gary pretended he wasn't interested" (Ch. 9).

Broca's Aphasia: a form of aphasia characterized by severe difficulties in the production of spoken speech; that is, the speech is hesitant, effortful, and distorted phonemically (contrast with **Wernicke's Aphasia**). The aphasia is due to damage in Broca's area, a region of the cortex next to a major motor control center (Ch. 10).

Brown–Peterson Task: a short-term memory task showing forgetting due to proactive interference (Ch. 4).

Bug: an incorrectly specified operation or procedure in a computer program that yields an error. In models of mental processing, a bug is an incorrectly learned or specified mental operation that yields an error; for example, a bug in a child's subtraction knowledge, which yields systematic errors on problems that are solved by that rule (Ch. 13).

Case Grammar: an approach in psycholinguistics in which the meaning of a sentence is determined by analyzing the semantic roles or cases played by different words, for example, which word names the overall *relationship* and which names the *agent* or *patient* of the action. Other cases include *time, location, and manner* (Ch. 8).

Case Roles (also Semantic Case): the various semantic roles or functions played by different words in a sentence; see also **Case Grammar** (Ch. 8).

Categorical Perception: the perception of similar language sounds as being the same phoneme, despite the minor physical differences among them; for example, the classification of the initial sounds of "cool" and "keep" as both being the /k/ (hard c) phoneme, even though these initial sounds differ physically (Ch. 8).

Central Executive: the major governing component in Baddeley's Working Memory; see also **Executive Control** (Ch. 4).

Cerebral Cortex: see **Neocortex**.

Cerebral Hemispheres (Left and Right): the two major structures in the neocortex. In most individuals, the left cerebral hemisphere is especially responsible for language and other symbolic processing, and the right for nonverbal, perceptual processing (Ch. 10).

Cerebral Lateralization: the principle that different functions or actions within the brain tend to be localized in one or the other hemisphere. For instance, motor control of the left side of the body is lateralized in the right hemisphere of the brain (Ch. 10).

Channel Capacity: an early analogy for the limited capacity of the human information processing system (Ch. 2).

Characteristic Feature: in the Smith et al. (1974) model of semantic memory, characteristic features are those features and properties of a concept that are common or frequent but are not essential to the meaning of the concept; for example, "eats worms" may be characteristic of BIRD, but the feature is not essential to the central meaning of the concept (contrast with **Defining Feature**) (Ch. 6).

Cherological: a term referring to the physical movements of the hands and arms in American Sign Language (ASL); two ASL signs are said to be cherologically similar if they involve similar physical movements (Ch. 4).

Chunk: a unit or grouping of information held in short-term memory (Ch. 4).

Clustering: the grouping together of related items during recall (e.g., recalling the words "apple, pear, banana, orange" together in a cluster, regardless of their order of presentation); see also **Organization** (Ch. 5).

Coarticulation: the simultaneous or overlapping articulation of two or more of the phonemes in a word (Ch. 8).

Cognition: the collection of mental processes and activities used in perceiving, remembering, thinking, and understanding, and the act of using those processes (Ch. 1).

Cognitive Economy: the principle, now largely discredited, that information is not stored redundantly in semantic memory if it can be inferred from already-stored information; under the principle, WINGS would only be stored with BIRD, rather than being stored repeatedly for ROBIN, SPARROW, EAGLE, and so on (Ch. 6).

Cognitive Science: a new term designating the study of cognition from the multiple standpoints of psychology, linguistics, computer science, and neuroscience (Ch. 1).

Competence: in linguistics, the internalized knowledge of language and its rules that fully fluent speakers of a language possess, uncontaminated by flaws in performance (contrast with **Performance**) (Ch. 8).

Computer Simulation: devising computer programs that imitate human mental processes, or devising psychological models of mental processes in the form of computer programs; largely synonymous with artificial intelligence nowadays; also, the computer program that imitates or models those mental processes (Ch. 13).

Computerized Cognition: a term referring to all computer simulation and artificial intelligence research in which human mental processes are understood by modeling or implementing them in computer programs; see also **Cognitive Science** (Ch. 13).

Conceptual Knowledge: the fourth level of analysis of language in Miller's scheme, roughly equivalent to semantic memory (Ch. 8).

Conceptually Driven Processing (also **Top–Down Processing**): mental processing is said to be conceptually driven when it is guided and assisted by the knowledge already stored in memory (contrast with **Data-Driven Processing**) (Ch. 2).

Conditional Reasoning: the form of reasoning in which the logical consequences of an IF–THEN statement and some evidence are determined; for example, given "If it rains, then the picnic will be canceled," the phrase "It is raining" determines whether or not the picnic is canceled (Ch. 11).

Confirmation Bias: in reasoning, the tendency to search for evidence that confirms a conclusion (Ch. 11).

Connectionist (also **Connectionism, Neural Net Modeling, PDP Modeling**): the terms refer to a recent development in cognitive theory, based on the notions (a) that the several levels of knowledge necessary for performance can be represented as massive, interconnected networks, (b) that performance consists of a high level of parallel processing among the several levels of knowledge, and (c) that the basic building block of these interconnected networks is the simple connection between nodes stored in memory. For instance, perception of spoken speech involves several levels of knowledge, including knowledge of phonology, of lexical information, of syntax, and of semantics. Processing at each level continually interacts with and influences processing at the other levels, in parallel. The "connections" in connectionist modeling are the network pathways both within and among the levels of knowledge (Ch. 2, 3, 10).

Conscious Attention: awareness; a slower attentional mechanism especially influenced by top–down processing (Ch. 3).

Conscious Processing: mental processing that is intentional, involves conscious awareness, and consumes mental resources (contrast with **Automatic, Automaticity**) (Ch. 2).

Consequent: in conditional reasoning, the consequent is the THEN statement; in "If it rains, then the picnic will be canceled," the consequent is "then the picnic will be canceled" (Ch. 11).

Content Accuracy: accuracy in recall, recognition, and so on, based on the content or meaning of the stimulus, rather than on the literal or verbatim stimulus that was presented (contrast with **Technical Accuracy**) (Ch. 7).

Contralaterality: the principle that control of one side of the body is localized in the opposite-side cerebral hemisphere. The fact that the left hand, for instance, is largely under the control of the right cerebral hemisphere illustrates the principle of contralaterality (Ch. 10).

Conversational Postulates: the rules, largely tacit, that govern our participation in and contributions to conversations (Ch. 9).

Cooperative Principle: the most basic of the conversational postulates, stating that participants cooperate by sharing information in an honest fashion (Ch. 9).

Corpus Callosum: the fiber of neurons that connects the left and right cerebral hemispheres (Ch. 10).

Costs: see **Inhibition**.

Data-Driven Processing (also **Bottom–Up Processing**): when mental processing of a stimulus is guided largely or exclusively by the features and elements in the pattern itself, this processing is described as being data-driven (contrast with **Conceptually Driven Processing**) (Ch. 2).

Data-Limited Performance: performance that is less than optimal because of limitations in the quality of the "data," that is, in the quality of the stimulus. Reading may be slowed down because of blurred, faint, or otherwise hard-to-perceive print, in which case the decline in performance would be described as data-limited (contrast with **Resource-Limited, Processing**) (Ch. 13).

Decay: simple loss of information across time, due presumably to some fading process, especially in sensory memory; also, an older theory of forgetting from long-term memory (Ch. 3, 4, 5).

Declarative Long-Term Memory (also **Declarative Knowledge**):

that portion of long-term memory in which facts and information are stored (contrast with **Procedural LTM** or **Procedural Knowledge**) (Ch. 2, 7, 13).

Deep Structure: in linguistics and psycholinguistics, the deep structure of a sentence refers to the meaning of the sentence; a deep structure is presumably the most basic and abstract level of representation of a sentence or idea (contrast with **Surface Structure**) (Ch. 8).

Default Value: the common or ordinary value of some variable. In script theory, default value refers to an aspect of a story or scene that conforms to the typical or ordinary state of affairs; for instance, MENU is the default value that fills the slot in a script in which customers find out what can be ordered in a restaurant (Ch. 7).

Defining Feature: in Smith et al.'s (1974) theory of semantic memory, a defining feature is a property or feature of a concept that is essential to the meaning of that concept; for instance, bearing live young is a defining feature of the concept MAMMAL (contrast with **Characteristic Feature**) (Ch. 6).

Dendrites: the branching, input structures of the neuron (Ch. 10).

Depth of Processing: see **Levels of Processing**.

Direct Theory: in conversation, a direct theory is an individual's appraisal of or informal theory about the other participant in the conversation, including information about that other person's knowledge, sophistication, and personal motives (contrast with **Second-Order Theory**) (Ch. 9).

Displacement: one of Hockett's (1960) linguistic universals, referring to the fact that language permits us to talk about times other than the immediate present; language thus permits us to "displace" ourselves in time, by talking about the past, future, and so on (Ch. 8).

Dissociations: patterns of abilities and performance, especially among brain-damaged patients, revealing that one cognitive process can be disrupted while another remains intact. In a double dissociation, two patients show opposite patterns of disruption and preserved function, further evidence that the cognitive processes are functionally and anatomically separate.

Distance Effect (also **Discriminability Effect**): an effect, seen particularly in reaction time, in which two distant or highly discriminable stimuli are more easily judged than two nearby or less discriminable stimuli; for instance, judgments are faster to "poor versus excellent" than to "good versus excellent" (Ch. 11).

Domain Knowledge: a general term referring to one's knowledge of a specific domain or topic, especially in problem solving (Ch. 12).

Downhill Change: in the simulation heuristic, a downhill change refers to an unusual or unexpected aspect of a story or situation that is changed to be more normal or customary. If a story character left work early and then was involved in a car accident, a likely downhill change would be to normalize the unusual characteristic and substitute a more customary aspect, such as leaving work on time (Ch. 11).

Dual-Coding Hypothesis: according to Paivio (1971), concrete words can be encoded into memory twice, once as verbal symbols, and once as image-based symbols, thus increasing the likelihood that they will be recalled or remembered (Ch. 5).

Dual Task Method: a method in which two tasks are performed simultaneously, such that the attentional and processing demands of one or both tasks can be assessed and then varied. Dual task methodology is commonly used in studies of attention and attention-dependent mental processing (Ch. 3).

Dysfluencies: errors, flaws, and irregularities in spoken speech (Ch. 8).

Echoic Memory: see **Auditory Sensory Memory**.

Ecological Validity: the principle, hotly debated, that research must resemble the situations and task demands that are characteristic of the real world, rather than rely on artificial laboratory settings and tasks, so that results will generalize to the real world, that is, will have ecological validity (Ch. 1).

Elaborative Rehearsal (also **Type II Rehearsal**): in the levels of processing framework, elaborative rehearsal involves any rehearsal activity that processes a stimulus into the deeper, more meaningful levels of memory; any rehearsal that involves meaning, images, and other complex information from long-term memory (contrast with **Maintenance Rehearsal**) (Ch. 2, 5).

Encode: to input or take into memory, to convert to a usable mental form, to store into memory. We are said to "encode" auditory information into sensory memory; if that information is transferred to short-term memory, then it is said to have been encoded into STM (Ch. 2).

Encoding Specificity: Tulving's hypothesis that the specific nature of an item's encoding, including all related information that was encoded along with it, determines how effectively the item can be retrieved. If you encode the word "bulb" along with the target item "light," then "bulb" has been encoded in specific relation to "light" and will serve as a better retrieval cue than some other word that was not encoded (Ch. 5).

Enhancement: in Gernsbacher's theory, the boosting of concepts' levels of activation during comprehension (Ch. 9).

Episodic Memory: Tulving's term for that portion of long-term memory in which personally experienced information is stored; one's autobiographical long-term memory (contrast with **Semantic Memory**) (Ch. 5).

Erasure: the masking or loss of information due to subsequent presentation of another stimulus; usually in sensory memory (see also **Masking**) (Ch. 3).

ERP (Event-Related Potentials): minute changes in electrical potentials in the brain, measured by EEG recording devices, and related specifically to the presentation of a particular stimulus; the research technique used for determining neural correlates of cognitive activity (Ch. 6).

Executive Control (also **Executive Controller, Central Executive**): in Baddeley's working memory system, that mechanism responsible for assessing the attentional needs of the different subsystems and furnishing attentional resources to those subsystems. Any executive or monitoring component of the memory system that is responsible for sequencing activities, keeping track of processes already completed, and diverting attention from one activity to another can be termed an executive controller (Ch. 4).

Expansion: in Schank's analysis of conversation, the additional information contained in a participant's remarks that elaborates on the conversational topic (Ch. 9).

Explicit Memory: long-term memory retrieval or performance requiring deliberate recollection or awareness (Ch. 2, 7, 10).

Eyewitness Memory: study of memory for personally experienced episodes with an emphasis on the accuracy or inaccuracy of the report as it relates to misinformation encountered since the original event (Ch. 7).

Facilitation (also **Benefits**): any positive or advantageous effect on processing, usually because of prior presentation of related information; in RT research, a speed-up of RT due to related information (Ch. 6).

False Alarm (also **False Positive**): an error in a recognition task in which a response of "yes" is made to a "new" stimulus; any "yes" response in recognition when a "no" response is correct (Ch. 7).

Familiarity Bias: in reasoning, the bias in the availability heuristic in which personal familiarity influences estimates of frequency, probability, and so on (Ch. 11).

Fast Process Task: Eysenck's (1982) term for those RT tasks requiring fairly simple decisions (e.g., yes/no), generally performed within a second or two by adult subjects, and generally composed of fairly automatic processes; for example, the lexical decision task (contrast with **Slow Process Task**) (Ch. 2).

Feature Detection (also **Feature Analysis**): a theoretical approach, most commonly in pattern recognition, in which stimuli (patterns) are identified by breaking them up into their constituent features (Ch. 3).

Feature List: see **Semantic Features**.

Filter Theories: especially in auditory perception, those theories that hypothesize some filtering or screening out of unwanted, unattended messages so that only the attended message is encoded into the central processing mechanism (e.g., Broadbent's filter theory) (Ch. 3).

Fixation: in visual perception, the pause during which the eye is virtually stationary and is taking in visual information; also, the visual point on which the eyes focus during the fixation pause (see also **Gaze Duration**) (Ch. 3, 9).

Flashbulb Memories: memories of specific, emotionally salient events, reported subjectively to be as detailed and accurate as a photograph, but now considered to be no different than any other highly accurate memory (Ch. 5).

Flexibility of Symbols: the characteristic that enables the meaning of a language symbol to be changed, and that enables new symbols to be added to the language (Ch. 8).

Focal Attention: Neisser's (1967) term for mental attention directed toward, for example, the contents of visual sensory memory, and therefore responsible for transferring that information into short-term memory (Ch. 3).

Forgetting: colloquially, losing information previously stored in memory. More technically, the term usually implies that the stored information is no longer in memory, that it is no longer available in the memory system (Ch. 5).

Formant: a concentration of physical energy in the spoken sounds of language, centered on one of several levels (e.g., in the spoken word "tool," the first formant, the concentration of energy at the lowest level, is centered at about 1000 cps) (Ch. 3, 8).

Fovea: the highly sensitive region of the retina responsible for precise, focused vision, composed largely of cones (Ch. 3).

Frames: in script theory, the slots or events in a stored script. In the restaurant script, for instance, there are frames for "How the customer gets the food" and "Who prepares the food" (Ch. 7).

Free Recall: the memory task in which the list items may be recalled in any order, regardless of their order of presentation (contrast with **Serial Recall**) (Ch. 4, 5).

Functional Fixedness: in problem solving, an inability to think of or consider any but the customary uses for objects and tools (Ch. 12).

Functionalism: the movement in psychology, closely associated with James, in which the functions of various mental and physical capacities were studied (contrast with **Structuralism**) (Ch. 1).

Fuzzy Boundaries: a characteristic of natural categories, in which the boundary of category membership is indistinct or fuzzy. For example, is CHICKEN a member of the BIRD or FARM ANIMAL category? (Ch. 6).

Garden-Path Sentence: a sentence in which an early word or phrase tends to be misinterpreted and thus must be reinterpreted after the mistake is noticed; for example, "After the musician played the piano was moved off the stage" (Ch. 8).

Gaze Duration: how long the eyes fixate on a specific word during reading, the principal measure of on-line comprehension during reading (Ch. 9).

Generativity: see **Productivity**.

Gestalt: a German term adopted into psychological terminology referring to an entire pattern, form, or configuration. The term always carries the connotation that decomposing a pattern into its components will in some way lose the essential "wholeness" of the cohesive pattern (Ch. 12).

Gist: general meaning, especially of a passage of text or prose (Ch. 7).

Goal: in problem solving, the end-point or solution to the problem, the ending state toward which the problem-solving attempt is directed (Ch. 12).

GPS (General Problem Solver): the first serious computer-based model of problem solving, by Newell, Shaw, and Simon (1958) (Ch. 12).

Grammar: in linguistics and psycholinguistics, a set of rules for forming the words and/or sentences in a language; optimally, the complete set of rules that characterizes a language, such that the rules will generate only acceptable or legal sentences and will not generate any sentences that are unacceptable (Ch. 8).

Hardware: in computers, the physical machinery of the computer (contrast with software, the programs that run on a computer); in humans, by metaphoric extension, the physical medium of mental processes, for example, the cerebral cortex and sensory mechanisms (contrast with mental "software," the learned skills and processes that operate within the physical system) (Ch. 2).

Headers: in script theory, the key phrases or words that activate a script; for example, "hungry" or "waitress" for the Restaurant script (Ch. 7).

Hemispheric Specialization: the principle that each of the cerebral hemispheres has specialized functions and abilities (Ch. 10).

Heuristic: an informal, "rule of thumb" method for solving problems, not necessarily guaranteed to solve the problem correctly, but usually considerably faster or more tractable than the correct algorithm (Ch. 11).

Hindsight Bias: in reasoning, the bias or attitude that some already completed event was in fact very likely to have had just that outcome (Ch. 11).

Hippocampus: an internal brain structure, just internal to the temporal lobes, strongly implicated in the storing of new information into long-term memory (Ch. 10).

Homunculous: the classic term for the unseen, internal "little man" who performs some mental task. The term generally has a negative connotation, since an explanation for some mental operation that falls back on the notion of a homunculous often endows the homunculous with exactly the characteristics that were originally to be explained (Ch. 2).

Horizontal Change: in the simulation heuristic, substituting one detail in a story or situation for another, where both are at the same level of generality or "commonness"; for example, changing "left work early" to "had a flat tire," both details being somewhat out of the ordinary (Ch. 11).

Icon: the contents of iconic (visual sensory) memory; the brief-duration visual image or record of a visual stimulus held in visual sensory memory (Ch. 3).

Iconic Memory: see **Visual Sensory Memory**.

Ill-Defined Problem: a problem in which the initial, intermediate, or final goal states are poorly or vaguely defined, and/or a problem in which the legal operators (moves) are not well specified (Ch. 12).

Implication: an unstated connection or conclusion that was nonetheless intended by a speaker (Ch. 9).

Implicit Memory: long-term memory performance affected by prior experience with no necessary awareness of the influence (Ch. 1, 2, 7).

Independent and Nonoverlapping Stages: in the strict information processing approach, the assumption that the several mental stages that must be performed are independent of one another, do not mutually influence one another's operation, and occur sequentially, that is, do not overlap in time as they are performed; a central assumption in the process model approach (Ch. 2).

Indirect Request: a question or statement that is not intended to be taken literally, but instead is a polite way of expressing the intended meaning; for example, "Do you have the time?" is an indirect way of asking "What time is it?" (Ch. 9).

Inference: drawing a conclusion based on some statement, for example, in conversation or reading (Ch. 9).

Inferred/Intended Topic: the idea inferred by the listener/intended by the speaker to be the conversational topic (Ch. 9).

Information: in the technical sense of the term, information refers to uncertainty, measured in "bits." To illustrate, it takes three bits of information to determine which of eight equally likely alternatives is the correct choice. More generally, the term refers to (stimulus) material, knowledge, and so on; for example, "to encode information into the sensory system" or "to retrieve information from long-term memory" (Ch. 2).

Information Processing Approach: broadly defined, the approach that describes cognition as the coordinated operation of active mental processes within a multicomponent memory system. As it was originally used, the term referred to mental processing as a sequence of mental operations, each operation taking in information, manipulating or changing it in some fashion, then forwarding the result on to the next stage for further processing. Nowadays, the term is taken to refer more generally to the fact that humans encode and process information (Ch. 2).

Inhibition (also **Costs**): any negative or disadvantageous effect on processing, usually because of prior presentation of some specific kind of information; in RT research, a slowing of RT due to the prior information (Ch. 6).

Insight/Illumination: said to be an essential step in creativity and problem solving, though little if any research supports this notion empirically (Ch. 12).

Interference: an explanation for "forgetting" of some target information, in which related or recent information competes with or causes the loss of the target information (Ch. 4, 5).

Internal Structure: natural categories are said to have internal structure, that is, to display members that differ in their degree of typicality or "goodness," as distinct from "all or none" membership in artificial categories (Ch. 6).

Intersection: in network models, the connecting pathway between two concepts, the location where activation from two separate nodes meets (Ch. 6).

Introspection: the largely abandoned method of investigation in which subjects "look inward" and describe their mental processes and thoughts; historically, the method of investigation promoted by Wundt and Titchener (Ch. 1).

Isa: in network models of semantic memory, the superordinate pathway or link; for instance, an "isa" pathway connects ROBIN and BIRD, as in "Robin *isa* Bird" (Ch. 6).

jnd (Just Noticeable Difference): in psychophysics, the amount by which two stimuli must differ in order that the difference can be perceived (Ch. 11).

Lag: in studies of mental processing, the number of intervening trials between a prime and a target (Ch. 6).

Language: a shared system for symbolic communication (Ch. 8).

Lesion: any damage to brain tissue, regardless of cause (e.g., from an accident, stroke, or surgery) (Ch. 10).

Levels of Processing (also **Depth of Processing**): Craik and Lockhart's (1972) alternative to the standard three-component memory model. Information subjected only to maintenance rehearsal is not being processed more deeply into the meaning-based levels of the memory system and therefore tends not to be recalled or recognized as accurately as information subjected to elaborative rehearsal (Ch. 5).

Lexical Ambiguity: the term refers to the fact that a word may have more than one meaning; for example, "bank" (Ch. 6).

Lexical Decision Task: a simple yes/no task in which subjects are timed as they decide if the letter string being presented is a word or not; sometimes called simply the word/nonword task (Ch. 2).

Lexicon: see **Mental Lexicon.**

Linguistic Intuitions: one's subjective judgments that a sentence is or is not "acceptable" or "correct"; the basis for most theorizing in linguistics (Ch. 8).

Linguistic Relativity Hypothesis: the hypothesis, credited to Whorf, that one's language determines—or at least influences strongly—what one can think about (Ch. 8).

Linguistics: the discipline that studies language as a formal system (Ch. 8).

Linguistic Universals: features and characteristics that are universally true of all human languages (see also **Displacement, Productivity**) (Ch. 8).

Location: the semantic case or argument in a proposition specifying the place or location of some event (Ch. 7).

Long-Term Memory (LTM): that portion of the memory system responsible for holding information for more than a period of seconds or minutes; virtually permanent storage of information (Ch. 2).

LTM: see **Long-Term Memory.**

Maintenance Rehearsal (also **Type I Rehearsal**): in the levels of processing approach, rehearsal that merely repeats, recycles, or "refreshes" information at a particular level via repetition, without processing it to deeper, more meaningful levels of storage (Ch. 5).

Mapping: in Gernsbacher's theory, drawing the connections between words and their meanings to the overall meaning of the sentence; in general, the process of determining the connections between two sets of elements (Ch. 9).

Masking: an effect, often in perception experiments, in which a mask or pattern is presented very shortly after a stimulus, and disrupts or even prevents the perception of the earlier stimulus (see also **Erasure**) (Ch. 3).

Means–End Analysis: a major heuristic in problem solving, assessing the distance between the current and the goal states, then applying some operator that reduces that distance (Ch. 12).

Memory: the mental processes of acquiring and retaining information for later retrieval; the mental storage system that enables these processes (Ch. 1).

Memory Impairment: a specific interpretation of early eyewitness memory results, in which a subsequent piece of information replaces a memory formed earlier, thus impairing memory for the original information (Ch. 7).

Memory Set: in any mental comparison or memory search task, the items held in memory (often short-term memory) so that a later probe or test item can be compared to them (Ch. 4).

Mental Lexicon: the "mental dictionary" of long-term memory, that is, that portion of long-term memory in which words and word meanings are stored (Ch. 6).

Mental Model: the mental representation of some situation or physical device; for example, an individual's mental model of the physical motion of bodies, or an individual's mental model of a home heating thermostat (Ch. 11).

Mental Rotation: mental manipulation of a visual short-term memory code that reorients the imaged object in space (Ch. 4).

Metacognition: awareness and monitoring of one's own cognitive state or condition; knowledge about one's own cognitive processes and memory system (Ch. 2, 5).

Metamemory: knowledge about one's own memory system and its functioning (Ch. 5).

Metatheory: a general theoretical framework, consisting of the assumptions made by practitioners of a science that guide the research activities of those practitioners (Ch. 2).

Method of Loci: a classic mnemonic device in which the to-be-remembered items are mentally placed, one by one, into a set of prememorized locations, with retrieval consisting of a mental "walk" through the locations (Ch. 5).

Misinformation Acceptance: the tendency to accept information presented after some critical event as being true of the original event itself; for example, accepting, then reporting, that a Yield sign had appeared in an earlier description of a traffic accident (Ch. 7).

Mnemonic Device: any mental device or strategy that provides a useful rehearsal strategy for storing and remembering difficult material; see **Method of Loci**, for instance (Ch. 5).

Modality Effect: in sensory memory research, the advantage in recall of the last few items in a list when those items have been presented orally rather than visually (Ch. 3).

Mood Congruence Effect: that memory for emotional information will be better if the learner was in the same emotional or mood state (Ch. 13).

Morpheme: smallest unit of meaning in language (Ch. 8).

Move: a turn in conversation; in problem solving, a single step, an action of a single problem-solving operator (Ch. 9, 12).

Naive Physics: a term referring to the study of people's misconceptions about the motion of physical objects, for example, a ball rolling off a cliff (Ch. 11).

Naming: the characteristic that human languages have names or labels for all the objects and concepts encountered by the speakers of the language (e.g., as opposed to most animal communication systems (Ch. 8).

Natural Categories: in research on categorization (see especially Rosch, 1975, 1978) in semantic memory, those groupings or clusters of objects and concepts that occur naturally in the world; that is, groups of objects that resemble one another, share common features and uses; as distinct from artificial categories such as "mammal," which rely on a technical definition for category membership (Ch. 6).

Negative Set: in problem solving, a tendency to become accustomed to a single approach or way of thinking about a problem, making it difficult to recognize or generate alternative approaches (Ch. 12).

Neocortex (also **Cerebral Cortex**): the top layer of the brain, newest (*neo-*) in terms of the evolution of the species, divided into left and right hemispheres; the locus of most higher-level mental processes (Ch. 10).

Network: a structure for information stored in long-term semantic memory, assumed by several popular models of mental processing. In most network models, concepts are represented as nodes that are interconnected by means of links or pathways; activation is presumed to spread from concept to concept along these connecting pathways (Ch. 6).

Neural Net Modeling: see **Connectionist**.

Neurocognition: a term referring to the neurological basis of cognition, and to the study of the combination of neurological and cognitive factors (Ch. 10).

Neuron: a specialized cell that conducts neural information through the nervous system, the basic building block of the nervous system (Ch. 10).

Neurotransmitter: the chemical substance released into the synapse between two neurons, responsible for either activating or inhibiting the next neuron in sequence (Ch. 10).

Node: especially in network models, a point or location in the long-term memory representation of knowledge; a concept or its representation in memory (Ch. 6).

Nonsense Syllable: a combination of letters, usually a consonant–vowel–consonant (C-V-C) pattern, that does not form a word or a meaningful pattern, used as list items in an experiment; the meaningless stimuli Ebbinghaus used in his research (Ch. 5).

Object: see **Patient**.

On-Line Comprehension Tasks: tasks in which measurements of performance are obtained as comprehension takes place; "on-line" means happening and being measured "right now" (Ch. 9).

Operator: in problem solving, a legal move or operation that can occur during solution of a problem; the set of legal moves within some problem space (e.g., in algebra, one operator is "multiply both sides by the same number") (Ch. 12).

Organization: especially in studies of episodic long-term memory, the tendency to recall related words together, or the tendency to impose some form of grouping or clustering on information being stored in/retrieved from memory; related to "chunking" or grouping in short-term memory (Ch. 5).

Paired-Associate Learning (P-A Learning): a task in which pairs of items, respectively the stimulus and response terms, are to be learned, so that upon presentation of a stimulus, the response term can be recalled; a favorite learning task during the verbal learning period of human experimental psychology (Ch. 5).

Pandemonium: Selfridge's early model of letter identification (Ch. 3).

Parallel Distributed Processing (PDP): see **Connectionist**.

Parallel Processing: any mental processing in which more than one process or operation is occurring simultaneously (Ch. 2).

Parse: to divide or separate the words in a sentence into logical or meaningful groupings (Ch. 8).

Partial Report: an experimental condition in Sperling's (1960) research in which only a randomly selected portion of the entire stimulus display was to be reported (contrast with **Whole Report**) (Ch. 3).

PAS (Precategorical Acoustic Storage): Crowder's (1972) hypothesized component of the auditory perceptual system, in which acoustic information is held temporarily in unanalyzed form; roughly synonymous with auditory sensory memory (Ch. 3).

Pathway: in network representations in long-term memory, the connecting link between two concepts or nodes (Ch. 6).

Patient: the object or recipient that receives the action in a sentence; one of the semantic cases in a case grammar approach (see also **Case Grammar**) (Ch. 8).

PDP Modeling: see **Connectionist**.

Peg-Word Mnemonic: the mnemonic device in which a prememorized set of peg-word connections is used to remember some new information; the peg words typically used are "One is a bun, Two is a shoe," and so on (Ch. 5).

Perception: the process of interpreting and understanding sensory information; the act of sensing and then interpreting that information (Ch. 3).

Performance: any observable behavior; in the context of linguistics, any behavior related to language (e.g., speech), influenced not only by linguistic factors but also by factors related to lapses in attention, memory, and so on (contrast with **Competence**) (Ch. 8).

Phoneme: a sound or set of sounds judged to be "the same" by speakers of a language (e.g., the initial sound in the words "cool" and "keep" for speakers of English). Note that because of categorical perception, we tend to judge some physically different sounds as "the same," and other different sounds as "different," that is, belonging to a different phoneme category (Ch. 3, 8).

Phonemic Competence: one's basic knowledge of the phonology of the language (Ch. 8).

Phonology: the study of the sounds of language, including how they are produced and how they are perceived (Ch. 8).

Phrase Structure: the underlying structure of a sentence in terms of the groupings of words into meaningful phrases; for example, [The young man] [ran quickly] (Ch. 8).

PI: see **Proactive Interference**.

Plan: in script theory, a mental structure derived from known scripts, enabling us to understand situations we've never encountered (Ch. 7).

Planning: (in psycholinguistics) the sequencing of various components necessary for uttering a spoken sentence; for example, translating the idea into words or adding stress and inflection (Ch. 8).

Plasticity: that the functions of a damaged region of the brain may be taken over by another region (Ch. 10).

Pragmatics: those aspects of language that are "above and beyond" the words, so-called extralinguistic factors. For instance, part of our pragmatic knowledge of language rules includes the knowledge that the sentence "Do you happen to know what time it is?" is actually an indirect request, rather than a sentence to be taken literally (Ch. 9).

Primacy Effect: in a recall task, the elevation of recall at the early positions of the list (contrast with **Recency Effect**) (Ch. 4, 5).

Prime: the first stimulus in a two-part, prime–target pair, intended to exert some influence on the second stimulus (see also **Priming**) (Ch. 6).

Priming: mental activation of a concept by some means, or the spread of that activation from one concept to another; also, the activation of some target information by action of a previously presented "prime"; sometimes loosely synonymous with the notion of "accessing" information in memory (Ch. 3, 6).

Proactive Interference (PI): interference or difficulty, especially during recall, because of some previous activity, often the stimuli learned on some earlier list; any interference in which material presented at one time interferes with material presented later (Ch. 4, 5).

Probe Item: in the Sternberg short-term memory paradigm, the probe item is the letter to be searched for in the memory set; it is the test item, to which subjects make a yes or no response (Ch. 4).

Problem of Invariance: in psycholinguistics, the problem that spoken sounds are *not* invariant, that they change depending on what sounds precede and follow in the word (Ch. 8).

Problem Space: the initial, intermediate, and goal states in a problem, along with the problem-solver's knowledge and any external resources that can be used to solve the problem (Ch. 12).

Procedural Knowledge: knowledge of "how to do" something; that part of Anderson's (1983) ACT* model dealing with knowledge of processes and procedures (e.g., how to add, how to ride a bicycle) (Ch. 2, 13).

Procedural LTM: see **Procedural Knowledge**.

Processing Efficiency: Eysenck and Calvo's (1992) hypothesis regarding the effects of anxiety on performance, that processing efficiency is the quality of performance divided by mental effort, where anxiety will have its main effects on effort (Ch. 13).

Process Model: a stage model designed to explain the several mental steps involved in performance to some task, usually implying that the stages occur sequentially and that they operate independently of one another (Ch. 2, 4).

Production, Production System: a production is a simple IF–THEN rule in models of memory processing, stating the conditions (IF) necessary for some action (THEN) to be taken, whether that action is a physical response or a mental step or operation. A production system is a large-scale model of some kind of performance or mental activity based on productions (see especially **ACT***) (Ch. 7).

Productivity (also **Generativity**): one of Hockett's (1960) linguistic universals, referring to the rule-based nature of language, such that an infinite number of sentences can be generated or produced by applying the rules of the language (Ch. 8).

Property Statements: simple statements in which the relationship being expressed is "X *has the property* or *feature* Y" (e.g., A robin has wings) (Ch. 6).

Proposition: a simple semantic relation between two concepts; a basic unit of meaning, expressing a simple relationship or idea; the representation of the meaning of an entire sentence, including all the relationships among all the words (Ch. 6, 7).

Prototype: the typical or average member of a category; the central or most representative member of a category. Note that a prototype may not exist for some categories, in which case the category's prototype would be some "average-like" combination of the various members (Ch. 6).

Psycholinguistics: the study of language from the perspective of psychology; the study of language behavior and processes (Ch. 8).

Psychophysics: the study of the relationship between physical stimuli and the perceived characteristics of those stimuli; the study of how perceptual experience differs from the physical stimulation that is being perceived (Ch. 11).

Reaction Time (RT): the elapsed time, usually measured in milliseconds, between some stimulus event and the subject's response to that event; a particularly common measure of performance in cognitive psychology (Ch. 1, 6).

Recall: see **Free Recall** and **Serial Recall**.

Recency Effect: in recall performance, the elevated recall of the last few items in a list, due presumably to the items being stored in and retrieved from short-term memory (contrast with **Primacy Effect**) (Ch. 4).

Recipient: see **Patient**.

Recoding: mentally transforming or translating a stimulus into another code or format; grouping items into larger units; for example, recoding a written word into an acoustic–articulatory code (Ch. 2, 4).

Recognition Task: any yes/no task in which subjects are asked to judge whether or not they have seen the stimulus before; more generally, any task asking for a simple yes/no (alternatively, true/false, same/different) response, often including a reaction time measurement of the time to respond (Ch. 5).

Reconstructive Memory: the tendency in recall or recognition to include ideas or elements that were inferred or related to the original stimulus but were not part of the original stimulus itself (Ch. 7).

Recursive: especially in problem solving, repeated application of an embedded set of moves or procedures (Ch. 12).

Reductionism: the scientific approach in which a complex event or behavior is broken down into its constituents, the individual constituents then being studied individually (Ch. 1).

Reference: in language, the allusion to or indirect mention of an element from elsewhere in the sentence or passage, for example, by using a pronoun or synonym (Ch. 9).

Rehearsal: the mental repetition or practicing of some to-be-learned material (Ch. 4, 5).

Rehearsal Buffer: the component of short-term memory that holds information currently being rehearsed (Ch. 4, 5).

Relation: in case grammar, the central idea or relationship being asserted in a sentence or phrase. For instance, in "Bill hit the ball with the bat," the central relation is HIT (see also **Case Grammar**) (Ch. 7, 8).

Relearning Task: an experimental task in which some material is learned, set aside for a period of time, and then relearned to the same criterion, in hopes that the relearning will require less time or effort to achieve the same level of accuracy; the task used by Ebbinghaus in his research on memory (Ch. 5).

Release from PI (Release from Proactive Interference): the sudden reduction in proactive interference when the material to be learned is changed in some fashion; for example, improved recall on a list of plant names after several trials involving animal names. The initial decline was due to proactive interference, and the improvement on the last trial is due to release from PI (Ch. 4).

Repetition Priming: a priming effect due to the exact repetition of a stimulus; often used in implicit memory tests (Ch. 7, 10).

Representation: a general term referring to the way information is stored in memory. The term always carries the connotation that we are interested in the format or organization of the information as it is stored (Is the information stored in a semantic representation? A sound-based representation?) (Ch. 2).

Representation of Knowledge: see **Representation**.

Representativeness Heuristic: a reasoning heuristic in which we judge the likelihood of some event by deciding how representative that event seems to be of the larger group or population from which it was drawn (Ch. 11).

Resource-Limited Processing: mental processing that is limited or less than optimal because of limitations in the mental resources that can be devoted to it; for instance, in a dual task procedure, where one task captures much of the available mental attention, flawed or less than optimal performance on the second task is said to be resource-limited (Ch. 13).

Retina: the layer of the eye covered with the rods and cones that initiate the process of visual sensation and perception (Ch. 3).

Retrieval Cue: any cue, hint, or piece of information that is used to prompt retrieval of some target information (Ch. 5).

Retroactive Interference: the interference from a recent event or experience that influences memory for an earlier event; for instance, trying to recall the items from list 1, but instead, recalling the items from list 2 (Ch. 4).

Rewrite Rules: in a phrase structure grammar, the rules that specify the individual components of a phrase; for example, a noun phrase is rewritten as a determiner, an adjective, and a noun, NP → det + (adj) + N (Ch. 8).

RI: see **Retroactive Interference**.

RT: see **Reaction Time**.

Saccade: the voluntary sweeping of the eyes from one fixation point to another (Ch. 3).

Salience, Vividness: sources of bias in the availability heuristic, in which a particularly notable or vivid memory influences judgments about the frequency or likelihood of such events (Ch. 11).

SAM (Script Applier Mechanism): Schank's model of comprehension based on scripted knowledge (Ch. 13).

Satisficing: finding an acceptable or satisfactory solution to a problem, even though the solution may not be optimal (Ch. 12).

Savings Score: in a relearning task, the score showing how much was saved on second learning, compared to original learning. For instance, if original learning took ten trials and relearning required only six trials, then savings would be 40%, $(10 - 6)/10 \times 100$ (Ch. 5).

Schema (plural—Schemata): in Bartlett's (1932) words, "an active organisation of past reactions or past experiences" (p. 201); a knowledge structure in memory (Ch. 7).

Script: Schank's term for a schema, a long-term memory representation of some complex event like "going to a restaurant" (Ch. 7).

Search Tree: the entire set of possible solutions to a problem that must be searched in some fashion in order to solve the problem (Ch. 12).

Second-Order Theory: in conversation, the informal theory we develop that expresses our knowledge of what the other participant knows about us, summarized by the phrase "what he/she thinks I know" (contrast with **Direct Theory**) (Ch. 9).

Self-Terminating: a description of mental processes, especially memory search processes, that end when the sought-for information is found (contrast with **Serial Exhaustive Search**) (Ch. 4).

Semantic Case (also **Case Roles**): in a case grammar approach, the particular case played by a word or concept is said to be that word's semantic case (see also **Case Grammar**) (Ch. 8).

Semantic Congruity Effect: in the mental comparison task, reaction time is speeded or judgments are made easier when the basis for a judgment is congruent or similar to the stimuli being compared; for instance, a congruent condition would be "choose the smaller of second versus minute," and an incongruent condition would be "choose the smaller of decade versus century" (Ch. 11).

Semantic Distance Effect: see **Semantic Relatedness Effect**.

Semantic Features (also **Feature List**): properties or characteristics stored in the mental representation of some concept, presumed by some theories to be accessed and evaluated in the process of making semantic judgments (Ch. 6).

Semantic Integration: the tendency to store related pieces of information into an integrated, unified representation (Ch. 7).

Semanticity: one of Hockett's (1960) linguistic universals, expressing the fact that the elements of language convey meaning (Ch. 8).

Semantic Memory: the long-term memory component in which general world knowledge, including knowledge of language, is stored (contrast with **Episodic Memory**) (Ch. 2, 6).

Semantic Relatedness Effect: in semantic memory tasks, reaction time is speeded up or judgments are made easier when the concepts are "closer together" in semantic distance, when they are more closely related. Note that the effect is reversed when the comparison is false; that is, RT is slower for the comparison "A whale is a fish" than for "A whale is a bird" (Ch. 6).

Semantics: the study of meaning (Ch. 8).

Sensation: the reception of physical stimulation and encoding of it into the nervous system (Ch. 3).

Sensory Memory: the initial mental storage system for sensory stimuli. There are presumably as many modalities of sensory memory as there are kinds of stimulation that we can sense (Ch. 2).

Sentence Verification Task: a task in which subjects must respond true or false to simple sentences (Ch. 6).

Sequential Stages of Processing: an assumption in most process models that the separate stages of processing occur in a fixed sequence, with no overlap among the stages (Ch. 2).

Serial Exhaustive Search: a search process in which all possible elements are searched one by one before the decision is made, even if the target is found early in the search process (contrast with **Self-Terminating** search) (Ch. 4).

Serial Position Curve: the display of accuracy in recall across the original positions in the to-be-learned list; often found to have a "bowed" shape, indicating lower recall in the middle of the list than in the initial or final positions (Ch. 4, 5).

Serial Processing: mental processing in which only one process or operation occurs at a time (Ch. 2).

Serial Recall: a recall task in which subjects must recall the list items in their original order of presentation (contrast with **Free Recall**) (Ch. 4).

Shadowing Task: a task in which subjects hear some spoken message and must repeat the message out loud at a very short lag; often used as one of the two tasks in a dual task method (Ch. 3).

Short-Term Memory (STM): that component of the human memory system that holds information for up to 20 seconds or so; the memory component where current and recently attended information is held; sometimes loosely equated with attention and consciousness (Ch. 2, 4).

Simulation Heuristic: a reasoning heuristic in which we predict some future event, or imagine a different outcome to completed events; a forecasting of how some event will turn out or how it might have turned out under another set of circumstances (Ch. 11).

Slow Process Task: any mental task requiring considerable time for completion (e.g., from several seconds up to several minutes or more), usually involving a fairly high degree of conscious processing (contrast with **Fast Process Task**) (Ch. 2).

SOA: see **Stimulus Onset Asynchrony**.

Software: in computer science, the programs that run on a computer. Metaphorically, "software" refers to learned procedures and processes that operate in the human cognitive system (Ch. 2).

Soma: the central portion of a neuron, containing the cell nucleus (Ch. 10).

Span of Apprehension (also **Span of Attention**): the number of simple elements (e.g., digits, letters) that can be heard and immediately reported in their correct order; a standard short-term memory task, appearing frequently on standardized intelligence tests (Ch. 3).

Split Brain: refers to patients in whom the corpus callosum has been severed surgically, and the resultant changes in their performance because of the surgery, or more generally, to research showing various specializations of the two cerebral hemispheres (Ch. 10).

Spotlight Attention: a rapid attentional mechanism operating in parallel and automatically across the visual field, especially for detection of simple visual features (Ch. 3).

Spreading Activation: the commonly assumed theoretical process by which long-term memory knowledge is accessed and retrieved. Some form of mental excitation or "activation" is believed to be passed or "spread" along the pathways that connect concepts in a memory network. When a concept has been activated, it has been retrieved or accessed within the memory representation. The process is loosely analogous to the spread of neural excitation within the brain (Ch. 6).

Stereotypes: in reasoning, bias in judgments related to the typical characteristics of a profession, type of person, and so on (Ch. 11).

Sternberg Task: the short-term memory scanning task devised by Saul Sternberg (Ch. 4).

Stimulus Onset Asynchrony (SOA): in priming studies, the interval of time separating the prime and the target, usually on the order of a few hundred milliseconds (Ch. 6).

STM: see **Short-Term Memory**.

Structuralism: the approach, most closely identified with Wundt and Titchener, in which the structure of the conscious mind—that is, the sensations, images, and feelings that were the elements of consciousness—was studied; the first major school of psychological thought, beginning with Wundt in the late 1800s (contrast with **Functionalism**) (Ch. 1).

Structure Building: the process of comprehension in Gernsbacher's theory, of building a mental representation of the meaning of sentences (Ch. 9).

Subgoal: in problem solving, an intermediate goal that must be achieved in order to reach some final goal (Ch. 12).

Subjective Organization: the grouping or organizing of items that are to be learned according to some scheme or basis devised by the subject (Ch. 5).

Suppression: in Gernsbacher's theory, the active process of reducing the activation level of concepts no longer relevant to the meaning of a sentence (Ch. 9).

Surface Structure: in linguistics and psycholinguistics, the actual form of a sentence, whether written or spoken (contrast with **Deep Structure**); the literal string of words or sounds present in a sentence (Ch. 8).

Syllogism (also **Categorical Syllogism**): a classical reasoning form composed of two premises and one conclusion, in which the logical truth of the conclusion must be derived from the premises (Ch. 11).

Symbolic Comparison: mental comparisons of symbols, for instance, digits, usually in a "choose smaller/larger" task (Ch. 11).

Symbolic Distance Effect: the result, in symbolic comparison tasks, in which two relatively different stimuli (e.g., 1 and 8) are judged more rapidly than two relatively similar stimuli (e.g., 1 and 2), because of greater symbolic distance between 1 and 8 (Ch. 11).

Synapse: the junction of two neurons; the small gap between the terminal buttons of one neuron and the dendrites of another; as a verb, to form a junction with another neuron (Ch. 10).

Syntax: the arrangement of words as elements in a sentence to show their relationship to one another; grammatical structure; the rules governing the order of words in a sentence (Ch. 8).

Tabula Rasa: Latin term meaning "blank slate." The term refers to a standard assumption of behaviorists, that learning and experience write a record on the "blank slate"; in other words, the assumption that learning, as opposed to innate factors, is the most important factor in determining behavior (Ch. 1).

Tachistoscope (also T-scope): an apparatus designed to present visual stimuli in a controlled position for a short period of time, usually on the order of milliseconds; nowadays, visual stimuli are often presented via computer, in tachistoscopic fashion (Ch. 3).

Tacit Knowledge: knowledge that is not openly expressed or consciously considered, but which affects performance nonetheless; inferred knowledge and relationships (Ch. 2).

Target: the second part of a two-part, prime–target stimulus (see **Priming**); any concept or material that is designated as being of special interest (Ch. 6).

Technical Accuracy: accuracy in recall or recognition that is scored according to verbatim criteria (contrast with **Content Accuracy**) (Ch. 7).

Template: a model or pattern. In theories of pattern recognition, a template would be the pattern stored in memory against which incoming stimuli would be compared in order to recognize the incoming patterns (Ch. 3).

Thalamus: a small structure in the brain through which most sensory information is relayed en route to the cerebral cortex (Ch. 10).

Thematic Effects: a "reconstructive memory" influence on recall or recognition when the individual's knowledge of the theme influences performance (see also **Content Accuracy**, **Reconstructive Memory**) (Ch. 7).

Top–Down Processing: see **Conceptually Driven Processing**.

TOT (Tip-of-the-Tongue) Effect: momentary retrieval failure, with the sense of being on the verge of retrieving the target concept (Ch. 5, 10).

Transformational Grammar: Chomsky's theory of the structure of language, a combination of a phrase structure grammar plus a set of transformational rules (Ch. 8).

Transformational Rules: in Chomsky's transformational grammar, the syntactic rules that transform an idea (a deep structure sentence) into its surface structure; for instance, rules that form a passive sentence or a negative sentence (Ch. 8).

Turing Test: a hypothetical test, named after Turing, in which one assesses the quality of a computer simulation/artificial intelligence program by trying to distinguish its output from a human's answers to the same questions (Ch. 13).

Type I/II Rehearsal: see **Maintenance** and **Elaborative Rehearsal**.

Typical (also Central, Focal): in semantic categories, the most representative, most commonly thought of, instance or member of the category; the central tendency of a category (Ch. 6).

Typicality Effect: in semantic memory research, the result that typical members of a category tend to be judged more rapidly than atypical members (Ch. 6).

Unauthorized: not intended, especially said of inferences drawn during a conversation (contrast with **Authorized**) (Ch. 9).

Unconscious Processing: mental processing outside of awareness (Ch. 2, 7).

Undoing: in the simulation heuristic, the changing of details or events in a story so as to alter the (unfortunate or undesirable) outcome (Ch. 11).

Unit: in short-term memory, a grouping or clustering of information together into a functional whole; the informational "packet" held in short-term memory (Ch. 4).

Uphill Change: in the simulation heuristic, changing a common or ordinary detail to an unusual one, so as to alter the outcome of the situation or story (Ch. 11).

Verbal Learning: the branch of human experimental psychology, largely replaced by cognitive psychology in the late 1950s and early 1960s, investigating the learning and retention of "verbal," that is, language-based, stimuli; influenced directly by Ebbinghaus's methods and interests (Ch. 1).

Verbal Protocol: in studies of problem solving, a word-for-word transcription of what the subject said aloud during the problem-solving attempt (Ch. 12).

Visual Imagery: the mental representation of visual information; the skill or ability to remember visual information (Ch. 5).

Visual Persistence: the perceptual phenomenon in which a visual stimulus still seems to be present even after its termination, usually on the order of a few hundred milliseconds to a few seconds (Ch. 3).

Visual Sensory Memory (also **Iconic Memory**): the short-duration memory system specialized for holding visual information, lasting no more than about 250–500 milliseconds (Ch. 3).

Visuo-Spatial Sketchpad: the visual/perceptual component of Baddeley's Working Memory model (Ch. 4).

von Restorff Effect: in a recall task, the elevated accuracy for an item that was noticeably different during list presentation, for instance, because it was written in a different color of ink (Ch. 5).

Well-Defined Problem: a problem in which the initial and final states and the legal operators are all clearly specified (Ch. 12).

Wernicke's Aphasia: one of two common forms of aphasia in which the language disorder is characterized by a serious disruption of comprehension, and the use of "invented" words as well as semantically inappropriate substitutions (contrast with **Broca's Aphasia**). The aphasia is due to damage in the region of the neocortex called Wernicke's area (Ch. 10).

Whole Report: especially in Sperling's (1960) research, the condition in which the entire visual display was to be reported (contrast with **Partial Report**) (Ch. 3).

Whorf's Linguistic Relativity Hypothesis: see **Linguistic Relativity Hypothesis**.

Word Frequency Effect: that frequent words in the language are processed more rapidly than infrequent words (Ch. 2).

Working Memory: the component, similar to short-term memory, in Baddeley and Hitch's (1974) theory in which verbal rehearsal and other conscious processing takes place; also, the component that contains the executive controller in charge of devoting conscious processing resources to the various other components in the memory system (Ch. 2, 4).

References

Aaronson, D., & Ferres, S. (1986). Reading strategies for children and adults: A quantitative model. *Psychological Review, 93,* 89–112.

Abbot, V., Black, J. B., & Smith, E. E. (1985). The representation of scripts in memory. *Journal of Memory and Language, 24,* 179–199.

Abelson, R. P. (1981). Psychological status of the script concept. *American Psychologist, 36,* 715–729.

Adamson, R. E., & Taylor, D. W. (1954). Functional fixedness as related to elapsed time and set. *Journal of Experimental Psychology, 47,* 122–216.

Adelson, B. (1985). Comparing natural and abstract categories: A case study from computer science. *Cognitive Science, 9,* 417–430.

Agnoli, F. (1991). Development of judgmental heuristics and logical reasoning: Training counteracts the representativeness heuristic. *Cognitive Development, 6,* 195–217.

Agnoli, F., & Krantz, D. H. (1989). Suppressing natural heuristics by formal instruction: The case of the conjunction fallacy. *Cognitive Psychology, 21,* 515–550.

Ahlum-Heath, M. E., & DiVesta, F. J. (1986). The effect of conscious controlled verbalization of a cognitive strategy on transfer in problem solving. *Memory & Cognition, 14,* 281–285.

Albrecht, J. E., & O'Brien, E. J. (1991). Effects of centrality on retrieval of text-based concepts. *Journal of Experimental Psychology: Learning, Memory, and Cognition, 17,* 932–939.

Allen, P. A., McNeal, M., & Kvak, D. (1992). Perhaps the lexicon is coded as a function of word frequency. *Journal of Memory and Language, 31,* 826–844.

Allport, A. (1989). Visual attention. In M. I. Posner (Ed.), *Foundations of cognitive science* (pp. 631–682). Cambridge, MA: Bradford.

Altmann, G. T. M., Garnham, A., & Dennis, Y. (1992). Avoiding the garden path: Eye movements in context. *Journal of Memory and Language, 31,* 685–712.

Anderson, J. R. (1976). *Language, memory, and thought.* Hillsdale, NJ: Erlbaum.

Anderson, J. R. (1980). *Cognitive psychology and its implications.* San Francisco: Freeman.

Anderson, J. R. (1982). Acquisition of cognitive skill. *Psychological Review, 89,* 369–406.

Anderson, J. R. (1983). *The architecture of cognition.* Cambridge, MA: Harvard University Press.

Anderson, J. R. (1985). *Cognitive psychology and its implications* (2nd ed.). New York: Freeman.

Anderson, J. R. (1989). A theory of human knowledge. *Artificial Intelligence, 40,* 313–351.

Anderson, J. R. (1990). *The adaptive character of thought.* Hillsdale, NJ: Erlbaum.

Anderson, J. R. (1992). Intelligent tutoring and high school mathematics. In *Proceedings of the Second International Conference on Intelligent Tutoring Systems* (pp. 1–10). Montreal, Quebec, Canada: Springer-Verlag.

Anderson, J. R. (1993). Problem solving and learning. *American Psychologist, 48,* 35–44.

Anderson, J. R., & Bower, G. H. (1973). *Human associative memory.* Washington, DC: Winston & Sons.

Anderson, J. R., Boyle, C. F., Corbett, A., & Lewis, M. W. (1990). Cognitive modelling and intelligent tutoring. *Artificial Intelligence, 42,* 7–49.

Anderson, J. R., & Pirolli, P. L. (1984). Spread of activation. *Journal of Experimental Psychology: Learning, Memory, and Cognition, 10,* 791–798.

Anderson, J. R., & Schooler, L. J. (1991). Reflections of the environment in memory. *Psychological Science, 2,* 396–408.

Antrobus, J. (1991). Dreaming: Cognitive processes during cortical activation and high afferent thresholds. *Psychological Review, 98,* 96–121.

Aram, D. M., & Eisele, J. (1992). Plasticity and recovery of higher cortical functions following early brain injury. In I. Rapin & S. J. Segalowitz (Eds.), *Handbook of neuropsychology: Vol. 6. Child neuropsychology* (pp. 73–92). Amsterdam: Elsevier.

Ashcraft, M. H. (1976). Priming and property dominance effects in semantic memory. *Memory & Cognition, 4,* 490–500.

Ashcraft, M. H. (1978a). Property dominance and typicality effects in property statement verification. *Journal of Verbal Learning and Verbal Behavior, 17,* 155–164.

Ashcraft, M. H. (1978b). Property norms for typical and atypical items from 17 categories: A description and discussion. *Memory & Cognition, 6,* 227–232.

Ashcraft, M. H. (1992). Cognitive arithmetic: A review of data and theory. *Cognition, 44,* 75–106.

Ashcraft, M. H. (1993). A personal case history of transient anomia. *Brain and Language, 44,* 47–57.

Ashcraft, M. H., & Faust, M. W. (1994). Mathematics anxiety and mental arithmetic performance: An exploratory investigation. *Cognition and Emotion.*

Ashcraft, M. H., Kellas, G., & Needham, S. (1975). Rehearsal and retrieval processes in free recall of categorized lists. *Memory & Cognition, 3,* 506–512.

Ashcraft, M. H., Yamashita, T. S., & Aram, D. M. (1992). Mathematics performance in left and right brain-lesioned children and adolescents. *Brain and Cognition, 19,* 208–252.

Atkinson, R. C., & Shiffrin, R. M. (1968). Human memory: A proposed system and its control processes. In W. K. Spence & J. T. Spence (Eds.), *The psychology of learning and motivation: Advances in research and theory* (Vol. 2, pp. 89–195). New York: Academic Press.

Atkinson, R. C., & Shiffrin, R. M. (1971). The control of short-term memory. *Scientific American, 225,* 82–90.

Atwood, M. E., & Polson, P. (1976). A process model for water jug problems. *Cognitive Psychology, 8,* 191–216.

Averbach, E., & Coriell, A. S. (1961). Short-term memory in vision. *Bell System Technical Journal, 40,* 309–328. (Reprinted in Coltheart, M. (1973). *Readings in cognitive psychology.* Toronto: Holt, Rinehart & Winston of Canada.)

Averbach, E., & Sperling, G. (1961). Short term storage and information in vision. In C. Cherry (Ed.), *Information theory* (pp. 196–211). London: Butterworth.

Baars, B. J. (1986). *The cognitive revolution in psychology.* New York: Guilford.

Baddeley, A. D. (1976). *The psychology of memory.* New York: Basic Books.

Baddeley, A. D. (1978). The trouble with levels: A reexamination of Craik and Lockhart's framework for memory research. *Psychological Review, 85,* 139–152.

Baddeley, A. D. (1981). The concept of working memory: A view of its current state and probable future development. *Cognition, 10,* 17–23.

Baddeley, A. D. (1986). *Working memory.* Oxford, England: Oxford University Press.

Baddeley, A. (1992a). Is working memory working? The Fifteenth Bartlett Lecture. *Quarterly Journal of Experimental Psychology, 44A,* 1–31.

Baddeley, A. (1992b). Working memory. *Science, 255,* 556–559.

Baddeley, A. D., & Hitch, G. (1974). Working memory. In G. H. Bower (Ed.), *The psychology of learning and motivation* (Vol. 8, pp. 47–89). New York: Academic Press.

Baddeley, A. D., & Lieberman, K. (1980). Spatial working memory. In R. Nickerson (Ed.), *Attention and performance VIII.* Hillsdale, NJ: Erlbaum.

Baddeley, A., Logie, R., Nimmo-Smith, I., & Brereton, N. (1985). Components of fluent reading. *Journal of Memory and Language, 24,* 119–131.

Baddeley, A. D., Thomson, N., & Buchanan, M. (1975). Word length and the structure of short-term memory. *Journal of Verbal Learning and Verbal Behavior, 14,* 575–589.

Baddeley, A., & Wilson, B. (1988). Comprehension and working memory: A single case neuropsychological study. *Journal of Memory and Language, 27,* 479–498.

Bahrick, H. P. (1983). The cognitive map of a city—50 years of learning and memory. In G. H. Bower (Ed.), *The psychology of learning and motivation: Advances in research and theory* (Vol. 17, pp. 125–163). New York: Academic Press.

Bahrick, H. P. (1984). Semantic memory content in permastore: Fifty years of memory for Spanish learned in school. *Journal of Experimental Psychology: General, 113,* 1–29.

Bahrick, H. P., Bahrick, P. C., & Wittlinger, R. P. (1975). Fifty years of memories for names and faces: A cross-sectional approach. *Journal of Experimental Psychology: General, 104,* 54–75.

Bahrick, H. P., & Hall, L. K. (1991). Lifetime maintenance of high school mathematics content. *Journal of Experimental Psychology: General, 120,* 20–33.

Balota, D. A., Boland, J. E., & Shields, L. W. (1989). Priming in pronunciation: Beyond pattern recognition and onset latency. *Journal of Memory and Language, 28,* 14–36.

Banaji, M. R., & Crowder, R. G. (1989). The bankruptcy of everyday memory. *American Psychologist, 44,* 1185–1193.

Banks, W. P. (1977). Encoding and processing of symbolic information in comparative judgments. In G. H. Bower (Ed.), *The psychology of learning and motivation* (Vol. 11, pp. 101–159). New York: Academic Press.

Banks, W. P., Clark, H. H., & Lucy, P. (1975). The locus of the semantic congruity effect in comparative judgments. *Journal of Experimental Psychology: Human Perception and Performance, 1,* 35–47.

Banks, W. P., Fujii, M., & Kayra-Stuart, F. (1976). Semantic congruity effects in comparative judgments of magnitude of digits. *Journal of Experimental Psychology: Human Perception and Performance, 2,* 435–447.

Bar-Hillel, M. (1980). What features make samples seem representative? *Journal of Experimental Psychology: Human Perception and Performance, 6,* 578–589.

Bartlett, F. C. (1932). *Remembering: A study in experimental and social psychology.* London: Cambridge University Press.

Bassok, M., & Holyoak, K. H. (1989). Interdomain transfer between isomorphic topics in algebra and physics. *Journal of Experimental Psychology: Learning, Memory, and Cognition, 15,* 153–166.

Bates, E., Masling, M., & Kintsch, W. (1978). Recognition memory for aspects of dialogue. *Journal of Experimental Psychology: Human Learning and Memory, 4,* 187–197.

Battig, W. F., & Montague, W. E. (1969). Category norms for verbal items in 56 categories: A replication and extension of the Connecticut category norms. *Journal of Experimental Psychology Monograph, 80* (3, Pt. 2), 1–46.

Baum, D. R., & Jonides, J. (1979). Cognitive maps: Analysis of comparative judgments of distance. *Memory & Cognition, 7,* 462–468.

Belli, R. F. (1989). Influences of misleading postevent information: Misinformation interference and acceptance. *Journal of Experimental Psychology: General, 118,* 72–85.

Benjamin, L. T., Jr., Durkin, M., Link, M., Vestal, M., & Acord, J. (1992). Wundt's American doctoral students. *American Psychologist, 47,* 123–131.

Benson, D. J., & Geschwind, N. (1969). The alexias. In P. Vincken & G. W. Bruyn (Eds.), *Handbook of clinical neurology* (Vol. 4, pp. 112–140). Amsterdam: North-Holland.

Berger, D. E., Pezdek, K., & Banks, W. P. (Eds.). (1986). *Applications of cognitive psychology: Problem solving, education, and computing.* Hillsdale, NJ: Erlbaum.

Berko Gleason, J. (Ed.). (1985). *The development of language.* Columbus, OH: Merrill Publishing.

Blakemore, C. (1977). *Mechanics of the mind.* Cambridge: Cambridge University Press.

Blaney, P. H. (1986). Affect and memory: A review. *Psychological Bulletin, 99,* 229–246.

Blom, J. P., & Gumperz, J. J. (1972). Social meaning in linguistic structure: Code-switching in Norway. In J. J. Gumperz & D. Hymes (Eds.), *Directions in sociolinguistics: The ethnography of communication* (pp. 407–434). New York: Holt.

Boas, F. (1911). Introduction to *The handbook of North American Indians.* Smithsonian Institution Bulletin 40, Part 1. (Reissued by the University of Nebraska Press, 1966)

Bock, J. K. (1982). Toward a cognitive psychology of syntax: Information processing contributions to sentence formulation. *Psychological Review, 89,* 1–47.

Bock, J. K. (1986). Meaning, sound, and syntax: Lexical priming in sentence production. *Journal of Experimental Psychology: Learning, Memory, and Cognition, 12,* 575–586.

Bock, K., & Miller, C. A. (1991). Broken agreement. *Cognitive Psychology, 23,* 45–93.

Boring, E. G. (1950). *A history of experimental psychology* (2nd ed.). New York: Appleton-Century-Crofts.

Bourne, L. E., Jr. (1982). Typicality effects in logically defined categories. *Memory & Cognition, 10,* 3–9.

Bourne, L. E., Jr., & Bunderson, C. V. (1963). Effects of delay of informative feedback and length of postfeedback interval on concept identification. *Journal of Experimental Psychology, 65,* 1–5.

Bousfield, W. A. (1953). The occurrence of clustering in the recall of randomly arranged associates. *Journal of General Psychology, 49,* 229–240.

Bousfield, W. A., & Sedgewick, C. H. W. (1944). An analysis of sequences of restricted associative responses. *Journal of General Psychology, 30,* 149–165.

Bowden, E. M. (1985). Accessing relevant information during problem solving: Time constraints on search in the problem space. *Memory & Cognition, 13,* 280–286.

Bower, G. H. (1970). Analysis of a mnemonic device. *American Scientist, 58,* 496–510.

Bower, G. H. (1986). Mood and memory. *American Psychologist, 36,* 129–148.

Bower, G. H., Black, J. B., & Turner, T. J. (1979). Scripts in memory for text. *Cognitive Psychology, 11,* 177–220.

Bower, G. H., Clark, M. C., Lesgold, A. M., & Winzenz, D. (1969). Hierarchical retrieval schemes in recall of categorical word lists. *Journal of Verbal Learning and Verbal Behavior, 8,* 323–343.

Bower, G. H., Gilligan, S. G., & Monteiro, K. P. (1981). Selectivity of learning caused by affective states. *Journal of Experimental Psychology: General, 110,* 451–473.

Bransford, J. D. (1979). *Human cognition: Learning, understanding and remembering.* Belmont, CA: Wadsworth.

Bransford, J. D., & Franks, J. J. (1971). The abstraction of linguistic ideas. *Cognitive Psychology, 2,* 331–350.

Bransford, J. D., & Franks, J. J. (1972). The abstraction of linguistic ideas: A review. *Cognition: International Journal of Cognitive Psychology, 1,* 211–249.

Bransford, J. D., & Johnson, M. K. (1972). Contextual prerequisites for understanding: Some investigations of comprehension and recall. *Journal of Verbal Learning and Verbal Behavior, 11,* 717–726.

Bransford, J. D., & Johnson, M. K. (1973). Considerations of some problems of comprehension. In W. G. Chase (Ed.), *Visual information processing* (pp. 383–438). New York: Academic Press.

Bransford, J. D., & Stein, B. S. (1984). *The ideal problem solver.* New York: Freeman.

Bransford, J. D., & Stein, B. S. (1993). *The ideal problem solver* (2nd ed.). New York: Freeman.

Breland, K., & Breland, M. (1961). The misbehavior of organisms. *American Psychologist, 16,* 681–684.

Bresnan, J. (1978). A realistic transformational grammar. In J. Bresnan, M. Halle, & G. Miller (Eds.), *Linguistic theory and psychological reality* (pp. 1–59). Cambridge, MA: MIT Press.

Bresnan, J., & Kaplan, R. M. (1982). Introduction: Grammars as mental representations of language. In J. Bresnan (Ed.), *The mental representation of grammatical relations* (pp. xvii–lii). Cambridge, MA: MIT Press.

Brewer, W. F., & Hay, A. E. (1984). Reconstructive recall of linguistic style. *Journal of Verbal Learning and Verbal Behavior, 23,* 237–249.

Bridgeman, B. (1988). *The biology of behavior and mind.* New York: Wiley.

Bridgman, P. W. (1927). *The logic of modern physics.* New York: Macmillan.

Broadbent, D. E. (1952). Speaking and listening simultaneously. *Journal of Experimental Psychology, 43,* 267–273.

Broadbent, D. E. (1958). *Perception and communication.* London: Pergamon Press.

Brooks, J. O. III, & Watkins, M. J. (1990). Further evidence of the intricacy of memory span. *Journal of Experimental Psychology: Learning, Memory, and Cognition, 16,* 1134–1141.

Brooks, L. R. (1967). The suppression of visualization by reading. *Quarterly Journal of Experimental Psychology, 19,* 289–299.

Brooks, L. R. (1968). Spatial and verbal components of the act of recall. *Canadian Journal of Experimental Psychology, 22,* 349–368.

Brown, A. L. (1975). The development of memory: Knowing, knowing about knowing, and knowing how to know. In H. W. Reese (Ed.), *Advances in child development and behavior* (Vol. 10, pp. 104–152). New York: Academic Press.

Brown, A. S., Neblett, D. R., Jones, T. C., & Mitchell, D. B. (1991). Transfer of processing in repetition priming: Some inappropriate findings. *Journal of Experimental Psychology: Learning, Memory, and Cognition, 17,* 514–525.

Brown, J. A. (1958). Some tests of the decay theory of immediate memory. *Quarterly Journal of Experimental Psychology, 10,* 12–21.

Brown, J. S., & Burton, R. R. (1978). Diagnostic models for procedural bugs in basic mathematical skills. *Cognitive Science, 2,* 155–192.

Brown, J. S., & VanLehn, K. (1980). Repair theory: A generative theory of bugs in procedural skills. *Cognitive Science, 4,* 379–426.

Brown, N. R., Rips, L. J., & Shevell, S. K. (1985). The subjective dates of natural events in very-long-term memory. *Cognitive Psychology, 17,* 139–177.

Brown, R., & Ford, M. (1961). Address in American English. *Journal of Abnormal and Social Psychology, 62,* 375–385.

Brown, R., & Kulik, J. (1977). Flashbulb memories. *Cognition, 5,* 73–99.

Brown, R., & McNeill, D. (1966). The "tip-of-the-tongue" phenomenon. *Journal of Verbal Learning and Verbal Behavior, 5,* 325–337.

Bruner, J. S. (1973). *Beyond the information given: Studies in the psychology of knowing* (J. Anglin, Ed.). New York: Norton.

Bruner, J. S., Goodnow, J. J., & Austin, G. A. (1956). *A study of thinking.* New York: Wiley.

Burke, A., Heuer, F., & Reisberg, D. (1992). Remembering emotional events. *Memory & Cognition, 20,* 277–290.

Burke, D. M., MacKay, D. G., Worthley, J. S., & Wade, E. (1991). On the tip of the tongue: What causes word finding failures in young and older adults? *Journal of Memory and Language, 30,* 542–579.

Campbell, J. I. D. (1987). Production, verification, and priming of multiplication facts. *Memory & Cognition, 15,* 349–364.

Campbell, J. I. D., & Graham, D. J. (1985). Mental multiplication skill: Structure, process, and acquisition. *Canadian Journal of Psychology, 39,* 338–366.

Caramazza, A. (1986). On drawing inferences about the structure of normal cognitive systems from the analysis of patterns of impaired performance: The case for single-patient studies. *Brain and Cognition, 5,* 41–66.

Caramazza, A., & McCloskey, M. (1988). The case for single-patient studies. *Cognitive Neuropsychology, 5,* 517–528.

Carlson, B. W. (1990). Anchoring and adjustment in judgments under risk. *Journal of Experimental Psychology: Learning, Memory, and Cognition, 16,* 665–676.

Carlson, R. A., Khoo, B. H., Yaure, R. G., & Schneider, W. (1990). Acquisition of a problem-solving skill: Levels of organization and use of working memory. *Journal of Experimental Psychology: General, 119,* 193–214.

Carr, T. H., & Dagenbach, D. (1986). Now you see it, now you don't: Relations between semantic activation and awareness. *The Brain and Brain Sciences, 9,* 26–27.

Carr, T. H., McCauley, C., Sperber, R. D., & Parmalee, C. M. (1982). Words, pictures, and priming: On semantic activation, conscious identification, and the automaticity of information processing. *Journal of Experimental Psychology: Human Perception and Performance, 8,* 757–777.

Carroll, D. W. (1986). *Psychology of language.* Monterey, CA: Brooks/Cole.

Case, R. (1992). The role of the frontal lobes in the regulation of cognitive development. *Brain and Cognition, 20,* 51–73.

Cavanaugh, J. P. (1972). Relation between the immediate memory span and the memory search rate. *Psychological Review, 79,* 525–530.

Cermak, L. S. (1975). *Improving your memory.* New York: Norton.

Cermak, L. S. (1982). *Human memory and amnesia.* Hillsdale, NJ: Erlbaum.

Challis, B. H., & Brodbeck, D. R. (1992). Level of processing affects priming in word fragment completion. *Journal of Experimental Psychology: Learning, Memory, and Cognition, 18,* 595–607.

Chang, T. M. (1986). Semantic memory: Facts and models. *Psychological Bulletin, 99,* 199–220.

Chase, W. G., & Ericsson, K. A. (1982). Skill and working memory. In G. H. Bower (Ed.), *The psychology of learning and motivation* (Vol. 16, pp. 1–58). New York: Academic Press.

Chase, W. G., & Simon, H. A. (1973). Perception in chess. *Cognitive Psychology, 4,* 55–81.

Cheng, P. W., Holyoak, K. J., Nisbett, R. E., & Oliver, L. M. (1986). Pragmatic versus syntactic approaches to training deductive reasoning. *Cognitive Psychology, 18,* 293–328.

Cherniak, C. (1984). Prototypicality and deductive reasoning. *Journal of Verbal Learning and Verbal Behavior, 23,* 625–642.

Cherniak, C. (1988). Undebuggability and cognitive science. *Communications of the ACM, 31,* 402–412.

Cherry, E. C. (1953). Some experiments on the recognition of speech, with one and with two ears. *Journal of the Acoustical Society of America, 25,* 975–979.

Cherry, E. C., & Taylor, W. K. (1954). Some further experiments on the recognition of speech with one and two ears. *Journal of the Acoustical Society of America, 26,* 554–559.

Chomsky, N. (1957). *Syntactic structures.* The Hague: Mouton Publishers.

Chomsky, N. (1959). A review of Skinner's *Verbal behavior. Language, 35,* 26–58.

Chomsky, N. (1965). *Aspects of a theory of syntax.* Cambridge, MA: Harvard University Press.

Chomsky, N. (1968). *Language and mind.* New York: Harcourt Brace Jovanovich.

Christianson, S. (1989). Flashbulb memories: Special, but not so special. *Memory & Cognition, 17,* 435–443.

Churchland, P. M. (1990). Cognitive activity in artificial neural networks. In D. N. Osherson & E. E. Smith (Eds.), *Thinking: An invitation to cognitive science* (Vol. 3, pp. 199–227). Cambridge, MA: MIT Press.

Clark, H. H. (1977). Bridging. In P. N. Johnson-Laird & P. C. Wason (Eds.), *Thinking: Readings in cognitive science* (pp. 411–420). Cambridge: Cambridge University Press.

Clark, H. H. (1979). Responding to indirect speech acts. *Cognitive Psychology, 11,* 430–477.

Clark, H. H., & Clark, E. V. (1977). *Psychology and language: An introduction to psycholinguistics.* New York: Harcourt Brace Jovanovich.

Clark, H. H., & Marshall, C. R. (1981). Context for comprehension. In J. Long and A. Baddeley (Eds.), *Attention and performance IX* (pp. 313–331). Hillsdale, NJ: Erlbaum.

Clark, H. H., & Wilkes-Gibbs, D. (1986). Referring as a collaborative process. *Cognition, 22,* 1–39.

Clifton, C., Jr., Frazier, L., & Connine, C. (1984). Lexical expectations in sentence comprehension. *Journal of Verbal Learning and Verbal Behavior, 23,* 696–708.

Coghill, G. E. (1929). *Anatomy and the problem of behavior.* Cambridge, MA: Cambridge University Press. (Reprinted by Hafner, New York, 1963)

Cohen, G. (1989). *Memory in the real world.* London: Erlbaum.

Collins, A. M., & Loftus, E. F. (1975). A spreading-activation theory of semantic processing. *Psychological Review, 82,* 407–428.

Collins, A., & Michalski, R. (1989). The logic of plausible reasoning: A core theory. *Cognitive Science, 13,* 1–49.

Collins, A. M., & Quillian, M. R. (1969). Retrieval time from semantic memory. *Journal of Verbal Learning and Verbal Behavior, 8,* 240–247.

Collins, A. M., & Quillian, M. R. (1970). Does category size affect categorization time? *Journal of Verbal Learning and Verbal Behavior, 9,* 432–438.

Collins, A. M., & Quillian, M. R. (1972). How to make a language user. In E. Tulving & W. Donaldson (Eds.), *Organization of memory* (pp. 309–351). New York: Academic Press.

Collins, A., Warnock, E. H., Aiello, N., & Miller, M. L. (1975). Reasoning from incomplete knowledge. In D. Bobrow & A. Collins (Eds.), *Representation and understanding: Studies in cognitive science* (pp. 383–415). New York: Academic Press.

Coltheart, M. (1973). *Readings in cognitive psychology.* Toronto: Holt, Rinehart & Winston of Canada.

Coltheart, M. (1983). Ecological necessity of iconic memory. *The Behavioral and Brain Sciences, 6,* 17–18.

Conrad, C. (1972). Cognitive economy in semantic memory. *Journal of Experimental Psychology, 92,* 149–154.

Conrad, R. (1964). Acoustic confusions in immediate memory. *British Journal of Psychology, 55,* 75–84.

Conway, M. A. (1991). In defense of everyday memory. *American Psychologist, 46,* 19–26.

Conway, M. A., Cohen, G., & Stanhope, N. (1991). On the very long-term retention of knowledge acquired through formal education: Twelve years of cognitive psychology. *Journal of Experimental Psychology: General, 120,* 395–409.

Cook, M. (1977). Gaze and mutual gaze in social encounters. *American Scientist, 65,* 328–333.

Cooper, E. H., & Pantle, A. J. (1967). The total-time hypothesis in verbal learning. *Psychological Bulletin, 68,* 221–234.

Cooper, L. A., & Shepard, R. N. (1973). Chronometric studies of the rotation of mental images. In W. G. Chase (Ed.), *Visual Information Processing* (pp. 75–176). New York: Academic Press.

Corballis, M. C. (1989). Laterality and human evolution. *Psychological Review, 96,* 492–505.

Coughlan, A. K., & Warrington, E. K. (1978). Word comprehension and word retrieval in patients with localised cerebral lesions. *Brain, 101,* 163–185.

Craik, F. I. M., & Lockhart, R. S. (1972). Levels of processing: A framework for memory research. *Journal of Verbal Learning and Verbal Behavior, 11,* 671–684.

Craik, F. I. M., & Tulving, E. (1975). Depth of processing and the retention of words in episodic memory. *Journal of Experimental Psychology, 104,* 268–294.

Craik, F. I. M., & Watkins, M. J. (1973). The role of rehearsal in short-term memory. *Journal of Verbal Learning and Verbal Behavior, 12,* 599–607.

Crick, F. H. C., & Asanuma, C. (1986). Certain aspects of the anatomy and physiology of the cerebral cortex. In D. E. Rumelhart, J. L. McClelland, & PDP Research Group (Eds.), *Parallel distributed processing* (Vol. 2, pp. 333–371). Cambridge, MA: MIT Press.

Crowder, R. G. (1970). The role of one's own voice in immediate memory. *Cognitive Psychology, 1,* 157–178.

Crowder, R. G. (1972). Visual and auditory memory. In J. F. Kavanaugh & I. G. Mattingly (Eds.), *Language by ear and by eye: The relationships between speech and reading* (pp. 251–276). Cambridge, MA: MIT Press.

Crowder, R. G., & Morton, J. (1969). Precategorical acoustic storage (PAS). *Perception and Psychophysics, 5,* 365–373.

Cummins, D. D., Lubart, T., Alksnis, O., & Rist, R. (1991). Conditional reasoning and causation. *Memory & Cognition, 19,* 274–282.

Dagenbach, D., Horst, S., & Carr, T. H. (1990). Adding new information to semantic memory: How much learning is enough to produce automatic priming? *Journal of Experimental Psychology: Learning, Memory, and Cognition, 16,* 581–591.

Dahlgren, K. (1985). The cognitive structure of social categories. *Cognitive Science, 9,* 379–398.

Darley, C. F., Tinklenberg, J. R., Hollister, L. E., & Atkinson, R. C. (1973). Marihuana and retrieval from short-term memory. *Psychopharmacologia, 29,* 231–238.

Darwin, C. J., Turvey, M. T., & Crowder, R. G. (1972). An auditory analogue of the Sperling partial report procedure: Evidence for brief auditory storage. *Cognitive Psychology, 3,* 255–267.

Dell, G. S. (1986). A spreading-activation theory of retrieval in sentence production. *Psychological Review, 93,* 283–321.

Dell, G. S., & Newman, J. E. (1980). Detecting phonemes in fluent speech. *Journal of Verbal Learning and Verbal Behavior, 20,* 611–629.

Dempster, F. N. (1985). Proactive interference in sentence recall: Topic-similarity effects and individual differences. *Memory & Cognition, 13,* 81–89.

DePaulo, B. M., & Bonvillian, J. D. (1978). The effect on language development of the special characteristics of speech addressed to children. *Journal of Psycholinguistic Research, 7,* 189–211.

Descartes, R. (1972). *Treatise on man* (T. S. Hall, Trans.). Cambridge, MA: Harvard University Press. (Original work published 1637)

Deutsch, G., Bourbon, T., Papanicolaou, A. C., & Eisenberg, H. M. (1988). Visuospatial tasks compared via activation of regional cerebral blood flow. *Neuropsychologia, 26,* 445–452.

Deutsch, J. A., & Deutsch, D. (1963). Attention: Some theoretical considerations. *Psychological Review, 70,* 80–90.

Dillon, R. F., & Reid, L. S. (1969). Short-term memory as a function of information processing during the retention interval. *Journal of Experimental Psychology, 81,* 261–269.

Donchin, E. (1981). Surprise! . . . Surprise? *Psychophysiology, 18,* 493–513.

Donders, F. C. (1969). Over de snelheid van psychische processen. Onderzoekingen gedann in het Psysiologish Laboratorium der Utrechtsche Hoogeschool (W. G. Koster, Trans.). In W. G. Koster (Ed.), Attention and Performance II. *Acta Psychologica, 30,* 412–431. (Original work published 1868)

Donley, R. D., & Ashcraft, M. H. (1992). The methodology of testing naive beliefs in the physics classroom. *Memory & Cognition, 20,* 381–391.

Dooling, D. J., & Christiaansen, R. E. (1977). Episodic and semantic aspects of memory for prose. *Journal of Experimental Psychology: Human Learning and Memory, 3,* 428–436.

Dooling, D., & Lachman, R. (1971). Effects of comprehension on retention of prose. *Journal of Experimental Psychology, 88,* 216–222.

Dosher, B. A., & Rosedale, G. (1989). Integrated retrieval cues as a mechanism for priming in retrieval from memory. *Journal of Experimental Psychology: General, 118,* 191–211.

Drachman, D. A. (1978). Central cholinergic system and memory. In M. A. Lipton, A. D. Mascio, & K. F. Killam (Eds.), *Psychopharmacology: A generation of process.* New York: Raven Press.

Dugas, J. L., & Kellas, G. (1974). Encoding and retrieval processes in normal children and retarded adolescents. *Journal of Experimental Child Psychology, 17,* 177–185.

Dunbar, K., & MacLeod, C. M. (1984). A horse race of a different color: Stroop interference patterns with transformed words. *Journal of Experimental Psychology: Human Perception and Performance, 10,* 622–639.

Duncan, E. M., & McFarland, C. E., Jr. (1980). Isolating the effects of symbolic distance and semantic congruity in comparative judgments: An additive-factors analysis. *Memory & Cognition, 8,* 612–622.

Duncan, J., & Humphreys, G. W. (1989). Visual search and stimulus similarity. *Psychological Review, 96,* 433–458.

Duncan, J., & Humphreys, G. W. (1992). Beyond the search surface: Visual search and attentional engagement. *Journal of Experimental Psychology: Human Perception and Performance, 18,* 578–588.

Duncan, S. (1972). Some signals and rules for taking speaking turns in conversations. *Journal of Personality and Social Psychology, 23,* 283–292.

Duncker, K. (1945). On problem solving. *Psychological Monographs, 58* (Whole No. 270).

Eastman, C. M. (1975). *Aspects of language and culture.* San Francisco: Chandler.

Ebbinghaus, H. (1885/1913). *Memory: A contribution to experimental psychology* (H. A. Ruger & C. E. Bussenius, Trans.). New York: Columbia University, Teacher's College. (Reprinted by Dover, New York, 1964)

Ebbinghaus, H. (1908). *Abriss der Psychologie.* Leipzig: Veit & Comp. (Also cited as 1910)

Eddy, D. M. (1982). Probabilistic reasoning in clinical medicine: Problems and opportunities. In D. Kahneman, P. Slovic, & A. Tversky (Eds.), *Judgment under uncertainty: Heuristics and biases* (pp. 249–267). Cambridge: Cambridge University Press.

Edridge-Green, F. W. (1900). *Memory and its cultivation.* New York: Appleton & Co.

Edwards, D., & Potter, J. (1993). Language and causation: A discursive action model of description and attribution. *Psychological Review, 100,* 23–41.

Egan, P., Carterette, E. C., & Thwing, E. J. (1954). Some factors affecting multichannel listening. *Journal of the Acoustic Society of America, 26,* 774–782.

Eimas, P. D. (1975). Speech perception in early infancy. In L. B. Cohen & P. Salapatek (Eds.), *Infant perception: From sensation to cognition: Vol. II. Perception of space, speech, and sound* (pp. 193–231). New York: Academic Press.

Ellis, A. W., & Young, A. W. (1988). *Human cognitive neuropsychology.* Hove, England: Erlbaum.

Ellis, H. C., & Ashbrook, P. W. (1988). Resource allocation model of the effects of depressed mood states on memory. In K. Fiedler & J. Forgas (Eds.), *Affect, cognition and social behavior: New evidence and integrative attempts* (pp. 25–43). Toronto: Hogrefe.

Ellis, H. C., & Hunt, R. R. (1993). *Fundamentals of cognitive psychology* (5th ed.). Madison, WI: William C. Brown.

Ellis, H. D. (1983). The role of the right hemisphere in face perception. In A. W. Young (Ed.), *Functions of the right cerebral hemisphere* (pp. 33–64). New York: Academic Press.

Ellis, N. C., & Hennelly, R. A. (1980). A bilingual word-length effect: Implications for intelligence testing and the relative ease of mental calculation in Welsh and English. *British Journal of Psychology, 71,* 43–52.

Epstein, W. (1961). The influence of syntactical structure on learning. *American Journal of Psychology, 74,* 80–85.

Epstein, W., Glenberg, A. M., & Bradley, M. M. (1984). Coactivation and comprehension: Contribution of text variables to the illusion of knowing. *Memory & Cognition, 12,* 355–360.

Erdelyi, M. H. (1974). A new look at the New Look: Perceptual defense and vigilance. *Psychological Review, 81,* 1–25.

Erdelyi, M. H. (1992). Psychodynamics and the unconscious. *American Psychologist, 47,* 784–787.

Erickson, T. D., & Mattson, M. E. (1981). From words to meanings: A semantic illusion. *Journal of Verbal Learning and Verbal Behavior, 20,* 540–551.

Ericsson, K. A., & Polson, P. G. (1988). An experimental analysis of the mechanisms of a memory skill. *Journal of Experimental Psychology: Learning, Memory, and Cognition, 14,* 305–316.

Ericsson, K. A., & Simon, H. A. (1980). Verbal reports as data. *Psychological Review, 87,* 215–251.

Eriksen, C. W., & Johnson, H. J. (1964). Storage and decay characteristics of non-attended auditory stimuli. *Journal of Experimental Psychology, 68,* 28–36.

Ernst, G. W., & Newell, A. (1969). *GPS: A case study in generality and problem solving.* New York: Academic Press.

Eysenck, M. W. (1982). *Attention and arousal: Cognition and performance.* Heidelberg: Springer-Verlag.

Eysenck, M. W. (1984). *A handbook of cognitive psychology.* Hillsdale, NJ: Erlbaum.

Eysenck, M. W. (1992). *Anxiety: The cognitive perspective.* Hove, England: Erlbaum.

Eysenck, M. W., & Calvo, M. G. (1992). Anxiety and performance: The processing efficiency theory. *Cognition and Emotion, 6,* 409–434.

Farah, M. J., Hammond, K. M., Levine, D. N., & Calvanio, R. (1988). Visual and spatial mental imagery: Dissociable systems of representation. *Cognitive Psychology, 20,* 439–462.

Farah, M. J., & McClelland, J. L. (1991). A computational model of semantic memory impairment: Modality specificity and emergent category specificity. *Journal of Experimental Psychology: General, 120,* 339–357.

Faust, M. W. (1992). *Analysis of physiological reactivity in mathematics anxiety.* Unpublished doctoral dissertation, Bowling Green State University, Bowling Green, OH.

Fechner, G. (1860). *Elements of psychophysics.* English ed. of Vol. 1. H. E. Adler (Trans.), D. H. Howes & E. G. Boring (Eds.). New York: Holt, Rinehart & Winston, 1966.

Feldman, D. (1992). *When did wild poodles roam the earth? An Imponderables™ book.* New York: HarperCollins.

Fillenbaum, S. (1974). Pragmatic normalization: Further results for some conjunctive and disjunctive sentences. *Journal of Experimental Psychology, 102,* 574–578.

Fillmore, C. J. (1968). Toward a modern theory of case. In D. A. Reibel & S. A. Schane (Eds.), *Modern studies in English* (pp. 361–375). Englewood Cliffs, NJ: Prentice-Hall.

Finke, R. A., & Freyd, J. J. (1985). Transformations of visual memory induced by implied motions of pattern elements. *Journal of Experimental Psychology: Learning, Memory, and Cognition, 11,* 780–794.

Fischhoff, B., & Bar-Hillel, M. (1984). Diagnosticity and the base-rate effect. *Memory & Cognition, 12,* 402–410.

Flavell, J. H. (1963). *The developmental psychology of Jean Piaget.* New York: Van Nostrand.

Flavell, J. H. (1970). Developmental studies of mediated memory. In H. W. Reese & L. P. Lipsett (Eds.), *Advances in child development and behavior* (Vol. 5, pp. 181–211). New York: Academic Press.

Flavell, J. H., & Wellman, H. M. (1977). Metamemory. In R. V. Kail and J. W. Hagen (Eds.), *Perspectives on the development of memory and cognition.* Hillsdale, NJ: Erlbaum.

Fletcher, C. R., & Bloom, C. P. (1988). Causal reasoning in the comprehension of simple narrative texts. *Journal of Memory and Language, 27,* 235–244.

Fodor, J. A. (1983). *The modularity of mind.* Cambridge, MA: MIT Press.

Fodor, J. A., Bever, T. G., & Garrett, M. F. (1974). *The psychology of language.* New York: McGraw-Hill.

Fodor, J. A., & Garrett, M. (1966). Some reflections on competence and performance. In J. Lyons & R. J. Wales (Eds.), *Psycholinguistic papers* (pp. 135–154). Edinburgh: Edinburgh University Press.

Fong, G. T., Krantz, D. H., & Nisbett, R. E. (1986). The effects of statistical training on thinking about everyday problems. *Cognitive Psychology, 18,* 253–292.

Fong, G. T., & Nisbett, R. E. (1991). Immediate and delayed transfer of training effects in statistical reasoning. *Journal of Experimental Psychology: General, 120,* 34–45.

Forgus, R. H., & Melamed, L. E. (1976). *Perception: A cognitive-stage approach.* New York: McGraw-Hill.

Foss, D. J., & Hakes, D. T. (1978). *Psycholinguistics: An introduction to the psychology of language.* Englewood Cliffs, NJ: Prentice-Hall.

Francik, E. P., & Clark, H. H. (1985). How to make requests that overcome obstacles to compliance. *Journal of Memory and Language, 24,* 560–568.

Franklin, M. B., & Barten, S. S. (1988). *Child language: A reader.* New York: Oxford University Press.

Frazier, L., & Rayner, K. (1982). Making and correcting errors during sentence comprehension: Eye movements in the analysis of structurally ambiguous sentences. *Cognitive Psychology, 14,* 178–210.

Frazier, L., & Rayner, K. (1990). Taking on semantic commitments: Processing multiple meanings vs. multiple senses. *Journal of Memory and Language, 29,* 181–200.

Frederiksen, C. H. (1975). Acquisition of semantic information from discourse: Effects of repeated exposures. *Journal of Verbal Learning and Verbal Behavior, 14,* 158–169.

Freedman, J. L., & Loftus, E. F. (1971). Retrieval of words from long-term memory. *Journal of Verbal Learning and Verbal Behavior, 10,* 107–115.

Freidman, A. (1978). Memorial comparisons without the "mind's eye." *Journal of Verbal Learning and Verbal Behavior, 17,* 427–444.

Freidman, A., & Polson, M. C. (1981). Hemispheres as independent resource systems: Limited-capacity processing and cerebral specialization. *Journal of Experimental Psychology: Human Perception and Performance, 7,* 1031–1058.

Freud, S. (1966). *Psychopathology of everyday life* (A. Tyson, Trans.). London: Benn. (Original work published 1901)

Fromkin, V. A. (1971). The non-anomalous nature of anomalous utterances. *Language, 47,* 27–52.

Fromkin, V. A. (1973). *Speech errors as linguistic evidence.* The Hague: Mouton.

Fulgosi, A., & Guilford, J. P. (1968). Short-term incubation in divergent production. *American Journal of Psychology, 81,* 241–246.

Gagne, E. D. (1985). *The cognitive psychology of school learning.* Boston: Little, Brown and Co.

Galanter, E. (1962). Contemporary psychophysics. In R. Brown, E. Galanter, E. H., Hess, & G. Mandler (Eds.). *New directions in psychology* (Vol. 1, pp. 87–156), New York: Holt, Rinehart & Winston.

Gallagher, M. (1985). Re-viewing modulation of learning and memory. In N. M. Weinberger, J. L. McGaugh, & G. Lynch (Eds.), *Memory systems of the brain* (pp. 311–334). New York: Guilford Press.

Gardner, H. (1985). *The mind's new science: A history of the cognitive revolution.* New York: Basic Books.

Garrett, M. F. (1975). The analysis of sentence production. In G. H. Bower (Ed.), *The psychology of learning and memory* (Vol. 9, pp. 133–177). New York: Academic Press.

Garrett, M. J. (1980). The limits of accommodation. In V. A. Fromkin (Ed.), *Errors in linguistic performance* (pp. 263–271). New York: Academic Press.

Geary, D. C. (1992). Evolution of human cognition: Potential relationship to the ontogenetic development of behavior and cognition. *Evolution and Cognition, 1,* 93–100.

Geary, D. C. (1993). Mathematical disabilities: Cognitive, neuropsychological, and genetic components. *Psychological Bulletin, 114,* 345–362.

Gentner, D. (1975). Evidence for the psychological reality of semantic components: The verbs of possession. In D. A. Norman & D. E. Rumelhart (Eds.), *Explorations in cognition* (pp. 211–246). San Francisco: Freeman.

Gentner, D. (1983). Structure-mapping: A theoretical framework for analogy. *Cognitive Science, 7,* 155–170.

Gentner, D., & Collins, A. (1981). Studies of inference from lack of knowledge. *Memory & Cognition, 9,* 434–443.

Gentner, D., & Toupin, C. (1986). Systematicity and surface similarity in the development of analogy. *Cognitive Science, 10,* 277–300.

Gernsbacher, M. A. (1985). Surface information loss in comprehension. *Cognitive Psychology, 17,* 324–363.

Gernsbacher, M. A. (1990). *Language comprehension as structure building.* Hillsdale, NJ: Erlbaum.

Gernsbacher, M. A. (1991). Cognitive processes and mechanisms in language comprehension: The structure building framework. In G. H. Bower (Ed.), *The psychology of learning and motivation* (Vol. 27, pp. 217–263). New York: Academic Press.

Gernsbacher, M. A. (in press). *Fundamentals of psycholinguistics.* Hillsdale, NJ: Erlbaum.

Gernsbacher, M. A., & Faust, M. E. (1991). The mechanism of suppression: A component of general comprehension skill. *Journal of Experimental Psychology: Learning, Memory, and Cognition, 17,* 245–262.

Gernsbacher, M. A., & Hargreaves, D. (1988). Accessing sentence participants: The advantage of first mention. *Journal of Memory and Language, 27,* 699–717.

Gernsbacher, M. A., Hargreaves, D., & Beeman, M. (1989). Building and accessing clausal representations: The advantage of first mention versus the advantage of clause recency. *Journal of Memory and Language, 28,* 735–755.

Gernsbacher, M. A., & Shroyer, S. (1989). The cataphoric use of the indefinite *this* in spoken narratives. *Memory & Cognition, 17,* 536–540.

Geschwind, N. (1967). The varieties of naming errors. *Cortex, 3,* 97–112.

Geschwind, N. (1970). The organisation of language and the brain. *Science, 170,* 940–944.

Gholson, B., & Barker, P. (1985). Kuhn, Lakatos, and Landon: Applications in the history of physics and psychology. *American Psychologist, 40,* 755–769.

Gibbs, R. W., Jr. (1986a). On the psycholinguistics of sarcasm. *Journal of Experimental Psychology: General, 115,* 3–15.

Gibbs, R. W., Jr. (1986b). What makes some indirect speech acts conventional? *Journal of Memory and Language, 25,* 181–196.

Gibbs, R. W., Jr. (1989). Understanding and literal meaning. *Cognitive Science, 14,* 243–251.

Gibbs, R. W., Jr. (1990). Comprehending figurative referential descriptions. *Journal of Experimental Psychology: Learning, Memory, and Cognition, 16,* 56–66.

Gibbs, R. W., Jr., & Nayak, N. P. (1991). Why idioms mean what they do. *Journal of Experimental Psychology: General, 120,* 93–95.

Gibson, E. J. (1965). Learning to read. *Science, 148,* 1066–1072.

Gick, M. L., & Holyoak, K. J. (1980). Analogical problem solving. *Cognitive Psychology, 12,* 306–355.

Gick, M. L., & McGarry, S. J. (1992). Learning from mistakes: Inducing analogous solution failures to a source problem produces later successes in analogical transfer. *Journal of Experimental Psychology: Learning, Memory, and Cognition, 18,* 623–639.

Giles, H., & Coupland, N. (1991). *Language: Contexts and consequences.* Pacific Grove, CA: Brooks/Cole.

Gilovich, T., Vallone, R., & Tversky, A. (1985). The hot hand in basketball: On the misperception of random sequences. *Cognitive Psychology, 17,* 295–314.

Glanzer, M. (1972). Storage mechanisms in recall. In G. H. Bower & J. T. Spence (Eds.), *The psychology of learning and motivation* (Vol. 5, pp. 129–193). New York: Academic Press.

Glanzer, M., & Cunitz, A. R. (1966). Two storage mechanisms in free recall. *Journal of Verbal Learning and Verbal Behavior, 5,* 351–360.

Glass, A. L., & Holyoak, K. J. (1975). Alternative conceptions of semantic memory. *Cognition, 3,* 313–339.

Glass, A. L., & Holyoak, K. J. (1986). *Cognition* (2nd ed.). New York: Random House.

Glass, A. L., Holyoak, K., & O'Dell, C. (1974). Production frequency and the verification of quantified statements. *Journal of Verbal Learning and Verbal Behavior, 13,* 237–254.

Glaze, J. A. (1928). The association value of nonsense syllables. *Journal of Genetic Psychology, 35,* 255–269.

Glenberg, A., & Adams, F. (1978). Type I rehearsal and recognition. *Journal of Verbal Learning and Verbal Behavior, 17,* 455–464.

Glenberg, A., Smith, S. M., & Green, C. (1977). Type I rehearsal: Maintenance and more. *Journal of Verbal Learning and Verbal Behavior, 11,* 403–416.

Glenberg, A. M., Wilkinson, A. C., & Epstein, W. (1982). The illusion of knowing: Failure in the self-assessment of comprehension. *Memory & Cognition, 10,* 597–602.

Glucksberg, S., & Danks, J. H. (1975). *Experimental psycholinguistics: An introduction.* Hillsdale, NJ: Erlbaum.

Glucksberg, S., & Keysar, B. (1990). Understanding metaphorical comparisons: Beyond similarity. *Psychological Review, 97,* 3–18.

Glucksberg, S., & McCloskey, M. (1981). Decisions about ignorance: Knowing that you don't know. *Journal of Experimental Psychology: Human Learning and Memory, 7,* 311–325.

Goldinger, S. D., Luce, P. A., & Pisoni, D. B. (1989). Priming lexical neighbors of spoken words: Effects of competition and inhibition. *Journal of Memory and Language, 28,* 501–518.

Goodglass, H., Kaplan, E., Weintraub, S., & Ackerman, N. (1976). The "tip-of-the-tongue" phenomenon in aphasia. *Cortex, 12,* 145–153.

Gorfein, D. S., & Hoffman, R. R. (Eds.). (1987). *Memory and learning: The Ebbinghaus Centennial Conference.* Hillsdale, NJ: Erlbaum.

Graesser, A. C. (1981). *Prose comprehension beyond the word.* New York: Springer-Verlag.

Graesser, A. C., & Nakamura, G. V. (1982). The impact of a schema on comprehension and memory. In G. H. Bower (Ed.), *The psychology of learning and motivation* (pp. 59–109). New York: Academic Press.

Graf, P., & Schacter, D. L. (1985). Implicit and explicit memory for new associations in normal and amnesic subjects. *Journal of Experimental Psychology: Learning, Memory, and Cognition, 11,* 501–518.

Graf, P., & Schacter, D. L. (1987). Selective effects of interference on implicit and explicit memory for new associations. *Journal of Experimental Psychology: Learning, Memory, and Cognition, 13,* 45–53.

Graf, P., Squire, L. R., & Mandler, G. (1984). The information that amnesic patients do not forget. *Journal of Experimental Psychology, 10,* 164–178.

Greenberg, J. H. (1978). Generalizations about numeral systems. In J. H. Greenberg (Ed.), *Universals of human language: Vol. 3. Word structure* (pp. 249–295). Stanford, CA: Stanford University Press.

Greene, J. M. (1972). *Psycholinguistics: Chomsky and psychology.* Harmondsworth, England: Penguin.

Greene, R. L. (1986). Effects of intentionality and strategy on memory for frequency. *Journal of Experimental Psychology: Learning, Memory, and Cognition, 12,* 489–495.

Greene, R. L. (1988). Generation effects in frequency judgment. *Journal of Experimental Psychology: Learning, Memory, and Cognition, 14,* 298–304.

Greene, R. L. (1990). Spacing effects on implicit memory tests. *Journal of Experimental Psychology: Learning, Memory, and Cognition, 16,* 1004–1011.

Greene, R. L., & Crowder, R. G. (1984). Modality and suffix effects in the absence of auditory stimulation. *Journal of Verbal Learning and Verbal Behavior, 23,* 371–382.

Greene, R. L., & Crowder, R. G. (1986). Recency effects in delayed recall of mouthed stimuli. *Memory & Cognition, 14,* 355–360.

Greeno, J. G. (1974). Hobbits and orcs: Acquisition of a sequential concept. *Cognitive Psychology, 6,* 270–292.

Greeno, J. G. (1978). Natures of problem-solving abilities. In W. K. Estes (Ed.), *Handbook of learning and cognitive processes: Vol. 5. Human information processing* (pp. 239–270). Hillsdale, NJ: Erlbaum.

Greeno, J. G., & Bjork, R. A. (1973). Mathematical learning theory and the new "mental forestry." *Annual Review of Psychology, 24,* 81–115.

Greenspan, S. L. (1986). Semantic flexibility and referential specificity of concrete nouns. *Journal of Memory and Language, 25,* 539–557.

Greenwald, A. G. (1992). New look 3: Unconscious cognition reclaimed. *American Psychologist, 47,* 766–779.

Grice, H. P. (1975). Logic and conversation. In P. Cole & J. L. Morgan (Eds.), *Syntax and semantics: Vol. 3. Speech acts* (pp. 41–58). New York: Seminar Press.

Griggs, R. A., & Cox, J. R. (1982). The elusive thematic-materials effect in Wason's selection task. *British Journal of Psychology, 73,* 407–420.

Gross, D., Fischer, U., & Miller, G. A. (1989). The organization of adjectival meanings. *Journal of Memory and Language, 28,* 92–106.

Gruneberg, M. M., Morris, P. E., & Sykes, R. N. (Eds.). (1978). *Practical aspects of memory.* London: Academic Press.

Haber, R. N. (1983). The impending demise of the icon: A critique of the concept of iconic storage in visual information processing. *The Behavioral and Brain Sciences, 6,* 1–54 (includes commentaries).

Haber, R. N., & Hershenson, M. (1973). *The psychology of visual perception.* New York: Holt, Rinehart & Winston.

Hall, J. F. (1971). *Verbal learning and retention.* Philadelphia: Lippincott.

Hampton, J. A. (1984). The verification of category and property statements. *Memory & Cognition, 12,* 345–354.

Hanson, C., & Hirst, W. (1988). Frequency encoding of token and type information. *Journal of Experimental Psychology: Learning, Memory, and Cognition, 14,* 289–297.

Hanson, V. L., Goodell, E. W., & Perfetti, C. A. (1991). Tongue-twister effects in the silent reading of hearing and deaf college students. *Journal of Memory and Language, 30,* 319–330.

Harley, T. A. (1984). A critique of top–down independent levels models of speech production: Evidence from non-plan-internal speech errors. *Cognitive Science, 8,* 191–219.

Harlow, H. F. (1953). Mice, monkeys, men and motives. *Psychological Review, 60,* 23–60.

Harris, G. J., & Fleer, R. E. (1974). High speed memory scanning in mental retardates: Evidence for a central processing deficit. *Journal of Experimental Child Psychology, 17,* 452–459.

Harris, R. J., & Monaco, G. E. (1978). Psychology of pragmatic implication: Information processing between the lines. *Journal of Experimental Psychology: General, 107,* 1–22.

Hasher, L., Stoltzfus, E. R., Zacks, R. T., & Rypma, B. (1991). Age and inhibition. *Journal of Experimental Psychology: Learning, Memory, and Cognition, 17,* 163–169.

Hasher, L., & Zacks, R. T. (1984). Automatic processing of fundamental information: The case of frequency of occurrence. *American Psychologist, 39,* 1372–1388.

Haugeland, J. (Ed.). (1981). *Mind design: Philosophy, psychology, artificial intelligence.* Cambridge, MA: MIT Press.

Haugeland, J. (1985). *Artificial intelligence: The very idea.* Cambridge, MA: MIT Press.

Hayes, J. R. (1989). *The complete problem solver* (2nd ed.). Hillsdale, NJ: Erlbaum.

Hayes, J. R., & Simon, H. A. (1974). Understanding written problem instructions. In L. W. Gregg (Ed.), *Knowledge and cognition* (pp. 167–200). Hillsdale, NJ: Erlbaum.

Hebb, D. O. (1961). Distinctive features of learning in the higher animal. In J. Dalafresnaye (Ed.), *Brain mechanisms and learning.* London: Oxford University Press.

Heilman, K. M., Schwartz, H. D., & Geschwind, N. (1975). Defective motor learning in ideomotor apraxia. *Neurology, 25,* 1018–1020.

Hell, W., Gigerenzer, G., Gauggel, S., Mall, M., & Muller, M. (1988). Hindsight bias: An interaction of automatic and motivational factors? *Memory & Cognition, 16,* 533–538.

Hellyer, S. (1962). Frequency of stimulus presentation and short-term decrement in recall. *Journal of Experimental Psychology, 64,* 650.

Helsabeck, F., Jr. (1975). Syllogistic reasoning: Generation of counterexamples. *Journal of Educational Psychology, 67,* 102–108.

Hembree, R. (1990). The nature, effects, and relief of mathematics anxiety. *Journal for Research in Mathematics Education, 21,* 33–46.

Hertel, P. T., & Rude, S. S. (1991). Depressive deficits in memory: Focusing attention improves subsequent recall. *Journal of Experimental Psychology: General, 120,* 301–309.

Hilgard, E. R. (1964). Introduction to Ebbinghaus, 1885, *Memory: A contribution to experimental psychology* (pp. vii–x). New York: Dover.

Hintzman, D. L. (1978). *The psychology of learning and memory*. San Francisco: Freeman.

Hirshman, E., Whelley, M. M., & Palij, M. (1989). An investigation of paradoxical memory effects. *Journal of Memory and Language, 28,* 594–609.

Hirshman, E., & Durante, R. (1992). Prime identification and semantic priming. *Journal of Experimental Psychology: Learning, Memory, and Cognition, 18,* 255–265.

Hirst, W., & Kalmar, D. (1987). Characterizing attentional resources. *Journal of Experimental Psychology: General, 116,* 68–81.

Hoch, S. J. (1984). Availability and interference in predictive judgment. *Journal of Experimental Psychology: Learning, Memory, and Cognition, 10,* 649–662.

Hoch, S. J. (1985). Counterfactual reasoning and accuracy in predicting personal events. *Journal of Experimental Psychology: Learning, Memory, and Cognition, 11,* 719–731.

Hoch, S. J., & Loewenstein, G. F. (1989). Outcome feedback: Hindsight *and* information. *Journal of Experimental Psychology: Learning, Memory, and Cognition, 15,* 605–619.

Hockett, C. F. (1960a). Logical considerations in the study of animal communication. In W. E. Lanyon & W. N. Tavolga (Eds.), *Animal sounds and communication* (pp. 392–430). Washington, DC: American Institute of Biological Sciences.

Hockett, C. F. (1960b). The origin of speech. *Scientific American, 203,* 89–96.

Hockett, C. F. (1966). The problem of universals in language. In J. H. Greenberg (Ed.), *Universals of language* (2nd ed., pp. 1–29). Cambridge, MA: MIT Press.

Hoffman, R. R., Bringmann, W., Bamberg, M., & Klein, R. (1987). Some historical observations on Ebbinghaus. In D. S. Gorfein & R. R. Hoffman (Eds.), *Memory and learning: The Ebbinghaus Centennial Conference* (pp. 57–75). Hillsdale, NJ: Erlbaum.

Hollan, J. D. (1975). Features and semantic memory: Set-theoretic or network model? *Psychological Review, 82,* 154–155.

Holyoak, K. J. (1985). The pragmatics of analogical transfer. In G. H. Bower (Ed.), *The psychology of learning and motivation* (Vol. 19, pp. 59–87). Orlando: Academic Press.

Holyoak, K. J., & Koh, K. (1987). Surface and structural similarity in analogical transfer. *Memory & Cognition, 15,* 332–340.

Holyoak, K. J., & Mah, W. A. (1982). Cognitive reference points in judgments of symbolic magnitude. *Cognitive Psychology, 14,* 328–352.

Holyoak, K. J., & Walker, J. H. (1976). Subjective magnitude information in semantic orderings. *Journal of Verbal Learning and Verbal Behavior, 15,* 287–299.

Horton, K. D., Smith, S. A., Barghout, N. K., & Connolly, D. A. (1992). The use of indirect memory tests to assess malingered amnesia: A study of metamemory. *Journal of Experimental Psychology: General, 121,* 326–351.

Hothersall, D. (1984). *History of psychology*. New York: Random House.

Hothersall, D. (1985). *Psychology*. Columbus: Merrill Publishing.

Howard, D. V. (1983). *Cognitive psychology: Memory, language, and thought*. New York: Macmillan.

Hubel, D. H., & Wiesel, T. N. (1962). Receptive fields, binocular interaction, and functional architecture in the cat's visual cortex. *Journal of Physiology, 160,* 106–154.

Hull, C. L. (1943). *Principles of behavior.* New York: Appleton-Century-Crofts.

Humphreys, M. S., & Revelle, W. (1984). Personality, motivation, and performance: A theory of the relationship between individual differences and information processing. *Psychological Review, 91,* 153–184.

Hunt, E. B. (1978). Mechanics of verbal ability. *Psychological Review, 85,* 109–130.

Hunt, E., & Agnoli, F. (1991). The Whorfian hypothesis: A cognitive psychology perspective. *Psychological Review, 98,* 377–389.

Hunter, W. S. (1923). *General psychology.* Chicago: University of Chicago Press.

Hyde, J. S., Fennema, E., Ryan, M., Frost, L. A., & Hopp, C. (1990). Gender comparisons of mathematics attitudes and affect: A meta-analysis. *Psychology of Women Quarterly, 14,* 299–324.

Hyman, I. E., Jr., & Rubin, D. C. (1990). Memorabeatlia: A naturalistic study of long-term memory. *Memory & Cognition, 18,* 205–214.

Inhoff, A. W. (1984). Two stages of word processing during eye fixations in the reading of prose. *Journal of Verbal Learning and Verbal Behavior, 23,* 612–624.

Irwin, D. E. (1991). Information integration across saccadic eye movements. *Cognitive Psychology, 23,* 420–456.

Irwin, D. E. (1992). Memory for position and identity across eye movements. *Journal of Experimental Psychology: Learning, Memory, and Cognition, 18,* 307–317.

Isaacs, E. A., & Clark, H. H. (1987). References in conversation between experts and novices. *Journal of Experimental Psychology: General, 116,* 26–37.

Iversen, L. L. (1979). The chemistry of the brain. In *The brain: A Scientific American book* (pp. 70–83). San Francisco: Freeman.

Jacoby, L. L., & Dallas, M. (1981). On the relationship between autobiographical memory and perceptual learning. *Journal of Experimental Psychology: General, 110,* 306–340.

Jaffe, J., & Feldstein, S. (1970). *Rhythms of dialogue.* New York: Academic Press.

James, W. (1890). *The principles of psychology.* New York: Dover.

Jarvella, R. J. (1970). Effects of syntax on running memory span for connected discourse. *Psychonomic Science, 19,* 235–236.

Jarvella, R. J. (1971). Syntactic processing of connected speech. *Journal of Verbal Learning and Verbal Behavior, 10,* 409–416.

Jenkins, J. G., & Dallenbach, K. M. (1924). Obliviscence during sleep and waking. *American Journal of Psychology, 35,* 605–612.

Jenkins, J. J. (1974). Remember that old theory of memory? Well forget it! *American Psychologist, 29,* 785–795.

Johnson, J. T., & Finke, R. A. (1985). The base-rate fallacy in the context of sequential categories. *Memory & Cognition, 13,* 63–73.

Johnson, N. F. (1970). The role of chunking and organization in the process of recall. In G. H. Bower (Ed.), *The psychology of learning and motivation* (Vol. 4, pp. 172–247). New York: Academic Press.

Johnson, W., & Kieras, D. (1983). Representation-saving effects of prior knowledge in memory for simple technical prose. *Memory & Cognition, 11,* 456–466.

Johnson-Laird, P. N. (1988). *The computer and the mind: An introduction to cognitive science.* Cambridge, MA: Harvard University Press.

Johnson-Laird, P. N., Legrenzi, P., & Legrenzi, M. S. (1972). Reasoning and a sense of reality. *British Journal of Psychology, 63,* 395–400.

Johnston, W. A., & Heinz, S. P. (1978). Flexibility and capacity demands of attention. *Journal of Experimental Psychology: General, 107,* 420–435.

Jones, G. V. (1989). Back to Woodworth: Role of interlopers in the tip-of-the-tongue phenomenon. *Memory & Cognition, 17,* 69–76.

Jonides, J., & Jones, C. M. (1992). Direct coding for frequency of occurrence. *Journal of Experimental Psychology: Learning, Memory, and Cognition, 18,* 368–378.

Joordens, S., & Besner, D. (1992). Priming effects that span an intervening unrelated word: Implications for models of memory representation and retrieval. *Journal of Experimental Psychology: Learning, Memory, and Cognition, 18,* 483–491.

Jusczyk, P. W., Smith, L. B., & Murphy, C. (1981). The perceptual classification of speech. *Perception and Psychophysics, 1,* 10–23.

Just, M. A. (1976, May). *Research strategies in prose comprehension.* Paper presented at the meetings of the Midwestern Psychological Association, Chicago.

Just, M. A., & Carpenter, P. A. (1980). A theory of reading: From eye fixations to comprehension. *Psychological Review, 87,* 329–354.

Just, M. A., & Carpenter, P. A. (1987). *The psychology of reading and language comprehension.* Boston: Allyn & Bacon.

Just, M. A., & Carpenter, P. A. (1992). A capacity theory of comprehension. *Psychological Review, 99,* 122–149.

Kahneman, D. (1968). Method, findings and theory in studies of visual masking. *Psychological Bulletin, 70,* 404–426.

Kahneman, D. (1973). *Attention and effort.* Englewood Cliffs, NJ: Prentice-Hall.

Kahneman, D., Slovic, P., & Tversky, A. (Eds.). (1982). *Judgment under uncertainty: Heuristics and biases.* Cambridge: Cambridge University Press.

Kahneman, D., & Tversky, A. (1972). Subjective probability: A judgment of representativeness. *Cognitive Psychology, 3,* 430–454.

Kahneman, D., & Tversky, A. (1973). On the psychology of prediction. *Psychological Review, 80,* 237–251.

Kahneman, D., & Tversky, A. (1982). The simulation heuristic. In D. Kahneman, P. Slovic, & A. Tversky (Eds.), *Judgment under uncertainty: Heuristics and biases* (pp. 201–208). Cambridge: Cambridge University Press.

Kaiser, M. K., Jonides, J., & Alexander, J. (1986). Intuitive reasoning about abstract and familiar physics problems. *Memory & Cognition, 14,* 308–312.

Kaiser, M. K., Proffitt, D. R., & Anderson, K. (1985). Judgments of natural and anomalous trajectories in the presence and absence of motion. *Journal of Experimental Psychology: Learning, Memory, and Cognition, 11,* 795–803.

Kanwisher, N., & Driver, J. (1992). Objects, attributes, and visual attention: Which, what, and where. *Psychological Science, 1,* 26–31.

Katz, J., & Fodor, J. A. (1963). The structure of a semantic theory. *Language, 39,* 170–210.

Kay, J., & Ellis, A. (1987). A cognitive neuropsychological case study of anomia: Implications for psychological models of word retrieval. *Brain, 110,* 613–629.

Keenan, J. M., MacWhinney, B., & Mayhew, D. (1977). Pragmatics in memory: A study of natural conversation. *Journal of Verbal Learning and Verbal Behavior, 16,* 549–560.

Keil, F. C. (1991). On being more than the sum of the parts: The conceptual coherence of cognitive science. *Psychological Science, 2,* 283–293.

Kellas, G., & Butterfield, E. C. (1971). Effect of response requirement and type of material on acquisition and retention performance in short-term memory. *Journal of Experimental Psychology, 88,* 50–56.

Kellas, G., McCauley, C., & McFarland, C. E., Jr. (1975a). Developmental aspects of storage and retrieval. *Journal of Experimental Child Psychology, 19,* 51–62.

Kellas, G., McCauley, C., & McFarland, C. E., Jr. (1975b). Reexamination of externalized rehearsal. *Journal of Experimental Psychology: Human Learning and Memory, 104,* 84–90.

Kempen, G., & Hoehkamp, E. (1987). An incremental procedural grammar for sentence formulation. *Cognitive Science, 11,* 201–258.

Kemper, S., & Thissen, D. (1981). Memory for the dimensions of requests. *Journal of Verbal Learning and Verbal Behavior, 20,* 552–563.

Kempton, W. (1986). Two theories of home heat control. *Cognitive Science, 10,* 75–90.

Keppel, G., & Underwood, B. J. (1962). Proactive inhibition in short-term retention of single items. *Journal of Verbal Learning and Verbal Behavior, 1,* 153–161.

Keren, G., & Wagenaar, W. A. (1985). On the psychology of playing blackjack: Normative and descriptive considerations with implications for decision theory. *Journal of Experimental Psychology: General, 114,* 133–158.

Kertesz, A. (1982). Two case studies: Broca's and Wernicke's aphasia. In M. A. Arbib, D. Caplan, & J. C. Marshall (Eds.), *Neural models of language processes* (pp. 25–44). New York: Academic Press.

Keysar, B. (1989). On the functional equivalence of literal and metaphorical interpretations in discourse. *Journal of Memory and Language, 28,* 375–385.

King, J., & Just, M. A. (1991). Individual differences in syntactic processing: The role of working memory. *Journal of Memory and Language, 30,* 580–602.

Kinsbourne, M., & Cook, J. (1971). Generalized and lateralized effects of concurrent verbalization on a unimanual skill. *Quarterly Journal of Experimental Psychology, 23,* 341–345.

Kintsch, W. (1970). *Learning, memory, and conceptual processes.* New York: Wiley.

Kintsch, W. (1974). *The representation of meaning in memory.* Hillsdale, NJ: Erlbaum.

Kintsch, W. (1977). *Memory and cognition* (2nd ed.). New York: Wiley.

Kintsch, W. (1985). Reflections on Ebbinghaus. *Journal of Experimental Psychology: Learning, Memory, and Cognition, 11,* 461–463.

Kintsch, W., & Bates, E. (1977). Recognition memory for statements from a classroom lecture. *Journal of Experimental Psychology: Human Learning and Memory, 3,* 150–159.

Kintsch, W., & Greeno, J. G. (1985). Understanding and solving word arithmetic problems. *Psychological Review, 92,* 109–129.

Kintsch, W., & Mross, E. F. (1985). Context effects in word identification. *Journal of Memory and Language, 24,* 336–349.

Klatzky, R. L. (1980). *Human memory: Structures and processes* (2nd ed.). San Francisco: Freeman.

Klatzky, R. L., & Atkinson, R. C. (1971). Specialization of the cerebral hemispheres in scanning for information in short-term memory. *Perception & Psychophysics, 10,* 335–338.

Klawans, H. L. (1988). *Toscanini's fumble.* Chicago: Contemporary Books.

Klayman, J., & Ha, Y.-W. (1989). Hypothesis testing in rule discovery: Strategy, structure, and content. *Journal of Experimental Psychology: Learning, Memory, and Cognition, 15,* 596–604.

Klieger, D. M. (1984). *Computer usage for social scientists.* Boston: Allyn & Bacon.

Koenig, O., Wetzel, C., & Caramazza, A. (1992). Evidence for different types of lexical representations in the cerebral hemispheres. *Cognitive Neuropsychology, 9,* 33–45.

Kohler, W. (1927). *The mentality of apes.* New York: Harcourt, Brace.

Kolb, B., & Whishaw, I. Q. (1990). *Fundamentals of human neuropsychology* (3rd ed.). New York: Freeman.

Kolers, P. A., & Roediger, H. L. III (1984). Procedures of mind. *Journal of Verbal Learning and Verbal Behavior, 23,* 425–449.

Kopelman, M. D. (1987). Crime and amnesia: A review. *Behavioral Sciences & the Law, 5,* 323–342.

Kosslyn, S. M. (1978). Imagery and internal representation. In E. Rosch & B. B. Lloyd (Eds.), *Cognition and categorization* (pp. 217–257). Hillsdale, NJ: Erlbaum.

Kosslyn, S. M. (1981). The medium and the message in mental imagery: A theory. *Psychological Review, 88,* 46–66.

Kosslyn, S. M., & Pomerantz, J. P. (1977). Imagery, propositions, and the form of internal representations. *Cognitive Psychology, 9,* 52–76.

Kotovsky, K., Hayes, J. R., & Simon, H. A. (1985). Why are some problems hard? Evidence from Tower of Hanoi. *Cognitive Psychology, 17,* 248–294.

Kounios, J., & Holcomb, P. J. (1992). Structure and process in semantic memory: Evidence from event-related brain potentials and reaction times. *Journal of Experimental Psychology: General, 121,* 459–479.

Kounios, J., Osman, A. M., & Meyer, D. E. (1987). Structure and process in semantic memory: New evidence based on speed–accuracy decomposition. *Journal of Experimental Psychology: General, 116,* 3–25.

Krauss, R. M., Morrel-Samuels, P., & Colosante, C. (1991). Do conversational hand gestures communicate? *Journal of Personality and Social Psychology, 61,* 743–754.

Kroll, N. E. A., Schepeler, E. M., & Angin, K. T. (1986). Bizarre imagery: The misremembered mnemonic. *Journal of Experimental Psychology: Learning, Memory, and Cognition, 12,* 42–53.

Kucera, H., & Francis, W. N. (1967). *Computational analysis of present day American English.* Providence, RI: Brown University Press.

Kuhn, T. S. (1962). *The structure of scientific revolutions.* Chicago: University of Chicago Press (2nd ed., 1970).

Kunda, Z., & Nisbett, R. E. (1986). The psychometrics of everyday life. *Cognitive Psychology, 18,* 195–225.

Lachman, R., Lachman, J. L., & Butterfield, E. C. (1979). *Cognitive psychology and information processing: An introduction.* Hillsdale, NJ: Erlbaum.

Lakoff, G., & Johnson, M. (1980). *Metaphors we live by.* Chicago: University of Chicago Press.

Larkin, J., McDermott, J., Simon, D. P., & Simon, H. A. (1980). Expert and novice performance in solving physics problems. *Science, 208,* 1335–1342.

Lashley, K. D. (1950). In search of the engram. *Symposia for the Society for Experimental Biology, 4,* 454–482.

Leahey, T. H. (1992a). *A history of psychology: Main currents in psychological thought* (3rd ed.). Englewood Cliffs, NJ: Prentice-Hall.

Leahey, T. H. (1992b). The mythical revolutions of American psychology. *American Psychologist, 47,* 308–318.

Leal, L., Crays, N., & Moely, B. E. (1985). Training children to use a self-monitoring study strategy in preparation for recall: Maintenance and generalization effects. *Child Development, 56,* 643–653.

Lehman, D. R., Lempert, R. O., & Nisbett, R. E. (1988). The effects of graduate training on reasoning. *American Psychologist, 43,* 431–442.

Leight, K. A., & Ellis, H. C. (1981). Emotional mood states, strategies, and state-dependency in memory. *Journal of Verbal Learning and Verbal Behavior, 20,* 251–266.

Lennie, P. (1980). Parallel visual pathways: A review. *Vision Research, 20,* 561–594.

Leonesio, R. J., & Nelson, T. O. (1990). Do different metamemory judgments tap the same underlying aspects of memory? *Journal of Experimental Psychology: Learning, Memory, and Cognition, 16,* 464–470.

Levine, M. (1988). *Effective problem solving.* Englewood Cliffs, NJ: Prentice-Hall.

Levine, M. W., & Schefner, J. M. (1981). *Fundamentals of sensation and perception.* London: Addison-Wesley.

Lewandowsky, S., Dunn, J. C., & Kirsner, K. (Eds.). (1989). *Implicit memory: Theoretical issues.* London: Erlbaum.

Lewis, J. L. (1970). Semantic processing of unattended messages using dichotic listening. *Journal of Experimental Psychology, 85,* 225–228.

Lewontin, R. C. (1990). The evolution of cognition. In D. N. Osherson & E. E. Smith (Eds.), *Thinking: An invitation to cognitive science* (Vol. 3, pp. 229–246). Cambridge, MA: MIT Press.

Libbey, R. (1981). *Accounting and human information processing: Theory and application.* Englewood Cliffs, NJ: Prentice-Hall.

Liberman, A. M. (1957). Some results of research on speech perception. *Journal of the Acoustical Society of America, 29,* 117–123.

Liberman, A. M. (1970). The grammars of speech and language. *Cognitive Psychology, 1,* 301–323.

Liberman, A. M., Harris, K. S., Hoffman, H. S., & Griffith, B. C. (1957). The discrimination of speech sounds within and across phoneme boundaries. *Journal of Experimental Psychology, 54,* 358–368.

Lindfors, J. W. (1987). *Children's language and learning* (2nd ed.). Englewood Cliffs, NJ: Prentice-Hall.

Lindsay, P. H., & Norman, D. A. (1977). *Human information processing: An introduction to psychology.* New York: Academic Press.

Lindsley, J. R. (1975). Producing simple utterances: How far ahead do we plan? *Cognitive Psychology, 7,* 1–19.

Linton, M. (1975). Memory for real-world events. In D. A. Norman & D. E. Rumelhart (Eds.), *Explorations in cognition* (pp. 376–404). San Francisco: Freeman.

Linton, M. (1978). Real world memory after six years: An in vivo study of very long term memory. In M. M. Gruneberg, P. E. Morris, & R. N. Sykes (Eds.), *Practical aspects of memory* (pp. 69–76). Orlando: Academic Press.

Litman, D. J., & Allen, J. F. (1987). A plan recognition model for subdialogues in conversation. *Cognitive Science, 11,* 163–200.

Loftus, E. F. (1979). *Eyewitness testimony.* Cambridge, MA: Harvard University Press.

Loftus, E. F. (1980). *Memory.* Reading, MA: Addison-Wesley.

Loftus, E. F. (1983a). Silence is not golden. *American Psychologist, 38,* 564–572.

Loftus, E. F. (1983b). Whose shadow is crooked? *American Psychologist, 38,* 576–577.

Loftus, E. F. (1991). Made in memory: Distortions in recollection after misleading information. In G. H. Bower (Ed.), *The psychology of learning and motivation* (Vol. 27, pp. 187–215). New York: Academic Press.

Loftus, E. F. (1991). Resolving legal questions with psychological data. *American Psychologist, 46,* 1046–1048.

Loftus, E. F., & Burns, T. (1982). Mental shock can reproduce retrograde amnesia. *Memory & Cognition, 10,* 318–323.

Loftus, E. F., Donders, K., Hoffman, H. G., & Schooler, J. W. (1989). Creating new memories that are quickly accessed and confidently held. *Memory & Cognition, 17,* 607–616.

Loftus, E. F., & Hoffman, H. G. (1989). Misinformation and memory: The creation of new memories. *Journal of Experimental Psychology: General, 118,* 100–104.

Loftus, E. F., & Palmer, J. C. (1974). Reconstruction of automobile destruction: An example of the interaction between language and memory. *Journal of Verbal Learning and Verbal Behavior, 13,* 585–589.

Loftus, G. R. (1983). The continuing persistence of the icon. *The Behavioral and Brain Sciences, 6,* 28.

Loftus, G. (1985). Johannes Kepler's computer simulation of the universe: Some remarks about theory in psychology. *Behavior Research Methods, Instruments, & Computers, 17,* 149–156.

Loftus, G. R., & Hanna, A. M. (1989). The phenomenology of spatial integration: Data and models. *Cognitive Psychology, 21,* 363–397.

Loftus, G. R., & Loftus, E. F. (1974). The influence of one memory retrieval on a subsequent memory retrieval. *Memory & Cognition, 2,* 467–471.

Loftus, G. R., & Loftus, E. F. (1976). *Human memory: The processing of information.* Hillsdale, NJ: Erlbaum.

Logan, G. D. (1990). Repetition priming and automaticity: Common underlying mechanisms? *Cognitive Psychology, 22,* 1–35.

Logan, G. D., & Klapp, S. T. (1991). Automatizing alphabet arithmetic: I. Is extended practice necessary to produce automaticity? *Journal of Experimental Psychology: Learning, Memory, and Cognition, 17,* 179–195.

Long, D. L., Golding, J. M., & Graesser, A. C. (1992). A test of the on-line status of goal-related inferences. *Journal of Memory and Language, 31,* 634–647.

Long, D. L., Golding, J., Graesser, A. C., & Clark, L. F. (1990). Inference generation during story comprehension: A comparison of goals, events, and states. In A. C. Graesser & G. H. Bower (Eds.) *The psychology of learning and motivation* (Vol. 25). New York: Academic Press.

Lorayne, H., & Lucas, J. (1974). *The memory book.* New York: Ballantine Books.

Lorch, R. F., Jr., Lorch, E. P., & Matthews, P. D. (1985). On-line processing of the topic structure of a text. *Journal of Memory and Language, 24,* 350–362.

Luchins, A. S. (1942). Mechanization in problem solving. *Psychological Monographs, 54* (Whole No. 248).

Luria, A. R. (1968). *The mind of a mnemonist.* New York: Basic Books.

MacDonald, M. C., & Just, M. A. (1989). Changes in activation levels with negation. *Journal of Experimental Psychology: Learning, Memory, and Cognition, 15,* 633–642.

MacDonald, M. C., Just, M. A., & Carpenter, P. A. (1992). Working memory constraints on the processing of syntactic ambiguity. *Cognitive Psychology, 24,* 56–98.

MacLeod, C. M. (1988). Forgotten but not gone: Savings for pictures and words in long-term memory. *Journal of Experimental Psychology: Learning, Memory, and Cognition, 14,* 195–212.

MacLeod, C. M. (1991). Half a century of research on the Stroop effect: An integrative review. *Psychological Bulletin, 109,* 163–203.

MacLeod, C. (1992). The Stroop task: The "gold standard" of attentional measures. *Journal of Experimental Psychology: General, 121,* 12–14.

MacWhinney, G. (1984). Topic and perspective as cognitive functions. *Monographs of the Society for Research in Child Development, 49* (5, Serial No. 208, pp. 66–71).

Madigan, S., & O'Hara, R. (1992). Short-term memory at the turn of the century: Mary Whiton Calkins's memory research. *American Psychologist, 47,* 170–174.

Maier, N. R. F. (1931). Reasoning in humans: II. The solution of a problem and its appearance in consciousness. *Journal of Comparative Psychology, 12,* 181–194.

Maki, R. H. (1989). Recognition of added and deleted details in scripts. *Memory & Cognition, 17,* 274–282.

Maki, R. H., & Berry, S. L. (1984). Metacomprehension of text material. *Journal of Experimental Psychology: Learning, Memory, and Cognition, 10,* 663–679.

Malt, B. C. (1985). The role of discourse structure in understanding anaphora. *Journal of Memory and Language, 24,* 271–289.

Malt, B. C. (1990). Features and beliefs in the mental representation of categories. *Journal of Memory and Language, 29,* 289–315.

Mandler, G. (1967). Organization and memory. In K. W. Spence & J. T. Spence (Eds.), *The psychology of learning and motivation* (Vol. 1, pp. 327–372). New York: Academic Press.

Mandler, G. (1972). Organization and recognition. In E. Tulving & W. Donaldson (Eds.), *Organization of memory* (pp. 139–166). New York: Academic Press.

Mandler, G. (1984). *Mind and body: Psychology of emotion and stress.* New York: Norton.

Mandler, G. (1985a). *Cognitive psychology: An essay in cognitive science.* Hillsdale, NJ: Erlbaum.

Mandler, G. (1985b). From association to structure. *Journal of Experimental Psychology: Learning, Memory, and Cognition, 11,* 464–468.

Mandler, G. (1989). Affect and learning: Causes and consequences of emotional interactions. In D. B. McLeaod & V. M. Adams (Eds.), *Affect and mathematical problem solving* (pp. 3–19). New York: Springer-Verlag.

Mandler, J. M., & Mandler, G. (1969). The diaspora of experimental psychology: The gestaltists and others. In D. Fleming & B. Bailyn (Eds.), *The intellectual migration: Europe and America, 1930–1960* (pp. 371–419). Cambridge, MA: Harvard University Press.

Marcel, A. J. (1980). Conscious and preconscious recognition of polysemous words: Locating the selective effects of prior verbal context. In R. S. Nickerson (Ed.), *Attention and performance VIII* (pp. 435–457). Hillsdale, NJ: Erlbaum.

Marcel, A. J. (1983). Conscious and unconscious perception: Experiments on visual masking and word recognition. *Cognitive Psychology, 15,* 197–237.

Marler, P. (1967). Animal communication signals. *Science, 35,* 63–78.

Marschark, M., & Cornoldi, C. (1990). Imagery and verbal memory. In C. Cornoldi & M. McDaniel (Eds.), *Imagery and cognition* (pp. 133–182). New York: Springer-Verlag.

Marschark, M., & Paivio, A. (1979). Semantic congruity and lexical marking in symbolic comparisons: An expectancy hypothesis. *Memory & Cognition, 7,* 175–184.

Marschark, M., Yuille, J. C. Richman, C. L., & Hunt, R. R. (1987). The role of imagery in memory: On shared and distinctive information. *Psychological Bulletin, 102,* 28–41.

Marslen-Wilson, W. D., & Tyler, L. K. (1980). The temporal structure of spoken language understanding. *Cognition, 8,* 1–71.

Marslen-Wilson, W. D., & Welsh, A. (1978). Processing interactions and lexical access during word recognition in continuous speech. *Cognitive Psychology, 10,* 29–63.

Martin, E., & Noreen, D. L. (1974). Serial learning: Identification of subjective subsequences. *Cognitive Psychology, 6,* 421–435.

Martin, L. (1986). "Eskimo words for snow": A case study in the genesis and decay of an anthropological example. *American Anthropologist, 88,* 418–423.

Martindale, C. (1991). *Cognitive psychology: A neural-network approach.* Pacific Grove, CA: Brooks/Cole.

Massaro, D. W. (1988). Some criticisms of connectionist models of human performance. *Journal of Memory and Language, 27,* 213–234.

Masson, M. E. J. (1984). Memory for the surface structure of sentences: Remembering with and without awareness. *Journal of Verbal Learning and Verbal Behavior, 23,* 579–592.

Matlin, M. (1983). *Cognition.* New York: Holt.

Maunsell, J. H. R., & Newsome, W. T. (1987). Visual processing in monkey extrastriate cortex. *Annual Review of Neuroscience, 10,* 363–401.

Mayer, R. E. (1981). *The promise of cognitive psychology.* San Francisco: Freeman.

Mayer, R. E. (1992). *Thinking, problem solving, cognition* (2nd ed.). New York: Freeman.

McCarthy, R. A., & Warrington, E. K. (1990). *Cognitive neuropsychology: A clinical introduction.* San Diego: Academic Press.

McClelland, J. L. (1979). On the time relations of mental processes: An examination of systems of processes in cascade. *Psychological Review, 86,* 287–330.

McClelland, J. L., & Elman, J. L. (1986). The TRACE model of speech perception. *Cognitive Psychology, 18,* 1–86.

McClelland, J. L., & Rumelhart, D. E. (1981). An interactive activation model of context effects in letter perception: Part 1. An account of basic findings. *Psychological Review, 88,* 375–407.

McClelland, J. L., & Rumelhart, D. E. (1986). *Parallel distributed processing: Explorations in the microstructure of cognition: Vol 2. Psychological and biological models.* Cambridge, MA: Bradford.

McClelland, J. L., Rumelhart, D. E., & Hinton, G. E. (1986). The appeal of parallel distributed processing. In D. E. Rumelhart, J. L. McClelland, & PDP Research Group (Eds.), *Parallel distributed processing* (Vol. 1, pp. 3–44). Cambridge, MA: MIT Press.

McCloskey, M. (1983). Naive theories of motion. In D. Gentner & A. L. Stevens (Eds.), *Mental models* (pp. 299–324). Hillsdale, NJ: Erlbaum.

McCloskey, M. (1991). Networks and theories: The place of connectionism in cognitive science. *Psychological Science, 2,* 387–395.

McCloskey, M. (1992). Cognitive mechanisms in numerical processing: Evidence from acquired dyscalculia. *Cognition, 44,* 107–157.

McCloskey, M., Caramazza, A., & Basili, A. (1985). Cognitive mechanisms in number processing and calculation: Evidence from dyscalculia. *Brain and Cognition, 4,* 171–196.

McCloskey, M., Caramazza, A., & Green, B. (1980). Curvilinear motion in the absence of external forces: Naive beliefs about the motion of objects. *Science, 210,* 1139–1141.

McCloskey, M., & Egeth, H. E. (1983a). A time to speak, or a time to keep silence? *American Psychologist, 38,* 573–575.

McCloskey, M., & Egeth, H. E. (1983b). Eyewitness identification: What can a psychologist tell a jury? *American Psychologist, 38,* 550–563.

McCloskey, M., & Kohl, D. (1983). Naive physics: The curvilinear impetus principle and its role in interactions with moving objects. *Journal of Experimental Psychology: Learning, Memory, and Cognition, 9,* 146–156.

McCloskey, M., & Lindemann, A. M. (1992). MATHNET: Preliminary results from a distributed model of arithmetic fact retrieval. In J. I. D. Campbell (Ed.), *The nature and origins of mathematical skills* (pp. 365–409). Amsterdam: North-Holland.

McCloskey, M., & Santee, J. (1981). Are semantic memory and episodic memory distinct systems? *Journal of Experimental Psychology: Human Learning and Memory, 7,* 66–71.

McCloskey, M., Washburn, A., & Felch, L. (1983). Intuitive physics: The straight-down belief and its origin. *Journal of Experimental Psychology: Learning, Memory, and Cognition, 9,* 636–649.

McCloskey, M., Wible, C. G., & Cohen, N. J. (1988). Is there a special flashbulb-memory mechanism? *Journal of Experimental Psychology: General, 117,* 171–181.

McCloskey, M., & Zaragoza, M. (1985). Misleading postevent information and memory for events: Arguments and evidence against memory impairment hypotheses. *Journal of Experimental Psychology: General, 114,* 1–16.

McDaniel, M. A., & Einstein, G. O. (1986). Bizarre imagery as an effective memory aid: The importance of distinctiveness. *Journal of Experimental Psychology: Learning, Memory, and Cognition, 12,* 54–65.

McGeoch, J. A. (1932). Forgetting and the law of disuse. *Psychological Review, 39,* 352–370.

McKoon, G., & Ratcliff, R. (1986). Inferences about predictable events. *Journal of Experimental Psychology: Learning, Memory, and Cognition, 12,* 82–91.

McKoon, G., & Ratcliff, R. (1989). Inferences about contextually defined categories. *Journal of Experimental Psychology: Learning, Memory, and Cognition, 15,* 1134–1146.

McKoon, G., & Ratcliff, R. (1992). Spreading activation versus compound cue accounts of priming: Mediated priming revisited. *Journal of Experimental Psychology: Learning, Memory, and Cognition, 18,* 1155–1172.

McKoon, G., Ratcliff, R., & Dell, G. S. (1985). The role of semantic information in episodic retrieval. *Journal of Experimental Psychology: Learning, Memory, and Cognition, 11,* 742–751.

McKoon, G., Ratcliff, R., & Dell, G. S. (1986). A critical evaluation of the semantic–episodic distinction. *Journal of Experimental Psychology: Learning, Memory, and Cognition, 12,* 295–306.

McNamara, T. P. (1992a). Priming and constraints it places on theories of memory and retrieval. *Psychological Review, 99,* 650–662.

McNamara, T. P. (1992b). Theories of priming: I. Associative distance and lag. *Journal of Experimental Psychology: Learning, Memory, and Cognition, 18,* 1173–1190.

McNeill, D. (1985). So you think gestures are nonverbal? *Psychological Review, 92,* 350–371.

McNeill, D. (1987). *Psycholinguistics: A new approach.* New York: Harper & Row.

Medin, D. L., Altom, M. W., Edelson, S. M., & Freko, D. (1982). Correlated symptoms and simulated medical classification. *Journal of Experimental Psychology: Learning, Memory, and Cognition, 8,* 37–50.

Medin, D. L., & Edelson, S. M. (1988). Problem structure and the use of base-rate information from experience. *Journal of Experimental Psychology: General, 117,* 68–85.

Mehler, J., Morton, J., & Jusczyk, P. W. (1984). On reducing language to biology. *Cognitive Neuropsychology, 1,* 83–116.

Melton, A. W. (1963). Implications of short-term memory for a general theory of memory. *Journal of Verbal Learning and Verbal Behavior, 2,* 1–21.

Mendelson, R. (1993). *Where did I put my glasses?* Cleveland: Segno Books.

Merikle, P. M. (1982). Unconscious perception revisited. *Perception & Psychophysics, 31,* 298–301.

Metcalfe, J. (1986). Feeling of knowing in memory and problem solving. *Journal of Experimental Psychology: Learning, Memory, and Cognition, 12,* 288–294.

Meyer, A. S., & Bock, K. (1992). The tip-of-the-tongue phenomenon: Blocking or partial activation? *Memory & Cognition, 20,* 715–726.

Meyer, D. E., & Schvaneveldt, R. W. (1971). Facilitation in recognizing pairs of words: Evidence of a dependence between retrieval operations. *Journal of Experimental Psychology, 90,* 227–234.

Meyer, D. E., Schvaneveldt, R. W., & Ruddy, M. G. (1975). Loci of contextual effects on visual word-recognition. In P. M. A. Rabbitt & S. Dornic (Eds.), *Attention and performance* (Vol. 5, pp. 98–118). London: Academic Press.

Micco, A., & Masson, M. E. J. (1991). Implicit memory for new associations: An interactive process approach. *Journal of Experimental Psychology: Learning, Memory, and Cognition, 17,* 1105–1123.

Miller, G. A. (1956). The magical number seven, plus or minus two: Some limits on our capacity for processing information. *Psychological Review, 63,* 81–97.

Miller, G. A. (1973). Psychology and communication. In G. A. Miller (Ed.), *Communication, language, and meaning: Psychological perspectives* (pp. 3–12). New York: Basic Books.

Miller, G. A. (1977). Practical and lexical knowledge. In P. N. Johnson-Laird & P. C. Wason (Eds.), *Thinking: Readings in cognitive science* (pp. 400–410). Cambridge: Cambridge University Press.

Miller, G. A. (1981). *Language and speech.* San Francisco: Freeman.

Miller, G. A. (1983). Introduction to James, W., *The principles of psychology* (1983 edition, pp. ix–xxi). Cambridge: Harvard University Press.

Miller, G. A., Galanter, E., & Pribram, K. H. (1960). *Plans and the structure of behavior.* New York: Henry Holt.

Miller, G. A., & Isard, S. (1963). Some perceptual consequences of linguistic rules. *Journal of Verbal Learning and Verbal Behavior, 2,* 217–228.

Milner, B., Corkin, S., & Teuber, H. L. (1968). Further analysis of the hippocampal amnesic syndrome: 14-year follow up study of H.M. *Neuropsychologia, 6,* 215–234.

Mitchell, D. C., & Holmes, V. M. (1985). The role of specific information about the verb in parsing sentences with local structural ambiguity. *Journal of Memory and Language, 24,* 542–559.

Mook, D. G. (1983). In defense of external invalidity. *American Psychologist, 38,* 379–387.

Moray, N. (1959). Attention in dichotic listening: Affective cues and the influence of instructions. *Quarterly Journal of Experimental Psychology, 11,* 56–60.

Moray, N., Bates, A., & Barnett, T. (1965). Experiments on the four-eared man. *Journal of the Acoustical Society of America, 38,* 196–201.

Morris, C. D., Bransford, J. D., & Franks, J. J. (1977). Levels of processing versus transfer appropriate processing. *Journal of Verbal Learning and Verbal Behavior, 16,* 519–533.

Morton, J. (1970). A functional model for memory. In D. A. Norman (Ed.), *Models of human memory* (pp. 203–254). New York: Academic Press.

Morton, J. (1979). Facilitation in word recognition: Experiments causing change in the logogen models. In P. A. Kolers, M. E. Wrolstad, & H. Bouma, (Eds.), *Processing of visible language* (Vol. 1, pp. 259–268). New York: Plenum Press.

Moscovitch, M. (1979). Information processing and the cerebral hemispheres. In M. S. Gazzaniga (Ed.), *Handbook of behavioral neurobiology: Vol. 2. Neuropsychology* (pp. 379–446). New York: Plenum Press.

Moyer, R. S. (1973). Comparing objects in memory: Evidence suggesting an internal psychophysics. *Perception and Psychophysics, 13,* 180–184.

Moyer, R. S., & Bayer, R. H. (1976). Mental comparison and the symbolic distance effect. *Cognitive Psychology, 8,* 228–246.

Murdock, B. B., Jr. (1962). The serial position effect of free recall. *Journal of Experimental Psychology, 64,* 482–488.

Murdock, B. B., Jr. (1985). The contributions of Herman Ebbinghaus. *Journal of Experimental Psychology: Learning, Memory, and Cognition, 11,* 469–471.

Murphy, G. L. (1985). Processes of understanding anaphora. *Journal of Memory and Language, 24,* 290–303.

Myles-Worsley, M., Johnston, W. A., & Simons, M. A. (1988). The influence of expertise on x-ray image processing. *Journal of Experimental Psychology: Learning, Memory, and Cognition, 14,* 553–557.

Nairne, J. S. (1983). Associative processing during rote rehearsal. *Journal of Experimental Psychology: Learning, Memory, and Cognition, 9,* 3–20.

Nakamura, G. V., Graesser, A. C., Zimmerman, J. A., & Riha, J. (1985). Script processing in a natural situation. *Memory & Cognition, 13,* 140–144.

Nauta, W. J. H., & Feirtag, M. (1979). The organization of the brain. *Scientific American, 241,* 88–111.

Nayak, N. P., & Gibbs, R. W., Jr. (1990). Conceptual knowledge in the interpretation of idioms. *Journal of Experimental Psychology: General, 119,* 315–330.

Neely, J. H. (1976). Semantic priming and retrieval from lexical memory: Evidence for facilitatory and inhibitory processes. *Memory & Cognition, 4,* 648–654.

Neely, J. H. (1977). Semantic priming and retrieval from lexical memory: Roles of inhibitionless spreading activation and limited-capacity attention. *Journal of Experimental Psychology: General, 106,* 226–254.

Neely, J. H., & Durgunoglu, A. Y. (1985). Dissociative episodic and semantic priming effects in episodic recognition and lexical decision tasks. *Journal of Memory and Language, 24,* 466–489.

Neely, J. H., Keefe, D. E., & Ross, K. L. (1989). Semantic priming in the lexical decision task: Roles of prospective prime-generated expectancies and retrospective semantic matching. *Journal of Experimental Psychology: Learning, Memory, and Cognition, 15,* 1003–1019.

Neill, W. R., Beck, J. L., Bottalico, K. S., & Molloy, R. D. (1990). Effects of intentional versus incidental learning on explicit and implicit tests of memory. *Journal of Experimental Psychology: Learning, Memory, and Cognition, 16,* 457–463.

Neisser, U. (1964). Visual search. *Scientific American, 210,* 94–102.

Neisser, U. (1967). *Cognitive psychology.* New York: Appleton-Century-Crofts.

Neisser, U. (1976). *Cognition and reality.* San Francisco: Freeman.

Neisser, U. (1978). Memory: What are the important questions? In M. M. Gruneberg, P. E. Morris, & R. N. Sykes (Eds.), *Practical aspects of memory* (pp. 3–24). London: Academic Press.

Neisser, U. (1981). John Dean's memory: A case study. *Cognition, 9,* 1–22.

Neisser, U. (1982). *Memory observed: Remembering in natural contexts.* San Francisco: Freeman.

Neisser, U. (1988). New vistas in the study of memory. In U. Neisser & E. Winograd (Eds.), *Remembering reconsidered: Ecological and traditional approaches to the study of memory* (pp. 1–10). Cambridge: Cambridge University Press.

Neisser, U. (1991). A case of misplaced nostalgia. *American Psychologist, 46,* 34–36.

Neisser, U., Novick, R., & Lazar, R. (1963). Searching for ten targets simultaneously. *Perceptual and Motor Skills, 17,* 955–961.

Nelson, D. L., Schreiber, T. A., & McEvoy, C. L. (1992). Processing implicit and explicit representations. *Psychological Review, 99,* 322–348.

Nelson, T. O. (1978). Savings and forgetting from long-term memory. *Journal of Verbal Learning and Verbal Behavior, 10,* 568–576.

Nelson, T. O. (1985). Ebbinghaus's contribution to the measurement of retention: Savings during relearning. *Journal of Experimental Psychology: Learning, Memory, and Cognition, 11,* 472–479.

Nelson, T. O. (1988). Predictive accuracy of the feeling of knowing across different criterion tasks and across different subject populations and individuals. In

M. Gruneberg, P. Morris, & R. Sykes (Eds.), *Practical aspects of memory: Current research and issues* (Vol. 1, pp. 190–196). New York: Wiley.

Nelson, T. O., & Leonesio, R. J. (1988). Allocation of self-paced study time and the "labor-in-vain effect." *Journal of Experimental Psychology: Learning, Memory, and Cognition, 14,* 676–686.

Nelson, T. O., McSpadden, M., Fromme, K., & Marlatt, G. A. (1986). Effects of alcohol intoxication on metamemory and on retrieval from long-term memory. *Journal of Experimental Psychology: General, 115,* 247–254.

Newell, A., Shaw, J. C., & Simon, H. A. (1958). Elements of a theory of human problem solving. *Psychological Review, 65,* 151–166.

Newell, A., & Simon, H. A. (1972). *Human problem solving.* Englewood Cliffs, NJ: Prentice-Hall.

Newport, E. L., & Bellugi, W. (1978). Linguistic expression of category levels in a visual-gestural language: A flower is a flower is a flower. In E. Rosch & B. B. Lloyd (Eds.), *Cognition and categorization* (pp. 49–71). Hillsdale, NJ: Erlbaum.

Nickerson, R. S., & Adams, M. J. (1979). Long-term memory for a common object. *Cognitive Psychology, 11,* 287–307.

Nisbett, R. E., Krantz, D. H., Jepson, C., & Kunda, Z. (1983). The use of statistical heuristics in everyday inductive reasoning. *Psychological Review, 90,* 339–363.

Nisbett, R., & Ross, L. (1980). *Human inference: Strategies and shortcomings of social judgment.* Englewood Cliffs, NJ: Prentice-Hall.

Nisbett, R. E., & Wilson, T. D. (1977). Telling more than we can know: Verbal reports on mental processes. *Psychological Review, 84,* 231–259.

Nissen, M. J., & Bullemer, P. (1987). Attentional requirements of learning: Evidence from performance measures. *Cognitive Psychology, 19,* 1–32.

Noble, C. E. (1952). The role of stimulus meaning (m) in serial verbal learning. *Journal of Experimental Psychology, 43,* 437–446.

Noordman, L. G. M., Vonk, W., & Kempff, H. J. (1992). Causal inferences during the reading of expository texts. *Journal of Memory and Language, 31,* 573–590.

Norman, D. A. (1976). *Memory and attention: An introduction to human information processing* (2nd ed.). New York: Wiley.

Norman, D. A. (1986). Reflections on cognition and parallel distributed processing. In J. L. McClelland, D. E. Rumelhart, & PDP Research Group (Eds.), *Parallel distributed processing: Explorations in the microstructure of cognition: Vol. 2. Psychological and biological models* (pp. 531–546). Cambridge, MA: MIT Press.

Norman, D. A., & Rumelhart, D. E. (Eds.). (1975). *Explorations in cognition.* San Francisco: Freeman.

Novick, L. R. (1988). Analogical transfer, problem similarity, and expertise. *Journal of Experimental Psychology: Learning, Memory, and Cognition, 14,* 510–520.

Novick, L. R., & Holyoak, K. J. (1991). Mathematical problem solving by analogy. *Journal of Experimental Psychology: Learning, Memory, and Cognition, 17,* 398–415.

O'Brien, E. J., & Albrecht, J. E. (1991). The role of context in accessing antecedents in text. *Journal of Experimental Psychology: Learning, Memory, and Cognition, 17,* 94–102.

O'Brien, E. J., & Myers, J. L. (1987). The role of causal connections in the retrieval of text. *Memory & Cognition, 15,* 419–427.

O'Brien, E. J., Plewes, P. S., & Albrecht, J. E. (1990). Antecedent retrieval processes. *Journal of Experimental Psychology: Learning, Memory, and Cognition, 16,* 241–249.

O'Brien, E. J., Shank, D. M., Myers, J. L., & Rayner, K. (1988). Elaborative inferences during reading: Do they occur on-line? *Journal of Experimental Psychology: Learning, Memory, and Cognition, 14,* 410–420.

Ojemann, G. A. (1982). Models of the brain organization for higher integrative functions derived with electrical stimulation techniques. *Human Neurobiology, 1,* 243–250.

Ojemann, G. A., & Creutzfeldt, O. D. (1987). Language in humans and animals: Contribution of brain stimulation and recording. In *Handbook of physiology: The nervous system* (Vol. 5). Bethesda: American Physiological Society.

Ornstein, R., & Thompson, R. F. (1985). *The amazing brain.* Los Altos, CA: ISHK Book Service.

Ortony, A. (1979). *Metaphor and thought.* New York: Cambridge University Press.

O'Seaghdha, P. G. (1989). The dependence of lexical relatedness effects on syntactic connectedness. *Journal of Experimental Psychology: Learning, Memory, and Cognition, 15,* 73–87.

Osterhout, L., & Holcomb, P. J. (1992). Event-related brain potentials elicited by syntactic anomaly. *Journal of Memory and Language, 31,* 785–806.

Owens, J., Bower, G. H., & Black, J. B. (1979). The "soap opera" effect in story recall. *Memory & Cognition, 7,* 185–191.

Paivio, A. (1971). *Imagery and verbal processes.* New York: Holt.

Palermo, D. S. (1978). *Psychology of language.* Glenview, IL: Scott, Foresman.

Paller, K. A., Mayes, A. R., Thompson, K. M., Young, A. W., Roberts, J., & Meudell, P. R. (1992). Priming of face matching in amnesia. *Brain and Cognition, 18,* 46–59.

Parker, L. M., Porter, M., & Finley, D. (1983, August). Halo effects and heuristics in the examination of audit evidence. *Proceedings of the American Accounting Association,* New Orleans.

Parkinson, S. (1977). *Information processing in the aged.* Paper presented at the Sandoz Conference on Aging, Batelle Memorial Institute, Seattle, Washington.

Patel, V. L., & Groen, G. J. (1986). Knowledge based solution strategies in medical reasoning. *Cognitive Science, 10,* 91–116.

Patel, V. L., Groen, G. J., & Arocha, J. F. (1990). Medical expertise as a function of task difficulty. *Memory & Cognition, 18,* 394–406.

Paul, S. T., Kellas, G., Martin, M., & Clark, M. B. (1992). Influence of contextual features on the activation of ambiguous word meanings. *Journal of Experimental Psychology: Learning, Memory, and Cognition, 18,* 703–717.

Penfield, W., & Jasper, H. H. (1954). *Epilepsy and the functional anatomy of the human brain.* Boston: Little, Brown & Co.

Penfield, W., & Milner, B. (1958). Memory deficit produced by bilateral lesions in the hippocampal zone. *Archives of Neurology and Psychiatry, 79,* 475–497.

Perfetti, C. A., Bell, L. C., & Delaney, S. M. (1988). Automatic (prelexical) phonetic activation in silent word reading: Evidence from backward masking. *Journal of Memory and Language, 27,* 59–70.

Peterson, L. R., & Peterson, M. J. (1959). Short-term retention of individual items. *Journal of Experimental Psychology, 58,* 193–198.

Peterson, L. R., Peterson, M. J., & Miller, A. (1961). Short-term retention and meaningfulness. *Canadian Journal of Psychology, 15,* 143–147.

Pezdek, K., Whetstone, T., Reynolds, K., Askari, N., & Dougherty, T. (1989). Memory for real-world scenes: The role of consistency with schema expectation. *Journal of Experimental Psychology: Learning, Memory, and Cognition, 15,* 587–595.

Piaget, J. (1967). *Six psychological studies* (A. Tenzer, Trans.). New York: Random House.

Pollack, I., & Pickett, J. M. (1964). Intelligibility of excerpts from fluent speech: Auditory vs. structural context. *Journal of Verbal Learning and Verbal Behavior, 3,* 79–84.

Pollatsek, A., Konold, C. E., Well, A. D., & Lima, S. D. (1984). Beliefs underlying random sampling. *Memory & Cognition, 12,* 395–401.

Polya, G. (1957). *How to solve it.* Garden City, NY: Doubleday/Anchor.

Posner, M. I. (1969). Abstraction and the process of recognition. In G. H. Bower & J. T. Spence (Eds.), *The psychology of learning and motivation* (Vol. 3, pp. 43–100). New York: Academic Press.

Posner, M. I. (1973). *Cognition: An introduction.* Glenview, IL: Scott, Foresman.

Posner, M. I. (1978). *Chronometric explorations of mind.* Hillsdale, NJ: Erlbaum.

Posner, M. I. (Ed.). (1989). *Foundations of cognitive science.* Cambridge, MA: MIT Press.

Posner, M. I., & Cohen, Y. (1984). Components of visual orienting. In H. Bouma & D. G. Bouwhuis (Eds.), *Attention and performance X* (pp. 531–556). Hillsdale, NJ: Erlbaum.

Posner, M. I., & Keele, S. W. (1967). Decay of visual information from a single letter. *Science, 158,* 137–139.

Posner, M. I., & Keele, S. W. (1968). On the genesis of abstract ideas. *Journal of Experimental Psychology, 77,* 353–363.

Posner, M. I., Kiesner, J., Thomas-Thrapp, L., McCandliss, B., Carr, T. H., & Rothbart, M. K. (1992, November). *Brain changes in the acquisition of literacy.* Paper presented at the meetings of the Psychonomic Society, St. Louis.

Posner, M. I., & Snyder, C. R. R. (1975). Facilitation and inhibition in the processing of signals. In P. M. A. Rabbitt & S. Dornic (Eds.), *Attention and performance V* (pp. 669–682). New York: Academic Press.

Postman, L., & Underwood, B. J. (1973). Critical issues in interference theory. *Memory & Cognition, 1,* 19–40.

Potts, G. R. (1974). Storing and retrieving information about ordered relationships. *Journal of Experimental Psychology, 103,* 431–439.

Potts, G. R., St. John, M. F., & Kirson, D. (1989). Incorporating new information into existing world knowledge. *Cognitive Psychology, 21,* 303–333.

Pressley, M., Levin, J. R., & Ghatala, E. S. (1984). Memory strategy monitoring in adults and children. *Journal of Verbal Learning and Verbal Behavior, 23,* 270–288.

Pritchard, R. M. (1961). Stabilized images on the retina. *Scientific American, 204,* 72–78.

Proffitt, D. R., Kaiser, M. K., & Whelan, S. M. (1990). Understanding wheel dynamics. *Cognitive Psychology, 22,* 342–373.

Quillian, M. R. (1968). Semantic memory. In M. Minsky (Ed.), *Semantic information processing* (pp. 216–270). Cambridge, MA: MIT Press.

Quillian, M. R. (1969). The teachable language comprehender: A simulation program and theory of language. *Communications of the ACM, 12,* 459–476.

Radvansky, G. A., Spieler, D. H., & Zacks, R. T. (1993). Mental model organization. *Journal of Experimental Psychology: Learning, Memory, and Cognition, 19,* 95–114.

Radvansky, G. A., & Zacks, R. T. (1991). Mental models and the fan effect. *Journal of Experimental Psychology: Learning, Memory, and Cognition, 17,* 940–953.

Raney, G. E. (1993). Monitoring changes in cognitive load during reading: An event-related brain potential and reaction time analysis. *Journal of Experimental Psychology: Learning, Memory, and Cognition, 19,* 51–69.

Raphael, B. (1976). *The thinking computer: Mind inside matter.* New York: Freeman.

Rappold, V. A., & Hashtroudi, S. (1991). Does organization improve priming? *Journal of Experimental Psychology: Learning, Memory, and Cognition, 17,* 103–114.

Ratcliff, R., & McKoon, G. (1978). Priming in item recognition: Evidence for the propositional structure of sentences. *Journal of Verbal Learning and Verbal Behavior, 17,* 403–418.

Ratcliff, R., & McKoon, G. (1988). A retrieval theory of priming in memory. *Psychological Review, 95,* 385–408.

Rayner, K., Carlson, M., & Frazier, L. (1983). The interaction of syntax and semantics during sentence processing: Eye movements in the analysis of semantically biased sentences. *Journal of Verbal Learning and Verbal Behavior, 22,* 358–374.

Rayner, K., & Frazier, L. (1989). Selection mechanisms in reading lexically ambiguous words. *Journal of Experimental Psychology: Learning, Memory, and Cognition, 15,* 779–790.

Rayner, K., Garrod, S., & Perfetti, C. A. (1992). Discourse influences during parsing are delayed. *Cognition, 45,* 109–139.

Rayner, K., Inhoff, A. W., Morrison, P. E., Slowiaczek, M. L., & Bertera, J. H. (1981). Masking of foveal and parafoveal vision during eye fixations in reading. *Journal of Experimental Psychology: Human Perception and Performance, 7,* 167–179.

Reber, A. S. (1989). Implicit learning and tacit knowledge. *Journal of Experimental Psychology: General, 118,* 219–235.

Reder, L. M., & Kusbit, G. W. (1991). Locus of the Moses illusion: Imperfect encoding, retrieval, or match? *Journal of Memory and Language, 30,* 385–406.

Reed, S. K. (1984). Estimating answers to algebra word problems. *Journal of Experimental Psychology: Learning, Memory, and Cognition, 10,* 778–790.

Reed, S. K. (1992). *Cognition: Theory and applications* (3rd ed.). Pacific Grove, CA: Brooks/Cole.

Reed, S. K., Dempster, A., & Ettinger, M. (1985). Usefulness of analogous solutions for solving algebra word problems. *Journal of Experimental Psychology: Learning, Memory, and Cognition, 11,* 106–125.

Reed, S. K., Ernst, G. W., & Banerji, R. (1974). The role of analogy in transfer between similar problem states. *Cognitive Psychology, 6,* 436–450.

Reed, S. K., & Saavedra, N. C. (1986). A comparison of computation, discovery, and graph procedures for improving students' conception of average speed. *Cognition and Instruction, 3,* 31–62.

Reich, P. A. (1986). *Language development.* Englewood Cliffs, NJ: Prentice-Hall.

Reinitz, M. T., Wright, E., & Loftus, G. R. (1989). Effects of semantic priming on visual encoding of pictures. *Journal of Experimental Psychology: General, 118,* 280–297.

Reiser, B. J., Black, J. B., & Abelson, R. P. (1985). Knowledge structures in the organization and retrieval of autobiographical memories. *Cognitive Psychology, 17,* 89–137.

Richardson, J. T. E. (1985). Integration versus decomposition in the retention of complex ideas. *Memory & Cognition, 13,* 112–127.

Rifkin, A. (1985). Evidence for a basic level in event taxonomies. *Memory & Cognition, 13,* 538–556.

Riley, K. P. (1989). Psychological interventions in Alzheimer's disease. In G. C. Gilmore, P. J. Whitehouse, & M. R. Wykle (Eds.), *Memory, aging and dementia.* New York: Springer.

Rips, L. J. (1975). Inductive judgments about natural categories. *Journal of Verbal Learning and Verbal Behavior, 14,* 665–681.

Rips, L. J., & Marcus, S. L. (1977). Supposition and the analysis of conditional sentences. In M. A. Just & P. A. Carpenter (Eds.), *Cognitive processes in comprehension* (pp. 185–220). Hillsdale, NJ: Erlbaum.

Rips, L. J., Shoben, E. J., & Smith, E. E. (1973). Semantic distance and the verification of semantic relations. *Journal of Verbal Learning and Verbal Behavior, 12,* 1–20.

Roediger, H. L. III (1990). Implicit memory: Retention without remembering. *American Psychologist, 45,* 1043–1056.

Roediger, H. L., & Blaxton, T. A. (1985). Testing psychological trivia. *Bulletin of the Psychonomic Society, 23,* 433–436.

Roediger, H. L. III, Stadler, M. L., Weldon, M. S., & Riegler, G. L. (1992). Direct comparison of two implicit memory tests: Word fragment and word stem completion. *Journal of Experimental Psychology: Learning, Memory, and Cognition, 18,* 1251–1269.

Rosch (-Heider), E. (1972). Universals in color naming and memory. *Journal of Experimental Psychology, 93,* 10–21.

Rosch, E. H. (1973). On the internal structure of perceptual and semantic categories. In T. E. Moore (Ed.), *Cognitive development and the acquisition of language* (pp. 111–144). New York: Academic Press.

Rosch, E. (1974). Linguistic relativity. In A. Silverstein (Ed.), *Human communication: Theoretical perspectives* (pp. 254–279). New York: Halsted Press.

Rosch, E. H. (1975). Cognitive representations of semantic categories. *Journal of Experimental Psychology: General, 104,* 192–233.

Rosch, E. H. (1978). Principles of categorization. In E. H. Rosch & B. B. Lloyd (Eds.), *Cognition and categorization* (pp. 27–48). Hillsdale, NJ: Erlbaum.

Rosch, E. H., & Mervis, C. B. (1975). Family resemblances: Studies in the internal structure of categories. *Cognitive Psychology, 7,* 573–605.

Ross, B. H. (1987). This is like that: The use of earlier problems and the separation of similarity effects. *Journal of Experimental Psychology: Learning, Memory, and Cognition, 13,* 629–640.

Ross, B. H. (1989). Distinguishing types of superficial similarities: Different effects on the access and use of earlier problems. *Journal of Experimental Psychology: Learning, Memory, and Cognition, 15,* 456–468.

Ross, J., & Lawrence, K. A. (1968). Some observations on memory artifice. *Psychonomic Science, 13,* 107–108.

Rubens, A. B., & Benson, D. F. (1971). Associative visual agnosia. *Archives of Neurology (Chicago), 24,* 305–316.

Rubin, D. C. (Ed.). (1986). *Autobiographical memory.* New Rochelle, NY: Cambridge University Press.

Rumelhart, D. E. (1989). The architecture of mind: A connectionist approach. In M. I. Posner (Ed.), *Foundations of cognitive science* (pp. 133–159). Cambridge, MA: MIT Press.

Rumelhart, D. E., & Abrahamson, A. A. (1973). A model for analogical reasoning. *Cognitive Psychology, 5,* 1–28.

Rumelhart, D. E., Lindsay, P. H., & Norman, D. A. (1972). A process model for long-term memory. In E. Tulving & W. Donaldson (Eds.), *Organization of memory* (pp. 197–246). New York: Academic Press.

Rumelhart, D. E., & McClelland, J. L. (1982). An interactive activation model of context effects in letter perception: Part 2. The contextual enhancement effect and some tests and extensions of the model. *Psychological Review, 89,* 60–94.

Rumelhart, D. E., & McClelland, J. L. (1986). *Parallel distributed processing: Explorations in the microstructure of cognition: Vol. 1. Foundations.* Cambridge, MA: Bradford.

Rumelhart, D. E., Smolensky, P., McClelland, J. L., & Hinton, G. E. (1986). Schemata and sequential thought processes in PDP models. In J. L. McClelland & D. E. Rumelhart (Eds.), *Parallel distributed processing* (Vol. 2, pp. 7–57). Cambridge, MA: MIT Press.

Rundus, D. (1971). Analysis of rehearsal processes in free recall. *Journal of Experimental Psychology, 89,* 63–77.

Rundus, D., & Atkinson, R. C. (1970). Rehearsal processes in free recall: A procedure for direct observation. *Journal of Verbal Learning and Verbal Behavior, 9,* 99–105.

Russo, J. E., Johnson, E. J., & Stephens, D. L. (1989). The validity of verbal protocols. *Memory & Cognition, 17,* 759–769.

Sachs, J. S. (1967). Recognition memory for syntactic and semantic aspects of connected discourse. *Perception & Psychophysics, 2,* 437–442.

Sacks, H., Schegloff, E. A., & Jefferson, G. (1974). A simplest systematics for the organization of turn-taking for conversation. *Language, 50,* 696–735.

Sacks, O. (1970). *The man who mistook his wife for a hat.* New York: Harper & Row.

Sakitt, B. (1975). Locus of short-term visual storage. *Science, 190,* 395–403.

Salame, P., & Baddeley, A. D. (1982). Disruption of short-term memory by unattended speech: Implications for the structure of working memory. *Journal of Verbal Learning and Verbal Behavior, 21,* 150–164.

Salthouse, T. A. (1984). Effects of age and skill in typing. *Journal of Experimental Psychology: General, 113,* 345–371.

Salthouse, T. A. (1992). *Mechanisms of age-cognition relations in adulthood.* Hillsdale, NJ: Erlbaum.

Sattler, J. M. (1982). *Assessment of children's intellectual and special abilities* (2nd ed.). Boston: Allyn & Bacon.

Schab, F. R. (1990). Odors and the remembrance of things past. *Journal of Experimental Psychology: Learning, Memory, and Cognition, 16,* 648–655.

Schacter, D. L. (1986). Amnesia and crime: How much do we really know? *American Psychologist, 41,* 286–295.

Schacter, D. L. (1987). Implicit memory: History and current status. *Journal of Experimental Psychology: Learning, Memory, and Cognition, 13,* 501–518.

Schacter, D. (1989). Memory. In M. I. Posner (Ed.). *Foundations of cognitive science* (pp. 683–725). Cambridge, MA: MIT Press.

Schacter, D. L. (1992). Understanding implicit memory: A cognitive neuroscience approach. *American Psychologist, 47,* 559–569.

Schacter, D. L., & Church, B. A. (1992). Auditory priming: Implicit and explicit memory for words and voices. *Journal of Experimental Psychology: Learning, Memory, and Cognition, 18,* 915–930.

Schank, R. C. (1972). Conceptual dependency: A theory of natural language understanding. *Cognitive Psychology, 3,* 552–631.

Schank, R. C. (1977). Rules and topics in conversation. *Cognitive Science, 1,* 421–441.

Schank, R. C., & Abelson, R. P. (1977). *Scripts, plans, goals and understanding.* Hillsdale, NJ: Erlbaum.

Schank, R. C., & Riesbeck, C. K. (1981). *Inside computer understanding: Five programs plus miniatures.* Hillsdale, NJ: Erlbaum.

Schegloff, E. A. (1972). Sequencing in conversational openings. In J. J. Gumperz & D. Hymes (Eds.), *Directions in sociolinguistics* (pp. 346–380). New York: Bobbs-Merrill.

Schmidt, S. R. (1985). Encoding and retrieval processes in the memory for conceptually distinctive events. *Journal of Experimental Psychology: Learning, Memory, and Cognition, 11,* 565–578.

Schneider, W., Noll, D. C., & Cohen, J. D. (1993). Functional topographic mapping of human visual cortex using conventional MRI. *Science,* in press.

Schneider, W., & Shiffrin. R. M. (1977). Controlled and automatic human information processing: I. Detection, search, and attention. *Psychological Review, 84,* 1–66.

Schnorr, J. A., & Atkinson, R. C. (1969). Repetition versus imagery instructions in the short- and long-term retention of paired associates. *Psychonomic Science, 15,* 183–184.

Schustack, M. W., Ehrlich, S. F., & Rayner, K. (1987). Local and global sources of contextual facilitation in reading. *Journal of Memory and Language, 26,* 322–340.

Schwanenflugel, P. J., & Shoben, E. J. (1985). The influence of sentence constraint on the scope of facilitation for upcoming words. *Journal of Memory and Language, 24,* 232–252.

Scoville, W. B., & Milner, B. (1957). Loss of recent memory after bilateral hippocampal lesions. *Journal of Neurology, Neurosurgery and Psychiatry, 20,* 11–21.

Scribner, S. (1975). Recall of classical syllogisms: A cross-cultural investigation of error on local problems. In R. J. Falmange (Ed.), *Reasoning: Representation and process* (pp. 153–173). Hillsdale, NJ: Erlbaum.

Segal, S. J., & Fusella, V. (1970). Influence of imaged pictures and sounds on detection of visual and auditory signals. *Journal of Experimental Psychology, 83,* 458–464.

Sehulster, J. R. (1989). Content and temporal structure of autobiographical knowledge: Remembering twenty-five seasons at the Metropolitan Opera. *Memory & Cognition, 17,* 590–606.

Seibert, P. S., & Ellis, H. C. (1991). Irrelevant thoughts, emotional mood states and cognitive task performances. *Memory & Cognition, 19,* 507–513.

Seidenberg, M. S., & McClelland, J. L. (1989). A distributed, developmental model of word recognition and naming. *Psychological Review, 96,* 523–568.

Seifert, C. M., Robertson, S. P., & Black, J. B. (1985). Types of inferences generated during reading. *Journal of Memory and Language, 24,* 405–422.

Sejnowski, T. J., & Churchland, P. S. (1989). Brain and cognition. In M. I. Posner (Ed.) *Foundations of cognitive science* (pp. 301–356). Cambridge, MA: MIT Press.

Selfridge, O. G. (1959). Pandemonium: A paradigm for learning. In *The mechanisation of thought processes.* London: H. M. Stationery Office.

Seron, X. (1982). Introduction: Toward a cognitive neuropsychology. *International Journal of Psychology, 17,* 149–156.

Shafir, E., & Tversky, A. (1992). Thinking through uncertainty: Nonconsequential reasoning and choice. *Cognitive Psychology, 24,* 449–474.

Shallice, T. (1988). *From neuropsychology to mental structure.* New York: Cambridge University Press.

Shallice, T., & Warrington, E. K. (1970). Independent functioning of the verbal memory stores: A neuropsychological study. *Quarterly Journal of Experimental Psychology, 22,* 261–273.

Shand, M. A. (1982). Sign-based short-term coding of American Sign Language signs and printed English words by congenitally deaf signers. *Cognitive Psychology, 14,* 1–12.

Shanks, D. R. (1991). Categorization by a connectionist network. *Journal of Experimental Psychology: Learning, Memory, and Cognition, 17,* 433–443.

Sharkey, N. E., & Mitchell, D. C. (1985). Word recognition in a functional context: The use of scripts in reading. *Journal of Memory and Language, 24,* 253–270.

Shelton, J. R., & Martin, R. C. (1992). How semantic is automatic semantic priming? *Journal of Experimental Psychology: Learning, Memory, and Cognition, 18,* 1191–1210.

Shepard, R. N., & Metzler, J. (1971). Mental rotation of three-dimensional objects. *Science, 153,* 652–654.

Shiffrin, R. M., & Schneider, W. (1977). Controlled and automatic human information processing: II. Perceptual learning, automatic attending, and a general theory. *Psychological Review, 84,* 127–190.

Shimamura, A. P., & Squire, L. R. (1989). Impaired priming of new associations in amnesia. *Journal of Experimental Psychology: Learning, Memory, and Cognition, 14,* 763–769.

Shoben, E. J., Sailor, K. M., & Wang, M.-Y. (1989). The role of expectancy in comparative judgments. *Memory & Cognition, 17,* 18–26.

Simon, H. A. (1975). The functional equivalence of problem solving skills. *Cognitive Psychology, 7,* 268–288.

Simon, H. A. (1979). *Models of thought.* New Haven: Yale University Press.

Simon, H. A. (1992). What is an "explanation" of behavior? *Psychological Science, 3,* 150–161.

Simpson, G. B. (1981). Meaning dominance and semantic context in the processing of lexical ambiguity. *Journal of Verbal Learning and Verbal Behavior, 20,* 120–136.

Simpson, G. B. (1984). Lexical ambiguity and its role in models of word recognition. *Psychological Bulletin, 96,* 316–340.

Simpson, G. B., Casteel, M. A., Peterson, R. R., & Burgess, C. (1989). Lexical and sentence context effects in word recognition. *Journal of Experimental Psychology: Learning, Memory, and Cognition, 15,* 88–97.

Singer, M. (1990). *Psychology of language: An introduction to sentence and discourse processes.* Hillsdale, NJ: Erlbaum.

Singer, M., Andrusiak, P., Reisdorf, P., & Black, N. L. (1992). Individual differences in bridging inference processes. *Memory & Cognition, 20,* 539–548.

Sitaran, N., Weingartner, H., Caine, E. D., & Gillin, J. C. (1978). Choline: Selective enhancement of serial learning and encoding of low imagery words in man. *Life Sciences, 22,* 1555–1560.

Skinner, B. F. (1957). *Verbal behavior.* New York: Appleton-Century-Crofts.

Skinner, B. F. (1984). The shame of American education. *American Psychologist, 39,* 947–954.

Skinner, B. F. (1990). Can psychology be a science of mind? *American Psychologist, 45,* 1206–1210.

Slamecka, N. J. (1966). Differentiation versus unlearning of verbal associations. *Journal of Experimental Psychology, 71,* 822–828.

Slamecka, N. J. (1985a). Ebbinghaus: Some associations. *Journal of Experimental Psychology: Learning, Memory, and Cognition, 11,* 414–435.

Slamecka, N. J. (1985b). Ebbinghaus: Some rejoinders. *Journal of Experimental Psychology: Learning, Memory, and Cognition, 11,* 496–500.

Slobin, D. I. (1979). *Psycholinguistics* (2nd ed.). Glenview, IL: Scott, Foresman.

Smith, D. A., & Graesser, A. C. (1981). Memory for actions in scripted activities as a function of typicality, retention interval, and retrieval task. *Memory & Cognition, 9,* 550–559.

Smith, E. E. (1978). Theories of semantic memory. In W. K. Estes (Ed.), *Handbook of learning and cognitive processes* (Vol. 6, pp. 1–56). Hillsdale, NJ: Erlbaum.

Smith, E. E., & Osherson, D. N. (1984). Conceptual combination with prototype concepts. *Cognitive Science, 8,* 337–363.

Smith, E. E., Rips, L. J., & Shoben, E. J. (1974). Semantic memory and psychological semantics. In G. H. Bower (Ed.), *The psychology of learning and motivation* (Vol. 8, pp. 1–45). New York: Academic Press.

Smith, E. E., Shoben, E. J., & Rips, L. J. (1974). Structure and process in semantic memory: A featural model for semantic decisions. *Psychological Review, 81,* 214–241.

Smith, L. C. (1984). Semantic satiation affects category membership decision time but not lexical priming. *Memory & Cognition, 12,* 483–488.

Smith, L., & Klein, R. (1990). Evidence for semantic satiation: Repeating a category slows subsequent semantic processing. *Journal of Experimental Psychology: Learning, Memory, and Cognition, 16,* 852–861.

Smith, S. M., & Rothkopf, E. Z. (1984). Contextual enrichment and distribution of practice in the classroom. *Cognition and Instruction, 1,* 341–358.

Snow, C. (1972). Mother's speech to children learning language. *Child Development, 43,* 549–565.

Snow, C., & Ferguson, C. (Eds.). (1977). *Talking to children: Language input and acquisition.* Cambridge, England: Cambridge University Press.

Sokol, S. M., McCloskey, M., Cohen, N. J., & Aliminosa, D. (1991). Cognitive representations and processes in arithmetic: Inferences from the performance of brain-damaged subjects. *Journal of Experimental Psychology: Learning, Memory, and Cognition, 17,* 355–376.

Spelke, E., Hirst, W., & Neisser, U. (1976). Skills of divided attention. *Cognition, 4,* 215–230.

Spellman, B. A., & Holyoak, K. J. (1992). If Saddam is Hitler then who is George Bush? Analogical mapping between systems of social roles. *Journal of Personality and Social Psychology, 62,* 913–933.

Sperling, G. (1960). The information available in brief visual presentations. *Psychological Monographs, 74* (Whole No. 48).

Sperling, G. (1963). A model for visual memory tasks. *Human Factors, 5,* 9–31.

Sperry, R. W. (1964). The great cerebral commissure. *Scientific American, 210,* 42–52.

Spieth, W., Curtis, J. F., & Webster, J. C. (1954). Responding to one of two simultaneous messages. *Journal of the Acoustical Society of America, 26,* 391–396.

Squire, L. R. (1987). *Memory and brain.* New York: Oxford University Press.

Squire, L. R. (1992). Memory and the hippocampus: A synthesis from findings with rats, monkeys, and humans. *Psychological Review, 99,* 195–231.

Srinivas, K., & Roediger, H. L. (1990). Classifying implicit memory tests: Category association and anagram solution. *Journal of Memory and Language, 29,* 389–412.

Steiner, R., Green, A., & White, N. (1992). Clarification of the dual task dilemma: Lateralized effects for perfunctory and purposeful tasks in left- and right-handed males. *Brain and Cognition, 19,* 148–171.

Sternberg, R. J. (1977). *Intelligence, information processing, and analogical reasoning.* Hillsdale, NJ: Erlbaum.

Sternberg, S. (1966). High-speed scanning in human memory. *Science, 153,* 652–654.

Sternberg, S. (1969). The discovery of processing stages: Extensions of Donder's method. In W. G. Koster (Ed.), Attention and performance II. *Acta Psychologica, 30,* 276–315.

Sternberg, S. (1975). Memory scanning: New findings and current controversies. *Quarterly Journal of Experimental Psychology, 27,* 1–32.

Stillings, N. A., Feinstein, M. H., Garfield, J. L., Rissland, E., Rosenbaum, D. A., Weisler, S. E., & Baker-Ward, L. (1986). *Cognitive science: An introduction.* Cambridge, MA: MIT Press.

Stroop, J. R. (1935). Studies of interference in serial verbal reactions. *Journal of Experimental Psychology, 18,* 643–662.

Stuss, D. T. (1992). Biological and psychological development of executive functions. *Brain and Cognition, 20,* 8–23.

Sulin, R. A., & Dooling, D. J. (1974). Intrusion of a thematic idea in retention of prose. *Journal of Experimental Psychology, 103,* 255–262.

Sussman, H. M. (1989). A reassessment of the time-sharing paradigm, with ANCOVA. *Brain and Language, 37,* 514–520.

Talland, G. A. (1967). Short-term memory with interpolated activity. *Journal of Verbal Learning and Verbal Behavior, 6,* 144–150.

Taraban, R., & McClelland, J. L. (1988). Constituent attachment and thematic role assignment in sentence processing: Influences of content-based expectations. *Journal of Memory and Language, 27,* 597–632.

Temple, C. M. (1991). Procedural dyscalculia and number fact dyscalculia: Double dissociation in developmental dyscalculia. *Cognitive Neuropsychology, 8,* 155–176.

Thomas, J. C., Jr. (1974). An analysis of behavior in the hobbits-orcs problem. *Cognitive Psychology, 6,* 257–269.

Thompson, C. P. (1982). Memory for unique personal events: The roommate study. *Memory & Cognition, 10,* 324–332.

Thompson, R. F. (1986). The neurobiology of learning and memory. *Science, 233,* 941–947.

Thomson, D. M., & Tulving, E. (1970). Associative encoding and retrieval: Weak and strong cues. *Journal of Experimental Psychology, 86,* 255–262.

Thorndike, E. L. (1914). *The psychology of learning.* New York: Teachers College.

Titchener, E. B. (1919). *A text-book of psychology.* New York: Macmillan.

Tolman, E. C. (1948). Cognitive maps in rats and men. *Psychological Review, 55,* 189–208.

Tomasello, M., & Mannle, S. (1985). Pragmatics of sibling speech to one-year-olds. *Child Development, 56,* 911–917.

Tourangeau, R., & Rips, L. (1991). Interpreting and evaluating metaphors. *Journal of Memory and Language, 30,* 452–472.

Treisman, A. M. (1960). Contextual cues in selective listening. *Quarterly Journal of Experimental Psychology, 12,* 242–248.

Treisman, A. M. (1964). Monitoring and storage of irrelevant messages in selective attention. *Journal of Verbal Learning and Verbal Behavior, 3,* 449–459.

Treisman, A. M. (1965). The effects of redundancy and familiarity on translating and repeating back a foreign and a native language. *British Journal of Psychology, 56,* 369–379.

Treisman, A. (1982). Perceptual grouping and attention in visual search for features and for objects. *Journal of Experimental Psychology: Human Perception and Performance, 8,* 194–214.

Treisman, A. (1988). Features and objects: The Fourteenth Bartlett Memorial Lecture. *Quarterly Journal of Experimental Psychology, 40A,* 201–237.

Treisman, A. (1991). Search, similarity, and integration of features between and within dimensions. *Journal of Experimental Psychology: Human Perception and Performance, 17,* 652–676.

Treisman, A. (1992). Spreading suppression or feature integration? A reply to Duncan and Humphreys (1992). *Journal of Experimental Psychology: Human Perception and Performance, 18,* 589–593.

Treisman, A., & Gelade, G. (1980). A feature integration theory of attention. *Cognitive Psychology, 12,* 97–136.

Treisman, A. M., Russell, R., & Green, J. (1975). Brief visual storage of shape and movement. In P. M. A. Rabbitt & S. Dornic (Eds.), *Attention and performance* (Vol. 5, pp. 699–721). New York: Academic Press.

Trigg, G. L., & Lerner, R. J. (Eds.). (1981). *Encyclopedia of physics.* Reading, MA: Addison-Wesley.

Tulving, E. (1962). Subjective organization in free recall of "unrelated" words. *Psychological Review, 69,* 344–354.

Tulving, E. (1972). Episodic and semantic memory. In E. Tulving & W. Donaldson (Eds.), *Organization of memory* (pp. 381–403). New York: Academic Press.

Tulving, E. (1983). *Elements of episodic memory.* Oxford, England: Clarendon Press.

Tulving, E. (1985). Ebbinghaus's memory: What did he learn and remember? *Journal of Experimental Psychology: Learning, Memory, and Cognition, 11,* 485–490.

Tulving, E. (1986). What kind of a hypothesis is the distinction between episodic and semantic memory? *Journal of Experimental Psychology: Learning, Memory, and Cognition, 12,* 307–311.

Tulving, E. (1989). Remembering and knowing the past. *American Scientist, 77,* 361–367.

Tulving, E. (1991). Memory research is not a zero-sum game. *American Psychologist, 46,* 41–42.

Tulving, E., & Donaldson, W. (Eds.). (1972). *Organization of memory.* New York: Academic Press.

Tulving, E., & Pearlstone, Z. (1966). Availability versus accessibility of information in memory for words. *Journal of Verbal Learning and Verbal Behavior, 5,* 381–391.

Tulving, E., Schacter, D., & Stark, H. (1982). Priming effects in word-fragment completion are independent of recognition memory. *Journal of Experimental Psychology, 8,* 336–342.

Tulving, E., & Thompson, D. M. (1973). Encoding specificity and retrieval processes in episodic memory. *Psychological Review, 80,* 352–373.

Turing, A. (1950). Computing machinery and intelligence. *Mind, 59,* 434–460.

Turvey, M. T. (1978). Visual processing and short-term memory. In W. K. Estes (Ed.), *Handbook of learning and cognitive processes* (Vol. 5, pp. 91–142). Hillsdale, NJ: Erlbaum.

Tversky, A., & Kahneman, D. (1971). Belief in the law of small numbers. *Psychological Bulletin, 76,* 105–110.

Tversky, A., & Kahneman, D. (1973). Availability: A heuristic for judging frequency and probability. *Cognitive Psychology, 5,* 207–232.

Tversky, A., & Kahneman, D. (1974). Judgment under uncertainty: Heuristics and biases. *Science, 185,* 1124–1131.

Tversky, A., & Kahneman, D. (1980). Causal schemas in judgments under uncertainty. In M. Fishbein (Ed.), *Progress in social psychology* (Vol. 1, pp. 49–72). Hillsdale, NJ: Erlbaum.

Tversky, A., & Kahneman, D. (1983). Extensional versus intuitive reasoning: The conjunction fallacy in probability judgment. *Psychological Review, 90,* 293–315.

Underwood, B. J. (1957). Interference and forgetting. *Psychological Review, 64,* 49–60.

Underwood, B. J., Keppel, G., & Schulz, R. W. (1962). Studies of distributed practice: XXII. Some conditions which enhance retention. *Journal of Experimental Psychology, 64,* 112–129.

Underwood, B. J., & Postman, L. (1960). Extraexperimental sources of interference in forgetting. *Psychological Review, 67,* 73–95.

Underwood, B. J., & Schulz, R. W. (1960). *Meaningfulness and verbal learning.* Philadelphia: Lippincott.

Utta, W. R. (1983). Don't exterminate perceptual fruit flies! *The Behavioral and Brain Sciences, 6,* 39–40.

Vallar, G., & Baddeley, A. D. (1984). Fractionation of working memory: Neuropsychological evidence for a phonological short-term store. *Journal of Verbal Learning and Verbal Behavior, 23,* 151–161.

Van der Linden, M., Coyette, F., & Seron, X. (1992). Selective impairment of the "central executive" component of working memory: A single case study. *Cognitive Neuropsychology, 9,* 301–326.

VanLehn, K. (1989). Problem solving and cognitive skill acquisition. In M. I. Posner (Ed.), *Foundations of cognitive science* (pp. 527–579). Cambridge, MA: MIT Press.

VanLehn, K. (1990). *Mind bugs: The origins of procedural misconceptions.* Cambridge, MA: Bradford.

Velten, E. (1968). A laboratory task for induction of mood states. *Behavior Research and Therapy, 6,* 473–482.

Wagenaar, W. A. (1986). My memory: A study of autobiographical memory over six years. *Cognitive Psychology, 18,* 225–252.

Wallas, G. (1926). *The art of thought.* New York: Harcourt, Brace.

Warren, R. M., & Warren, R. P. (1970). Auditory illusions and confusions. *Scientific American, 223,* 30–36.

Warrington, E. K., & McCarthy, R. (1983). Category specific access dysphasia. *Brain, 106,* 859–878.

Warrington, E. K., & Shallice, T. (1969). The selective impairment of auditory verbal short-term memory. *Brain, 92,* 885–896.

Warrington, E. K., & Shallice, T. (1984). Category specific semantic impairments. *Brain, 107,* 829–854.

Warrington, E. K., & Weiskrantz, L. (1968). New method of testing long-term retention with special reference to amnesic patients. *Nature, 277,* 972–974.

Warrington, E. K., & Weiskrantz, L. (1970). The amnesic syndrome: Consolidation or retrieval? *Nature, 228,* 628–630.

Warrington, E. K., & Weiskrantz, L. (1982). Amnesia: A disconnection syndrome? *Neuropsychologia, 20,* 233–248.

Wason, P. C., & Johnson-Laird, P. N. (1972). *Psychology of reasoning: Structure and content.* Cambridge, MA: Harvard University Press.

Wasow, T. (1989). Grammatical theory. In M. I. Posner (Ed.), *Foundations of cognitive science* (pp. 161–205). Cambridge, MA: MIT Press.

Watkins, M. H., Peynircioglu, Z. F., & Brems, D. J. (1984). Pictorial rehearsal. *Memory & Cognition, 12,* 553–557.

Watkins, M. J., & Sechler, E. S. (1988). Generation effect with an incidental memorization procedure. *Journal of Memory and Language, 27,* 537–544.

Watkins, M. J., & Tulving, E. (1975). Episodic memory: When recognition fails. *Journal of Experimental Psychology: General, 104,* 5–29.

Watkins, O. C., & Watkins, M. J. (1980). The modality effect and echoic persistence. *Journal of Experimental Psychology: General, 109,* 251–278.

Watson, J. B. (1913). Psychology as the behaviorist sees it. *Psychological Review, 20,* 158–177.

Watson, J. B. (1924). *Behaviorism.* New York: Norton. (2nd ed., 1930).

Watson, R. I. (1968). *The great psychologists from Aristotle to Freud.* New York: Lippincott.

Waugh, N. C., & Norman, D. A. (1965). Primary memory. *Psychological Review, 72,* 89–104.

Webster's New World Dictionary of the American Language. (1980). 2nd College Edition. Cleveland: William Collins Publishers.

Weisberg, R. (1993). *Creativity: Beyond the myth of genius* (2nd ed.). New York: Freeman.

Weldon, M. S. (1991). Mechanisms underlying priming on perceptual tests. *Journal of Experimental Psychology: Learning, Memory, and Cognition, 17,* 526–541.

Werner, H. (1935). Studies on contour. *American Journal of Psychology, 47,* 40–64.

West, R. F., & Stanovich, K. E. (1986). Robust effects of syntactic structure on visual word processing. *Memory & Cognition, 14,* 104–112.

Whaley, C. P. (1978). Word-nonword classification time. *Journal of Verbal Learning and Verbal Behavior, 17,* 143–154.

Wheeler, D. D. (1970). Processes in word recognition. *Cognitive Psychology, 1,* 59–85.

Wheeler, M. A., & Roediger, H. L. III (1992). Disparate effects of repeated testing: Reconciling Ballard's (1913) and Bartlett's (1932) results. *Psychological Science, 3,* 240–245.

Whitney, P., Ritchie, B. G., & Crane, R. S. (1992). The effect of foregrounding on readers' use of predictive inferences. *Memory & Cognition, 20,* 424–432.

Whorf, B. L. (1956). Science and linguistics. In J. B. Carroll (Ed.), *Language, thought, and reality: Selected writings of Benjamin Lee Whorf* (pp. 207–219). Cambridge, MA: MIT Press.

Wickelgren, W. A. (1965). Acoustic similarity and retroactive interference in short-term memory. *Journal of Verbal Learning and Verbal Behavior, 4,* 53–61.

Wickelgren, W. (1973, November). *Single trace theory of associative memory dynamics.* Paper presented at the meetings of the Psychonomic Society, St. Louis.

Wickelgren, W. A. (1974). *How to solve problems.* San Francisco: Freeman.

Wickens, C. D. (1984). *Engineering psychology and human performance.* Columbus, OH: Charles E. Merrill.

Wickens, D. D. (1972). Characteristics of word encoding. In A. W. Melton & E. Martin (Eds.), *Coding processes in human memory* (pp. 191–215). New York: Winston.

Wickens, D. D., Born, D. G., & Allen, C. K. (1963). Proactive inhibition and item similarity in short-term memory. *Journal of Verbal Learning and Verbal Behavior, 2,* 440–445.

Wilkes-Gibbs, D., & Clark, H. H. (1992). Coordinating beliefs in conversation. *Journal of Memory and Language, 31,* 183–194.

Winograd, E., & Killinger, W. A., Jr. (1983). Relating age at encoding in early childhood to adult recall: Development of flashbulb memories. *Journal of Experimental Psychology: General, 112,* 413–422.

Winston, P. H. (1984). *Artificial intelligence* (2nd ed.). Reading, MA: Addison-Wesley.

Wixted, J. T. (1991). Conditions and consequences of maintenance rehearsal. *Journal of Experimental Psychology: Learning, Memory, and Cognition, 17,* 963–973.

Wixted, J. T., & Ebbesen, E. B. (1991). On the form of forgetting. *Psychological Science, 2,* 409–415.

Woltz, D. J. (1990). Repetition of semantic comparisons: Temporary and persistent priming effects. *Journal of Experimental Psychology: Learning, Memory, and Cognition, 16,* 392–403.

Wood, F., Taylor, B., Penney, R., & Stump, B. (1980). Regional cerebral blood flow response to recognition memory versus semantic classification tasks. *Brain and Language, 9,* 113–122.

Woods, B. T. (1980). Observations on the neurological basis for initial language. In D. Caplan (Ed.), *Biological studies of mental processes* (pp. 149–158). Cambridge, MA: MIT Press.

Woodworth, R. S., & Schlosberg, H. (1954). *Experimental psychology* (rev. ed.). New York: Holt, Rinehart & Winston.

Yantis, S., & Meyer, D. E. (1988). Dynamics of activation in semantic and episodic memory. *Journal of Experimental Psychology: General, 117,* 130–147.

Yates, F. A. (1966). *The art of memory.* Chicago: University of Chicago Press.

Yuille, J. C., & Paivio, A. (1967). Latency of imaginal and verbal mediators as a function of stimulus and response concreteness-imagery. *Journal of Experimental Psychology, 75,* 540–544.

Zaragoza, M. S., & Koshmider, J. W. III (1989). Misled subjects may know more than their performance implies. *Journal of Experimental Psychology: Learning, Memory, and Cognition, 15,* 246–255.

Zaragoza, M. S., McCloskey, M., & Jamis, M. (1987). Misleading postevent information and recall of the original event: Further evidence against the memory impairment hypothesis. *Journal of Experimental Psychology: Learning, Memory, and Cognition, 13,* 36–44.

Zbrodoff, N. J., & Logan, G. D. (1986). On the autonomy of mental processes: A case study of arithmetic. *Journal of Experimental Psychology: General, 115,* 118–130.

Zola-Morgan, S., Squire, L., & Amalral, D. G. (1986). Human amnesia and the medial temporal region: Enduring memory impairment following a bilateral lesion limited to field CA1 of the hippocampus. *The Journal of Neuroscience, 6,* 2950–2967.

Credits

Photo Credits:

All photos not credited are the property of Scott, Foresman and Company.

Cover: © Elle Schuster; **p. 2:** Scott Mutter; **p. 17:** The Bettmann Archive; **p. 19:** The Bettmann Archive; **p. 20:** By permission of the Houghton Library, Harvard University; **p. 30:** Donna Coveney/The MIT Museum; **p. 40:** Andy Zito/The Image Bank; **p. 47:** Jon Riley/Tony Stone Images; **p. 57:** Tony Freeman/Photo Edit; **p. 60:** NASA; **p. 74:** Ron James; **p. 80:** Sidney Harris; **p. 84:** Scott Mutter; **p. 90:** Tom Ives; **p. 92:** Estate of Sybil Shelton/Peter Arnold, Inc.; **p. 124:** Jean-Claude LeJeune; **p. 131:** Mark Antman/The Image Works; **p. 136:** Courtesy of IBM; **p. 194:** Elle Schuster; **p. 238:** Alan Carey/The Image Works; **p. 241:** Spencer Grant/The Picture Cube; **p. 244:** Michael Evans/The White House; **p. 247:** NASA; **p. 252:** Scott Mutter; **p. 256:** Bill Rieter/CSU News Bureau; **p. 308:** Scott Mutter; **p. 318:** Shostal; **p. 360:** Elle Schuster; **p. 368:** Michael Newman/Photo Edit; **p. 376:** Sidney Harris; **p. 388:** David Young-Wolff/Photo Edit; **p. 414:** Scott Mutter; **p. 430:** Richard Hutchings/Photo Edit; **p. 438:** Sybil Shelton/Peter Arnold, Inc.; **p. 468:** Elle Schuster; **p. 477:** From "The Organization of the Brain," by Walle J. H. Nauta and Michael Fertag. Copyright © 1979 by *Scientific American, Inc.* All rights reserved; **p. 478:** Sidney Harris; **p. 486:** From Penfield, W. "The Excitable Cortex in Conscious Man," Liverpool University Press, 1958.; **p. 489:** J. Croyle/Custom Medical Stock Photo. All rights reserved; **p. 490:** Custom Medical Stock Photo. All rights reserved; **p. 519:** Andy Zito/The Image Bank; **p. 532:** Pictor/DPI/Uniphoto; **p. 546:** John Neubauer/Photo Edit; **p. 574:** Scott Mutter; **p. 579:** Courtesy Herbert A. Simon; **p. 581:** Plate IV from Kohler, "The Mentality of Apes," 1925. Reprinted in 1973 by Routledge & Kegal Paul Ltd.; **p. 615:** Joel Gordon Photography; **p. 620:** Myron Davis/*Life Magazine*/Time Warner Inc.; **p. 630:** Mark Antman/The Image Works; **p. 634:** Movie Still Archives; **p. 647:** Robert Kalman/The Image Works.

Figures:

p. 46: From D. M. Klieger, *Computer Usage for Social Scientists.* Copyright © 1984 by Allyn and Bacon. Reprinted by permission. **p. 51:** From Human memory: A proposed system and its control processes by R. C. Atkinson and R. M. Shiffrin, *The Psychology of Learning and Motivation,* vol. 2, 93. Copyright © 1968 by Academic Press. Reprinted by permission. **p. 73:** Adapted with the permission of Macmillan Publishing Company from *Cognitive Psychology: Memory, Language and Thought,* Second Edition by Darlene V. Howard. Copyright © 1993 by Macmillan Publishing Company. **p. 74:** Copyright Ron James. **p. 94:** From Short term storage of information in vision by E. Averbach and G. Sperling. Copyright © 1960. Reprinted by permission. **p. 101:** From *Principles of Psychology* by R. H. Price. Copyright © 1987 by Scott, Foresman and Company. Reprinted by permission. **p. 102:** Ulric Neisser, *Cognitive Psychology,* Copyright © 1967, p. 174. Reprinted by permission of Prentice-Hall, Englewood Cliffs, New Jersey. And from H. Fletcher, *Speech and Hearing,* Van Nostrand, 1929 edition. **p. 104:** From

An auditory analogue of the Sperling partial report procedure: Evidence for brief auditory storage by C. J. Darwin et al., *Cognitive Psychology, 3,* 259. Copyright © 1972 by Academic Press. Reprinted by permission. **p. 106:** From The role of one's own voice in immediate memory by R. C. Crowder, *Cognitive Psychology, 1,* 166. Copyright © 1970 by Academic Press. Reprinted by permission. **p. 108:** From Visual and auditory memory by R. C. Crowder, in Kavanaugh and Mattingly (eds.), *Language By Ear and By Eye,* 262. Copyright © 1972 by MIT Press. Adapted by permission. **p. 112:** From Pandemonium: A paradigm for learning by O. G. Selfridge, in Teddington Symposium, *Mechanization of Thought Processes,* 517. Copyright © 1959 National Physical Laboratory, Teddington, England. **p. 115:** From Visual search by Ulric Neisser. Copyright © 1964 by Scientific American, Inc. All rights reserved. **p. 121:** From The appeal of parallel distributed processing by J. L. McClelland and D. Rumelhart, *Parallel Distributed Processing,* vol. 1, 23. Copyright © 1986 by MIT Press. Reproduced by permission. **p. 127:** From A. M. Treisman, Selective attention in man, *British Medical Bulletin,* 1964, vol. 20, pp. 12–16. Reprinted by permission. **p. 128:** Figure adapted from *Human Information Processing, An Introduction to Psychology,* Second Edition by Peter H. Lindsay and Donald A. Norman. Copyright © 1977 by Harcourt Brace & Company. Reprinted by permission of the publisher. **p. 136:** Courtesy of AT&T Archives. **p. 150:** From Short-term retention of individual items by L. R. Peterson, *Journal of Experimental Psychology, 58,* 195. Copyright © 1959 by the American Psychological Association. Reprinted by permission. **p. 153:** From Primary memory by N. C. Waugh and D. A. Norman, *Psychological Review, 72,* 91. Copyright © 1965 by the American Psychological Association. Adapted by permission. **p. 155:** From Proactive inhibition and item similarity in short-term memory by Wickens et al., *Journal of Verbal Learning and Verbal Behavior, 2,* 442. Copyright © 1963 by Academic Press. Reprinted by permission. **p. 157:** Panel A: From The serial position effect in free recall by B. J. Murdock, *Journal of Experimental Psychology, 64,* 486. Copyright © 1962 by the American Psychological Association. Adapted by permission. Panels B and C: From Two storage mechanisms in free recall by M. Glanzer and A. R. Cunitz, *Journal of Verbal Learning and Verbal Behavior, 5,* 354, 358. Copyright © 1966 by Academic Press. Reprinted by permission. **p. 161:** From Effect of response requirement and type of material on acquisition and retention performance in short-term memory by G. Kellas, *Journal of Experimental Psychology, 88,* 52, 53. Copyright © 1971 by the American Psychological Association. Adapted by permission. **p. 162:** From Developmental aspects of storage and retrieval by G. Kellas, *Journal of Experimental Child Psychology, 104,* 58. Copyright © 1975 by Academic Press. Reprinted by permission. **p. 166:** Adapted by permission of *American Scientist,* journal of Sigma Xi, the Scientific Research Society. **p. 171:** From Mechanics of verbal ability by E. Hunt, *Psychological Review, 85,* 119. Copyright © 1978 by the American Psychological Association. Reprinted by permission. **p. 173:** Reprinted by permission of Hemisphere Publishing Corporation, Washington, D.C. **p. 175:** Copyright 1968. Canadian Psychological Association. Reprinted with permission. **p. 176:** From Mental rotation of three-dimensional objects by R. N. Shepard, *Science, 171,* 702. Copyright © 1971 by the AAAS. Reprinted by permission. **p. 188:** From Working memory by A. D. Baddeley and G. Hitch, *The Psychology of Learning and Motivation,* vol. 8, 56. Copyright © 1974 by Academic Press. Adapted by permission. **p. 212:** From Frequency of stimulus presentation and short-term decrement in recall by S. Hellyer, *Journal of Experimental Psychology, 64,* 650. Copyright © 1962 by the

American Psychological Association. Reprinted by permission. **p. 213:** From Analysis of rehearsal processes in free recall by D. Rundus, *Journal of Experimental Psychology, 89,* 66. Copyright © 1971 by the American Psychological Association. Reprinted by permission. **p. 222:** From Hierarchical retrieval schemes in recall of categorized word lists by G. H. Bower et al., *Journal of Verbal Learning and Verbal Behavior, 8,* 324. Copyright © 1969 by Academic Press. Reprinted by permission. **p. 226:** From *Memory & Cognition, 12,* 553–557. Reprinted by permission of Psychonomic Society, Inc. **p. 230:** Adapted by permission. **p. 242:** From Fifty years of memory for names and faces by H. P. Bahrick et al., *Journal of Experimental Psychology, 104,* 66. Copyright © 1975 by the American Psychological Association. Reprinted by permission. **p. 246:** From On the very long-term retention of knowledge acquired through formal education: Twelve years of cognitive psychology by M. A. Conway et al., *Journal of Experimental Psychology: General, 120,* 401. Copyright © 1991 by the American Psychological Association. Reprinted by permission. **p. 263:** From Theories of semantic memory by E. E. Smith, in W. K. Estes (ed.), *Handbook of Learning and Cognitive Processes,* vol. 6. Copyright © 1978 by Lawrence Erlbaum Associates, Inc. Reprinted by permission. **p. 263:** From Structure and process in semantic memory by E. E. Smith et al., *Psychological Review, 81,* 222. Copyright © 1974 by the American Psychological Association. Adapted by permission. **p. 267:** From Retrieval time from semantic memory by A. Collins and M. R. Quillian, *Journal of Verbal Learning and Verbal Behavior, 8,* 240–247. Copyright © 1969 by Academic Press. Adapted by permission. **p. 272:** From Structure and process in semantic memory by E. E. Smith et. al., *Psychological Review, 81,* 235. Copyright © 1974 by the American Psychological Association. Adapted by permission. **pp. 276 and 277:** From Structure and process in semantic memory by J. Kounios and P. J. Holcomb, *Journal of Experimental Psychology: General, 121,* 468, 469. Copyright © 1992 by the American Psychological Association. Reprinted by permission. **p. 287:** From *Memory & Cognition, 2,* 467–471. Reprinted by permission of Psychonomic Society, Inc. **p. 289:** From Cognitive representations of semantic categories by E. Rosch, *Journal of Experimental Psychology: General, 104,* 204. Copyright © 1975 by the American Psychological Association. Reprinted by permission. **p. 293:** From *Memory & Cognition, 4,* 648–654. Reprinted by permission of Psychonomic Society, Inc. **p. 295:** From Semantic priming and retrieval from lexical memory by J. H. Neely, *Journal of Experimental Psychology: General, 106,* 233. Copyright © 1977 by the American Psychological Association. Adapted by permission. **p. 298:** From Meaning dominance and semantic context in the processing of lexical ambiguity by G. B. Simpson, *Journal of Verbal Learning and Verbal Behavior,* 20, 126. Copyright © 1981 by Academic Press. Reprinted by permission. **p. 303:** From *Cognitive Psychology: A Neural-Network Approach* by Colin Martindale. Copyright © 1991 by Wadsworth, Inc. Reprinted by permission of Brooks/Cole Publishing Company, Pacific Grove, California, 93950. **p. 319:** From Creating new memories that are quickly accessed and confidently held by Loftus et al., *Memory & Cognition,* 17, 607–616, 1989. Reprinted by permission of the Psychonomic Society, Inc. **p. 323:** From The abstraction of linguistic ideas by J. D. Bransford and J. J. Franks, *Cognitive Psychology,* 2, 346. Copyright © 1971 by Academic Press. Reprinted by permission. **p. 329:** From Long-term memory for a common object by R. S. Nickerson and M. J. Adams, *Cognitive Psychology,* 11, 297. Copyright © 1979 by Academic Press. Reprinted by permission. **pp. 332–334:** From *Human Associative Memory* by J. R. Anderson and G. H.

Bower. Copyright © 1973 by Lawrence Erlbaum Associates, Inc. Adapted by permission; and from *Representation of Meaning in Memory* by W. Kintsch. Copyright © 1974 by Lawrence Erlbaum Associates, Inc. Adapted by permission. **p. 336:** From: *Cognitive Psychology and its Implications* by John R. Anderson. Copyright © 1980 by W. H. Freeman and Company. Reprinted with permission. **p. 347:** From *Scripts, Plans, Goals, and Understanding* by R. C. Schank and R. P. Abelson. Copyright © 1977 by Lawrence Erlbaum Associates, Inc. Adapted by permission. **p. 356:** From On the relationship between autobiographical memory and perceptual learning by L. Jacoby and M. Dallas, *Journal of Experimental Psychology: General, 110,* 311. Copyright © 1981 by the American Psychological Association. Adapted by permission. **p. 367:** From Linguistic expression of category levels by E. L. Newport and U. Bellugi, in E. Rosch and B. B. Lloyd (eds.), *Cognition and Categorization.* Copyright © 1978 by Lawrence Erlbaum Associates, Inc. Redrawn by permission. **p. 380:** Figure adapted from *An Introduction to Language* by Victoria A. Fromkin and Robert Rodman. Copyright © 1974 by Holt, Rinehart & Winston, Inc.. Reprinted by permission of the publisher. **p. 382:** From *Perception and Psychophysics, 30,* 10–23. Reprinted by permission of Psychonomic Society, Inc. **p. 383:** From The discrimination of speech sounds within and across phoneme boundaries by A. M. Liberman et al., *Journal of Experimental Psychology, 54,* 358–368. Copyright © 1957 by the American Psychological Association. Reprinted by permission. **p. 385:** From Some results of research on speech perception by A. M. Liberman, *Journal of the Acoustic Society of America, 29,* 117–123. Copyright © 1957. Reprinted by permission. **p. 386:** From The grammars of speech and language by A. M. Liberman, *Cognitive Psychology, 1,* 301–323. Copyright © 1970 by Academic Press. Reprinted by permission. **p. 390:** Donald J. Foss/David T. Hakes, *Psycholinguistics: An Introduction to the Psychology of Language,* Copyright © 1978, p. 77. Reprinted by permission of Prentice Hall, Englewood Cliffs, New Jersey. **p. 393:** From *Psychology of Language* by David W. Carroll. Copyright © 1986 by Wadsworth, Inc. Reprinted by permission of Brooks/Cole Publishing Company, Pacific Grove, California, 93950. **p. 394:** From *Cognitive Psychology and Information Processing: An Introduction* by R. Lachman et al. Copyright © 1979 by Lawrence Erlbaum Associates, Inc. Reprinted by permission. **p. 402:** From Event-related brain potentials elicited by syntactic anomaly by L. Osterhout and P. J. Holcomb, *Journal of Memory and Language, 31,* 790. Copyright © 1992 by Academic Press. Reprinted by permission. **p. 405:** From *Cognitive Psychology and Information Processing: An Introduction* by R. Lachman et al. Copyright © 1979 by Lawrence Erlbaum Associates, Inc. Adapted by permission. **p. 408:** From Making and correcting errors during sentence comprehension: Eye movements in the analysis of structurally ambiguous sentences by L. Frazier and K. Rayner, *Cognitive Psychology, 14,* 193. Copyright © 1982 by Academic Press. Adapted by permission. **p. 420:** From *Psychonomic Science, 19,* 235–236. Reprinted by permission of Psychonomic Society, Inc. **p. 424:** From Accessing sentence participants: The advantage of first mention by M. A. Gernsbacher and D. Hargreaves, *Journal of Memory and Language, 27,* 703. Copyright © 1988 by Academic Press. Adapted by permission. **p. 425:** From Building and accessing clausal representations: The advantage of first mention versus the advantage of clausal recency by M.A. Gernsbacher et al., *Journal of Memory and Language, 28,* 742. Copyright © 1989 by Academic Press. Reprinted by permission. **p. 438:** From Marcel A. Just and Patricia A. Carpenter, *The Psychology of Reading and Language Comprehension.* Copyright © 1987 by Allyn and Bacon. Reprinted by permission. **pp. 439 and 443:** From A theory of reading: From eye fixations to comprehension by M. A. Just and P. A. Carpenter, *Psychological Review, 87,* 330, 331. Copyright © 1980 by the American Psychological Association. Reprinted by permission. **p. 458:** Adapted with permission from Ablex Publishing Corporation. **p. 476:** From Certain aspects of the anatomy and physiology of the cerebral cortex by F. H. C. Crick and C. Asanuma, in J. L. McClelland and D. Rumelhart (eds.), *Parallel Distributed Processing,* vol. 2, 338. Copyright © 1986 by MIT Press. Reprinted by permission. **p. 486:** From *The Excitable Cortex in Conscious Man:* Wilder Penfield, Liverpool University Press, 1958. Reprinted by permission. **pp. 489:** From Functional topographic mapping of the cortical ribbon in human vision with conventional MRI scanners by W. Schneider et al., *Nature, 365,* 150. Copyright © 1993 Macmillan Magazines Ltd. Reprinted with permission from *Nature.* **pp. 489, 490, and 491:** From Robert L. Solso, *Cognitive Psychology,* 3rd edition. Copyright © 1991 by Allyn and Bacon. Adapted by permission. **p. 493:** From Remembering and knowing the past by E. Tulving, *American Scientist, 77,* 364. Copyright © 1989 by American Scientist. Reprinted by permission. **p. 497:** Reprinted by permission. **p. 504:** From *Mechanics of the Mind* by C. Blakemore. Copyright © 1977 by Cambridge University Press. Reprinted by permission. **pp. 513 and 514:** From A computational model of semantic memory impairment by M. J. Farah and J. L. McClelland, *Journal of Experimental Psychology: General, 120,* 343, 345. Copyright © 1991 by the American Psychological Association. Reprinted by permission. **p. 528:** From *Cognitive Psychology and its Implications* by John R. Anderson. Copyright © 1980 by W. H. Freeman and Company. Reprinted with permission. **p. 534:** From The locus of the semantic congruity effect in comparative judgments by W. P. Banks et al., *Journal of Experimental Psychology: Human Perception and Performance, 104,* 38. Copyright © 1975 by the American Psychological Association. Reprinted by permission. **p. 536:** From Encoding and processing of symbolic information in comparative judgments by W. P. Banks, *Psychology of Learning and Motivation, 11,* 106. Copyright © 1977 by Academic Press. Reprinted by permission. **p. 538:** From *Perception and Psychophysics, 13,* 180–184. Reprinted by permission of Psychonomic Society, Inc. **p. 540:** From Cognitive reference points in judgments of symbolic magnitude by K. J. Holyoak and W. A. Mah, *Cognitive Psychology, 14,* 334. Copyright © 1982 by Academic Press. Redrawn by permission. **pp. 563, 564, and 565:** From Naive theories of motion by M. McCloskey, in D. Gentner and A. L. Stevens (eds.), *Mental Models.* Copyright © 1983 by Lawrence Erlbaum Associates, Inc. Redrawn/reprinted by permission. **p. 580:** Panel D: From Margaret Matlin, *Perception.* Copyright © 1983 by Allyn and Bacon. Reprinted by permission. **p. 583:** From Verbal behavior and problem solving by S. Glucksberg and R. W. Weisberg, *Journal of Experimental Psychology, 71,* 659–664. Copyright © 1966 by the American Psychological Association. Reprinted by permission. **p. 591:** From Analogical problem solving by M. L. Gick and K. J. Holyoak, *Cognitive Psychology, 12,* 312. Copyright © 1980 by Academic Press. Reprinted by permission. **pp. 598 and 622:** From *How to Solve Problems* by Wayne Wickelgren. Copyright © 1974 by W. H. Freeman and Company. Reprinted with permission. **p. 611:** From *Cognition* by A. L. Glass and K. J. Holyoak. Copyright © 1986 by McGraw Hill, Inc. Reprinted by permission. **p. 612:** From Hobbits and Orcs: Acquisition of a sequential concept by J. G. Greeno, *Cognitive Psychology, 6,* 282. Copyright © 1974 by Academic Press. Reprinted by permission. **p. 639:** Reprinted by permission of the publishers from *The Architecture of Cognition* by J. R.

Anderson, Cambridge, Mass.: Harvard University Press. Copyright © 1983 by the President and Fellows of Harvard College. **p. 646:** From Emotional mood states, strategies, and state-dependency in memory by J. A. Leight and H. C. Ellis, *Journal of Verbal Learning and Verbal Behavior, 20,* 259. Copyright © 1981 by Academic Press. Reprinted by permission. **p. 649:** From Anxiety and performance: The processing efficiency theory by M. Eysenck and M. G. Calvo, *Cognition and Emotion, 6,* 409–434. Copyright 1992 by Lawrence Erlbaum Associates. Adapted by permission. **p. 653:** From The use of indirect memory tests to assess malingered amnesia by K. D. Horton et al., *Journal of Experimental Psychology: General, 121,* 331. Copyright © 1992 by the American Psychological Association. Reprinted by permission.

Tables:

p. 123: From Auditory illusions and confusions by R. M. Warren and R. P. Warren, *Scientific American, 223,* 32. Copyright © 1970. **p. 184:** From Working memory by A. D. Baddeley and G. Hitch, *The Psychology of Learning and Motivation,* vol. 8, 51, 53. Copyright © 1974 by Academic Press. Adapted by permission. **p. 216:** From The role of rehearsal in short-term memory by Craik and Watkins, *Journal of Verbal Learning and Verbal Behavior, 12,* 600, 601. Copyright © 1973 by Academic Press. Adapted by permission. **p. 223:** From Hierarchical retrieval schemes in recall of categorized word lists by G. H. Bower et al., *Journal of Verbal Learning and Verbal Behavior, 8,* 326. Copyright © 1969 by Academic Press. Adapted by permission. **pp. 237–238:** From *The Ideal Problem Solver* by Bransford and Stein. Copyright © 1984 by W. H. Freeman and Company. Reprinted with permission. **p. 255:** From How to make a language user by A. Collins and M. R. Quillian, in Tulving and Donaldson (eds.), *Organization of Memory,* 327–328. Copyright © 1972. Reprinted by permission of Academic Press. **p. 292:** From Facilitation in recognizing pairs of words: Evidence of a dependence between retrieval operations by D. E. Meyer and R. W. Schvaneveldt, *Journal of Experimental Psychology, 90,* 229. Copyright © 1971 by the American Psychological Association. Adapted by permission. **p. 299:** From Meaning dominance and semantic context in the processing of lexical ambiguity by G. B. Simpson, *Journal of Verbal Learning and Verbal Behavior, 20,* 128. Copyright © 1981 by Academic Press. Reprinted by permission. **p. 312:** From *Remembering: A Study in Experimental and Social Psychology* by F. C. Bartlett. Copyright © 1967 by Cambridge University Press. Reprinted by permission. **p. 318:** From Reconstruction of automobile destruction: An example of the interaction between language and memory by E. F. Loftus and J. C. Palmer, *Journal of Verbal Learning and Verbal Behavior, 13,* 586. Copyright © 1974 by Academic Press. Reprinted by permission. **pp. 321 and 322:** From Remember that old theory of memory? Well, Forget it! by J. J. Jenkins, *American Psychologist, 29,* 791. Copyright © 1974 by the American Psychological Association. Adapted by permission. **p. 339:** From Recognition memory for syntactic and semantic aspects of connected discourse by J. S. Sachs, *Perception and Psychophysics,* 437–442. Reprinted by permission of the Psychonomic Society, Inc. **p. 341:** From Priming in item recognition: Evidence for the propositional structure of sentences by R. Ratcliff and G. McKoon, *Journal of Verbal Learning and Verbal Behavior, 17,* 414. Copyright © 1978 by Academic Press. Reprinted by permission. **p. 347:** From *Human Memory and Cognition: Learning, Understanding and Remembering,* by John D. Bransford. Copyright © 1979 by Wadsworth, Inc. Reprinted by permission of Brooks/Cole

Publishing Company, Pacific Grove, California, 93950. **p. 365:** Copyright © 1960 by the American Institute of Biological Sciences. Reprinted by permission. **p. 379:** From *Experimental Psycholinguistics: An Introduction* by S. Glucksberg and J. H. Danks. Copyright © 1975 by Lawrence Erlbaum Associates, Inc. Reprinted by permission. **p. 399:** From *Psychology of Language* by David W. Carroll. Copyright © 1986 by Wadsworth, Inc. Reprinted by permission of Brooks/Cole Publishing Company, Pacific Grove, California, 93950. Original source Language by W.A. Fromkin (1971). **p. 421 and 423:** From *Language Comprehension as Structure Building* by M. A. Gernsbacher. Copyright © 1990 by Lawrence Erlbaum Associates, Inc. Reprinted by permission. **p. 433:** From Types of reference and implication by H. H. Clark, in Johnson-Laird and Wason (eds.), *Thinking: Readings in Cognitive Science,* 414–419. Copyright © 1977 by Cambridge University Press. Adapted by permission. **pp. 442 and 445:** From A theory of reading: From eye fixations to comprehension by M. A. Just and P. A. Carpenter, *Psychological Review, 87,* 348. Copyright © 1980 by the American Psychological Association. Reprinted by permission. **p. 460:** From Explorations in Cognition by Donald A. Norman and David E. Rumelhart. Copyright © 1975 by W. H. Freeman and Company. Reprinted with permission. **p. 483:** From *Fundamentals of Human Neuropsychology* by Bryan Kolb and Ian Q. Whishaw. Copyright © 1990 by W. H. Freeman and Company. Reprinted with permission. **p. 496:** From *Cognitive Neuropsychology: A Clinical Introduction* by R. A. McCarthy and E. K. Warrington. Copyright © 1990 by Academic Press. Adapted by permission. **p. 498:** From Neural models of language processes by Kertesz in M. A. Arbib et al. (eds.), *Neural Models of Language Processes,* 25–44. Copyright © 1982 by Academic Press. Adapted by permission. **p. 526:** Reprinted with the permission of Macmillan Publishing Company from *Cognitive Psychology: Memory, Language, and Thought,* Second Edition by Darlene V. Howard. Copyright © 1993 by Macmillan Publishing Company. **p. 527:** Reprinted by permission of the publishers from *Psychology of Reasoning: Structure and Content* by P.C. Wason and P. N. Johnson-Laird, Cambridge, Mass.: Harvard University Press. Copyright © 1971 by P. C. Wason and P.N. Johnson-Laird. **p. 558:** From Simulation heuristic story and table of data in Kahneman et al. (eds.), *Judgment Under Uncertainty,* 204–206. Copyright © 1982 by Cambridge University Press. Adapted by permission. **p. 584:** Adapted from Mechanization in problem solving by A. Luchins, *Psychological Monographs,* 1942, 1. Redrawn by permission. **p. 585:** From *The Ideal Problem Solver* by Bransford and Stein. Copyright © 1984 by W. H. Freeman and Company. Reprinted with permission. **pp. 588, 589, and 590:** From Analogical problem solving by M. L. Gick and K. J. Holyoak, *Cognitive Psychology, 12,* 311, 335, 352. Copyright © 1980 by Academic Press. Reprinted by permission. **p. 619:** From Feeling of knowing in memory and problem solving by J. Metcalfe, *Journal of Experimental Psychology: Learning, Memory and Cognition, 12,* 294. Copyright © 1986 by the American Psychological Association. Reprinted by permission. **p. 638:** From *Scripts, Plans, Goals, and Understanding* by R. C. Schank and R. P. Abelson. Copyright © 1977 by Lawrence Erlbaum Associates, Inc. Reprinted by permission. **p. 645:** Reprinted from *Behaviour Research and Therapy, 6,* E. Velten, A laboratory task for induction of mood states, 473–482. Copyright © 1968, with kind permission from Pergamon Press Ltd, Headington Hill Hall, Oxford OX3 0BW, UK.

Subject Index